CRIMINOLOGICAL THOUGHT
PIONEERS PAST AND PRESENT

CRIMINOLOGICAL THOUGHT
PIONEERS PAST AND PRESENT

Robert J. Mutchnick
Randy Martin
W. Timothy Austin
Indiana University of Pennsylvania

Prentice Hall
Upper Saddle River, New Jersey
Columbus, Ohio

Library of Congress Cataloging-in-Publication Data

Mutchnick, Robert J.
  Criminological thought : pioneers past and present / Robert J. Mutchnick, W. Timothy Austin,
Randy Martin. — 1st ed.
    p. cm.
  Previous ed. entered under: Martin, Randy,
  Includes index.
  ISBN-13: 978-0-13-119046-7
  ISBN-10: 0-13-119046-6
  1. Criminologists—Biography. 2. Criminology—Methodology—History. I. Austin, W. Timothy.
II. Martin, Randy, 1956- III. Martin, Randy, Criminological thought. IV. Title.
  HV6023.M37 2008
  364.01—dc22

2008017864

Vice President and Executive Publisher: Vernon R.
Anthony
Acquisitions Editor: Tim Peyton
Editorial Assistant: Alicia Kelly
Production Manager: Wanda Rockwell

Creative Director: Jayne Conte
Cover Designer: Margaret Kenselaar
Cover art: Getty Images, Inc.
Director of Marketing: David Gessell

Pearson Prentice Hall™ is a trademark of Pearson Education, Inc.
Pearson® is a registered trademark of Pearson plc
Prentice Hall® is a registered trademark of Pearson Education, Inc.

Pearson Education Ltd., London
Pearson Education Singapore Pte. Ltd.
Pearson Education, Canada, Ltd.
Pearson Education–Japan
Pearson Education Australia Pty, Limited

Pearson Education North Asia Ltd.
Pearson Educación de Mexico, S.A. de C.V.
Pearson Education Malaysia, Pte. Ltd.
Pearson Education, Upper Saddle River, New Jersey

Prentice Hall
is an imprint of

www.pearsonhighered.com

ISBN-13: 978-0-13-119046-7
ISBN-10:   0-13-119046-6

Dedicated to
Mom, Barbara, Kathryn, Sarah
Jamie, Lane, Tyler
Betty, Philip

CONTENTS

PREFACE

To The Reader:

When individuals decide to write a book, they often do so for a wide variety of reasons. Some of these are readily apparent; some are not so obvious. All the individuals involved in the writing of this book have taught theory classes both in the field of criminology and in their degree-specific disciplines. Each has, in discussion with the others, admitted some dissatisfaction with the books currently available. In the spirit of the academic discussion, it was suggested, "Why don't we write a book that would fill this void?" After further deliberation, it was agreed that an attempt would be made to bring together those ideas and people whom we believed were instrumental in the understanding and development of criminological thought.

In undertaking this project, we want to provide the reader the opportunity to get to know something about the people who have helped shape the discipline and have influenced our thinking about criminal behavior. It is our belief that knowledge of these pioneers enhances our understanding of their theories and key ideas. By placing all of this within an historical context, the interaction between the evolution of human philosophical and scientific thought and the specific content of criminology should become clearer.

This book is also unique in that it is a complete collaboration—each of us contributed to the development of this work at every step of the process. What the reader discovers in the following pages represents the combined efforts of three individuals who have come to criminology via different routes. Our degrees represent the disciplines of psychology, criminology, and sociology. Each of us brings to this book our own perspective on the developments of criminological thought. It is our expectation that through an integration of different backgrounds and orientations we can contribute to an understanding of the development of key ideas and theory in criminology. In addition, through our own preferences and interests, we take a holistic approach that allows us to introduce several pioneers not traditionally discussed in criminology texts. In addition, we also take a new look at some of the old standards.

This book follows a rather specific and original format for scrutinizing the contributors. Each of the presentations in the book is organized around five subheadings. The first subheading is the biographical sketch. We believe strongly that this aspect of these eminent writers has been glossed over in other texts. Accordingly, a careful, personal, and historical discussion enables the reader to more easily comprehend the pioneer's individual contributions within the overall chronology of the discipline. For example, the fact that Cesare Lombroso and Charles Darwin were contemporaries or that Sigmund Freud's deterministic theory was an outgrowth of the positivistic movement become critical points in understanding the contributions of these pioneers. At times, setting the stage is as important as the characters themselves.

Each chapter also provides the reader with a synopsis of the pioneer's basic assumptions. These assumptions refer to the fundamental concepts or principles that provide the foundations for how each pioneer looks at the world. For some of these pioneers, such basic assumptions are more straightforward and highly documented, as in the case of Cesare Beccaria. For others, this particular aspect of the presentation is more obscure and challenging, but certainly no less important.

The third subheading of each presentation pertains to the "Key Ideas" of the pioneers. It is at this juncture that we offer a discussion of the pioneer's major contributions to criminology. In some cases, the reader finds the contributor's life-works focused primarily on criminology, as exemplified by the writings of Edwin Sutherland and William Sheldon. More often, however, we find that the major writers have not been discipline-specific, and in some instances have been indirectly or marginally concerned with criminology, with an impact not fully realized. This can undoubtedly be said of such a pioneer as Erving Goffman.

Fourth, a part of each presentation is discussed under the subheading "Critique." An important aim of this text is to offer the reader a succinct review of criticism and support directed toward the pioneers over the years. It becomes apparent that any writer who is farsighted enough to create significant breakthroughs in the discipline must, for the same reason, be prepared to submit their key ideas to careful examination. Consequently, influential writers and their works are scrutinized by their contemporaries, as well as by subsequent pioneers who have thought further the ideas of these earlier scholars.

If one is working from the assumption that science is a process of critical analysis, then no apology need be made if several pioneers are found to have as their primary contribution the stimulation of others to question and challenge. Therefore, the history of criminology, not unlike other sciences, may be seen as a long series of critical dissections and faultfinding. We often reach a point, as in the case of Cesare Lombroso, where a most prominent pioneer is rarely lauded for his original findings but is much praised for his methodology. Similarly, William Sheldon is often scoffed at for insisting, even into the 1950s, that there are causal links between body type and temperament. Nevertheless, his work provided a stepping-stone, frequently through peer review, that allows one to understand more clearly the continuum between biological and social determinism. Moreover, the reader finds that the present pioneers are not immune to active debate, as can be seen in the presentations regarding Sigmund Freud, Cesare Beccaria, or the conflict theorist Richard Quinney.

The "References and Bibliography" section of each presentation forms the fifth subheading and should be seen as an integral part of the text. Although the book does not pretend to be encyclopedic, it directs the reader logically to appropriate related works. Furthermore, a complete name and subject index is provided at the end of the book.

This second edition waited the best part of two decades before being realized. When the first edition was released in 1990, we clearly felt that more needed to be said and included in a subsequent edition. We knew this even before the first edition hit the bookstores. However, the years drifted by much too quickly. As authors, we moved in different directions with our academic careers and research interests even while remaining as faculty in the Department of Criminology at Indiana University of Pennsylvania. Finally, several years ago we pulled ourselves together to rethink our earlier volume on *Criminological Thought: Pioneers Past and Present.*

Do our former decisions regarding which scholars to include in the first volume still make sense today, years later? What changes occurred in the lives of some of the contemporary scholars that require adjustments in the original chapters? Earlier pioneers in criminology may have died since the first edition, and this must be noted. In a number of cases, there have been more modern critiques of the earlier pioneers that can provide fresh insights into a scholar's life and work. In addition, has the discipline of criminology altered so much over the past several decades that it has an impact on our identification of modern-day pioneers? Indeed, has criminology fluctuated to such an extent to require a reshuffling of our earlier decisions? When we were compiling the first edition in the late 1980s, the Internet had yet to make its way into faculty offices. Today, bibliographic searches are nearly instantaneous, allowing the update of important citations to relevant information not easily accessed in earlier years. Even with our realization that this second edition was not going to be a quick fix, we remained convinced that it was doable and worth the effort.

Fortunately, from an historical perspective, as much as things have changed in criminology, more things have remained the same. Most of the earlier chapters remain intact, but with minor adjustments or clarifications. Those chapters of the first edition portraying living scholars require somewhat more effort than others. For instance, fewer adjustments are required for Cesare Lombroso or Walter Reckless than for scholars who remained active in their careers after the first edition.

Readers will see several new chapters in our list of present-day pioneers. After some banter and debate, we included separate sections for Travis Hirschi and for Marcus Felson. Clearly, as in the earlier edition, and with the ever-expanding number of criminologists, we were confounded with the overwhelming increase of worthy scholars deserving special attention. We wanted to include a larger number of new chapters, but agreed to go with this new version and not to wait so long before again rethinking the pioneers in subsequent years.

As with the first edition, the reader may follow the life and work of a particular pioneer, past or present, from either a chronological or a theoretical perspective. That is, the chapters continue to follow a close chronological order, beginning with earlier scholars such as Beccaria and Lombroso and ending with contemporaries such as Hirschi and Felson. At the same time, one may also skip to specific theoretical viewpoints and focus; for example, on particular traditions in criminology such as Social Ecology, Strain, Conflict, or Control.

As with every project of this nature, it could not be accomplished without the support of a multitude of individuals. We thank Howard Becker, Albert Cohen, Robert Merton, Lloyd Ohlin, Richard Quinney, Gresham Sykes, Travis Hirschi, and Marcus Felson for providing us with valuable information that helped us prepare their chapters. In addition, we acknowledge the materials provided on Walter Reckless by Mrs. Martha Reckless and Simon Dinitz of Ohio State University. James Byrne of the University of Lowell assisted by providing materials on Richard Quinney, while Yves Winken of Universite de Liege provided materials on Erving Goffman.

We would be remiss if we did not recognize the vision and contributions of our editor, Tim Peyton, who has consistently provided his encouragement, support, good counsel, and friendship as we prepared this edition. The completion of this second edition was assisted by a number of doctoral students who deserve recognition—Keith Johnson, Keith Bell, Tony Bezich, and Byung Jun Cho.

Finally, we would like to recognize Indiana University of Pennsylvania for bringing us all together as faculty in the Department of Criminology. Without this serendipitous occasion, this book would most likely not have been written.

Robert Mutchnick
Randy Martin
W. Timothy Austin
July 2008

CHAPTER 1
CESARE BECCARIA: 1738–1794

I. BIOGRAPHICAL SKETCH

Cesare Bonesara, Marchese di Beccaria, is credited as the author of one of the most influential eighteenth-century publications related to the reform of the criminal justice system. Described by those who knew him as quiet, reserved, and dedicated to the contemplative life, Beccaria was a very private individual who continually shied away from publicity and public appearances; as a consequence, very little is known about his personal life. He was born in Milan, Italy, on March 15, 1738, the son of aristocratic parents, and attended the Jesuit College in Parma, where he did nothing to distinguish himself academically. He dabbled in a number of areas, showing a particular interest in mathematics but not formally pursuing the subject. In 1758, he graduated from the University of Pavia, where he had studied law (Monachesi 1973, 36).

After his college career he returned to Milan. His first marriage was strongly opposed by his father, who did everything he could to prevent it. Ignoring this, Beccaria married and had two children by his first wife. Beccaria married a second time in 1774, three months after the death of his first wife. His second marriage produced a son (Phillipson 1970, 22).

Once he returned to Milan after college, Beccaria joined a group of individuals who called themselves the *Accademia dei Transformati* (Bondanella and Bondanella 1979), a very fashionable literary group. During this period, Beccaria read and was very strongly influenced by Montesquieu's *Persian Letters* and developed "a devotion to social philosophy with a view to effecting reform in many parts of the existing constitution of society" (Phillipson 1970, 4). In addition, Beccaria read the works of Helvetius, d'Alembert, Diderot, Buffon, and Hume, all contemporaries and influential individuals of the day (Beccaria 1963).

It was while he was a member of the Accademia that he met and became friends with Pietro Verri, a noted Italian economist. Impressed with Verri's views, Beccaria left the Accademia dei Transformati to join the *Accademia dei Pugni,* or the "academy of the fists" (Beccaria 1963, xii). Verri and his brother, Alessandro, a creative writer of some note, led the group, and the Accademia met regularly in the Verri household to discuss important issues of the day. At these meetings, members adopted the names of noted individuals, and Beccaria used the name Titus Pomponius Atticus (Phillipson 1970, 5). This new discussion group assumed a stronger political stance, and Beccaria joined because he, like the other members, was unhappy with the "economic organization" of his country (Phillipson 1970). Members wrote on various topics of interest, producing essays designed to challenge the existing structure of eighteenth-century Italian society.

Cesare Beccaria produced his first published work in 1762 entitled *Del Disordine e de' Rimedi delle Monete nello Stato di Milano nell' anno 1762 (The Disorder and Remedies of the Economy in Milan, 1762*) (Monachesi 1973, 37), a monograph that addressed remedies for problems in Milan's monetary system. This monograph, although an important statement, did not receive the acclaim that would be showered on his later work on penal reform.

Writing apparently wasn't an easy task for Beccaria. He would write for a short period, stop to discuss his thoughts with his colleagues in the Accademia, and then often go to sleep rather than return to his pen. Perhaps mental activity of this sort was a strain on his physical being; or perhaps, as Pietro Verri recounted, it was simply that "Beccaria tended to be lazy and easily discouraged. He needed prodding and even had to be given assignments upon which to work" (Monachesi 1973, 38), and it was Pietro Verri who assigned Beccaria the task of writing about penal reform. Alessandro Verri held the formal position of Protector of Prisoners and regularly traveled into the prisons. Alessandro informed the members of the Accademia with what he had seen and heard while on official business, and members were so incensed that Pietro Verri urged Beccaria to write about it. Alessandro Verri took Beccaria into some of the prisons so that he could view the situation for himself, and in March 1763, Beccaria began work on what would eventually be his most famous essay. He completed the essay in January 1764, and its first edition was published anonymously in July of that same year.

There is some speculation that the completed work, entitled *Dei Delitti e delle Pene* (*On Crimes and Punishments*), might not have been written by Beccaria. When questioned about his role in the production of the monograph, Pietro Verri staunchly maintained that Cesare Beccaria was the author. In a letter, Pietro Verri stated, "I suggested the topic to him, and most of the ideas came out of daily conversations between Beccaria, Alessandro, Ambertenghi and myself" (Beccaria 1963, xiii), but he insisted that the essay "is by the Marquis Beccaria" (Beccaria 1963, xiii). Even though Pietro Verri, in this instance, supported the commonly held belief that Beccaria was the author of *On Crimes and Punishments*, in another communication Pietro Verri indicates that the task of writing is "so laborious for him [Beccaria], and costs him so much effort that after an hour he collapses and can't go on. When he had amassed the materials, I wrote them out, arranged them in order, and thus made a book out of them" (Paolucci 1963, xiv). It has been suggested that Pietro Verri was disappointed with his own literary career and jealous of the success that he himself had helped Beccaria to achieve.

Given the description of Beccaria's work habits, his lack of knowledge of the penal system, the speed with which he finished the essay, and the fact that he produced nothing else of note in his career, the speculation about actual authorship actually provides us with circumstantial support. It appears that it might have been more appropriate if both Beccaria and Pietro Verri had been listed as co-authors of the essay. The issue of authorship, however, in no way affects the importance of the work and the influence it exercised over the justice system. It has also been suggested that the essay was published anonymously because its "contents were designed to undermine many if not all of the cherished beliefs of those in position to determine the fate of those accused and convicted of crime" (Monachesi 1973, 38). Whatever degree of validity this second supposition might have, Beccaria was listed as the author beginning with the second printing of the work.

Although he published nothing else of outstanding note, Beccaria was a regular contributor to *Il Caffe*, a journal modeled on Joseph Addison's *Spectator* (Beccaria 1963, xii), published by the Accademia dei Pugni every ten days. Beccaria was involved in writing for this journal until May 1766, when it ceased publication and the Accademia dei Pugni disbanded, apparently because of internal conflicts among the members (Phillipson 1970).

By this time, Beccaria's essay had been widely distributed and read. He had already received much critical acclaim, and invitations to speak and assist with the revision of criminal codes were logged regularly. In October 1766, Beccaria traveled to Paris to meet with a group of writers known as the *Encyclopaedists*. Voltaire, a member of the group who had read Beccaria's essay, had himself extended two invitations to Beccaria to visit Paris and lecture to his group (Phillipson 1970). In fact, Voltaire based his famous work "Commentary" on Beccaria's essay. Beccaria, however, was not one to seek the limelight; in Paris he soon grew homesick, and after a short period of time he returned to Milan. Beccaria was also invited by the Empress Catherine II to St. Petersburg, Russia, to help with the development of a new criminal code; however, because of his disappointing experience in Paris, Beccaria decided not to travel abroad and declined the invitation.

Beccaria thereafter stayed in Milan, accepting the position of Professor of Political Economy in the Palatine School in 1768. He held this position for two years; then, in April 1771, was appointed "counselor of state and a magistrate" (Phillipson 1970, 22). For the next twenty-three years, Beccaria apparently returned to the quiet, reserved, and contemplative life until his death of apoplexy on November 28, 1794, at the age of fifty-five.

II. BASIC ASSUMPTIONS

At the time Beccaria was writing, the historical ideology was represented by the "theology of the Church Fathers and the doctrine of the divine right of kings" (Vold and Bernard 1986, 19). This historical ideology was being challenged by the forces of reform. The Naturalists, a group of philosophers, posited that society was ordered and that this order "was separate from religious revelation" (Williams and McShane 1988, 14). According to some of the reformers, the mixture of ideas that were the basis of the society during this time included that when people originally developed they lived in what has been described a state of grace. In this state of grace, or innocence, individuals had "free will" to make whatever choices they so desired. In the state of grace, the only form of regulation that existed was what Vold and Bernard (1986) refer to as "psychological reality." Out of necessity, a state emerged that attempted to control behavior through fear of pain. Punishment was the primary method used to instill fear. States could legitimately transfer control of an individual to a "political state" for the purpose of punishment and, in extreme cases, execution.

Part of this viewpoint included the reform orientation of the social contract that Beccaria embraced. In addition to accepting the concept of the social contract as espoused by Hobbes and Rousseau, Beccaria also based many of his ideas concerning crime and punishment on the philosophy of the greatest good for the greatest number. Although the concept is most closely associated with the writings of Jeremy Bentham on utilitarianism, it was Beccaria who influenced Bentham. The concept of *utilitarianism*, although not specifically identified as such, was first used by Beccaria and appeared first in his work. It is likely that Bentham developed the term as a result of his reading of Beccaria's work. In his *An Introduction to the Principles of Morals and Legislation* (1789), "Bentham not only repeats the concept of the greatest happiness for the greatest number, but he further develops the notion of a hedonistic calculus" (Bondanella and Bondanella 1979, 42).

It is important to understand Beccaria's notion of society and the existence of laws as influenced by the concept of the social contract. For Beccaria,

> [L]aws are the conditions whereby free and independent men united to form society. Weary of living in a state of war, and enjoying a freedom rendered useless by the uncertainty of its perpetuation, men willingly sacrifice a part of this freedom in order to enjoy that which is left in security and tranquillity. The sum of all the portions of the freedom surrendered by each individual constitutes the sovereignty of a nation, deposited in and to be administered by a legitimate sovereign. It was not, however, alone sufficient to create this depository from private usurpation of every man who would want not only that portion of the sovereignty that he individually had contributed but also that which had been contributed by all others. . . . It is because of this that punishments were established to deal with those who transgress against the laws. (Beccaria 1963, 11–12)

The criminal law of eighteenth-century Europe was in general considered barbaric and repressive. Its administration permitted and encouraged incredibly arbitrary and abusive practices. Prosecutors and judges were allowed tremendous latitude in their decision making, and corruption was rampant. Secret accusations and torture were not uncommon, and individuals were often imprisoned on the flimsiest of evidence. Judges had autonomy to the degree that they were afforded unlimited discretion in the punishment of criminals (Monachesi 1973, 39). The "standing" of a person in the community had a direct and overt influence on the handling he could expect from the justice system. Justice, to all intents and purposes, was "relative."

Referring to the situation as it existed during the last half of the eighteenth century, Phillipson writes that "while offering a climate for change [the century] still saw the existence of the old criminal jurisprudence with all its unmitigated ferocity and lack of reason was still in existence" (1970, 27). With regard to Italy during this time, Phillipson also indicates the period was seen as a time of "recuperation" (1970, 27).

Beccaria understood that it was the responsibility of the legislature to pass laws and determine punishments, and the responsibility of the magistrate or judge to apply the punishment prescribed by law. However, his concern went beyond this basic regimen: "Beccaria, following Montesquieu, warns that every punishment which is not founded upon absolute necessity is tyrannical" (Monachesi 1973, 41). How much punishment is "necessary"? From Beccaria's perspective, using the principle of hedonism, what is necessary is to outweigh the pleasure one derives from an act with just enough pain to make in not worthwhile to engage in the criminal act.

Beccaria's basic philosophy grew out of the Enlightenment. Probably one of the central tenets of his thinking was that "the rights of man had to be protected against the corruption and excesses of existing institutions" (Taylor, Walton, and Young 1973, 1). Beccaria was convinced that the social contract, although restricting a citizen's behavior, did so in the best interests of society:

> The view that each citizen should have within his power to do all that is not contrary to the laws, without having to fear any other inconvenience than that which may result from the action itself—this is the political dogma that

should be believed by the people and inculcated by the supreme magistrates with the incorruptible guardianship of the laws. (Beccaria 1963, 67)

III. KEY IDEAS

An understanding of Beccaria's ideas is best gleaned from a detailed review and analysis of his only work that is devoted to the topic of criminal justice, *On Crimes and Punishments.* First published in 1764 in Italian and translated into English in 1768, it is his foremost publication. It is important to recognize that Beccaria did not specifically set out to develop a theory pertaining to crime and justice, but rather simply wanted to delineate the parameters of a just system of dealing with criminals. Whether he intended to or not, Beccaria developed an outline for a theory of justice.

Beccaria divided his text into forty-two short chapters, some of which were less than a page in length and the longest no more than five pages. Phillipson, in his review of Beccaria's work, reduces the forty-two chapters into six general categories:

1. The measures of crimes and punishments
2. The certainty of punishment and the right of pardon
3. The nature and division of crimes and relative punishments
4. A consideration of certain punishments
5. Procedures, including secret accusations and torture
6. The prevention of crimes (1970, 56).

These categories provide the reader with a general sense of the subject matter that Beccaria included in his essay.

Beccaria indicates to the reader that it was his intention not to "diminish legitimate authority"; instead, his text "must serve to increase it" (Beccaria 1963, 4). However, he also believed that the need to increase legitimate authority should be accompanied by a search for truth. He believed that the existing legal system was archaic and needed to have its legal codes updated. It was Beccaria's contention that "a people's customs and laws are always, in point of merit and propriety, a century behind its actual enlightenment" (Phillipson 1970, 57).

LAW AND PUNISHMENT

On the origins of punishment, Beccaria posits that legitimate punishment must emanate from the law. Lasting laws represent the wishes of humankind—if laws do not represent humankind, they will ultimately be changed. Laws must be made by a legislative body, not by individuals, if they are to be impartial. In those places where a sovereign exists, magistrates are necessary because a sovereign should not both make the laws and enforce them. "There must . . . be a third party to judge the truth of the fact. Hence the need for a magistrate whose decisions, from which there can be no appeal, should consist of mere affirmations or denials of particular facts" (Beccaria 1963, 14). For Beccaria, there is no interpretation of the law, only its application. If one were to "consult the spirit" of the law, discretion would be an integral part of the process and corruption would therefore run rampant.

Although the state has the right to punish, the punishment must be proportionate to the offense and no greater than necessary to preserve the peace and security of society. "Punishments that exceed what is necessary for protection of the deposit of public security are by their very nature unjust" (Beccaria 1963, 13). When applying punishment, it is necessary that the punishment

> should be the same for the greatest citizen as for the humblest. If it be said that a certain punishment imposed equally on a noble and on a commoner is not really the same by reason of their different education and of the disgrace spread over an illustrious family, the answer is that the measure of punishment is not the sensibility of the particular delinquent, but the public injury, and that is all the greater when committed by a man placed in more favorable circumstances. (Phillipson 1970, 61)

PROOF OF GUILT

Beccaria identifies two types of proofs of guilt—perfect and imperfect. *Perfect guilt* applies to those cases "that exclude the possibility of innocence," whereas *imperfect guilt* applies to

> those that do not exclude it. Of the first, a single [proof] suffices for condemnation; of the second, as many [proofs as] are necessary to form a single perfect one; in other words, such that, though each separately does not exclude the possibility of innocence, their convergence on the same subject makes innocence an impossibility. (Beccaria 1963, 21)

The distinction between these two proofs is an important one for our present-day justice system. Usually, we do not have a perfect proof. More often than not, we have an imperfect proof with many pieces of evidence that when considered individually are not sufficient to establish guilt, but when taken collectively are able to acceptably establish guilt. It is this understanding of proof as delineated by Beccaria that is related to our present-day concepts of "probable cause" and "beyond a reasonable doubt."

THE JURY

On the subject of jury, Beccaria called for a panel of peers. Beccaria suggests that "in crimes involving the offense of one citizen against another one-half of those who try the case should be peers of the accused and one-half [should] be peers of the person offended" (Monachesi 1973, 47). Beccaria posited that a jury made up evenly of peers of the accused and peers of the victim would produce a proper balance (Beccaria 1963, 22). During jury selection, the defendant should have the right to reject a potential juror on the grounds of suspicion regarding his impartiality. The division of jurors into peers of the accused and peers of the victim is designed to create a final jury that is as nearly as possible impartial.

WITNESSES

On the subject of the reliability of a witness, the issue of credibility, according to Beccaria, "must diminish in proportion to the hatred, or friendship, or close connections between him and the accused" (Beccaria 1963, 23). The number of witnesses was important to Beccaria. If each side, the prosecutor and the defendant, produced the same number of witnesses it would be very difficult, if not impossible, for a magistrate to determine guilt. It was therefore necessary for one side to have one more witnesses than the other so that a judgment could be reached. Beccaria also considered it inappropriate to exclude women from serving as witnesses.

SECRET ACCUSATIONS AND TORTURE

As indicated in the Basic Assumption section, secret accusations and torture were a regular part of the justice system up to the late 1700s. These abuses of power were not confined to Italy. Torture, secret accusations, and other barbarisms were found throughout most of Europe. Beccaria believed that if secret accusations were being used, it was because of a "weakness of government" (1963, 25).

When addressing the subject of torture, Beccaria was very clear about his position. Torture was an inappropriate measure to be taken against suspected criminals because individuals were not criminals until they had been convicted of a crime in a court of law. "Every difference between guilt and innocence disappears by virtue of the very means one pretends to be using to discover it" (Beccaria 1963, 32). If tortured, a weak but innocent individual could be forced to confess to a crime he or she did not commit. However, a strong but guilty individual might be able to withstand the torture and thereby be set free.

> Of two men, equally innocent or equally guilty, the strong and courageous will be acquitted, the weak and timid condemned, by virtue of this rigorous rational argument: "I, the judge, was supposed to find you guilty of such and such a crime; you the strong, have been able to resist the pain, and I therefore absolve you; you, the weak, have yielded, and I therefore condemn you. I am aware that a confession wrenched forth by torments ought to be of no weight whatsoever, but I'll torment you again if you don't confirm what you have confessed." (Beccaria 1963, 32–33)

The use of torture prior to the determination of guilt is unfair to the person who is innocent and inappropriate for the individual who is guilty. The use of torture is particularly inappropriate because, instead of using evidence as the basis for determining truth, pain and suffering become the guiding principles (Monachesi 1973).

> A strange consequence that necessarily follows from the use of torture is that the innocent person is placed in a condition worse than that of the guilty, for if both are tortured, the circumstances are all against the former. Either he confesses the crime and is condemned, or he is declared innocent and has suffered a punishment he did not deserve. The guilty man, on the contrary, finds himself in a favorable situation; that is, if, as a consequence of having firmly resisted the torture, he is absolved as innocent, he will have escaped a greater punishment by enduring a lesser one. Thus the innocent cannot but lose, whereas the guilty may gain. (Beccaria 1963, 33)

INTERROGATIONS

Interrogation was another topic that Beccaria addressed in his *On Crimes and Punishments*. For Beccaria,

> [A] person who under examination obstinately refuses to answer the questions
> asked of him deserves a punishment that should be fixed by law, and of the
> severest kind, so that men may not thus fail to provide the necessary example
> which they owe to the public. This punishment is not necessary when the guilt
> of the accused is beyond doubt. For in that case interrogations are useless in
> the same way that a confession of the crime is useless when other proofs are
> enough to establish guilt. This last case is the commonest, for experience shows
> that in most trials the accused deny their guilt. (Beccaria 1963, 28)

Beccaria expected individuals to deny their guilt; given the procedures used by the
justice system, it was in the best interest of the individual to deny involvement in a
criminal act. It followed that oaths were useless because they did not in some way compel individuals to tell the truth (Beccaria 1963, 29).

RIGHT TO APPEAL

Related indirectly to our present-day appeal process, Beccaria believed that a convicted individual should have the right to present new evidence that would support his
contention of innocence.

> After proofs of a crime have been introduced and its certainty determined, the
> criminal must be allowed opportune time and means for his defense—but
> time so brief as not to interfere with that promptness of punishment which we
> have seen to be one of the principal checks against crime. (Beccaria 1963, 37)

The issue of promptness was important because Beccaria believed that the punishment should be closely associated with the offense for maximum impact on the public.
Beccaria did not specify what procedures should be used or who should underwrite the
expense of the identification and introduction of new evidence. In fact, Beccaria did
not specify how much time the convicted individual should be allowed before the sentence is carried out. This rudimentary use of the concept of "appeal" was based in part
on and consistent with Beccaria's notion of the search for truth.

PROMPTNESS OF PUNISHMENT

For Beccaria, the "more promptly and the more closely punishment follows the commission of a crime, the more just and useful will it be" (Beccaria 1963, 55). The utility of
the punishment is related to the deterrent effect it has on the public.

> The promptness of punishments is more useful because when the length of
> time that passes between the punishment and the misdeed is less, so much
> stronger and more lasting in the human mind is the association of these two
> ideas, crime and punishment; they then come insensibly to be considered, one
> as the cause, the other as the necessary inevitable effect. (Beccaria 1963, 56)

The key to assuring justice and utility, then, is to make sure that the two, the crime
and the punishment, are "intimately linked."

MILDNESS OF PUNISHMENTS

Using the concept of *hedonism*, Beccaria prescribes only that punishment which is necessary to prevent new or additional crime.

The purpose can only be to prevent the criminal from inflicting new injuries on [society's] citizens and to deter others from similar acts. Always keeping due proportions, such punishments and such method of inflicting them ought to be chosen, therefore, which will make the strongest and most lasting impression on the minds of men, and inflict the least torment on the body of the criminal. (Beccaria 1963, 42)

According to Beccaria, the overall scale of punishment is relative to the developmental stage of the country. As countries develop, the types and range of punishments must change. Beccaria posited in 1764 that "[t]he severity of punishment itself emboldens men to commit the very wrongs it is supposed to prevent; they are driven to commit additional crimes to avoid the punishment for a single one" (1963, 43). Evidence of this can be seen today in cases wherein mandatory and exceedingly harsh sentences are handed down for certain offenses. It has been suggested by some that if the potential penalty for an offense is harsh enough, it could prompt suspects to kill victims so that there are no witnesses. This has specifically been identified as an issue for individual defendants who would be "three-time losers." "For a punishment to attain its end, the evil which it inflicts has only to exceed the advantage derivable from the crime" (Beccaria 1963, 43).

CERTAINTY OF PUNISHMENT

The concept of *certainty of punishment* holds that certainty is more important than intensity. According to Beccaria, "[t]he certainty of a punishment, even if it be moderate, will always make a stronger impression than the fear of another which is more terrible but combined with the hope of impunity" (1963, 58). This concept is consistent with much of the learning theory material that has been developed in recent decades. Operant learning theory includes six basic principles: (1) positive reinforcement; (2) negative reinforcement; (3) positive punishment; (4) negative punishment; (5) discriminative stimuli; and (6) schedules. It is the schedule aspect of learning theory that most closely associates with Beccaria's position on certainty of punishment. *Schedule* refers to "the frequency with which and probability that a particular consequence will occur as well as the length of time it occurs after the behavior" (Williams and McShane 1988, 121). The more immediately after a behavior the punishment occurs the greater the impact. In addition the greater the probability of the punishment occurring the greater the impact it will have. If a person believes that he or she is not likely to be punished or that he or she can talk his or her way out of the punishment, then the fear of the occurrence of punishment is not sufficient to deter someone from committing a crime. It now seems that the inevitability of punishment is a necessity if the system as designed is to deter individuals from engaging in criminal activity.

"The right to inflict punishment is a right not of an individual, but of all citizens, or of their sovereign. An individual can renounce his own portion of right, but cannot annul that of others" (Beccaria 1963, 58) or of society. This belief that it is the state that has the right and obligation to punish is an outgrowth of the social contract, and is based on the premise that it is necessary to ensure the continued existence of society. There are parallels between this concept as put forth in 1764 by Beccaria and our present-day justice system.

THE DEATH PENALTY

In vogue at the time Beccaria was writing, the death penalty was used as a punishment for a host of offenses. Although he argued for individuals to accept responsibility for their behavior, Beccaria was in opposition to the death penalty. In *On Crimes and Punishments* he indicates that the sentence of death was "the war of a nation against a citizen whose destruction it judges to be necessary or useful" (Beccaria 1963, 45). Using the social contract as a partial basis for his position, Beccaria states, "Life is the greatest of all human good and no man willingly gives another man the authority to deprive him of his life" (Monachesi 1973, 45). Therefore, man did not consign his right to life to the sovereign when he entered into the social contract.

Beccaria can understand and accept the death sentence only if it is "the only real way of restraining others from committing crimes" (Beccaria 1963, 46). In support of his opposition to the sentence of death, he raises the issue of duration versus intensity of sentence. For Beccaria, "our sensibility is more easily and more permanently affected by slight but repeated impressions than by a powerful but momentary action" (1963, 47). A relatively current example of the application of Beccaria's thinking on this point is the Scared Straight program, which began in Rahway, New Jersey. The program was designed to take inner-city youths who were identified as delinquents and potential delinquents and take them to visit a maximum-security prison. The premise of the program was to expose these juveniles to the vile and distasteful conditions as well as the type of people housed in a maximum-security institution and therefore deter the juveniles from becoming involved in delinquent and eventually criminal behavior. The juveniles taken on the tour of the maximum-security facility had the opportunity to meet some of the inmates who would attempt to "scare" the juvenile about what would happen to them if they were sent to the prison. The program had a strong short-term effect, but the long-term results were far more negligible. Many of the juveniles were duly impressed when they visited the prison, and from every indication they wanted to make sure they never became a resident of the facility. The further the juveniles physically got from the facility and the inmates and the more time that passed from their visit, the less impact the visit and tour had. Juveniles who participated in the program were often found, weeks after the program, to be boasting that they were too smart to get caught and wind up in prison. This coincides with the thinking of Beccaria, who believed that the duration of the punishment as opposed to the intensity would have the best long-term effect. Some modern-day criminologists make the argument that this is one reason that the sentence of death is, in fact, not a general deterrent.

For Beccaria to consider a punishment just, it had to "consist of only such gradation of intensity as to deter men from committing crimes" (1963, 47). He based this conclusion on the fact that

> the person does not exist who, reflecting upon it, could choose for himself total and perpetual loss of personal liberty, no matter how advantageous a crime might seem to be. Thus the intensity of the punishment of a life sentence of servitude, in place of the death penalty, has in it what suffices to deter any determined spirit. (1963, 47–48)

Beccaria closes this chapter of *On Crimes and Punishments* by stating that "[i]t seems . . . absurd that the laws, which are an expression of the public will, which detest and punish public homicide, should themselves commit it, and that to deter citizens from murder, they order a public one" (Beccaria 1963, 50).

CLASSIFICATION OF CRIME

Three general categories of crime were identified by Beccaria. The first type, is the most serious, threatens the existence of society. An example of this type of crime would be high treason. For Beccaria, "crimes of 'lese majeste'" (high treason) were the most serious because "every crime, even of a private nature, injures society, but it is not every crime that aims at its immediate destruction" (1963, 68). The second classification covers crimes that injure the security and property of individuals. The third classification recognized by Beccaria included crimes that are disruptive of the public peace and tranquility. Examples of this third category include, but are not limited to, rabble rousing and inciting disorder (Monachesi 1973).

In addition to the classification of crimes into three major categories, Beccaria also singled out specific crimes for discussion, including injuries to honor, theft, and smuggling. According to Beccaria, the act that causes injury to honor should be punished with disgrace. In cases of theft, he suggests that fines be used as the appropriate punishment. Beccaria was considerably ahead of his time when he suggested that "the most suitable punishment will be that kind of servitude which alone can be called just—the temporary subjection of the labors and person of the criminal to the community, as repayment, through total personal dependence for the unjust despotism usurped against the social contract" (1963, 74). Translated into our present-day parlance, Beccaria is suggesting that restitution is the appropriate punishment for individuals convicted of theft. Smuggling, a crime of the second magnitude for Beccaria, "is a real crime that injures both the sovereign and the nation, but its punishment should not involve infamy, for it is itself not infamous in public opinion" (1963, 75). One reason for Beccaria's position in this regard is that in his opinion, those who participate in smuggling are not fully aware of the damage that can result from the act because the consequences are remote.

THE MEASURE OF CRIMES

An important point for Beccaria that has become a cornerstone of the Classical School of criminology is that the actions of an individual are of utmost importance. What is the actual degree of injury or harm that is done to society by the criminal act? Beccaria did not consider the issue of the *intent* of the individual to be important. "They were in error who believed that the true measure of crimes is to be found in the intention of the person who commits them" (Beccaria 1963, 65), a major point that distinguishes the Classical School from its successor, the Positive School.

CONCLUSION

To sum up the essence of his penal doctrine, Beccaria presents the following grand conclusion: "In order that every punishment may not be an act of violence committed by one man or by many against a single individual, it ought to be above all things public, speedy, necessary, the least possible in the given circumstances, proportioned to its crime, dictated by the laws" (Phillipson 1970, 82).

IV. CRITIQUE

Even though more than 200 years have elapsed since the initial publication of Beccaria's *On Crimes and Punishments,* the number of critiques of his work is limited. At the time Beccaria wrote, secret accusations, torture, and generally barbaric treatment were in keeping with the general practice and tone of the day. Beccaria's work posited a system of justice based on the concepts of the social contract and utilitarianism that was in direct opposition to the operation of the day. Of those reviews of his work that were published, it is not surprising that many of them were not supportive. Those who perceived themselves to be victims of the existing system were advocates of Beccaria's proposal, whereas those who controlled the system were interested in maintaining the status quo and therefore rejected Beccaria's penal doctrine. From our modern, more objective viewpoint, Beccaria's work is usually acknowledged as having had "more practical effect than any other treatise ever written in the long campaign against barbarism in criminal law and procedure" (Barnes and Becker 1952, 551–552).

As noted earlier, Beccaria did not put forth a "theory" to explain criminal behavior; instead, he presented a philosophy of justice that he applied to the system. If there has been a criticism of Beccaria, it has not come in a formal fashion, but instead in the development of competing schools or ideologies. Probably the most important development that shifted attention away from the system Beccaria proposed came approximately 100 years after his essay was first published. The decline of interest in Beccaria is best represented by the development of the Positive School of thought. It is possible that one reason the Positive School developed when it did was that the issues that were first raised by Beccaria, and that became the basis of the Classical School, were inculcated into the system at that time.

The true test of the impact of Beccaria's essay can be judged by the influence it has had over time on our justice system. "Many of the reforms Beccaria advocated had been proposed by others, but rather because it constituted the first successful attempt to present a consistent and logically constructed penological system—a system to be substituted for the confusing, uncertain, abusive and inhuman practices inherent in the criminal law and penal system of the world" (Monachesi 1973, 48). It had a lasting impact.

In addition to his contribution of *On Crimes and Punishments*, Beccaria is also credited with being a founder of what has come to be known as the Classical School of Criminology. Although this may not have been his conscious intention, Beccaria had a profound long-term effect on the development of criminology. A brief summary of Beccaria's basic tenets is in order:

1. Beccaria was of the mind that all people are liable to commit crimes, and that there is a need for society to protect not only the physical well-being of its members, but the property that they have come to rightfully own as well.
2. There is a clear sense of the need for the social contract, whereby all people give up some of their rights to the state to preserve the peace. Hand in hand with this is the idea that punishment can be used where appropriate to protect the peace that everyone agrees they want.
3. Beccaria and the Classical School caution that punishment must be proportional to the crime committed. From Beccaria's perspective, we are to use punishment for just that, punishment, not for purposes of reformation of the criminal. Members of society are responsible for their actions, and therefore it logically follows that there are no mitigating circumstances or excuses that are acceptable.

There are many specific influences that Beccaria's work had on our present-day justice system. The notion of free will was a guiding principal of the Classical School. The concept of free will—that individuals were responsible for their own behavior and therefore punishment was an appropriate response if a person transgressed the law—has helped develop the due process model, the right to counsel, the determination of guilt, and the use of punishment for those found guilty. Although citizens give up certain rights to the state in exchange for certain services provided by the state (the essence of the social contract), citizens still retain a "natural" right of life. Beccaria was therefore opposed to the use of the death penalty, and this argument of the "natural right to life" was taken up by many and has been considered by the Supreme Court. If a citizen violates a criminal law promulgated by a legislature, the victim of the offense is considered a representative of society rather than an individual. The purpose of punishment is to deter both the individual who transgressed the law and the other citizens of society from similar behavior in the future. This approach to deterrence includes specific (the individual transgressor) and general (society at large) forms. Our society has incorporated the use of the concept of deterrence in our justice system today.

The Classical School was the dominant approach for approximately 100 years, with a tentative resurgence in the late 1960s, when a shift back to Classical School ideology was demonstrated in part by the adoption of determinate sentencing tactics and the reduction of emphasis on rehabilitation. Even though the Classical School of criminology is not in the forefront of the development of criminological thought today, it has left behind a legacy that we see in almost every aspect of our present-day justice system.

References

Barnes, Harry Elmer, and Howard Becker. 1952. *Social thought from lore to science.* Washington, DC: Dover Publications, Inc.

Beccaria, Cesare. 1963. *On crimes and punishments,* Henry Paolucci (trans.). New York: The Bobbs–Merrill Company Inc.

Bondanella, Peter, and Julia Bondanella. 1979. *Dictionary of Italian literature.* Westport, CT: Greenwood Press.

Monachesi, Elio. "Cesare Beccaria" in Hermann Mannheim (Ed.), *Pioneers in criminology.* 2nd ed. Montclair, NJ: Patterson Smith.

Paolucci, Henry (trans.). 1963. *On crimes and punishments,* by Cesare Beccaria. New York: The Bobbs–Merrill Company Inc.

Phillipson, Coleman. 1970. *Three criminal law reformers.* Montclair, NJ: Patterson Smith.

Taylor, Ian, Paul Walton, and Jock Young. 1973. *The new criminology.* New York: Harper and Row Publishers.

Vold, George B., and Thomas J. Bernard. 1986. *Theoretical criminology.* 3rd ed. New York: Oxford University Press.

Supplemental Readings

Jenkins, Philip. Varieties of enlightenment criminology: Beccaria, Godwin, de Sade. *Br. J. Criminol.* 24(2):112–30.

Maestro, Marcello. 1942. *Voltaire and Beccaria as reformers of criminal law.* New York: Columbia University Press.

———. 1973. *Cesare Beccaria and the origins of penal reform.* Philadelphia: Temple University Press.

Monroe, Paul (ed.). 1911. *A cyclopedia of education.* New York: The Macmillan Company.

Rothman, David J. 1971. *The discovery of the asylum.* Boston: Little, Brown and Company.

Venturi, Franco. 1972. *Italy and the Enlightenment.* New York: New York University Press.

Walker, David M. 1980. *The Oxford companion to law.* New York: Oxford University Press.

Williams, Frank P., and Marilyn D. McShane. 1988. *Criminological theory.* Englewood Cliffs, NJ: Prentice Hall.

CHAPTER 2
CESARE LOMBROSO: 1835–1909

INTRODUCTION

Although today many of Cesare Lombroso's ideas have fallen on hard times, he is still credited with making extensive and major contributions to the development of criminological thought. A close examination of his work—as well as the works of his pupils, collaborators, and supporters—reveals the extraordinary and long-reaching influence of his ideas. Lombroso caused a shift of focus from that of the crime, which the theorists of the Classical School emphasized, to that of the criminal, the focus of the Positive School. The magnitude of this contribution should not be underestimated—Lombroso was at the forefront of a radical development in criminological thought. If Lombroso contributed little else, he has still earned the right to be recognized as one of the pillars of criminological thought.

I. BIOGRAPHICAL SKETCH

Born in Verona, Italy, in 1835, Cesare Lombroso was the second of five children born to Aron Lombroso, whose family can be "traced back to a colony of North African Jews" (Kurella 1910, 1), and Zefira Levi, who came from a "rich family engaged in the higher branch of industrial life" (Kurella 1910, 3). At the time of Lombroso's birth, Verona was under Austrian rule. This was a fortuitous situation for the Lombroso family; because of Austrian rule, Cesare was permitted to attend the Gymnasium, a school operated by the Jesuits. Had Verona been under Italian rule, it is likely that as a Jew, Lombroso would not have been able to attend school.

From the evidence concerning his family, it appears that his mother was the dominant parental force in his life. Zefira Lombroso was an extremely ambitious individual who placed great emphasis on education for all her children (Wolfgang 1973, 233). Cesare did not disappoint his mother and pursued his education with vigor. By the time he was fifteen, he had written two papers demonstrating his interest in history: the first, entitled "Essay on History of the Roman Republic," and the second, "Sketches of Ancient Agriculture in Italy" (Wolfgang 1973, 233). He attended the University of Pavia from 1852 to 1854 and the University of Vienna from 1855 to 1856. In 1858, he received his medical degree from the University of Pavia, and in 1859, his specialty degree in surgery from the University of Genoa (Wolfgang 1973). Even though he was a good student, he did not readily embrace the accepted doctrines of the day. Possessing what has been described as a "distinctive temperament" (Kurella 1910, 4) that is believed to have stemmed from his youth, Lombroso often opposed the doctrines that were "professed at the Universities by the sons of the well-to-do" (Kurella 1910, 4).

At thirty-four, Lombroso married his first wife, Alexandra, with whom he had two daughters, Gina and Paola. Not much has been written about Alexandra, but it is known that Paola was named after Lombroso's close friend and mentor Paola Marzolo, who influenced Lombroso to go to medical school. Paola married M. Carrara, a professor and physician. Lombroso's other daughter, Gina, was responsible for a translation of his *L'Uomo Delinquent* (*Criminal Man,* written in English specifically for an American audience), for which Lombroso wrote a preface. Gina married William Ferrero, the author of *History of the Roman Empire,* who in part because of his relationship with Cesare Lombroso, collaborated with him to write *The Female Offender.*

During the course of his life, Lombroso held numerous positions, including army physician, alienist (forerunner of the modern-day psychiatrist), and university professor in the fields of medical jurisprudence, psychiatry, and, just before his death, anthropology. Soon after his graduation from medical school, Lombroso volunteered for a career in the army as a physician. It was during his work in the army that he arrived, albeit indirectly, at his theory of criminal anthropology. Because he had considerable time on his hands as an army physician, Lombroso began measuring and observing more than 3,000 soldiers. His original intent was to determine if there were any significant differences in the soldiers that might be traced to the regions of Italy they came from. Ultimately, however, his investigation took an unanticipated turn. During the course of his observations (Wolfgang 1973), he found that there was a positive correlation between soldiers who had tattoos and soldiers who were involved in violation of military and civilian rules and laws. When Lombroso developed his theory of criminal behavior, this apparent correlation between tattooing and unlawful behavior became part of that theory.

Wolfgang reports that when Lombroso was stationed in Pavia during his stint as an army physician, he received permission to "study clinically the mental patients in the hospital of St. Euphemia" (1972, 235). His work as an alienist at St. Euphemia was later incorporated into his lectures on mental illness.

Lombroso received his first professorial appointment in legal medicine and public hygiene at the University of Turin in 1876. In 1880, he established the journal *Archivio di Psichiatria e Anthropologia Criminale* with Garofalo and Ferri, and in 1896, he received an appointment as professor of psychiatry and clinical psychiatry. His final professorial appointment, in 1906, was in the field of criminal anthropology (Wolfgang 1973). That same year, Lombroso was honored by the French Government with the Legion of Honor Medal.

In the United States, Lombroso was held in high regard. In 1908, Professor John Wigmore, first president of the American Institute of Criminal Law and Criminology, offered Lombroso the position of Harris Lecturer at Northwestern University for the academic year 1909–10. However, because of his age and ill health, Lombroso was unable to accept the position (Wolfgang 1973).

On October 19, 1909, at 5 A.M., Lombroso died as a result of cardiac complications. As he had requested, his body was taken to the University of Turin, where an autopsy was performed and "his brain . . . placed in the Institute of Anatomy" (Wolfgang 1973, 241).

II. BASIC ASSUMPTIONS

Lombroso grew up at a time when many of the basic assumptions under which humankind had been operating were being questioned. From the middle to the late 1800s, society was undergoing a period of great intellectual growth. As an avid student, Lombroso was exposed to many of the new ideas through some of his contacts as well as through many of the works he read.

One of the earliest individuals, outside of his immediate family, to have a strong, positive influence on his intellectual development and career was Paola Marzolo, a philosopher and physician. In 1851, Marzolo and Lombroso met because of a review Lombroso had written about Marzolo's book, *An Introduction to Historical Monuments Revealed by an Analysis of Words.* Lombroso's review was brought to the attention of Marzolo, who was so impressed with the review that he decided to visit Lombroso, only to be surprised to discover that Lombroso was a mere child of sixteen. A friendship grew between the boy and Marzolo, and because of the respect and friendship each felt for the other, Lombroso was influenced to pursue a career in medicine.

While in attendance at different universities in pursuit of his education, Lombroso came across two professors who helped mold and focus his thinking. At the University of Pavia, Lombroso was influenced by a Professor Bartolome Panizza, who, early in his career, had been an army surgeon and was now "widely known as a tetratologist and comparative anatomist" (Kurella 1910, 7). When Lombroso continued his studies at the University of Vienna, he met Professor Skoda, a "specialist in internal medicine" (Wolfgang 1973, 234). It was while studying at Vienna that Lombroso first established his interest in the subject of psychology.

Outside of the classroom, Lombroso's thinking was profoundly affected by a group of individuals he discovered mainly through reading, one of whom was Auguste Comte, credited with introducing the term *sociology.* Two works by Comte, *Positive Philosophy* (1830–42) and *Positive Polity* (1851–54), based in part on biology and in part on some of the work of F.J. Gall, were published during Lombroso's developmental years. Shortly afterward, Herbert Spencer published *First Principles* (1862), which tied the writings of the evolutionists to social thought (Wolfgang 1973).

Lombroso was also familiar with the writings of some of the followers of F.J. Gall, whose work was concerned with the qualities of the human skull. Gall was "the originator of the principles of the localization of the function of the brain and gave the first impulse to the scientific study of criminals" (Kurella 1910, 14). Included in this group were Despine, a French physiologist and physician; Morel, a French psychiatrist; Prichard, an English psychiatrist and anthropologist; and Nicolson and Thomson, English prison surgeons (Kurella 1910). Despine "made a thorough study of the psychology of the criminal and showed that the principal characteristics of the habitual criminal are idleness, irresolution, and lessened sensibility, both mental and physical" (Kurella 1910, 14). B.A. Morel's *Traite des Degenerescences* (*Treatise on Degeneracy*) was published in 1859. Although his work "lacked thorough analysis and was also destitute of a firm biological foundation" (Kurella 1910, 14), it did provide us with the concept and term *degeneration.* A second work by Morel, *Formation of Typology in Degeneracy* (1864), extended Morel's 1859 work on the relationship between heredity and environment. Prichard "was the first to detect what is typical in the outward appearance of old 'goal-birds,' and put forward, in explanation of confirmed criminality, the conception of moral insanity" (Kurella 1910, 16). Through their work in the field of criminal anthropology, these individuals helped develop some basic assumptions about "criminal man."

Still others influenced Lombroso, including the work of American Benjamin Rush, in which one finds the roots of the concept of moral insanity. Rush, a physician and one of the signers of the *Declaration of Independence,* wrote *The Influence of physical causes upon The Moral faculty in 1789, in which he discussed micronomia* (a weekend moral faculty) and *anomia* (the lack of moral faculty) (Lomboroso 1910, viii).

There has been considerable speculation as to what role, if any, Quetelet played in the development of Lombroso's thinking. Kurella points out that he has been unable to "ascertain precisely to what extent Lombroso was influenced by Quetelet" (1910, 10). Kurella speculates that Lombroso was probably not directly influenced by Quetelet, but that Quetelet's ideas reached Lombroso through the publication *Moral Statistik* by von Oettingen, which Lombroso was most likely familiar with. A Belgian, Quetelet was the first to take advantage of the criminal statistics that were beginning to become available in the 1820s. Quetelet challenged the concept of free will and, through his works, published in 1831, *Research on the Law of Growth in Man* and *Research on the Propensity for Crime at Different Ages* argued that group factors were important. Quetelet suggested that man is determined. Sir Leon Radzinowicz, in his work *Ideology and Crime,* discusses three other individuals who, most likely through their writings, contributed to Lombroso's intellectual development: Paul Broca, working in the field of anthropology, identified what was then a new area of study—the "natural history of man" (1966); Rudolf Virchow, who, in 1856, wrote *Cellular Pathology,* in which he "spoke of the evolution of man from lower animals, of organic regression, and of the fact that individuals may revert on a moral level to standards of lower animals, or at least to the stage of man's pre-history" (Wolfgang 1973, 243). Virchow created the term *thermorophism,* defined as "the presence in man of certain bodily peculiarities of one of the lower animals" (Kurella 1910, 12), which helped to draw Lombroso's attention to the idea of organic and moral regression of man. Finally, according to Radzinowicz, Lombroso was influenced by Hackel's work in the area of evolution. Hackel developed the evolutionary "law of recapitulation, according to which ontogeny recapitulates phylogeny" (Radzinowicz 1966, 48). By this, Hackel was indicating his belief that in an individual one can identify the developmental stages of more primitive forms of man, and that we can trace the development of man by studying the physical characteristics of his descendants. Published in 1856, *The Human Physiognomy,* written by Jean Baptists della Porte was one of the first to draw attention to the relationship between behavior and the physical characteristics of an individual. An example of the relationship described by Jean Baptists della Porte is that "a thief may be identifiable by his characteristically small ears and nose, bushy eyebrows, mobile eyes and sharp vision, lips that are large and remain open, plus long and slender fingers" (Jones 1986, 82). Although it is not possible to determine if Lombroso had ever read this work, or was even familiar with its particular conclusions, it probably had some influence on the thinking of the day and indirectly helped formulate some of Lombroso's basic assumptions about man. Along these same lines, in 1775, approximately 100 years before Lombroso wrote his first edition of *Criminal Man,* Hohan Casper Lavater published *Physiognomical Fragments.* In this four-volume text, Lavater addressed the issue of the "relationship between the parts of a person's face and their behavior" (Jones 1986, 82).

One basic assumption that it is clear Lombroso accepted and that helped direct much of his work was that man was determined. Lombroso did not accept the Classical School approach that assumed man has free will. "During his student days Lombroso found himself increasingly in disagreement with the free-will philosophy then current in academic circles" (Wolfgang 1973, 234). The assumption that man is determined would find its way into Lombroso's thinking as he expanded his intellectual base and began developing his own theoretical perspective. His disagreement with the notion of free will found its expression in his idea that "a man's mode of feeling, and therewith the actual conduct of his life, are determined by his physical constitution; and, on the other hand, that his constitution must find expression in his bodily structure" (Kurella 1910, 18). *Determinism,* a concept accepted by such prominent individuals as Schopenhauer and Quetelet, was also consistent with the materialist conception of history that was popular at the time; it is therefore not surprising that many of "his most distinguished pupils and collaborators" (Kurella 1910, 107) were supporters of Marxist doctrine.

Charles Darwin was one of the major influences on Lombroso's thinking and the formulation of his basic assumptions. As Radzinowicz puts it, "not least he was affected by the discoveries of Darwin himself" (1966, 48). Charles Darwin's work dramatically changed the medical and biological sciences. His *On the Origin of the Species,* published in 1859, advanced the theory of natural selection and survival of the fittest both between and within species. "He shocked the world with this declaration, because the Bible maintains that God created each order of life separately" (Jones 1986, 82). Darwin's second book, *The Descent of Man,* published in 1871, expanded Darwin's thinking as it related to evolution and linked man to the most primitive forms of life. This was even more of a shock, because "religious leaders . . . maintained God had created man in His own image" (Jones 1986, 82). *Expression of Emotion in Man and Animals,* published in 1872, was an extension of *The Descent of Man.* Darwin first used the term *atavistic man* that Lombroso developed into a cause of crime.

At the time that Darwin was writing there were other individuals who had developed thoughts along the same lines. Even if Lombroso had not been influenced by Darwin, which he must have been (Radzinowicz 1966), he could have been influenced by the work of T.H. Huxley. In 1863, Huxley wrote *Man's Place in Nature,* in which he stated that "the structural differences which separate Man from the Gorilla and the Chimpanzee are not so great as those which separate the Gorilla from the lower apes" (Wolfgang 1973, 243). The message of the time was clear: The concept of evolution was, at the least, widely talked about and debated, if not accepted. It is quite evident in Lombroso's work that he accepted many of the basic assumptions about man and evolution.

The contributions of Enrico Ferri and Raffaele Garofalo, two of Lombroso's students, to the development of positive criminology had a great influence on Lombroso: not only did Lombroso teach them, but they also, in turn, taught him. The nature of this intellectual relationship is evident in the fact that Lombroso focused on the anthropological aspects of the development of the Positive School, while Garofalo worked on the legal component and Ferri specialized in the sociological aspects. The work of these three men complemented each other and helped present a more cohesive and complete picture of the Positive School.

III. KEY IDEAS

Given the breadth and depth of Lombroso's writing, space limits the discussion here to present and discuss only a few of his key ideas. During the course of his professional career, he developed a number of important concepts, including the application of Darwin's concept of atavism to crime and the development of a typology. Arguably, Lombroso's most important contribution was that he helped shift the focus of investigation from the crime to the criminal, thereby influencing hundreds of individuals in their scholarly pursuits. When examining his key ideas, bear in mind the fact that Lombroso's thinking can be characterized as having changed and expanded over time, as shown with the increased size of each edition of *L'Uomo Delinquente.* When first published in 1876 it contained 252 pages. With each succeeding edition, the number of pages grew to the point that in 1896, with the fifth edition, there were three volumes covering almost 2,000 pages. To the fifth and final edition, Lombroso added 527 pages in the form of *Crime: Its Causes and Remedies,* a publication in its own right, but considered by some to be another volume of, or an appendix to, *L'Uomo Delinquente.*

In 1859, when Lombroso had finished his medical studies, he joined the Italian army as a physician. Stationed at Calabria, he was not very taxed by his work and had time to engage in pursuits of interest. During the four years he spent at Calabria, he studied approximately 3,000 soldiers, systematically measuring and observing each. It was because of these observations that Lombroso identified a relationship between those soldiers who had tattoos and those who engaged in criminal behavior. The identification of this relationship helped to stimulate Lombroso to continue his systematic observations of individuals.

From 1864 to 1872, Lombroso worked at various mental hospitals throughout Italy. He systematically observed mental patients in much the same way he had observed the soldiers. In 1876, he published the first edition of *L'Uomo Delinquente,* which had a resounding impact all over Europe. In *L'Uomo Delinquente,* Lombroso details his original thinking as it relates to the physical constitution of an individual and his behavior.

ATAVISM

Cesare Lombroso used the term *atavism* to characterize those individuals who had not fully evolved, individuals he called *throwbacks.* Darwin refers to *atavism,* or *throwbacks,* when he says that "some of the worst dispositions which occasionally without any assignable cause make their appearance in families may perhaps be reversions to a savage state, from which we are not removed by very many generations" (Wolfgang 1973, 247). Based on Lombroso's investigations and observations on criminals, he found that

> in the skulls and brains of criminals, but also in other parts of the skeleton, in the muscles, and in the viscera, we find anatomical peculiarities, which in some cases resemble the characters of the few authentic remnants of the earliest prehistoric beings, in other cases correspond to the characters of still extant lower races of mankind, and in yet others, correspond to the characters of some or all of the varieties of monkey. (Kurella 1910, 21)

Organic in nature, heredity, Lombroso concludes, is the principal cause of criminal tendencies. He addresses two forms of heredity, indirect and direct. *Indirect heredity* is the result of being born into a "generically degenerate family" (Lombroso 1918, 136). Examples of the manifestations of indirect heredity are insanity, deafness, syphilis, epilepsy, and alcoholism. *Direct heredity,* as used by Lombroso, is when one is born into a family with criminal parentage. Direct heredity can be aggravated by the environment as well as the education a person receives. As well as the physical anomalies that a person evidences, there is also the demonstration of primitive man mentality. Wolfgang points out in his work on Lombroso that

> [t]he concept of atavism (from Latin: *atavus*, ancestor, great-great-grandfather's father; from *avus*, grandfather) postulated a reversion to a primitive or subhuman type of man, characterized physically by a variety of inferior morphological features reminiscent of apes and lower primates, occurring in the more simian fossil men and to some extent preserved in modern "savages." (1972, 246)

TYPES OF CRIMINALS

Lombroso developed a typology of criminals that included four general types: the born criminal, the criminal by passion, the insane criminal, and the occasional criminal. Within the category of occasional criminal Lombroso delineated four subgroups—the pseudo-criminal, the criminaloid, the habitual criminal, and the epileptoid. In addition to his discussion of each of the types of criminals, Lombroso offered some observations about criminals in general, positing that in terms of "natural affections, the criminal rarely, if ever experiences emotions of this kind and least of all regarding his own kin . . . . On the other hand, he shows exaggerated and abnormal fondness for animals and strangers" (Lombroso 1911, 27). Without the normal emotions of affection for his kin, the criminal "is dominated by a few absorbing passions: vanity, impulsiveness, desire for revenge, [and] licentiousness" (Lombroso 1911, 28). Criminals do not repent or show remorse unless there is some advantage to be gained by it.

The Born Criminal

Although Lombroso used and made familiar the term *born criminal,* credit goes to Enrico Ferri for originating the term. According to Gina Lombroso-Ferrero, who translated some of her father's work, born criminals represent approximately one-third of all offenders (1911), and the born criminal is both a moral imbecile and an epileptic: "The connection between epilepsy and crime is one of derivation rather than identity. Epilepsy represents the genus of which criminality and moral insanity are the species" (Lombroso-Ferrero 1911, 69). According to Lombroso, the born criminal has the same "anatomical, skeletal, physiognomical, psychological, and moral characteristics peculiar to the recognized forms of epilepsy, and sometimes also its motorial phenomena although at rare intervals" (Lombroso-Ferrero 1911, 69).

The Criminal by Passion

Although Lombroso's criminal by passion is more likely to be female than male, this category is distinguished not by gender, but by the high level of impetuousness and ferocity. This type of criminal commits a crime because she or he is "urged to . . . by a pure spirit of altruism" (Lombroso-Ferrero 1911, 115). Two examples of this type of criminal are the wife who kills her unfaithful husband and the brother who kills the man who raped his sister. Lombroso points out that criminals by passion often commit suicide after their crimes, and in this category, "homicide forms 91.0% of the criminality" (Lombroso-Ferrero 1911, 121). In terms of punishment, Lombroso argues, "[t]he true criminal of passion suffers more from remorse than from any penalty the law can inflict" (1911, 186).

The Insane Criminal

Those best qualified to be labeled *insane criminals* are kleptomaniacs, nymphomaniacs, habitual drunkards, and pederasts. Insane criminals commit crimes because of a "consequence of an alteration of the brain [which] makes them unable to discriminate between right and wrong" (Lombroso 1911, 74). For Lombroso, these individuals are truly insane and without "responsibility for their actions" (1911, 74). As he does with many of the other categories of criminals, Lombroso identifies a number of types of the insane criminal: the idiot, the imbecile, those experiencing melancholia and dementia, and those "afflicted with general paralysis" (1911, 74–75).

The Occasional Criminal

The broadest and most inclusive category for Lombroso is the *occasional criminal*, which includes four types: the pseudo-criminal, the criminaloid, the habitual criminal, and the epileptoid. The category of occasional criminal is extremely broad and encompasses a large number of criminal types. In *Crime: Its Causes and Remedies*, Lombroso characterizes occasional criminals as "those who do not seek the occasion for the crime, but are almost drawn into it, or fall into the meshes of the code for very insignificant reasons" (1918, 376). For Lombroso, individuals who fall into this category may not show signs of atavism or epilepsy.

Pseudo-criminals   An example of the pseudo-criminal is one who kills in self-defense. The pseudo-criminal can also be called the *juridical criminal*—someone who is not really a criminal in the sense that most of the other types are. Juridical criminals "break the law, not because of any natural depravity, nor owing to distressing circumstances, but by mere accident" (Lombroso 1911, 115). In the case of the pseudo- or juridical criminal, there is a deficiency in the law that allows or causes the individual to be labeled a criminal. In general, these individuals do not cause a great concern for society.

Criminaloid   *Criminaloids* are epileptoids who "suffer from a milder form of the disease so that without some adequate cause criminality is not manifested" (Lombroso 1911, 101). Individuals with weak natures who can be swayed to good or evil depending on the circumstances are potential criminaloids, and often show hesitation "before committing a crime, especially the first time" (Lombroso 1911, 105). When apprehended, these individuals are quick to confess without much pressure being placed on them, and often "manifest deep repugnance towards common offenders" (Lombroso 1911, 105). Depending on circumstances, criminaloids can become habitual criminals. Lombroso suggests that in the case of the criminaloid, and especially when the offense is minor, a fine is the appropriate punishment. If the offender is unable to afford the fine, then some form of compulsory labor would be appropriate. Lombroso is opposed to any term of imprisonment for the criminaloid who is convicted of a minor offense; instead, he believes that bringing "this type of offender into contact with habitual criminals not only does not serve as a deterrent, but generally has an injurious effect, because it tends to lessen respect for the law, and in the case of recidivists to rob punishment of all its terror" (1911, 187).

Habitual Criminals   *Habitual criminals* are defined as "individuals who regard systematic violation of the law in the light of an ordinary trade or occupation and commit their offenses with indifference" (Lombroso 1911, 111). Examples of this type of criminal include those convicted of theft, fraud, arson, forgery, and blackmail. Lombroso suggests if the individuals who commit these crimes are insane, they must be placed in lunatic asylums; otherwise, deportation is an appropriate punishment.

Toward the end of his publishing career, Lombroso showed how his thinking had evolved when he stated that "[e]very crime has its origins in a multiplicity of causes, often intertwined and confused, each of which we must in obedience to the necessities of thought and speech, investigate singly" (Lombroso 1918, 1). On the subject of crime prevention, in the introduction to *Crime: Its Causes and Remedies*, Lombroso states,

> [t]he statesman . . . , who wishes to prevent crime ought to be eclectic and not limit himself to a single course of action. He must guard against the dangerous effects of wealth no less than against those of poverty, against the corrupting influence of education not less than against that of ignorance. (1918, xxxv)

In addition to atavism as the basis for crime, Lombroso expanded his thinking to include degeneracy. In fact, Lombroso "even admitted that an entirely normal person could become a criminal by passion or a pseudo-criminal under exceptional circumstances" (Jones 1986, 87).

RAFFAELE GAROFALO AND ENRICO FERRI

Two of Lombroso's students, Enrico Ferri and Raffaele Garofalo, became famous in their own right. Each of these men joined Lombroso and studied with him; in the end, the three became colleagues, learning from and teaching each other. As indicated earlier, Garofalo generally viewed things from a legalistic perspective, Ferri primarily from a sociological perspective, and Lombroso from an anthropological perspective.

Raffaele Garofalo

Baron Raffaele Garofalo was born in 1852 in Naples, to a family of Spanish origin, and was educated to become a magistrate. During the course of his life, Garofalo held positions as a lawyer, prosecutor, and magistrate. In addition, Garofalo served as professor of criminal law and procedure at the University of Naples. By 1909, Garofalo had published five books, the best known being his 1885 work, *Criminology,* which was originally begun as a brochure entitled "Concerning a Positive Criterion of Punishment" (1880). Garofalo is the individual who "pioneered the concept of social defense" (Jones 1986, 94), and the concept of "natural crime." He posited that when the initial sentencing of an offender is to take place, it is necessary to determine if the "offender's 'elimination' is necessary for the safety of the community and, if so, if it has to be permanent or only temporary" (Jones 1986, 94). For Garofalo, elimination included death, transportation and imprisonment, as well as exclusion from the offender's trade or profession. This last was thought to be useful in reducing recidivism if the offense was something like embezzlement.

In *Criminology,* Garofalo indicates that there is a quandary because of the "task of definition [of crime] they have left to the jurists, without attempting to say whether or not criminality from the legal standpoint is coterminous with criminality from the sociologic point of view" (1914, 3–4). Garofalo suggests that it would be more fruitful if one pursued "the sociologic notion of crime" (1914, 4), because all that the jurists have done is lump together some behaviors and identified them as crimes. Garofalo calls for the concept of *natural crime,* which he defines as

> that which is not conventional, of that which exists in a human society independently of the circumstances and exigencies of a given epoch or the particular views of the lawmakers. . . . [N]atural crime . . . designate[s] those acts which no civilized society can refuse to recognize as criminal and repress by means of punishment. (1914, 4–5).

Garofalo calls for a definition of natural crime that transcends individual human variations, that is not dependent on a particular situation, and is not susceptible to economic or political factors. One should use sentiments, not facts, to determine which acts are natural. According to Garofalo, if one uses facts as evidence that a specific act was always viewed or not always viewed as a crime, one must abandon the concept of natural crime, because it would be impossible to demonstrate the existence of natural crime. Every act, regardless of how offensive, has at least at one time been considered not only acceptable behavior, but appropriate. In *Criminology,* Garofalo cites as numerous examples acts of murder that were indeed accepted as appropriate. Therefore, to be able to use the concept of natural crime, it is necessary to use the concept of an offense to the elementary moral sentiment of society as the identifying factor of eligibility. Of course, those acts that are defined as *crimes* by a government are far greater in number than those included in his definition of natural crime. Garofalo's definition of *natural crime* can therefore be criticized for defining crime in a way that is too limiting. In part, Garofalo averts this criticism because of the specific function he identifies for his concept. "[T]he chief function of the natural crime concept is to delimit the area of conduct of major, perhaps exclusive, concern to the scientific criminologist" (Allen 1973, 322).

For an act to be a crime in the concept of natural crime, it is necessary that the crime be clearly harmful to society, as well as offensive to the basic moral sentiments of pity and probity. *Pity* is the "repugnance to acts which produce physical pain" (Garofalo 1914, 23). As for the sentiment of *probity,* Garofalo finds this in "as the adult persons of a civilized race . . . [who] possess generally, as a result of heredity and tradition, a certain instinct which restrains them from taking by fraud or violence that which does not belong to them" (1914, 31). For Garofalo, pity and probity are sentiments as universal as any that one can identify. Specifically, in terms of the level of these moral sentiments that must be offended for the offense to be included as a natural crime, Garofalo speaks to the average person of society.

Although Lombroso and Ferri emphasized physiological anomalies in their work, Garofalo chose to focus on psychic anomalies. For Garofalo, the criminal was "one who lacked the proper development of the altruistic sensibility—a sensibility that has an organic basis and is not the result of environmental or economic factors" (Pelfrey 1980, 9). Garofalo identified four types of criminals: (1) murderers, (2) violent criminals, (3) criminals deficient in probity, and (4) lascivious criminals.

In the first type, murderers, there is absolutely no altruism of any kind. In fact, what is present is complete egoism, to the extent that there can be no altruism. Because the sentiment for justice exists at a higher level than that of pity and probity, this sentiment is not evident in these individuals. Garofalo writes that the murderer kills "to satisfy his greed for money, . . . to put out of the way an incriminating witness, to avenge a fancied or insignificant wrong, or even to exhibit his physical dexterity, his sure eye, . . . to display his contempt for the police, or his hatred for men of another class" (1914, 111–12). Garofalo's scale peaks with the murderer, also known as the *assassin*. Jones (1986) describes this class of individuals as extreme criminals who are "wholly destitute of moral sense . . . too improvident, too brutalized, of too little sensibility, to appreciate the disgrace of prison or to feel the suffering, moral rather than physical, which loss of liberty entails" (1986, 95).

Garofalo separates the second type, violent criminals, into two subtypes: the endemic criminals and the passional criminals. Violent criminals, both the endemic and passional subtypes, are "characterized by lack of benevolence or pity" (Garofalo 1914, 112). The *endemic criminal* is one involved in those crimes that are specific to a geographic region. Garofalo cites the "vendettas of the Neopolitan Camorrists or the political assassinations of the Russian Nihilists" (1914, 112). For Garofalo, the environment exerts a strong influence on this type of criminal. One example he cites is in *Criminology*: "In the South of Italy there are people who believe that sexual intercourse with a virgin is a cure for venereal disease. It is this belief which accounts for many cases of rape" (Garofalo 1914, 114). In another instance, Garofalo points out that "[i]n France, within a comparatively recent period, it became quite common for women betrayed by their lovers to have recourse to vitriol for the purposes of disfigurement—a practice which at times seems to have assumed the proportions of an epidemic" (1914, 114). In terms of this specific type of criminal, Garofalo acknowledges that imitation plays a role. Although on this point he does not reference Gabriel Tarde as a source, it is clear that he is aware of Tarde and some of Tarde's work, because at an earlier point in *Criminology,* he refutes some statements made by Tarde. Garofalo is of the opinion that it was possible that "harsh punishments for this class of offender may be counterproductive" (Jones 1986, 96).

Garofalo suggests that the second type of violent criminals, those who commit crimes under the influence of passion, may be habitual criminals, or their crimes "may be the result of external causes, such as alcoholic liquors, high temperature, or even circumstances of a really extraordinary nature which are calculated to arouse the anger of any person" (1914, 115–16). Although these external factors can have a role in causing one to be a passional criminal, it is still the case that "there is always present in the instincts of the true criminal, a specific element which is congenital or inherited, or else acquired in early infancy and become inseparable from his psychic organism" (Allen 1973, 327).

For the third type of criminal, those deficient in probity (crimes against property), "social factors are much more influential" (Garofalo 1914, 125) than in murderers and violent criminals. Even though the influence of environmental factors is great, the existence "in the criminal's organism [of] an element which preexists any effect of environmental influence" (Garofalo 1914, 125–26) is most probable.

Lascivious criminals constitute Garofalo's fourth type of criminal. This class of criminals commits crimes because of sexual impulse. Garofalo points out that often these individuals are identified as violent criminals, but if "an extreme degree of lasciviousness is the sole motive of the offense" (Garofalo 1914, 130), then the individual would be classified as this fourth type. According to Garofalo, lascivious criminals commit crimes because of a "lack of moral energy rather than [an] absence of [the] sentiment of pity" (1914, 130).

In addition to formulating his typology, Garofalo also wrote about the value of juries. He was in opposition to the use of trial juries. Garofalo believed that a trial should be held only before a judge, and that the judge, not a jury, is in the best position to evaluate the evidence and render a just decision. Juries, however, often represent "popular biases and ignorance" (Jones 1986, 96). Sometimes juries, in spite of overwhelming evidence of guilt, return a verdict of not guilty. Garofalo was cognizant of this, and viewed it as a possible protest against government. For Garofalo, "the only way to reform the jury is to abolish it" (Jones 1986, 97).

Enrico Ferri

Ferri was born on February 25, 1856, in San Benedetto Po, Mantua, Italy. His family was not as well off as Garofalo's; Ferri's father was a shopkeeper, a seller of tobacco and salt. Ferri distinguished himself in his early educational years, but did so almost in spite of himself. He studied only those subjects that interested him. At one point in his education, Ferri expressed a desire to change schools, but initially failed the entrance exams and was denied transfer. When he did successfully transfer, he was regularly truant and was threatened with expulsion. Ferri's father took him out of school and "threatened to put him to manual labor" (Sellin 1973, 362). Enrico got the message and went back to school (the Liceo Virgilio) after one week. Although he apparently avoided the threat of expulsion, Ferri still maintained much of his independence and still studied only that which interested him. Ferri followed this approach to the extent that "he simply ignored the requirement in Greek and was forced to cheat in his final examination for the diploma" (Sellin 1973, 363).

As for Ferri's intellectual stimulation, while he was at the Liceo Virgilio, Robert Ardigo, a philosopher who had given up the ministry, probably was his greatest influence. Ardigo had recently published a book entitled *Psychology as a Positive Science.*

For the first two years of college at the University of Bologna, Ferri behaved much as he had at the Liceo Virgilio. He missed classes, and spent most of his time involved in "extracurricular" activities. However, Ferri became a student of Pietro Ellero, a professor of criminal law, and finally, in his third year, he began serious study. It was during this time that he developed his thesis topic on the subject of free will. It was Ferri's contention that "the concept of free will, implicit in the current criminal law, was a fiction" (Sellin 1973, 363). For Ferri, it was the concept of social or legal responsibility that should take precedence over free will. Based on the quality of the defense of his thesis, Ferri was awarded a scholarship that he used to study under Francesco Carrara at the University of Pisa. Proud of his thesis, in 1879, Ferri sent a copy of it to Lombroso, who, on reviewing it, proclaimed that it was not positive enough (Jones 1986, Sellin 1973).

The defense of his thesis brought Ferri a "traveling scholarship," which took him to France to study in Paris. While in Paris, Ferri published *Studies of Criminality in France from 1826–1878.* In addition, he published a review of Lombroso's *L'Uomo Delinquente* in *Revista Europea.* In 1879, Ferri returned to Italy and began his studies under Lombroso's tutelage at the University of Turin. Although his stay at Turin was brief, Ferri developed a lasting relationship with Lombroso that was to influence him throughout the remainder of his life.

Staying only one year in Turin, Ferri left to accept an appointment as a professor of Criminal Law at the University of Bologna, his alma mater. In 1882, he accepted an appointment as a professor at the University of Siena, a position he held for four years. While at Siena, Ferri published *The Homicide* in 1884 and did the majority of the revision work on *I Nuovi Orrizonti del Diritto e della Procedura Penale (The New Right and Criminal Proceedings in Orrizonti).* Published as a second edition in 1884, he changed the title to *Criminal Sociology* (Jones 1986) and made one of his most important contributions: the concept of *the law of criminal saturation,* which Ferri defined as "the level of crime each year is determined by the different conditions of the physical and social environment combined with the congenital tendencies and accidental impulses of individuals, in accordance with a law, which, in analogy to the law of chemistry" (Jones 1986, 99).

In 1884, Ferri married Camilla Guarnieri and they had two sons and a daughter. In 1886, Ferri defended a number of individuals from his home province of Mantua who "were being prosecuted for incitement to civil war" (Sellin 1973, 373). Two months after his presentation in court won the acquittal of his clients, Ferri was elected to the Italian Parliament. He moved to Rome with his family and continued to serve in Parliament until 1924. By this time Ferri, according to his own later analysis, had accepted and incorporated many aspects of Marxist doctrine into his thinking, writing, and presentations. In 1925, when reviewing his 1886 defense speech, Ferri concluded that "already then, in 1886, I was a Marxist without knowing it" (Sellin 1973, 373).

In 1890, Ferri was offered and accepted the chair of criminal law at the University of Pisa. Ferri was to replace Francesco Carrara, a man with whom Ferri had had numerous intellectual debates when he was a student of Carrara's at Pisa. While holding the chair, Ferri started a journal entitled *La Scuola Positiva,* and held the position of editor or served on the editorial board until his death. The journal served as a vehicle for the publication of positivist manuscripts. Because of his Marxist views, however, Ferri held the chair for only three years before he was forced out.

Ferri set forth his doctrine of criminal causation in 1881 with the publication of his *Studies in Criminality in France in 1876–1878.* The doctrine "consists of the recognition of three different sets of factors in crime: namely those in the physical or geographical environment, those in the constitution of the individual, and those in the social environment" (Ferri 1917, xxxi). Ferri's three categories of criminal causation have been referred to as the anthropological, the physical, and the social. The anthropological factors include sex, age, race, organic constitution, and anomalies, whether physical or mental, acquired or hereditary. Physical factors are represented by climate, temperature, fertility of the soil, meteorical conditions, and so on. For social factors, Ferri included economic and civil status, profession, social rank, density of population, customs, religion, education, and so on.

Originally, in *The Homicide–Suicide,* Ferri outlined four types of criminals. To the original four, Ferri added fifth and sixth types of criminals when he published later editions of *Criminal Sociology.* The original four types, which were very similar to those of Lombroso, were born or instinctive criminal, the insane criminal, the passional criminal, and the occasional criminal (Jones 1986). The fifth type of criminal, the habitual criminal, was added soon after Ferri presented his original four types. The sixth type of criminal, the involuntary criminal, was not added to the classification system until the fifth edition of *Criminal Sociology.* These six criminal types each had distinctive features.

Born Criminal   The *born criminal,* a term coined by Ferri but popularized by Lombroso, is someone who, because of an unfortunate situation regarding his or her parents who are criminals or alcoholics, is more likely to respond to criminal stimuli.

Insane Criminal The *insane criminal* suffers from "mental disease or a neuropsychopathic condition" (Sellin 1973, 369).

Passional Criminal There are two varieties of the *passional criminal;* the first is the criminal by passion, someone who suffers from a "prolonged and chronic mental state" (Sellin 1973, 369). The second type of passional criminal is one who suffers from the sort of emotional outburst that is "explosive and unexpected" (Sellin 1973, 369).

Occasional Criminal For Ferri, the *occasional criminal* represents the vast majority of those who commit crimes. These individuals commit crimes because of "family and social milieu" (Sellin 1973, 369). These individuals, in terms of their psychological makeup, are not very different from those who do not commit crimes.

Habitual Criminal The *habitual criminal* commits crimes because of the social environment. For the habitual criminal, the commission of crime becomes an acquired habit. From an early age, the individual grows up in an environment that is represented by poverty, poor education, and bad companions. When this individual first enters jail, he or she has contact with individuals who are considerably worse in terms of criminal behavior, and he or she acquires the habits of criminals. Because of the problems associated with reintegration, oftentimes these individuals decide to make crime their trade.

Involuntary Criminal Ferri does not discuss the sixth criminal type, the *involuntary criminal,* extensively. It appears that this type was not fully integrated into the text because Ferri failed to change references in other places in the text to reflect the addition of a sixth criminal type. In the one location he did identify the involuntary criminal, he indicated that they "are pseudo-criminals who cause damage and peril by their lack of foresight, imprudence, negligence or disobedience of regulations rather than through malice" (Sellin 1973, 370).

It should be noted that although they are both classified as positivists, Garofalo did not agree with the classification system proposed by Ferri. In Rome in 1885, at the first Congress of Criminal Anthropology, Garofalo stated that Ferri's "classification is without scientific basis and lacks homogeneity and exactness" (Garofalo 1914, 132). Garofalo also questioned the existence of a criminal type labeled *habitual criminal.* The criticism was based on the belief that "from the anthropologic point of view, it may be said that there is no such thing as a class of habitual offenders" (Garofalo 1914, 132). Needless to say, Ferri was relatively undaunted by Garofalo's criticisms.

The concept of criminal saturation and his classification system were built on the premise that man does not have "free will." Ferri was a strong proponent of the idea that man is determined and that free will is not an operative concept. When it came to the corrections system, Ferri believed that prisons needed to be places where "the obligation to work must be universal and absolute" (Jones 1986, 103). Prisons were not to be places of ease.

Toward the end of his career, Ferri was tapped by Ludovico Mortara, the Minister of Justice, to develop a new criminal code for Italy. Mortara was a former schoolmate of Ferri's at the Liceo Virgilio. Heading the commission gave Ferri the opportunity to put into practice many of the thoughts he had concerning positivist criminal justice. When the final product was placed before the Italian Chamber of

Deputies for consideration in 1921, it was rejected because it differed sharply from Beccaria's doctrines. It should be noted that Benito Mussolini came to power in 1922, and shortly after Mussolini became prime minister, the Ferri Draft failed. "With the failure of the Ferri Draft in 1922, one may argue, the Italian school of positivist criminology ceased to have much of an impact except among its most ardent proponents" (Jones 1986, 105).

IV. CRITIQUE

There have been numerous critiques of the works of the positivists, particularly those of Lombroso. Whereas some of the criticisms are based on methodological flaws, others are grounded in basic philosophical disagreements. One criticism that has been echoed by many who have read Lombroso's works is that he did not use a control group (Shoemaker 1984). The failure to use a group of noncriminals for comparison purposes is a flaw that brings into question many of Lombroso's findings. Lombroso also did not demonstrate adequately that there are any "direct connections between physical features and criminality" (Shoemaker 1984, 16).

One of the critiques identified by many who question the positive school is *The English Convict: A Statistical Study,* by Charles Buckman Goring, published in 1913. Goring criticized the methods used by Lombroso more than he did the theoretical base. The statistical analysis completed by Goring had no theoretical base of its own. The study was designed solely for the purpose of testing Lombroso's conclusions. To this end, Goring tested a substantial number of variables and their relation to crime. Goring concluded that Lombroso's work represented "an organized system of self-evident confusion whose parallel is only to be found in the astrology, alchemy, and other credulities of the Middle Ages" (Jones 1986, 107).

Goring writes that "[t]he preconceived, and in our opinion, totally unfounded, Lombrosian notion that criminality is a specific condition of mind or soul: is a definite state of psychical instability" (1972, 15). For Goring, the rejection of Lombroso's work is

> directed not against conclusions, but against the methods by which they were reached. We cannot presuppose, at the outset, the invalidity of these dogmas, nor make any judgment upon the extent of their falsity or their truth: we can only assert that, since they were arrived at by unscientific means, they must not be accepted without further investigation. (1972, 19)

It should be noted that E.A. Hooton attacked Goring's work and in turn was a proponent of Lombroso's work. As would be expected, Hooten's work has also been questioned, leaving the definitive answer unformulated at this time.

Thorsten Sellin, writing later, suggested that some of the difficulty with the tenets of the Positive School were the result of the "ease with which it fits into totalitarian patterns of government" (Vold and Bernard 1986, 42). Generally, at the time the positivists were writing, specifically Ferri, the shift toward socialism was gaining momentum. The fact that the similarities in thinking between the two orientations were so great did not enhance the acceptance of the Positive School.

Leonard Savitz "maintained that Lombroso's theories met with such great success because they coincided with the rise of Social Darwinism which justified racism and inequality on the basis of evolutionary principles" (Vold and Bernard 1986, 40).

In summary, most modern theorists have given short shrift to Lombroso's work and the works of the other members of the Positive School. Lombroso is covered in all criminology theory texts, but only because of his place in the development of criminological thought, not for any contribution that is relevant today. In fact, the work of people like Ferri, Garofalo, and Lombroso has had both a large and a direct impact on the function of the criminal justice system. A deterministic approach that called for the use of the indeterminate sentence, the concern for treatment, and the social definition of crime are hallmarks of the Positive School. If one looks at the concepts of probation and parole and their origins, they can be viewed as results of the influence of the Positive School. The whole focus on treatment/rehabilitation with specific programs in job training, remedial education, alcoholism and drug counseling, and therapy are all examples of the direct impact the Positive School has had on our justice system. In addition, the development of the juvenile court as a separate entity from adult criminal court and a minimum age necessary to be charged with a criminal act are outgrowths of the work of Lombroso, Ferri, and Garofalo. It is the opinion of this author that one of the most important contributions, if not the most important, by Lombroso is that he caused a shift in focus from the study of the crime to the study of the criminal. This shift has dominated theoretical orientations since it was first promulgated.

It was Thorsten Sellin who best sums up Lombroso's work: "[A]ny scholar who succeeds in driving hundreds of fellow students to search for the truth and whose ideas after half a century possess vitality, merits an honorable place in the history of thought" (1937, 896–97).

References

Allen, Francis A. 1973. Raffaele Garofalo. In *Pioneers in criminology.* 2nd ed. Hermann Mannheim (ed.). Montclair, NJ: Patterson Smith.

Ferri, Enrico. 1917. *Criminal sociology.* Boston: Little, Brown and Company.

Garofalo, Raffaele. 1914. *Criminology.* Robert Millar (trans.). Boston: Little, Brown and Company.

Goring, Charles. 1972. *The English convict: A statistical study.* Montclair, NJ: Patterson Smith. (First published in 1913 by His Majesty's Stationary Office, London, England.)

Jones, David A. 1986. *History of criminology: A philosophical perspective.* New York: Greenwood Press.

Kurella, Hans. 1910. *Cesare Lombroso: A modern man of science.* M. Eden Paul (trans.). New York: Rebman Company.

Lombroso, Cesare. 1918. *Crime: Its causes and remedies.* Henry P. Horton (trans.). Boston: Little, Brown and Company.

———. 1910. *Criminal man (L'uomo delinquente).* Gina Lombroso-Ferrero (trans.). Montclair, NJ: Patterson Smith (republished 1972).

Lombroso, Cesare, and William Ferrero. 1958. *The female offender.* New York: Philosophical Library Inc.

Pelfrey, William. 1980. *The evolution of criminology.* Cincinnati: Anderson Publishing Company.

Radzinowicz, Sir Leon. 1966. *Ideology and crime.* New York: Columbia University Press.

Sellin, Thorsten. 1973. Enrico Ferri. In *Pioneers in criminology.* 2nd ed. Hermann Mannheim (ed.). Montclair, NJ: Patterson Smith.

———. 1937. Letter to the editor. *Am. J. Sociol.* 42:6, 896–99.

Shoemaker, Donald J. 1984. *Theories of delinquency.* New York: Oxford University Press.

Vold, George B., and Thomas J. Bernard. 1986. *Theoretical criminology.* 3rd ed. New York: Oxford University Press.

Wolfgang, Marvin E. 1972. Cesare Lombroso. In *Pioneers in criminology.* 2nd ed. Hermann Mannheim (ed.). Montclair, NJ: Patterson Smith.

Supplemental Readings

Bryant, Christopher G.A. 1975. Positivism reconsidered. *Sociolog. Rev.* 23:2.

Ferri, Enrico. 1877. *The theory of imputability and the denial of free will.*

_____. 1879. *Studies of criminality in France from 1826 to 1878.*

_____. 1881. *I nuovi Orizzonti del diritto e della procedura penale.*

_____. 1883. *La scuola positiva di diritto criminale.* (Trans. Kerr, Chicago, 1906 © The Positive School of Criminology)

_____. 1884. *The homicide.*

_____. 1884. *Criminal sociology.*

_____. 1887. *Polemica in difesa della scuola criminale positive.*

_____. 1888. *Variations thermometriques et criminalite.*

_____. 1889. *Delitti e delinquenti nella scienza e nella vita.*

_____. 1895. *L'omicidio nell' antropolgia criminale.* (2 vols.)

_____. 1904. *Studi sulla criminalita ed altri saggi.*

_____. 1906. *Les criminels danss l'art et la literature.* 2nd ed. Paris.

Garofalo, Raffaele. 1880. *Di un criteri positivo della penalita.* Naples, Italy.

_____. 1882. *Il tentativo criminoso con mezzi inidonei.* Turin, Italy: Loescher.

_____. 1882. *Cio che dovrebbe essere un giudizion penale.* Turin, Italy: Loescher.

_____. 1885. *Criminology,* first Italian edition. Naples, Italy,

_____. 1885. *Riparazione alle vittime del delitto.* Turin, Italy: Boca.

_____. 1895. *La superstition socialiste.* Paris, France: F. Alcan.

_____. 1909. *De la solidarite des nations dans la lutte contre la criminalite.* Paris, France: Giard et Briere.

Johnson, Herbert A. 1988. *History of criminal justice.* Cincinnati: Anderson Publishing Co.

Lindesmith, Alfred, and Yale Levin. 1937. Rejoinder. *Am. J. Soc.* 42:6, 899.

_____. 1937a. The Lombrosian myth in criminology. *Am. J. Soc.* 42:5, 653–71.

Lombroso, Caseare. 1863. *Archives of psychiatry, criminal anthropology and kindred sciences.* Thirty-two volumes. Turin, Italy: Fratelli Bocca.

_____. 1871. *L'uomo bianco e l'uomo di colore.* Padua, Italy: Sacchetto.

_____. 1888. *Troppo presto! Appunti al nuovo codice penale.* Turin, Italy: Fratelli Bocca.

_____. 1890. *Il delitto politico le rivoluzioni.* With R. Laschi. Turin, Italy: Fratelli Bocca.

_____. 1893. *Le piu recenti scoperte ed applicazioni della psichiatria ed antropolgia criminale.* Turin, Italy: Fratelli Bocca.

_____. 1894. *Gli anarchici.* Turin, Italy: Fratelli Bocca.

_____. 1895. *The female offender.* With William Ferrero. London, England: Fisher Unwin.

_____. 1896. *Criminal man (L'uomo delinquente).* 5th ed. Turin, Italy: Fratelli Bocca.

_____. 1888. *Palimsesti del carcere.* Turin, Italy: Fratelli Bocca.

_____. 1890. *Pazzi e anrmali.* Citta di Castello, Italy: Lapi.

_____. 1890. *Trattato profilattico e clinico della pellagra.* Turin, Italy: Fratelli Bocca.

_____. 1891. *The man of genius (L'uomo di genio).* London, England: Walter Scott.

_____. 1894. *L'antisemitismo e le scienze moderne.* Turin, Italy: Roux.

_____. 1895. *Grafologia.* Milan, Italy: Ulrich Joepli.

_____. 1897. *La delinquenza e la rivoluzione Francese.* Milan, Italy: Treve.

_____. 1897. *Criminal anthropology.* New York.

_____. 1898. *In Calabria.* Catania Sicily, Italy: Niccolo Giannotta.

_____. 1899. *Luccheni e l'antropologia criminale.* Turin, Italy: Fratelli Bocca.

_____. 1900. *Lezioni di medicina legale.* Turin, Italy: Fratelli Bocca.

_____. 1902. *Nuovi studi sul genio.* Two volumes, Palermo, Italy: Remo Sandron.

_____. 1905. *La perizia psichiatrico-legale.* Turin, Italy: Fratelli Bocca.

_____. 1905. *Il caso olivo.* With A.G. Bianchi. Milan, Italy: Liberia Editrice Internazionale.

_____. 1905. *Il momento attuale in Italia.* Milan, Italy: Casa Editrice Nazionale.

_____. 1906. *Problemes du jour.* Paris, France: Flammarion.

_____. 1908. *Genio e degenerazione.* Palermo, Italy: Remo Sandron, Second edition.

_____. 1909. *Ricerche sui fenomeni ipnotici e spiritici.* Turin, Italy: Unione Tip. Edit.

Mannheim, Hermann. 1971. *Group problems in crime and punishment.* 2nd enlarged ed. Montclair, NJ: Patterson Smith.

Schafer, S. 1969. *Theories in criminology.* New York: Random House.

Williams, Frank P., and Marilyn D. McShane. 1988. *Criminological theory.* Englewood Cliffs, NJ: Prentice Hall.

CHAPTER 3
DAVID EMILE DURKHEIM: 1858–1917

———✦✦✦———

I. BIOGRAPHICAL SKETCH

David Emile Durkheim was born on April 15, 1858, in Epinal, the capital of the mountainous province of Lorraine in northeast France. With an elder brother and two older sisters, young Emile grew up in a Jewish family of modest income. His father was the local rabbi and his mother worked in the family home as an embroiderer. Durkheim's grandfather and great-grandfather had also been rabbis, and it was not surprising that Emile was placed in a local rabbinical school where it was presumed he would follow in his forefathers' footsteps.

Throughout most of his life, Durkheim was a recluse. His living style has been characterized as stoical, devoid of humor, and with a near-total devotion to study and scholarly pursuits. Like Immanuel Kant, one of his predecessors, it has been said that a watch could be set according to Durkheim's punctuality and disciplined study habits. Such an intellectual, even one whose writing would be of such monumental importance, was not quick to inspire biographers. Durkheim's intellectual life was anything but humdrum, but his everyday life probably was. For this reason, until rather recently, there is some difficulty tracing his early history (see LaCapra 1972, and Lukes 1972, for perhaps the best descriptions of Durkheim's youth).

Durkheim's personal values were unquestionably shaped by the rigid and disciplined way of life characteristic of Jewish traditions in rural France. Life was austere and puritanical—only hard work produced anything worthwhile, and earthly pleasures were experienced with the requisite accompanying guilt. It is noteworthy that Durkheim realized, and subsequently appreciated, an extreme sense of family and community cohesion. Such family and neighborhood bonds, so close in part because he was a member of a persecuted religious minority, most likely influenced his future research interests in social science and welfare. This is particularly noticeable in his concern with the impact of community instability on various social ills in France, which included crime only incidentally.

Although the reasons are unclear, Durkheim did not accept Judaism (later referring to himself as agnostic) and completed his early schooling not in rabbinical preparation, but in letters and sciences. When he was only sixteen and already possessing a baccalaureate degree, he became infatuated with the moral philosophers of mid-nineteenth-century Europe, and most clearly with the recently published works of a fellow Frenchman, Auguste Comte, the acknowledged founder of sociology.

Durkheim's early adulthood was fraught with great anxiety about the state of national affairs. France was still undergoing convulsions resulting from the French Revolution, the defeat of Napoleon, and losses in the Franco-Prussian campaigns. From about 1850 to about 1890, France was struggling to regain composure and a lost sense of national pride (*Encyclopedia Britannica* 1910, 168). Not only had numerous military battles been waged in the land, but the social and cultural aspects of life were also in disarray. Rapid fluctuation in migration patterns accompanying the move from a feudal–agricultural economy to an industrial economy could be observed. It is not surprising that a sensitive and studious French scholar would turn his attention to understanding and explaining societal influences on morality, religion, deviance, and the general breakdown of traditional social institutions.

Compounding these national emergencies surrounding Durkheim were a series of personal crises that arguably further molded the direction and subject matter of his professional career as a philosopher–educator and early sociologist. Throughout his life, Durkheim was confronted with death, and he suffered poor health; as a result, he relied on medical concepts and analogies to explain social issues. Durkheim's father died an untimely death, leaving the younger Durkheim to lead the family when he was not much more than a teenager. It has been suggested that Durkheim's personal insecurities regarding his own intellectual abilities led to a debilitating and perhaps psychosomatic skin illness that caused him a great deal of difficulty during his early college education. Twice he failed the entrance examination to the Parisien Ecole Normale Superieure, where he would later receive his doctorate in philosophy. His closest friend and roommate in college committed suicide, an engrossing topic of concern and study for Durkheim for the rest of his life. Decades after this initial shock, during World War I, more than half of the student body of the Ecole Normale were killed. Moreover, Durkheim's only son was killed in battle during the same war, which, according to Durkheim's contemporaries, literally caused him to die of a broken heart a few years later.

Neither Durkheim's professional nor his personal life went smoothly during early adulthood. His own insecurities led him to be something of a social outcast, and he found it necessary to teach in several small local schools before he finally received the doctorate at the age of thirty-five. In 1887, he received his first professorship at the University of Bordeaux, married, and finally settled down to his most productive years as a writer and scholar. All of his well-known book-length works were published in the last twenty-four years of his life. Although available photographs all appear to show Emile Durkheim as an elderly man, in fact, he died at only fifty-nine.

A most important factor to observe in Durkheim's biography is the relationship it reveals between his tumultuous life and times and the subject matter of his major works. His first principal work (his Ph.D. dissertation) was *The Division of Labor in Society,* first published as *De la Division du Travail Social* (1893). In this work, Durkheim presents a theoretical explanation of order and disorder in modern societies. His concept of *anomie* is introduced in this work as one of the pathological states of rapidly changing society. While at the University of Bordeaux, he quickly followed up his first book with two others, both as seminal as his first. In 1895, *The Rules of Sociological Method* (*Les Regles de la Methode Sociologique*) appeared in print. This work, with a rather misleading title, outlines, among many other things, the functions of crime in society.

Two years later Durkheim published the far-reaching work *Suicide* (1897), which reveals most convincingly an astute use of the scientific method for studying social problems. In that suicide has been defined as a crime throughout much of modern history, the direct relevance of the work to criminology, as well as to scientific methodology generally, is evident.

This scholarly productivity, three works destined to become classics within a period of four years, is hardly matched among early pioneers in social science. Such a prolific output apparently resulted from his final attainment of professorial status at the University of Bordeaux and the coincident settling qualities of married life. It also seems plausible that his relatively late achievement of academic acceptance at middle-age allowed him to accumulate a sizeable pool of notes and papers from which the major works were to appear abruptly crystallized.

Following the publication of *Suicide,* twelve years elapsed until his next and last major book-length treatise appeared: *The Elementary Forms of Religious Life* (1912). This work was published in French under the title *Les Formes Elementaires de la Vie Religieuse, le Systeme Totemique en Australie.* On occasion, this last book has been characterized as Durkheim's most important work (Parsons 1968, 317). Its contribution to criminology may be only an indirect one. Nonetheless, for an in-depth analysis of the origins of morality and moral symbols from a cross-cultural perspective, it should not be overlooked.

During the twelve-year hiatus between books, Durkheim turned his attention to developing and editing *L'Annee Sociologique.* The volumes so produced contain one of the most fruitful and influential collections of late nineteenth- and early twentieth-century European journal articles on social issues and problems. As the editor, Durkheim either wrote or had direct influence over hundreds of articles, some of which were directly pertinent to early criminological theory. This collection of volumes helped bring French sociology to full acceptance as a social science, and provided a launching point for the emergence of the then infant discipline of criminology.

After his death in 1917, Durkheim's accomplishments lay dormant, with interest in them generally limited to French-speaking Europeans. An exception is an early doctoral dissertation regarding Durkheim's work written at Columbia University (Gehlke 1915). However, as Durkheim's works began to be translated into English in the 1930s, his full stature and impact on social science began to be realized—first as a sociologist and anthropologist, and only later, and then indirectly, as a criminologist.

II. BASIC ASSUMPTIONS

The basic assumptions of Emile Durkheim must be viewed in the context of his major writings and in reference to the state of social science of that era. Because much of his work predates the appearance of criminology as an organized discipline of study, we must examine his world view accordingly, not in reference to theoretical criminology per se, but in reference to human behavior and social disorganization in general. As regards criminology, at least five assumptions appear to stand out in Durkheim's work, on which are couched his various analyses of behavior and society:

1. Like Cesare Lombroso, a contemporary, Emile Durkheim was a positivist, but with a social rather than a biological focus. Durkheim argued that an explanation of personal behavior must take into account the various social forces surrounding the individual. Constitutional or biological factors were insufficient, apart from the influence of group and community dynamics to serve as determinates.

2. Another most important feature of Durkheimian thought is the assumption that *social facts* are quantifiable and measureable things, and may compose the ingredients of scientific analysis. Such social facts, as opposed to individual phenomena, may include such features as customs, obligations, laws, morality, and religious beliefs.

3. As societies develop from simple and homogeneous populations to advanced states with division of labor, any explanations of deviance must also change. Consequently, an interpretation of various social pathologies such as suicide, divorce, or crime, for example, varies from one state of community development and organization to another and from one time to another.

4. A most logical and fruitful method for understanding and explaining social features would involve historical and comparative analysis. How have social phenomena fluctuated from one decade to another and from one society to another?

5. The application of theory to effect planned change is a justifiable function of social science and specifically of sociology. Durkheim was an early advocate of applied sociology and criminology.

III. KEY IDEAS

Although Durkheim's works are voluminous, spanning a period of nearly thirty years and a wide range of topics, four specific principles pertain clearly to criminology. These features of his thought are regarded here as representative of his key ideas in criminology, although other elements of his publications also have relevance to various themes in the study of crime and the offender.

The first key idea is contained in a brief but often reprinted selection translated as "The normalcy of crime," excerpted from *The Rules of Sociological Method*. A second key idea comes from Durkheim's earliest major work and doctoral thesis, *The Division of Labor in Society*, in which he describes, in a most definitive way, the differing nature of social bonds between people in rural, traditional villages and the social bonds typical among people in more modern, urban areas. Here Durkheim considers how polar types of society may be seen as functional, and at the same time, as representative of several pathological characteristics.

A third, and perhaps most famous conceptual contribution to criminology, is Durkheim's development of *anomie*. This rather simple French term has inspired a sizeable amount of opinion and research since first used by Durkheim in several of his early publications. The concept was used to refer to a specific form of societal disharmony and to consequent individual pathology.

A fourth key idea of particular importance to criminology is Durkheim's analysis of suicide in society. He presents a methodologically rigorous study of this specific type of social deviance. Although suicide was his chosen subject, it becomes clear that other forms of social deviance could well have been used as topics for his analysis. This work provides one of the earliest classifications or conceptual schemes for interpreting suicide in various social environments.

Although these four key ideas are, for purposes of this short summary, given separate treatment, it should be understood that each idea is closely aligned with every other. We might, for instance, discuss the normalcy of criminal behavior in various types of society, either rural or urban, or how an anomic society might generate a specific type of suicide or other social malady.

NORMALCY OF CRIME

Whereas writing styles and changes in language often make reading turn-of-the-twentieth-century treatises on social philosophy difficult to grasp, Durkheim's handling of the normalcy of crime offers a fresh, clear, and logical commentary. This short essay should be, and often is, required reading in both beginning and advanced criminology courses, and is often found as the leading article in various anthologies of criminology (see Dressler 1964).

Durkheim's exposition on the normalcy of crime, or in fact of conflict or deviance in general, is best approached from two viewpoints. First, why might one presume that criminal behavior is, in fact, normal? Second, in what specific ways does Durkheim see criminal behavior as being functional or necessary for the efficient existence and progression of society?

Emile Durkheim is at his philosophical best when he explains that crime is normal because it is impossible to conceive of or to find a locale totally devoid of behavior defined as crime. If crime exists everywhere, he states, it cannot be viewed as abnormal. Although one may understandably detest abnormal forms and amounts of crime, its existence is normal—certainly in a statistical sense.

Durkheim draws his famous analogy between society in general and a society of saints. He argues that even if crime, as it might be known outside a convent, does not exist among the residents of the institution, other forms of norm-breaking and infractions would be found inside the walls, and would be elevated there to a position similar to that of crimes more common outside the walls.

The reason some type of deviance must persist is that total social consensus is impossible. Such a condition would require, according to Durkheim, a total understanding of the rules themselves, as well as total agreement in the degree of acceptance of the rules. The most important factor is that no two people are ever exactly alike in their interpretation of environmental stimuli. Durkheim argues that this is true, if for no other reason than that people occupy different portions of space.

Probably more attention has been given to the second aspect of this key idea, that crime is functional or necessary. Crime, or interpersonal conflict, is functional in at least four ways. The first is what might best be called the *progress explanation*—that is, a primary source of social change must be individual deviation from the social norm. A single individual may choose to follow a path different from that taken by the majority, and in so doing may be coincidently defined as a lawbreaker. Simultaneously, however, the individual deviant may inspire others to follow suit. In some historic cases society itself is transformed, as in the celebrated cases of Socrates, Galileo, William Harvey, or Martin Luther King. All were, in their time, treated as criminals and all were instrumental in altering society's course for the better—or, in other words, toward progress. The problem lies in the fact that at the time of the deviation, society is unable to foretell which of the criminal acts will result in progress and which will not; for example, many may be influenced to follow social offenders such as Charles Manson, Timothy Leary, or the Reverend Jones of Guyana.

A second functional quality of crime may be referred to as the *warning-light aspect*. For example, because the assessment of crime rates over time allows the researcher a bird's-eye view of social behavior, concerned citizens and policymakers may be alerted and can zero in on high-crime areas to administer whatever treatment may be necessary to bring the ailing portion of society back into the fold. Again, it should be noted that although some criminal behavior is functional and necessary, abnormally large amounts are dysfunctional. The warning-light function has its counterpart in medicine where Durkheim suggests that pain, like crime, is normal and necessary—and provides patient and physician a chance to probe more accurately for ultimate causes of disease. By the same argument, a heart-attack victim may reassess earlier lifestyles and live a long life, thanks, in part, to the original attack.

By clarifying boundaries, crime may be viewed as necessary in a third way. The view that a rule becomes most vivid with its occasional transgression was an important observation of Durkheim. Accordingly, he was an early proponent of *general deterrence theory.* He did not elaborate on the nature or degree of particular crimes that might allow others to witness and learn from the consequent punishment, but he saw a small percentage of social deviants as beneficial for boundary maintenance of the larger community. Correspondingly, a small child can never totally understand behavioral expectations if not permitted to occasionally violate the rules.

Finally, the fact that the larger group may, in the face of rule breakers, be drawn more closely together attests to the ability of crime, like war, to generate cohesiveness for the larger society. This quality is discussed later under the topic of mechanical solidarity.

SOCIAL ORDER AND DISORDER

The Division of Labor in Society was Durkheim's first major work, and his most fundamental treatise. There seems little question that many of his other ideas are derivatives of those in this early book. Again, in regard to criminology, it must be observed that Durkheim's development of mechanical and organic models of society pertains only indirectly to deviation and law breaking. Indeed, following in the paths of Toennies and Spencer, who also wrote eloquently of community structure and organization, Durkheim was concerned with macro-level understanding of nineteenth-century European society. How can the sociologist best account for the transition of folk-level communities to modern, urban areas? How has this massive rural–urban transition affected the quality of life, and specifically, individual alienation? Building on the works of several contemporaries (most notably Toennies' *Gemeinschaft and Gesellschaft*), Durkheim contrasted two extremes of society that he perceived in the aftermath of the French Revolution.

Table 1 provides an interpretation of the basic features of what Durkheim labels *mechanical* (i.e., simple, rural) and *organic* (i.e., complex, urban) societies.

TABLE 1: Features of Mechanical vs. Organic Societies

Mechanical (Rural)	*Organic (Urban)*
Small population	Large population
Slight division of labor	Extreme division of labor
Isolation (social and geographic)	Non-isolation
Slight mobility	Extreme mobility
Cultural homogeneity	Cultural heterogeneity
Harmony based on consensus	Harmony based on mutual dependence or contract
Altruism/esprit de corps	Apathy/anomie
Tradition oriented	Change oriented

In a near-perfect mechanical society, the rate of deviation from expected behavior is slight. By definition, most of the members of the community are in a state of social consensus.

Concurrence with the rules is widespread in smaller population, most of whom engage in the same kind of specialty (typically agriculture), and with very little outside interference. Modern-day Amish villages of Pennsylvania represent near-perfect mechanical-type communities. It appears clear, however, that increase in mobility is met with an increase in norm-breaking simply because the adherence to a single set of rules and beliefs becomes increasingly difficult with movement of people and the advent of strangers. Whereas Toennies was more concerned with the personality attributes of persons in extreme folk communities (that is, with community will or *gemeinschaft*), Durkheim focused more on group obligation to follow the rules. Vold and Bernard (1986, 147) state, "To the extent that a particular society is mechanical, its solidarity will come from the pressure for uniformity exerted against diversity."

As noted, some deviation is expected. However, insofar as there is enforcement of the rules, it is most likely in the form of informal pressure from the majority of community members. In such traditional and stable societies, the various social institutions (e.g., family, church, school) remain solidly intact, providing informal pressure to conform. Children grow up to be cultural clones of their parents unless acted on by some outside force.

Organic society presents a totally different picture. Diversity becomes the norm and individuals, out of necessity, must learn to live in a continual state of mutual dependence. Many, if not most, persons occupy specialized occupational positions. Because traditional institutions are greatly modified and reduced from their earlier forms, people and groups must respect each other for the functions each provides, even if such functions are carried out among individuals in a purely impersonal manner. There is a much greater reliance on the more formal means of social control—that is, when deviance occurs, which is bound to happen more frequently given the lesser degree of cultural homogeneity, formal regulatory agencies must be established to maintain the ever-growing and fluctuating organic society. A dilemma occurs if the division of labor is so rapid that various regulatory agencies cannot keep up with the increasing demands made on them. The proliferation of work strikes, slowdowns, and labor violence are indications of a runaway division of labor, according to Durkheim. The degree to which people become alienated from each other, or from the various remnants of social institutions still lingering on, is the degree to which a condition of anomie exists in the society.

As clearly noted by Vold and Bernard (1986, 145), no society is purely mechanical or purely organic, but is in a state of transition from one to the other. Generally, the trend has been toward advanced urban states, which ideally experiences considerable organic solidarity. Some modern states appear to have been reasonably successful in maintaining low levels of social pathology in the midst of advanced population size and density and increasing mobility. Japan and Singapore are, perhaps, good examples (see Adler 1983, Austin 1987).

Durkheim was always very much interested in the application of sociological theory to alleviate some of the social turmoil in France during his day. Although he was not precise in outlining systems of social rehabilitation, he wrote extensively, but hypothetically, about the necessity of establishing regulatory welfare agencies and upgrading the basic social institutions that appear to falter with extreme urbanism.

ANOMIE

Because it is impossible to discuss Durkheim's *The Division of Labor in Society* or *Suicide* without addressing anomie, the concept deserves separate scrutiny in its own right. The literal translation from the Greek of the French term *anomie* (i.e., *a nomos* or *anomique*, meaning without norms or normlessness), although popularly used by sociologists, is, in reality, inappropriate—that is, it appears illogical to presume that any society or community could persist with an "absence of norms." Similarly, to assume an individual would suffer an absence of any norms is fallacious. Since we are, as it were, stuck with the term, we should search for an interpretation of the word which fits the way it is used (see Simpson 1960, ix).

It is first necessary to distinguish between *anomie* and *anomia*. The former applies to a state of society, and the latter to a psychological condition of an individual. The term *anomie*, as it pertains to a societal condition (i.e., an *anomic society*), was first used by Durkheim in *The Division of Labor in Society* (1893). Indeed, some of his critics argue that, at least in his early writings, he slighted the social-psychological aspects of behavior by not being generally concerned, as a sociologist, with individual pathology while being too exclusively concerned with social pathology.

Social thinkers have used at least three interpretations of *anomie,* all of which are defensible and arise from Durkheim's concept of organic society.

Anomie as Norm Saturation or Superfluity

Rather than assume *anomie* simply means normlessness, one may view it as that which results from an abundance of societal rules. A saturation of rules may predictably result in social confusion. The problem is not so much with an absence of norms as it is with the difficulty in assimilating a multitude of rules or norms. As society becomes increasingly pluralistic in function, the rules of behavior, including laws, increase in abundance, making recall of particular norms difficult, if not impossible.

The United States is, perhaps, a legalistic society to the point that no single individual can know all, or be expected to know all, the norms and laws. The adage that "Ignorance of the law is no excuse" becomes a rather inappropriate axiom with the increasing proliferation of legal codes. By the same token, in a mechanical, ruralistic community, one finds a simplicity of rules and laws and a condition whereby individuals are more easily made aware of all norms.

Anomie as Confusion of Particular Norms

A more common interpretation of *anomie,* if not a more appropriate one, is the confusion regarding "particular" or "specific" norms resulting from the abundance of rules and legal codes. In other words, it logically follows that a particular rule of behavior may become unclear as a society becomes increasingly modern and urban (i.e., organic). In this regard, Durkheim was noticeably disturbed with what he saw as a loss of meaning of traditional values—that is, with confusion regarding what is the expected way to behave in terms of morality, integrity, or duty.

Also, more specific to legal codes, the definitions of particular crimes (e.g., theft, assault) may become unclear and difficult to define in a highly complex, heterogeneous, and mobile society. Again, in that organic society is associated with cultural change, it is not surprising that the rules and laws become muddled as they evolve, fluctuate, and, in some cases, dissolve.

Anomie as Difficulty in Achieving Goals

Perhaps the most noted interpretation of *anomie* is the one associated with the frustration resulting from the difficulty of achieving goals or success in a society beset by normative complexity and a breakdown of traditional social institutions. This interpretation is expanded by Merton (1949, 131–94) in what is now often noted as the "goals–means" conceptual scheme or theory. Durkheim was critically concerned with the fact that traditional means of achieving goals become increasingly deficient or confusing in a society undergoing rapid transition to organic styles of organization. The various adaptations to an anomic society are dealt with in this volume in the section on Robert K. Merton.

In all of these interpretations, the focus is on "confusion" of the rules of society. Additionally, following Durkheim's early thesis, such confusion is the natural result of organic society. The problem is not that it exists, but what to do to adapt to such confusion successfully.

SUICIDE AS DEVIANT BEHAVIOR

There appears to be no doubt that Durkheim's most famous single empirical work was his study of suicide (see Nisbet 1974, 226), which established Durkheim as a premier researcher, and is used today, more than ninety years later, as a clear model of the relationship between theory and research. Furthermore, *Suicide* demonstrated that in order to fully understand self-demise, one must focus not on the individual, but on the larger society. Historical and comparative methods emphasizing social forces are required, according to Durkheim, to best explain the fluctuating suicide rates in a society.

Durkheim found "social facts," notably religious affiliation, family integrity, and community cohesion and support, were found to be directly related to the frequency of suicide in a society. Although it is no longer appropriate to think of suicide as criminal behavior, it is clear that the same social factors that may influence one to take his or her own life may also motivate one toward other types of deviance, including some crimes. With the exception of the relationship between anomie and suicide, Durkheim's analysis of suicide has not been given much coverage by criminology texts. However, from the standpoint of crime causality, Durkheim's well-documented conceptual scheme of the four categories of suicide provides a relevant launching point for analyzing not only social influences on suicide, but also on crime or other types of interpersonal conflict. Briefly, the following are the four conceptual categories of suicide (or criminal behavior) first discussed by Durkheim in 1897.

Altruism

The quality of altruism is probably the least common of social influences leading to suicide. As the world becomes increasingly urban and modernized, according to Durkheim's earlier arguments, the world also becomes less prone to altruism. As a consequence, the likelihood today that an individual may give up his or her life out of a sense of loyalty, honor, commitment, or self-sacrifice is less than in earlier days, when a larger proportion of the population lived in small, homogeneous communities.

Given the various features of mechanical society, individual residents of the classic village community have very little control over personal destiny. It is correct to say that the individual is subordinated to the collective or the community at large. Furthermore, each individual is obligated to the larger whole that guides, conditions, and sets goals for the individual. Ascription, rather than individual achievement, characterizes altruistic community life. If a community resident, out of duty or honor, chooses to sacrifice his or her life (as dramatically portrayed by the Japanese Kamikaze pilot), the suicide could be characterized as "altruistic." Depending on one's perspective, such extreme integration into community life may be seen either as a positive or a negative quality.

By the same token, it is consistent to suppose that an individual may place loyalty to family or community over loyalty to the state. Devotion to the state may be seen as an obligation to adhere to formal legal norms of higher government systems. Thus, an individual may choose to defy government laws and commit crimes out of group or community loyalty. Theft to feed one's family is the most obvious example. Also, loyalty to one's group or gang may lead one to turn away from obedience to the law in favor of group faithfulness, as in group vandalism, vigilantism, and violence (see Sykes and Matza 1957 for similar rationalizations).

Egoism

Durkheim saw egoism as the opposite of altruism. Thus, a society characterized by a preponderance of egoistic individuals is, by definition, a society lacking in high degrees of community integration. Thus, one finds gratification of self-interest, or selfishness, to be the rule. Again, Durkheim looked on egoism primarily as a social, rather than a personal, phenomenon. An egoistic society is one in which individual activities take precedence over communal obligations of allegiances. Accordingly, persons become detached from various community support groups and pursue their own individualistic destinies. In the absence of community groups, should one fail in egoistic pursuits aimed at self-aggrandizement, one might resort to suicide. For example, ending one's life by leaping from a building after the 1929 stock market crash may be seen as an egoistic suicide.

Although Durkheim did not develop his idea of the relevance of egoism to interpersonal conflict or criminal behavior, the connection appears clear. Egoism is closely aligned with, if not synonymous with, greed. The likelihood that a society of greed-oriented individuals would predictably step on and over their fellows in pursuit of a personal mission is not surprising. In this view, it is not difficult to imagine a wide range of criminal activities motivated by the condition of greed or egoism. Recall that Durkheim saw such a condition in the post-revolutionary days of France when individuals lost traditional family and community bonds, and followed personal aims with little apparent consideration of others (Durkheim 1897).

Anomism

Anomic and egoistic suicide are no doubt often confused. The difference is that, whereby *egoism* is associated with a greedy pursuit of personal goals, *anomism* is the striving for community-accepted goals, albeit goals in a state of confusion. An anomic society, therefore, need not be a greedy one. As discussed earlier, anomie suggests a societal condition of unclear rules or regulations in regard to how one could succeed in life. Success could be defined in economic terms, as in striving to enter a particular profession, or in family or community terms, as in striving to raise a family. Again, in a war-torn society, the various support groups that typically allow one to view more clearly the routes of upward mobility, if not happiness, are absent or confused. This particular suicide-conducive condition of society has been most fully developed as an influencing feature of crime and delinquency (see, e.g., Chapter 9).

The relevance of all this to criminal behavior is fairly obvious. Lower-status, poor individuals, striving against seemingly all odds to get ahead in an anomic society, might understandably find in their plight sufficient motivation to violate laws. In essence, the traditional routes toward success lose meaning under anomic conditions, making criminal behavior easier to rationalize.

Fatalism

Although not elaborated on by Durkheim, a final category of fatalistic suicide completes the conceptual scheme. *Fatalistic suicide* is the opposite of anomic suicide, in that the society that induces it disallows individual expression or pursuit of goals through excessive regulation. Here we have a condition whereby community members may wish to pursue individualistic goals, but are not permitted to do so. Thus, futures are blocked and passions choked by oppressive discipline (Smelser and Warner 1976, 164).

Whereas in an anomic condition routes are unclear toward reaching community-accepted goals, we find in a fatalistic society that such routes are often purposefully blocked. In extremely regimented and dictatorial societies one can see how an individual might choose suicide or crime out of extreme integration and altruism. However, someone might see the same society as frustrating and fatalistic, and this perception might lead to the same outcome of taking one's own life or that of another. Also, it is plausible to view fatalistic society as an eventual motivating condition of terrorism and revolt, both commonly viewed as illegal, at least by the original dominant society.

IV. CRITIQUE

As is the case with early late-nineteenth-century pioneers in criminology, Durkheim was not without critics. Steven Lukes (1972, 497) writes:

> Durkheim's ideas never ceased to be the center of intense controversy. It was not merely that they were new, often extreme, and pungently and dogmatically expressed. They challenged academic and religious orthodoxies, disputing the methodologies of the former and discounting the supernatural justifications of the latter.

Durkheim's four major works, published during his lifetime and referenced in this chapter, are sufficient to ensure a lasting place of honor among the pioneer thinkers. However, we must keep in mind that at least nine further book-length treatises were published after his death, some translated from the Latin or French as recently as 1972 (see Giddens 1972). Some of his more obscure articles are yet to be translated into English.

Because much of Durkheim's work is only indirectly pertinent to criminology, we should limit our criticism to what is reported in this chapter. Suffice it to say, for example, that much criticism of Durkheim's work was in reference to his analysis of fundamental religious ideas, not given close attention here. Although Durkheim's concept of anomie and its associated ills has remained comparatively untarnished, the same cannot be said of several underlying principles of mechanical and organic society. Simply put, not all of Durkheim's contemporaries, or present writers, are convinced that mechanically organized communities necessarily lead to social harmony or personal contentment.

Durkheim presumed that crime, like suicide, would intensify as society became increasingly modernized and anomic. However, as noted by Vold and Bernard (1986, 156), crime data were not presented by Durkheim to demonstrate such a conclusion. In fact, several researchers (e.g., Lodhi and Tilly 1973, 297–318) argue that crime rates actually either remained constant or in some cases declined during Durkheim's era (Zehr 1981, 136–37).

Although such a revelation may appear to cast a giant shadow on Durkheim's major thesis, we must recall the difficulty, even today, of defining exactly what is meant by *criminal behavior* and what should be documented as crime by those who keep the statistics. It is likely that today Durkheim would agree that sweeping generalizations about rising crime rates in society would have to give way to more tailored assumptions of specific types of crimes in more specific environments. As again suggested by Vold and Bernard (1986, 156), Durkheim's major theories may become more clear in the context of later developments in theories of ecology, strain, and social control.

Today, early or so-called primitive societies are not generally believed to have been as harmonious and crime-free as Durkheim suggested. Durkheim may have been correct in the short-run of history, seeing increases in crime during his own life. However, more recently, the thesis is set forth that crime rates may have actually decreased over the millennia as a result of advanced strategies of maintaining social control. Consequently, the criticism persists that Durkheim may have been a bit shortsighted, although the jury is still out (see Gurr 1981, 340–46). In Durkheim's defense, LaCapra (1972, 293) notes that Durkheim "saw modern society as passing through a transitional period which confronted men with the problems of anomie . . . especially pronounced in the economy." It is likely that his concepts of mechanical and organic solidarity are more "ideal types," in the Weberian sense, and are never fully observed in reality.

At a more general level of criticism, Durkheim's methodological approach was severely attacked by late-nineteenth-century philosophers. This is understandable, given the evolving nature of scientific thought of the day. Several contemporaries of Durkheim included Charles Darwin and Cesare Lombroso, themselves not without critics. With Durkheim, we see the unswerving social determinist. Durkheim was a staunch positivist and received substantial assaults from "free-will" advocates. Such criticism came most loudly regarding his sociological explanation of religion and morality (Lukes 1972, 498, 500–505). Durkheim appeared to disregard the self or mental aspects of life in favor of the more empirically quantifiable traits of society. Rauch (1904, 359–62) argued, "Durkheim misdescribed the nature of moral judgements, making them purely cognitive, and he concentrated on the external, immobile shell of social life, missing its active and living reality."

Durkheim's conceptualization of the four types of socially induced suicide remains intact, with relatively little criticism. Although the statistical data collected regarding suicide in nineteenth-century France may leave a bit to be desired by today's standards, Durkheim's logical deductions attributing social causes to personal ailments are as potent today as they were a century ago. Regarding his philosophical commentary on the normalcy and necessity of crime, little criticism can be noted outside of a series of rather caustic debates with Gabriel Tarde, another criminological pioneer (for discussion, see Lukes 1972, 302–13).

In summary, Durkheim's productivity and contributions to the empirical study of social forces far outweigh any shortcomings criticism may conjure. Although Emile Durkheim must be shared with sociologists and anthropologists, he nonetheless occupies a prominent place in the early evolution of the discipline of criminology.

References

Adler, Freda. 1983. *Nations not obsessed with crime*. Littleton, Colorado: Rothman and Company.

Austin, W. Timothy. 1987. Crime and custom in an orderly society: The Singapore prototype. *Criminology*, 25(2), 279–94.

Dressler, David (ed.). 1964. *Readings in criminology and penology*. 2nd ed. New York: Columbia University Press.

Durkheim, Emile. 1893. *De la Division du Travail Social: Etude sur L'Organisation des Societes Superieues*. Paris: Felix Alcan. *The division of labor in society* (G. Simpson, Trans.). New York: Macmillan, 1933.

———. 1895. *Les Regles de La Methode Sociologique*. Paris: Felix Alcan. *The rules of sociological method* (S. A. Solovay and J. H. Mueller, Trans.) Chicago: University of Chicago Press, 1938.

———. 1897. *Le Suicide: Etude de Sociologie*. Paris: Felix Alcan. *Suicide: A study in sociology*. (J. A. Spaulding and G. Simpson, Trans.). Glenco, IL: Free Press, 1951.

——— 1912. *Les Formes Elementaires de la Vie Religieuse: Le Systeme Totemique en Australie*. Paris: Felix Alcan. *The elementary forms of religious life*. (J. W. Swain, Trans.). London: George Allen and Unwin, 1915.

Encyclopedia Britannica. 1910. New York: The Encyclopedia Britannica. 11th ed.

Gehlke, Charles Elmer. 1915. *Emile Durkheim's contributions to sociological theory*. Ph.D. dissertation. Columbia University.

Giddens, Anthony (ed). 1972. *Emile Durkheim: Selected writings*. Cambridge: Cambridge University Press.

Gurr, Ted Robert. 1981. *Historical forces in violent crime*. In Michael Tonry and Norval

Morris (eds.), *Crime and justice*. Chicago: University of Chicago Press.

LaCapra, Dominick. 1972. *Emile Durheim: Sociologist and philosopher*. Chicago: University of Chicago Press.

Lodhi, A. Q., and Tilly, Charles. 1973. Urbanization, crime and collective violence in 19th century France. *Am. J. Soc.* 79:296–318.

Lukes, Stephen. 1972. *Emile Durkheim: His life and work*. New York: Harper and Row.

Merton, Robert K. 1949. *Social theory and social structure*. London: Glencoe.

Nisbet, Robert A. 1974. *The sociology of Emile Durkheim*. New York: Oxford University Press.

Parsons, Talcott. 1968. Emile Durkheim. In David L. Sills (ed.), *International encyclopedia of the social sciences*. New York: Macmillan.

Simpson, George. 1960. Introduction. *The division of labor in society*. New York: Macmillan.

Smelser, Neil J., and Warner, R. Steven. 1976. *Sociological theory: Historical and formal*. Morristown, NJ: General Learning Press.

Sykes, G. M. and David, Matza. 1957. Techniques of neutralization: A theory of delinquency. *Am. Soc. Rev.* 22:664–70.

Toennies, Ferdinand. 1887. *Gemeinschaft und gesellschaft* (*Community and society*). C.P. Loomis, Trans.) East Lansing: Michigan State University, 1957.

Vold, George, and Bernard, Thomas J. 1986. *Criminological theory*. 3rd ed. New York: Oxford University Press.

Zehr, Howard. 1981. The modernization of crime in Germany and France, 1930–1913. In Louise I. Shelley (ed.), *Readings in comparative criminology*. Carbondale, IL: Southern Illinois University Press.

Supplemental Readings

Rauch, F. 1904. Science et conscience. *Rev. Philosoph.* 57:359–67.

Wallwork, Ernest. 1972. *Durkheim: Morality and milieu*. Cambridge, MA: Harvard University Press.

CHAPTER 4
SIGMUND FREUD: 1856–1939

I. BIOGRAPHICAL SKETCH

Sigmund Freud was born on May 6, 1856, in Friedburg, Moravia (now Czechoslovakia), of Jewish extraction. He was the first child of Jacob Freud and his second wife Amalie Nathanson, who was nineteen years younger than Jacob. When Freud was four years old, financial difficulties prompted his father, a wool merchant of modest means with a large family, to move to Vienna, where Freud was to spend the rest of his life.

As a youngster, Freud was well behaved and consistently at the top of his class in school. Given the age difference between his parents, the fact that he was Amalie's first child, and his high level of achievement at an early age, it is not difficult to see how young Sigmund (or "Siggie," as he was referred to by his family and friends) became his mother's favorite. His preferential position persisted throughout his relationship with his parents, especially with his mother, and he was indulged constantly. Freud (1935) cites examples of such favoritism in his own works: he had his own room even though he, his parents, and his five siblings lived in a crowded apartment; he also had an oil lamp to study by, whereas everyone else made do with candles.

As a young man, Freud was uncertain about his career, but he was always more inclined toward the social or human sciences than the natural sciences (Jones 1953). Given the prevailing anti-Semitic climate of late-nineteenth-century Austria, all professional careers except medicine and law were closed to him. He considered law for a time, but finally, having been influenced by the works of Darwin and Goethe, he chose medicine, entering the University of Vienna in 1873 (Fadiman and Frager 1976). However, by his own admission, he was never a doctor in the usual sense of the term (Freud 1935).

Two major things happened at the University of Vienna that had a great and prolonged impact on both Freud the man and Freud the scientist. Because he was Jewish, Freud was treated as an "inferior and an alien." According to him, this experience increased his capacity to withstand criticism and pursue independent ideas (Freud 1935). Second, Freud found himself very attracted to the role of "basic scientist." This attraction was the result of his work in the laboratory of Dr. Ernst Brucke, one of the leading physiologists of the time (Jones 1953). The association with Brucke was undoubtedly a major influence on Freud's faith in and dependence on biological conceptualizations and his positivistic orientation.

While working in Brucke's laboratory, Freud conducted histological studies and published articles on neurology and anatomy. He earned a minor reputation by devising a method for staining cells for microscopic studies. However, a turn of events brought an end to his short career as a university scholar. Freud aspired to fill the next open position in the laboratory, but there were two well-qualified assistants already ahead of him. He also had fallen in love with and wished to marry a young woman named Martha Bernays. In 1882, on the advice of Dr. Brucke, Freud completed his medical degree and sought to enter private practice (Rychlak 1973).

Freud worked first as a surgeon and then moved into general medicine, eventually becoming a "house physician" at one of the more prestigious hospitals in Vienna. By 1885, Freud had gained the highly coveted position of lecturer at the University of Vienna (Fadiman and Frager 1976). It was during this time that he began to move into the realm of what we would now call *neuropsychiatry,* taking a course in psychiatry and forming a relationship with Joseph Breuer, a well-established neurologist who was instrumental in helping Freud establish a practice and ultimately in the development of psychoanalysis (Rychlak 1973). Also during this time, Freud began his infamous research on cocaine, extolling its virtues to all who would listen as a treatment for a wide variety of psychological problems. He later regretted this stance as cocaine's potentially harmful effects began to become more apparent.

In 1895, Freud traveled to Paris on the grant that Brucke had helped him obtain. There he studied under the flamboyant and controversial French psychiatrist Jean Charcot, who was experimenting with hypnosis as a treatment for hysteria. In hysteria, Freud found physical symptoms that were anatomically impossible, and determined that it was a physical disorder with a psychological source (Fadiman and Frager 1976). The exposure to Charcot, his relationship and work with Breuer, and another trip to France in 1889 to observe Bernheim propelled Freud into the psychodynamic perspective, of which he was to become the cutting edge for the time.

From 1887 until just after the turn of the twentieth century, Freud sketched out his theoretical ideas; the 1890s were particularly productive. In 1893, he coauthored *Studies on Hysteria* with Breuer. In 1895, Freud states that the "secret of dreams" was revealed to him. The term *psycho-analysis* was coined in 1896, and in 1897, he began his now famous "self-analysis." This decade of productive thought culminated with the publication of Freud's two monumental initial statements of his theory, *The Interpretation of Dreams* and *The Psycho-Pathology of Everyday Life*, in 1900 and 1901, respectively (Rychlak 1973, Fadiman and Frager 1976).

These works received very little attention at first, but as Freud's stature grew and the word spread, he began to attract a group of "disciples," and many of whom, Alfred Adler, Carl Jung, Otto Rank, Sandor Ferenczi, and Ernest Jones among them, became famous in their own rights. These individuals formed the core of the Psychoanalytic Society, and the doctrine was spread.

Freud's associations with his followers were often stormy. He was dogmatic and tyrannical, showing little tolerance for those who deviated from his views. One by one, Breuer, Adler, Jung, Ferenczi, and Rank (among others) were ejected or sought to leave the society because of their disagreements with Freud (Rychlak 1973, Fadiman and Frager 1976).

Freud made only one trip to the United States. In 1909, G. Stanley Hall invited both Freud and Jung to speak at Clark University (Jones 1957). This invitation was an indication that people around the world were beginning to hear about and be intrigued by the work of Sigmund Freud; Western thought was never to be the same. Freud was a true scientist, and like all positivists he fully expected to find the "cause" for all behavior (Maddi 1980), and he devoted his life to the creation and evolution of psychoanalytic theory in an attempt to do so. In the process, he wrote prodigiously. His collect works fill twenty-four volumes (two full feet on a book shelf) and contain his efforts to cover the entire gamut of human personality and behavior. Freud's goal was to find the truth and, in so doing, develop a theory that would outlive him (Fadiman and Frager 1976).

The more widely known Freud's work became, the more criticism it (and he) received. In fact, the later years of his life were not easy ones either professionally or personally. In 1923, he contracted cancer of the mouth and jaws (probably from smoking twenty cigars a day), which kept him in considerable pain until his death in 1939. Also, during this time, Freud was constantly embroiled in conflict over the validity and utility of psychoanalytic theory and psychoanalysis. In 1933, the Nazis targeted Freud (and many other academicians) as a destructive influence and publicly burnt his books. This event prompted Freud to exhibit his rather sharp wit. He is quoted by Earnest Jones (1957) as having said, "What progress we are making. In the Middle Ages, they would have burned me, nowadays they are content with burning my books." The Nazi movement into Austria was in full swing by 1938. Freud was given permission to emigrate to London, where he finally succumbed to cancer in 1939 at the age of 83.

In Freud's case, the man and his theory are inseparable, probably more so than is the case with any other major theorist in any discipline. He certainly is the most well known and often cited of all psychologists (Siegel, 1986). In fact, he is considered by many to be the father of psychology. As Vold and Bernard (1986) point out, psychiatry is as old as medicine, but psychology (psychoanalysis) is relatively recent; it is Freud.

Everyone concedes that Freud is a famous psychologist and personality theorist, but his influence goes far beyond psychology. Philip Reiff (1961) sees him as a major force in the moral revolution of our time. Scroggs (1985) observes that Freud is often cited, along with Darwin and Marx, as one of the greatest shapers of Western thought. Larry Siegel (1986), in his introductory text on criminology, calls Freud's concepts "pioneering." The psychoanalytic perspective has proved to be one of the most influential theories of human functioning of our times (Gibbons 1982), especially in the first half of the twentieth century (Vold and Bernard 1986). The true impact of Freud and his ideas was summed up best by Richard Wolheim (1971, ix) when he said, "Sigmund Freud, by the power of his writings and by the breadth and audacity of his speculations, revolutionized the thought, the lives, and the imagination of an age. . . . It would be hard to find in the history of ideas, even in the history of religion, someone whose influence was so immediate, so broad, or so deep." Freud looms as such a giant that it is difficult for either his advocates or his opponents to see him objectively in our time (Maddi 1980).

II. BASIC ASSUMPTIONS

It is exceedingly difficult to present succinctly the basic assumptions of psychoanalytic theory and still provide the necessary depth and complexity in the present format. However, understanding the discussion of criminality that comes later is inextricably linked to understanding the fundamental postulates of the theory. The presentation here should in no way be considered a complete picture of Freudian theory, but, rather a thumbnail sketch of what these authors believe to be the most complex and sweeping theory of human behavior ever formulated. The information that follows constitutes a general synthesis of Freud's major ideas and assumptions; but over the course of their development, Freud and his theory evolved considerably. In a brief presentation such as this, it is not possible to address all of the subtle changes.

Freud was not merely a psychologist; he was a scholar of humanity and human development *in toto,* a philosopher addressing questions about the human place in the world (Freud 1961a) and in the cosmos (Reiff 1961). His is a "metapsychological" theory, but this does not mean that it goes beyond psychology. Rather, it means that Freud "psychologized" everything (Freud 1963). There was almost no question about personality or human conduct that Freud did not attempt to answer (Scroggs, 1985). He psychologized the commonly held belief of human rationality into an evolutionary theory of individual metamorphosis from narcissism to mature "libidinal sociality" (Reiff 1961). Vehemently denying Beccaria's rational model of choice, Freud postulated that maximum pleasure (id) manifests itself unless controlled by the conscious reality principle (ego) (Allen et al. 1981). Even though Freud offered a rather dramatic departure from the rationality model, one can see some synchronicity between his "pleasure vs. reality principle" and Bentham's "hedonistic calculus" (Vetter and Silverman 1986). The fundamental difference is the source of the input, with Freud's emphasis being on the unconscious (nonrational) component.

Psychoanalytic theory, as originated by Sigmund Freud, is an individual and psychodynamic approach to understanding behavior. However, the theory draws heavily on sociobiological concepts. Freud perceived the inseparable connections between the individual and society, stating, "Individual psychology is from the very first the same as social psychology" (Freud 1959, 2). The mental life of the individual analogizes social phenomena; the individual manifests the conditions of his or her society, and both (individual and society) manifest the conditions of nature. If people are corrupt and aggressive, society must be as well; and if violence exists in society, then it also exists in the universe. For Freud (1963), the science of human behavior is a social science composed of a multidimensional continuum of nature, the individual, and society.

To flesh out Freud's philosophy of human nature, we can examine briefly three of his major theoretical contributions: levels of consciousness (unconscious motivation); stages of development (childhood influence on adult personality); and, the conflict model of motivation (instincts and pansexualism).

LEVELS OF CONSCIOUSNESS (UNCONSCIOUS MOTIVATION)

Freud believed that "being conscious cannot be the essence of what is mental. It is only the quality of what is mental and an unstable quality at that—one that is far oftener absent than present" (Freud 1963, 221). Prior to the ascension of Freudian thought, it was generally assumed that the nature of mental existence was being conscious, and consequently, that human motives were conscious or rational (e.g., Beccaria, Bentham). Freud argued that mental processes are arranged structurally and actually take place on three independent levels. These levels he named the conscious, the preconscious, and the unconscious.

The *conscious (C),* as conceived by (Freud 1965a, 1962) deals with that which we typically think of when we consider mentation. It is the level of the psyche that deals with everyday, real-world affairs of which we are immediately aware. The *preconscious (PC)* has two primary functions. It is a storage area (memory, if you will), housing that which is not in immediate awareness but can be brought into C when desired. The PC also acts as a buffer zone between C and the *unconscious (UC).*

It was the UC that intrigued Freud most, and he believed that it constituted the bulk of mental activity and motivation. In the UC dwell our most basic and primitive desires, drives, instincts, and needs. It also serves as repository for those events (memories) from our lives, especially childhood, that have proved to be in some way too traumatic to be dealt with on a C level. The UC is a veritable fountain of psychic energy that we can never be fully conscious of and cannot ever totally control or direct. Freud, like all positivists, held deterministic beliefs, but for him, the determinism was psychic. The UC dictates all behavior (Freud 1961, 1962, 1965a).

The levels of consciousness provide the basic structure for Freud's model of psychic existence, but his theory is *psychodynamic,* which means that the psyche exhibits great life and energy. To explain the dynamic workings, Freud (1962) developed three components of personality—the id, the ego, and the superego. The *id* is present at birth, dwells permanently in the UC, and is a reservoir of undifferentiated instinctual and psychic energy. It consists of our most basic strivings and needs and operates on the pleasure principle, knowing only that it needs and wants. The id is neither aware of nor concerned with outside factors and forces, and consequently imposes no self-restriction on the attempt to satisfy these needs (primary process thinking). The id should not be considered as in any way evil, as it has often been portrayed in the popular media; it is amoral; morality does not apply. The id constantly operates below the level of conscious awareness and cannot be directly affected by the laws and rules of external reality. The id is the continually "immature" component of our personality, by society's standards (Freud 1961a, 1962).

The exact process by which the ego develops is somewhat confusing, but simply put, as the id comes into contact with the external world and its demands, conflict quickly arises. The real world holds many impediments to the satisfaction of the id's (UC) desires, but the id is incapable of dealing with them. This situation forces a small portion of the reservoir of energy to break off and form the *ego* (Freud 1959, 1962, 1965a), which represents a compromise between the unbridled wants of the id and the often unyielding demands of society and the world. It operates on the reality principle and uses secondary process thinking. In other words, unlike the id, the ego is in constant interaction with the outside world, and its functioning is subject to all of the rules and laws of reality. The ego is saddled with the awesome task of trying to balance the unrelenting cravings of the id with the realities of life in society; it becomes a mediator and a go-between, often struggling not to become a victim.

The last component to develop is the *superego.* A part of the ego becomes specialized in a sense, focusing on moral and ethical concerns. The superego evolves as standards and expectations from parents and other authority figures become internalized. Basically, it is the process of adopting the norms, values, and ideals of society (Freud 1962). Gibbons (1982) calls the superego the "personal-police," because it represents the rules and metes out the punishment in the form of guilt (a concept that, as we discuss later, is very important in the psychoanalytic interpretation of criminality).

The interaction between the three components holds tremendous possibilities for conflict. Ideally, Freud says, they should function in relative harmony, with each having fairly equal input. However, as it is the ego that deals with both internal and external demands, for the sake of mental well-being, it should be somewhat dominant. Disharmony among the components or excessive dominance by one results in psychic problems, which manifest themselves as a variety of aberrant behaviors, including criminal and other dissocial acts (Aichhorn 1935).

STAGES OF DEVELOPMENT (CHILDHOOD INFLUENCE ON ADULT PERSONALITY)

Freud (1965a, 1965b) postulates five universal psychosexual stages of development. A lengthy discourse on these and their specific natures is far beyond our purposes here. Suffice it to say that each of the stages is characterized by a unique set of problems pertaining to satisfaction of various basic needs. The extent to which these gratification dilemmas are not resolved determines the amount of psychic energy (libido) that is repressed into the UC and psychologically remains at that stage of development (fixated). On occasions later in life, when the finite store of conscious psychic energy grows low, these repressed reserves may be drawn upon. The price that is paid for the use of this libido is the expression of behaviors representative of the unsatisfied wishes from that earlier stage. For example, smoking or eating when under stress is oral behavior emanating from unsatisfied wishes or needs during the oral stage of development. Freud believed that, as a result of the process of fixation, most of our personalities are determined by the age of six and remain virtually unchanged throughout our lives (Maddi, 1980).

More simply put, within the psychoanalytic model, unresolved childhood problems continue to be problems (e.g., neurosis, antisocial behavior) into adulthood.

CONFLICT MODEL OF MOTIVATION (INSTINCTS AND PANSEXUALISM)

Freud (1965a) once called the mind a seething cauldron of conflict. Within his model of personality, there are a great many possibilities for conflict, which is the major motivational construct in psychoanalytic theory. To understand the multidimensional implications for conflict, we must first understand Freud's use of the term *instincts*.

In the literature, most people classify Freud's approach as an *instinctive theory* (see Megargee 1972, Bandura 1973, Maple 1973, Wrightsman and Deaux 1981), but we are more inclined toward an interpretation similar to Fromm's (1973, 6), who finds that "identification of Freudian theory with instinctivism . . . is very much open to doubt." According to Fromm, Freud actually was investigating the realm of human passions—love, hate, ambition, greed, guilt, jealousy, and envy. The confusion and subsequent misinterpretation seem to have resulted primarily from the fact that Freud could not help but conceive of his new findings and insights in terms of the concepts and terminology of his day. Also, given his medical background and apparent inability to free himself totally from the materialism of his mentors, he felt compelled to find a way to disguise the fact that he was dealing with human passions. This, coupled with the Darwinian spirit of the times, made his adoption of "instinctive" language inevitable (Fromm 1973, Megargee 1972).

Instincts, for Freud, were the mental representations of somatic processes; consequently, all were rooted in biological functioning. This observation leads Monte (1980) to conclude that Freud's treatment of instincts was the precursor to the "need—drive—behavior" conceptualization of motivation. However, Freud perceived of it as less a conscious and more a primitive process than did those who came later. According to Redl and Toch (1979), what Freud actually described was a *drive* (usually defined as the psychological component of a physiological/biological need) and the term *instinct*, they believe, is the result of poor or incorrect translation.

In clearing up what we see as misconceptions, it is crucial to address the "infamous" issue of *pansexualism*, which is the notion that all human behavior is motivated by sexual instincts (Scroggs 1985). It is certainly true that sexual motivation has played a dominant role in psychoanalytic theory, especially in earlier versions, but it is also true that the definition applied to *sexual* when interpreting Freud's theory has often been considerably more narrow than he intended. All positive affect and pleasurable experiences are sexual by the Freudian definition (Redl and Toch 1979). The reason for elevating sexual motivation to the dominant position was not some perverted sense of reality, which Freud's critics have often attributed to him, but the influence of the Darwinian approach. The primary instinct in all organisms is seen as sexual, in the form of preservation of the species (Scroggs 1985). Putting these metatheoretical issues aside, we can examine the evolution of instincts within psychoanalytic theory, especially those more relevant to criminality.

In its original form, Freud's theory assumed that human behavior was regulated by two opposing sets of instincts, sexual instincts (libido) and self-preservative or ego instincts. However, certain behavioral phenomena, such as sadisms and self-destructive actions, could not be adequately understood in this dichotomous approach (Bandura 1973). Freud (1920) initially believed that aggression was a "primary response" to the thwarting of instincts from these two sets, but as he modified his theory of motivation, his conceptualization of aggression exhibited marked change.

In *Beyond the Pleasure Principle* (1920/1961a), *The Ego and Id* (1923/1962), and his later writings (1933/1965a), Freud postulated a new dichotomy between Eros (life instincts), aimed at prolonging and enhancing life, and Thanatos (death instinct) that constantly strives for self-destruction and a return to one's original inanimate state. The wide range of potential human behaviors results from the complex interaction of these two instinctive motivational systems. Within this dichotomy, aggression is no longer merely a response to frustration of sexual or social needs but is built in as a result of the presence of the death instinct. Aggression is no longer a secondary emotion, but as Reiff (1961) puts it, is as "original as sin." By this, he does not mean to suggest that it is inherently evil, but that it is natural.

The idea of a death instinct may be very unpalatable; it was to many of Freud's contemporaries and is to many who wrestle with his ideas today. However, the relationships between Thanatos and aggression become important components in many psychoanalytic interpretations of criminal behavior. According to Freud (1963), the difference between life and death is that death has no character. There is no name for the energy of the death instinct (like *libido* for life). Aggression is not an energy; it is more pervasive and basic than that.

In one of his last works, *Civilization and Its Discontents*, Freud (1930/1961b) observed that humans are not gentle creatures that want to be loved, but, on the contrary, are creatures who possess a powerful level of instinctive aggressiveness. For humans, their neighbor is not only a potential helper and love object, but also someone who tempts satisfaction of aggressive urges to misuse and abuse sexually; to seize possessions; to humiliate, torture, and kill. Fortunately, cruel aggression usually awaits some provocation or finds itself in the service of some other purpose whose goal often can be attained by milder measures. Nevertheless, this inherent hostility constantly threatens civilization, as instinctive passions are stronger than reasonable interests (Freud, 1961b). So prevalent was the role of aggressive instinct in Freud's later writings that Reiff (1961) saw it as filling the same role as "free-will" in Christian Psychology.

The central point to understanding the Freudian position on instincts and their impact on behavior is that they emanate from the UC (id); the wishes and emotions of the id are deeply self-centered and are not subject to any social refinements. As people are virtually at the mercy of the UC, individuals are basically selfish and uncivilized. Society is a necessary evil to "elevate progenesis over self enhancement" (Monte 1980). It is also important to keep in mind that the complexity of instinctive interaction and the resulting behavioral manifestations is immense. The potential for conflict arising out of these interactions is compounded by the fact that we can never fully master nature, and our organism is part of nature. Our own organism remains at some level a "transient structure with limited capacity for adaptation and achievement" (Freud 1961b).

In Freud's theory, instincts and conflict form the foundation of all human motivation, and subsequently, they are the source of all behavior (psychic determinism) within the psychoanalytic model. With this in mind there is one more arena of conflict that must be discussed to further clarify the Freudian conceptualization of psychic conflict. The dynamic components of the personality, the id, the ego, and the superego, actually represent the central players in Freud's passion play. The id, given the nature of its functioning (primary process thinking), frequently finds itself at odds with the external world. Also, as the ego and superego reflect the outside world, they are often in conflict with the id. The potentially tyrannical superego (Horney 1945) may leave the ego in a moral quagmire, inundated with guilt. Then, of course, the ego must confront reality, which is not always cooperative or receptive to individual needs.

The ego thus finds itself in a rather precarious position, being literally in the midst of all conflicts. It is the ego that suffers from the anxiety, guilt, and other negative emotions generated by psychic disharmony. It is this disharmony that is manifested as various types of problematic and dissocial behavior.

III. KEY IDEAS

Freudian theory applied to criminology focuses on explaining criminal acts through psychoanalytic concepts and interpretations, and there are certain key ideas in Freudian theory that are most relevant to thinking about criminal behavior.

Freud had no direct contact with criminal types. Consequently, in the twenty-four volumes of his collected works, there is only a smattering of direct references to crime or criminals (Vold and Bernard 1986, Vetter and Silverman 1986). In *A General Selection from the Works of Sigmund Freud* (1957), which is an extensive index and glossary of Freudian ideas and concepts from 1910 to 1923, only a few pages relate to criminality. In reading Freud, one is more likely to encounter in-depth discourse on a variety of behaviors reflecting UC drives, which in turn represent social and greater universal conditions. Freud was a generalist. What follows is a progression, from a more purely Freudian interpretation of the etiology of criminal behavior through the various modifications and applications of others.

The most direct fit between "true Freudian" theory and criminal conduct is in the area of violence. In fact, Megargee (1973) says that the single most important aspect of Freud's theory is that it is truly a theory of violence, not simple aggression. As stated earlier, aggression is a dominant instinct in the psychoanalytic model. It was originally conceived of as a response to a thwarting of the pleasure principle (Freud 1961a), but later, Freud (1965a) reconstructed his theory, making aggression a direct outgrowth of Thanatos (the death instinct). Murder or other acts of criminal violence can result from Eros (the life instinct) redirecting Thanatos outwardly (Monte 1980), or a lack of socially acceptable avenues for aggressive catharsis, or from inadequate ego control and repression mechanisms (Bartol 1980). Generally, psychiatric studies of homicide have concentrated on individual cases, usually of extreme forms, and can typically be characterized as being preoccupied with the "medicolegal implications" and motivated by an overwhelming desire to prove Freudian orthodoxy (Bartol 1980). Subsequently, little has been done in the way of developing comprehensive general theories of criminal violence or other criminal conduct from the psychoanalytic perspective.

In light of this rather narrow focus, a more fruitful line of theorizing to pursue, in regard to a general psychoanalytic interpretation of criminal conduct, relates to Freud's emphasis on guilt. For Freud, the sense of guilt is the most important problem in the development of civilization; it is the key element in understanding the destructive instinct. He postulated two origins of the sense of guilt: fear of authority and, later, fear of the superego. *Fear of authority* relates to the insistence (from others) that instinctive satisfactions be renounced. *Fear of the superego* includes this same insistence, but it also demands punishment, as the individual cannot conceal from himself the continuance of forbidden wishes (Freud, 1961a).

In *The Ego and the Id*, Freud (1962) states that in many criminals, especially youthful ones, it is possible to detect a powerful sense of guilt that existed prior to the criminal transgression. Guilt, then, is the motive and not the result; relief comes from fastening it to something real. These individuals suffer from oppressive guilt feelings of which they do not know the origin. Only after committing a misdeed is the oppression mitigated, as it is only then that the guilt can be consciously accounted for. The criminal commits crimes to provide punishment from authority in an attempt to justify pre-existing guilt; the act reflects a need to hurt the self (Reiff 1961). The major culprit in such a scenario is an overdeveloped superego. It produces constant and excessive feelings of guilt that serve to motivate a desire to be punished, which affords the only escape, albeit temporary (Vold and Bernard 1986). Of course, guilt cannot become a motive until the capacity to experience it is acquired. This process entails the internalization of society's rules and standards (Monte 1980).

Unlike many who proposed religious explanations, Freud viewed guilt as a motive for bad behavior, not as a response to it. To Freud, guilt is not natural but pathological: a guilty conscience may not (and often does not) imply a turn to the good, but may actually bring about the most heinous of crimes (Reiff 1961). Most criminal acts in adulthood, then, result from the mental relief accompanying a forbidden act (Freud 1959). Crimes are *sublimations*, a defense mechanism involving the rechanneling of energy associated with an emotion or event into a seemingly unrelated activity. They serve to mitigate guilt by bringing punishment. The evolution of this process on an individual level is intricately interwoven with the development of society and civilization, and it becomes quite complex as explained by Freud. A sortie into the anthropologic origins (as seen by Freud) of the punishment–guilt connection is beyond our scope; for an in-depth explication, see *Totem and Taboo* (Freud 1950).

There are other Freudian concepts besides guilt that have been used in the explanation of criminal behavior. One of the more prominent concepts that has been associated with various types of criminal behavior is the Oedipal or Electra conflict. Very briefly, the Oedipal conflict in males or Electra in females occurs during the third (phallic) of Freud's five stages of development. At this time, the boy begins to fantasize himself as his mother's lover and his father's rival (and the girl fantasizes herself as her father's lover and her mother's rival). This conflict is generally resolved by the age of five, when the child realizes that it is impossible to posses the mother/father and that continued rivalry is not worth the risk, given the obvious power of the adversary. Consequently, the child chooses to identify with the same-sex parent and tries to become as much like him or her as possible. (This is the foundation for gender identification in Freudian theory.) Once this conflict is resolved, the child enters the latency period of middle childhood, and sexual urges do not reemerge as major motivational factors until puberty (genital stage) (Freud 1965b).

If this conflict is not resolved adequately through identification with the same-sex parent, later in life the repressed (UC) aspects will come back to influence behavior. Unresolved Oedipal/Electra conflicts have been offered as explanations for various types of prostitution and sexual promiscuity, as well as hostility toward (male) authority and running away (Bartol 1980, Gibbons 1982, Hagan 1986).

Sexual motivation has also been theoretically linked to sadistic behavior (Freud 1959, Fromm 1973) and to problems such as pyromania (Abrahamsen 1960, Gold 1962). However, such explanations are always post hoc, and they are quite vague on the way the relationships between these acts and sexual gratification really develop (Bartol 1980).

To examine what is arguably the most productive, reasonable, and defensible line of criminological theorizing to evolve out of the psychoanalytic perspective, some ideas presented earlier must be examined. First, a few questions about the connection between guilt–punishment and society are apropos. What is the ultimate source of both guilt and punishment? The source is in the communal requirements of society. Who are the most frequent transgressors of these requirements? The young are, of course. Who most often levies the punishment of the transgressions? Parents do. The nature of the experiences shared by children and parents is crucial within the psychoanalytic perspective. As noted earlier, Freud's observation that childhood experience has an impact on adult personality and behavior is considered to be one of his major theoretical contributions.

The earliest and most prominent application of this notion to criminological theory was made by August Aichhorn (1935) in his famous work on delinquency *Wayward Youth* (to which Freud, incidentally, wrote the Foreword). Aichhorn was an Austrian psychiatrist and director of a correctional facility for juveniles (Gibbons 1982). His basic line of reasoning has been elaborated by various theorists such as Friedlander (1947) and Abrahamsen (1960).

Dr. Aichhorn (1935) was not at all convinced, as were many of his contemporaries, that the environment could be the whole cause of delinquent behavior. Instead, he believed that there first must be a "predisposition to delinquency," concluding that societal stress alone could not result in a life of crime. This predisposition or latent delinquency could be manifested in youngsters' personalities by requiring them to seek immediate gratification (impulsivity), by forcing them to adopt a more hedonistic and egoistic approach to the world, or as a poorly developed superego (lack of guilt). In Freudian terms, any or all of these characteristics are present in a personality dominated by the id (Siegel 1986).

In the psychoanalytic interpretation of criminal and delinquent behavior, the central concern is with disturbances or disharmony between the ego and superego or a lack of control of the id (Allen, Friday, Roebuck, and Sagarin 1981, Vold and Bernard 1986). According to Warren and Hindelang (1979), such disturbances manifest as criminal behavior when there is a failure in effective personal controls stemming from problematic early learning and parental neglect. Problems experienced (and not adequately resolved) in the first few years of life make it impossible for the child to control impulses, arresting psychological development to the point that the individual remains sort of an "aggrandizing infant" who never fully develops the ego (reality principle) (Redl and Toch 1979). Kate Friedlander (1947) postulates that faulty early development leads to the establishment of an antisocial character structure that is not capable of handling reality properly.

These ideas are direct derivatives of both original Freudian and Aichhornian conceptualizations. Aichhorn (1935) believed that delinquent behavior is the result of early psychic trauma or injury and repressed experiences from childhood. This psychological condition constitutes his "predisposition to delinquency" discussed earlier. In *Civilization and Its Discontents*, Freud (1961b) theorizes that, in delinquent children brought up without love, tension between the ego and superego is lacking, which serves to direct the whole of the aggressive instinct outward. Both Freud (1961b) and Aichhorn (1935) placed heavy emphasis on the nature of childrearing. Both believed that two main types of pathogenic styles of upbringing were possible: overstrictness and spoiling. Overstrictness hampers the development of the superego while also instilling hostility. Spoiling causes the formation of an overly severe superego, because constant unconditional love allows no outlet for aggression, hence turning it inward. Considerable empirical support has been garnered for the connection between problematic behavior and improper parenting styles (see Hoffman and Saltzstein 1967, Hoffman 1970, Baumrind 1970).

Another very prevalent psychodynamic explanation of criminality that can be viewed as an extension of our preceding discussion of problems created by bad parenting relates to the role played by psychological maladjustment. The type of psychological disorder that has been (and continues to be) most associated with criminality is the psychopathic personality. One of the early psychoanalytic interpretations of psychopathic personality disorder that holds clear implications for criminal behavior comes from neo-Freudian Karen Horney (1945). In brief, Horney postulates three "neurotic styles" for dealing with others: moving toward, moving away, and moving against. The moving against style is characterized by aggressiveness and hostility, and she portrayed this individual as seeing life as a "free-for-all." Horney refers to this style as a "psychopathic type" characteristic. The person believes in power and force, and any need for approval or affection that is present is in the service of aggressive goals. Feelings are choked off unless they serve a function in enhancing power, and there is not great concern or feeling for others. The major cause of this and other types of maladjusted coping strategies is most often what Horney (1937) calls the "basic evil," bad parenting.

Psychopathy has been extensively covered in the literature (for good treatments, see Cleckley 1976, Hare 1978). Basically, it is a bit of a departure from the traditional Freudian reliance on guilt as a prime motivator of criminal behavior in that it relies on the opposite, no guilt. This model postulates a weak superego and an ego that seems incapable of checking the impulsivity of the id, but that is strong in the sense that it can locate temptations, enlist allies, and create alibis (Redl and Toch 1979). Whether it is an ego overcome by and in the service of the id or one that is overwhelmed by the oppressive guilt heaped on it by an overzealous superego, from the psychoanalytic perspective, the source of criminality is never quite where it seems. It is only the ego that manifests it, and it is the ego that pays the price. However, the ego does not bear the bulk of the blame.

In summary, Redl and Toch (1979) identify five basic psychoanalytic interpretations of crime:

1. Criminal behavior is a form of neurosis (or other maladjustment) not fundamentally different from other types. It is an attempt to restore psychic order.
2. Crime is the result of a compulsive need for punishment to alleviate guilt and anxiety from the UC.
3. Criminal behavior is a means for obtaining substitute gratification of needs and desires not met in the family.
4. Criminal behavior is a direct result of intrusions into consciousness of traumatic repressed memories.
5. Criminal conduct represents displaced hostility.

A few comments on Freud's views on the criminal justice system are in order. As is the case with criminality, his observations relating to the criminal justice system are sparse and are often buried within more general discussions of societal institutions. The most relevant observations for our purposes relate to punishment in response to crime. The earliest human penal systems can be traced to the concept of *taboo*. As society evolved, it took over punishment for certain transgressions, punishment previously considered automatic and left to divine intervention. Violation of a taboo makes the offender taboo, which means that he or she is contagious and to be shunned. Furthermore, according to Freud, if the violations were not to be avenged by other group members, it would force into their awareness that they too really want to transgress in the same way. If one person succeeds in gratifying the repressed desire, the same desire will inevitably be kindled in others (Freud 1950).

In order to quell temptation, transgressors must not be allowed to reap the ill-gotten fruits of their enterprise. Also, punishment often provides those who administer it the opportunity to commit the same outrage "under the colour of expiation" (Freud 1950). The very foundation of the human penal system is based on the notion that the same prohibited impulses are present in criminals and in the punishing community. Society hopes to prevent brutal violence by exercising the exclusive right to use violence against criminals, but unfortunately, the law is not capable of grasping the more refined manifestations and cautious applications of human aggressiveness (Freud 1961b). It should be clear that Freud was not surprised at the general ineffectiveness of correctional approaches. The failures are inherent in the human condition, as the system serves the same master as the behavior it seeks to control and deter.

IV. CRITIQUE

The coverage of Freud's theory and its various applications has been, by necessity, condensed and rudimentary. Also, whereas the basic integrity of those thoughts may have been maintained, some loss is inevitable when the broader picture is not totally represented. Unfortunately, there is no way to give the whole picture here, even if the entire book were devoted to psychoanalytic theory and its impact. At some point, a careful reading of Freud and some of the others discussed should be undertaken to provide a better feel for the true depth and complexity of the psychoanalytic perspective. Tempered by this aside, the following critical discussion of the psychoanalytic orientation and its concepts is offered.

It has been stated that few views in the social sciences have evoked stronger reactions, theoretically or emotionally, or provided as much controversy as have Freud's (Redl and Toch 1979). Over the course of time, Freud and his ideas have been ignored, revered, ostracized, rebelled against, ridiculed, defied, modified, remodified, discarded, and resurrected. It is inconceivable that any other theory has had greater heuristic impact across the disciplines in the social sciences or has crept deeper into the fabric of the lay conception of human nature. Despite this widespread influence, in their recent book *Crime and Human Nature*, Wilson and Herrnstein (1985) state that criminologists have been reluctant historically to accept such psychological conceptualizations, preferring a more sociological orientation. Some possible reasons for this lack of acceptance can be gleaned from criticisms commonly levied against the psychoanalytic approach. In the following, basic criticisms (positive and negative) of psychoanalytic theory in general are offered and then considered more narrowly as they are specifically applicable to criminological thought.

One of the most frequent complaints against Freud's model of personality/behavior is that it is too philosophical and clinical, or, in other words, it is not empirically testable. The problem of empirical evaluation is not a statement against internal validity. Freud's theory is for the most part extremely tight and logically ordered, but it leaves serious questions unanswered concerning external validity. Freud relied on the patients that he treated in his private practice, most of whom were upper-middle-class and upper-class women, as a source of data for developing and testing his theory. This situation poses several potential threats to external validity, as it raises questions about Freud's methodology and his ability to assess his theoretical concepts objectively and about the representativeness of his sample and subsequent generalizability of his conclusions. Research that has been done professing to test empirically, and more often than not support, Freudian interpretations are actually ad hoc explanations (Vold and Bernard 1986) of observed behavior, usually in clinical settings. Freudians tend to interpret subjective states of individuals undergoing psychotherapeutic treatment rather than accumulate and statistically analyze aggregate behavioral samples (Wilson and Herrnstein 1985). Psychoanalysis is first and foremost a therapeutic technique, and the quest for criminal personality typically is only an element of the therapeutic goal, not a systematic empirical endeavor to identify general causal factors in criminal behavior (Hagan 1986). Psychoanalysis is primarily an attempt to separate private affections/passions from their neurotic displacements onto society's institutions and public authority (Reiff 1961). Philosophically and scientifically, this is a very different goal than the desire to develop a general and grounded theory of criminal behavior.

One very important reason for the inability to subject psychoanalytic concepts to empirical scrutiny is Freud's exclusive reliance on UC processes as the source of behavior. By his definition, it is not possible to isolate and measure such processes objectively. Instead, we must provide them with an avenue for expression, such as dream interpretation, free association, or projective devices, and then interpret their existence through the symbolic content of the response—post hoc, of course. This issue of UC dominance surfaces again when we discuss the pessimism/responsibility criticisms and also the exaggerated role for biology/instincts accusation.

The expansion of psychoanalytic theory into the newly evolving discipline of criminology led to an emphasis on maladjustment as a factor in criminality, but the maladjustment approach to explaining criminal behavior has not been unanimously well received. Many criminologists (and psychologists) have aptly pointed out that all of those labeled as criminally deviant are not necessarily mentally disturbed; they are "just" criminals (McMahon and McMahon 1983). From our own combined experiences, we must concur; most offenders are not, like Charles Manson, a walking *Diagnostic and Statistical Manual* (the handbook of clinical diagnosis). There are those who argue that the Freudian approach can account for only a few crimes, especially those of a more bizarre or violent nature (McNamara and Sagarin 1977, Allen et al. 1981, Siegel 1986). However, Redl and Toch (1979) state that the belief that psychoanalytic theory is relevant only when offenders are suffering from a psychobiological disorder is a myth. Justification for their conclusion lies in an understanding of the Freudian context of maladjustment. Simply put, because of the dominant role of the UC within psychoanalytic theory, everyone is by definition maladjusted to some extent. The real focus is not on the maladjustment per se, but on the UC source of the behavior.

One is well advised not to become too extreme in either direction on this issue. It certainly does not seem tenable that the UC dictates all behavior, and that all of us are maladjusted because of the skeletons of trauma and unresolved desires buried there; by the same token, the psychoanalytic interpretation certainly has done more than simply account for criminal behavior in a few fringe cases. If nothing else, it has drawn our attention to psychodynamic processes.

A second area of criticism is of a philosophical rather than an empirical nature. The great grievance against Freud by the Humanists (e.g., Rogers 1961) and others has been that he is far too pessimistic in his view of human motivation and potential. Freud saw people as being dominated by selfish and uncivilized needs, desires, and psychic processes (Monte 1980), believing that no matter how much we are able to master nature and its forces, we still cannot attain the satisfactions we really want (Freud 1961a).

It is true that Freud did not see humans through rose-colored glasses, but maybe one can interpret his view more as a form of hardened realism than unbounded pessimism and negativism. In *The Ego and the Id*, he did say that humans are far more immoral than is generally believed, but he also said that we are far more moral than we have any idea of. A look at Freud's life is relevant here. The seemingly excessive pessimism that characterized his writing, and especially his later writings, can be attributed at least partially to the human catastrophes that Freud had experienced and witnessed (e.g., World War I, cancer, the rise of Nazi Germany, the beginnings of World War II). The dramatic and often destructive lengths to which Freud saw individuals and whole societies go to satisfy their desires led him to conclude that, at the very best, civilization can only reach a balance of discontents (Reiff 1961).

In determining why humans are like this, Freud laid the blame largely in the lap of civilization. Maladjustment, he said, comes from an inability to cope with the continual frustrations and conflict heaped on us by civilization (Freud 1961b). Society is seen as a necessary but definite evil, serving to elevate progenesis over self-enhancement (Monte 1980). However, for there to be conflict, there must be opposing sides. Within the psychoanalytic model, the extremely powerful opposing force to civilization is the UC (the repository of unresolved conflicts and traumas from childhood, and the container of our unfettered and most primitive instinctive desires), which, according to the principle of psychic determinism, actually dictates all behavior. There is another potential problem with the "Freudian human being." It seems that Freud's being cannot be held accountable for his or her own actions. After all, UC instinctive desires are genetically determined, civilization is forced on us, and a child cannot be held responsible for the traumas that they experience. However, linking adult behavior or problems to past events is not necessarily equivalent to absolution from responsibility. The fact that behavior is understandable by psychic, even UC motives, in no way justifies it or makes it any more acceptable to society (Redl and Toch 1979). What the Freudian view offers is a potential explanation.

Freud has often been accused of being too biological and has been soundly criticized for his heavy reliance on instincts as motivators. The Humanists and even some of Freud's own students (e.g., Erich Fromm) have felt that he likened us too much to (other) animals. Fromm (1941) believes that there is a distinction between animal and human nature. Animal nature consists of the biochemical and physiological mechanisms for physical survival and is the least important aspect of psychological existence. Humans are the only organism possessing human nature (Fromm 1941, Rogers 1961, Maslow 1971), which is characterized more by emotional and cognitive abilities.

Two instincts more than any others have served as fodder for scathing attacks on Freudian theory: sex and death. The fundamental problem with death instinct is that it runs contrary to commonly held conceptions of human nature. We have no problem with Eros. A drive or even an instinct for survival seems reasonable, but not an instinct to cease to live. Attitudes also account for a significant part of the uneasiness expressed over the psychoanalytic "preoccupation" with sexual motivation. Given the sexually repressive atmosphere that prevailed in Victorian-era Vienna, it is not hard to see why Freud's ideas drew derision. Misinterpretation and translation problems have also fueled and continue to fuel criticism over sexual motivation.

Another problem with the attributes assigned to sexual instincts is that, as mentioned earlier, the connections between them and the variety of behaviors said to emanate from them are often quite vague. This is a problem, whether they are being used to explain criminal behavior or any other type of behavior. The connection between the death instinct and aggression/violence is more readily apparent, but alternative explanations for such behaviors are at least equally feasible. Dollard and coworkers (Dollard, Miller, Doob, Mowrer, and Sears, 1939), in their classic work *Frustration and Aggression*, attribute aggression not to an instinct, but to frustration. Fromm (1973) cites numerous examples of instrumental aggression as acts of aggression motivated by other needs. He further argues that the anthropologic data demonstrate that an instinctive interpretation of destructiveness is untenable, as destruction and cruelty are minimal kin many societies, especially the least civilized.

Destructiveness, according to Fromm (1973), is not an isolated factor but is part of a syndrome. The fact that this syndrome is not a biological or instinctive part of human nature does not imply that destruction is not widespread and intense. To explain the pervasiveness of aggression, Fromm (1973) and many others (e.g., Bandura, Ross, and Ross 1961, Binswanger 1963, Bandura 1973) have used more social and interpersonal factors. Fromm (1941, 1973), the existentialists (e.g., Kierkegaard, Nietzsche), and Durkheim (1960) make much of the breakdown of human relations in (modern) industrialized society, using concepts such as *mass-man, inauthenticity,* and *anomie.*

The last major criticism of Freudian theory is his neglect of social factors. Philip Reiff (1961) concluded that Freud was never a social psychologist in the true sense of the term; rather, he always portrayed society as a mirror of the individual. Considerable attention is paid at throughout this book to sociological explanations of crime; comparisons and conclusions in regard to this criticism are left to the reader.

In summary, psychoanalytic and other psychological explanations are often reproached for making the causation of behavior too complex. Statistically, it does seem that most human behavior (criminal not excepted) is probably fairly rational, goal-oriented, direct, based in the present, and reasonably uncomplicated, but there certainly are times when ignoring the depth to which psychology goes can produce distorted views of crime and initiate inappropriate reactions to offenders. So, even though we might not adopt the extreme UC—nonrational—instinctive explanation of the etiology of criminal behavior that characterizes true Freudianism, we certainly must acknowledge that there are offenders whose actions are not clearly reflective of the underlying motives (Redl and Toch 1979). In such cases, focusing only on the criminal act itself creates a serious gap in our understanding of crime and criminality.

If most behavior is explainable by current happenings and is seldom the result of deep-seated psychological processes, then what has been the real contribution of psychoanalytic theory? The answer must be that the heuristic impact of Freudian psychology stands above everything else. His theory has generated immeasurable amounts of productive thought and research that extend far beyond psychology and into all of the social sciences. Besides the widespread impact of his ideas in science, the Freudian view of human functioning has crept into the fabric of Western thought, permeating the beliefs of laypersons as well as social scientists. These factors make Freud and his theory a force beyond compare in contemporary thought, and actually guarantees him what we believe he most wanted—immortality.

References

Abrahamsen, D. 1960. *The psychology of crime.* New York: Columbia University Press.

Aichhorn, A. 1935. *Wayward youth.* New York: The Viking Press.

Allen, H.E., Friday, P.D., Roebuck, J.B., and Sagarin, E. 1981. *Crime and punishment: an introduction to criminology.* New York: The Free Press.

Bandura, A. 1973. *Aggression: a social learning analysis.* Englewood Cliffs, NJ: Prentice-Hall.

Bandura, A., Ross, D., and Ross, S.A. 1961. Transmission of aggression through imitation of aggressive models. *J. Person. Soc. Psych.* 63:575–82.

Bartol, C.R. 1980. *Criminal behavior: a psychosocial approach.* Englewood Cliffs, NJ: Prentice-Hall.

Baumrind, D. 1970. Socialization and instrumental competence in young children. *Young Child.* 26(2):104–19.

Binswanger, L. 1963. *Being-in-the-world* (J. Needham, Trans.). New York: Basic Books.

Cleckley, H. 1976. *The mask of sanity.* 5th ed. St. Louis: C.V. Mosby.

Dollard, J., Miller, N.E., Doob, L.W., Mowrer, O.H., and Sears, R.R. 1939. *Frustration and aggression.* New Haven: Yale University Press.

Durkheim, E. 1960. *The division of labor in society.* Glencoe, IL: The Free Press. (Original work published 1893).

Fadiman, J., and Frager, R. 1976. *Personality and personal growth.* New York: Harper and Row.

Freud, S. 1920. *A general introduction to psychoanalysis.* New York: Bonni and Liveright.

————. 1935. *Autobiography.* New York: W.W. Norton and Company.

————. 1950. *Totem and taboo.* London: Routledge and Keagan Paul. (Original work published 1913.)

————. 1959. *Group psychology and the analysis of the ego.* New York: W.W. Norton and Company. (Original work published 1921.)

————. 1961a. *Beyond the pleasure principle*. New York: W.W. Norton and Company. (Original work published 1920.)

————. 1961b. *Civilization and its discontents*. New York: W.W. Norton and Company. (Original work published 1930.)

————. 1962. *The ego and the id*. New York: W.W. Norton and Company. (Original work published 1923.)

————. 1963. *General psychological theory papers on metapsychology*. New York: Collier Books.

————. 1965a. *New introductory lectures on psycho-analysis*. New York: W.W. Norton and Company.

————. 1965b. *Three essays on the theory of sexuality*. New York: Aron Books. (Original work published 1905.)

————. 1969. *The psychopathology of everyday life*. New York: W.W. Norton and Company. (Original work published 1901.)

Fromm, E. 1941. *Escape from freedom*. New York: Aron Books.

————. 1973. *The anatomy of human destructiveness*. New York: Holt, Rinehart and Winston.

Gibbons, D.C. 1982. *Society, crime and criminal behavior*. 4th ed. Englewood Cliffs, NJ: Prentice-Hall.

Gold, L.H. 1962. Psychiatric profile of the firesetter. *J. Forens. Sci.* 7:404–17.

Hagan, F.E. 1986. *Introduction to theories, methods, and criminal behavior*. Chicago: Nelson Hall.

Hare, R.D. 1978. Psychopathology and crime. In L. Otten (Ed.), *Colloquium on the correlates of crime and the determinants of criminal behavior*. Rosslyn, VA: Mitre Corporation.

Hoffman, M.L. 1970. Moral development. In P.H. Mussen (Ed.), *Carmichael's manual of child psychology* (Vol. 2, 3rd ed.). New York: John Wiley and Sons.

Hoffman, M.L., and Saltzstein, H.D. 1967. Parent discipline and the child's moral development. *J. Person. Soc. Psych.* 5:45–57.

Horney, K. 1937. *The neurotic personality of our time*. New York: W.W. Norton and Company.

————. 1945. *Our inner conflicts*. New York: W.W. Norton and Company.

Jones, E. 1953. *The life and work of Sigmund Freud: the formative years and the great discoveries* (Vol. 1). New York: Basic Books.

————. 1957. *The life and work of Sigmund Freud: the last phase* (Vol. 3). New York: Basic Books.

Maddi, S.R. 1980. *Personality theories: a comparative analysis*. 4th ed. Homewood, IL: The Dorsey Press.

Maple, T. 1973. Introduction to the scientific study of aggression. In T. Maple (Ed.), *Aggression, hostility, and violence: nature or nurture?* (pp. 1–10). New York: Holt, Rinehart and Winston.

Maslow, A.H. 1971. *The farther reaches of human nature*. New York: The Viking Press.

McMahon, F.B., and McMahon, J.W. 1983. *Abnormal behavior: psychology's view*. Homewood, IL: The Dorsey Press.

McNamara, D.E.J., and Sagarin, E. 1977. *Sex, crime, and the law*. New York: The Free Press.

Megargee, E.I. 1972. *The psychology of violence and aggression*. (Reprint from a report prepared for the National Commission on the Causes and Prevention of Violence.) Morristown, NJ: General Learning Press.

Monte, C.F. 1980. *Beneath the mask: an introduction to theories of personality*. 2nd ed. New York: Holt, Rinehart and Winston.

Redl, F., and Toch, H. 1979. The psychoanalytic perspective. In H. Toch (Ed.), *Psychology of crime and criminal justice* (pp. 183–197). New York: Holt, Rinehart and Winston.

Reiff, P. 1961. *Freud: the mind of the moralist*. Garden City, NJ: Doubleday Anchor Books.

Rogers, C.R. 1961. *On becoming a person*. Boston: Houghton Mifflin.

Rychlak, J.F. 1973. *Introduction to personality and psychotherapy: a theory construction approach*. Boston: Houghton Mifflin.

Scroggs, J.R. 1985. *Key ideas in personality theory*. New York: West Publishing.

Siegel, L.J. 1986. *Criminology*. 2nd ed. New York: West Publishing.

Vetter, H.J., and Silverman, I.J. 1986. *Criminology and crime: an introduction*. New York: Harper and Row.

Vold, G.B., and Bernard, T.J. 1986. *Theoretical criminology.* 3rd ed. New York: Oxford University Press.

Wilson, J.Q., and Herrnstein, R.J. 1985. *Crime and human nature: the definitive study of the causes of crime.* New York: Simon and Schuster.

Wolheim, R. 1971. *Sigmund Freud.* New York: The Viking Press.

Wrightsman, L.S., and Deaux, K. 1981. *Social psychology in the 80s.* 3rd ed. Monterey, CA: Brooks/Cole Publishing.

Supplemental Readings

Abrahamsen, D. 1960. *The psychology of crime.* New York: Columbia University Press.

Ellison, K.W., and Buckhout, R. 1981. *Psychology and criminal justice.* New York: Harper and Row.

Freud, S. 1920. *A general introduction to psycho-analysis.* New York: Bonni and Liveright.

———. 1935. *Autobiography.* New York: W.W. Norton and Company.

———. 1961. *Civilization and its discontents.* New York: W.W. Norton and Company.

———. 1965. *New introductory lectures on psycho-analysis.* New York: W.W. Norton and Company.

Fromm, E. 1973. *The anatomy of human destructiveness.* New York: Holt, Rinehart and Winston.

Jones, E. 1953. *The life and works of Sigmund Freud* (Vol. 1). New York: Basic Books.

———. 1955. *The life and works of Sigmund Freud* (Vol. 2). New York: Basic Books.

———. 1957. *The life and works of Sigmund Freud* (Vol. 3). New York: Basic Books.

Maddi, S.R. 1980. *Personality theories: a comparative analysis.* 4th ed. Homewood, IL: The Dorsey Press.

Monte, C.F. 1980. *Beneath the mask: an introduction to theories of personality.* 2nd ed. New York: Holt, Rinehart and Winston.

Redl, F., and Toch, H. 1979. The psychoanalytic perspective. In H. Toch (Ed.), *Psychology of crime and criminal justice* (pp. 183–97). New York: Holt, Rinehart and Winston.

Reiff, P. 1961. *Freud: the mind of the moralist.* Garden City, NJ: Doubleday Anchor Books.

Rickman, J. (Ed.). 1957. *A general selection from the works of Sigmund Freud.* Garden City, NJ: Doubleday Anchor Books.

Rychlak, J.F. 1973. *Introduction to personality and psychotherapy: a theory construction approach.* Boston: Houghton Mifflin.

Vold, G.B., and Bernard, T.J. 1986. *Theoretical criminology.* 3rd ed. New York: Oxford University Press.

CHAPTER 5
ROBERT EZRA PARK:
1864–1944

—◦◦◦—

I. BIOGRAPHICAL SKETCH

Perhaps more than any of the pioneers in this volume, Robert Ezra Park arrived late in life as a critical player in the development of social science and criminology. He was already fifty years old when he began teaching at the university, establishing for himself significant long-term relationships with colleagues as well as carrying out research projects destined to become benchmark studies in sociology, and subsequently, in criminology.

Park was born near the small town of Shickshinny (Luzerne County), Pennsylvania, on February 14, 1864. At the end of the Civil War, his father—a Union soldier—and his mother—Vermont woman cultured in art and literature—moved to another rural town, Red Wing, Minnesota. His father opened a grocery business, and the family settled in to northern rural life. Young Robert remained in this rather stark environment until he graduated from high school in 1882.

Only brief comments are available regarding Park's early schooling. He was reportedly an average student, with geometry a favorite subject and with an avid appetite for reading dime novels (Matthews 1977, 3). Although it is not clear how or why he first developed a flair for writing, which was later to become his livelihood, it is known that he edited his high school newspaper and later a college newspaper at the University of Michigan.

As an undergraduate student, Park was not particularly absorbed with scholarship. The University of Minnesota, which he briefly attended, and the University of Michigan, where he spent the remainder of his undergraduate years, offered more than intellectual pursuits. College athletics, Greek fraternal organizations, and student activism were not foreign to U.S. campuses in the period just prior to what became known as the "gay nineties." Park played football, at least for a period of time, and kept quite busy in extracurricular activities. In fact, toward the end of his undergraduate years, his out-of-class activities caused him to fail a required course in Greek, and his graduation was on the verge of being delayed. Only at the last minute did the faculty decide to permit his graduation because he had completed extra courses in contemporary humanities (Matthews 1977, 6). However, Park maintained a growing fascination with the world of ideas and was ever curious to find answers to abstract issues. It was not surprising that he was lured into the social sciences and humanities and away from engineering, his initial choice of study.

In 1883 he graduated with a bachelor's degree in philosophy and with a reasonable knowledge of German. While at the University of Michigan, Park had taken a number of courses from a young professor named John Dewey. Through Dewey, who became a close friend, Park gained an appreciation for philosopher and sociologist

Herbert Spencer and a view of the world as an interrelated framework of organic forms that includes various social structures. It was also Dewey who first exposed Park to the importance of understanding communications as a social institution and who made him especially aware of the function and impact of the telegraph and the newspaper on society.

During this era, the United States was working its way through the Reconstruction period following the Civil War, and the nation was in the midst of a technological and industrial revolution. The inventions of electricity and the telephone, soon to be joined by the automobile, were rapidly altering the way people related to each other. Park was able to experience these major shifts somewhat as an outsider, having been reared in small, Midwestern-town culture. However, rather than to withdraw after college into the security and calm of rural life, as his father wished him to do, he packed his bags and set off to see the world, experience its glamour, and seek his fortune. This Horatio Alger–attitude was undoubtedly acted on in a similar manner by many young men of the period who were guided by a strong Protestant ethic and disenchantment with rural life.

On graduation, Park's combining of good times with enough study to get by did not leave him much of an impetus toward any particular vocation. In fact, for most of his life he was preoccupied, if not obsessed, with finding his occupational "calling." After a very brief semester or two of teaching secondary school, he set out to explore the larger urban areas of the Northeast. He did this in a way that changed his life and later shaped his thinking as a social scientist. He became a newspaper reporter.

Undoubtedly, a most memorable aspect of Park's nonacademic life was his nearly twelve years in various phases of newspaper journalism. Beginning in 1885 as a reporter with the *Minneapolis Journal* and later with the *Detroit Tribune* and the *New York Journal*, he ended this rather colorful and eye-opening early career with the *Chicago Tribune* in 1898. During this period he covered the gamut of newspaper function, beginning as a novice street reporter, to writing feature editorials for the Sunday edition of the *New York World*, to being city editor of the *Detroit Tribune*.

It would not be much of an overstatement to say that Park experienced all aspects of urban life, especially because he also saw city life from the "behind-the-scenes" vantage point of a police-beat reporter (for the *New York Journal*). Matthews suggests that Park loved New York City, "warts and all" (1977, 11). He enjoyed telling stories of working his way into opium dens in order to report on the seamier side of turn-of-the-twentieth-century New York City (Matthews 1973, 254). It is important to note that during this same time, the discipline of sociology, still in its infancy, was increasingly identified with the study of urbanization and its subsequent effects on citizen and social life (see Chapter 3 on Durkheim), and both Park and the fledgling discipline were examining the same subject matter, although from differing perspectives.

Whereas classroom sociology was yet a rather sterile and intellectual armchair pursuit, Park's sidewalk observations and reporting of everyday life depicted city life literally from the ground up. Although by 1898 the classroom was in need of an injection of reality, and Park was becoming frustrated with newspaper life, exotic though it was, the union of Park with academic sociology was still sixteen years away.

Although Park later spoke nostalgically of the newspaper days, he admitted that he had never thought of the newspaper business as his chosen profession. The lingering question of what he should do with his life continued to bother him, particularly after his marriage to the aristocratic daughter of a Michigan Supreme Court judge. He began to feel the newspaper business was insufficiently fulfilling for him and provided inadequate support for his family. Consequently, he decided to return to university life to pursue graduate study, this time taking with him a sizable pocketful of life experiences.

By age thirty-four, Park had completed a master's degree in philosophy at Harvard, where he was influenced greatly by the pioneer psychologist William James. It was James who helped Park appreciate the interplay between human consciousness and the environment. Park also learned from James the important role of emotion in the overall attempt to understand others: one cannot discount the value of empathy in any attempt to reach total understanding. This especially appealed to Park, whose feelings had figured significantly in much of what he had written as a news reporter. Later, as a sociologist, he would appreciate the value of participant observation with the analysis of case histories as an effective scientific methodology.

At the turn of the century, Europe—particularly Germany—was still considered the center of scholasticism. With the financial support of his father, Park moved with his family to Berlin. He attended the University of Berlin for a brief time and later enrolled at the University of Heidelberg, where he graduated in 1904 with a Ph.D. in philosophy. His doctoral dissertation, of which he was not particularly proud, was titled "Masse und Publikum: Eine Methodologische und Soziologische Untersuchung" ("The Crowd and the Public: A Methodological and Sociological Examination"). Following the wake of August Comte, European sociology was still in its formative stages, and writers such as Emile Durkheim, Ferdinand Toennies, and Herbert Spencer were concerned with explaining social disorganization associated with war and revolution. Park's book on crowd behavior falls into this intellectual tradition by its concern with the impact of urban decay on citizenry. While in Berlin, Park studied under Georg Simmel, a professor whose conceptualization of the city was to have lasting influence on the younger scholar. It was from Simmel that Park received his only direct university exposure to sociology, and it is the influence of Simmel, especially his views on "self-perception" in complex society, which can be detected in Park's later writings. This is particularly vivid as Park develops a fascination with the intimate interaction between individual and society, or *social psychology* as it came to be known. Park's work was closely aligned with the ideas of George Herbert Mead, and are recognizable in later years, in much of the works of Erving Goffman (see Chapter 13). With a new doctorate in hand in 1904, Park spent the next two years combining his interests in journalism with a yet unfulfilled appetite for seeing the world and immersed himself in real-world problems. He worked as a correspondent with the Congo Reform Association and published reports from the African Congo that outlined in exposé style the turmoil and oppression of black Africans by King Leopold of Belgium (see, e.g., Park 1906, 763–72). Although Park never considered himself a reformer, and certainly not a missionary, he did, in fact, embrace the plight of the Africans pushed into slavery in their own land. This was the beginning of Park's lifelong focus on race relations and cultural conflict. Then in his early forties, Park developed a first-hand understanding of the sociopolitical conflict involving oppressed peoples. The plight of black and immigrant populations became a primary topic of concern, although still more from a journalistic or political point of view than from a sociological one. In order to better understand problems of black populations in Africa and the United States as well as possible educational solutions, Park visited Booker T. Washington, the principal of the Tuskegee

Institute in Alabama. The collaboration between Park and Washington resulted in Park accepting a position in 1905 as Washington's press secretary, a position Park held for seven years. Booker T. Washington was a renowned educator, and by associating with him, Park's career orientation began to move in the direction of academic life. In 1912, Park happened to meet sociologist W. I. Thomas during a conference at the Tuskegee Institute. Thomas was impressed with Park's research interests and convinced him to visit the University of Chicago during the winter of 1914 to teach a course on the American Negro. Park agreed to the visit and remained until his retirement nineteen years later in 1933. It was during these last two decades of university life in Chicago that Park surfaced as the central figure of what became known as the "Chicago School" of sociology. This school encompassed a theoretical and methodological perspective that spawned a wide range of projects and student theses of direct relevance to social science and, in a most straightforward way, to criminology.

II. BASIC ASSUMPTIONS

Given Park's relatively advanced age before he entered formal academic life, it is difficult to pinpoint the assumptions that underlie his thought and work. As noted, his introduction to scholarship may be seen as early as 1883, when he came under the influence of John Dewey. In the late 1900s he met and admired Georg Simmel, and from 1900 to 1914 was certainly influenced by Booker T. Washington, Albion Small, and W. I. Thomas. However, even given this rather extensive time period and these significant figures in his life, at least five general areas appear to crystallize as "basic assumptions."

1. As with other pioneers in criminological thought, Park was a strong advocate of the scientific method. The philosophical foundation of his work is represented most clearly by the "positivistic organicism" tradition (see Martindale 1960, 81). There is no question that Park considered himself a positivist, and as social science was breaking away from philosophy, he was quick to vocalize his believe in the value of science (Park 1929, 3–49; 241). As a positivist, he rejected metaphysics in favor of a scientific orientation to reality, and forcefully advocated a social analysis based on empirically verifiable facts and relationships.

2. In the tradition of Comte, Spencer, Durkheim, and Toennies, Park was also guided by the principle that society was organismic in character. Thus, he was a strong advocate, even throughout his Chicago period, of identifying and clarifying the bio-organismic nature of society and social forces. Consequently, Park saw a society (e.g., the city) as a system of interrelated parts or organs that were functionally dependent on one another. Like others of his contemporaries, Park may be seen as a functionalist. In his early study of the crowd, including mob and riot behavior, he did not see such collective behavior necessarily as undesirable, but as a segment of social life that did not appear out of nothing and could best be seen as a functional or natural aspect of the overall society (Martindale 1960, 253–55).

3. From the influence of sociologist Georg Simmel, which Park admits and his later work demonstrates, a further basic assumption can be detected. It is Park's consistent conception that dissecting society into its various subparts or "forms" allows for more precise descriptions. Most likely borrowing from Simmel, Park felt comfortable with such concepts as social process, types of interaction, social relations, and social differentiation as areas of study. Like Simmel and later George H.

Mead, the process of atomistically reducing social behavior to smaller parts for more careful conceptualization and study became second nature to Park.

It appears plausible that much of Park's professional journalism entailed more than just reporting the news. He previously argued for a system of "scientific reporting" whereby the reporter, in essence, would use the methods of social science by probing deeply to reach the ultimate facts and relationships (Bidwell, 1973, p. 254). Park was a master of description in the early part of the twentieth century in a style similar to that which Goffman championed in later decades.

4. In addition to Park's belief in reductionism and scientific reporting was his presumption that sociology was inextricably intertwined with history. This belief, perhaps reinforced if not inspired by Simmel, led to the contention that the real business of sociology was the social interpretation of historical phenomena (see Wolff 1950, xxxi). Designated the *historical method*, or, more appropriately, *comparative history*, this was a prevalent procedure followed by early social scientists, such as Comte and Durkheim, among others. Park was not far removed from this tradition and, in fact, was convinced early in his career that the news reporter (i.e., and the sociologist) may influence history, if not create it. He may seem to be claiming too much credit for the reporter, but Park was simply saying that the individual who describes, interprets, and records social events and relationships, provides the written substance of which history is comprised, and which may subsequently influence the behavior of others. Later in his life, Park became a central proponent of the "life history" method of interpreting social facts.

5. Park's life spanned the period in American history associated with a comparatively open-door policy toward immigration. Even during his early life in Minnesota he was closely aware of migrant populations and with their special problems (Raushenbush 1979, 3–14). Also, through his travels and work with African and American blacks, he was intimately cognizant of the worldwide dilemma of interracial conflict. At a time when one might have predicted that Park would have strong leanings toward reform (especially as a result of his years with Booker T. Washington), one finds instead more of a "live and let live" philosophy of passive humanitarianism. He detested what he called "do-gooder" reformists, and consistently stressed explanation and understanding of culture conflict over social change in any particular direction (Raushenbush 1979, 96).

Such a view most likely resulted from his acceptance of a philosophy of social Darwinism held by many early twentieth-century sociologists. From a social Darwinian perspective, conflict, change, and even crime, for example, would have to be seen simply as "processes" that may alter the ecological makeup of society irrespective of any value assessment of the process. Social movements, revolutions, and riots that change society occur, and such phenomena are expected in any vibrant social organism. Although Park was an advocate of social Darwinism, he apparently vacillated somewhat in the strength of his belief. Park did comment that he wished the blacks would at least win "some" of the riots (Matthews 1977, 189).

III. KEY IDEAS

Notwithstanding Park's pioneering abilities as a creative thinker, one is forced to conclude in his case that timing and circumstances helped push him to stardom as a sociologist. In 1914, the University of Chicago was a new private institution with heavy backing from the Rockefeller family. With little worry about money, the various departments could afford to hire some of the best faculty and could recruit the choice students. Surely Park had the advantage of long-lasting personal relationships, with similarly motivated faculty, in the budding Chicago academic atmosphere.

Furthermore, a listing of the graduate students who passed through Park's classes and office door reads as a who's who among American sociologists and criminologists in the 1920s and 1930s (see especially Faris 1967). If there is a golden era of Chicago sociology, it most likely coincides with the Park years (1914–1933). What is to this day referred to as the "Chicago School" or the "Ecology School" of sociology (or of criminology) must be a blend of Park, his colleagues, and, to a substantial extent, his students. It becomes quite difficult to isolate one from the other in outlining the "Chicago" tradition. In this chapter, emphasis is limited primarily to Park's work, whether individual or coauthored. However, in several cases, some attention must be given to the projects conducted by Chicago graduate students under Park's supervision.

For purposes of examining Park's key ideas, his contributions may be grouped into three general categories: human ecology, methodology, and sponsored research.

HUMAN ECOLOGY

Although ecological perspectives were proposed and debated long before Park entered the academic scene, the early writings tended to center around explanations of nonhuman life. Consequently, plant and animal ecology predominated around the turn of the twentieth century. Even prior to the rise of American sociology, naturalists and ecologists were beginning to analyze social interaction patterns, and group and community networks, as they pertained to lower organic forms. In fact, a plausible argument can be made that sociology evolved out of ecology as much as from any other scientific discipline. It is not much of an exaggeration to say that most of the major subunits of sociology can find their counterpart in the research of ecologists of the early 1900s. This is particularly evident in works on various social pathologies, including group conflict, overpopulation, community disorganization, and deviance. Such phenomena can be addressed among nonhuman populations (Darwin 1859, Warming 1909, Wheeler 1911, Clements 1916).

It was Park, however, who coined the term *human ecology*, and who presented voluminous writings synthesizing ecological explanations of human conduct (Faris 1944). Although some of Park's very early essays, including his doctoral dissertation, incorporated ecological thinking, his most seminal work on the topic appeared in 1921 with the publication of *Introduction to the Science of Sociology*, coauthored with Ernest W. Burgess. This work, known reverently by students at the University of Chicago in the early 1920s as the "Green Bible," is still claimed today to rank among the most important treatises ever written in sociology (Martindale 1960, 256; Raushenbush 1979, 84). Burgess was an office mate of Park, and the two collaborated closely on the book. However, the text was primarily Park's project, clearly so because many of Park's earlier essays appear throughout the work. Park wrote the lengthy introductory chapter and included thirteen of his earlier articles or essays in the text. No chapters are credited specifically to Burgess, who is referenced in the extensive index only three times, compared to thirty-one times for Park. Burgess had been an earlier graduate student at Chicago and was academically junior to Park. Nonetheless, Park and Burgess became one of the more famous author duos in all of sociology. Later, Burgess was to become associated with criminology in his own right. The book continues to be useful as a historical anthology of early sources pertinent to human ecology and as an authoritative account of how human societies can be explained using the concepts derived from plant and animal ecology.

Although it is true that the Park and Burgess volume is remembered as a basic sociology text, when viewed from the perspective of ecological theory, it serves well as a general explanation of human social problems. Indeed, whereas the work addresses crime only indirectly, its ecological theme is immediately relevant throughout. Perhaps what makes the work so useful is its clarity of presentation. Even though by today's standards, its more than 1000 pages would be considered lengthy, a review of selected chapters is especially worthwhile for anyone wishing a cogent picture of human ecology. The work appears to be a compilation of Park's own views of the social world, as philosopher, sociologist, and natural observer, and sets the stage for many of the projects he and his Chicago colleagues would inspire others to undertake.

Given the composite nature of the treatise, a review of the book's format and content introduces the reader to much of Park's more general interests and ideas as a human ecologist.

Isolation

No doubt Park and Burgess were among the first to include a chapter on isolation as an important feature in understanding human social life. Most sociology texts tended to concentrate foremost on the "interactional" aspects of human life. However, the authors define isolation of people and societies and examine the functional as well as dysfunctional aspects of social seclusion. Beginning with biology, the values of social isolation are explored with shelter, security, and self-protection from predators being most emphasized. Park introduces his own conception of the way the process of urbanization ironically led to social isolation, or "segregation" of entire groups into neighborhoods. Such a process proved to be a double-edge sword, in that the evolution of neighborhoods created, at least for some, the value of community cohesion, but at the same time, distanced or isolated one group or neighborhood from another.

Having spent a portion of his life studying race relations, Park was much concerned with what he saw as a spontaneous establishment of segregated and isolated communities within the larger city. From ecological perspectives this isolation was a natural process, and part of social, or human, evolution. To Park, the social forces of economic competition, generated by the increase of population and the division of labor, naturally pushed people into segmented groups (Park and Burgess 1921, cf. Park 1915). Similar thinking was voiced by Durkheim (See Chapter 3) and Marx. It should be remembered that all of Park's writing was strongly rooted in the Darwinian perspectives of evolution and "survival of the fittest." Park was an advocate of "social Darwinism" and was one of the last scholars to employ such a concept in an attempt to develop, through ecology, a holistic theory of human behavior.

By focusing on isolation as a social process, Park and Burgess were able to introduce a variety of potential social pathologies for scrutiny. Some of the earliest discussions of the effects of isolation on individual behavior are offered, including the significance of considering "feral" individuals as topics of study. Furthermore, the text elaborated on "isolation and the rural mind," and "isolation as an explanation of national, and racial, differences" (Park & Burgess 1921, 247).

Park and Burgess provided a series of topics for student themes at the end of each chapter in *Introduction to the Science of Sociology*. These suggested themes offer a more clear idea of the authors' own thinking during the early 1920s and show the relevance of isolation, for example, to theoretical perspectives of deviance and crime. They suggest, for example, written themes on "isolation, segregation, and the physical defective"; "isolated areas and cultural retardation"; and "moral areas, isolation, and segregation: city slums, vice districts, breeding places of crime" (see Park & Burgess 1921, 226; 268).

Social Contact and Interaction
The authors present contact and interaction as logical sequels to social isolation. Drawing upon early writings of Charles Darwin (1873), Georg Simmel (see Wolff 1950), Albion Small (1905), and W.G. Sumner (1906), Park and Burgess describe human social life and contrast it with animal societies. Here, Park introduces primary and secondary contacts and considers the association of impersonal, secondary contacts of city life with the increased probability of deviant types. Both the "genius" and the "criminal" have an opportunity to blossom in the metropolis (Park & Burgess 1921, 314).

It is here that the first widespread English translation of Simmel's "The Sociological Significance of the Stranger" (1908) is presented and considered. As a type of secondary contact associated with urbanization, the connection between the stranger and crime is highlighted and continues to this day as a prominent topic of consideration in criminology. Suggested theme topics for students included "Mobility and Social Types: The Gypsy, the Nomad, and the Hobo" (see Park, "The Mind of the Hobo," 1925). Park and Burgess similarly suggest the theme "Attempts to Revive Primary Groups in the City, as in the Social Center and the Settlement." Recall that, according to Durkheim, one way to alleviate the disruption of an anomic society is to rebuild personal and community relationships, even in the metropolis (see Chapter 3).

Social Forces
Park and Burgess insert a short chapter on the various internal forces that motivate human behavior. These forces include attitudes, interests, and sentiments. Here, the authors come closest to social psychological perspectives of behavior causation, but point out that even these personal motives are influenced by "individual differences in original nature," suggesting a larger ecological scheme. That is, if a particular trait persists, it must provide some significant ecological function in the environment of the group. It is here that the authors introduce as psychological attributes or social forces the "four wishes" of W.I. Thomas. Park saw the wishes simply as a clear way to "classify" the nature of social behavior. Thus, the wish for "security," the wish for "new experience," the wish for "response," and the wish for "recognition" are permanent and fundamental motives. Interestingly, Park and Burgess also put the wishes into spatial perspectives. They show how each wish varies across space. Accordingly, the wish for "security" may be represented by position, or mere immobility; the wish for "new experience" by the greatest possible freedom of movement and constant change of position; the wish for "response" by the number and closeness of points of contact; and the wish for "recognition" by the level desired or reached in the vertical plane of super or subordination (Park & Burgess 1921, 442).

Other themes of relevance to a study of criminology and criminal justice included "Institutions as organizations of social forces: An analysis of a typical institution, its organization and dominant personality"; and "Personal and social disorganization from the standpoint of the four wishes."

Competition and Conflict

Park's ecological orientation is most evident when he outlines the significance of competition and conflict among human societies. Again, the authors carefully, almost unnoticeably, analyze human social problems by using concepts and models directly borrowed from animal ecology. At this point, the relevance of the treatise to crime and criminology is more straightforward. In these chapters Park and Burgess extend the ecological argument to such topics as "inter-racial" competition, economic competition, and the rivalry of small groups, as in gang conflict.

The authors also include war as an ultimate form of natural competition and conflict. The themes outlined in these chapters pertain to criminology in a variety of ways, and suggest topics that are precursory to later research projects. Among such topics are, "Types of conflict: war, duels, litigation, gambling, and the feud," and "Conflict groups, gangs, labor organizations, sects, parties, nationalities," as well as subtler forms of conflict such as "rivalry, emulation, jealousy, and aversion." The authors also suggest a study of "popular justice" pointing to turn-of-the-twentieth-century vigilante groups such as the Molly Maguires and the Night Riders, as pertinent topics for further investigation (Park & Burgess 1921, 661).

Accommodation and Assimilation

Park and Burgess round out their ecological analysis of human societies by focusing on the adaptive mode of life forms. The writers present the evolution of "social hierarchy," for example, as a logical and natural means of adjusting to conflict and competition. The resulting state of rigid social classes and caste systems is made understandable and expected from the standpoint of ecological accommodation. It becomes clear that crime may be naturally contained, as in the highly stratified society of India, where interaction between castes is strictly proscribed. Similarly, Park draws on his earlier work regarding race relations, and considers slavery and segregation as forms of accommodation that ultimately may conclude in social control. The suggestion that racial competition may have been naturally accommodated through slavery and segregation may have tarnished the image of Robert Park, who persisted in taking a conservative "social Darwinian" view toward race relations in the early 1920s (see Matthews 1977, 157–74).

The conceptual importance of human ecology to cultural and subcultural conflict should be noted (compare with Cohen, Chapter 10). Also, even though a system of tight, rank-ordering of classes may evolve and result in social control through subordination and segregation, the possibility of conflict between classes is simultaneously established. Park and Burgess were well aware of the fragile balance between war and peace among various strata, and suggested race riots, for example, as a topic of scientific study. Notably, the Park and Burgess text has one of the first sociological treatments of the immigration process and its subsequent relevance as a topic of concern to students of culture conflict. The discussion of the immigrant in human ecological terms incorporates Park's earlier writings on the immigrant (see, particularly, Park 1922, cf. Hughes 1950).

Natural Areas

Park and Burgess examine the topic of human collective behavior in *Introduction to the Science of Sociology* by incorporating patterns of flock, herd, and pack behavior among lower animals. Indeed, they generalized from animal to human aggregates and finally to the formation of cities. However, the innovative ecological concept of "natural areas" among human societies is not developed until 1925 with the publication by

Park, Burgess, and McKenzie of *The City*. This equally classic work is, in fact, a collection of ten rather brief essays, six written by Park, two by Burgess, and one each by R. D. McKenzie and Louis Wirth.

Park introduces the concept of the natural area in the opening essay by discussing the territorial pattern of population segregation. The forming of segregated populations is a normal outgrowth of the earlier processes of competition, conflict, accommodation, and assimilation. The social evolution of territoriality, like that of rank ordering into social classes, can be seen as a natural ecological survival mechanism. As a result, spatial areas within a city may appear well defined, and the population of people who happen to dwell in the segregated territories or neighborhoods may also develop or assimilate distinct characteristics.

In other words, particular territories or natural areas have survival value for certain people. Poor people, for example, naturally emerge or migrate into specific segments of the city, and the well-to-do into another. In time, the distinct ecological niches may appear to have a life of their own, and diverse populations or nationalities that move in and out of the segmented communities have, at least for a time, minimal impact on the natural area.

Accordingly, some natural areas seem to be high crime or vice areas, regardless of the characteristics or nationality of the people dwelling within the area. Stated differently, no matter which group or nationality of people move into a certain area, the crime rate will remain high in that area. Faris (1967, 57) sums up the natural area concept:

> The Chicago research . . . showed that with few exceptions, each racial or national population that poured into the slum areas of the city experienced the same severe disorganization, and that as each of these populations in time prospered and migrated outward into more settled residential districts, the symptoms of disorganization declined. The human behavior pathologies thus were found to be consistently associated with the type of urban area and not with the particular ethnic group which inhabited it.

The essay by Burgess titled "The Growth of the City: An Introduction to a Research Project" (Park, Burgess, & McKenzie 1925) offers a portrayal of the natural urban areas or zones of the city of Chicago in the early 1920s. This rather simplistic depiction of five concentric zones was destined to become a hallmark contribution to sociological and criminological theory. The original zones reflected natural areas for ghettos, working-class homes, single-family dwellings, residential hotels, and immigrant settlements. Also, zones were demarcated as bright light, underworld, or vice areas. With the zone theory, vice and crime activity could be associated with spatial areas. Thus in the 1920s, a social–ecological explanation was effectively introduced that, at least in part, offset the prevalent perspectives of biological determinism popular at that time.

The source of the original concept of natural areas must go to both Park and Burgess. It is clear that Park had worked with geographic plotting of events as a news reporter, and with the concept of natural areas. However, the Burgess essay includes the actual drawing of the concentric zones. As office mates, the two colleagues must have had substantial influence on each other. Park had the reputation of being more the rigid social scientist and field researcher, whereas Burgess's reputation was one of being the one more interested in social problems from humanitarian or social work perspectives (see Matthews 1977, 104–5).

METHODOLOGY

Park's theoretical ideas in regard to human ecology seem in hindsight to overshadow his methodology. However, his innovative procedures for going about doing social research are legendary for the Chicago School era. It is probably fair to say that his particular methods of conducting research cannot easily be separated from his primary topic of study at Chicago, the "ecological examination of the city and city life." It is difficult to discern which came first, Park's interest in the city or his special method for looking at the world. Certainly, his fascination with human ecology and his early and continual adoption of the methods of the city-beat news reporter in his academic work paralleled each other.

Park's methodological contributions can be categorized under the broad headings of participant observation, social survey, and life history.

Participant Observation

Surely, Park did not invent or discover participant observation as a tool of social research. Anthropologists, among others, had long engaged in participant observation, although typically while exploring foreign cultures. However, it was Park, as an early American social researcher concerned with local city life, who emerged as a first and major patron of participant observation for a generation of sociology graduate students at the University of Chicago. The value of immersing oneself in the data was probably first realized by Park from his early contacts as a philosophy student with William James. Park overheard James remark, "The most real thing is a thing that is most keenly felt rather than a thing most clearly conceived" (see Matthews 1977, 33). Such a philosophical acceptance of subjective realism remained with Park throughout his various careers.

Park was one of the first scholars to remove sociology, and only incidentally, criminology, from the world of armchair philosophizing to the street, first as a reporter, and later as a scholar at the University of Chicago. The importance of this move by sociologists into the community—to study people where they live—is even more momentous because the University of Chicago housed the first sociology department in the United States and became a model for much of the nation. Matthews (1977, 33) summarizes Park's research orientation by stating, "The outsider who merely observed could only partially understand; any real understanding demanded an imaginative participation in the life of others; insight demanded empathy as well as observation."

Park had little regard for mathematics or statistics; he was not interested in the simple collection of historical facts or in statistically analyzing them. Instead, he was absorbed with the various meanings certain facts had for the people at the ground level. To acquire these meanings he believed one had to speak the same language of, or at least try to stand in the shoes of, the person one was trying to understand. For this reason, Park is often mentioned as an early advocate of symbolic interactionism and of the investigation of personality (Faris 1944). Because a majority of Park's research projects are based on personal interviews, his commitment to encouraging in-depth interviewing and rapport building with people on the streets or sidewalks where they reside is clear.

Park is quite explicit in demanding that students get their hands and the seats of their pants dirty in conducting field research. If necessary, he says, "Sit in the hotel lounges, on the doorsteps of the flophouses, and visit the dance halls" (Bulmer 1984, 97). After more than fifty years, this imperative may seem self-evident, but it must be recalled that Park began his career in sociology at a time when anthropometric measures of offenders were still being given substantial credence as bases for explaining behavior.

From the standpoint of research methods, Park saw a sizable amount of overlap between news reporting and sociological investigation. He wrote:

> It was . . . while I was a city editor and a reporter that I began my sociological studies . . . . In the article I wrote about the city (1915) I leaned rather heavily on the information I had acquired as a reporter regarding the city. Later on, as it fell to my lot to direct the research work of an increasing number of graduate students, I found that my experience as a city editor in directing a reportorial staff had stood me in good stead. Sociology, after all, is concerned with problems in regard to which newspapermen get a good deal of firsthand knowledge. Besides that, sociology deals with just those aspects of social life which ordinarily find their most obvious expression in the news and in historical and human documents generally. One might fairly say that a sociologist is merely a more accurate, responsible, and scientific reporter. (Quoted in Bulmer 1984, 91)

Social Survey

In reference to the advent of the social survey, Park must be recognized not so much for a methodological invention as for making good use of being well situated in time and place. The nation was changing rapidly from a rural to an urban society, and the various social problems long associated with city life began to be felt by Chicago politicians and citizens alike. There was a need to address community problems, and the newly established, research-oriented university was a logical place to turn to. Park was more interested in trying to understand the precise nature and characteristics of the city than in finding solutions to social problems. However, with the assistance of colleagues like Burgess, he was able to combine purely scientific research with humanitarian and social-work goals. With a tight rein on the theoretical view of the city as a social organism, Park set out with his students to describe, explain, and literally to survey the social ways of the city of Chicago. In 1910, the Census Bureau had begun to divide the city of Chicago into 600 census tracts. For the first time, this allowed sociologists to map various social characteristics according to the population base of a specific census tract. Thus, rates of social behavior and activities were collected for the entire Chicago area, and area maps could be constructed showing the distribution of people and social activities. Students augmented the census tract information with their own data gained from interview surveys and the files of local community service agencies. These included police and court records, as well as reports reflecting the characteristics of patrons of dance halls, movie theaters, speakeasies, rooming houses, and businesses of many kinds.

Although Park tended to favor the in-depth, open-ended interview, it was not long before more structured schedules were administered in an attempt to record social characteristics of city dwellers and to gauge various group activities. By the mid-1920s, courses in social statistics were being offered in the Department of Sociology, resulting in a more quantitative social survey of Chicago. However, even though Park was instrumental in seeing social surveys conducted, he is generally associated with the more qualitative assessments of social life.

Life Histories

As with the social survey, Park was not the first to use life or case histories as a technique of social research. However, given his conviction that a subjective understanding of the individual being studied is paramount, the life history approach logically fitted his research objectives. In developing life histories, the investigator, rather than survey-ing characteristics of the larger group or aggregate, extensively reconstructs through in-depth interviews or autobiographical documents the personal and social-life ways of a specific individual.

In reality, the researcher will often do both, combining the collection of both social and individual characteristics. This may be seen in *The Hobo*, wherein Anderson (1925), one of Park's master's students, explores the ecological distribution of hobo populations throughout Chicago, as well as compiles life histories on individual va-grants. Similarly, when Cressey (1929) conducted his master's thesis research on taxi-dance halls in Chicago, he also compiled life-history data on several individual dancers.

Park seems always to have been at the right place at the right time. This is espe-cially evident in the timeliness of his close personal friendship with W.I. Thomas who, along with Florian Znaniecki, published *The Polish Peasant in Europe and America* (1918–1920). The monumental, five-volume work did not maintain popularity over the years, as did many of the Chicago School projects, but it was perhaps the first study in sociology to set forth a methodology based on case histories. Park and Thomas were not only good friends, but also became strong advocates of each other's research aims and methods. When Thomas was forced to resign from the university in 1918, Park was left to carry on and build on the case-history method and other subjective methods, which he willingly did until his retirement from the department.

SPONSORED RESEARCH

A most plausible way to understand more about a professor's key ideas is to focus on the students and student projects inspired by the professor. Park's influence on students, as with others in the small Department of Sociology at Chicago, was effected through the classroom and the supervision of theses and dissertations. Also, a course in field re-search, which was so popular that it was jointly taught by Park and Burgess throughout the 1920s, allowed the professors to direct student projects continuously (Raushenbush 1979, 96; Bulmer 1984, 95). Consequently, it is again often difficult to separate the con-tributions of these two prodigious scholars and to draw clear distinctions regarding each man's particular impact on graduate students and criminology. To make historical analy-sis of these professors more complex, it is found that they served on many of the same theses committees throughout the height of the Chicago School era.

Nonetheless, careful scrutiny of the growing number of biographical documents and the listing of theses and dissertations recorded by Faris (1967) permits one to iso-late student research supervised primarily by Park. This research tends to cluster into four categories representing his chief areas of interest: race relations, the city, the crowd and revolution, and the newspaper as an institution. Any of these categories may be approached either theoretically or methodologically from a Parkian tradition.

At least ten graduate students wrote theses or dissertations that were later pub-lished as books with Park's foreword or introduction. Each reveals Park's fascination with race and nationality and the broader issue of cultural conflict and ecological as-similation. Examples include Jesse F. Steiner, *The Japanese in America* (1913); Maurice T. Price, *Protestant Missions as Culture Contact* (1924); Andrew Lind, *Racial Invasion in Hawaii* (1931); Pauline V. Young, *The Pilgrims of Russian-town* (1932); Charles S. Johnson, *Shadow of the Plantation* (1934); Romanzo Adams, *Interracial Marriage in Hawaii* (1937); and Bertram Doyle, *The Etiquette of Race Relations in the South* (1937).

Also representative are Everett Stonequist, *The Marginal Man* (1937), and Donald Pierson, *The Negro in Brazil* (1938).

Park was equally as productive in supervising field studies aimed at exploring the various natural areas of Chicago, particularly as they pertained to aspects of social disorganization. Some of these early theses or dissertations resulted in book manuscripts that have been in continuous print since the mid-1950s. Anderson's *The Hobo* (1923) and Frederic Thrasher's *The Gang: A Study of 1,313 Gangs in Chicago* (1926) are good examples. Several earlier projects include Kimball Young's *Sociological Study of a Disintegrated Neighborhood* (1918), and Roderic D. McKenzie's *The Neighborhood: A Study of Local Life in Columbus, Ohio* (1921). Also illustrative of natural areas are Norman S. Hayner's *The Sociology of Hotel Life* (1923), Walter C. Reckless's *Natural History of Vice Areas in Chicago* (1925), and Paul Cressey's *The Closed Dance Hall in Chicago* (1929). Furthermore, Louis Wirth's study *The Ghetto: A Study in Isolation* (1926) has received wide recognition.

Although Park was intrigued with the social–psychological behavior of crowds and the related concept of social revolution, only two student projects appear to directly apply. These are E. T. Hiller's "The Strike as Group Behavior" (1924), and L. P. Edward's *The Natural History of Revolution* (1927). Similarly, Park had a long-standing interest in the social character and function of the news media and specifically in the newspaper. He directed seven student projects in this area. Two dissertations that Park supervised in his later years were C.D. Clark's "News: A Sociological Study" (1931), and Helen M. Hughes "News and the Human Interest Story" (1938). His last student projects reflect once again his earlier news reporting orientations.

If it is agreed that the success of one's students is a plausible measure of the professor, then one must elevate Park to a high level of academic stature. Eight of his students became president of the American Sociological Association, and Park himself was president in 1925–26. The names of some of his students are directly and prominently connected with the later development of criminology, and include Clifford Shaw and Frederick Zorbaugh (1929), Ruth Shonle Cavan (1928), and Walter C. Reckless (1925). Other students developed illustrious careers in subdisciplines of sociology other than criminology. Even here, however, the works of many of these scholars were expressly pertinent to the theoretical understanding of human social behavior, including theoretical deviance (see, e.g., Louis Wirth 1938; Redfield 1942; 1960; and Blumer 1969).

In Park's brief twenty years as a member of the sociology faculty, he directed more than thirty theses or dissertations, certainly a prodigious accomplishment by standards of any era. It is likely that he had at least an indirect influence on most of the seventy-seven doctoral dissertations completed during his Chicago years (see Raushenbush 1979, 192).

IV. CRITIQUE

It becomes apparent that for one to critique Park, one must also critique the Chicago, or Ecological, school of sociology, which is beyond the scope of this chapter. The heyday of the Chicago tradition, about 1914 to 1934, closely coincides with Park's presence in the department. Certainly, Park was part of a team; but, with the clarity of hindsight, we can feel secure in naming Park the leader of the team. This is true because the Chicago tradition during the formative years was directly associated with human ecology, eventually the city, and with subjective methodologies, areas with which Park was most intimately identified.

If a critique is meant to examine the pros and cons of a work or an individual, then the Parkian legacy can be historically judged, with very few exceptions, in a positive light. Four major biographical sources of Park and the Chicago School attest to this assessment, pointing out the numerous accolades and tributes due Robert Park, and voicing very few negative comments (see, e.g., Faris 1967; Matthews 1977; Raushenbush 1979; and Bulmer 1984). These writers, among others, conclude that Park's key ideas and methods were breakthroughs in sociology, particularly given the time frame and setting in which they emerged. That Park's work rather obviously bore fruit in the works of many of his students is witness to the longevity of some of his ideas.

However, there is no question that the so-called Chicago School or the Parkian tradition no longer flourishes as it did during the first quarter of the twentieth century. The decline of the Chicago School, which happens to coincide with Park's retirement, results from a number of factors, only one of which is the departure of Park. First, other theories of social life that reached the United States successfully competed with ecological theory. These included Durkheimian theory, which was slow in being translated from the French; Weberian sociology; Marxian theory; and the emerging influence of the works of Sigmund Freud, to name but a few.

Second, the influx of theoretical ideas, conceptual schemes, indeed, of information generally, gave impetus to a rapid growth of departments of sociology and centers of graduate study, other than Chicago. Third, social science began to depart rather dramatically from Park's view of value-free research, and entered an era of research activity geared more toward the specific solving of social problems. Government-sponsored programs and various private funding agencies, aimed at finding practical solutions to social ills, began to thrive (Matthews 1977, 183). One impact of World War II was to give increased credence to humanitarian and problem-oriented research goals. Pure or basic research, directed toward describing and examining a behavioral phenomena "for its own sake," began to take a back seat to political and social problem issues, until the resurgence of phenomenology and ethnomethodology in the late 1960s.

Fourth, the utility and popularity of subjective methodologies began to move aside for the more technical methodology of data collection and analysis. As early as the mid-1930s, statistical techniques began to prosper in sociology departments and overshadow more qualitative methods. Science began to be associated in increasing degrees with quantitivity. The use of case histories and participant observation did not disappear, but was seen less frequently in graduate programs, including the one at Chicago. Toward the end of the 1930s, ecological mapping and the isolation and examination of various natural areas was less in vogue as a conceptual scheme in the Department of Sociology at Chicago.

Besides the specific key ideas associated with Park, his tenure in academic sociology also illustrates a consistent union of theory and research. As noted, a sizable amount of social science research during the early years of the twentieth century was highly theoretical and speculative. Park, with his feet planted very much on the ground, may be credited as much as anyone for insisting on and enforcing a test of social theory with real-world data collection.

Surely, he was vigorous in his application of human ecology to seemingly any social pattern. In so doing, Park became one of the last major social scientists to attempt to explain all social behavior under the umbrella of a single theoretical scheme. His persistence in trying to incorporate a "grand theory" approach, even to explain microlevel interaction, has been criticized (see especially Alihan 1939, 243–48), though such criticism has been countered by one or more of Park's supporters (Matthews 1977, 181). One should consult Chapter 17 on Marcus K. Felson for interesting extensions of Robert Park's research themes.

After retiring from the University of Chicago in 1933, Park was enticed by Charles S. Johnson, one of his former students, to accept a visiting professorship at Fisk University in Nashville, Tennessee. Johnson was then president of the university. Park accepted, and for several years combined travel and a leisurely teaching schedule with assisting Fisk University in the development of its social science department—a struggle that took place during the later years of the Depression.

In Nashville, on February 7, 1944, just prior to his eightieth birthday, Robert E. Park suffered a stroke and died.

References

Adams, Romanzo. 1937. Interracial marriage in Hawaii. PhD diss., University of Chicago.

Alihan, Milla Aissa. 1939. *Social ecology: A critical analysis*. New York: Columbia University Press.

Anderson, Nels. 1923. *The hobo*. Chicago: University of Chicago Press (Sociological Series).

———. 1925. The hobo. Master's thesis, University of Chicago.

Blumer, Herbert. 1969. *Symbolic interactionism: Perspective and method*. Englewood Cliffs, NJ: Prentice Hall.

Bulmer, Martin. 1984. *The Chicago School of Sociology*. Chicago: University of Chicago Press.

Clark, C. D. 1931. News: A sociological study. PhD diss., University of Chicago.

Clements, Frederick E. 1916. *Plant succession*. Washington, DC: Carnegie Institution.

Cressey, Paul G. 1929. *The closed dance hall in Chicago*. Master's thesis, University of Chicago.

Darwin, Charles. 1873. *The expression of the emotions in man and animals*. New York: John Murray.

———. 1859. *On the origin of the species by means of natural selection*. London: John Murray.

Doyle, Bertram. 1937. Etiquette of race relations. PhD diss., University of Chicago.

Edward, Lyford. 1927. *The natural history of revolution*. Chicago: University of Chicago Press.

Faris, Ellsworth. 1944. Robert E. Park: 1864–1944. Obituary. *Am. Soc. Rev.* 9 (June): 322–25.

Faris, Ellsworth. 1967. *Chicago sociology: 1920–1932*. San Francisco: Chandler Publishing Company.

Hayner, Norman S. 1923. *The sociology of hotel life*. PhD diss., University of Chicago.

Hiller, E. T. 1924. The strike as group behavior. PhD diss., University of Chicago.

Hughes, Everett C., ed. 1950. *Race and culture* (the collected papers of R. E. Park, vol. 1). Glencoe: The Free Press.

Hughes, Helen M. 1938. News and the human interest story. PhD diss., University of Chicago.

Johnson, Charles S. 1934. Shadow of the plantation. PhD diss., University of Chicago.

Lind, Andrew. 1931. Racial invasion in Hawaii. PhD diss., University of Chicago.

Martindale, Don. 1960. *The nature and type of sociological theory*. Boston: Houghton Mifflin.

Matthews, Fred H. (1977). *Quest for an American sociology: Robert E. Park and the Chicago School*. Montreal: McGill-Queen's University Press.

McKenzie, Roderick D. 1921. The neighborhood: A study of local life in Columbus, Ohio. PhD diss., University of Chicago.

Park, Robert E. 1906. The terrible story of the Congo. *Everybody's Mag.* December: 763–72.

———. 1915. The city: Suggestions for the investigation of behavior in the city environment. *Am. J. Soc.* 20: 577–612.

———. 1922. *The immigrant press and its control.* New York: Harper.

———.1925. The mind of the hobo: Reflections upon the relation between mentality and locomotion. In *The city,* ed. Robert E. Park, Ernest W. Burgess, and R. D. McKenzie. Chicago: University of Chicago Press.

———. 1929. Sociology. In *Research in the social sciences,* ed. Wilson Gee. New York: Macmillan.

Park, Robert E., and Ernest W. Burgess. 1921. *Introduction to the science of sociology.* Chicago: University of Chicago Press.

Park, Robert E., Ernest W. Burgess, and Roderic D. McKenzie. 1925. *The city.* Chicago: University of Chicago Press.

Pierson, Donald. 1938. The negro in Brazil. PhD diss., University of Chicago.

Price, Maurcie T. 1924. Protestant missions as culture contact. PhD diss., University of Chicago.

Raushenbush, Winifred. 1979. *Robert E. Park: Biography of a sociologist.* Durham: Duke University Press.

Reckless, Walter C. 1925. Natural history of vice areas in Chicago. PhD diss., University of Chicago.

Redfield, Robert. 1942. *The folk culture of Yucatan.* Chicago: University of Chicago Press.

———. 1960. *The little community and peasant society and culture.* Chicago: University of Chicago Press.

Shaw, Clifford R., and Frederick Zorbaugh. 1929. *Delinquency areas.* Chicago: University of Chicago Press.

Simmel, Georg. 1908. *Sociologie.* Excerpts translated by Albion W. Small and published in *Am. J. Soc.* XV: 296–98 (originally published in 1887).

Small, Albion W. 1905. *General sociology.* Chicago: University of Chicago Press.

Steiner, Jesse F. 1913. The Japanese in America. PhD diss., University of Chicago.

Stonequist, Everett. 1937. The marginal man. PhD diss., University of Chicago.

Sumner, William G. 1906. *Folkways: A study of the sociological importance of usages, manners, customs, mores and morals.* Boston.

Thomas, W. I., and Florian Znaniecki. 1918–1920. *The Polish peasant in Europe and America* (5 vols). Chicago: University of Chicago Press.

Thrasher, Frederic. 1926. The gang: A study of 1,313 gangs in Chicago. PhD diss., University of Chicago.

Warming, Eugene. 1909. *Ecology of plants.* Oxford University Press.

Wheeler, W. M. 1911. The ant-colony as an organism. *J. Morph.* vol. XXII.

Wirth, Louis. 1926. The ghetto: A study in isolation. PhD diss., University of Chicago.

———. 1938. Urbanism as a way of life. *Am. J. Soc.* XLIV (July): 1–24.

Wolff, Kurt H. 1950. *The sociology of Georg Simmel.* Toronto: The Free Press.

Young, Kimball. 1918. Sociological study of a disintegrated neighborhood. Master's thesis, University of Chicago.

Young, Pauline V. 1932. The pilgrims of Russiatown. PhD diss., University of Chicago Press.

Supplemental Readings

Bidwell, Charles E. 1973. Life history: Robert E. Park. *Am. J. Soc.* 79 (September): 251–61.

Hughes, Everett C., ed. 1950. *Race and culture* (vol. I). Glencoe, Illinois: The Free Press.

———. 1952. *Human communities: The city and human ecology* (vol. II). Glencoe, Illinois: The Free Press.

———.1955. *Society* (vol. III). Glencoe, Illinois: The Free Press.

Shaw, Clifford R., and Henry D. McKay. 1942. *Juvenile delinquency and urban areas: A study of rates of delinquents in relation to different characteristics of local communities in American cities.* Chicago: University of Chicago Press.

CHAPTER 6
WILLIAM HERBERT SHELDON: 1898–1977

I. BIOGRAPHICAL SKETCH

Some might wonder at the inclusion of William Sheldon as one of the pioneers of criminological theory. His ideas have always been on the very periphery of the discipline, and some would argue they were not scientific at all. However, perhaps more than other thinkers, Sheldon represents the last of the trendsetters who carried on the work of early twentieth century biological determinists and never really wavered in their belief in a direct link between biology and personality. Also, William Sheldon's concepts became almost household words and continue to be so when conversations turn to the evolution of criminological thought.

Sheldon was born and reared in Warwick, Rhode Island, and spent much of his childhood on a farm. Although not much is recorded of his father, William Herbert, or his mother, Mary Abby Greene, it is clear that young William had a comfortable and quite happy, if not idyllic, early life (see the preface to Sheldon's *Early American Cents* 1971). His father was a naturalist, a hunting guide, and a professional judge of hunting dogs. Indeed, in the tradition of the naturalist, the senior Sheldon, through painstaking direct observation, studied and wrote one of the authoritative books on the life-history of moths (Nasso 1971). The naturalist's practice of careful observation and classification was to become a distinct trademark of the young Sheldon's later career.

Several of William Sheldon's occupations during high school years and during summer breaks from college included working as an assistant ornithologist, an oilfield scout, and as a wolf hunter for a New Mexico sheep ranch. He obviously enjoyed the outdoors, and early in his life came to view animal behavior patterns as being simply an extension of the more basic biological or genetic foundations. The idea that function, including personality, is a continuance of, or directly associated with, structure or morphology among animals and humans was to shape Sheldon's thinking for the rest of his life.

Although the social connection is unclear, Sheldon's father was a close friend of William James, the prominent American psychologist. In fact, when the senior Sheldon died leaving behind a twelve-year-old son, it was William James who apparently became young Sheldon's second father and teacher (Osborne 1979). The inquiring mind of such a formidable figure as James, on top of the senior Sheldon's influence, must have had a profound impact on William Sheldon, who soon entered college and pursued psychology as his career choice.

Sheldon remained in Rhode Island to complete a bachelor's degree in 1918 at Brown University. Immediately thereafter he entered the U.S. Army at the end of WWI, attaining the rank of 2nd Lieutenant. After the army, he traveled west to the University of Colorado, where he completed studies for a master's degree in 1923.

Two years later he was awarded the PhD in psychology at the innovative and still young University of Chicago. As is often the case with doctoral students, Sheldon began as a classroom teacher even prior to receiving the PhD. He was an instructor of sociology and psychology at the University of Texas for several years, and while a doctoral student at Chicago, he taught as an instructor and later as assistant professor of psychology. Afterward, with PhD degree in hand, Sheldon entered the University of Wisconsin's Department of Psychology as assistant professor, where he remained until 1931.

His interests were not limited to psychology. Throughout his career, he maintained that personality could not be looked on separately from influences of the body. Accordingly, to fully understand the intricacies of the mind, Sheldon took the logical step of studying medicine, as had Sigmund Freud. Sheldon returned to the University of Chicago, and in 1933 was awarded a degree in medicine.

By the age of thirty-five, Sheldon's most significant works, which were to include eleven volumes, were still ahead of him. In addition to his father and William James, several others had greatly influenced him, although much of the impact of such influence was still dormant. At James' suggestion, Sheldon, while still an undergraduate at Brown University, attended a seminar at Harvard taught by Martin Peck, a former student of William James and Sigmund Freud. It was Peck, a great admirer of Freud, who planted the seed with Sheldon that psychology was in need of a classification scheme. Peck "considered Freud the foremost emancipator of mankind but emphasized that the job was still only half done; that somebody now must bring descriptive order to comprehending the constitutional patterns underlying the psychiatric patterns" (Osborne 1979, 715, c.f. Sheldon, Lewis, and Tenney 1968).

Even as a young college student Sheldon carried with him this life mission—to classify personality patterns according to constitution or physiological form and structure. Early influences on Sheldon, including those of his father, had a long-standing effect on his life's task of classifying a wide range of temperaments according to body size and shape. Through Sheldon's research, an even earlier idea, that delinquent and criminal offenders were somehow physiologically different from non-offenders, was to gain a most prominent and vocal advocate throughout the mid-twentieth century.

As Sheldon set out to satisfy Peck's mandate for a new classification scheme, the circles of scientific thought in the first third of the twentieth century were still replete with strong advocates of biological over social or cultural influences. Even with the criticism levied against the earlier ideas of Cesare Lombroso, other researchers were picking up the torch and presenting findings that they believed demonstrated the link between physiology and temperament, and that accounted for deviant and criminal behavior.

After finishing medical studies, Sheldon visited Europe on a traveling fellowship from the National Council on Religion in Higher Education. During this period, from 1933 to 1934, Sheldon was influenced by Ernst Kretschmer, who, in 1921, had published *Korperbau und Charakter* (*Physique and Character*). The Kretschmer work that addressed the issue of criminal biological types lacked the conceptual precision later attributed to Sheldon's work. In 1938, Sheldon worked as a full-time researcher in physical anthropology and psychology at Harvard University. While there, he met and was influenced by Ernest Hooton, who had published controversial findings on the constitutional inferiority of criminals (Hooton 1939b, c.f. Vold and Bernard 1986).

Sheldon not only believed that biology formed the basis for psychology and psychiatry but was also convinced that religion had its roots in biology. Such a philosophical perspective drew on the works and visions of William James and, later, on Carl Jung, whom Sheldon sought out for intellectual stimulation and corroboration of his own ideas. Sheldon's continual insistence that body, mind, and the spiritual world were really one was to form the philosophical foundation of Alcoholics Anonymous (AA). Sheldon had met the founder of AA while on the traveling fellowship in England at a time when the original doctrine of the organization was being developed (see Gellman 1964, Osborne 1979).

Sheldon continued to travel widely, and worked out of several university offices on both coasts of the United States (i.e., Harvard University, Columbia University, and the University of California at Berkley). However, he spent the largest part of his professional life (1951–1970) at the University of Oregon, where he eventually was named distinguished professor.

Whereas William Herbert Sheldon is best known for his classification of body types with temperament, his fascination with precise taxonomy extended beyond psychology and criminology. It is clear that even as a small boy, Sheldon was intrigued with coin collecting and soon developed one of the most impressive collections of large early American pennies. In fact, much of his college education was funded by trading and selling coins. By age 50, he wrote one of the most authoritative accounts of early American pennies in *Early American Cents* (Sheldon 1949). Ironically, his ability to identify and classify blemishes on the busts and figures on the face of coins stemmed from the same tireless energy used to study differences and defects of human form as they were reportedly correlated with temperament.

After a long and notable career, William Sheldon died of heart failure in Cambridge, Massachusetts, at age seventy-eight.

II. BASIC ASSUMPTIONS

Sheldon's thinking and the direction of his research were shaped by the times in which he was reared and the several mentors he strove to emulate. At least four features are noteworthy in regard to basic assumptions underlying his work.

SCIENTIFIC TRADITION

Sheldon readily accepted the basic tenets of scientific inquiry and did not question the cause and effect relationship as a fundamental truism of science. Not only did he accept the foundations of the positive school of criminology but adopted the primary thrust of strict Lombrosianism. Here he departed from the mainstream of the social science of his day. Whereas Durkheim had already made inroads in sociology long before Sheldon, and the Chicago School was experiencing its golden era during Sheldon's college years, he nonetheless was steadfast in adhering to principles of biological determinism. This appears to have been the case almost to the point of his ignoring altogether some of the most basic tenets of social psychology and sociology. Even while teaching early in his career in various departments of social science, he was apparently looked on as something of an extremist or renegade (see Osborne 1979).

SOCIAL DARWINISM

Although Sheldon's writings do not explicitly acknowledge social Darwinism, it is clear that his thinking and research were guided by such principles. Sheldon accepted the inevitability of "survival of the fittest" not only for physical life forms, but also for various psychological patterns that to Sheldon must provide survival value if they are to persist. Here he was likely influenced by William James, who also argued for the survivability, in evolutionary terms, of certain forms of consciousness (Rothenberg 1981). Furthermore, the institution of religion, which, according to Sheldon, was made realizable by the evolvement of the large frontal lobes of the human brain (making possible conceptions of past and future), also allowed human societies to better survive. Consequently, to Sheldon, the spiritual nature of humans cannot be separated from human biology. A change in one should have a subsequent impact on the other. Such a "holistic" approach to health (although Sheldon did not use the term) was the apparent reason his earliest writings are mentioned as being instrumental in the development of a philosophical rationale for Alcoholics Anonymous (Osborne 1979).

NATURE–TEMPERAMENT CONNECTION

Sheldon's major theoretical assumption held that physique or body type can be classified along a continuum, from flawed or imperfect to the more normal and well balanced. He saw a natural beauty to the normal physical forms, and any deviation from the norm was reputed to be associated with a variety of personality deviations, if not abnormalities. Both the temperament and the diversity of physique were constitutional or genetically based (Sheldon and Stevens 1942, c.f. Samuel 1981). Accordingly, the so-called perfect human form would possess perfect or well-balanced temperament and would represent, among other qualities, the non-criminal or non-delinquent type.

From the benefits of hindsight, it is understandable how such a theoretical position would be met with some emotional disenchantment in the 1940s and 1950s, especially given the philosophical rationalization used to justify world war by Adolph Hitler (see Abramson 1980).

NATURALIST METHODOLOGY

As noted in the biographical sketch, Sheldon was undoubtedly swayed, purposely or not, by his father to follow the naturalist tradition of directly observing life forms under study. Because those who research non-human animals or plant life cannot interact verbally with their objects of study, various precise techniques had to be invented to exactly code and describe behavior in its natural state. Early classifiers of plant and animal life had to be careful observers of the highest dedication and order (see, e.g., Warming 1909, Schjelderup-Ebbe 1935).

There is no question that Sheldon was introduced to these meticulous observational techniques, given his relationship with his naturalist father and his early employment as an assistant ornithologist. The scientific trait of pure description was refined to an art by early naturalists, and in coding human forms and personality traits during the mid-twentieth century, Sheldon was possibly unmatched.

III. KEY IDEAS

To a certain extent, Sheldon had a one-track mind. A review of his major writings in behavioral science reveal a fixation on demonstrating the need to combine biology with psychology to understand deviant behavior. More specifically, Sheldon focused on the relationship between body size and shape and any associated traits of temperament. Unlike other pioneers in this volume, Sheldon restricted himself to this area of study, and it is for this that his name is synonymous with the search for constitutional links to crime and delinquency. His key ideas include first an extension of the principles of Cesare Lombroso, and second the development of a precise technique for somatotyping.

EXPANSION OF LOMBROSIANISM

Although the modern era of the study of crime causation has primarily emphasized social–environmental factors, such has not always been the case. Indeed, from the inception of the Positive School of criminology to today, a biological thread can be discerned, even though in more recent years it has become nearly invisible. After Cesare Lombroso, biological assumptions about the nature of the criminal remained for a time at the forefront. Indeed, throughout the first third of the twentieth century they competed handily, especially in Europe, with the growing prominence of the Ecology School of criminology and with social learning theories.

After Lombroso, three historically prominent researchers preceded Sheldon in carrying on the tradition of biological inquiry, all of whom hold memorable places in the history of biological determinism: Charles Goring, E. A. Hooton, and Ernst Kretchmer. Because it is primarily from these earlier researchers that Sheldon received the torch to continue the Lombrosian theme, they deserve brief discussion.

Charles Goring set out as a young man to study medicine, not behavioral science and certainly not the criminal offender. However, his life overlapped with that of Cesare Lombroso, and as a young physician in England, Goring was employed in several large prisons as a medical officer. Goring had earlier proved himself, even as a student, a top scholar, and had received numerous prestigious awards in science and philosophy, unusual at that time for a medical student.

Just prior to the turn of the twentieth century, Lombroso found himself immersed in great controversy regarding the validity of the principle of the "born criminal." He had, in fact, angrily argued that if anyone could prove the fallaciousness of the born criminal concept, he would retract his theory. Although Goring did not apparently set out to disprove Cesare Lombroso's doctrines, his work did, in fact, fail to substantiate the existence of a physical criminal type. Goring is remembered, and rightfully so, for his extensive application of statistical techniques to test the relationships among variables. His vast list of independent variables, which were correlated with criminal offenders, extends the full range of biological and social characteristics.

After a decade of data compilation, Goring, with the help of statistician Karl Person, published *The English Convict: A Statistical Study* (1913). This work was monumental not only in timeliness and topic, but also in sheer size and weight. The single book is 530 pages and is an oversized volume with a full foot of printed matter per page. The work reported measurements of 3,000 English convicts that were compared with measurements of control groups of non-criminal Englishmen. The offender population was composed entirely of incarcerated recidivists; consequently, Goring was better able to argue they represented criminal types. His control population included university undergraduates from Oxford and Cambridge as well as hospital patients and British military personnel. Goring's primary concern was to determine whether criminal populations differed significantly from the non-criminal population. He did not try, as Lombroso had, to differentiate between born criminals and persons with only a propensity toward crime.

Goring's study was more methodologically sound than Lombroso's and attempts were made to rely on variables that could be measured objectively—at least by standards of the day. Lombroso had argued earlier that it was often impossible to measure the physical anomalies of criminals accurately, although they could be detected by the trained eye. Such a subjective qualification enabled Lombroso to get out of the box, should later investigators find inconclusive differences between criminal and noncriminal populations (see Vold 1958, c.f. Vold and Bernard 1986).

After analyzing hundreds of statistical tables, graphs, and charts, Goring concludes that there was no distinct criminal type. However, he believed avidly in a genetic base of physiology and behavior, and accordingly did admit to finding a positive correlation between physique and the criminal. The recidivist group was several inches shorter and three to seven pounds lighter than the control groups. According to Goring, the offenders also were found to be inferior in mental ability as a result of hereditary influence.

Goring's analysis was to have mixed reviews. Lombrosian proponents were quick to argue that beneath some of the heavy statistical manipulations were indeed some positive relationships between the criminal population and specific physiological traits. Goring, it was argued, was too anxious to disprove Lombroso (see Mannheim 1972). Even as Goring clearly states that one criminal type was not significantly different from another, the point remained, according to some protagonists, that Goring might have been less than honest by making his statistics reveal what he wished them to reveal.

There appears to be little doubt that Goring found it easier than Lombroso to theorize that one may simply be "selected out," as a result of social characteristics, to engage in crime; and Goring did not have to resort, as did Lombroso, to a nonmeasurable and innate atavistic quality to explain criminal character. Goring's work would likely be relatively palatable to modern-day criminologists.

However, the Lombrosianists were not yet prepared to admit defeat, and found another strong advocate in Earnest Albert Hooton, a young and rather brash instructor of physical anthropology at Harvard University in 1916, about the time Goring's work was making in-roads in the United States. Hooton sought to improve on Goring's research, which Hooton saw as being full of statistical errors if not outright measurement dishonesty. Furthermore, there appears no question that Hooton was not satisfied with Goring's general conclusions. He admits that he conducted his twelve years of anthropological calculations with the thought of disproving Goring while vindicating Cesare Lombroso. A reading of the introduction to Hooton's first major work, *Crime and the Man* (1939a), suggests he was angered by Goring's methods and conclusions in that fourteen pages are devoted to severely criticizing Goring.

Hooton's research was extensive, very well financed, and involved many collaborators from major universities around the country. In addition, the study had the stamp of approval of Harvard University, which eventually published Hooton's massive statistical calculations in three volumes. Hooton examined 17,000 individuals in ten different states. This sample included 14,000 prisoners and 3,000 who were the non-criminal control group. As might be expected, Hooton, as a physical anthropologist, was meticulous in recording great anthropometric detail of his subjects, and included most physical traits suggested as being pertinent by earlier proponents of Lombroso.

Of particular note, however, is that Hooton took much more time developing comparisons between different types of criminal offenders, an exercise omitted by Goring. Moreover, Hooton gave special attention to geographic background of the sample as well as to nationality and race. When Hooton was conducting his study, sociology was well under way in the United States, and certainly sociological theory was a topic of major discussion at Harvard. During the same time, the University of Chicago was placing major emphasis on human ecology and social–psychological perspectives of behavior causation. Nonetheless, although Hooton addressed social variables including occupation, religion, marital status, and education, he did not, as had Durkheim, make the creative assumption that aberrant behavior could be explained as a consequence of social and cultural characteristics apart from biological features (Hooton 1939b, 257). Instead, after reporting correlations between physical traits and his criminal population, Hooton chose to ignore any potential social explanations.

Hooten emphatically asserts that the criminal is a physically inferior type, thus taking a strong biological determinist stance. He argues,

> Differences in constitutional type, whether of racial origin or due to familial
> or individual factors of endocrine or other causation undoubtedly are agents
> in determining the choice of offense. But in any case these constitutional and
> environmental factors operate upon the physical and mental inferiors. . . .
> Criminals are organically inferior . . . It follows that the elimination of crime
> can be effected only by the extirpation of the physically, mentally, and
> morally unfit, or by their complete segregation in a socially aseptic environment. (Hooton 1939b, 308–09)

As with other social Darwinists of the era, Hooton found himself writing not only on the very question of the organic inferiority of one people over another, but at a time when WWII was spreading across Europe and into North America, being fought in part on the grounds that there was or should be a preferred hereditary type of individual. His work was destined to become embroiled in controversy. Ironically, Hooton was faulted from purely scientific perspectives, just as he had earlier faulted Goring, and for some of the same reasons.

In great detail, Hooton argues, often through cartoon-like illustrations, that one type of criminal is organically different from another. His data reflect that murderers should look different from rapists, and robbers different from simple thieves; murderers and robbers are tall and skinny, and tall, heavy men not only kill, but also perpetrate forgery and fraud. Burglars tend to be smaller, and short, squatty men are more often associated with assault, rape, and other sexual crimes (Hooton 1939a, 376–78).

Hooton received a good amount of criticism for presuming that a particular physical trait, even if correlated with criminality, was necessarily an indication of inferiority. This same type of criticism has been levied against other biological determinists, beginning with Lombroso. If a particular physical characteristic is to be evidence of inferiority, then major segments of the Earth's population must be deemed inferior. Obviously, as common sense dictates, brilliant minds and careers have been and are represented by all sizes and shapes of people on all continents.

As Vold and Bernard point out (1986, 57), Hooton also tends to ignore or discount a number of social and cultural differences (e.g., degree of rurality, occupation) between criminal and non-criminal groups. This suggests a bias by Hooton away from social science and toward organic differences. Both Hooton and Goring argued that physical inferiority was inherited, but were unable to demonstrate or validate such a claim with hard evidence.

Whereas both Goring and Hooton helped form an early intellectual and research tradition within which Sheldon was to develop his own studies purporting a link between physique and temperament, it was Ernst Kretschmer who provided the closest model on which Sheldon's classification scheme was based (Kretschmer 1921). Kretschmer, a professor of psychiatry at the University of Tubingen (Germany), built on the works of Emil Kraeplin by associating various mental disorders according to constitutional types. Kretschmer was basically a typologist (see Vold 1958, 68, c.f. Schafer 1969), and tended to pigeonhole people into categories without much concern for degree of fit.

Following Kraeplin's classification of mental disorders (1883), Kretschmer argued that there was an association among specific body shapes. By observing more than 4,000 mentally ill patients, he arranged his subjects into *cyclothymes, schizothymes,* and a mixed group of *displastics,* which included *epileptoids* and *hysterics.* The cyclothyme personality type supposedly lacked sophistication, informality, and spontanaity and wavered between gaiety and sorrow. Later psychiatric definitions simply referred to *cyclothemia* as a mild fluctuation of the manic–depressive type (Hinsie and Campbell 1960). As criminals, cyclothymes tended to commit more intellectual and less serious crimes. "Less serious" apparently meant less violent to Kretschmer, who, from a purely physical point of view, saw cyclothymic individuals as being a *pyknic* types, or round, soft, plump figures with little muscle and medium or short in height.

Schizothymes were further characterized as hypersensitive, strongly insensitive, or apathetic. When involved in criminal acts, they leaned toward serious and often violent offenses. Physically, schizothymes were either asthenic (i.e., thin, lean, or flat) or athletic (i.e., wide, muscular, and strong). Kretschmer's category of epileptoids and hysterics did not fit any particular physical type, but because they were highly emotional and not always in control of their passions, Kretschmer attributed to them various sexual crimes.

The pre-Sheldon history of constitutional types of personality and criminals is long and diverse. Criminal or deviant body appearances are referred to in the Bible and are discussed in writings of Hippocrates. Lombroso attempted to provide such ideas with an aura of scientific credibility. It would be left to Sheldon to afford such argumentative theoretical ideas with their greatest typological precision.

SOMATOTYPING

Sheldon, like earlier theorists, believed in the basic presumption that the primary determinants of behavior were constitutional and inherited. He never digressed from this basic proposition and argued concerning it in his first book *Psychology and the Promethean Will* (1936). Although no one has ever been able to test the validity of biological determinist assumptions adequately, Sheldon was convinced, even after the criticism of earlier researchers, that one could at least indirectly assess biological influence by simply measuring the body. Sheldon seemed determined to resurrect the earlier fundamental practices of Italian anthropometry.

Furthermore, Sheldon continued to hold that body physique was a reliable indicator of personality. Ultimately, it was as short a leap of the imagination for him as it was for his predecessors to generalize from certain types of temperament to delinquent or criminal tendencies (see, e.g., Sheldon and Stevens 1942).

No matter how one judges Sheldon from theoretical perspectives, he was first and foremost a consummate taxonomist. His expertise in classification and his somatotypes continue to appear even today in any comprehensive treatise in criminology, if only as historical conceptual dinosaurs. Sheldon's first task was to classify physique. Following the procedures of any rigorous naturalist, he began by examining his subjects in their natural state. In order to avoid the distractions to observation of dress, background, and social setting, Sheldon chose to examine photographs of individual male subjects, standing completely nude on a small pedestal from a full, front, profile, and back positions. His first research of body classification was titled *The Varieties of Human Physique* (Sheldon, Stevens, and Tucker 1940), and reports of his success in categorizing 4,000 male college students who had volunteered for his project. Students were photographed in departments of student health in five universities (Chicago, Wisconsin, Northwestern, Oberlin, and Harvard). Sheldon was concerned in this initial project with whether he could effectively code and categorize a large sample of men and reduce the results to a small number of basic body types. He believed that the early study by Kretschmer was faulty as a result of its basis on a sample of mental patients of disparate ages; Sheldon's first research fixed only on college-age males.

The findings isolated three primary structures of human physique: endomorphy, mesomorphy, and ectomorphy. These basic types approximated Kretschmer's earlier classification. The *endomorph,* similar to the pyknic, is a type with a relative predominance of soft roundness throughout the various regions of the body. In Sheldon's words,

> When endomorphy predominates, the digestive viscera are massive and highly developed, while the somatic structures are relatively weak and undeveloped. Endomorphs are of low specific gravity. They float high in the water. Endomorphs are usually fat but they are sometimes seen emaciated. In the latter event they do not change into mesomorphs or ectomorphs any more than a starved mastiff will change into a spaniel or a collie. They become simply emaciated endomorphs. (Sheldon and Stevens 1942, 8)

> *Mesomorphy,* like Kretschmer's athletic type, is characterized by a preponderance of muscle, bone, and connective tissue. The mesomorphic physique is normally heavy, hard, and rectangular in outline. As Sheldon put it,

> When mesomorphy predominates, the somatic structures (bone and muscle) are in the ascendancy. The mesomorphic physique is high in specific gravity and is hard, firm, upright, and relatively strong and tough. Blood vessels are large, especially the arteries. The skin is relatively thick, with large pores, and it is heavily reinforced with underlying connective tissue. The hallmark of mesomorphy is uprightness and sturdiness of structure, as the hallmark of endomorphy is softness and sphericity. (Sheldon and Stevens 1942, 8)

The *ectomorph,* like the asthenic, is thin and delicate. Sheldon writes,

> Ectomorphy means fragility, linearity, flatness of the chest, and delicacy throughout the body. There is relatively slight development of both the viscera and somatic structures. The ectomorph has long, slender, poorly muscled extremities with delicate, pipestem bones, and he has, relative to his mass, the greatest surface area and hence the greatest sensory exposure to the outside world. His nervous system and sensory tissue have relatively poor protection. (Sheldon and Stevens 1942, 8)

Sheldon was convinced the analysis of photographs was an improvement over earlier direct observational approaches. He later argued a reliability coefficient of .90 was attainable among personnel using his classification scheme (Sheldon, Dupertuis, and McDermott 1954). An actual detailed measurement on each photograph was completed for five regions of the body: head–neck, chest–trunk, arms, stomach–trunk, and legs. Moreover, fifteen separate traits of each body segment were also assessed from photo analysis. Ultimately, by averaging individual assessments on all five major body regions, the investigator (or *somatotyper*) arrived at three distinct scores of endomorphy, mesomorphy, and ectomorphy. The highest score attainable for any one of the three basic somatotypes was seven, and the lowest was one. An extremely obese individual might receive a 7–1–1, high in endomorphy and low in the remaining categories.

By using a seven-point scale it was possible to arrive at 343 combinations or body types (e.g., 5–1–1, 5–1–2, 5–1–3). In Sheldon's original study of 4,000 males, he found only 76 different somatotypes, but in later years increased the distinct types to 88, and most recently to 267 (Sheldon, Lewis, and Tenney 1969). These body types were to remain relatively constant even with some fluctuation in nutrition. Modern athletes and dieters would undoubtedly disagree with this point (see Abramson 1980, 153).

Sheldon's first volume in what was called the "Human Constitution Series" was devoted entirely to determining physique and arriving at somatotypes (see Sheldon, Stevens, and Tucker 1940). His second major volume published in the same year guided the reader through an assessment of various personality temperaments that were matched accordingly with physiques of one kind or another (see *The Varieties of Human Temperament,* 1942).

Sheldon readily admits he wished to add scientific rigor to the street wisdom that fat men were jolly and that so-called Scrooge-like men were dour (see Sheldon and Stevens 1942, 1). He began with an accumulation of 650 recorded personality traits, apparently gathered from texts available during his time. These he reduced to fifty more basic clusters of temperament. With those fifty types, he devised a survey incorporating the aid of thirty-three male graduate students, young instructors, and "other academic people" gathered from around Harvard University. Over a period of one year, each member of the sample underwent what Sheldon referred to as an "academic interview," and was also directly observed over the course of the year in daily routines and in social relationships (Sheldon and Stevens 1942, 13).

Each member of the sample was assessed by matching observed characteristics with the fifty types of temperament determined previously. The researchers reported that only twenty-two specific traits were verified and that these fell into three major clusters or groups: six in group I, called *viscerotonia;* seven in group II, called *somatotonia;* and nine in group III, called *cerebrotonia*. To the investigators, the conclusion quickly became obvious as the three primary clusters of temperament fitted neatly into place and could be superimposed over the three basic somatotypes.

Sheldon writes,

> Viscerotonia, in its extreme manifestation is characterized by general relaxation, love of comfort, sociability, conviviality, gluttony for food, for people, and for affection. The viscerotonic extremes are people who "suck hard at the breast of mother earth" and love physical proximity with others. The motivational organization is dominated by the gut . . . and the personality seems to center around the viscera. The digestive tract is king, and its welfare appears to define the primary purpose of life. (Sheldon and Stevens 1942, 10)

By *somatotonia*, Sheldon means

> a predominance of muscular activity and of vigorous bodily assertiveness. The motivational organization seems dominated by the soma. These people have vigor and push. The executive department of their internal economy is strongly vested in their somatic muscular systems. Action and power define life's primary purpose. (Sheldon and Stevens 1942, 10)

Finally, Sheldon writes that *cerebrotonia*

> is roughly a predominance of the element of restraint, inhibition, and of the desire for concealment. Cerebrotonic people shrink away from sociality as from too strong a light. They repress somatic and visceral expression, are hyperattentional, and sedulously avoid attracting attention to themselves. Their behavior seems dominated by the inhibitory and attentional functions of the cerebrum. (Sheldon and Stevens 1942, 10–11)

Sheldon believed he had shown that endomorphs were more viscerotonic, mesomorphs more somatotonic, and ectomorphs more cerebrotonic. With these features, as in all of Sheldon's work, an inherited or genetic biological base of all behavior is argued. Temperament and physique are simply different levels of genetic expression.

Sheldon more directly overlaps into criminology with a third volume in the Human Constitutional Series entitled *Varieties of Delinquent Behavior* (1949). In this work, Sheldon, Hartl, and McDermott, not unlike Goring and Hooton in method, entered the Hayden Goodwill Inn (an early Boston reformatory for youthful males) to further test his theories. This last study in the series more closely replicates the work of earlier biological determinists by analyzing the behavior of so-called abnormal members of the population (e.g., mental patients, criminals).

Over the course of several years, Sheldon was able to somatotype 200 youthful males of the reformatory. He found high correlation between his various predetermined categories and his confined population. Basically, Sheldon analyzed the youth in case-study fashion. His methods included direct observation, interviews with staff members regarding the youth, and examination of previously recorded medical and social histories. The 200 males fell into a mix of classifications, including (1) mental deficient, (2) psychopath, (3) alcoholic, (4) gynandrophrene (feminine characteristics), (5) primary criminal, and (6) nondelinquent (i.e., the chaplain's unit). As the temperaments already associated with somatotypes predicted, Sheldon found criminal types to be more meso-morphic and somatotonic—that is, they were aggressive, possessed a need for action when troubled, loved physical adventure, and dominated others.

This volume of the series is 900 pages long and provides seemingly endless detail not only in photographs, but also in graphs, charts, and tables. Five years after the pub-lication of *Varieties of Delinquent Behavior,* Sheldon published a last book of somato-types entitled *Atlas of Men: A Guide for Somatotyping the Adult Male at All Ages* (Sheldon, Dupertuis, and McDermott 1954). This final work appears to be composed largely of photographs (samples from a total of 46,000 photographs), with little theo-retical explanation or justification. Sheldon wished to include a later book on the so-matotyping of women; as it turned out, he had difficulty arranging for volunteers to pose for the required photographs. However, he did include a variety of hand-drawn il-lustrations of his conception of the way women would appear were they to undergo the full somatotyping process (Sheldon 1940, 281–89.)

IV. CRITIQUE

Not all the memorable personages of science or philosophy are necessarily honored for their well-received contributions, and certainly not all are respected for the validity of their ideas. It seems that in science, we at times need a few good "bad" examples to help show us which way not to go.

Sheldon was perhaps the last of the great believers in the all-importance of consti-tutional or biological determinism, and in the subordinance of social–environmental features. The history of criminological thought marched past Sheldon as it had past Goring, Hooton, and Kretschmer. Sociologically, three major theoretical perspectives were simply too powerful to allow for the continuance of biological determinism on such a scale as that suggested by Sheldon.

First, Emile Durkheim's fundamental arguments demonstrated that phenomena apparently caused by biologic or psychical deficiencies (e.g., suicide) can be explained through purely social variables. Sheldon should have been aware of Durkheim's seminal ideas, especially given the time of his writing. However, he rarely took his at-tention from his specific research mission and never quoted Durkheim or any other major sociologists of the era.

Second, Sheldon managed to ignore the human ecology school of thought developed by Robert Park and his associates at the University of Chicago that helped forge crimi-nology as a discipline and push it farther from pure biological determinism. A primary theme of the Ecological School of thought was that crime rates continued to be high in some areas of the city irrespective of the race, nationality, or type of person dwelling in the area. The Human Ecological School of sociology and of criminology dealt a near fatal blow to the idea that biology was a significant factor explaining crime or delinquency. Yet Sheldon never acknowledged such a major school of thought, or even if he was aware of it. Shaw and McKay's major works, which examined "delinquency areas" from ecological vantage points, were having their heaviest impact in 1942, the same year that Sheldon's three volumes in the Human Constitution Series were marketed.

Third, the period from the early 1950s to the present marks the ascendancy of mod-ern conflict theory, which all but extinguishes the earlier fire of biological causation of criminal behavior. Simply put, biological features can hardly explain the occurrence of fluctuating crime rates when it is obviously possible for crime itself to be variously defined and enacted into law by legislators from one day to the next, and from one jurisdiction to another.

Finally, it must be candidly stated that Sheldon did not improve on the general research methodology over that of Goring or Hooton. He did, indeed, devise a rather highly refined technique of taxonomy of the human physique. Nevertheless, his scientific rigor appears to have ended with his descriptive technique.

Historically, Sheldon's rather dramatic works will always be tarnished by his nearly exclusive fixation on somatotyping. However, it should be recalled that his first and last books dealt not with physical classification, but with the need to include biologic, psychiatric, and social elements in a holistic, almost religious approach to the study of the human behavior. Although these works are exceedingly abstract, some of the principles have been noteworthy, especially in the development of philosophical foundations of such organizations as Alcoholics Anonymous.

References

Abramson, Paul R. 1980. *Personality.* New York: Holt.

Gellman, Irving Peter. 1964. *The sober alcoholic.* New Haven: College and University Press.

Goring, Charles, and Karl Person. 1913. *The English convict: A statistical study.* London: His Majesty's Stationery Office.

Hinsie, L.E., and R.J. Campbell. 1960. *Psychiatric dictionary.* 3rd ed. New York: Oxford University Press.

Hooton, Earnest Albert. 1939a. *Crime and the man.* Cambridge: Harvard University Press.

———. 1939b. *The American criminal: An anthropological study.* Cambridge: Harvard University Press.

Kretschmer, Ernst. 1921. *Korperbau und charakter (Physique and character).* Berlin: Springer-Verlag.

Mannheim, Hermann. 1972. *Pioneers in criminology.* 2nd ed. Montclair NJ: Patterson Smith. (Originally published by the *J. Crim. Law Crimin. Police Sci.* 1960).

Nasso, Christine (ed.). 1971. William H. Sheldon. In *Contemporary authors.* Vol. 25, 655–56.

Osborne, Richard H. 1979. William H. Sheldon. In *The international encyclopedia of the social sciences.* Vol. 18, 715. Christine Nasso (ed.). New York: The Free Press.

Rothenberg, Michael. 1981. *The encyclopedia of psychology.* Guilford CT: DPG Reference Publications, Inc.

Samuel, William. 1981. *Personality: Searching for the source of human behavior.* New York: McGraw-Hill.

Schafer, Stephen. 1969. *Theories in criminology.* New York: Random House.

Schjelderup-Ebbe, T. 1935. Social behavior of birds. In A. Murchison (ed.). *A handbook of social psychology.* Worcester MA: Clark University Press.

Sheldon, William H. 1936. *Psychology and the Promethean will.* New York: Harper and Brothers.

———. 1949. *Early American cents: 1793–1814.* New York: Harper and Brothers.

Sheldon, William H., C.W. Dupertuis, and E. McDermott. 1954. *Atlas of men: A guide for somatotyping the adult male at all ages.* New York: Gramercy Publishing Company.

Sheldon, William H., Emil M. Hartl, and Eugene McDermott. 1949. *Varieties of delinquent youth.* New York: Harper and Brothers.

Sheldon, William H., N.D.C. Lewis, and A.M. Tenney. 1969. *Psychotic patterns and physical constitution: A thirty year follow-up of thirty-eight hundred psychiatric patients in a New York hospital.* Hicksville NY: PJD Publications.

Sheldon, William H., and S.S. Stevens. 1942. *The varieties of temperament.* New York: Harper and Row.

Sheldon, William H., S.S. Stevens, and W.B. Tucker. 1940. *The varieties of human physique.* New York: Harper and Row.

Vold, George B. 1958. *Theoretical criminology.* New York: Oxford University Press.

Vold, George B., and Thomas J. Bernard. 1986. *Theoretical criminology.* New York: Oxford University Press.

Warming, Eugene. 1909. *Ecology of plants.* New York: Oxford University Press.

Supplemental Readings

Alcoholics Anonymous. 1955. *Alcoholics Anonymous: The story of how many thousands of men and women have recovered from alcoholism.* New York: AA Publications, Inc.

———. 1975. *Prometheus revisited: A second look at the religious function in human affairs, and a proposal to merge religion with a biologically grounded social psychiatry.* Cambridge: Schenkman Publishing Company.

CHAPTER 7
EDWIN HARDIN SUTHERLAND: 1883–1950

I. BIOGRAPHICAL SKETCH

Edwin Sutherland was many things to many people, from ardent critic to "messiah," but most would certainly agree that he was the leading criminologist of his generation. Given the tremendous and widespread impact that his works and ideas have had on the discipline, it is appropriate to place him among the most prominent, if not as the most prominent, of American criminologists. (Sutherland would resist such plaudits, as he believed knowledge to be a collective whose development was not at all dependent on specific individuals.) The stature that Sutherland has attained is all the more noteworthy because he took only one criminology course (in 1906), taught only one criminology course per year from 1913–21, and, by his own admission, he did not begin his organized work in criminology until 1921 (Sutherland 1973b). Sutherland is portrayed as very much a gentleman and a scholar. He is said to have been sincere, objective, soft-spoken, gentle, and respectful and to have possessed a kind of "paternal wisdom" (Geis and Goff 1983, Snodgrass 1972). However, he was not above anger when some of his convictions were challenged, as is evidenced in his final major work, *White Collar Crime* (1949), and in some of his critiques of research and theory that did not measure up to his high standards. He once referred to a book by William Sheldon as being "primarily crap" (Snodgrass 1972). Sutherland's basically gentle demeanor, coupled with his tenaciousness in pursuing his convictions and his penchant for pushing the discipline to the limits, led Snodgrass (1972) to call him the "gentle and devout iconoclast."

Not a lot of information is available about Sutherland's personal life, especially his childhood and youth; he was not given to talking about such things. Consequently, in some ways he is not as well known as some of the other prominent American criminologists (Geis and Goff 1983, Snodgrass 1972). He was born the fourth child in a family of five boys and three girls on August 13, 1883, in Gibbon, Nebraska. His parents were George Sutherland and Lizzie J. (Pickett) Sutherland. When Edwin was one year old, his family moved to Kansas, where his father was the head of the history department at Ottawa College, a position he held for nine years (Geis and Goff 1983).

In 1893, George Sutherland moved the family to Grand Island, Nebraska (population 6,000), where he became the president of the Nebraska Baptist Seminary, and Edwin attended school there, where he played football (the dream of so many young Nebraska boys) and was awarded an A.B. in 1904 from Grand Island College (the former Nebraska Baptist Seminary; Geis and Goff 1983). Sutherland was born, raised, and educated in a religious and academically oriented Midwestern setting (Schuessler 1973), a combination that was to have great impact on his later research and theorizing.

George Sutherland was a religious fundamentalist who believed in strict adherence to the Baptist faith, an austere existence, and stern discipline (Snodgrass 1972). His works, which include three book-length manuscripts, show him to be highly intellectual, often critical of himself, and very critical of those whose work failed to measure up to his rigorous standards. George is characterized as possessing a strong personality, and as being assertive and quite conceited, a trait Edwin did not share (Geis and Goff 1983).

George's commitment to higher education certainly influenced his children. Four of them, including Edwin, became involved in higher education. His religiosity also seems to have affected Edwin (Geis and Goff 1983), although it is thought that Edwin ultimately broke with the church (Snodgrass 1972). Just as his father was religious about the Baptist faith, "Edwin retained the ethics of his upbringing and became religious about his sociology" (Geis and Goff 1983, xix). A prominent and overt expression of his moralistic side appears in *White Collar Crime* (1949), where Sutherland calls for something other than a strict legal definition of acceptable behavior.

After receiving his A.B. in 1904, Edwin tried for a Rhodes Scholarship nomination; when he was not awarded it, he accepted a position at Sioux Falls College, a sister Baptist institution to Grand Island. There, he taught Greek, Latin, and shorthand from 1904 to 1906. More important, while at Sioux Falls, Edwin enrolled in a home-study course in sociology (although his intent at the time was to pursue history) through the University of Chicago (Geis and Goff 1983).

Edwin left Sioux Falls in 1906 for the University of Chicago and signed up for three courses in the Divinity School. At the urging of Dr. Annie Marion MacLean, he took a course called "Social Treatment of Crime." Shortly thereafter, he shifted his focus to sociology and began to slowly develop his interest in criminal behavior (Geis and Goff 1983, Gaylord and Galliher 1988). It was during this time that Sutherland was exposed to some of the most prominent sociologists of the day: Charles Henderson, Albian Small, and W.I. Thomas (Schuessler 1973). He stayed at Chicago until 1909, and then left for two years to teach sociology and psychology back at Grand Island (Geis and Goff 1983).

In 1911, Sutherland returned to Chicago intent on finishing his degree; however, he became disenchanted with the sociology department because he felt that the discipline (or at least the department) was too far removed from the problems that the theories were supposed to be addressing and that the methods lacked objective rigor, which led to nothing more than empty moralizing (Gaylord and Galliher 1988). He moved to the department of political economy, where he had previously taken a course from Thorsten Veblen (Geis and Goff 1983); although by this time Veblen had left the university. Once in political economy, Sutherland came under the tutelage of Robert Hoxie, a Veblen protégé. It is Hoxie whom Sutherland credits with exerting more "constructive influence" on his thinking than any of the sociologists, and it is this exposure to political economy that very possibly ignited the spark that was eventually to become *White Collar Crime*. Hoxie supervised Sutherland's Ph.D., granted under a double major in sociology and political economy, and Sutherland graduated magna cum laude in 1913 (Geis and Goff 1983).

On receiving his degree, Sutherland was offered a position in the sociology department of William Jewell College, another Baptist institution, in Missouri. Even though Sutherland was there for six years (1913–19), he really did not seem to fit in well. The president of the school was looking for a "political evangelist," and the benefactor of the chair that Sutherland occupied was hoping for a socialist; Edwin was neither. Other than his marriage in 1918 to Myrtle Crews, with whom he later had a daughter, Betty, very little happened during his tenure at William Jewell. Sutherland published only one article in six years (Geis and Goff 1983).

In 1919, Sutherland left William Jewell for the University of Illinois and began what was to be a sort of sojourn through the "Big Ten." While at Illinois, Sutherland's interests shifted from labor problems to criminology. Edward Carey Hayes was chairman of the sociology department and also served as an editor for the Lippincott Sociology Series. It was he who suggested that Sutherland write a criminology text (Schuessler 1973), but it is doubtful that he could have foreseen the impact that the relatively simple suggestion would ultimately have. Sutherland took Hayes' advice and wrote a book entitled *Criminology*, which was published in 1924, and three revisions were published by Sutherland in 1934, 1939, and 1947. After Sutherland's death, Donald Cressey, one of Sutherland's last doctoral students and leading proponents, published six more editions before his own death in 1987. The book became the dominant text of its time and set the standard for all those that followed. It also served as the primary vehicle for the presentation of many of Sutherland's major theoretical ideas.

In 1926, Sutherland once again moved, this time to the University of Minnesota, where he really began to develop a philosophy of research and to hone his skills. Sutherland's stay at Minnesota was short-lived, as he left in 1929 to assume a position in the Bureau of Social Hygiene in New York City. During the year that followed, Sutherland also spent some time in England doing research on the British Correctional System. This brief stint was to be the last time in his career that Sutherland would be employed in a location outside of the Midwest. In 1930, he left New York for the University of Chicago (Schuessler 1973, Geis and Goff 1983).

At Chicago, he did not occupy a regular faculty position. He was in what was referred to as a "research professorship," the primary responsibility of which was to carry out funded research, but Sutherland did offer a seminar that he taught at his home. The research performed while he was at Chicago led to the publication of two books, *Twenty Thousand Homeless Men* (Sutherland and Locke 1936) and *The Professional Thief* (1937). The reasons for Sutherland's leaving Chicago are not entirely clear, but it appears that he was not considered University of Chicago material or that there was a personality clash with Ellsworth Farris, the sociology chair (Gaylord and Galliher 1988). In 1935, he went back to the Big Ten to stay, accepting a position at Indiana University (Snodgrass 1972, Schuessler 1973, Geis and Goff 1983).

Prior to moving to Indiana, Sutherland was known only for his text, which had just come out in its second edition. Nonetheless, he was named as the first head of the newly established criminology department, a post he held until 1949, when poor health forced him to step down. Sutherland spent the remaining fifteen years of his career and life at Indiana University. This was a very productive time for Sutherland. The impact of his work and ideas had begun to spread, and by the time of his death, he was recognized as the premier criminologist of his day. Edwin Sutherland died of a stroke while walking to work on October 11, 1950 (Vold 1951, Snodgrass 1972).

Before closing this brief biography of Dr. Sutherland, a few general comments on him as a teacher and researcher are in order. Snodgrass (1972) states that Sutherland was not a terribly efficient researcher, but he was "compulsively thorough." His files were laden with lengthy typed quotes from books, newspaper clippings, outlines, and notes. When one compares the volume of Sutherland's published work with that of other pioneers of similar stature, the amount might seem to be a bit modest; however, the works that he did publish have consistently garnered high praise (Snodgrass 1972). Sutherland was also prone to passing his work out to his students and colleagues rather than submitting it for publication.

It has been variously claimed that, on the one hand, Sutherland was a great graduate level teacher (Geis and Goff 1983) and that, on the other hand, he was not a dynamic teacher, and his lectures were dull and delivered in a monotone. These statements may not be as inconsistent as they appear. According to accounts by his graduate students, Sutherland really shone in seminars and outside discussions, which he conducted in an informal, collaborative, egalitarian, and supportive manner (Snodgrass 1972). His greatest strength as a teacher was not his ability in the classroom, but rather in his willingness to take his students seriously as scholars; he was able to pull even beginning Masters students into the process of advancing criminology (Gaylord and Galliher 1988). It has also been reported that his students loved him (Geis and Goff 1983), which is no doubt true for many; but other reports indicate he was not perfect, that he played favorites, and leveled reprisals and recriminations when breaks occurred (Snodgrass 1972).

Edwin Sutherland has indeed been many things to many people, from fervent critic, to mentor, to friend. He was a highly regarded scientist, and like so many great thinkers, he was no less a moral philosopher (albeit a quieter one than some). Above all else, as the sections that follow demonstrate, Edwin Sutherland was a pioneer in criminological thought.

II. BASIC ASSUMPTIONS

SOURCES OF INFLUENCE

The most obvious and direct sources of influence, and those most often cited, on the thinking and theorizing of Edwin Sutherland were several sociologists from the University of Chicago. Sutherland and Henry McKay were close friends, and Shaw and McKay's work (1969) provided part of the foundation and much of the background for Sutherland's theorizing (Williams and McShane 1988, Snodgrass 1972). Sutherland was also influenced by W.I. Thomas and George Herbert Mead (Schuessler 1973, Williams and McShane 1988, Vold and Bernard 1986), as well as Louis Wirth and Thorsten Sellin. Consequently, themes from three major Chicago School theoretical orientations run through Sutherland's work: ecological and cultural transmission theory, symbolic interactionism, and cultural conflict theory.

The influence of the sociological tradition on Sutherland's theory has been widely discussed and is, for the most part, easily recognized, but there are less obvious sources of input that warrant exploration. The possible relationships of his concepts to psychological theories have not been very fully developed in the literature. Although one may not disagree with Vold's (1951) contentions that Sutherland is America's best-known and most singularly consistent criminologist and that he was "always the sociologist" when examining the phenomenon of crime, one can also legitimately conceptualize aspects of Sutherland's work as social–psychological.

From many of his works, such as the criticisms of the Gluecks (Schuessler 1973, Snodgrass 1972), the criticism of Sheldon (1951), his discussion of IQ (1931), and his sexual psychopath work (1950a, 1950b), it can be seen that Sutherland was generally not inclined to focus on internal causal agents of crime, or at least, he was not impressed by the "internal theories" that were in vogue at the time. It is also clear from his statement in the preface to the first edition of *Criminology* (1924) that he did not place great faith in psychological explanations, which he said account for a "very slight part of understanding" the criminal. One can surmise that this lack of enthusiasm for psychological interpretations developed early in his career; at least one of those who influenced him, W.I. Thomas, was very anti-Freudian (Schuessler 1973).

However, despite this apparent dislike for depth or individual psychology, when one looks closely at differential association theory, strong social–psychological overtones can be identified. In fact, Shoemaker (1984, 148) characterizes Sutherland's theory as social–psychological, stating that it places "the primary cause of delinquency with the individual but not within." Vold (1951) claims that Sutherland rejected Watson's behaviorism in favor of a "meaningful social psychology." Such descriptions become more supportable when one realizes that the history of social psychology has been characterized by a lack of conceptual unity. Even today, the majority of social psychologists receive their degrees in either psychology or sociology, merely specializing in social–psychological as a subarea of their broader disciplines (McCall and Simmons 1982). Meltzer (1961) called attention to the dual nature of social–psychological, stating that "sociological social psychology" stresses group variables whereas "psychological social psychology" emphasizes the impact of individual variables. At this point, it might be concluded that if Sutherland's theory is (somewhat) social psychological, it surely must be of the "sociological" ilk. However, in light of Allport's (1968, 3) description of psychological social psychological as "an attempt to understand and explain how the thought, feeling, and behavior of individuals are influenced by the actual, imagined, or implied presence of other human beings," such a conclusion becomes questionable.

Sutherland (1973b) said that the most difficult and important issue in criminological theory is the relationship of personal traits to cultural patterns in the genesis of criminal behavior. The "basic explanatory concept" used in social psychological to account for individual thought, feeling, or behavior is the personal trait (McCall and Simmons 1982). (It should also be noted that Sutherland taught psychology at Grand Island College from 1909 to 1911.)

Now that the case has been made for characterizing Sutherland's theory as social–psychological (at least at some level), the next question that arises is, what type of social–psychological interpretation did he offer? Most generally put, Sutherland's theory is a learning theory, but there are many variations of learning theory. The task becomes to trace the specific roots of learning theory "a la Sutherland."

During the time that Sutherland was formulating his ideas about human behavior, there were four prominent schools of thought in psychology: structuralism, functionalism, psychoanalytic theory, and behaviorism. The learning orientation, to a significant extent, precludes heavy Freudian influence, which would also be unlikely given Sutherland's relationship with W.I. Thomas. If Vold (1951) is correct in his observation that Sutherland rejected Watson's psychology (and it appears that he is), then behaviorism is out.[1] Looking at differential association theory, it is evident that Sutherland

---

[1]It is interesting to note that Watson was the recipient of the first Ph.D. in psychology awarded by the University of Chicago (Samuel 1981) in 1913, the same year that Sutherland received his doctorate in sociology.

did not adhere to the behavioristic tenet that subjective processes should not be included in theories of behavior. Structuralism reputedly started in 1879 in Austria, but the ideas were brought to the United States by many individuals, most notably Edward Titchener at Cornell. Structuralism is based on identifying the elements of human experience and establishing how those elements combine to form feelings and thoughts. The fourth approach, functionalism, was developed in the United States by William James. The focus was on the way in which mental processes function to fill needs. The structuralist would ask, "What is thinking?" whereas the functionalist would ask, "What is it for?" (Worchel and Shebilske 1983).

There is no indication at all that Sutherland was influenced by structuralism, either in the literature or in his concepts, but there is reason to believe that functionalism may have had some impact on his ideas. John Dewey, a leading proponent of functionalism, was at the University of Chicago from 1894 to 1904. Although he left there before Sutherland arrived, it is conceivable that a situation similar to that with Veblen and Hoxie might have been operating; those who had contact with Dewey passed his ideas on to later students. In addition, Sutherland (1947) makes numerous references to the works of Dewey, and Vold (1951) specifically states that Sutherland accepted Dewey's approach.

In the introduction to *On Analyzing Crime*, Schuessler (1973) says that if Sutherland were working today, he might have availed himself of B.F. Skinner's theory of operant conditioning. Although this is consistent with the earlier statement that Sutherland's theory is generally a learning theory, it is highly doubtful that this is a defensible conclusion. First, Skinner and Sutherland were contemporaries; in fact, they were at Indiana at the same time, so it seems likely that Sutherland would have been aware of Skinner's work. Also, Skinner first published the statement of his theory in 1938 in a book entitled *The Behavior of Organisms*. Sutherland did not publish the formal statement of differential association theory until 1939, and he certainly had ample opportunity to revise it in the direction of operant conditioning in later editions of his book *Principles of Criminology*. It should be reiterated that Sutherland did not pick up on the behaviorism of Watson in formulating early versions of his theory, despite having taken a class with him (Gaylord and Galliher 1988). Although Watson's and Skinner's behaviorisms are not exactly the same, their general orientations are quite similar.

If Sutherland's learning theory is not behavioristic, then what type of theory is it, and from where did he draw the impetus to formulate it? The first half of the question is easy enough to answer, once one examines the theory; it is a social learning theory. Sutherland (1973b) said that differential association was an attempt to explain crime via learning, interaction, and communication. The second half of the question need not pose any great mystery either, even if one accepts the presence of functionalist influence. The principles of functionalism are quite consistent with learning theory. In fact, one of the great applications of functionalist concepts was made in the area of education. Sutherland's emphasis on social interaction as the process of learning can be traced most directly to the symbolic interactionism tradition and to the cultural transmission notion of Shaw and McKay, two sources that Sutherland readily acknowledged. However, there is another learning theory with which differential association bears a rather striking resemblance—Gabriel Tarde's "imitation" theory.

Tarde was born in France in 1843 and died in 1904. He was a provincial magistrate, a researcher, a philosopher, a psychologist, a sociologist, and a criminologist (Allen,

Vine 1973, Friday, Roebuck, and Sagarin 1981). Like Sutherland after him, he rejected biological approaches, preferring instead what Vine (1973) called a "happy marriage of psychological and sociological." Tarde was one of the first to contend that criminal behavior is learned, and stressed the social nature of the learning process. For Tarde, criminality was not an inherited characteristic or a disease to be contracted; it was an occupational lifestyle (a "profession") learned through interaction with others. The central concept in Tarde's social learning explanation was imitation (Haskell and Yablonsky 1978, Vine 1973), but he never clearly defined the concept. He also placed a great deal of importance on the role of close friends in the learning process (Vine 1973).

Of imitation, Tarde (1912) said, "Men imitate one another in *proportion* as they are close in contact. The superior is imitated by the inferior to a greater extent than the inferior by the superior. Propagation from the higher to the lower in every sort of fact: language, dogma, furniture, ideas, needs" (p. 326, emphasis not in original). He stated further that the example of any man "radiates" around him, with an *intensity* that weakens as "distance of the men touched by his ray increases." In this case, *distance* is not merely geometric, but more "especially in the psychological sense" (Tarde 1912, 326).

Vine (1973) concludes that it was a "short step" from Tarde's view to the prevailing theories of the day in U.S. criminology, citing Sutherland's differential association theory as being "reminiscent" of Tarde. Haskell and Yablonsky (1978) refer to differential association as one of the most systematic attempts to explain crime in terms of imitation. Despite the attention that has been called to the similarities between differential association and Tarde's social learning approach, Sutherland (1973b) insisted that differential association takes into account not only imitation but all processes of learning. In the first edition of *Criminology* (1924), Sutherland made three references to Tarde, none of which related to imitation. This situation did not change in later editions. Of course, the assumption that imitation occurs and is a mechanism of learning is at least as old as Aristotle (Langer 1969). Nonetheless, Mannheim (1965) concludes that Sutherland should have more fully acknowledged his indebtedness to Tarde, but this issue is debatable and will be left for further consideration as Sutherland's key ideas are addressed later in the chapter.

GENERAL PHILOSOPHY AND THEORY OF BEHAVIOR

Sutherland's work reflects a reaction to the biological and psychological determinism espoused by the positivists of his day (Shoemaker 1984, Vold 1951). Sutherland was striving for a level of abstraction beyond the individual—his or her traits or surrounding environmental conditions (Vold 1951); but in a kind of paradoxical manner, he too was something of a positivist and determinist. Like the positivists before him, Sutherland focused on proximate causes, but unlike many of his predecessors, especially the symbolic interactionists, he made a great effort to integrate more immediate causes with input from distal sources. In this sense, Sutherland presented an interactionist approach (although he professed dislike and distrust of multifactor theories), which places his approach somewhere between positivism and the free will approaches of the classicists.

Sutherland emphasized process rather than structure (Williams and McShane 1988). He was basically opposed to "macro-level theories" because he believed that they did not provide the mechanism for translating environmental factors into individual motives and behaviors (Shoemaker 1984). In his quest for the proper balance of factors, Sutherland used a level of abstraction beyond, but never totally out of touch with, the individual. Drawing heavily on his symbolic interactionism roots, Sutherland's process involved tracing the development of individuals as they assigned meaning to their experiences and to the events in their environment. The source of these meanings was interaction with others, and it is these meanings or ideas that become the actual causes of behavior. Drawing further from his Chicago School background, and especially from his contact with Louis Wirth (Gaylord and Galliher 1988), Sutherland also incorporated a conflict philosophy into his work. Meanings can and often do come into conflict with each other, and these "normative and cultural conflicts" exert influence over behavior (Cressey 1979).

Sutherland's intellectual development, to a great extent, recapitulates the history of theoretical development in American criminology. Early in his career, he was oriented toward multifactor theories, then moved in the direction of social disorganization and cultural conflict approaches, and finally evolved his own social psychological theory. The major thrust of his later work was to develop a theory that transcended the fragmented and arbitrary quality of the prevalent multifactor interpretations of his day. This goal was not a statement against the existence of multiple factors; rather, it represented a criticism of inadequate attempts to organize them (Snodgrass 1972). Sutherland was generally critical of any theory that stretched to accommodate every possible factor, and said that such approaches should not be called *theories* at all (Schuessler 1973). In light of the contention that Sutherland's theory is interactionistic, this apparent rejection of multifactor explanations might seem a bit paradoxical. However, it could have been that he was expressing a concern similar to that raised later by Hirschi (1979), who warned against fusing our theories together end-to-end or side-to-side in an attempt to integrate them, as such strategies result in linkages of partial theories with limited applicability.

Sutherland's interpersonal explanation of behavior is based on three major assumptions:

- Human behavior is flexible, not fixed, and changes based on the situation (i.e., all behavior is learned).
- Learning occurs primarily in small and informal groups.
- The learning of behavior occurs through collective experiences as well as through specific situations.

The interpersonal nature of assumptions two and three is consistent with symbolic interactionism, functionalism, and the cultural transmission orientations. It is important to note that such an interpretation is very much a process approach. Although the specific content of what is learned is obviously important, within this framework how learning occurs becomes equally important, if not more so. The focus of the theory (differential association) is really on the social and mental aspects of the learning process and not on the occurrence of any specific behavior(s). Sutherland (1973b) states explicitly that it is not only the techniques of behavior that are learned, but more importantly, the evaluations of behavior and definitions of situations (i.e., meaning). This heavy emphasis on the symbolic aspects of the learning process serves to place Sutherland's theory among what have more recently been called *cognitive–social learning approaches*. This observation should come as no surprise given the extensive influence of symbolic interactionism and of the functionalist school in psychology. William James, the originator of functionalism, is often recognized as an early cognitive theorist because of the central position that consciousness and conscious processes occupied in his theory.

Donald Cressey (1960), in an introduction to differential association theory, refers to the dual nature of Sutherland's theory. When applied to the individual, the theory is social–psychological; when applied to the larger group, it is sociological. In psychology, the unit of analysis is the individual. When Sutherland's principles regarding behavior based on learning or acquiring meanings from others are used to explain a given act by a specific individual, those principles constitute a social–psychological explanation. However, when the theory is used to explain how meanings that have been transmitted from person to person within a group can come into conflict with those of another group (i.e., normative or cultural conflict), the explanation is sociological. The extent to which one acknowledges the ability of Sutherland's differential association to explain both processes is the extent to which one would conclude that he was able to correct the problem he saw with macrolevel and multifactor theories. His success in this area is better addressed after differential association theory is examined in more detail (see the following section). Sutherland's theory of criminal behavior was being formulated when American criminology was struggling to define itself as a discipline. Generally, at the time, criminological theories were still heavily dependent on instinct approaches or their derivatives. There was also a strong reliance on abnormal perspectives for explaining criminality. Sutherland helped pull criminology into focus (Sykes 1967) and bring it more up to date (Mannheim 1965). Vold and Bernard (1986) state that Sutherland's theory, more than any other, was responsible for freeing criminology from the deterministic grip of biological and abnormal orientations.

Owing in part to the (apparent) rise in gang violence in the 1950s and to the arrival of a newer and more sociologically oriented group of criminologists, the emphasis on the family and other more immediate sources of criminality began to diminish. By the mid-1950s, a perspective was focusing on forces external to the family had ascended to dominance (Wilson and Herrnstein 1985). One of the major catalysts in the early stages of this theoretical movement was Sutherland's theory of differential association, which stated that "a person becomes delinquent because of an excess of definitions favorable to violations of the law over definitions unfavorable to violations of the law" (Sutherland and Cressey 1966, 30). In Sutherland's scheme of things, the family was only one possible source of such definitions; there were many more potential external sources, most notably peers, that could be responsible for altering attitudes and values and for modifying rewards (Wilson and Herrnstein 1985).

The core of Sutherland's theory of criminality is the interaction and communication between individuals (Sutherland 1973b). His theory of criminal behavior represents an adaptation of W.I. Thomas' interactional–social approach (Schuessler 1973). It is an interpersonal theory, but, as did others who had been exposed to the works of people like Shaw and McKay, Wirth, and Sellin, Sutherland (1929) also incorporated value conflict into his theoretical framework. He wrote that crime is conflict, but it is part of a "process of conflict" of which law and punishment are other parts. The main objective of Sutherland's attention to conflicting values was to explain how normative or cultural conflicts influence the learning of criminal behavior (Williams and Mc-Shane 1988). Even though there were rather strong conflict overtones built into his theory, Sutherland was generally skeptical of class and economic explanations of crime and delinquency. He felt, as his later work in white-collar crime would demonstrate, that crime was basically independent of class and economic circumstances. Crime is relatively equally distributed across all of the social economic levels; what varies is the nature of the acts (Snodgrass 1972), how the acts are perceived, and the meanings attached to them.

In addition to his contact with the major thinkers in the discipline at Chicago, insights derived from the general cultural backdrop of the 1920s and 1930s contributed to the development of Sutherland's ideas and theory. The Depression was leading many into crime who might not otherwise have become involved. It also provided those in a position to exploit the system with even greater opportunities to do so. During this time, the Uniform Crime Report was first published, and early data painted a picture of the dispersal of crime that was consistent with the arguments of the Ecological School, that certain segments of society were more likely to be involved in criminal conduct than others (Williams and McShane 1988).

Drawing on these various sources, Sutherland developed a theoretical orientation that is a combination of the interpersonal (symbolic interactionism) and situational (cultural transmission and cultural conflict) theories of his day. Shoemaker (1984) offers some generic assumptions of interpersonal and situational theories:

- Human behavior is flexible. It is not fixed but changes based on the situation.
- Neither the delinquent/criminal nor the society in which he or she lives is deviant or bad.
- Most delinquent behavior is committed in a group or gang context.

For his blending of interpersonal and situational concepts, Sykes (1967) credits Sutherland with developing a theory of criminality that focuses on the "social milieu" in which it occurs. Sutherland (1937) said that criminal behavior is learned through all of the same mechanisms by which any behavior is learned, but he also pointed out that crime must be viewed in the context of political and social conflict (Vold and Bernard 1986). By addressing both the immediate and the wider origins of crime, Sutherland expanded symbolic interactionism and cultural conflict approaches by integrating them. In doing so, he was able to make sense out of both carrying crime rates and the processes by which the individual becomes criminal.

DEFINITION AND CONCEPTUALIZATION OF CRIME AND CRIMINALS

"The problem in criminology," says Sutherland (1947, 4), "is to explain the criminality of behavior not the behavior as such. The problem of criminal behavior is precisely the problem of differentiating one class of behaviors from another." Given his conceptualization of the problem facing criminology, Sutherland was not prone to making generalizations about criminals beyond the fact that they had been found guilty of a violation of the law. He believed that all humans commit crimes but that there are differences between "systematic and occasional offenders" (Sutherland 1924). This is a stance that he later relinquished to some extent, but it does not appear that he ever completely abandoned it.

Snodgrass (1972) believes that Sutherland fluctuated between a consensual and a conflict definition of crime, and reading the various statements made by Sutherland at different points in his career seems to support this contention. However, a more careful examination leads one to realize that Sutherland's apparently changing definitions are really a reflection of the possibility of defining crime at different levels, depending upon one's purposes. Sutherland (1949, 30) states, "the criminologist who is interested in a theory of criminal behavior needs to know only that a certain class of acts is legally defined as crime and that a particular person has committed an act out of this class." Therefore, if one's main concern is the criminal act and not the criminal actor, the definition is reasonably sufficient. However, he did caution that "neither different naming nor different procedures" used by a court make one behavior any less criminal than another instance of the same behavior.

Sutherland also believed that criminologists who search for the causes of crime find it hard to operate within a purely legalistic definition such as those used by the classical theorists (Vold and Bernard 1986). Sutherland (Sutherland and Cressey 1974, 21) states that, "obviously, legal definitions should not confine the work of the criminologist; he should be completely free to push across the barriers of legal definitions wherever he sees noncriminal behavior which resembles criminal behavior." These (apparent) definitional inconsistencies might be interpreted as delineating the difference between a theory that attempts to describe criminal behavior and how it comes to be viewed as such and a theory that attempts to explain criminals and how they become so. The latter was the overall focus of Sutherland's differential association theory. In the tenth edition of *Principles of Criminology*, Cressey (Sutherland and Cressey 1978) qualifies the previous quote by stating that such behaviors should not be called *crimes*. This qualifier may, at one level, ring true, but the essential question is, should those performing such acts be considered criminal? From his treatment of such issues in *White Collar Crime*, it seems that Sutherland's (1949) answer to this question would be yes. Haskell and Yablonsky (1978) support this conclusion, stating that Sutherland rejected traditional legal definitions based on official statistics because they were distorted by two factors: (1) The upper class was frequently able to escape arrest or conviction because money and social position gave them the power to do so; and (2) the laws that apply exclusively to business and professionals are not often dealt with in criminal courts.

As one examines Sutherland's work, it is clear that his primary concern was with the causes of criminality, but his collected papers also indicate strong interests in penology and other practical and policy concerns (Cohen, Lindesmith, and Schuessler 1956). Schuessler (1973, ix), in the introduction to *Edwin H. Sutherland on Analyzing Crime*, states that Sutherland's goal was to formulate an "internally consistent sociological explanation of crime with implications for both social policy and social practice." The Key Ideas section focuses on the crime causation aspects of Sutherland's work, but it is important to keep in mind that Sutherland was not only a complete thinker and criminologist, but also a reformist and moralist.

PHILOSOPHY OF SCIENCE

In developing his philosophy of science and research, Sutherland used the two main methods that developed out of the Chicago School, statistical information and life histories (Williams and McShane 1988). However, as was to become his trademark, he took these methods and put his own stamp on them. They became statistics and life history "a la Sutherland."

A quote from W.I. Thomas' (1923, 244) *The Unadjusted Girl*, which appears in all four of the Sutherland editions (1924, 81; 1934, 57; 1939, 62; 1947, 61) of *Criminology*, sums up his position on the use of statistics rather concisely. "Taken in themselves, statistics are nothing more than symptoms of unknown causal processes." According to Vold (1951), adherence to such a notion does not at all constitute a disavowal of statistics on the part of Sutherland. Rather, it represents an insistence upon keeping priorities properly ordered. It was doing just this that enabled Sutherland to look beyond the official statistics and expand his definition and theory of crime. His perspective on the use and value of statistics also kept Sutherland from becoming involved in "accumulating long lists of minutiae of tests and measurements relating to individual criminals so common in textbooks in criminology" (Vold 1951, 6).

In regard to the second method, life history, there is some debate in the literature as to whether Sutherland used it. Snodgrass (1972) argues that Sutherland avoided the subjective "natural history" approach of the Chicago tradition and that he did not attempt "subjectivism" as a method for understanding the offender. This conclusion cannot be entirely correct. Given Sutherland's (1937) publication of *The Professional Thief,* he obviously did not totally avoid the life history method. However, Sutherland's painstaking attempts to cross-validate and corroborate the information provided by Chic Conwell (the thief) serves as a commentary on his concern for not becoming overly dependent on the subjective.

As a researcher, Sutherland was well aware of the need for objectivity. However, he was not so dogmatic that he could not be flexible in his attempts to gain useful information. He possessed what could be called a healthy combination of the quantitative and the qualitative in his approach to research.

III. KEY IDEAS

Reviewing the literature generated by Sutherland, either directly or indirectly, is an awesome task. Schuessler (1973) has written that Sutherland had something to say about every criminological topic that arose between 1925 and 1950. Much of this work Sutherland published, but a considerable amount was also disseminated to his colleagues and students as unpublished papers. Since his death, these unpublished works have found their way into print. Along with his own writings, there is a plethora of material about him, critiquing his work and expanding his ideas. Obviously, it is not possible in one brief chapter to explore or even touch on all of the contributions and ideas of such a productive and influential scholar. Coverage, therefore, is necessarily restricted to what are considered by most to be his major contributions (i.e., key ideas).

Sutherland is best known for three works: differential association theory, *White Collar Crime,* and *The Professional Thief.* The bulk of the coverage is devoted to differential association, as it constitutes his general theory of criminality. Some space is also allotted to white-collar crime, a concept that Sutherland spent twenty-five years developing. Treatment of *The Professional Thief* is limited to references to it as appropriate in discussing other key ideas.

DIFFERENTIAL ASSOCIATION THEORY

Sutherland adopted an interpersonal–situational approach to explaining criminal behavior; more simply put, he believed that crime, like other behaviors, is learned. His theory, *differential association* (actually short for "differential association with criminal and anti-criminal behavior patterns" according to Cressey 1962) is considered one of the best known and most systematic and influential of the interpersonal theories (Haskell and Yablonsky 1978, Wilson and Herrnstein 1985, Shoemaker 1984, Sykes 1967). The theory was presented in the third (1939) and fourth (1947) editions of Sutherland's highly popular text, *Principles of Criminology*.

The theory states, "A person becomes delinquent because of an excess of definitions favorable to violations of the law over definitions unfavorable to violations of the law" (Sutherland 1947, 6). The process of acquiring definitions of what is desirable in reference to the law Sutherland (1939) called *differential association*, so called because what is learned in association with criminal behavior patterns differs in nature from what is learned in association with anti-criminal behavior patterns. The first suggestion of differential association theory appears in the second edition of *Principles of Criminology* in 1934, but at that time, the concept had not been developed fully. In fact, Sutherland (1973b) says that he was quite surprised by Henry McKay's reference to his theory of criminal behavior in 1935. He reports being reluctant to state a theory as such, as "every criminological theory which had lifted its head had been cracked down by everyone except its authors" (Sutherland 1973b, 17). However, at the urging of his friends and colleagues, Sutherland made the first formal statement of the theory in a chapter entitled "A Theory of Criminality" in the third edition of *Principles of Criminology*, which came out in 1939. The statement of this theory marked an important change in his thinking. He realized that concrete conditions could not cause crime and that a theory of criminal behavior must abstract from varying concrete conditions (Sutherland 1973b). With differential association, Sutherland was trying to create a general theory of criminality in response to a 1933 report by Jerome Michael and Mortimer J. Adler that severely criticized the state of criminological theory (Vold and Bernard 1986). Differential association emerged as a "tentative explanation" that sought to abstract common elements from multifactor theories and to combine their relationships into some reasonably concise and coherent theoretical model (Snodgrass 1972).

The theory of differential association, like many theories, went through a variety of changes. However, since the fourth edition of *Principles of Criminology* in 1947, the theory has remained virtually unchanged, except for "clarifications" by Cressey.

ASSUMPTIONS, CONCEPTS, AND PROPOSITIONS

The central assumption of differential association is that criminal behavior is learned in the process of interaction with others in the context of intimate personal groups. What is learned is not just the techniques for committing acts but also motives, drives, rationalizations, and attitudes that are favorable to criminal conduct (Haskell and Yablonsky 1978). For Sutherland, crime is normal learned behavior (Vold and Bernard 1986) acquired through interaction with others in a "pattern of communication" (Cressey 1960).

Shoemaker (1984) identifies two key concepts in Sutherland's theory, differential association itself and differential social organization. Differential association refers to the process by which criminal acts are committed in response to an excess of attitudes favoring law or norm violation at a given time. This excess is attained through association with others. Differential social organization represents Sutherland's contention that there is some level of organization in all social settings. He disagreed with Shaw and McKay's (1969) postulate that some areas are disorganized and contended instead that different areas may be organized differently.

To outline his theory, Sutherland adopted an unusual approach. He utilized a series of propositions. As they relate to theory construction, propositions are statements that address the relationships between or among concepts. There were originally (1939) seven propositions, and in the fourth edition of *Principles of Criminology* (1947), the list was revised to nine. Sutherland presented the propositions in approximately two pages with little elaboration and offered them as an explanation of both criminal and delinquent behavior and the distribution of crime and delinquency rates (Cressey 1960). The propositions are:

- Criminal behavior is learned.
- Criminal behavior is learned in interaction with other persons in a process of communication.
- The principle part of the learning of criminal behavior occurs within intimate personal groups.
- When criminal behavior is learned, the learning includes (a) techniques of committing the crime, which are sometimes very complicated, and sometimes very simple; (b) the specific direction of motives, drives, rationalizations, and attitudes.
- The specific direction of motives and drives is learned from definitions of the legal codes as favorable or unfavorable.
- A person becomes delinquent because of an excess of definitions favorable to violation of law over definitions unfavorable to violation of law.
- Differential associations may vary in frequency, duration, priority, and intensity.
- The process of learning criminal behavior by association with criminal and anti-criminal behavior patterns involves all of the mechanisms that are involved in any other learning.
- Although criminal behavior is an expression of general needs and values, it is not explained by those general needs and values because non-criminal behavior is an expression of the same needs and values. (Sutherland 1947, 6–8)

To more fully understand the theory, three integral elements must be fleshed out: differential association, differential social organization, and cultural conflict. As stated previously, Sutherland (1939) postulated that persons become criminal/delinquent when they acquire an "excess of definitions" that are conducive to violations of the law. The acquisitional process is referred to as *differential association,* as the individual may associate differently with criminal and anti-criminal behavior patterns. Vold and Bernard (1986) point out that there are two essential aspects of this conceptualization: content and process. *Content* is what is learned: behaviors, techniques, rationalizations, attitudes, and so on; *process* is the way the learning occurs. Both elements derive from symbolic interactionism theory. The content component is quite similar to Mead's "meanings," which he believed were of central importance in explaining behavior. Mead argued that it was not social or psychological conditions but the definitions of them by individuals that determine behavior. These definitions or meanings are acquired or derived through the process of social interaction. Sutherland characterized this social interaction process as being a process of differential associations.

A key characteristic of both criminal and anti-criminal associations is that they may vary in terms of frequency, duration, intensity, and priority (Sutherland 1939). Consideration of such qualitative variation is quite important, as Sutherland did not intend for excess to be interpreted simply or absolutely. *Excess* refers to the weight of the definitions as determined by the quality and intimacy of the interaction. Individuals operate on a balance or ratio of potential good to potential bad behavioral definitions (Williams and McShane 1988). The situation most conducive to the development of criminality is that in which there is association with criminal behavior patterns and an absence of associations with anti-criminal patterns.

Sutherland (1924, 605; 1934, 566; 1939, 595; 1947, 595) stated, "The essential reason why persons become criminals is that they have been isolated from the culture of the law abiding group." This isolation/association concept formed the core of differential association theory from its inception, but the conceptualization of the relationship between isolation and association changed over time, evolving along two lines. The isolation concept changed from an individual being isolated within a neighborhood to the isolation of a whole group from the larger community. The nature of association changed, from associations among one another in the isolated group and direct relationships with those committing criminal acts to associations with those in and out of the group who communicated "criminal behavior patterns." The changes reflect a shift in focus from the person doing the associating to the nature of the associations themselves (Snodgrass 1972).

Perhaps it was this shift in focus from the criminal and his or her actions to the meaning, rationalizations, and attitudes communicated by those expressing criminal behavior patterns that led Sutherland (1973b) to insist that differential association was not merely a restatement of Tarde's imitation. If imitation is considered mainly a mimicking of behavior, then Sutherland is correct in his claim; however, it seems that such an interpretation of Tarde's conceptualization of imitation is not accurate.

Sutherland's (1973a) differential association presented criminal behavior as a closed system: differential association is both a necessary and sufficient cause—necessary because no person would enter the system of criminal behavior unless he or she had associations with criminal behavior patterns, and sufficient because all persons who have had such associations participate in criminal behavior unless inhibited by associations with anti-criminal patterns. The key becomes the ratio between criminal associations and anti-criminal associations. Other factors are causal only to the extent that they affect the differential association process (Sutherland 1973a). The ability of differential association to satisfy the criteria of causality is discussed in the critique section.

In Sutherland's model, cultural conflict also plays a role. Criminality is seen as a consequence of conflicting values. An individual may exhibit behaviors that are approved within his or her "culture" but are disapproved of (possibly as illegal) in the eyes of the larger culture or society. While working with differential association theory after Sutherland's death, Cressey (1968) replaced *cultural conflict* with *normative conflict*. *Norms* refer to socially acceptable rules of conduct, and different groups may hold different norms that can and often do come into conflict. Cressey states that he sees this change not as a revision of differential association theory, but only as a clarification.

Although differential association, with its emphasis on learning via interaction and its attention to cultural (or normative) conflict, is similar to Shaw and McKay's (1969) cultural transmission theory, there is a very important difference between these two approaches. Shaw and McKay claimed that what fosters crime in lower-class neighborhoods is social disorganization. Initially, Sutherland (1939) also described the general social conditions underlying the differential association process in terms of cultural conflict and social disorganization, but in the final version of the theory (1947), he replaced social disorganization with differential social organization, which exists in a multigroup type of social structure. In such an organizational structure, various groups espouse alternatives and inconsistent standards of conduct. Members of one group have a greater probability of learning to use legal means for achieving success, whereas members of other groups may deny the importance of success, or accept success but promote illicit means for its achievement (Cressey 1960). In summary, the theory basically states that in situations of differential social organization and normative conflict, different behaviors (criminal or noncriminal) arise because of differential associations (Vold and Bernard 1986).

When one analyzes the relationships among the three central components of the theory, it shows that differential association theory actually operates on more than one level, with the two most overt levels being the individual and the group. The concept of differential association is an attempt to explain how an individual becomes criminal; at this level, the theory is social–psychological; differential social organization is an attempt to account for the uneven distribution of crime throughout different groups in society. These two explanations must, of course, be consistent (Cressey 1960, Snodgrass 1972). There is a third level, the normative level, represented by Sutherland as cultural conflict. According to Sutherland (1973b), differential association and differential social organization are definitely subordinate to cultural conflict.

WHITE-COLLAR CRIME

The concept of white-collar crime is today ingrained in the layperson's perception of corporations, politicians, and so on, and it has been and continues to be the subject of considerable empirical attention. It has become such an integral part of both the general and social scientific perspectives on our world that its origins as a concept are seldom contemplated. The concept of white-collar crime was originated and pioneered by Edwin Sutherland and did not attract much attention until the publication of *White Collar Crime* in 1949, and was the culmination of twenty-five years of work. In their introduction to *White Collar Crime: The Uncut Version*, Geis and Goff (1983) state that there are only sparse clues regarding the route by which Sutherland came to study the subject. He was fifty-six when he presented "The White Collar Criminal" at the 1939 meeting of the American Sociological Society. Then, in 1940, he published a journal article entitled "White Collar Criminality," and in 1941, "Crime and Business." The complete and final statement on the concept was made in the 1949 book.

Gresham Sykes (1967) states that *White Collar Crime* is a "pioneer work" and has remained "controversial and provocative." He also called it an ingenious study based on a simple hypothesis. A detailed explication of Sutherland's entire treatment of white-collar crime is beyond the scope of this chapter, but given the impact that it has had on thinking in and out of criminology, an outline and some discussion is imperative. Sutherland (1949, 112) defined *white-collar crime* as "a violation of criminal law by a person of the upper socioeconomic class in the course of his occupational activities"; in other words, he was focusing on crimes committed by persons of respectability and position that were "in accordance with their normal business ideals and practices." Such offenses include violations of antitrust laws, patent infringements, and misrepresentations in advertising.

Sutherland was skeptical of official statistics; he felt that crime is actually more evenly distributed across the social strata than the official data indicate. White-collar crime is the concept he used to test this idea. He compiled a list of the seventy largest nonfinancial business firms in the United States in 1929 and set about gathering information on all the convictions brought against them for committing criminal acts. He found a total of 980 convictions, with an average of fourteen per firm. Most of the violations recorded were for restraint of trade, formation of monopolies, and misappropriation of corporate funds. There has been some debate over the inclusion of certain violations in the analysis, as it appears that some of them were of federal administrative regulations (Sykes 1967).

Geis and Goff (1983) indicate that the book published in 1949 contained softened language compared to earlier forms of the manuscript. Originally, the names of the corporate offenders had been included, but Sutherland was pressured by the publisher and Indiana University to remove them and to make some other changes for reasons of legal liability and other potential repercussions. The uncut version, published in 1983, includes the names.

Although Sutherland, like most people, viewed crime in general as harmful to society, there is evidence that he believed that white-collar crime was a greater danger than many forms of street crime. Snodgrass (1972) reports that Sutherland purportedly held greater respect for the professional thief and conventional offender than for white-collar criminals, whom he saw as deceiving themselves and the public about their conduct. It was not the financial losses associated with white-collar offenses that concerned Sutherland, but the damage to social relations, public morale, and the general social structure and organization that he thought constituted the greatest loss. He believed that in these ways white-collar crime has a far more destructive impact on society than has ordinary crime (Reckless 1973).

In a foreword added to the 1961 edition of Sutherland's original version of *White Collar Crime*, Donald Cressey says, "This book has had an important effect on criminological thought" (p. iii). Sutherland's address on white-collar crime to the American Sociological Society in 1939 included several targets: He ridiculed both broken-home/poverty and Freudian theoretical orientations, citing the pronounced existence of white-collar crime as evidence against them. He discussed the link between the media and those guilty of corporate crime, saying that the media focused attention on heinous street crime and away from white-collar crimes. Given the rather broad net of criticism for which Sutherland used white-collar crime as a foundation and the apparent far-reaching implications he saw for the concept, Cressey's (1961) statement seems reasonable. The concept is certainly prevalent in the average person's perceptions of business; and, since Sutherland's statement in 1939, the media has not only become much more sensitive to the issue of white-collar crime, but, in fact, at times seems to revel in its exposure.

Along with these more macrolevel, societal impacts, *White Collar Crime* has had considerable influence within criminology itself. Vold (1951) called it the most definitive application of Sutherland's overall theory to the redefinition of the study of crime and to the reform of criminological theory, and Cohen, Lindesmith, and Schuessler (1956) refer to it as a logical extension of Sutherland's earlier critical approach. In his preface to the book, Sutherland (1949) calls it "a study in the theory of criminal behavior," referring to the book as an attempt to reform theory of criminal behavior and nothing else.[2] The book has been characterized primarily as just that—an attempt to

---

[2]This latter claim should be debated if one believes that Sutherland was as much a moral philosopher and social reformer as a scientist.

reform and extend the discipline of criminology, most notably by demonstrating that criminological theory does not and should not be solely dependent on the Uniform Crime Report (UCR) and other official sources for data and statistics (Cressey 1961).

Cressey (1961) argues that an expansion of the definition of crime itself was not part of Sutherland's reform movement, as there is only one definition—the legal one. Sutherland, according to Cressey, was making the argument that white-collar crime is a violation of criminal law. However, questions have been raised about some of the instances that Sutherland included as violations of the law (Tappan 1947, Caldwell 1958, Sykes 1967). The basis for these questions is the claim that not all of the acts referred to as white-collar crimes are technically violations of the criminal law. Sutherland (1949), addressing this very issue, stated that one behavior does not become less of a crime than another example of the same behavior simply because it has a different label or because different legal procedures are used to deal with it. Getting to the heart of this problem, Mannheim (1965) says that the white-collar crime controversy is really a debate between lawyers and social scientists over which is more appropriate, a legal or a social definition of crime. More specifically, it is a disagreement over whether prosecution in a criminal court makes a person a criminal (as Tappan 1947 advocates) or whether conduct alone suffices, irrespective of legal action.

Whether Cressey (1961) is correct or not, the controversy surrounding the conceptualization of white-collar crime has forced academicians, criminal justice practitioners, and people at large to reevaluate their definitions of crime and their determinations of who is a criminal. The lasting merit of the work is not its demonstration that corporations and highly placed individuals engage in crime, but its demonstration that a pattern of criminal behavior can be found outside of the focus of the public and scientific investigators (Cressey 1961).

It is clear that the concept of white-collar crime has had a direct general and practical impact on the entire field of criminology. The book has been in print for half a century, with the uncut version released in 1983. It has also been translated into several languages and has gained international prominence. Most standard criminology texts include some discussion of white-collar crime. The work also influenced several scholars who went on to become significant contributors to the discipline in their own rights, such as Marshal Clinard, Frank Hartung, and, most notably, Donald Cressey (see 1953, 1965, and 1969 for examples of his extensions of Sutherland's ideas on white-collar crime). The concept continues to be expanded, and now includes such areas as tax violations, social security fraud, improper use of credit cards, and a variety of computer scams (Haskell and Yablonsky 1978).

CONCLUDING REMARKS

There is no doubt that Sutherland's key ideas and general impact are of great importance. Differential association was an attempt to "bridge the gap" between the atomistic individual explanations that were dominant at the turn of the twentieth century and the newly evolving situational approaches of the 1920s and 1930s (Shoemaker 1984). Sutherland's work can also be seen, at least to some extent, as a reaction to the overly deterministic orientation that characterized both the biological and psychological theories of the period. Ironically, differential association is in its own manner a deterministic theory. Sutherland (1973a) presented differential association as both a necessary and a sufficient cause. In addition, like the other situational approaches, differential association theory has "mechanical undertones," relying on concepts like weights and ratios (Snodgrass 1972).

There are, however, some identified and important differences between differential association and its learning theory contemporaries. It did not rely on the simple stimulus–response model, like the theories from the Watsonian and Skinnerian traditions. Differential association theory is an attempt to explain criminal behavior via learning, but it is learning rooted in the process of interaction and communication, not in direct reinforcement or simple imitation. The focus is really on mental aspects, not on the overt relationships among stimulus, behavior, and consequence. Sutherland's theory is much more active than reactive; it is a cognitive, social learning theory.

Gresham Sykes (1967) observed that it is not clear whether Sutherland saw learned criminal behavior primarily as an integral part of the deviant subcultures or as a more isolated trait that could be found anywhere in society, or both. If one looks at *The Professional Thief* and *White Collar Crime*, the answer must be both. The subculture perspective certainly was part of the heritage of differential association, but Sutherland's insistence that crime occurred at all levels of society was equally important.

One final comment, as aptly offered by Cohen, Lindesmith, and Schuessler (1956), is that, although Sutherland's theoretical contributions in terms of differential association and white-collar crime are extremely influential in the historical development of criminology, his critical appraisals of theories, research, and other matters in penology and criminology have also been of considerable importance to the discipline. His evaluations were always carefully thought out, and his judgments were "widely appreciated and profoundly respected" (Cohen, Lindesmith, and Schuessler 1956) by both academicians and practitioners.

IV. CRITIQUE

There are a great many articles, old and new, addressing the value and validity of Sutherland's work, especially differential association. Among these, one finds a wide array of criticisms coming from "the right and the left" (Snodgrass 1972); but one also encounters studies reporting support for many of Sutherland's concepts. Although the literature ranges widely, differential association has received the lion's share of the attention.

One of the most scathing attacks on Sutherland's differential association theory came from Sheldon Glueck (1956), whose own research was severely criticized by Sutherland. Glueck argues that differential association, contrary to what its proponents claim, is, like its predecessors, a unilateral theory of causation. He further remonstrates that the theory fails to organize and integrate valid and relevant research findings and is at best so "general and puerile" that it adds nothing to the explanation, treatment, and prevention of delinquency. The theory, Glueck says, "adds nothing but excess baggage of confusing terminology to what is already well known and explainable" (92).

More common than such general and emotionally charged assaults are the variety of specific criticisms directed against differential association. Cressey (1962) identified five common types or categories of criticisms:

1. There are behavioral exceptions to the theory.
2. The theory does not adequately incorporate personality factors.

3. The theory emphasizes the social process of transmission but minimizes the process of reception.

4. Ratios of learned behavior patterns used to explain criminality cannot be determined with accuracy in specific cases.

5. The theory oversimplifies the process by which criminal behavior is learned.

According to Cressey (1962) and Shoemaker (1984), the most damaging of all the criticisms is the accusation that the theory of differential association is generally too broad to quantify and test (Mannheim 1965, Glueck 1956). More specifically, it has been stated that key concepts such as frequency, duration, priority, and intensity are hard to operationalize and that attempts to examine these as well as concepts like the ratio of law abiding to delinquent attitudes empirically have not fared well at all (Shoemaker 1984, Vold and Bernard 1986, Cressey 1960, Mannheim 1965).

Sharp criticisms have also been focused on the contention that criminal behavior is learned. Some question the claim itself, whereas others are skeptical of Sutherland's explication of the learning process. However, two other elements of the learning question pose critical problems: One obvious problem for the process component of the theory relates to those who become criminal but have had no interactions with criminals (Vold and Bernard 1986). The other element represents the other end of the continuum. Glueck (1956) contends that if the theory is carried out to its quantitative extreme, then the biggest criminals of all should be prison guards, professors of criminology, and so on.

A third type of criticism relates to the focus of differential association theory. Many have argued that Sutherland did not give sufficient attention to internal/individual factors (Wilson and Herrnstein 1985, Vold and Bernard 1986, Cressey 1962, Glueck 1956, Schuessler 1973). A variety of such factors are mentioned, ranging from IQ to sexual desire, but, generally speaking, the crux of this criticism comes from the psychological orientation that bases its complaints on two primary grounds: (1) Sutherland's view of learning is dependent (simplistically) on external contact; and (2) the theory neglects personality factors completely (Schuessler 1973). The neglect of personality factors is considered quite serious, as it constitutes the exclusion from theoretical consideration of some important determinant factors of crime and criminality. According to Glueck (1956), this neglect creates two shortcomings: First, all people are treated as if the environment exerts equal influence over them; and second (and more important), by emphasizing the definition of the situation, differential association circumvents the essential question of what makes a delinquent, or what causes him or her to define a situation in a manner that is favorable to law violation. Differential association presents a tautological scenario in which crime begets crime.

The last type of criticism refers to conceptual ambiguity, inconsistency, and lack of clarity. Of course, the issues raised here are not independent from others raised earlier, such as the difficulty with operationalizing concepts, for example. Cressey (1960) acknowledges that the statement of differential association theory is "neither precise nor clear." There are instances in Sutherland's work, he says, of circular reasoning and of inconsistency. The lack of precision and inconsistency referred to questions raised about Sutherland's actual definition of the concept of white-collar crime and some of the examples he cited. An example of lack of precision also appears in *The Professional Thief,* in which references are made to the background of Chic Conwell and the role of certain factors in his life of crime, although Sutherland does not actually supply much real information.

Sutherland's definitions of concepts are at times inconsistent, even within the same work (e.g., see the definitions of crime offered in the third edition of *Principles of Criminology*), and Sutherland is also guilty of incomplete definitions. He never fully identifies what constitutes a definition favorable or unfavorable to violation of the law, or explains how a definition favorable to one person might be unfavorable to another (Cressey 1962). He never explains why differential association actually occurs, or why different levels of commitment and different values develop (Haskell and Yablonsky 1978). He attempts to address such problems with the concepts of intensity, priority, duration, and frequency, but these concepts are themselves never clearly defined, resulting in the operationalization problems discussed earlier.

There are a wide variety of other specific criticisms that have appeared in the literature, and there is much more detail that could be offered on those covered. However, time and the purpose at hand preclude a more in-depth treatment at this point. For more detail on criticisms of Sutherland's works see Cressey (1962), Snodgrass (1972), Vold and Bernard (1986), and Wolfgang, Savitz, and Johnston (1962).

RESPONSES AND SUPPORT (AND ADDITIONAL CRITICISMS)

There have been numerous attempts to validate Sutherland's ideas empirically, especially with juveniles. It has been documented that most delinquency occurs in a group context (Shoemaker 1984, Jensen and Rojeck 1980), but most of the studies reporting this finding have not addressed such concepts excess of definitions, intensity, and so on directly; consequently, the temporal criterion of causality has not been satisfied. In other words, the data indicate a relationship between delinquent behavior and interaction with others, but they do not demonstrate that it is, in fact, the contact with these certain others that causes the behavior. Causal sequence is not established, nor are other potential causal factors ruled out.

James Short (1957) attempted to assess more specific aspects of differential association using delinquents. He operationalized *priority* as the first friend that could be remembered, *frequency* as the friends most associated with, *duration* as those friends associated with longest, and *intensity* as best friends. He then compared the delinquent conduct of the various categories of friends with that of the respondent. In a later work, Short (1960) focused on the quality of *intensity*, trying to characterize it in terms of whether best friends produced or inhibited delinquency. Short (1960) concludes that his work was generally supportive of differential association theory, but acknowledges that it was limited in its application. He also points out that isolated sets of consistent findings do not necessarily validate a theory. Reiss and Rhodes (1964) found less support for intensity as a causal factor in criminality. Given the difficulties with operationalizing and subsequently testing Sutherland's concepts, efforts have been made to reformulate his theory into operant conditioning concepts (e.g., Burgess and Akers 1966, Adams 1973). Some believe that the operant conditioning paradigm provides a more objective, precise, and quantifiable framework than does differential association. However, Halsbach (1979) contends, based on the observation that differential association theory allows for influence from emotions and interpersonal feedback, whereas the operant approach does not, that the conversion is not necessarily productive, and concludes that Sutherland's theory may succeed where its reformulations fail. This same debate prevailed in psychology for quite some time concerning the utility of operant as opposed to social learning/cognitive approaches; right now, it appears that the verdict favors the cognitive social learning interpretations.

Not only has differential association been accused of presenting an oversimplified conceptualization of learning, but it has also been charged with not allowing for other types of learning or accounting for behavior that is "independently invented." Cressey (1962) accepts these as legitimate criticisms (to an extent), but he also points out that generally criticizing the theory on such grounds is one thing, whereas it is quite another to clearly specify what other types of learning fit where and how. Remember also that Sutherland (1973b) said that the process of learning criminal or anti-criminal behavior involves all the mechanisms of learning.

Differential association has been portrayed by some as emphasizing the social process of transmission but as minimizing the individual process of reception; in other words, the theory does not take into account the meaning of the process to the recipient (Cressey 1962). The validity of this criticism becomes suspect when one recognizes the strong influence that symbolic interactionism had on Sutherland. In fact, Cressey (1962) says that differential association itself accounts for "differential response patterns" or "receptivity" to the criminal behavior pattern presented.

Another criticism that Sutherland and Cressey (1978) find erroneous is the charge that differential association fails to account for why people have the associations they have. They rebut this claim on two grounds: (1) The concept of differential social organization accounts for this, but research concerning differential association virtually ignores this component of the theory; and (2) the individual aspect of the theory is self-contained and does not necessarily have to account for why or how associations develop.

Sutherland was severely reproached for ignoring psychological/personality variables in his explanation of criminal behavior; however, it is possible that this criticism has been overstated and is founded, to some extent, on misinterpretation. Cressey (1962) claims that a theory explaining social behavior in general or any specific kind of social behavior should have two distinct but consistent aspects: (1) a statement that explains the statistical distribution of behavior in time and space (epidemiology), and (2) the ability to (at least) imply the process by which individuals come to exhibit the behavior in question. He goes on to say that Sutherland's theory has been largely ignored for its epidemiological aspects and viewed primarily as an alternative to psychiatric theories. The implication is that this one-sided focus in examining the theory has led to an intensified amount of attention to psychological factors and subsequently to exaggerated criticisms about the inadequacy of the theory in this area.

Despite the potential for misinterpretation in this criticism, Sutherland took it seriously. In addressing the problem, he found what he believed to be a fundamental flaw in the argument of his critics. He pointed out that *personality traits* and *personality* are words that merely specify a condition without showing a relationship between the condition and criminality. When used with no further elaboration, such words are synonymous for *unknown conditions* (Cressey 1962). Based on this conclusion, Sutherland ultimately answered the questions of the personality advocates with three questions of his own:

- What personality traits should be regarded as significant?
- Are these traits supplements, or are they already included in differential association?
- Can differential association, which is essentially a process of learning, be combined with personality traits, which are essentially the product of learning? (Cressey 1962)

One final point relating to the complaint by the personality proponents is that they apparently ignored the fact that differential association theory deals not only with actual contacts or associations with criminal behavior, but it also addresses the role of attitudes and values connected with behavior patterns as well (Shoemaker 1984). This component of the theory provides a strong social learning and cognitive element, which certainly places differential association as an interactionistic theory (i.e., the interaction between internal cognitive and perceptual factors with a variety of external factors to produce criminal behavior). In addition, Halsbach (1979) observes that differential association does allow for the influence of emotion and other forms of interpersonal feedback. So, if variables other than "traits" are acceptable as reflective of personality, Sutherland's theory cannot be accused of totally neglecting such factors.

In summary, differential association appears to offer a reasonable explanation of individual crime/delinquency within environmental and social contexts, but there are valid criticisms in terms of its logic and scope. Short (1960) referred to differential association as a "principle," and as such, it can have great value for future research and theory, even if its own specific hypothesis cannot be derived and tested. Whether one puts more faith in the data that are supportive, or in those that are nonsupportive or refutive, the fact is that despite the intense scrutiny and criticism visited on it, differential association has not been abandoned. In fact, it continues to generate considerable amounts of thought and research.

HEURISTIC IMPLICATIONS

The overall impact of Sutherland's work cannot be accurately assessed or expressed by examining only the data relating to the validity of specific concepts. The verdict on the validity of many of his concepts is not yet in, and many of the issues may never be fully resolved. However, even if it should turn out that not one of his concepts ultimately withstands empirical analysis, Sutherland's contribution to criminology would in no way be diminished. To see that his ideas permeate the entire discipline requires but a skimming of the literature. Virtually any work dealing with a general view of the discipline or with theory devotes considerable space to Sutherland. As more specific statements of theory or reports of research are perused, one invariably comes across innumerable direct and indirect references to his ideas and concepts. Space does not permit a detailed explication of the magnitude of this widespread impact; therefore, what follows is a brief and general discussion of the heuristic implications of the work of Edwin H. Sutherland.

Much of the value of Sutherland's theory and ideas lies in the fact that there has been so much debate about them. Cressey (1960) states that the theory has had an important effect on thought about crime and criminals, if for no other reason than it has been the center of controversy. He further contends that, at a minimum, the theory is valuable as an organizing tool for research. A review of the literature demonstrates that the most accurate predictors in criminological prediction research are deducible from differential association theory, whereas the least accurate are not.

A great deal of contemporary criminological theory and research is traceable to Sutherland's original formulation. They state that a substantial portion of modern criminologists have done work in response to a question that Sutherland asked years ago: Why are the normal learned behaviors of some groups defined as criminal, whereas the normal learned behaviors of other groups are defined as legal? Their claim serves not only as testimony to the timelessness of Sutherland's influence, but also to its range. However, the best barometer of Sutherland's true impact on the field is the people he influenced. The list of his students and others who credit his influence reads like a "Who's Who in Criminology": Albert Cohen, Marshal Clinard, Donald Cressey, Lloyd Ohlin, Fred Strodtbeck, C. Ray Jeffery, George Vold, Richard Quinney, Alfred Lindesmith, Karl Schuessler, Frank Hartung, James Short, Donald Glaser, and very certainly a host of others less well known or yet to become so. It may very well be this living legacy, more than any other contribution, that elevates Edwin Sutherland to a special place in the history and development of criminological thought.

References

Adams, L.R. 1973. Differential association and learning principles revisited. *Soc. Prob.* 20: 458–70.

Allen, H.E., P.C. Friday, J.B. Roebuck, and E. Sagarin. 1981. *Crime and punishment: An introduction to criminology.* New York: The Free Press.

Allport, G.W. 1968. The historical background of modern social psychology. In G. Lindzey and E. Aronson (Eds.), *The hand book of social psychology.* 2nd ed., vol. 1. Reading, MA: Addison-Wesley, pp. 1–80.

Burgess, R.L., and R.L. Akers. 1966. A differential association–reinforcement theory of criminal behavior. *Soc. Prob.* 14: 128–47.

Caldwell, R.G. 1958. A re-examination of the concept of white collar crime. *Fed. Prob.* 22: 30–6.

Cohen, A., A. Lindesmith, and K. Schuessler. 1956. Introduction. In A. Cohen, A. Lindesmith, and K. Schuessler (Eds.), *The Sutherland papers.* Bloomington, IN: Indiana University Press, pp. 1–4.

Cressey, D.R. 1953. *Other people's money.* New York: The Free Press.

———. 1960. The theory of differential association: An introduction. *Soc. Prob.* 8: 2–6.

———. 1961. Foreword. In E.H. Sutherland, *White collar crime* (originally published 1949). New York: Holt, Rinehart and Winston.

———. 1962. The development of a theory: differential association. In M.E. Wolfgang, L. Savitz, and N. Johnston (Eds.), *The sociology of crime and delinquency.* New York: John Wiley and Sons, pp. 81–90.

———. 1965. The respectable criminal. *Trans-Action.* 2: 13.

———. 1968. Culture, conflict, differential association, and normative conflict. In M.E. Wolfgang (Ed.), *Crime and culture.* New York: John Wiley and Sons, pp. 43–54.

———. 1969. *Theft of the nation.* New York: Harper and Row Publishing.

———. 1979. Fifty years of criminology. *Pacif. Sociolog. Rev.* 22: 457–80.

Gaylord, M.S., and J.F. Galliher. 1988. *The criminology of Edwin Sutherland.* New Brunswick, NJ: Transaction Books.

Geis, G., and C. Goff. 1983. Introduction. In E.H. Sutherland, *White collar crime: The uncut version.* New Haven: Yale University Press.

Glueck, S. 1956. Theory and fact in criminology: a criticism of differential association. *Br. J. Deling.* 7: 92–109.

Halsbach, K. 1979. Differential reinforcement theory examined. *Criminology.* 17: 217–29.

Haskell, M.R., and L. Yablonsky. 1978. *Crime and delinquency.* 3rd ed. Boston: Houghton Mifflin.

Hirschi, T. 1979. Separate and unequal is better. *J. Res. Crime Deling.* 16: 34–8.

Jensen, G.F., and D.G. Rojeck. 1980. *Delinquency.* Lexington, MA: D.C. Heath.

Langer, J. 1969. *Theories of development.* New York: Holt, Rinehart, and Winston.

Mannheim, H. 1965. *Comparative criminology.* Boston: Houghton Mifflin.

McCall, G.J., and J.L. Simmons. 1982. *Social psychology: a sociological approach.* New York: The Free Press.

Meltzer, L. 1961. The need for a dual orientation in social psychology. *J. Soc. Psych.* 55: 43–47.

Reckless, W.C. 1973. *The crime problem*. 5th ed. Pacific Palisades, CA: Goodyear Publishing Company.

Reiss, A.J., Jr., and A.L. Rhodes. 1964. An empirical test of differential association theory. *J. Res. Crime Delinq*. 1(1): 5–18.

Samuel, W. 1981. *Personality: Searching for the sources of human behavior*. New York: McGraw-Hill.

Schuessler, K. 1973. Introduction. In K. Schuessler (Ed.), *Edwin H. Sutherland on analyzing crime*. Chicago: University of Chicago Press, pp. 1–12.

Shaw, C.R., and H.D. McKay. 1969. *Juvenile delinquency and urban areas*. Rev. ed. Chicago: University of Chicago Press.

Shoemaker, D.J. 1984. *Theories of delinquency: an examination of explanations of delinquent behavior*. New York: Oxford University Press.

Short, J.F., Jr. 1957. Differential association and delinquency. *Soc. Prob*. 4: 233–239.

_____. 1960. Differential association as a hypothesis: problems of empirical testing. *Soc. Prob*. 8: 14–25.

Skinner, B.F. 1938. *The behavior of organisms*. New York: Appleton-Century-Crofts.

Snodgrass, J. 1972. The American criminologist tradition: Portraits of the men and ideology in a discipline. Unpublished doctoral dissertation, University of Pennsylvania.

Sutherland, E.H. 1924. *Criminology*. Philadelphia: J.B. Lippincott Company.

_____. 1929. Crime and the conflict process. *J. Juv. Res*. 13: 38–48.

_____. 1931. Mental deficiency and crime. In K. Young (Ed.), *Social attitudes*. New York: Henry Holt and Company, pp. 357–375.

_____. 1934. *Principles of criminology*. 2nd ed. Philadelphia: J.B. Lippincott Company.

_____. 1937. *The professional thief*. Chicago: University of Chicago Press.

_____. 1939. *Principles of criminology*. 3rd ed. Philadelphia: J.B. Lippincott Company.

_____. 1940. White-collar criminology. *Am. Sociol. Rev*. 5: 2–3.

_____. 1941. Crime and business. *Ann. Am. Acad. Pol. Soc. Sci*. 217: 112–18.

_____. 1947. *Principles of criminology*. 4th ed. Philadelphia: J.B. Lippincott Company.

_____. 1949. *White collar crime*. New York: Holt, Rinehart, and Winston.

_____. 1950a. The diffusion of sexual psychopath laws. *Am. J. Sociol*. 56: 142–48.

_____. 1950b. The sexual psychopath laws. *J. Crim. Law Criminol*. 41: 543–54.

_____. 1951. Critique of Sheldon's varieties of delinquent youth. *Am. Sociolog. Rev*. 16: 10–13.

_____. 1956. Critique of the theory. In A. Cohen, A. Lindesmith, and K. Schuessler (Eds.), *The Sutherland papers*. Bloomington, IN: Indiana University Press, pp. 30–41.

_____. 1973a. Critique of the theory. In K. Schuessler (Ed.), *Edwin H. Sutherland on analyzing crime*. Chicago: University of Chicago Press, pp. 30–41.

_____. 1973b. Development of the theory. In K. Schuessler (Ed.), *Edwin H. Sutherland on analyzing crime*. Chicago: University of Chicago Press, pp. 13–29.

_____. 1983. *White collar crime: The uncut version*. New Haven: Yale University Press.

Sutherland, E.H., and D.R.Cressey. 1966. *Principles of criminology*. 7th ed. Philadelphia: J.B. Lippincott Company.

_____. 1974. *Principles of criminology*. 9th ed. Philadelphia: J.B. Lippincott Company.

_____. 1978. *Principles of criminology*. 10th ed. Philadelphia: J.B. Lippincott Company.

Sutherland, E.H., and H.J. Locke. 1936. *Twenty thousand homeless men*. Chicago: University of Chicago Press.

Sykes, G.M. 1967. *Crime and society*. 2nd ed. New York: Random House.

Tappan, P.W. 1947. Who is the criminal? *Am. Sociolog. Rev*. 12: 96–102.

Tarde, G. 1912. *Penal philosophy* (R. Howell, Trans.). Boston: Little, Brown.

Thomas, W.I. 1923. *The unadjusted girl*. Boston: Little, Brown.

Vine, M.S.W. 1973. Gabriel Tarde. In H. Mannheim (Ed,), *Pioneers in criminology*. 2nd ed. Montclair, NJ: Patterson Smith.

Vold, G.B. 1951. Edwin Hardin Sutherland: Sociological criminologist. *Am. Sociolog. Rev*. 16: 3–9.

Vold, G.B., and T.J. Bernard. 1986. *Theoretical criminology*. 3rd ed. New York: Oxford University Press.

Williams, F.P., III, and M.D. McShane. 1988. *Criminological theory*. Englewood Cliffs, NJ: Prentice-Hall.

Wilson, J.Q., and R.J. Herrnstein. 1985. *Crime and human nature: The definitive study of the causes of crime*. New York: Simon and Schuster.

Wolfgang, M.E., L. Savitz, and N. Johnston. (Eds.). 1962. *The sociology of crime*. New York: John Wiley and Sons.

Worchel, S., and W. Shebilske. 1983. *Psychology: Principles and applications*. Englewood Cliffs, NJ: Prentice-Hall.

The Complete Works of Edwin Hardin Sutherland

Books

Sutherland, E.H. 1924. *Criminology*. Philadelphia: J.B. Lippincott Company.

———. 1934. *Principles of criminology*. 2nd ed. Philadelphia: J.B. Lippincott Company.

———. 1937. *The professional thief*. Chicago: University of Chicago Press.

———. 1939. *Principles of criminology*. 3rd ed. Philadelphia: J.B. Lippincott Company.

———. 1947. *Principles of criminology*. 4th ed. Philadelphia: J.B. Lippincott Company.

———. 1949. *White collar crime*. New York: Dryden Press.

Sutherland, E.H., and H.J. Locke. 1936. *Twenty thousand homeless men*. Philadelphia: J.B. Lippincott Company.

Articles and Other Items

Sutherland, E.H. 1914. Unemployment and public employment agencies. In *Rep. (Chicago) Mayor's Commiss. Unemploy.* 95–175.

———. 1916. What rural health surveys have revealed. Proc. Missouri Conf. Soc. Welfare. In *Month. Bull. State Board Charit. Correc.* 9: 31–7.

———. 1922. The isolated family. *Inst. Quart.* 13: 189–92.

———. 1924. Report on the work of the national council for social studies. Proc. High School Conf. November 24, 1923. In *Univ. Ill. Bull.* 21: 384–386.

———. 1924. Public opinion as a cause of crime. *J. Appl. Soc.* 9: 50–6.

———. 1925. Murder and the death penalty. *J. Crim. Law Crimin.* 15: 522–29.

———. 1925. Administration of justice in the modern city and county. *Muni. Index* 192–94.

———. 1926. Capital punishment. In *Nelson's encyclopedia*.

———. 1926. The biological and sociological processes. *Am. J. Soc.* 32(1): 58–65.

———. 1927. Report of an investigation of probation in Minnesota. *Proc. Minn. Conf. Soc. Work*, 219–29.

———. 1927. Criminology, public opinion, and the law. *National Conference of Soc. Work* 168–75.

———. 1927. Is there undue crime among immigrants? *National Conference of Soc. Work* 572–79.

———. 1927. Social aspects of crime. *Proc. Conf. Natl. Crime Commiss.* 156–57.

———. 1928. Is experimentation in case work processes desirable? *Soc. Forces* 6: 567–69.

———. 1929. Crime and the conflict process. *J. Juv. Res.* 13: 38–48.

———. 1929. The person versus the act in criminology. *Cornell Law Quart.* 14: 159–67.

———. 1929. Neue Ameritanische Kriminalwissenschaftlische Literatur. *Monatsschrift fur Kriminalpsychologie und Strafrechtsreform* 19: 228–36.

———. 1929. Edward Carey Hayes: 1868–1928. *Am. J. Soc.* 35: 93–9.

———. 1930. The content of the introductory courses for prospective social workers. *Soc. Forces* 8: 503–07.

———. 1930. Prognose von Evflog oder Fehlschlag bei Bewuhrungsfrist. *Monatsschrift fur Kriminalpsychologie und Strafrechtsreform* 21: 507–13.

———. 1931. The Missouri crime survey. In S.A. Rice (Ed.), *Scientific methods in the social sciences: a case book*. Chicago: University of Chicago Press, pp. 528–40.

_____. 1931. Mental deficiency and crime. In K. Young (Ed.), *Social attitudes.* New York: Henry Holt and Company, pp. 357–75.

_____. 1931. The prison as a criminological laboratory. *Ann. Am. Acad. Pol. Soc. Sci.* 157: 131–36.

_____. 1931. Research work in prisons. *Proc. Am. Prison Assoc.* 426–33.

_____. 1932. Social processes in behavior problems. *Pub. Am. Socio. Soc.* 26: 55–61.

_____. 1933. Parole in relation to the institution. *Proc. Am. Prison Assoc.* 305–11.

_____. 1934. The decreasing prison population of England. *J. Crim. Law Crimin.* 24: 880–900.

_____. 1935. L'interdiction aux personnes condemmnees l'exercise de cette profession. *Congress Penal Et Penitentiare International, Troisieme Section, Deuxieme Question,* pp. 1–9.

_____. 1936. Wie der Befursdieb der Bestrafung entgeht. *Monatsschrift fur Kriminalpsychologie und Strafrechtsreform* 27: 449–56.

_____. 1937. Report on ecological survey of crime and delinquency in Bloomington, Indiana. State Director of NYA Indianapolis.

_____. 1937. Die Bekampfung des Berufsdiebes in den Vereinigten Staaten von Nordamerika. *Monatsschrift fur Kriminalbiologie und Strafrechtsreform* 28: 401–06.

_____. 1937. The professional thief. *J. Crim. Law Crimin.* 28: 161–63.

_____. 1937. The person and the situation in the treatment of prisoners. *Proc. Am. Prison Assoc.* 145–50.

_____. 1938. Parole in Indiana. *News Bull. Osborne Assoc.* 9: 1–2.

_____. 1938. Parole. *Pub. Welf. Indiana* 48: 4–6.

_____. 1940. White collar ciminality. *Am. Socio. Rev.* 5: 1–12.

_____. 1941. Imprisonment. *Hill Topics* (Indiana State Prison), April 10, pp. 6–7.

_____. 1941. Do severe penalties reduce crime? *Bourne* (Indiana State Prison), May.

_____. 1941. Conviction and probation. In *Eng. Stud. Crim. Sci.* 24–6.

_____. 1941. Crime and business. *Ann. Am. Acad. Pol. Soc. Sci.* 217: 112–18.

_____. 1942. The development of the concept of differential association. *Ohio Vall. Sociolog.* 15: 3–4.

_____. 1944. War and crime. In W.F. Ogburn (Ed.), *American society in wartime.* Chicago: University of Chicago Press, pp. 185–206.

_____. 1945. Is "white collar crime" crime? *Am. Sociolog. Rev.* 10: 132–39.

_____. 1945. Prevention of delinquency. *Pub. Welf. Indiana* 55: 5–15.

_____. 1945. What we expect from our prisons. In *83rd Annu. Rep. Indiana State Prison: 1942–1943*, pp. 26–7.

_____. 1945. Social pathology. *Am. J. Soc.* 50: 429–35.

_____. 1945. Free enterprise and overpopulation. *Ohio Vall. Sociolog.* 16: 2–3.

_____. 1946. Discussion of Norman Hayner's 'criminogenic zones in Mexico City. *Sociolog. Rev.* 11: 437–38.

_____. 1950. The sexual psychopath laws. *J. Crim. Law Crimin.* 41: 543–54.

_____. 1950. The diffusion of sexual psychopath laws. *Am. J. Soc.* 56: 142–48.

_____. 1951. Critique of Sheldon's varieties of delinquent youth. *Am. Sociolog. Rev.* 10: 10–13.

Sutherland, E.H., and C.E. Gehlke. 1933. Recent social trends in crime. *Rec. Soc. Trends* 2: 1115–1135.

Sutherland, E.H., and T. Sellin. (Eds.). 1931. Prisons of tomorrow. *Ann. Am. Acad. Pol. Soc. Sci.* 157: 1–262.

Sutherland, E.H., and C.C. Van Vechten, Jr. 1934. The reliability of criminal statistics. *J. Crim. Law Crimin.* 25: 10–20.

(Complete Works taken from Vold, G.B. 1951. Edwin Hardin Sutherland: Sociological Criminologist. *Am. Sociolog. Rev.* 16: 3–9.)

CHAPTER 8
WALTER CADE RECKLESS: 1899–1988

—⋘∾⋙—

I. BIOGRAPHICAL SKETCH

Walter Cade Reckless was born in Philadelphia, Pennsylvania, on January 19, 1899. His father was in the textile industry and was able to provide a rich cultural environment for Walter and his two sisters; music and the arts played dominant roles in the family's life. Walter had a deep love for the arts, especially music, and he started singing in the church choir at the age of six. He also became an accomplished violinist, thinking seriously at one point about a musical career as a concert violinist. However, while attending the University of Chicago, Walter was involved in a terrible automobile accident that left him with a slight but permanent limp, and he lost the tip of a finger on his bowing hand, ending his aspirations to become a violinist but not dampening his love for music. Throughout his life, Reckless enjoyed nothing more than participating in string quartets and hosting musicales at his home. These events attracted some of the finest musicians in the area, and an invitation to a Reckless musicale was considered a great honor.

After finishing high school, Reckless entered the social science program at the University of Chicago, majoring in history. Shortly thereafter, he was inducted into the military, but was deferred from active duty until the completion of his degree; however, by that time, World War I had ended. The social science program was a very broad one, and early in his college career Reckless developed interests in Middle Eastern archaeology, Egyptology, and comparative religion. In fact, Professor Breasted, an authority on ancient history, invited him to participate in an expedition to explore the tomb of Tutankhamen. However, Robert Park and Ernest Burgess, who offered him a graduate assistantship in the sociology program and a chance to get involved in their studies of vice in Chicago, lured him away from the expedition. Yet Reckless' interest in these other areas never totally waned as, even years later, he would often reflect "on the 'staying power' of various religious groups and sects and their ability to 'insulate' themselves and their children against crime and deviance." The concept of insulation against deviance was to become a central aspect of Reckless' theory of delinquency.

Reckless stayed on at the University of Chicago and entered the graduate program in sociology. Because of his association with Robert Park, he began getting involved in participant observation research. Reckless played his "fiddle" in some of the roadhouses operated by the Mob during Prohibition, and in his research, he explored the illegitimate and legitimate social structure of these roadhouses, observed the clientele, and became especially interested in the careers of the prostitutes who worked these "joints." His research ultimately led to a doctoral dissertation and was published as the book *Vice in Chicago* in 1933, which was recognized as one of the classic studies of the Chicago School and became a standard for qualitative research in occupational deviancy.

Reckless' close relationship with Park and his experiences in the roadhouses around Chicago influenced him to insist that all of his graduate students "get their feet wet" by observing deviance in real settings. In addition, it was Park's ecological approach that first got him interested in the distribution of crime, and his exposure to the "seamier side of life" in the roadhouses solidified his interest in crime and deviance.

Reckless left Chicago in 1924, the year before he received his Ph.D., to accept a position at Vanderbilt, where he remained until 1940. While there, he wrote prolifically, producing numerous articles, chapters, and reports, but his books were his most notable publications. He produced two books in 1931, the first text published on *Juvenile Delinquency* (with M. Smith) and the second text published in *Social Psychology* (with E. T. Krueger). Along with his research and writing, Reckless found the time to build a very successful undergraduate criminology program at Vanderbilt. In 1936, he married Martha Washington, who had been his student and with whom he raised a son and spent the remaining years of his life. His impressive scholarship and programmatic accomplishments at Vanderbilt did not go unnoticed, and in 1940, Dr. Reckless moved to Ohio State University to build a Criminology–Corrections program.

At Ohio State, Reckless was originally attached to the College of Social Work, with a joint appointment in sociology. He moved to the Department of Sociology full time in 1958, and remained there until his mandatory retirement in 1969. Over the thirty years that he was at Ohio State, Reckless accomplished a tremendous amount. He nurtured OSU's fledgling graduate and undergraduate programs in criminology, setting the curriculum, teaching all of the various courses, recruiting graduate students, and placing graduates in a wide variety of academic and federal, state, and local agency positions. Of course, he continued to conduct research and write. In 1950, he published the first of what were to be seven editions of the widely adopted text, *The Crime Problem* (1950). Many other books followed, including *The Prevention of Juvenile Delinquency: An Experiment* (1972) and *American Criminology: New Directions* (1973). During the late 1950s and into the 1960s, Reckless and his associates (most notably Simon Dinitz) conducted the now famous "good boy–bad boy" studies, which examined the role of self-concept as an "insulator" against delinquency, and this research led to the development of containment theory (the focus of the Key Ideas section). In addition, in the early 1960s, Reckless helped revive the American Society of Criminology, serving three terms as its president.

There was also an applied or practical side to Reckless' work. He was interested in "translating theory into action," as is evidenced by his extensive work in the development of delinquency prevention programs. In addition to his interests in the delinquency area, he was heavily involved in the professionalization of probation and parole and the juvenile court system, and he led the fight to remove adult corrections and the Department of Youth Services from under the umbrella of the Ohio Public Welfare Department. He spent endless hours in meetings and testifying on these and other matters affecting correctional policies, programs, and budgets. Just as Dr. Reckless' achievements during his academic tenure were not restricted to the academic arena, so they did not cease when he retired at the age of seventy from Ohio State. He was a consultant to the Social Defense Section (Crime Prevention) of the United Nations and spent considerable time shuttling back and forth to Europe, the Far East, and the Middle East presenting lectures, setting up training programs, and inspecting and evaluating jails, prisons, and facilities for juveniles. Moreover, he continued to pound "his ancient typewriter with two fingers seven days a week."

Dr. Reckless received many honors and awards during his long and illustrious career. He was an early recipient of the Sutherland Award, and he was also named as the Chair of the Criminology Section of the American Sociological Association. One of his most cherished honors was awarded to him in 1981, when he received the Ohio State Distinguished Service Award.

In the mid-1970s, Dr. Reckless began to succumb to the effects of Alzheimer's disease. From that time on, it became difficult for him to continue his research program; he ceased all writing after 1973, when he returned from his final semester of teaching (at the University of Ottawa). Walter Reckless died quietly in his sleep at his home on September 20, 1988. In the words of his long-time friend and colleague Simon Dinitz, "Walter Reckless made a difference. Not many of us are privileged to lead such interesting, productive and useful lives or to leave so impressive a legacy as a scholar, teacher and public figure."[1]

II. BASIC ASSUMPTIONS

According to Quinney and Wildeman (1977), theoretical developments in criminology during the post-WWII period, at least up to the mid-1960s, consisted mainly of extensions of perspectives formulated in the 1930s, and they cite Walter Reckless' work of as an example. Gibbons (1976) concurs, referring to Reckless' theory as "old wine in a new bottle," a theory that offered a new set of terms to replace old ones. To some extent, these claims are true—certainly, Reckless' theory drew on a variety of earlier ideas. It combined aspects of symbolic interactionism with elements from social disorganization and with Durkheim's notions of social integration. However, in combining the various aspects from these earlier conceptualizations, it offered a different perspective on crime and delinquency. The theory focused explicitly on the role of self-concept in the etiology of both non-delinquent and delinquent behavior. Because of its ties to Durkheim and the Chicago School, Reckless' theory is usually classified as a social control theory (Gibbons 1981, Williams & McShane 1988), but some argue that it can be more accurately characterized as a theory of personal control. Shoemaker (1984) claims that, other than psychoanalytic theory, the containment perspective developed by Reckless has probably attracted the greatest attention as a personal control theory of delinquency. Regardless of specific type, the theory is clearly a control theory, and the central thesis of control theory is that individuals are restrained from lawbreaking as the result of some type of containment factors (Gibbons 1976). In *The Prevention of Juvenile Delinquency: An Experiment*, Reckless and Dinitz (1972) criticize subcultural and other structural approaches for failing to account for the "obvious fact" that most adolescents, even those in the highest delinquency areas, manage to avoid involvement with the criminal justice system. To address this fact, they say, criminology must move beyond structural factors and look at who succumbs and who does not to the various structural pressures and strains. Control theories generally attempt to combine theories of conformity with theories of deviance. From this perspective,

---

[1]All materials contained in the Biographical Sketch were adapted from a memoriam by Dr. Simon Dinitz written for *The Criminologist*, from information provided by Dr. Dinitz in personal communications on November 23 and December 8 and 14, 1988, and from a personal communication with Mrs. Martha Reckless on May 18, 1989.

deviance is caused not so much by forces as by the failure to prevent it. Most theories assume that conformity represents the natural order and requires no explanation, but control theory reverses this reasoning, claiming that it is conformity, not deviance, that needs to be explained (Clinard & Meier 1985). In other words, the question asked by control theory is the opposite of that asked by most other theories of criminality. It asks why people *aren't* criminal, rather than why people *are* criminal.

Control theory assumes that everyone is motivated to commit deviant acts and that they will act on this motivation if restraints are absent. There are two specific assumptions that relate to this general notion: (1) Human nature is on the "bad" side of neutral (naturally egocentric, etc.); and (2) A decrease in prolegal controls (internal and external) allows delinquency/criminality to occur (Clinard & Meier 1985). Another assumption of control theory is that there is a common system of values that makes explicit to everyone what is and is not deviant (Williams & McShane 1988, Clinard & Meier 1985). This assumption, however, should not be interpreted as a claim that deviance is learned; the behavioral variations found across individuals are not the result of what is learned, but to the controls that are present.

Control theory occupies an intermediate, intervening position between delinquency and the plethora of potential preconditions. The stance of control theories is that it is more appropriate and fruitful to focus on the immediate precursors to crime and delinquency than on those (structural) conditions that are more removed (Shoemaker 1984). Whereas strain and subcultural theories are concerned with distal causes, control theory focuses on the proximal causes.

Reckless (1961) devised a control or containment theory in which he attempted to integrate a variety of concepts from earlier theories into a general theory of crime and delinquency. He claimed that all individuals are affected by a host of internal and external forces that drive them toward criminal or delinquent conduct and a variety of other forces that restrain them from such activity. He maintained that his containment theory was a general theory that was better equipped to explain crime and deviance than were other theories that had focused on specific "pushes and pulls." Reckless' approach "cuts into the reality" of criminal and delinquent conduct at a different point than did Sutherland's or similar theories.

Reckless is not interested in explaining why one society rather than another generates a certain kind of self-concept in its citizens, or why persons in different social positions commit different amounts and kinds of crime. In addition, unlike Sutherland, he is not interested in the process by which forces of containment are learned. Rather, he is concerned with developing a paradigm that allows the identification of the immediate forces acting within and on an individual at any given moment, permitting an understanding of the form of behavior that the person is apt to exhibit (Bloch & Geis 1970).

In the first formal statement of his containment theory, Reckless (1961) criticizes Differential Association and Cohen's subcultural approach for not explaining who does and who does not adopt a delinquent pattern of behavior and internalize delinquent values. He accuses Cloward and Ohlin and the "psychogenic" theories of being relevant only to the "fringes" of criminality. He acknowledges that the Glueck's identification of five distinguishing characteristics of delinquents and non-delinquents is interesting but calls their method "the buckshot approach," shooting out in all directions to explore and discover. With containment theory, Reckless was attempting to keep the best aspects of the structural theories while using more process-oriented concepts to address what he saw as the essential and individual etiological question, a question that the structural theories had left unanswered. It has been argued that the main advantage of containment theory is its merging of psychological and sociological approaches, which facilitates the analysis of inner, personal forces that allow or push a person to commit a crime and at the same time permits the examination of sociocultural forces that shape motivation and personality (Yablonsky & Haskell 1988). Reckless really rejected psychological interpretations and was opposed to the "psychologizing" of processes, preferring instead a more strictly symbolic interactionistic conceptualization of self-concept and its development, in the tradition of Mead, Cooley, and Blumer.

Containment theory acknowledges the general etiological role of the types of "pressures" that Cloward and Ohlin talked about, and it addresses the same types of "pulls" that Sutherland dealt with in differential association. In addition, like differential association, containment is linked strongly to self-concept, but the focus is on the personalized feelings of the youths rather than on their associations (Shoemaker 1984). Along with the emphasis on self-concept and other individualized variables, containment theory makes some assumptions similar to those of psychoanalytic theory, in the form of the motivation to be deviant and the need for some external restraint. Too much, however, should not be made of this similarity; Reckless was not an advocate of psychoanalytic theory, seeing it as basically untestable. Therefore, although Reckless' work may be portrayed as using the social–psychological perspective in attacking the question of crime/delinquency, it would be inaccurate to characterize his approach as being primarily psychological; he was primarily a sociologist (Dinitz, personal communication, December 8 and 14, 1988). Within the framework of containment theory, the delinquent or predelinquent is someone who is trying to resolve problems in terms of his or her own "personal equation." From this perspective, delinquency is a research problem in the social process (Schwartz & Tangri 1965). In *The Prevention of Juvenile Delinquency*, Reckless and Dinitz (1972) begin with the need to view delinquency and other forms of deviance as being inherent parts of the social system. Containment theory presents a paradigm in which delinquency is treated as part of the social system, but in a way that allows an individual orientation to be maintained and pursued.

As support for his containment interpretation, Reckless (1961) cites the works of Albert Reiss (1951) on delinquency and the failure of social and personal controls, Jackson Toby (1957) on social disorganization and conformity, F. Ivan Nye (1958) on family relations and delinquency, and his own research with Dinitz and others (see the Supplemental Readings) on self-concept in "good" and "bad" boys in high-delinquency areas. Drawing from these various sources, Reckless' containment theory rests on three specific assumptions:

- Delinquency is the result of a poor self-concept. (It should be noted that this assumption is in direct contrast to the labeling perspective [see Howard Beck chapter] which says that poor self-concept is the result of being labeled delinquent.)
- A boy's positive view of self provides "insulation" against pressures and pulls toward delinquency, regardless of social class or other environmental conditions.
- Behavior is "multifaceted"; people are composed of several layers of drives, pressures, pulls, and insulators/buffers, all of which affect the individual simultaneously. The most important of these forces is the internal insulator, self-concept. (Shoemaker 1984)

III. KEY IDEAS

Although Walter Reckless has not necessarily received the same level of acclaim as many of the other individuals in this book, his work in its own right was pioneering. He is one of the "fathers of control theory," laying the groundwork for the "more sophisti-cated" later versions of scholars like Travis Hirschi (Dinitz, personal communication, December 8, 1988), and he was one of the first sociologists/criminologists to focus em-pirically on self-concept as a controlling factor in delinquency. Reckless' containment theory was developed in opposition to the strain perspective. He was never satisfied with the structural focus that dominated the sociological theories of the time, nor with the "usual psychological trait or clinical perspectives." He saw delinquency resulting from failure in the socialization process, especially in the "under the roof culture" (family, neighborhood) and was interested in the "insulating" elements that deflected most juveniles, even in adverse conditions, from developing deviant behavior patterns (Dinitz, personal communication, December 8, 1988).

In *The Prevention of Juvenile Delinquency*, Reckless and Dinitz (1972) address the need to view delinquency as an inherent part of the social system. They refer to delin-quency as a "social pathology" and discuss the role of factors that weaken social control and facilitate "norm erosion," most importantly those within the family. Expressing con-cern over the breakdown of family, they cite this process as a significant factor in the eti-ology of delinquency, especially in the lower class. They claim that the high rates of family dissolution, maladjustment, and pathology adversely affect socialization of the young and "create a cadre of adolescents" freed of external restraints and often internal control as well. The central focus of Reckless' model of delinquency is really on the fac-tors that prevent or contain it, and his theory is built around those elements that are re-sponsible for "insulating" young persons from the pushes and pulls to be delinquent.

Although it is true that Walter Reckless had far-reaching interests in both crimi-nology and sociology, certainly his greatest interest was in delinquency, and his greatest contribution is considered to be his theorizing in that area.

THE ROOTS OF CONTAINMENT THEORY

It is interesting to note that there is no direct reference to the notion of containment in the second edition of Reckless' book *The Crime Problem* (1955), and the only mention of self-concept is a brief comment in the chapter on "The Criminality of Women." These observations are important, because they indicate that although the seeds of containment theory were in Reckless' discontent with existing sociological and psy-chological theories of crime and delinquency, the major part of the substance of the theory evolved from a research program undertaken by Reckless and his colleagues in 1955, a program that would ultimately span fifteen years. The fundamental purpose of this program was to look for differences between "good" and "bad" boys in high delin-quency areas in Columbus, Ohio, in the hopes of isolating factors that contained or pre-vented the occurrence of delinquency. The initial phase of the research identified boys, through ratings by teachers and school administrators, who were not considered to be delinquent and were not expected to become so (i.e., "good boys"). These boys were followed over time (1960) and later compared to a group of "bad" boys (1958), who were also followed over time (1962). (The purpose here is not to provide a detailed review of the various studies that made up this program, but to demonstrate that the theoretical concepts that Reckless and his colleagues ultimately came up with were empirically based. For good summaries of the research program, see Reckless and Dinitz's (1967) article "Pioneering with Self-Concept as a Vulnerability Factor in Delinquency" and *The Prevention of Juvenile Delinquency: An Experiment,* by Reckless and Dinitz (1972). (For a complete listing of the articles published as a result of the program, see the Supplemental Readings at the end of the chapter.)

Two key concepts emerged from this research program: (1) *containment*—which refers to the process by which the drives and pulls toward delinquency are kept in check; and (2) *self-concept*—which refers to the image of self in relation to others (Shoemaker 1984). It is the latter concept that was to become the core of containment theory, as it represented the "differences in outlook" that were found between the "good and bad boys" (Reckless & Dinitz 1972).

Containment theory is an explanation of conforming behavior as well as of deviancy (Reckless 1961). The development of such an approach addressed one of the central problems that plagued many of the theories of the day, most notably differential association. Conformity is the result of the containment factors propelling individuals in that direction and reinforcing them for acceptable action (Bloch & Geis 1970). There are two reinforcing aspects: the inner control system and the outer control system. "The assumption is that strong inner and reinforced outer containment constitutes insulation against normative deviance (not constitutional or psychological) that is a violation of sociological concept norms" (Reckless 1961, 42). Although containment is offered as a general and complete explanation of conforming behavior, the breakdown of containment, from Reckless' (1961) perspective, cannot explain the entire spectrum of delinquency and crime. It cannot explain crime resulting from strong inner pushes such as personality disorders and phobias or from organic impairments or neurotic mechanisms. It also cannot explain criminal or delinquent acts that are part of "normal" or "expected" roles or such activities within families or communities (i.e., within specific subcultures). Containment theory is a "midrange" theory that falls between these two extremes, but as such it can explain the bulk of crime and delinquency, as two thirds to three fourths of all officially reported cases and unreported cases are representative of this range of activity. "Containment theory points to the regulation of normative behavior through resistance to deviance as well as through direction toward legitimate social expectations" (Reckless 1961, 45). Most of the regulation is in the form of "defense or buffer against deflection." The inner and outer containments occupy the "central core" position between the pressures and pulls of the external environment and the inner pushes. Reckless (1961) proposed that internal and external containment can be assessed and approximated; strengths and weaknesses can be specified for research and can be measured through some standardized means. Containment theory seeks to ferret out the specific inner and outer controls over normative behavior, since one way to get closer to an understanding of crime and delinquency is by focusing on the components that regulate conduct.

CONTAINMENT

Reckless (1967) identified four types of containments and pressures:

- Outer or social pressures and pulls
- External containments

- Inner containments
- Inner (organic and psychological) pushes

In vertical order, pressures and pulls from the environment are at the top or side of the containing structure, whereas pushes follow inner containment (Reckless 1961). More specifically, at the top of the arrangement, impinging on the individual, is a layer of social pressures that can drive the individual toward crime or delinquency and pull factors that can draw them away from accepted norms. Immediately surrounding the individual is a structure of variably effective or ineffective external containment. The next layer is inner containment, and the bottom layer consists of inner pushes (Yablonsky & Haskell 1988). In this model, outer and inner containments are intervening variables between a variety of internal pushes and external pressures and pulls and behavior. If the containments, either in conjunction or independently, are of sufficient strength then some type of conforming behavior is exhibited, but if the containments are not strong enough, then the behavior performed is deviant.

Pressures, Pulls, and Pushes

External pressures refer to an array of "living conditions" consisting of aspects of the social structure and the situation within the family. Structural conditions that exert pressures are poverty, deprivation, unemployment, limited access to opportunities, minority group status, and discrimination; familial pressures take the form of instability, conflict, and discord within the family unit. The *external pulls* are the things that become distractions for acceptable roles and conduct and attractions for deviant roles and conduct. These are the temptations and inducements encountered in associations with bad companions or gangs, in observing deviant role models and other carriers of delinquent and criminal patterns and through the mass media. Inner pushes are represented by a variety of ordinary drives and motives such as frustration, restlessness, rebellion, hostility and aggressiveness, feelings of inferiority, and the need for immediate gratification; but they also include organic conditions such as brain damage and psychological states such as psychoses. It should be noted that these latter pushes are abnormal and are therefore not controllable (Reckless 1961).

External Containment

Containment theory concentrates on two dimensions of the individual's situation to determine "crime-proneness": "inner controls" and "outer controls." Outer controls are "structural buffers" in the immediate social world that act to keep the individual's behavior within acceptable limits. These buffers generally take the form of the presentation of a consistent moral front to the individual; institutional reinforcements of norms; goals, expectations, effective supervision and discipline; and the opportunity for acceptance, identity, and belongingness (Block & Geis 1970). Although society offers a variety of external constraints on behavior, the most important sources are the *nuclear groups*: family and community ties (Reckless 1967); it is in these groups that the structure of roles and expectations are acquired and opportunities for acceptance and belongingness are most readily available. A stable family environment and solid ties to the community provide "insulation" against delinquency in an ongoing process that provides the vehicle for the internalization of nondelinquent values and opportunities for conforming to the expectations of significant others (Reckless, Dinitz, & Murray 1956). A lack of outer containment manifests as ill-defined limits to behavior, a breakdown of rules, an absence of definitive roles, and a general failure of the family to present adequate limits and roles to the youth (Yablonsky & Haskell 1988). If outer containments are weak, then the various pressures, pulls, and pushes must be handled by inner containment (Reckless 1961).

Inner Containment

Inner containment, then, is the last line of defense; if breached, delinquency will occur. Inner containment is the most important type of containment within Reckless' theoretical framework, especially in industrialized societies where external controlling factors are not as powerful as in other types of societies (Shoemaker 1984). Inner containment is the product of good or poor internalization of non-deviant attitudes (Reckless, Dinitz, & Murray 1956, Yablonsky & Haskell 1988). Reckless (1973, 65) sees inner containments as consisting mainly of self-components that he describes as "self-control, good self-concept, ego strength, well-developed super-ego, high frustration tolerance, high resistance to diversions, high sense of responsibility, goal orientation, ability to find substitute satisfactions, tension reducing rationalizations, etc." In addition to these elements, Shoemaker (1984) points out that "norm commitment and retention" are important aspects of inner containment. It is inner containment, in the form of a well-developed and prosocial self-concept, that plays the major role in insulating the person from the multitude of pressures, pulls, and pushes that are constantly impinging on him or her, thereby preventing delinquency. The role of the self as a containment factor is especially crucial in those societies in which external control is not as prevalent or as strong (Shoemaker 1984).

SELF-CONCEPT

Containment theory, while addressing a variety of factors, focuses primarily on self-concept and the processes and functions related to it. Reckless and his colleagues' findings concerning differences in self-concept between good and bad boys in high-delinquency areas were interpreted as support for Albert Reiss' (1951) earlier work, and provided a starting point for Reckless' own version of control theory, especially the emphasis on inner containment. In an early study, Reckless, Dinitz, and Murray (1956) concluded that the concept of self might work negatively to attribute certain abstract characteristics and predictions of delinquency to certain individuals or groups that might influence these individuals to accept the ascribed role and to act out self-fulfilling prophecies. In other words, applying a label such as *juvenile delinquent* does not help a person think well of his or her "self." Such an occurrence would be quite detrimental in the end, because the key to an individual's ability to maintain a non-delinquent approach is a high self-image; a "socially acceptable" concept of self acts as an "insulator" against delinquency. It was further postulated that this "good-boy self-concept" is what keeps middle-class and upper-class boys out of delinquency. This initial study did not indicate how it was that some boys in high-delinquency areas acquire a good self-concept, but the point remained that a strong self-concept could insulate boys in high-delinquency areas from involvement in a delinquent lifestyle.

A second study was undertaken by Reckless, Dinitz, and Kay (1957) to further examine the preventive role of self-concept and to explore potential sources of the "good-boy self-concept" in high-delinquency areas. The first study had shown that a good self-concept could insulate against delinquency. Similarly, it could be concluded that adverse concepts of self might set the tone for delinquency, as such views of self represent a lack of internalized resistance to "bad components in the environment." Following the same procedure as in the first study, the second study compared teacher/administrator-nominated boys to similarly nominated bad boys. The results supported earlier findings: significant differences were found in the self-concepts of the good boys and the bad (potentially delinquent) boys. The boys nominated as potentially delinquent were more likely to think that they would have trouble with the law, less likely to place importance on avoiding such trouble, less concerned about what their parents expected of them, and so forth. Reckless et al. (1956) conclude from the data that one precondition of both law-abiding and delinquent conduct can be found in self-concept and the conception of others that one acquires in primary group relationships. The conception of self and others is a differential response component that helps explain why some individuals succumb to the pressures, pulls, and pushes toward delinquency whereas others do not. The concept of self contains the "impact of life" as it has been internalized by the individual. This process represents a "normal or modal" acquisition, not a pathological one.

The source of the differing self-concepts, as conceived by Reckless and his colleagues, is in differing individual socialization experiences, especially those within the family and other intimate groups, and the internalization of these experiences. "Reckless, like most Chicago School sociologists, but even more so, owed his intellectual heritage to the symbolic interactionists. He never ceased being one and was a practicing disciple of C. H. Cooley, G. H. Mead and, of course, Herbert Blumer" (Dinitz, personal communication, December 8, 1988). The source of self-concept is interaction with others and the internalization of the feedback about self that they provide. This interpretation was supported by the findings that juveniles selected as good boys by teachers and administrators were also well regarded by their mothers and exhibited positive self-concepts. Bad boys, however, were on poorer terms with their parents had more negative self-concepts (Gibbons 1976).

Self-concept is the central component of Reckless' theory not only in a figurative sense, but in a spatial sense as well. Reckless (1967) conceptualizes the four types of pressures and containments that he postulated as circles or layers emanating outward from the self-concept. The self is the central core and serves as a container of internal pushes. Its prosocial contents act as "buffers" against external pressures and containers against external pulls (Shoemaker 1984). Reckless and Dinitz (1967, 522) conclude that "a good self-concept, undoubtedly a product of favorable socialization, veers slum boys away from delinquency, while a poor self-concept, a product of unfavorable socialization, gives the slum boy no resistance to deviancy, delinquent companions, or delinquent sub-culture."

TRANSLATING THEORY INTO PRACTICE

Simon Dinitz (personal communication, December 8, 1988) describes Walter Reckless as "an activist in all things." He sees Reckless as "one of the founders of scientific criminology in the United States," stating that he was interested in prediction and longitudinal research, the application of sophisticated (for the time) statistical methods and in *translating theory into action* (emphasis by Dinitz). Dinitz further states that Reckless was one of only two prominent criminologists of his time (the other being Lloyd Ohlin) who was program oriented. It is not surprising, then, that Reckless devoted considerable time and effort to testing his theoretical notions about delinquency by putting them into practice in the form of preventive programs. The chance to translate the concepts from containment theory into action came in 1959 when the Columbus, Ohio, school system asked Reckless to attempt some practical application of his findings.

An extensive program was developed (for details, see *The Prevention of Juvenile Delinquency: An Experiment,* Reckless & Dinitz 1972) to discover whether the appropriate presentation of realistic models of behavior in the classroom could "beef up" a vulnerable boy's self-concept (Reckless & Dinitz 1967). During the 1959–60 school year a pilot study using a limited number of boys was conducted. The pilot continued into the 1960–61 school year, and in 1961–62, it expanded to four schools in high-delinquency areas. The three years of demonstration projects yielded some encouraging results, and so a large-scale project was developed and implemented in 1963. Vulnerable boys were randomly assigned to either special or regular classes and control groups were established. The special classes provided, in addition to the normal curriculum, instruction and role models designed to enhance the self-concepts of the potentially delinquent boys in the class. It was hoped that such a program would serve to insulate the boys from future involvement in delinquent conduct. Unfortunately, the program was not as successful as had been hoped; the special classes did not have any significant impact on the likelihood of future delinquency (Reckless & Dinitz 1972).

Reckless was also an important figure in the development of the Buckeye Boys Ranch, a dynamically oriented private facility for troubled youths (Dinitz, personal communication, December 8, 1988).

CONCLUSION

Containment theory was offered as an "overarching perspective" for the explanation of criminality and delinquency (Gibbons 1976), but it has attracted the most attention as a theory of delinquency. It has been claimed that one of the strengths of the theory is that it integrated concepts from the psychodynamic approaches of its day with the sociological concepts from the Chicago tradition. Although it is true that Reckless "bought into" some of the practices flowing from the psychodynamic perspectives, he did not accept most of their major propositions and tenets. He was very familiar with the psychoanalytic perspective because of his long association with Dr. Hugh Missildine, a child psychiatrist who was one of Reckless' closest friends and a member of the research and program development team for the delinquency prevention studies. He was also aware of the work of Carl Rogers and the other "psychological social psychologists," but their theories played only a minor role in the development of containment theory. He also did not much appreciate the work of his contemporaries in the psychology department at OSU, George Kelly and Julian Rotter, who were involved in the early development of more cognitively oriented theories—personal construct theory and social learning theory, respectively. Reckless was so deeply committed to the Chicago School that he could not accept the internal focus that characterized all of the prominent psychological theories of his day. He believed that external factors provided a more productive ground for explaining behavior and had trouble with the untestable nature of the psychodynamic concepts (Dinitz, personal communications, December 8 and 14, 1988).

According to Simon Dinitz (personal communication, December 8, 1988), Walter Reckless' greatest contributions were providing the germ for the subsequent control theories (like that of Travis Hirschi); calling attention to the socialization process, especially the internalization of norms and values; and the development of scales and instruments used in the study of delinquency. Throughout his career, Reckless never moved far from these concerns. Even though he did broaden his focus to include some work testing strain theories, the containment perspective "dominated his intellectual life, and he never gave up his search for ways to test for and redirect negative self-images."

IV. CRITIQUE

Reckless (1967) claims that containment is a better explanation of delinquency than other theories because

1. It can be applied to particular individuals.
2. The various external and internal constraints can be observed and measured, qualitatively and quantitatively.
3. It explains both deviant and conforming behavior.
4. It explains a wide variety of criminal and delinquent activity.
5. It provides a basis for treatment and prevention of delinquency.

The ultimate question, of course, is how well the theory actually realizes these claims. The answer to this multidimensional and difficult question lies somewhere in between the support and criticism of the theory that has appeared in the literature.

CONTAINMENT THEORY ASSUMPTIONS

Containment, like most control theories, is based on two fundamental and debatable assumptions:

1. There is a common set of values that makes explicit to everyone what is and is not deviant (Clinard & Meier 1985, Williams & McShane 1988).
2. Crime and delinquency are naturally and equally motivated in everyone (Clinard & Meier 1985, Bloch & Geis 1970).

The potential problems with the first assumption are discussed elsewhere in this book (e.g., the Critique section of Lloyd E. Ohlin chapter), and it has been stated that there is not considerable empirical support for the existence of such a value set (Williams & McShane 1988, Clinard & Meier 1985).

The second assumption also leaves room for serious questions. The contention that humans are naturally motivated to be aggressive and destructive has an old and dubious history. Freud has been heavily criticized for making such claims (Sigmund Freud chapter), as have others. Clinard and Meier (1985) and Nettler (1984) argue that it is diversity, not similarity, that is the most striking characteristic of humans, and consequently any assumption of uniformity is highly disputable. Williams and McShane (1988) apparently sidestep this problem by claiming that control theories do not necessarily assume deviant motivations but instead assume "neutrality." However, the assumption of neutrality does not totally clarify the problem, as it seems to carry with it the implication that deviance is then somehow learned or acquired, an implication that is inconsistent with control theory, which claims that deviance is the result of variations, not in what is learned, but in the controls themselves (Clinard & Meier 1985).

DEFINITIONAL AND METHODOLOGICAL PROBLEMS

One of the reasons that control theories supplanted strain theories and became popular among criminologists is that they are "very testable" (Vold & Bernard 1986). One of the big advantages of the approach is that it provides a framework within which factors can be abstracted, tested, and quantified. It is possible to develop measures of the various containment factors, thereby making empirical testing of the theory possible (Bloch & Geis 1970).

Not everyone, however, holds these views in regard to the empirical adaptability of containment theory. Schrag (1971) points out that key terms are vague; pressures and pulls are defined only by asserting their functions and providing a list of illustrations, making it difficult to identify which variables belong in which categories. Without clearly defined concepts and variables, it is extremely difficult to develop the operational definitions on which to base appropriate empirical assessments of the theory.

Orcutt (1970) offers similar criticisms concerning the lack of clear definitions and identifies some methodological problems with the studies from which containment evolved. He claims that the sampling procedures were faulty; hence, many of the boys actually came from areas where delinquency was uncommon and consequently had little to be "insulated" against by positive self-concept. He also questions the validity of the procedure of using teachers and school administrators to identify potentially delinquent boys. The critical question is the accuracy of the predictions. Reckless and Dinitz (1972) in their longitudinal study of delinquency prediction report that, of the more than 1,000 predicted delinquents, more than forty percent had had no police contact within four years. If nominations/predictions of future delinquency are to be used as primary measures of delinquency, there must be consistent and substantial agreement between predicted and subsequent behavior for the procedure to be acceptable (Shoemaker 1984). Of course, the use of official records as outcome measures of delinquency is also a questionable practice (Reckless & Dinitz 1972, Gibbons 1976).

SELF-CONCEPT AND DELINQUENCY

The most tested and most criticized aspect of containment theory is the notion of self-concept itself. There are two areas of controversy; one relates to the methods used by Reckless and his colleagues in their series of studies on self-concept as an insulator against delinquency, and the other centers on the predicted relationships between self-concept and delinquent behavior patterns.

Schwartz and Tangri (1965, 923), in one of the more frequently cited criticisms of Reckless et al.'s self-concept studies, state that "his treatment of self-concept is not at all clear." Too many factors (questions) are treated as being indicative of or related to self-concept, a circumstance that does not provide a meaningful definition of the variable. Gibbons (1976), from his review of the research, concludes that many of the questionnaire and test items used as measures of self-concept appear to be "invalid indicators." In addition, Reckless assumes that mothers and teachers are significant others whose evaluations the boys incorporated into their own self-concepts. In other words, there was no distinction between individuals' knowledge of others' expectations as matters of fact and those expectations that became part of self-evaluation. It has been argued that cross validating personally expressed self-concept with teachers' and mothers' judgments confuses the issue between what a person actually thinks of self and what he or she thinks others expect from him or her (Schwartz & Tangri 1965, Orcutt 1970).

In an attempt to address this problem, Schwartz and Tangri (1965) looked at self-concept using a semantic differential procedure. Juveniles were asked to rate themselves on a "good–bad" continuum along several dimensions. These ratings were then correlated with judgments of how the respondents felt mothers, friends, and teachers would rate them. The results lend some support to containment, as good boys had higher self-concepts than did bad boys. However, the comparisons of self-concept with the judgments of others' perceptions indicated that self-image was correlated with different significant others, and these significant others varied between good and bad boys.

The implications from these findings are that who is significant in the development of self-concept varies across individuals, for a variety of reasons, and not all of what others "say" about one's self is relevant to one's own evaluation of self. Dinitz (personal communication, December 8, 1988) points out that Schwartz and Tangri were "supercritical" of Reckless' scales and procedures, but they fared no better overall in their own efforts at assessing the role of self-concept in delinquency; "they are best known for their criticisms of our self-concept studies and not at all for their research."

Another interesting point raised about Reckless' work is that a "theoretical link" is missing; the theory does not explain why poor self-concept should leave an individual vulnerable to delinquency. It might be argued that it would be as likely to produce conformity to the demands of significant others. Alternatively, it could lead to the rejection of the rejecters and attribution of significance to others (i.e., delinquent peers) who prove more rewarding (Schwartz & Tangri 1965).

In regard to the connection between the development of a negative self-concept (through interactions with others) and delinquent behavior patterns, Shoemaker (1984) argues that it has been "fairly uniformly established." He claims that empirical research has demonstrated that predicted delinquents have lower self-concepts than do predicted non-delinquents, and this pattern holds up from the ages of twelve to thirteen on up through adolescence. As support, Shoemaker cites the various studies of Reckless and his colleagues (see Reckless et al. 1956, 1957, Scarpitti, Murray, Dinitz, & Reckless 1960, Dinitz, Scarpitti, & Reckless 1962). However, others conclude that their work is actually less conclusive than first appearances suggest. Critics have presented evidence exhibiting only moderate correlations between the self-concept displayed by juvenile boys and their perceptions of the opinions of them held by others (Schwartz & Tangri 1965, 1967, Gibbons 1976). Hirschi (1969) found that increased involvement in conventional activities was related to increased delinquency, the opposite of what control theory predicts. In addition, although such a prediction may not be directly attributable to containment theory, it is possible to argue that increased involvement in conventional activity is not consistent with the development of a negative self-concept. Of course, it could also be argued that this finding is quite consistent with a negative self-concept, as increasing one's involvement in conventional activity may be seen as an avenue for enhancing one's image with others, especially parents and teachers. Some inconsistent results have been found with adults. Social integration was not found to be a buffer against heavy drinking, and in fact, high levels of socialization into conventional activities is related to heavy drinking (Seeman & Anderson 1983). It must be kept in mind, however, that these were adults and that drinking is linked to many positively viewed conventional roles. There is also the "sickness" notion that has been associated with alcoholism, and Reckless was very clear that his theory did not account for pathological behavior.

Along with the conceptual and methodological concerns that have been raised about containment theory, some have questioned its relative importance. The general conclusion is that self-concept measures can distinguish between delinquents and non-delinquents, but other factors may play a more dominant role in the etiology of delinquency. A variety of studies (e.g., Voss 1969, Jensen 1973, Rankin 1977) find that inner containment may be less powerful as an explanation of delinquency than other factors such as peer group association, family relations, and social class. These data suggest that self-concept or containment appears to possess less explanatory power than do some other factors related to delinquency, especially when official records are used to assess its occurrence (Shoemaker 1984).

As Wells (1978) concludes, it cannot be denied that self-concept has an effect on behavior, deviant or non-deviant, delinquent or non-delinquent. However, it also seems reasonable to conclude, as did Schwartz and Tangri (1965), that self-concept is a more complex aspect of human functioning than as portrayed in the Reckless studies. The issues relating to the measurement of self-concept and its application to delinquency are clearly multiple and largely perplexing, but are also clearly important. The work that has been done on self-concept and delinquency is not yet complete, and, whereas the work of Reckless and his associates has its shortcomings, it certainly seems that their conceptualization of self-concept and vulnerability may still hold the seeds for further productive inquiry and study. One fruitful avenue of inquiry may lie in the area of cognitive processes and structure, which may provide a fertile ground for assessing self-concept and its relationships to various behaviors as intervening variables between delinquency and salient social experiences (for examples of the use of cognitive variables in the assessment of self-concept and its relationship to criminal behavior, see Martin 1985 and Heilbrun 1982). Dinitz (personal communication, December 8, 1988) cites Howard Kaplan's (1980) *Deviant Behavior in Defense of Self* as an example of work that has "moved the area quite far along both theoretically and empirically." In addition, of course, there is the work of other control theorists in criminology, most notably Travis Hirschi, who have extended Reckless' ideas mainly in the direction of attachment and social bonding.

THE SEED FOR LATER THEORIZING

Simon Dinitz (personal communication, December 8, 1988) concedes that "as originally postulated, containment theory has nothing much to offer now." However, he says, "as the kernel of control theory, it is very much alive and viable." Not everyone, however, shares Dinitz's interpretation of the role of Reckless' theory. In their highly regarded book on criminological theory, Vold and Bernard (1986) give no special attention to Reckless' views, devoting only about two pages to the discussion of early control theories. They claim that containment did not add anything to already existing control-type theories, and it has problems because the dimensions it proposes are not very precise. Its only real contribution to control theory has been the attention it focused on the concepts of internal and external containment. However, there are those who agree with Dinitz's appraisal, crediting the personality-oriented social control theories like those of Reiss and Reckless with setting the stage for contemporary approaches to explaining crime and delinquency (Williams & McShane 1988). Shoemaker (1984), in his book *Theories of Delinquency*, gives considerable attention to the role of containment theory as a predecessor to later control theories like Hirschi's. The authors of this book take a similar stance, seeing Reckless' containment theory as a cornerstone in the foundation of contemporary control theory and agreeing with Shoemaker that the work of Travis Hirschi, which has become synonymous with control theory, constitutes an extension of Reckless' ideas into broader social contexts. It is beyond the focus of this chapter to provide a detailed discussion of Hirschi's work, but Hirschi, like Reckless, conceives of delinquency from the perspective of both process and structure, and both talk about the process by which certain people are freed from controls and come to commit delinquent acts (Clinard & Meier 1985). (For a complete discussion of Hirschi's social bond theory, see his 1969 book, *Causes of Delinquency*).

THE YOUTH DEVELOPMENT PROGRAM: AN APPLICATION OF CONTAINMENT THEORY

Given that a rather extensive application of the principles and concepts of containment theory was conducted in the form of the Youth Development Program that Reckless and his associates designed and implemented for the Columbus, Ohio, school system, it seems appropriate that the results of the program should be discussed as part of any critique of containment theory. Reckless and Dinitz (1972) offer a variety of conclusions concerning the outcomes of the project.

1. There were no significant differences between the experimental subjects (potential delinquents exposed to the special classes designed to "beef up" self-concept) and the controls on any of the outcome variables, a finding "most painfully evident" in school performance and police contact data.

2. Police involvement of both experimentals and controls increased with age, as did the seriousness of offenses.

3. School performance of both groups deteriorated with age.

4. The same trends applied to good boys, but they maintained their overall superiority to the bad boys.

5. Attitudinal dimensions paralleled the behavioral data; there were no significant differences between the groups.

6. In follow-ups of the 1964 and 1965 cohorts, interviewers were more impressed with the experimental boys and felt that they were not as likely to be having legal or school problems. The hard data, however, did not support their conclusions.

7. The boys and the teachers like the (special) classes.

Based on these conclusions, it is clear that the program, which was designed to "beef up" the self-concepts of the experimentals in order to "insulate" them from delinquency, was a failure.

Reckless and Dinitz (1972) offer some possible explanations for the lack of success of the program:

1. The "medicine" was not strong enough. The models presented and/or the format for presenting them were not sufficient to have the necessary impact.

2. The teachers and administrators were not as good predictors as the researchers anticipated. Consequently, many boys were included who were not actually predelinquent.

3. The role model exposure was not intensive enough.

4. The role model lesson plans could have lacked significance for thirteen-year-old inner-city boys; maybe the models were too middle class.

5. There were a multitude of general measurement problems. The study was forced to rely on official records for outcome measures, with the follow-up studies being especially susceptible to such problems.

Despite the very disappointing outcome of their experimental delinquency prevention program, Reckless and Dinitz (1972) urge that the results should not dissuade future attempts. They also do not see these data as necessarily invalidating containment theory, as they contend that the consistent superiority exhibited by the good boys provides additional confirmation for the general thesis concerning the nature of insulation against delinquency. The problems for them lie more with the program itself and with the available means for assessing the relevant variables.

CONCLUSION

Vold and Bernard (1986) conclude, despite claims to the contrary, that neither the empirical evidence from general research on human behavior nor that of a specific criminological nature is overly supportive of containment theory. They do acknowledge that control theories may adequately explain delinquency in juveniles who spend only a few hours per year engaged in it, but whether they can explain delinquency among "boys like Cohen's delinquents" (Albert Cohen chapter) is another question. Control theories, they say, have been generally supported by one type of data, self-report surveys, and they are good explanations of one type of criminal conduct, less serious delinquency. However, control theories do not provide good explanations of adult criminality or more serious delinquency. Clinard and Meier (1985) support these general conclusions, claiming that there are other theories that present stronger empirical arguments than do control theories.

In assessing these conclusions, several factors must be considered. First, it cannot be overlooked that Reckless (1961) calls containment theory a "middle range" theory and says it is designed to explain the bulk of criminal behavior and delinquency, which consists of acts that fall within the "middle range of norm violation." In addition, although it is true that there are various conceptual and methodological problems that characterize containment theory and attempts to test it, there are those who interpret the empirical evidence as being generally supportive of control theory (e.g., Shoemaker 1984, Hirschi 1969, Wiatrowski, Griswold, & Roberts 1981, Gibbs 1982). Shoemaker (1984) further concludes that the evidence gathered to date warrants continued development of control approaches, and Williams and McShane (1988) evidently concur, arguing that control theories represent the immediate future in criminological theory. One major barrier facing containment theory and control theories in general "lies in the excruciatingly complex problem of balancing the various items in some manner that will allow a predictive statement to be made on the basis of a particular mixture of controls" (Bloch & Geis 1970, 100). This obstacle, however, is not insurmountable from Reckless' (1967) perspective, as he argues that further research would ultimately distinguish one or two basic inner and outer regulators. The verdict is not yet in on this issue, but Dinitz (personal communication, December 8, 1988) believes that progress is being made in the area.

The debate continues, and although it may be true that containment theory as originally presented has little to offer today, it is also true that the value of a theory does not lie solely in its literal applicability at any given point in time. Likewise, the impact of a theorist cannot be measured entirely by the final verdict handed down on his or her theory. If it is true that containment theory is nothing more than "old wine in a new bottle," then it is a wine that reached its time under Walter Reckless. His statement of containment theory attracted attention and directed it toward some very important issues: the value of looking beyond the immediately observable in our explanations of behavior, and the need to address the inner life of the individual; the inappropriateness of developing theories of criminality that treat it like a unique and (possibly) pathological realm of human functioning; and his approach was interwoven with an inherent optimism that is all too often missing from the sterile models of the human condition that evolve out of the quest to be scientific. At the very least, Reckless' work provided a framework within which many theories of crime and delinquency can be viewed (Vold & Bernard 1986). Moreover, Walter Reckless provided a model for action-oriented scientific research in criminology from which we all can benefit.

References

Bloch, H. A., and G. Geis. 1970. *Man, crime and society*. 2nd ed. New York: Random House.

Clinard, M. B., and R. F. Meier. 1985. *Sociology of deviant behavior*. 6th ed. New York: Holt, Rinehart & Winston.

Dinitz, S., S. R. Scarpitti, and W. C. Reckless. 1962. Delinquency and vulnerability: A cross group and longitudinal analysis. *Am. Socio. Rev.* 27:515–17.

Gibbons, D. C. 1976. *Delinquent behavior*. 2nd ed. Englewood Cliffs, NJ: Prentice Hall.

Gibbs, J. P. 1982. Testing the theory of status integration and suicide rates. *Am. Socio. Rev.* 47:227–37.

Heilbrun, A. B., Jr. 1982. Cognitive models of criminal violence based upon intelligence and psychopathy levels. *J. Consult. Clin. Psych.* 50:546–57.

Hirschi, T. 1969. *Causes of delinquency*. Berkeley, CA: University of California Press.

Jensen, G. F. 1973. Inner containment and delinquency. *J. Crim. Law Criminol.* 64:464–70.

Kaplan, H. B. 1980. *Deviant behavior in defense of self*. New York: Academic Press.

Martin, R. 1985. Perceptions of self and significant others in assaultive and nonassaultive criminals. *J. Police Crim. Psych.* 1:2–13.

Nettler, G. 1984. *Explaining crime*. 3rd ed. New York: McGraw-Hill.

Nye, F. I. 1958. *Family relationships and delinquent behavior*. New York: John Wiley.

Orcutt, J. D. 1970. Self-concept and insulation against delinquency: Some critical notes. *Sociolog. Quart.* 2:381–90.

Quinney, R., and J. Wildeman. 1977. *The problem of crime: A critical introduction to criminology*. 2nd ed. New York: Harper & Row.

Rankin, J. H. 1977. Investigating the interrelations among social control variables and conformity. *J. Crim. Law Criminol.* 67:470–80.

Reckless, W. C. 1955. *The crime problem*. 2nd ed. New York: Appleton-Century-Crofts.

———. 1961. A new theory of delinquency and crime. *Fed. Prob.* 25:42–6.

———. 1967. *The crime problem*. 4th ed. New York: Appleton-Century-Crofts.

———. 1973. *The crime problem*. 5th ed. New York: Appleton-Century-Crofts.

Reckless, W. C., and S. Dinitz. 1967. Pioneering with self-concept as a vulnerability factor in delinquency. *J. Crim. Law Criminol. Police Sci.* 58:515–23.

———. 1972. *The prevention of juvenile delinquency: An experiment*. Columbus: Ohio State University Press.

Reckless, W. C., S. Dinitz, and B. Kay. 1957. The self component in potential delinquency and potential non-delinquency. *Am. Sociolog. Rev.* 22:566–70.

Reckless, W. C., S. Dinitz, and E. Murray. 1956. Self concept as an insulator against delinquency. *Am. Sociolog. Rev.* 21:744–46.

Reiss, A. J., Jr. 1951. Delinquency as the failure of personal and social controls. *Am. Sociolog. Rev.* 16:196–206.

Scarpitti, F. R., E. Murray, S. Dinitz, and W. C. Reckless. 1960. The "good boy" in a high delinquency area: 4 years later. *Am. Sociolog. Rev.* 25:555–58.

Schrag, C. 1971. *Crime and justice: American style*. Washington, DC: U.S. Government Printing Office.

Schwartz, M., and S. S. Tangri. 1965. A note on self-concept as an insulator against delinquency. *Am. Sociolog. Rev.* 30:922–26.

———. 1967. Delinquency research and the self-concept variable. *J. Crim. Law Criminol. Police Sci.* 18:182–90.

Seeman, M., and C. S. Anderson. 1983. Alienation and alcohol: The role of work mastery and community in drinking behavior. *Am. Sociolog. Rev.* 48:60–77.

Shoemaker, D. J. 1984. *Theories of delinquency: An examination of explanations of delinquent behavior*. New York: Oxford University Press.

Toby, J. 1957. Social disorganization and stake in conformity: Complementary factors in predatory behavior of hoodlums. *J. Crim. Law Criminol. Police Sci.* 48:12–17.

Vold, G. B., and T. J. Bernard. 1986. *Theoretical criminology*. 3rd ed. New York: Oxford University Press.

Voss, H. L. 1969. Differential association and containment theory: A theoretical convergence. *Soc. Forces* 47:381–91.

Wells, L. E. 1978. Theories of deviance and the self-concept. *Soc. Psych.* 41:189–204.

Wiatrowski, M. D., D. B. Griswold, and M. K. Roberts. 1981. Social control theory and delinquency. *Am. Sociolog. Rev.* 46:525–41.

Williams, F. P., III, and M. D. McShane. 1988. *Criminological theory*. Englewood Cliffs, NJ: Prentice Hall.

Yablonsky, L., and M. R. Haskell. 1988. *Juvenile delinquency*. 4th ed. New York: Harper & Row.

Supplemental Readings

The Good Boy–Bad Boy Series
(in chronologic order)

Reckless, W. C., S. Dinitz, and E. Murray. 1956. Self concept as an insulator against delinquency. *Am. Sociolog. Rev.* 21:744–56.

———. 1957. Teacher nominations and evaluations of "good boys" in high delinquency areas. *Elem. School J.* 57:221–23.

Dinitz, S., B. Kay, and W. C. Reckless. 1957. Delinquency proneness and school achievement. *Edu. Res. Bull.* 36:131–36.

Reckless, W. C., S. Dinitz, and E. Murray. 1957. The "good boy" in a high delinquency area. *J. Crim. Law Criminol. Police Sci.* 48:18–25.

Reckless, W. C., S. Dinitz, and B. Kay. 1957. The self component in potential delinquency and potential non-delinquency. *Am. Sociolog. Rev.* 22: 566–570.

Dinitz, S., B. Kay, and W. C. Reckless. 1958. Group gradients in potential delinquency and achievement scores of sixth graders. *Am. J. Orthopsych.* 28:598–605.

Dinitz, S., W. C. Reckless, and B. Kay. 1958. A self gradient among potential delinquents. *J. Crim. Law Criminol. Police Sci.* 49:230–33.

Reckless, W. C., and S. Dinitz. 1958. Hunting for an insulator against delinquency. *Grad. School Rec.* Ohio State University, 13:20–22.

Simpson, J., S. Dinitz, B. Kay, and W.C. Reckless. 1960. Delinquency potential of pre-adolescents in high delinquency areas. *Br. J. Delinq.* 10:211–15.

Scarpitti, S. R., E. Murray, S. Dinitz, and W. C. Reckless. 1960. The "good boy" in a high delinquency area: 4 years later. *Am. Sociolog. Rev.* 25:555–58.

Lively, E. L., S. Dinitz, and W. C. Reckless. 1962. Self-concept as a predictor of juvenile delinquency. *Am. J. Orthopsych.* 32:159–68.

Dinitz, S., S. R. Scarpitti, and W. C. Reckless. 1962. Delinquency and vulnerability: A cross group and longitudinal analysis. *Am. Sociolog. Rev.* 27:515–17.

Landis, J. R., S. Dinitz, and W. C. Reckless. 1963. Implementing two theories of delinquency: Value orientation and awareness of limited opportunity. *Sociol. Soc. Res.* 47:409–16.

_____. 1964. Differential perceptions of life changes: A research note. *Sociolog. Inq.* 34:60.

Reckless, W. C., and S. Dinitz. 1967. Pioneering with self-concept as a vulnerability factor in delinquency. *J. Crim. Law Criminol. Police Sci.* 58:515–23.

_____. 1972. *The prevention of juvenile delinquency: An experiment.* Columbus: Ohio State University Press.

Other Works

Reckless, W. C. 1928. Suggestions for the sociological study of problem children. *J. Edu. Sociol.* 2:156–71.

_____. 1929. *Six boys in trouble.* Monograph. Ann Arbor, MI: Edward Brothers.

_____. 1933. *Vice in Chicago.* Chicago: University of Chicago Press.

_____. 1940. *Criminal behavior.* New York: Appleton-Century-Crofts.

_____. 1943. A sociologist looks at prostitution. *Fed. Proba.* 7:12–16.

_____. 1946. How to treat women prisoners. *Surv. Midmon.* 82:259–61.

_____. 1946. The democracy of probation and parole. In *Yearbook.* New York: National Probation Association, 101–03.

_____. 1947. Prostitution in the U.S. In M. Fishbein and E. W. Burgess, Eds., *Successful marriage.* Garden City, NJ: Doubleday, 433–47.

_____. 1952. *Jail administration in India.* Monograph. New York: Technical Assistance Administration, United Nations.

_____. 1958. The small residential treatment institution in perspective. In H. A. Weeks, Ed., *Youthful offenders at Highfields.* Ann Arbor, MI: University of Michigan Press, 157–64.

_____. 1961. A new theory of delinquency and crime. *Fed. Proba.* 25:42–46.

Reckless, W. C., and L. S. Selling. 1937. A sociological and psychiatric interview compared. *Am. J. Orthopsych.* 7:533–36.

Reckless, W. C., and C. Newman. 1965. Interdisciplinary problems of criminology. *Papers Am. Soc. Criminol.*

Reckless, W. C., and S. Dinitz, S. 1968. *Critical issues in the study of crime.* Boston: Little, Brown.

Special thanks to Dr. Simon Dinitz of Ohio State University for his invaluable assistance in preparing this bibliography.

CHAPTER 9
ROBERT KING MERTON: 1910–2003

I. BIOGRAPHICAL SKETCH

Robert Merton rose from very humble beginnings to become one of the premier sociologists of our day. Meyer R. Schkolnick (his birth name) was born on July 5, 1910, the second of two children to Jewish-immigrant parents who lived above the family's dairy-products store. Merton's father, who was of Eastern European origin, scraped out a living as a carpenter and truck driver in the slums of south Philadelphia, Pennsylvania. A member of a juvenile gang, young Merton "participated with zest" (Bierstedt 1981, 441) in the street fights that Merton admits were more ceremonial than physical. Most of the "gang warfare" consisted of throwing rocks and bottles from a safe distance. By age eight, Merton had developed a definite affinity for books, spending much of his time reading and exploring the library. Although Merton's reading interests at this time are best described as eclectic, he often chose to read biographies of important people (Hunt 1961).

Around age twelve, Merton discovered the art of prestidigitation when he began taking lessons from his next-door neighbor and soon found that he could earn between five and ten dollars per engagement performing for neighborhood groups as "Robert Merlin." It is possible that, had a problem not developed at one performance because of his finale, the Houdini needle trick, the world would have had Robert Merlin the Magician rather than Robert Merton the Sociologist. According to Morton M. Hunt's January 28, 1961, column in *The New Yorker* entitled "Profiles: How Does It Come to Be So?" a few hundred Sunday-school children watched Merton as he was performing his finale, which consisted of his "seeming to swallow several needles plus a length of black thread, washing them all down with a glassful of water, and then pulling the thread out of his mouth with the needles neatly strung on it" (57). Merton apparently was so convincing in the performance of this trick that a number of the children who witnessed him perform it attempted to duplicate his efforts. Calls from concerned parents helped influence Merton to seek a "less harrowing" (57) career.

In February 1927, Merton graduated from South Philadelphia High School for Boys, won a scholarship, and entered Temple University. It was at this time that he changed his name to Merton. During his freshman year, he majored in philosophy and became a protégé of James Dunham, the dean of Temple and a professor of philosophy. During his sophomore year, Merton took an introductory course in sociology from a young instructor named George E. Simpson. Within a very short period, Merton became a disciple of Simpson and sociology. According to Merton's recollection, "[i]t wasn't so much the substance of what Simpson said that did it ... it was more the joy of discovering that it was possible to examine human behavior objectively and without using loaded moral preconceptions" (Hunt 1961, 57). Merton became Simpson's research assistant and, in addition to his research responsibilities, spent much time conversing and drinking with Simpson, who was single and lived on campus. Hunt reports from his interview with Merton that Simpson "all but adopted Merton" (1961, 57). In concert with the opportunity to develop his keen interest in sociology, Temple also provided Merton with the opportunity to engage in extracurricular activities. Merton became fairly knowledgeable in classical music, as well as proficient at dancing the foxtrot and playing tennis. The development of these social graces helped identify Merton as a "comer" when he entered Harvard in 1931 to pursue his graduate education.

While a graduate student at Harvard, Merton was an industrious individual who was able to survive on five hundred dollars a year, "a feat he achieved in part by subsisting for long stretches on sandwiches and milkshakes and by making his own whiskey" (Hunt 1961, 58).

During one summer, Merton traveled to all of the Hoovervilles and hobo jungles in the Boston area, interviewing the homeless individuals who inhabited these make-shift communities. Merton wanted to know who these people were and where they had come from. At another point in his graduate career, Merton worked daily for approximately five months in the basement of the Widener Library on the Harvard campus, cataloging the tens of thousands of patents issued by the U.S. government between 1860 and 1930. Merton's purpose was to "chart fluctuations in the rate of invention within each industry and to relate these fluctuations to changing social conditions" (Hunt 1961, 59). To prepare for his dissertation, Merton read 6,034 biographies in the *Dictionary of National Biography*. Merton turned these three projects into manuscripts he submitted to various discipline-based journals; all three were accepted for publication.

In 1933, Merton began work on his dissertation, entitled "Sociological Aspects of Scientific Development in Seventeenth Century England," which he completed in 1935. His dissertation related technological progress in Great Britain to its changing social conditions. During the two years that Merton worked on his dissertation, he found time to court and marry Suzanne M. Carhart, a social worker, who attended Temple during the years Merton was a student there. They were married on September 8, 1934, once Merton had become an instructor at Harvard. They had three children: Stephanie, Robert, and Vanessa.

In 1936, Merton was awarded the Ph.D. in sociology from Harvard, and published an article entitled "The Unanticipated Consequences of Purposive Social Action." From 1936 through most of 1939, Merton remained at Harvard, where he served as a tutor and instructor. During his tenure as instructor, Merton had such individuals as Bernard Barber, Albert K. Cohen, Albert Damon (a future anthropologist), Glenn Frank, J.R. Pitts, and H.W. Riecken as students in his classes. In 1938, he published his dissertation in *Osiris* under the title *Science, Technology and Society in Seventeenth-Century England*.

In 1939, Merton accepted an offer for a position as Associate Professor of Sociology at Tulane University. Merton told an interesting story to Caroline Hodges Persell (1984) about how he interviewed for the position. The Depression caused Harvard University to pass a policy that called only for the replacement of vacated tenure positions. No new positions were to be added. Merton was an instructor and, at this point in his career, had been one for three years. Talcott Parsons had been an instructor for nine years before he was promoted to the rank of Assistant Professor. This, coupled with the fact that Pitirim Sorokin was the oldest member of the Department of Sociology at fifty, made it appear that at least for quite a while there were not going to be any openings in the department. In addition, Merton had an interest in living in another part of the country so that he could experience a culture different from those in Philadelphia and Boston. Only two areas of the country held any interest for Merton—San Francisco and New Orleans. The chances of going to San Francisco were greatly diminished by the fact that at this time the University of California at Berkeley had no sociology department. New Orleans, however, held promise.

One day, Merton received a call from the president of Tulane asking if he was interested in a position. Ironically, Merton had only fantasized about a position in New Orleans; he had not discussed it with anyone, nor had he applied to any universities in New Orleans. Merton and the president of Tulane agreed to meet in New York at the Astor Hotel for breakfast to discuss the position. In partial preparation for his interview, Merton read about the culture of New Orleans and discovered it was a "hard-drinking" one. When the time for the interview arrived and Merton and the president were seated on the rooftop restaurant, with a waiter waiting, the president asked what Merton would like to drink. Merton paused for a moment and, thinking that his choice of drink might give some indication of his ability to fit into the New Orleans culture, he ordered a scotch—straight. The president then ordered a tomato juice. In spite of this *faux pas*, Merton was offered the position, which he attributed to the "interpretation of the president's question [as] the by-product of [his] thorough ethnographical research on the New Orleans subculture" (Persell 1984, 378). Merton spent two years at Tulane, becoming chair of the department and receiving a promotion to the rank of full professor.

Two years later, in 1941, he joined the faculty at Columbia University as an assistant professor, and began a love affair with the school that has lasted until this day. In 1979, he was appointed University Professor Emeritus after twenty-eight years of service. In 1941, Columbia University had a Department of Sociology that had a reputation as one of the most active in the country. Individuals such as Robert Lynd, the explorer of Middletown, and the scholarly Robert MacIver (Hunt 1961, 61) were in residence. The choice for Merton to leave Tulane and join the faculty at Columbia was not a difficult one. This time, in an interview with Morton Hunt, Merton explains how he came to be offered the position at Columbia "almost as much for his symbolic value as for his ability" (1961, 59). The Department of Sociology at Columbia University had been split into two major factions—the empiricists and the theorists. For a number of years, the rift between these two groups had been so great that they were unable to agree on a candidate for a faculty position. Finally, in a compromise, each faction was given the opportunity to select an individual for appointment. The empiricist faction selected Paul F. Lazarsfeld, while the theorist faction chose Robert Merton. In 1944, Merton was promoted to the rank of associate professor, and in 1947 to full professor. In 1963, Merton was appointed Giddings Professor of Sociology, a position he held until 1974, when he was cited for his contributions and appointed a University Professor, a position he held for five years. In 1979, he was appointed Special Service Professor as well as University Professor Emeritus. Although Merton served as Special Service Professor for only five years, he continues to hold the title of University Professor Emeritus, and since 1979 has been a resident scholar at the Russell Sage Foundation.

Robert Merton received more than twenty honorary degrees from such institutions as Oxford University, Yale University, Harvard University, and the University of

Chicago. In addition to his numerous honorary degrees, Merton has been recognized for his outstanding achievements and contributions by many societies, organizations, and foundations. Most recently, in 1986, he received the George Sarton Medal in the History of Science from the University Ghent, Belgium. In 1962, he was a Guggenheim Fellow, and in 1979, he was made a Foreign Member of the Royal Swedish Academy of Sciences. From 1983 to 1988, he was a MacArthur Prize Fellow, and in 1984, he was selected as the first *Who's Who in America* Achievement Award in the Social Sciences and Social Policy.

In addition to the numerous honorary degrees and awards Merton received, he delivered many invited lectures both in the United States and abroad, and has served or serves on too many editorial boards, committees, and commissions at the local, state, and federal levels to list here. These recognitions, awards, and appointments are the result of his many decades of teaching and scholarship. Merton published thirty-one books, edited an additional twelve books and countless articles. The number of reprints of his work in English as well as other languages would run too many pages to list. [For a complete listing of Merton's work up to 1976, the reader is referred to "The Writings of Robert K. Merton: A Bibliography" by Mary Wilson Miles, Merton's research secretary, published in *The Idea of Social Structure: Papers in Honor of Robert K. Merton*, edited by Lewis Coser (1975).]

Morton Hunt reports, after a visit to Merton's study, that in addition to those books and articles Merton published, there are "[s]tacked on a shelf . . . in neat brown leather binders . . . are the typescripts of enough completed books and finished research to make a respectable bibliography—if he could only be persuaded to release them" (1961, 61).

II. BASIC ASSUMPTIONS

Understanding the time from which Merton draws his intellectual roots, the Depression of the 1930s, sheds considerable light on his orientation. "An entire generation of sociologists could observe the collapsing and deregulation of social traditions and the effect that it had upon both individuals and the institutions of society" (Williams and McShane 1988, 60–61). Merton identifies many persons who played an important role in his intellectual development, including George Simpson, Pitirim Sorokin, L.J. Henderson, E.F. Gay, George Sarton, Gilbert Murray, Talcott Parsons, Paul F. Lazarsfeld, Emile Durkheim, and Georg Simmel.

In terms of sociology, the 1930s was a very exciting time to be at Harvard. Admitted in 1931, Merton was a member of the first cadre of students accepted to study in the Sociology Department, founded by Pitirim Sorokin only the year before. In addition to Sorokin, George Sarton, the historian of science, and L.J. Henderson, the biochemist and sometime sociologist, were members of the faculty at Harvard.

Relatively unknown at the time Merton entered Harvard, a young assistant professor by the name of Talcott Parsons had recently joined the faculty. Merton describes Parsons as a "mentor" not only for himself, but for many of the graduate students as well. Merton characterizes the sense of Parsons in the following manner: "The students came to study under Sorokin, but stayed to study under Parsons" (Merton 1980, 69). Merton was part of a group of students who "induced [Parsons] to form what we, not he, immodestly called the Parsons Sociological Group. That group met for some years in his tutorial quarters in Adams House—as I remember, in G-34—which inevitably became tagged as the Parsonage" (Merton 1980, 70). Merton's relationship with Parsons would eventually change from one of student and teacher to one of colleagues because, as Merton informs us, "our teacher as a reference figure, accorded us intellectual respect, because he took us seriously; we, in strict accord with Meadian theory, came to take ourselves seriously. We had work to do. Soon, we were less students than younger colleagues—fledgling colleagues to be sure, but colleagues for all that" (1980, 70).

Sorokin opened Merton's thinking to European social thought. Sorokin's book *Contemporary Sociological Theories* "called attention to Durkheim's use of the term anomic suicide" (Williams and McShane 1988, 61). L.J. Henderson "taught [Merton] something about the disciplined investigation of what is first entertained as an interesting idea" (228). Merton was greatly influenced by the writings of Emile Durkheim and Georg Simmel as well. In describing his relationship with Durkheim, Merton says, "I chose to adopt the position of my master-at-a-distance, Durkheim. . . . Durkheim repeatedly changed the subjects he chose to investigate" (228).

In 1941, when Merton moved to a faculty position at Columbia, he had an opportunity to work with many well-known individuals, including MacIver and Lazarsfeld, and his students, including Gouldner, the Blaus, Selznick, Lipset, the Rossis, and the Cosers, who would eventually establish themselves as major movers in the field of sociology, continually stimulated and challenged him. The government's efforts at restructuring society through the New Deal had a profound impact on Merton's thinking, and many of his students were politically motivated and anxious to help rearrange society. The move was "away from the narrower applications of sociology and toward an examination of the social structure as a whole" (Williams and McShane 1988, 61).

Although Merton's relationship with Paul F. Lazarsfeld at Columbia University was more professional than social, they considered themselves close friends. Both were hired at Columbia at the same time in what amounted to a compromise, and the two supposedly represented different schools of sociological thought—Merton was to be the theorist component, whereas Lazarsfeld was to represent the methodological or empiricist component. Hanan Selvin, a student of both Merton and Lazarsfeld, writes of herself and other graduate students as "satellites, not of one sun, but of two, for Robert K. Merton and Paul F. Lazarsfeld so dominated Columbia during these three decades that no lesser figure of speech will do" (Sills 1987, 269–70). In a Festschrift for Lazarsfeld, Merton identifies Lazarsfeld as a "brother." "Their students and colleagues know that these words only hint at the depth and complexity of their intellectual and personal companionship" (Sills 1987, 271). Writing in 1975, Lazarsfeld echoes the sentiments expressed by Merton and Selvin when he characterizes his relationship with Merton.

During an interview with Morton Hunt, Merton describes his first true social contact with Lazarsfeld as one that moved quickly from what was supposed to be dinner at the Lazarsfeld home to a working research project at a radio station. Lazarsfeld, being the older of the two, took it on himself to invite Merton and his wife to dinner. On the day of the dinner, Lazarsfeld, who was the Director of the Rockefeller Foundation project to study the social effects of radio, received an urgent call; he had to do some audience-reaction testing that evening. When Merton and his wife arrived at the Lazarsfeld apartment, Lazarsfeld met them at the door and told Merton not to take off his coat, that he had a "sociological surprise" (Hunt 1961, 56), and whisked Merton to a radio studio to observe a reaction test of the audience to the radio program. Merton became very interested once the questioning started, and began passing notes to Lazarsfeld about the theoretical shortcomings of the process. They talked until long after midnight in what was the beginning of a long-lasting professional relationship. Merton became involved with Lazarsfeld in a project that was eventually to become the Bureau of Applied Social Research at Columbia.

III. KEY IDEAS

When Merton taught at Columbia, it was in part because he was viewed as a theorist, an identification he enjoyed. It has been because of his theoretical orientation to sociology that Merton was able to avoid the kind of subject specialization that has become (and, in his opinion, has for the most part rightly become) the order of the day in sociology, as in other evolving disciplines. For Merton, the need to study a wide variety of subjects was and is still essential, and included in his broad-based theoretical approach has been the study of such topics as social stratification, housing, the self-fulfilling prophecy, the interrelationship of science and religion, the sociology of science, the transmission of authority, the effects of radio propaganda, the mass media, reference group theory, and, of course, his major contribution to the development of criminological thought, anomie. Space and the focus of this book preclude the examination of all his research and contributions, and those included here are the subjects that are directly and indirectly related to the development of criminological thought: the science of sociological theory as it relates to history and theories of the middle range, the concept of the self-fulfilling prophecy, reference group theory, and anomie.

In his book *On Theoretical Sociology: Five Essays Old and New* (1967), Merton reprints in an expanded form two essays from *Social Theory and Social Structure* and adds three new essays that he groups into a category called Sociological Theory. In the first chapter, Merton addresses the distinction between "the history of sociological theory on the one hand and the systematic substance of current sociological theory on the other" (Bierstedt 1981, 449). Bierstedt quotes Merton from his first chapter: "The rationale for the history of science is to achieve an understanding of how things came to develop as they did in a certain science or in a complex of sciences" (1981, 449). Merton would have us understand that it is important to know the roads theorists have traveled in arriving at their conclusions. Sociology develops in an incremental pattern, building on what has come before. Merton believes we should "stand on the shoulders of giants" who have come before us to be able to get a better view.

For Merton, reading and rereading the classics in sociology serves five distinct functions:

1. If we are aware of what has already been discovered, we can avoid the time-consuming process of reinventing the wheel.
2. Classical sociological theory also helps formulate ideas clearly, especially those we are not clear about to begin with.
3. It allows us to question our ideas to make sure they will stand up to the challenges of what has come before.
4. It provides a model and guidelines to follow in the development of our own theories.
5. It is important to read and reread classical sociological theory because we glean different things each time it is read. As we grow and reread classical sociological theory, it changes based on changes in our perceptions and knowledge base.

Merton's definition of sociological theory is relatively simple and straightforward: It is "logically interconnected sets of propositions from which empirical uniformities can be derived" (Merton 1967, 39). Merton primarily addresses those theories that are of the "middle range," those "that lie between the minor but necessary working hypotheses that evolve in abundance during the day-to-day research and the all-inclusive systematic efforts to develop a unified theory that will explain all the observed uniformities of social behavior, social organization and social change" (1967, 39). In a footnote, Merton, using a definition by James B. Conant (1947), in his work *On Understanding Science*, explains what he means by a working hypothesis: the "common-sense procedure used by all of us every day. Encountering certain facts, certain alternative explanations come to mind and we proceed to test them" (1967, 39).

The theories of the middle range in Merton's opinion hold the greatest promise. In 1961, Merton suggested that "[o]ur major task today is to develop special theories, applicable to limited ranges of data-theories, for example, of deviant behavior, or the flow of power from generation to generation, or the unseen ways in which personal influence is exercised" (Hunt 1961, 42). Once we have developed these "middle-range" theories, we must "[c]onsolidat[e] them some day into theories of a higher level of generality" (Bierstedt 1981, 456).

Although Merton's work in the area of reference group theory is not what he is best known for, two chapters in *Social Theory and Social Structure* are related to the topic. His contributions to understanding reference group theory are important because of the foundation reference group theory provides for those theories that follow. Two of the theories influenced in their development by reference group theory are *labeling theory* and *conflict theory*.

One of the chapters in *Social Theory and Social Structure*, "Contributions to the Theory of Reference Group Behavior," is coauthored with Alice S. Rossi and discusses the work of Samuel Stouffer on *The American Soldier*. Whereas Stouffer does not write about reference group theory in his work, Merton and Rossi analyze all the cases Stouffer includes that bear on reference group theory. For Merton and Rossi, *reference group theory* is defined as that which "aims to systematize the determinants and consequences of those processes of evaluation and self-appraisal in which the individual takes the values or standards of other individuals and groups as a comparative frame of reference" (Merton 1957, 234). Merton and Rossi are interested to determine "under which conditions are associates within one's own groups taken as a frame of reference for self-evaluation and attitude-formation and under which conditions do out-groups or non-membership groups provide the significant frame of reference" (Merton 1957, 233). As to the extent of membership and nonmembership reference groups, "any of the groups of which one is a member, and these are comparatively few, as well as groups of which one is not a member, and these are, of course, legion, can become points of reference for shaping one's attitudes, evaluations and behaviors" (Merton 1957, 233).

Merton and Rossi build in part on Herbert Hyman's work and question the work of Tamotsu Shibutani. In addition, George Herbert Mead's *Mind, Self, and Society* in general and the concept of the "looking-glass self" specifically serve as part of the foundation for the development of reference group theory. Merton studied the concept of *reference group*, first developed in the field of social psychology, because he believed that it "has a distinctive place in the theory of sociology" (1957, 281).

First published in the *Antioch Review* in 1948, Merton's chapter is one of his most important. Merton created the term *self-fulfilling prophecy* to describe a concept that has had an impact on many disciplines, including criminology. Although the chapter devoted to this concept in *Social Theory and Social Structure* is short, it has played a large and key role in the development of our thinking about how individuals act based on their perceptions of themselves. Merton starts with W.I. Thomas' theorem that "if men define situations as real, they are real in their consequences" (1968, 421). Merton provides a parable about the failure of the Last National Bank to illustrate Thomas' theorem. The bank fails because of rumor of its insolvency. Enough depositors believe the rumor and withdraw their funds, thereby causing the bank to fail.

> The stable financial structure of the bank had depended upon one set of definitions of the situation: belief in the validity of the interlocking system of economic promises men live by. Once depositors had defined the situation otherwise, once they questioned the possibility of having these promises fulfilled, the consequences of this unreal definition were real enough. (Merton 1957, 422)

The concept of the self-fulfilling prophecy is one that everyone can understand even if unaware of the term that identifies it. An example might be the failing college student. A student who is having difficulty in a class spends more time worrying about passing an exam than actually studying for it. If this process dominates, the student's self-induced anxiety becomes a legitimate fear. Merton states, "The self-fulfilling prophecy is, in the beginning, a false definition of the situation evoking a new behavior which makes the originally false conception come true" (1957, 423). A vicious cycle begins that is very difficult—if not impossible—to extricate oneself from. "The specious validity of the self-fulfilling prophecy perpetuates a reign of error" (Merton 1957, 423). How the application of this concept contributes to our understanding of some of the aspects of deviance, delinquency, and criminal behavior is obvious. The concept of the self-fulfilling prophecy understood from sociological and psychological perspectives helps establish, in part, the necessary groundwork for the development and popularity of labeling theory.

Anomie theory, most often associated with the work of two men—Emile Durkheim (Emile Durkheim chapter) and Robert Merton—used the term in very different ways, with Merton building on Durkheim's initial work, expanding its orientation and attempting to make it more specific in application (Clinard 1964).

Durkheim used the term *anomie* in two distinct ways: In his book *The Division of Labor in Society* (1893), *anomie* was an abnormal form of the division of labor. According to Durkheim, the increasing complexity of society could lead to three abnormal forms of the division of labor, of which the anomic was one type. For Durkheim, the anomic form of division of labor exists because there is "a lack of integration or mutual adjustment of functions growing out of industrial crises, conflicts between labor and capital, and increasing specialization of science. Anomie arises because the division of labor fails to produce sufficiently effective contacts between societies' members and adequate regulations of social relationships" (Clinard 1964, 4).

Durkheim saw humans as naturally insatiable in their desires and appetites. Thus, they require laws or norms to regulate these appetites. In *Suicide* (1897), published four years after *The Division of Labor in Society*, Durkheim uses the term *anomie* to refer to a form of suicide where there has been a sudden an unexpected upheaval in the norms of society. "[T]he concept of anomie referred to a condition of relative normlessness in a society or group" (Merton 1957, 161). For the person in society who is able to function within an existing normative structure, the sudden upheaval causes a dissonance that the person cannot cope with, and thus if suicide is committed, Durkheim classifies it as anomic.

In his most reprinted publication, "Social Structure and Anomie" (1938), Merton first discussed, in publication form, his use of the term *anomie*. Robert Merton was only twenty-seven when this publication gained him immediate national attention, and he later expanded on this initial effort when he published *Social Theory and Social Structure,* which he compiled for publication from a number of pieces he had written previously. The primary aim of his 1938 article was "to discover how some social structures exert a definite pressure upon certain persons in the society to engage in nonconforming conduct rather than conformist conduct" (Merton 1938, 672). From a theoretical standpoint, the "immediate . . . problem was to find a way of construing systematically the character of anomie in terms of social and cultural variables and of construing systematically rather than in ad hoc descriptive fashion, the types of behavioral responses to anomie" (Merton 1964, 215). Merton's work in anomie theory has been classified as the first "strain" theory approach, and although it is a general attempt to explain crime, many of the strain theories that followed Merton's lead have been more specific in nature, such as the strain theories presented in the works of Cloward and Ohlin (1960) and Albert K. Cohen (1955).

Merton, in contrast to Durkheim, does not view humans as having naturally insatiable appetites, but sees human appetites as strongly influenced by culture, which tells us what things we should want and how much we should desire them. Culture tells us what goals we should desire and also prescribes the legitimate means of achieving them. In order for society to enter into a state of anomie, certain conditions must be present. First, there must be a goal that everyone is culturally expected to desire and obtain (e.g., Merton's financial success goal). Second, there must be an imbalance in the emphasis placed on the goal; that is, obtaining the goal is more important than how it is obtained. Third, there are social structural blocks to obtaining the goal that prevent a portion of the population from obtaining the goal through legitimate means. The resulting strain is what makes the society anomic.

More specifically, Merton begins by separating culturally defined goals from the social structure, a dichotomy that he admits is arbitrary (Clinard 1964). The cultural goals act as "a frame of aspirational reference" (Merton 1938, 672), whereas the social structure "defines, regulates and controls the acceptable modes of achieving these goals" (1938, 672–73). Although there is a relationship between the culturally defined goals and the normative structure, the relationship is not a constant one. "The emphasis upon certain goals may vary independently of the degree of emphasis upon institutional means" (Merton 1938, 673). For Merton, "parents serve as a transmission belt" (1957, 137), providing children with values and goals specific to their social class, or the class they identify with. In a formal setting, the schools are the primary purveyors of the prevailing values. "[S]train toward anomie, i.e., the inability to achieve the goals of society by available means, will be differentially distributed through a social system and . . . different modes of deviant adaptation will be concentrated in varying social strata" (Clinard 1964, 13).

In his 1938 article, Merton described *aberrant behavior* "as a symptom of dissociation between culturally defined aspirations and socially structured means" (674). When the dissociation between the norms and the means is so pervasive and extensive, anomie can result. In his 1957 edition of *Social Theory and Social Structure*, Merton defines *anomie* as a "breakdown in the cultural structure, occurring particularly when there is an acute disjunction between the cultural norms and goals and the socially structured capacities of members of the group to act in accord with them" (1957, 162).

Two types of general responses can result from dissociation: one that places greater emphasis on the goals and a second that places greater emphasis on the means. For the first general response, the emphasis is on goals and can be so great that whatever method is of greatest efficiency and expediency in obtaining the goal is used. The degree of the illegitimacy of the method is irrelevant. Merton points out that if everyone in society adopts this posture, "the integration of society becomes tenuous and anomie ensues" (1938, 674). An important question for those who violate the rules is, do they know the rules before they violate them? Merton is of the opinion that the rules are known, "but that the emotional supports of these rules are largely vitiated by cultural exaggeration of the success goal" (1938, 675). The second general type of response occurs when individuals have internalized the norms to the extent that they are prevented from violating them. These individuals find comfort in routines in which they have abandoned or reduced their expectations and fit Merton's ritualism adaptation.

Five adaptations—that is, conformity, innovation, ritualism, retreatism, and rebellion— are identified that people can engage in, depending on how they perceive the goals and the means available to obtain the goals and the emphasis placed on each. Merton wants no mistake made: "These categories refer to behavior, not personality, and the same person may use different modes of adaptation in different circumstances" (Bierstedt 1981, 463). The terms of the adaptation and the relationship between cultural goals and institutionalized means are presented in Table 1.

TABLE 1:

	Cultural Goals	Institutionalized Means
I. Conformity	+	+
II. Innovation	+	−
III. Ritualism	−	+
IV. Retreatism	−	−
V. Rebellion	−/+	−/+

According to Merton, "[n]one of these adaptations . . . is deliberately selected by the individual or is utilitarian, but rather, since all arise from strains in the social system, they can be assumed to have a degree of spontaneity behind them" (Clinard 1964, 16).

CONFORMITY

In this adaptation, the most widely practiced of the five, the individual accepts and follows the cultural goals as well as the institutionalized means provided to obtain the goals. If conformity were not the most prominent adaptation, society would tend to become unstable. Because those who accept the cultural goals and adhere to the institutionalized means are in the vast majority, the behavior exhibited in this category contributes to the stability of society. Because the behavior exhibited by conformity is law abiding and non-deviant in nature, Merton does not devote much space to its discussion.

INNOVATION

When the individual accepts the emphasis on cultural goals but has not accepted equally the institutionalized means available for obtaining the goals, the individual is classified as an *innovator*. Merton posits that the "greatest pressures toward deviation are exerted upon the lower strata" (1957, 144). Class structure places limits on the avenues available to members of the lower strata to obtain the cultural goals, and "it is the combination of the cultural emphasis and the social structure which produces intense pressure for deviation" (Merton 1957, 145). Pressures cause a reduction in the attempt to succeed using legitimate means while also causing an expansion in the use of illegitimate methods. What individuals, especially those in the lower strata, are experiencing is a disjuncture between the goals and the means available to obtain them. Merton presents his discussion of the modes of adaptation in terms of financial success. The goal of wealth has been emphasized as desirable but the available legitimate means structure prevents many from obtaining this goal. "For the unsuccessful and particularly for those among the unsuccessful who find little reward for their merit and their effort, the doctrine of luck serves the psychological function of enabling them to preserve their self-esteem in the face of failure" (Merton 1957, 149). For those in the lower strata, defined in economic terms, the cultural norms and the institutionalized means available present incompatible demands. Members of these strata are "asked to orient their conduct toward the prospects of large wealth, but . . . they are . . . denied effective opportunities to do so institutionally" (Merton 1957, 146). Innovation adaptation as a response to this incompatibility is the one most closely associated with expression of deviant, delinquent, and criminal behavior. The emphasis is still strongly on the goals regardless of the means used to obtain them.

RITUALISM

Ritualism represents a scaling down or abandonment of the cultural goals with a continued adherence to the institutionalized means. "[T]hough one rejects the cultural obligation to attempt 'to get ahead in the world,' though one draws in one's horizons, one continues to abide almost compulsively by institutional norms" (Merton 1957, 149–50). Individuals in the ritualistic mode of adaptation tend to follow routines mapped out or provided by their roles. In our society, where our status is determined by our achievements, we expect to find a large number of individuals adapting in a ritualist manner. Merton suggests that the competitiveness that is inherent in our society causes acute anxiety. "One device for allaying these anxieties is to lower one's level of aspirations—permanently" (Merton 1957, 150). Fear of failure produces inaction. Safety from anxiety and fear of failure are enhanced when one scales down aspirations.

It has been argued that this is actually not a form of deviant behavior because the individual involved continues to follow the available legitimate means. Merton counters that this is a form of deviant behavior because members of society are culturally "obliged to strive actively . . . to move onward and upward in the social hierarchy" (1957, 150) and the ritualist does not do this.

RETREATISM

Retreatism is the least frequently used form of adaptation. Merton characterizes people who retreat as, strictly speaking, "in the society, but not of it" (1957, 153). The range of individuals who fall into this category of adaptation is quite broad, including drunkards, drug addicts, autists, vagrants, and psychotics. Retreatism is most likely to occur when an individual accepts both the cultural goals and the institutionalized means but acceptable institutional mechanisms are unavailable. The deviant in this category is nonproductive, sees no value in the success goal, and pays little attention to the institutional practices. The retreatist "is free from conflict because he has abandoned the quest for security and prestige, and is resigned to the lack of any claim to virtues or distinction" (Merton 1957, 154). Retreatism is not a collective mode of adaptation; it "is largely private and isolated rather than unified under the aegis of a new cultural code" (Merton 1957, 155). Retreatists are the "socially disinherited," and while they do not have many of the rewards of society, they have few of the frustrations. These individuals often exist on very little food, indulge in excessive amounts of sleep, and develop no discernible, respectable pattern of behavior. In some extreme cases, retreatists "finally succeed in annihilating the world by killing themselves" (Merton 1964, 219).

REBELLION

In rebellion, individuals go completely outside of the social structure in order to modify it, rejecting the conventional social structure and attempting to create a new one, or at the very least to make major alterations in the existing structure. Rebellion "arises when the institutional system is regarded as a barrier to the satisfaction of legitimized goals" (Clinard 1964, 17). A parable that helps to explain this form of adaptation comes from Aesop's Fables: The fox who cannot have the grapes states that they are probably sour anyway. The fox's frustration in not being able to obtain the desired grapes leads to full denunciation by the fox of that which was previously prized. Merton points out that rebellion is an adaptation that is on a clearly different plane from the others; "it represents a transitional response seeking to institutionalize new goals and new procedures to be shared by other members of the society" (1957, 140).

According to Clinard, Merton altered his perception of the rebellion adaptation in a later publication, indicating that Merton "divided deviant behavior into two types, non-conforming and aberrant behavior, on the basis of social structure and consequences for the social system" (1964, 18). These two types of deviant behavior are very different. Simply, *aberrant behavior* is either a delinquent or a criminal act, whereas *nonconforming behavior* is more complex than aberrant behavior because it involves public dissent. The nonconformist questions the legitimacy of the norms of the social structure, often appeals to a higher morality, and "draws upon the ultimate basic values of society for his goals" (Clinard 1964, 18). The people who engage in aberrant behavior tend to acknowledge the legitimacy of the norms being violated, but still try to hide their delinquent or criminal behavior. These individuals are interested in serving their own interests, and their goals are private and self-centered.

ANOMIA

Here we must pause to make a distinction between the terms *anomie* and *anomia*. *Anomie* "refers to a property of a social system, not to the state of mind of this or that individual within the system. It refers to a breakdown of social standards governing behavior and so also signifies little social cohesion" (Merton 1964, 226). *Anomia,* however, "appears as a response to the personal discovery that the attainment of a long sought-after goal is no stable stopping point. What appeared from below as the end of the road becomes, in the actual experience, only another way station" (Merton 1964, 221).

Leo Srole (1956) proposed the term *anomia* to represent the anomic state of the individual, and presents a five-item scale that measures an individual's sense of anomia:

1. Community leaders are indifferent to the individual's needs
2. Little can be accomplished in a society that is seen as unpredictable and lacking order
3. Life goals are receding rather than being realized
4. Life holds little meaning and small prospect for one's children
5. One cannot count on associates for social and psychological support (Merton 1964, 228)

IV. CRITIQUE

Merton's work in the area of anomie theory has had a tremendous impact on the field of criminological thought, and it has been combined with another theoretical approach to create opportunity theory, which was the basis for the government program Mobilization for Youth in the 1960s. Numerous "spin-offs" evolved based on Merton's original work and modes of adaptation. Although Merton has received accolades from many quarters, he has also been subjected to serious criticism from others. The space necessary to address the studies, both theoretical and empirical, that have examined, expanded, and challenged the credibility of Merton's anomie theory is not available here. A small sample of the work, primarily theoretical, that has examined the theory of anomie must suffice. [For a thorough review of both theoretical and empirical studies on the subject of anomie, see Stephen Cole and Harriet Zuckerman (1964) in Marshall B. Clinard's *Anomie and Deviant Behavior* that presents a complete list and proper citations for each study in this area.]

When Merton's anomie theory specifically and strain theory in general are criticized, the criticism often begins with the charge that the theory, while appealing and interesting, is very difficult if not impossible to verify scientifically Vold, George B., & Bernard, Thomas J (1986). An examination of a few of the criticisms and the resultant extensions of Merton's theory include an article by Robert Dubin (1959), in which he suggests that Merton's adaptations must be expanded to fourteen. Dubin begins with a discussion of a difficulty associated with Merton's schematic presentation of innovation, which Merton diagrammed as an adaptation in which the individual accepted the cultural goals but rejected the institutionalized means. Dubin contends that the diagram of the adaptation is incorrect and that it should actually depict people who accept the cultural goals, reject the given institutionalized means, and substitute their own means, in this case usually illegitimate in nature. Dubin's examination innovation provides insight suggesting that Dubin is correct, and Merton's discussion of innovation logically supports the revision of the diagram. Once Dubin established this premise, he then divides innovation into behavioral innovation, which is Merton's original concept, and value innovation, which is Dubin's addition. Dubin also divides ritualism into behavioral ritualism, again Merton's original concept, and value ritualism, Dubin's addition. Once Dubin has completed this preliminary division, he expanded the modes of adaptation to six. Table 2 shows Dubin's first extension of Merton's modes of adaptation.

TABLE 2:

Mode of Adaptation	Cultural Goals	Institutionalized Means
Behavior innovation	+	+/−
Value innovation	+/−	+
Behavior ritualism	−	+
Value ritualism	+	−
Retreatism	−	−
Rebellion	+/−	+/−

+ = acceptance
− = rejection
+/− = rejection and substitution (active rejection)

(Dubin, R. 1959. Deviant behavior and social structure: continuities in social theory. *Am. Sociolog. Rev.* 24(2):148.)

From this first extension, Dubin continues by separating institutionalized norms from institutionalized means. Dubin acknowledges that Merton incorporated the distinction between norms and behavior in his typology, but did not introduce it in this extensive manner. Institutionalized norms are the "boundaries between prescribed behaviors and proscribed behaviors in a particular institutional setting" (Dubin 1959, 149). These norms set the parameters of legitimate behavior in a specific situation; outside the limits set by institutionalized norms is illegitimate behavior. Institutionalized means "are the specific behaviors, prescribed or potential that lie within the limits established by institutional norms" (Dubin 1959, 149) and are the actual behaviors of individuals. Incorporating institutional norms and means into his first extension of Merton's modes of adaptations, Dubin produces fourteen modes of adaptation, as shown in Table 3.

TABLE 3:

Type of Deviant Adaptation	Cultural Goals	Mode of Attachment to	
		Institutional Norms	Means
Behavioral innovation			
Institutional invention	+	+/−	+/−
Normative invention	+	+/−	+
Operating invention	+	+	+/−
Value innovation			
Intellectual invention	+/−	+	+
Organization invention	+/−	+/−	+
Social movement	+/−	+	+/−
Behavioral ritualism			
Leveling of aspirations	−	+	+
Institutional moralist	−	+	−
Organization automaton	−	−	+

Value ritualism			
Demagogue	+	−	−
Normative opportunist	+	−	+
Means opportunist	+	+	−
Retreatism	−	−	−
Rebellion	+/−	+/−	+/−

+ = acceptance
− = rejection
+/− = rejection and substitution (active rejection)

(Dubin, R. 1959. Deviant behavior and social structure: continuities in social theory. *Am. Sociolog. Rev.* 24(2):148.)

Drawing from all aspects of life, Dubin provides a number of examples of each of the extended categories in his model. Behavioral innovation is seen as a form of invention, a context he believes Merton ignores. As identified previously, behavioral innovations are generally viewed as constructive. Collective bargaining is an example of institutional invention, as are employer-supported health and welfare funds. Drag racing on controlled tracks represents a "normative invention . . . which gave to an already developed activity the moral sanction of legitimacy by surrounding it with an acceptable justification" (Dubin 1959, 152). Using Cohen's example of the wanton destructive behavior of gang members, Dubin posits that if the gang member has institutional norms that include internal competition and a need for the mutual interdependence of the members, the gang members' behavior can represent this adaptation.

There are numerous examples of the intellectual invention adaptation, one of which relates to the work of Sigmund Freud (Sigmund Freud chapter)—the subconscious, especially in Freud's analysis of the role of the subconscious in human behavior. Organization invention is exemplified in the development of the Air Force because the original Air Corps was unable to respond to the change in function created with the beginning of World War I. "Social movements are characterized by an active search for new cultural goals and modification of existing institutional means" (Dubin 1959, 156), for example, women's rights and the civil rights movement.

Dubin's adaptation of leveling of aspirations is the equivalent of Merton's adaptation of ritualism. The individual continues to accept the means but scales down his or her goals or, in Dubin's case, aspirations. The institutional moralist "centers his over-conforming behavior on the norms of the institution in which he acts" (Dubin 1959, 157). If the institutional moralist obtains an official position within an organization, this can give organizational legitimacy to his or her ritualistic viewpoints, for example, a clergyman or a labor executive. In the organization automaton adaptation, the individual, according to Dubin, is most likely to evidence anomic deviant behavior. Dubin cites the "barracks room lawyer whose text is Army Regulations" (1959, 158). The legitimacy of institutional means is the only thing that controls the range of behaviors for the organization automaton.

The demagogue makes use of society's strongly held beliefs in the cultural goals, and absolute priority of goals is their hallmark. Dubin cites the late Senator Joseph McCarthy, who draped himself him the flag and identified "Americanism" as the ultimate goal, as a demagogue.

The normative opportunist tends to reject temporarily the institutional norms that are of a limiting nature. When the crisis is over, the normative opportunist can return to conforming behavior. The means opportunist, however, temporarily rejects the institutional means in favor of illegitimate means, rationalizing that it is "for this one time only."

Dubin makes no substantive changes in the modes of adaptation of retreatism and rebellion, as outlined earlier in this chapter, and has been criticized for selectively expanding the adaptation categories originally developed by Merton. His answer to this criticism can be found in his 1959 article on the subject of expanded modes of adaptation. Dubin explains that he does not include the conformity adaptation because it is not a deviant adaptation, and he does not expand the adaptations of retreatism and rebellion because the norms and the means as proposed by Merton are in sync, obviating the need for expansion.

Richard Cloward, in an article published at the same time Dubin's, takes a very different approach to expanding Merton's work on anomie. Cloward attempts to merge two major theoretical approaches—the first represented by Durkheim's and Merton's work on anomie, and the second best evidenced by people like Sutherland and Shaw and McKay that has been called the differential association/cultural transmission approach.

From Durkheim's perspective, the individual in society has physical needs regulated by the organic structure and moral needs evidenced by social desires. According to Durkheim, nothing in an individual's make-up is capable of controlling social desires; therefore, laws are necessary so that individuals understand the acceptable limits of their behaviors. When the external sources controlling the individual are disrupted, their social desires are no longer kept in check, something Durkheim describes as a state of anomy and identifies three states in which anomy can exist. The first is created when a sudden depression occurs. When an individual is suddenly and usually without warning cast into a lower social stratum, adjustments are not easily made and anomy can result. The second is when there is sudden prosperity and the individual is thrust into a higher social stratum. The third state is an ongoing one and is brought on by rapid technological change. With the existence of vast unexplored markets and the developments that new technology brings, there are seemingly limitless possibilities. For Durkheim, the rapid changes of this sort result in a chronic state of anomie. Cloward adds Merton's work in this area to Durkheim's. To recap briefly, Merton's concept of anomie is a breakdown of the cultural structure that often occurs when there is a severe disjunction between goals and means.

Cloward is of the opinion that Durkheim and Merton addressed only one opportunity structure, the one that is legitimate. Cloward posits that just because people do not have access to the legitimate opportunity structure does not mean they automatically have access to the illegitimate opportunity structure. Access to the illegitimate opportunity structure is not freely available. The legitimate and illegitimate opportunity structures are separate and distinct. Anomie theory, specifically that of Merton, assumes that people, depending on their position in the social strata, have varying degrees of access to the legitimate opportunity structure. Cloward suggests that the same holds true for the illegitimate opportunity structure.

> The availability of illegitimate means . . . is controlled by various criteria in the same manner that has long been ascribed to conventional means. Both systems of opportunity are (1) limited, rather than infinitely available, and (2) differentially available depending on the location of persons in the social structure. (Cloward 1959, 168)

When Cloward uses the term *means,* whether legitimate or illegitimate, two things are assumed: (1) that there are learning structures to educate people as to the methods, and (2) that there are opportunity structures to discharge their role once they have learned the techniques. (For a more complete explanation and treatment of the work of Cloward and Ohlin and delinquency and opportunity theory, see Lloyd Ohlin chapter on Ohlin, with Cloward's comment.)

Robert Merton commented on both Dubin's and Cloward's work as it relates to the expansion of anomie theory. It is Merton's opinion that "[b]oth papers . . . move toward a more adequate sociological theory of deviant behavior" (1959, 177). What Dubin and Cloward are doing is in keeping with Merton's views on the development of sociological theory. For Merton, sociological theory proceeds in increments, building on what has come before. As individuals examine and test theory, they uncover gaps in the theory; the set of ideas is found to be not discriminating enough to deal with aspects of phenomena to which it should apply in principle. In some cases, it is proposed to fill the gap by further differentiation of concepts and propositions that are consistent with the earlier theory, which is regarded as demonstrably incomplete (Merton 1959, 177).

Merton views Dubin's and Cloward's work as theoretically sound and appropriate. He finds Dubin's work expansion of the deviant adaptations to be "sound in principle and productivity" (1959, 178), and also finds merit in developing the typology in light of the distinction between attitudes toward social norms and actual behavior. Merton's review of Dubin's work suggests that Dubin perhaps inadvertently helped develop the typology of conformity. "Although Dubin has undertaken to differentiate types of deviant behavior, it turns out that by implication, he begins also to differentiate important types of conforming behavior" (Merton 1959, 180). Although Merton identifies ambiguities based on the discrepancies between Dubin's explicit and implicit programs, Merton believes that they provide valuable direction for "inquiry into the relations between conforming and nonconforming behavior" (1959, 178). The distinction that Dubin makes, from Merton's perspective, is not between a norm and a behavior, but between the attitudes toward a norm and behavior. Dubin's effort is very different from that of Merton. The general focus of Dubin's work is the identification of subtypes of socially deviant adaptations. Cloward and Merton differ from Dubin in that they attempt to identify social and cultural conditions that cause different rates of deviant behavior for people in different social strata. For Cloward and Merton, the typology is intended to help reach this end, and is not the end in and of itself.

Merton finds his own work much more in tune with that of Cloward, who he perceives is interested in the sources of behavior. Although Merton focuses on illegitimate behavior as a result of pressure because of emphasis on cultural goals, Cloward raises the question of access to the illegitimate structure. (For a complete explanation and critique of access to the illegitimate opportunity structure, see Cloward's comments on Ohlin in Lloyd Ohlin chapter.)

More recently, Ivan Chapman, writing in the *Quarterly Journal of Ideology*, takes Merton to task for what Chapman calls the "social engineering" aspects of his development of adaptations. Chapman believes that the "prerogative assigned by Merton to culture in his paradigm" (1977, 14) is inadmissible. The question for Chapman is, if social action is made up of three elements—that is, person, society, and culture—"does the same one of these elements always have the prerogative of defining legitimate and normal social action?" (1977, 14). It is incorrect, Chapman says, to allow a single element to control social action in a permanent way. Chapman states that Merton's typology

violates and damages the social process of reciprocal interaction of the three major elements of social action. . . . This violation takes the form of a permanent domination of the person and other forms of social action by a single cultural construct elevated to the place of deity and given total defining power over social thought and action. (1977, p. 17)

Chapman uses a model based on Sorokin's interaction matrix that includes the person, society, and culture, and develops the following combinations:

1. Personal goals and personal means
2. Social goals and personal means
3. Cultural goals and personal means
4. Personal goals and social means
5. Social goals and social means
6. Cultural goals and social means
7. Personal goals and cultural means
8. Social goals and cultural means
9. Cultural goals and cultural means

A comparison of Merton's typology of cultural goals and cultural means represents only one of Chapman's combinations. For Chapman, the nine possible combinations represent normal social processes of interaction. Chapman concludes his critique of Merton's typology by stating, "Merton's modes of adaptation are modes of submission to modes of dominance" (1977, 18). Chapman's perspective is from an orientation entirely different from Merton's, and has the benefit of the development of conflict theory that did not exist as a theoretical orientation when Merton wrote *Social Theory and Social Structure*.

The examples of criticism and expansion of Merton's theory of anomie discussed here represent a microcosm of the literature on this subject. The materials cited are intended only as a demonstration of how Merton's theory has been received and responded to, and in no way are intended to suggest the full range of responses to his theory.

When Merton retired from his regular position as a faculty member of the Department of Sociology at Columbia University, he was still extraordinarily active as a scholar, researcher, and lecturer. Up until his death, he continued to write and publish at a pace that most young academicians would be proud of. On addressing the retirement of his friend and colleague Herbert Hyman, Merton said that when one retires, "[t]hen comes the joy of relaxed concentration—so different from the lesser joy of concentrated relaxation. There's nothing else quite like it" (Merton 1988, 175). It appears from Merton's activity that even in retirement, only when he was researching, writing, and publishing was he in a state of relaxed concentration.

References

Bierstedt, Robert. 1981. *Robert K. Merton. American sociological theory: A critical history*. New York: Academic Press.

Chapman, Ivan. 1977. A critique of Merton's typology of modes of individual adaptation. *Quart. J. Ideol.* 1:13–18.

Clinard, Marshall B. 1964. The theoretical implications of anomie and deviant behavior. In Marshall B. Clinard (Ed.), *Anomie and deviant behavior*. New York: The Free Press of Glencoe, pp. 1–56.

Cloward, Richard. 1959. Illegitimate means, anomie, and deviant behavior. *Am. Sociolog. Rev.* 24:164–76.

Cloward, Richard, and Lloyd E. Ohlin. 1960.*Delinquency and opportunity: A theory of delinquent gangs.* New York: The Free Press of Glencoe.

Cohen, Albert K. 1955. *Delinquent boys: The culture of the gang.* New York: The Free Press of Glencoe.

Cole, Stephen, and Harriet Zuckerman. 1964. Inventory of empirical and theoretical studies of anomie. In Marshall B. Clinard (Ed.), *Anomie and deviant behavior.* New York: The Free Press of Glencoe, pp. 243–314.

Conant, James B. 1947. *On understanding science.* New Haven, CT: Yale University Press.

Coser, Lewis A. (Ed.). 1975. Merton's uses of the European sociological tradition. In Lewis A. Coser (Ed.). *The idea of social structure: Papers in honor of Robert K. Merton.* New York: Harcourt Brace Jovanovich, pp. 85–102.

Dubin, Robert. 1959. Deviant behavior and social structure: Continuities in social theory. *Am. Sociolog. Rev.* 24:147–64.

Hunt, Morton M. 1961. Profiles: How does it come to be so? *New Yorker*, 36(Jan. 28):39–63.

Lazarsfeld, Paul F. 1975. Working with Merton. In Lewis A. Coser (Ed.), *The idea of social structure: Papers in honor of Robert K. Merton.* New York: Harcourt Brace Jovanovich, pp. 35–66.

Merton, Robert K. 1936. Civilization and culture. *Sociol. Soc. Res.* 21:103–13.

―――. 1936. The unanticipated consequences of purposive social action. *Am. Sociolog. Rev.* 1:894–904.

―――. 1938. Social structure and anomie. *Am Sociolog. Rev.* 3:672–82.

―――. 1945. Sociological theory. *Am. J. Sociol.* 50:462–73.

―――. 1948. The self-fulfilling prophecy. *Antioch Rev.* Summer:193–210.

―――. 1957. *Social theory and social structure.* New York: The Free Press of Glencoe.

―――. 1959. Social conformity, deviation, and opportunity-structures: A comment on the contributions of Dubin and Cloward. *Am. Sociolog. Rev.* 2(2):177–88.

―――. 1961. Social problems and sociological theory. In Robert K. Merton and Robert A. Nisbet (Eds.), *Contemporary social problems.* New York: Harcourt, Brace and World.

―――. 1964. Anomie, anomia, and social interaction: Contexts of deviant behavior. In Marshall B. Clinard (Ed.), *Anomie and deviant behavior.* New York: The Free Press of Glencoe, pp. 213–42.

―――. 1967. *On theoretical sociology: Five essays old and new.* (Rev. Ed.). New York: The Free Press of Glencoe.

―――. 1968. *Social theory and social structure.* New York: The Free Press of Glencoe.

―――. 1980. Remembering the young Talcott Parsons. *Am. Sociol.* 15:68–71.

―――. 1981. Our sociological vernacular. *Columbia Mag. Columbia Uni.* November:42–44

―――. 1988. Reference groups, invisible colleges and deviant behavior in science. In Hurbert J. O'Gorman (Ed.), *Surveying social life: Papers in honor of Herbert H. Hyman.* Middletown, CT: Wesleyan University Press.

Miles, Mary Wilson. 1975. The writings of Robert K. Merton: A bibliography. In Lewis A. Coser (Ed.). *The idea of social structure: papers in honor of Robert K. Merton.* New York: Harcourt Brace Jovanovich, pp. 497–522.

Persell, Caroline H. 1984. An interview with Robert K. Merton. *Teach. Soc.* 11(4):355–86.

Sills, David L. 1987. Paul F. Lazarsfeld: 1901–1976. *Biographical memoirs*, Vol. 56. Washington, D.C.: The National Academy Press.

Srole, L. 1956. Social integration and certain corollaries: An exploratory study. *Am. Sociolog. Rev.* 21: 709-716.

Vold, George B. and Thomas J. Bernard. 1986. *Theoretical criminology.* 3rd ed. New York: Oxford University Press.

Williams, Frank P., and Marilyn D. McShane. 1988. *Criminological theory.* Englewood Cliffs, NJ: Prentice Hall.

Supplemental Readings

Abraham, Gary A. 1983. Misunderstanding the Merton thesis: A boundary dispute between history and sociology. *ISIS.* 74:368–87.

Campbell, Colin. 1982. A dubious distinction? An inquiry into the value and use of Merton's concepts of manifest and latent function. *Am. Sociolog. Rev.* 47:29–44.

Caplovitz, David. 1977. Review symposium of the ideas of social structure: Papers in honor of Robert K. Merton. *Contemp. Soc.* 6(2):142–50.

Coleman, James S. n.d. *Robert K. Merton as teacher.* Unpublished manuscript.

Cooper, Adam, and Jessica Cooper (Eds.). 1985. Robert K. Merton. *The social science encyclopedia.* London: Routledge and Kegan Paul, pp. 522–23.

Coser, Lewis A., and Robert Nisbet. 1975. Merton and the contemporary mind: an affectionate dialogue. In Lewis A. Coser (Ed.). *The idea of social structure: Papers in honor of Robert K. Merton.* New York: Harcourt Brace Jovanovich, pp. 3–10.

Cullen, Francis T. 1988. Were Cloward and Ohlin strain theorists? Delinquency and opportunity revisited. *J. Res. Crime Delinq.* 25(3):214–41.

Cullen, Francis T., and Steven F. Messner. 1987. The making of criminology revisited: An interview with Robert K. Merton. Unpublished manuscript presented at the American Society of Criminology meetings, Montreal, Canada.

Evory, Ann (Ed.). 1974. Merton, Robert K(ing) 1910—*Contemporary authors*, Vol. 41–44. Detroit: Gale Research Co.

Garfield, Eugene. 1977. Robert K. Merton: Among the giants. *Curr. Comm.* 28:5–7.

———. 1983. Robert K. Merton—author and editor extraordinare. Part I. *Curr. Comm.* 39:5–11.

———. 1983a. Robert K. Merton—author and editor extraordinare. Part II. *Curr. Comm.* 40:5–15.

Merton, Robert K. 1934. Recent French sociology. *Soc. Forces.* 12:537–45.

———. 1934. Durkheim's division of labor in society. *Am. J. Soc.* 40:319–28.

———. 1935. Fluctuations in the rate of industrial invention. *Quart. J. Econ.* 49:454–70.

———. 1936. Civilization and culture. *Sociol. Soc. Res.* 21:103–13.

———. 1936. Puritanism, pietism and science. *Sociolog. Rev.* 28:1–30.

———. 1936. The unanticipated consequences of purposive social action. *Am. Sociolog. Rev.* 1:894–904.

———. 1937. The sociology of knowledge. *ISIS.* 27:493–503.

———. 1938. Science and the social order. *Philos. Sci.* 5:321–27.

———. 1938. Social structure and anomie. *Am. Sociolog. Rev.* 3:672–82.

———. 1939. Bureaucratic structure and personality. *Soc. Forces.* 18:560–68.

———. 1945. Sociological theory. *Am. J. Sociol.* 50:462–73.

———. 1948. The bearing of empirical research upon the development of sociological theory. *Am. Sociolog. Rev.* 13:505–15.

———. 1948. The self-fulfilling prophecy. *Antioch Rev.* Summer:193–210.

———. 1948. The position of sociological theory. *Am. Sociolog. Rev.* 13:64–168.

———. 1949. Social structure and anomie: Revisions and extensions. In Ruth N. Anshen (Ed.), *The family: Its function and destiny.* New York: Harper and Brothers, pp. 226–57.

———. 1949. *Social theory and social structure.* New York: The Free Press.

———. 1965. *On the shoulders of giants: A Shandean postscript.* New York: The Free Press.

———. 1967. *On theoretical sociology: Five essays, old and new.* New York: The Free Press.

———. 1976. *Sociological ambivalence and other essays.* New York: The Free Press.

———. 1980. Remembering the young Talcott Parsons. *Am. Sociolog.* 15:68–71.

———. 1982. Alvin W. Gouldner: Genesis and growth of a friendship. *Theory Soc.* 11:915–38.

———. 1983. Florian Znaniecki: A short reminiscence. *J. Hist. Behav. Sci.* 10:123–26.

————. 1985. George Sarton: Episodic recollections by an unruly apprentice. *ISIS*. 76:470–86.

Merton, Robert K., Leonard Broom, and Leonard S. Cottrell, Jr. 1959. *Sociology today: Problems and prospects*. New York: Basic Books.

Merton, Robert K., James Coleman, and Peter H. Rossi. 1979. *Qualitative and quantitative social research: Papers in honor of Paul F. Lazarsfeld*. New York: The Free Press.

Merton, Robert K., Marjorie Fiske, and Patricia L. Kendall. 1956. *The focused interview*. New York: The Free Press.

Merton, Robert K., and Patricia L. Kendall. 1944. The boomerang response. *Channels, Natl. Publ. Counc. Health Welfare Serv.* 21:1–7.

————. 1946. The focused interview. *Am. J. Sociol.* 51:541–57.

Merton, Robert K., and Paul F. Lazarsfeld (Eds.). 1950. *Continuities in social research: Studies in the scope and method of "The American Soldier."* New York: The Free Press.

Merton, Robert K., and M. F. Ashley Montagu. 1939. Crime and the anthropologist. *Am. Anthropol.* 42:384–408.

Merton, Robert K., and Robert A. Nisbet. 1961. *Contemporary social problems*. New York: Harcourt Brace Jovanovich.

————. 1966. *Contemporary social problems*. 2nd ed. New York: Harcourt Brace Jovanovich.

————. 1971. *Contemporary social problems*. 3rd ed. New York: Harcourt Brace Jovanovich.

————. 1976. *Contemporary social problems*. 4th ed. New York: Harcourt Brace Jovanovich.

Merton, Robert K., and Pitirim A. Sorokin. 1937. Social time: A methodological and functional analysis. *Am. J. Sociol.* 42:615–29.

Parsons, Talcott. 1951. *The social system*. New York: The Free Press of Glencoe.

Ritzer, George. 1983. *Sociological theory*. New York: Alfred Knopf.

Sztompka, Piotr. 1986. *Robert K. Merton: An intellectual profile*. London: Macmillan Education Ltd.

CHAPTER 10
ALBERT KIRCIDEL COHEN:
B. 1918

I. BIOGRAPHICAL SKETCH

Albert Kircidel Cohen was born in Boston on June 15, 1918, and represents one of criminology's more contemporary pioneers and, because he remained active as a writer and university professor into his senior years, he has seen the intellectual shifts from the late 1930s until the present. He represents, perhaps more so than others discussed in this book, a modern-day synthesizer of the works of a number of earlier pioneers with whom he was directly associated, as is clear in his ability to unite both environmental and personal explanations of crime and deviance.

With only a few exceptions, Cohen, as with most of our pioneers, spent the greater part of his life in university towns. However, unlike, for example, Robert Park or William Sheldon, Cohen was apparently not inclined to be a migratory scholar. For most of his life, he remained in the immediate Massachusetts or Connecticut areas, or in Bloomington, Indiana, all areas closely associated with university life.

Having spent his early youth in the Boston area, Cohen completed undergraduate education at Harvard in 1939 at twenty-one years old. It is a reasonable assumption that he was influenced by several prominent Harvard sociology scholars of the day, including Talcott Parsons and Pitirim Sorokin, both of whom published works instrumental to the development of criminological thought in the mid-1930s. It is also likely that while Cohen was an undergraduate student at Harvard he first became acquainted with Robert K. Merton, a young instructor at the time in the department of sociology.

Although Cohen was later to return to Boston, he chose Indiana University in Bloomington for early graduate training. Three years after receiving the bachelor's degree from Harvard, Cohen graduated with a master's degree in sociology. While at Indiana University, Cohen came under the tutelage of Edwin H. Sutherland, another pioneer in criminology who, like Parsons and others at Harvard, had substantial impact on Cohen's later writing as a sociologist.

At age twenty-four and with a master's degree in hand, Cohen worked for a brief period as Director of Orientation at the Indiana Boys' School in Plainfield. It is not clear what attracted Cohen to work in a correctional institution for youth; however, it is likely that while there, his thinking was further shaped regarding the cultural background of delinquent youth, which he was later to write about so eloquently.

During this period, the United States was actively engaged in World War II, and between 1942 until shortly after the end of the war in 1946, Cohen interrupted his work and further graduate study to serve in the Chemical Warfare Service in the Army, where he reached the rank of First Lieutenant. On occasion, Cohen draws on his military experience to provide examples of group conduct and deviance (1965, 78–79).

The period immediately following the war was a most active time for graduate education throughout the nation as millions of troops returned home eager to get on with their lives and careers. There is some truth to the suggestion that the early 1950s was a golden era for education, as the returning students hit the books and classrooms with unforeseen gusto, and Cohen was one of the many modern scholars in sociology that appeared as an outgrowth of this wartime cohort. He returned to Harvard, where he enrolled in the doctoral program in sociology. He received his Ph.D. in sociology from Harvard in 1951 with an unpublished dissertation entitled *Juvenile Delinquency and the Social Structure*. There is little doubt that Cohen's later book, *Delinquent Boys: The Culture of the Gang* (1955), was a direct byproduct of his early writing. In addition, an occasional excerpt from the dissertation appeared in various anthologies or articles (e.g., Wolfgang, Savitz, and Johnston 1962). Nonetheless, the 1955 work on delinquent boys established Cohen permanently as a major figure in sociology and subsequently in criminological thought.

Cohen returned to the University of Indiana in 1947 as an instructor in sociology even prior to receiving his Ph.D. from Harvard. He eventually attained the academic rank of professor of sociology, remaining at Indiana University for eighteen years. In 1965, at forty-seven, Cohen returned to the New England area, this time to Storrs, where he spent more than two decades as a professor of sociology at the University of Connecticut. He continued an already rather prolific career as a writer, and most of his more notable works built on his long-time association with juvenile delinquency and sociological theories of deviance.

Although he considered Indiana University and the University of Connecticut to be his home-base institutions, Cohen contributed to a variety of other institutions from the mid-1970s onward. For example, in 1960 and 1961, he was a visiting professor at the University of California at Berkeley. Immediately thereafter, from 1961 to 1962, he was designated a Fellow of the Center for Advanced Study in Behavioral Sciences at Stanford, California. In addition, from 1968 to 1969, he was a visiting professor at the University of California at Santa Cruz, and from 1972 to 1973, he was a visiting professor at the Institute of Criminology, Cambridge, England. Consequently, in his more senior years, he compensated for the stationary posts he held all the years at Indiana University and in Connecticut.

Cohen was the editor of the *American Sociological Review* in 1967, and was the president of the Society for Study of Social Problems from 1970 to 1971. Although his stature as a pioneer in criminological thought stems primarily from his seminal work on the culture of the gang, later scholarly writings addressed social problems of the university (1973); the concept of criminal organization (1977); and, more recently, delinquency patterns in Asia Tokuoka, Hideo, & Albert K. Cohen (1987). In 1987, he received a Senior Fulbright Award to the Philippines, where he continued to study and lecture on patterns of delinquent behavior.

II. BASIC ASSUMPTIONS

It makes common sense to assume that the basic assumptions underlying the works of our more contemporary pioneers would extend over a wider range of ideas and of years than those of eighteenth- and nineteenth-century writers. For example, whereas Durkheim's work was shaped in part by the novel scientific method emerging during his day, the more-modern scholars such as Cohen most likely take such methodology as a given. Furthermore, in the field of criminology, the work and ideas of the more-modern scholars have been built on the products of earlier pioneers and contemporaries alike.

Because he was heavily influenced by both sociological and psychological perspectives of behavior causation, Cohen represents a clear example of a recent synthesis of divergent philosophies and methods. Furthermore, from a methodological point of view, his writings demonstrate that the naturalistic field studies, making up much of social science in the 1930s and 1940s, had major impact on his thinking. Four earlier intellectual traditions converge in Cohen's work: human ecology, learning theory, psychology, and anomie theory.

HUMAN ECOLOGY

Although as a student Cohen did not benefit from direct classroom contact with the early scholars at the University of Chicago, he draws heavily on their research and theoretical viewpoints, particularly concerning human ecology. Cohen's writing on the culture of delinquent youth directly integrates the human ecological research of Shaw and McKay, whom he liberally quotes (e.g., Cohen 1955, 185, 187). It was Robert Park, Ernest Burgess, and Shaw and McKay who helped paved the way for Cohen to write, twenty-five years later, of a subculture of delinquency. Cohen expanded on these early ecologists by analyzing the competitive relationship between different social levels, especially between the middle and working classes, that give rise to differently oriented youth.

It is also fitting that Cohen embraces the works of Frederick Thrasher, who, as a student of Park and Burgess at the University of Chicago, studied the ecological distribution of delinquent gangs (Thrasher 1927, cf. Cohen 1955, 27–28). Moreover, William Foote Whyte's (1943) celebrated research into the social organization of a lower-class Boston neighborhood clearly helped direct Cohen's thinking of delinquent subcultures of urban males (Cohen 1955, 104–5), and it is probable they crossed paths as students at Harvard University.

LEARNING THEORY

Given Cohen's likely association with sociologists Talcott Parsons, Pitirim Sorokin, and George Homans at Harvard, as well as Edwin Sutherland at Indiana University, it is not surprising that he followed in the tradition of learning theory. His writing suggests that he accepts the basic premise that one's behavior forms primarily because of direct interaction with the social environment—that is, an individual's behavior is fashioned through interaction with persons with whom one associates from an early age. Culture is thus transmitted to another through the process of interaction. Various symbols, including language patterns, are learned as part of one's culture. As Sutherland's colleague, Cohen was predictably well acquainted with principles of differential association that were, in fact, extensions of cultural transmission theory discussed earlier by George Herbert Mead and Shaw and McKay, among others, at the University of Chicago (see Cohen 1955, 181).

PSYCHOLOGY

Few sociologists or criminologists have risked trying to integrate conceptual schemes of psychology directly with the more straightforward and safer cultural transmission theory. Against this general trend, Cohen's research on the culture of delinquent boys boldly unites the contrasting perspectives. He succinctly compares cultural transmission theory with psychology's concept of inborn aggressive (i.e., criminal) tendencies and comes up with a third alternative—that delinquency may also be a symptom of an individual who is subconsciously trying to cope with some underlying social problem.

ANOMIE THEORY

Cohen's development of delinquent subcultures, and especially his conclusions regarding the culture of working-class boys, links directly with earlier Chicago School themes and with Merton's early work on anomie theory, as shown most clearly when Cohen addresses the question of how working-class boys might adapt to frustrations resulting from the inability to compete successfully with middle-class boys in the school setting. Cohen no doubt was influenced directly by Merton's earliest work on anomie (1938) as well as by his larger volume, *Social Theory and Social Structure* (1949). It is clear that Merton also detected the theoretical connection between his work and Cohen's. The second edition of Merton's 1949 volume incorporates portions of Cohen's writings on delinquent boys (Merton 1957, 177–79). In addition, in 1965, ten years after the publication of *Delinquent Boys: The Culture of the Gang* (1955), Cohen published a lengthy essay on anomie theory that provides insights into the directions of strain theory as well as suggestions as to how his own work fit into Merton's conceptual scheme.

III. KEY IDEAS

By the time Cohen began his doctoral work, and certainly by the late 1940s and early 1950s, most of the major theoretical ideas in the sociology of deviance and criminology were already posited, at least in rough form. The task remained for scholars to refine the work of others or to rearrange earlier ideas in novel ways in order to better explain and cope with modern issues in criminology. Cohen was well suited in time and place to integrate the work of his predecessors who had already helped shape the basic philosophical assumptions underlying his approach to sociology and criminology. Four of Cohen's key ideas—the theory of subcultures, delinquent gangs, the middle class, and theoretical refinements—deserve special comment.

THEORY OF SUBCULTURES

Cohen is remembered primarily for his writings on juvenile delinquency, especially for *Delinquent Boys: The Culture of the Gang* (1955), which provides the reader not only with Cohen's specific explanation for the existence of delinquent gangs, but also with a more general theory of subcultures. A careful reading of the book reveals that Cohen was concerned with deviance generally, not just with juvenile delinquency. Furthermore, he was fascinated by the broader question of behavior causation and the various links between social structure and individual cultural patterns.

Cohen clearly borrows from his mentors and early scholars to construct a straightforward and coherent statement on the nature of subcultures. His own writing is remarkably unpretentious and jargon-free. Thus, further simplification or description of his already precise summation is difficult. Nevertheless, his comments on "subcultures" tend to fall into five categories: prevalence, origins, process, purpose, and problem (Cohen 1955, 49–72).

Prevalence

Before Cohen discusses a theory of subcultures, he spends considerable time outlining the state of research regarding the prevalence and distribution of delinquency across the nation. He is concerned with determining if delinquency emerges more from the working-class than from the middle-class sector of society. This question, still confronting researchers today, is discussed at length in Cohen's work. Cohen acknowledges that juvenile delinquency arises in all social strata. Nonetheless, based on available data in the early 1950s, he reasoned that poor regions of the city and nation were more delinquency prone. Such a conclusion was logical given the situational and ecological features prevalent in poor areas that were conducive to deviance according to Chicago School advocates—that is, there are clear reasons why we would expect the poorer segments of society to be represented as more deviant and norm-breaking than we would the more prosperous segments. Such a conclusion rests directly on the human ecological foundations posited first by Thrasher (1927), and later by Whyte (1937) and Shaw and McKay (1942).

To Cohen, there was little question that delinquency was not distributed randomly throughout the nation. In addition, the fact that delinquent areas tended to be more prevalent in zones of transition was more than a consequence of a biased justice system targeting poor regions. People at the lower end of the socioeconomic scale simply had a more pressing motivation to commit delinquent acts than their less-oppressed counterparts.

Following in the traditions of Durkheim and Merton, Cohen concluded that some groups were more stress ridden and anomic than others. Accordingly, he adhered to a social-strain or structural model in theorizing about the nature of delinquency—that is, the social system in which an individual was located influenced him or her to deviate or not to deviate.

Origins

Understanding why subcultures evolve in the first place is obviously important to a full understanding of their nature. Cohen argues that all human action may be viewed as an ongoing series of efforts to solve problems. He assumes that the world, beset on all sides with conflicts of one sort or another and characterized by a continuous struggle for survival, shows his acceptance of socioecological presuppositions. Every human social act may be seen as involving a conscious decision aimed at responding to some task. Such tasks may range from the near innocuous, like deciding how much sugar to put in coffee or which tie to wear, to more problematic tasks involving career-goal decisions. Many of the problems confronting humans are solved quickly and efficiently with little conscious efforts, whereas others may involve varying amounts of distress or anxiety; yet others persist, nag, and press for novel solutions (Cohen 1955, 50).

To Cohen, all social problems may be seen in the context of interaction between an actor's frame of reference and the situation confronting the actor. The frame of reference is composed of preconceptions, goals, aspirations, stereotypes, and personality attributes. Such individual cultural and personality features operate within situational environments that include natural surroundings, finite time and energy, and other individuals. Cohen contends that a solution to problems may require altering one's frame of reference (i.e., changing one's point of view), such as deciding a particular goal is not feasible, whereas other solutions may require more direct interaction with the outside world.

According to Cohen, we are all faced with pressures to conform to the standards and expectations of the larger group or society, a basic problem confronting all humans. Conformity reaps its own reward in the form of acceptance, recognition, and respect. Experiencing social approval is better than experiencing social disapproval; consequently, it is logical to presume that human groups strive toward an achievement of group consensus. However, given the fact that people are different from one another, entry into the larger group is not always easy or smooth. If an individual finds assimilation into a larger and dominant culture problematic, he or she may search for alternate routes to the desired recognition and respect. Such a new quest is made easier if one associates with others who are experiencing similar rejection. As individuals experiencing similar stress congregate, new subcultures emerge.

Process

Cohen wonders how it is possible for subcultures to emerge while each of the participants in the culture is so powerfully motivated to conform to what is already established. As noted, a critical condition for the emergence of new cultural forms is the existence of a number of actors with similar problems of adjustment. Before a new group is actually configured, the members must learn that their withdrawal from the traditions of the larger group will be met with at least a modicum of approval and support. Cohen writes, "But how does one know whether a gesture toward innovation will strike a responsive and sympathetic chord in others or whether it will elicit hostility?" (Cohen 1955, 60). Cohen theorizes that an actor tests the waters by a series of minute exploratory gestures. "By a casual, semi-serious, non-committal or tangential remark I may stick my neck out just a little way, but I will quickly withdraw it unless you by some sign of affirmation stick yours out" (Cohen 1955, 61).

Social deviance is thus produced primarily through successions of trials and errors by multiple actors each demonstrating a nearly imperceptible amount of rule bending. The final product may, indeed, differ from the original pattern of any single actor. Nonetheless, a new cultural process or subculture evolves through such incremental postures and represents a blend of similar but diverse actors.

Cohen suggests the process is one of mutual conversion, in which the initial motivation to deviate is as much or more a result of the response of others as it is a response to some felt need within ourselves. Gaining support from others is necessary in order to accept our own definition of self as a rule-breaker. Cohen provides analogies of such social conversion or "mass psychoneurosis" by drawing on his own experience in World War II, when soldiers would occasionally break away from the larger company if they perceived they had the mutual support of others (Cohen 1955, 61–62). The influence of earlier social interactionist theorists on Cohen is detectable at this point (see particularly Mead 1934, Sutherland 1947, and Thomas 1909). The formation of subcultures is closely likened to crowd behavior, and even to mob-action. However, such collective outbursts as means of problem solving are short lived. Subcultures, once established, tend to persist over time.

Purpose

The reason for the existence of a subculture must be that, through the solving of particular problems by the collective, the individual survives more efficiently—that is, the subculture allows the individual to derive psychological benefits of recognition and respect. Consequently, the member of the subculture gains in self-esteem and in social status. Cohen emphasizes the importance of group status, and only through a continuing process of positive reinforcement does the status remain intact. At this point, Cohen includes numerous subcultures in his theory, including religious sects, political extremist groups, and delinquent gangs.

Problem

As subcultures evolve and increase in status, they necessarily pull farther away from the original group or culture. Consequently, relationships between the new and old cultures are as pronounced as ever. Because no group can live entirely unto itself, and must at least on occasion rely on interaction outside the group, collision courses inevitably appear. Members of the new culture find they must repudiate outsiders if they are to continue to justify their own deviation specified when the new group was formed. Cohen says:

> The new subculture of the community of innovators comes to include hostile and contemptuous images of those groups whose enmity they have earned. Indeed, this repudiation of outsiders, necessary in order to protect oneself from feeling concerned about what they may think, may go so far as to make nonconformity with the expectations of the outsiders a positive criteria of status within the group. Certain kinds of conduct . . . become reputable precisely because they are disreputable in the eyes of the out-group. (1955, 68)

Thus the establishment of subcultures, itself a normal process, must necessarily generate a heightened sense of conflict between cultures (i.e., subcultural conflict).

DELINQUENT GANGS

Whereas Cohen outlines a general theory of subcultures, the bulk of his work pertains to a specific subculture—the delinquent gang. The prevalence of youthful gangs in metropolitan centers of the United States had been known for decades before Cohen published *Delinquent Boys*. However, with his work, a detailed explanation was set forth providing a comprehensive explanation of such gangs. It had been generally accepted by researchers, including Cohen, that deviance and lawbreaking persisted in all social classes. It was also accepted that the nature of deviance and crime differed from one class to another. Certainly upper-class youth engaged in delinquency, but not of the same type or in the same manner as that engaged in by lower-class youth. It appears, for example, that working-class boys are more likely to engage in lawbreaking as an offshoot of organized gang behavior than are their middle- and upper-class counterparts.

Cohen uses his theory of subcultures to account for the formation of male working-class gangs. Regarding the culture of the gang, three features must be addressed: class differences, the middle-class measuring rod, and adaptation to status frustration.

Class Differences

Although Cohen was describing and analyzing American cultures from a post–World War II, early 1950s vantage point, his reasoning as to differences between the middle and working classes continues to be widely quoted. Cohen argues that middle- and lower-class children are reared in different cultures that stress contrasting values and lifestyles. At least nine different aspects of social life were outlined by Cohen in comparing youth from the two distinct social classes (Table 1).

TABLE 1: Contrasting Patterns of Socialization Between Middle-
and Working-Class Boys

Cultural Trait	Middle Class	Lower Class
Drive and ambition	High	Low
Individual responsibility	High	Low
Success in the classroom	High	Low
Deferred gratification	High	Low
Long-range planning	High	Low
Cultivation of etiquette	High	Low
Nonviolence	High	Low
Wholesome leisure activity	High	Low
Respect for property	High	Low

Drive and Ambition   On the surface, it seems unusual to presume that one social class would possess more ambition than another. In the short run, especially with regard to daily desires, various classes may not greatly differ. However, Cohen refers in this case to the long-term aspiration, characteristic of middle-class children, to "make something of themselves." This might have been best illustrated in the early 1950s by the small child already saving nickels from a weekly allowance for a college education. Drive and ambition is more clearly associated with what Merton referred to as the "American Dream" (1949, 136, 137). Cohen flatly considered ambition a middle-class virtue, and its absence a defect and a sign of maladjustment (1955, 88).

Individual Responsibility   Although it sounds contrary to ideals embodied in the concept of community, Cohen finds that the middle-class youngster is taught to strive for independence. Such an aspiration is part of the longer-range goal of ultimately leaving home, or of going out after high school to seek one's fortune. Such an ethic of individual responsibility applauds resourcefulness and self-reliance. At this point, one can see Cohen's evolving argument that middle-class children develop a distaste for near total dependence on peer groups or gangs. Responsibility for self is seen as even more pressing than helping others.

> Although middle-class society recognizes, as does every society, a certain virtue in generosity, it minimizes the obligation to share with others, even with one's own kin, especially insofar as this obligation is likely to interfere with the achievement of one's own goals. If one's first obligation is to help, spontaneously and unstintingly, friends and kinsmen in distress, a kind of minimum security is provided for all, but nobody is likely to get very far ahead of the game. (Cohen 1955, 89)

Success in the Classroom   The middle-class culture stresses the cultivation of skills, especially those that might better enable the individual to achieve later occupational rewards. For this reason, emphasis is given to academic achievement even at a very early age. Cohen acknowledges athletic skill as an admired trait, but notes that academic advancement is placed on a high plateau.

Deferred Gratification   Middle-class youth, Cohen contends, are conditioned to subordinate temptations of immediate satisfaction and self-indulgence in favor of emphasis on the careful planning of long-term objectives. The working class, however, is more likely to stress living for the moment under the adage "Eat, drink, and be merry, for tomorrow you may die," perhaps because daily survival is usually more of an issue to the working-class child.

Long-Range Planning   The middle-class child must not only defer gratification, but must also be taught rationality. Nothing can be left up to chance, certainly not when the stakes are one's own life goals. Thus, great care must be given the "conscious planning, budgeting of time, and the allocation of resources in the most economic way" (Cohen 1955, 90). Planning for college when one is in junior high school would be a good example of rational long-range planning.

Cultivation of Etiquette   Cohen makes it clear that the definition, possession, and cultivation of manners, courtesy, and personality are oriented around social class. The middle-class child grows up in a world where a mastery of numerous norms of etiquette is of crucial importance. It is felt that a deep understanding of the social graces is necessary if one is to get along with people, on the job and off. Making friends and influencing people becomes an important aspect of long-range goals, and demands the acquiring of etiquette skills along with the development of patience and self-control. Armed with manners and good grooming, the middle-class child could best present himself or herself to friend or stranger.

Nonviolence   Control of physical aggression accompanies courtesy and personality, Cohen points out. Showing aggression corrupts proper social relationships, and also disallows an emphasis on other, more proper, forms of competition—those involving intellectual and social skills. The assumption that the pen is mightier than the sword then becomes a middle-class tenet.

Wholesome Leisure Activity   To the middle class, Cohen says, leisure time should be used wisely and constructively. Rather than the haphazard kicking of a ball in the street, emphasis is placed on the development of skills that may have longer-range payoffs, as is the acquisition of specialized knowledge. Accordingly, Cohen states, middle-class youth pursue "hobbies" of one kind or another more so than do working-class youth.

Respect for Property   Respect for property is a middle-class feature that pertains to the goal of individual responsibility. Being responsible in a socioeconomic world, especially if one accepts the traits already enumerated, logically requires the ability to distinguish and respect another's property. The middle-class culture lends itself well to this value, because children are typically reared in a home where objects of one's labor are relatively numerous and prominent and are things to be cherished. Cohen writes:

> The middle-class home is, to a great extent, a carefully ordered museum of artifacts for display, representing a great deal of "congealed labor." Their function for conspicuous consumption depends upon the preservation of their original state and upon ready recognition of their value, and the middle-class children are trained to respect such objects and the order in which they have been lovingly arranged. (Cohen 1955, 93)

Middle-Class Measuring Rod

The middle-class child internalizes the nine cultural features outlined in Table 1. It is not so much a conscious effort as a simple mimicry of models set by the child's immediate social milieu. The working-class child has a more difficult time of it. Day-to-day problems often pertain to economic survival. Long-range goals receive less attention, and apply only marginally to developing and polishing skills of etiquette. Street life generally acquires more consequence than the organized wholesome use of leisure time associated with the middle classes. In the late 1940s and early 1950s, for example, opportunities to join Little League baseball groups or the Boy Scouts were fairly exclusively left to middle-class youth.

According to Cohen, the working-class boy found himself ill-prepared to compete on the same footing as the middle-class boy. This might have been less of a dilemma if the two factions had remained in separate worlds. However, the United States, and certainly its urban centers, is a country characterized by extreme transience. People of all ages were on the move. Walter Reckless, writing about the same time as Cohen, recalls that mobility was in the form of ideas as well as of geographic movements (1950, 43–66). Thus the working-class youth, although situated within a different cultural system, was at the same time thrust intermittently into the realm of the middle class.

Nowhere was this so evident as in the public school system, where both cultures necessarily congregated. Middle-class culture was the prevailing culture of 1950s society. Certainly, as Cohen relates, the school system remained entrenched in middle-class values and social networks. School boards were middle class, as were principals and teachers. Textbooks remained directed toward middle-class cultural models. School success logically entailed the ability to accept and to maintain middle-class values and aspirations. Student progress was gauged according to middle-class standards.

Working-class youth had to compete with middle-class boys according to a middle-class measuring rod. The former were ill-equipped to compete on such biased foundations. It should come as no surprise that working-class boys suffered a loss of status in groups of mixed social class. Frustrated expectations led to status loss and to diminished self-esteem.

Adaptation to Status Frustration

A number of options remain open to the working-class boy suffering loss of status and self-esteem. Discussion of how the working class adapts to such hard times is perhaps the most memorable aspect of Cohen's theoretical statements. Three distinct alternatives are offered.

First is the "college-boy" route of upward mobility. Even with the difficulty brought about by the clash of cultures, some working-class boys pursue a middle-class goal embarking on college careers. This route is taken against almost impossible odds. Success likely requires divorcing themselves from working-class associations, and riding the fence between the two classes while attempting to meet expectations of both results in extreme frustration. Cohen also notes:

> It is hard at best to be a college-boy. . . . It entails great effort and sacrifice to the degree that one has been indoctrinated in what we have described as the working-class socialization process; its rewards are frequently long-deferred; and for many working-class boys it makes demands which they are, in consequence of their inferior linguistic, academic and social skills, not likely ever to meet.

Nevertheless, a certain portion of working-class boys accept the challenge of the middle-class status system and play the status game by middle-class rules. (1955, 128)

Cohen does not offer statistical proportions as to the size of college-boy responses. Also, he admits the reasons some choose one route over another remain obscure. Having spent a number of years as a colleague to Sutherland, it is likely Cohen's thinking was in part shaped by differential association theory (see Edwin Sutherland chapter). A second adaptation to status frustration felt by the working-class youth is the "corner-boy" response. Borrowing somewhat from Whyte's *Street Corner Society* (1943), Cohen describes how a substantial number of youth adapt by socially withdrawing from close association with middle-class representatives. Such a response places the working-class boy in a relatively stable position. He simply declines to compete, and resorts to gaining social support from similarly situated peers. They do not rid themselves entirely of stress, because they realize the outside world is basically middle class. They find shelter and solace among the clusters of youth hanging out on the neighborhood corner. The youth who adopts this form of response appears similar to Merton's "ritualist," who adapts to anomie by choosing not to compete for the American Dream, but who at the same time does not radically deviate from the legitimate means of getting along in society. That is, the "corner boy" would not typically be an "innovator" of illegal behavior; he simply finds more comfort not with middle-class youth, and relegates himself to more passive and stable working-class aspirations. The corner-boy response "represents a preference for the familiar, with its known satisfactions and its known imperfections, over the risks and uncertainties as well as the moral costs of the college-boy response" (Cohen 1955, 129).

Third, a working-class boy may adapt by resorting to membership in a delinquent subculture or gang. Cohen emphatically states that the delinquent subculture represents the explicit and wholesale repudiation of middle-class standards and the adaptation of their antithesis. As a member of a delinquent gang, the working-class boy may gain a heightened sense of social status. In the gang, the youth is provided the recognition and approval not available in direct confrontation with the middle class. The delinquent gang response reflects a more severe break with middle-class values and indeed, incorporates deviant and law-breaking activity.

Cohen reports that the delinquent response embraces three behavior features far removed from middle-class orientations, including negativistic, malicious, and nonutilitarian behavioral patterns that openly contest middle-class values. The behavior of the delinquent subculture is not just different from the middle class; it is the opposite of it. Thus, Cohen suggests,

It would appear at least plausible that the delinquent subculture is defined by its negative polarity to middle-class norms. That is, the delinquent subculture takes its norms from the larger culture but turns them upside-down. The delinquent's conduct is right by the standards of his subculture, precisely because it is wrong by the norms of the larger culture. (1955, 28)

Working-class boys find satisfaction and a regaining of self-esteem by convincing themselves that they do not need the middle class. If one finds difficulty attaining a goal, a sure solution is to deny the legitimacy or worth of the goal—that is, one redefines the mission as not being worth the effort. Cohen contends that this disavowal of

middle-class values and aspirations takes the form of a psychological reaction formation, or a kind of subconscious survival mechanism. The pain felt by not competing
successfully in a middle-class world becomes masked by an excessive and inflexible
demonstration of an opposite trait or attitude. Consequently, the working-class boy really wants to enjoy the rewards of middle-class culture, but, experiencing failure, finds
pleasure in doing the opposite.

Accordingly, the working-class delinquent boy typically demonstrates maliciousness
ness or an enjoyment in the discomfort of others. Following Thrasher's analysis of
gangs (1927), Cohen writes: "Apart from its more dramatic manifestations in the form
of gang wars, there is keen delight in terrorizing 'good' children, in driving them from
playgrounds and gyms . . . and in general in making themselves obnoxious to the
virtuous" (1955, 28).

Cohen points out that much of the delinquency was nonutilitarian, not for profit.
Stealing became extremely prevalent within the working-class delinquent gang, but
much of the theft was from pure spite, or simply for the "hell of it," rather than for any
economic gain.

THE MIDDLE CLASS

Although Cohen concentrates strongly on the working-class subculture as a source of
delinquency, the possibility of middle-class delinquency is not disregarded altogether,
and he offers several comments to help account for this. First, some families may technically appear middle class after an assessment of income, but not when cultural traditions
and child rearing are evaluated. Cohen argues that some mislabeled middle-class youth
may actually suffer the same status frustration experienced with working-class communities. Thus, the same set of theoretical principles accounting for working-class delinquency may help understand some middle-class delinquency.

Furthermore, according to Cohen, it is theoretically possible, but not probable,
that a similar delinquent subculture may arise in the middle classes in response to different but "functionally equivalent" sets of conditions. In other words, middle-class
boys may find frustration and loss of status and self-esteem in striving to live up to
upper-class standards. Although the idea is not developed, Cohen suggests that differences in lawbreaking patterns among boys from various class levels are qualitative as
well as quantitative, and upholds the assumption that delinquency expectedly erupts
more readily among the working class and is distinct in style compared to that found
among middle-class youth. Other research upholds this idea (Chambliss 1973; c.f.
Wattenberg and Balistrieri 1950).

THEORETICAL REFINEMENTS

For better or worse, Cohen will be remembered primarily for the now classic 1955
Delinquent Boys, the relatively small volume that forged a permanent place for him in
sociology. However, other activities and intellectual enterprises occupied his time as
well. Cohen's subsequent writing, and even some of his very early publications prior to
1955, bears a resemblance to the theoretical dialog incorporated in his theory of subculture. At least five other publications deserve note. First are several of his earliest
writings on the place of "themes" and "kindred concepts" in social theory (1946, 1948).

Although by contemporary standards the language seems archaic and a bit tedious, Cohen offers further analysis of "cultural patterns" identifiable in any society.

Following in the wake of Pitirim Sorokin (1937) and Morris Opler (1945, 1946), Cohen elaborates on the need to better understand and use as a conceptual tool the basic themes, patterns, or fundamental values of a culture. When Merton discusses the American Dream as something to be striven for, and as a goal whose absence may result in personal stress, he relies on what Cohen refers to as a *cultural theme* or *kindred concept*. Likewise, Cohen addresses the *cultural standards, ethos,* or *spirit of being* identified either as middle or working class. Cohen believed that these fundamental cultural themes or premises, even though they ring of mysticism, must be carefully understood and conceptualized in order to comprehend a fully integrated cultural system.

Second, in 1965, a decade after the first release of *Delinquent Boys*, Cohen published *The Sociology of the Deviant Act: Anomie Theory and Beyond.* This work carefully outlines several areas left untended by social strain theorists. Cohen ultimately seeks a general theory of deviance, using Merton's anomie theory as a departure point, but recognizes imperfections and gaps in the earlier theory. Cohen agrees that some disenfranchised individuals may suffer strain or anomie, but contends the process had not been clearly described from a microsociological perspective. Exactly when does a disjuncture between goals and means, as discussed by Merton, actually begin to generate stress or strain? What is the precise role of social interaction as ego enters situations destined to result in anomia?

Presuming an individual may adapt to strain by choosing illegitimate means, as Merton suggests, precisely how is such a process described? Cohen provides further clarification of anomie, especially regarding microlevel movements and gestures of actors in the production of deviance. His responses build on earlier explanations and from his understanding of how deviant subcultures emerge.

Third, in 1966, Cohen introduced *Deviance and Control.* A relatively slender book of 120 pages, it was destined to become, if not a classic test, certainly a memorable one. Published during a time when the discipline of criminology was enjoying a rapid rise in popularity, it developed a reputation as a concise summary of deviance theories and was widely adopted as a supplemental text in sociological and criminological theory courses. Following his earlier mission, he focused on integrating the wide-ranging explanations of norm violation, and outlined clearly the necessity of incorporating all the various ingredients of behavior in order to arrive at a general theory of deviance. Cohen constructed his theory on four fundamental sources of action:

1. Emphasis on the action itself
2. Emphasis on the situation
3. Conjunctive theories (combined influence of actor and situation)
4. Emphasis on the interaction process

In 1973, while a visiting professor at the Institute of Criminology in Cambridge, England, Cohen presented a lecture subsequently printed under the title *The Elasticity of Evil* (1974). An essay of about forty pages and one not widely disseminated, it revealed Cohen's adeptness at microsociological analysis of precise behavior features underlying deviance or fluctuations in deviance. In this publication, Cohen does not actually invent new ways of examining deviance. Instead, he imaginatively enhances earlier perspectives of others, and elaborates on, among other things, Durkheim's concern with the normalcy of crime.

In *The Elasticity of Deviance*, Cohen presents identity theory in simplistic language. Everyone wants to "be someone" or to identify with something special. The process of being someone special depends to a great extent on how we decide, in the first place, that one thing is more worthy than another. The definition of deviance changes depending on the needs of some people either to avoid being defined as deviant or to acquire particular labels of worthiness. Cohen outlines in exacting fashion the interaction process of becoming or avoiding deviant stereotypes, and discusses the way definitions of deviance change to fit the situation (1974, 9–10).

Also, in 1977, as a result of his association with the Cambridge Institute of Criminology Cohen published *The Concept of Criminal Organization*, which analyzes the sociological features of criminal organization in general. Cohen focuses on patterns of criminal relationships, the scope of criminal organization, and the implication of the legitimate social order in the criminal enterprise. Furthermore, the concept of "trust" in both legal and illegal organizations is analyzed sociologically, and Cohen clarifies that a functional analysis can be appropriate to any organization—legitimate or criminal.

IV. CRITIQUE

As a general rule, social scientists have been comparatively kind to Cohen's key ideas. Social theory analysts credit him with launching the subculture theory of delinquency, especially true in regard to the 1950s era of theorizing, which benefited from the early Ecology School and several decades of psychological research. Certainly any discussion of subculture delinquency and status frustration must reckon with Cohen's *Delinquent Boys*. Whereas his explanation of delinquent subcultures has withstood the test of time and is given substantial coverage in contemporary delinquency textbooks, Cohen's ideas have not been immune to rather heated reviews. The following criticisms of *Delinquent Boys* appeared in the *American Sociological Review* (Kitsuse and Dietrick 1959).

1. Cohen does not present adequate support, either in theory or in fact, for his explanation of the delinquency subculture.
2. The methodological basis of the theory renders it inherently untestable.
3. The theory is ambiguous concerning the relationship between the emergence of the subculture and its maintenance.
4. The theory should include an explanation of the persistence of the subculture if it is to meet an adequate test.

With the advantage of hindsight, the criticisms, although no doubt written in earnest in 1959, seem curious today. First, the idea that Cohen does not present adequate support for his theory is a matter of perspective. Most likely the critics hoped for new sets of data to demonstrate the theoretical directions followed by Cohen. Instead, he depended heavily on previous ethnography.

The criticism of methodology has some merit, but basically only if the book is viewed as a thesis or dissertation. It is true that Cohen does not acquaint the reader with the procedures used to arrive at the theoretical conclusions. Along the same line as Merton's *Social Theory and Social Structure*, we find a theoretical exposition slighted by methodological technique. The notion that Cohen's theory of subcultures is not amenable to test seems odd at best. To the contrary, the work appears to have provided abundant new concepts and variables for future exploration and critical analysis (see Shoemaker 1984 for further discussion of Cohen's impact).

The third criticism, that the theory is ambiguous, appears to lose its force when applied as well to other comparable subcultural theories of the era that lacked Cohen's descriptive detail. If Cohen's work is in any way to be considered vague, it is in reference to the inclusion of psychogenic perspectives of gang behavior. Granted, psychological features such as "reaction formations" may prevail as explanations, but they are difficult to operationalize and demonstrate.

Also, criticizing the theory by asserting it does not do enough (i.e., explain the persistence of subcultures) appears to beg the question—that is, few theoretical statements can do everything. Cohen set out to explain further the nature of working- and middle-class culture and to address why one group seems to involve itself in certain kinds of misbehavior more than another.

A further criticism must be noted. Is it necessary to accept Cohen's basic premise that working-class youth naturally strive to acquire middle-class cultural traits? This fundamental argument is questioned by Walter B. Miller in his own exemplary research on urban, lower-class culture (1958). Miller contends that factors other than "frustrated expectations" may account for the emergence of delinquent gangs among lower-class males.

The 1950s and 1960s saw the rapid expansion of delinquency theory, and Albert K. Cohen's work holds a prominent place among important advances in criminological thought.

References

Chambliss, William. 1973. The saints and the roughnecks. *Society.* 11:24–31.

Cohen, Albert K. 1946. An evaluation of "themes" and kindred concepts. *Am. J. Sociol.* 52:41–42.

———. 1948. On the place of themes and kindred concepts in social theory. *Am. Anthro.* 50:436–43.

———. 1955. *Delinquent boys: The culture of the gang.* New York: The Free Press of Glencoe.

———. 1965. The sociology of the deviant act: Anomie theory and beyond. *Am. Sociolog. Rev.* 30(1):5–14.

———. 1966. *Deviance and control.* Englewood Cliffs, NJ: Prentice Hall.

———. 1973. The social problems of the university: Two crises of legitimacy. *Soc. Prob.* 20:265–83.

———. 1974. *The elasticity of evil: Changes in the social definitions of deviance.* Oxford, England: Oxford University Penal Research Unit.

———. 1977. The concept of criminal organization. *Br. J. Criminol.* 17(2):97–111.

Kitsuse, John, & David C. Dietrick. 1959. Delinquent boys: A critique. *Am. Sociolog. Rev.* 24:208–15.

Manheim, Herman. 1956. Juvenile delinquency (review article). *Br. J. Criminol.* 7:148–52.

Mead, George Herbert, 1934, *Mind, Self, and Society,* Chicago: University of Chicago Press.

Merton, Robert K. 1938. Social structure and anomie. *Am. Sociolog. Rev.* 3:672–82.

———. 1949. *Social theory and social structure.* Glencoe: The Free Press.

Miller, Walter B. 1958. Lower-class culture as a generating milieu of gang delinquency. *J. Soc. Iss.* 14(3):5–19.

Opler, Morris E. 1945. Themes as dynamic forces in culture. *Am. J. Sociol.* 52:43–44.

Reckless, Walter C. 1950. *The crime problem.* New York: Appleton-Century-Crofts.

Shaw, Clifford R., & Henry D. McKay. 1942. *Delinquency and urban areas.* Chicago: The University of Chicago Press.

Shoemaker, Donald J. 1984. *Theories of delinquency: An examination of explanations of delinquent behavior.* New York: Oxford University Press.

Sorokin, Pitirim. 1937. *Social and cultural dynamics.* New York: American Book Company.

Sutherland, Edwin H., 1947, *Principles of Criminology*, Philadelphia: J.B. Lippincott.

Thomas, W.I. (editor), 1909, Source Book for Social Origins: *Ethnological materials, Psychological Standpoint, Classified and Annotated Bibliographies for the Interpretation of Savage Society,* Chicago: University of Chicago Press.

Thrasher, Frederick M. 1927. *The gang: A study of 1,313 gangs in Chicago.* Chicago: The University of Chicago Press.

Tokuoka, Hideo, & Albert K. Cohen. 1987. Society and delinquency. *Internatl. J. Comparat. Appl. Crim. Jus.* 11(1):13–22.

Wattenberg, William W., & James J. Balistrieri. 1950. Gang membership and juvenile misconduct. *Am. Sociolog. Rev.* 15:744–52.

Whyte, William Foote. 1937. *Street corner society.* Chicago: The University of Chicago Press.

Wolfgang, Marvin, Leonard Savitz, & Norman Johnston. 1962. *The sociology of crime and delinquency.* New York: Wiley.

CHAPTER 11
LLOYD E. OHLIN: B. 1918
WITH COMMENTS ON
RICHARD CLOWARD (1927–2001)

I. BIOGRAPHICAL SKETCH

Lloyd Ohlin was born in Belmont, Massachusetts, on August 27, 1918, the second of four boys to Emil and Elise (Nelson) Ohlin, Swedish immigrants who had met after coming to the United States. His father operated a reasonably successful bakery, which allowed the Ohlins to lead a very normal middle-class life. He and his brothers were very active and spent a lot of time at a nearby town field. Lloyd differed from his brothers, however, in his passion for reading and his studiousness. He reports that he made great use of the town library and constantly had "his nose in a book." Lloyd attended Belmont High School, where he not only excelled in the classroom, but also participated in track, running the quarter mile. He says that he preferred track to football or other sports because it did not require as much of his time.

Lloyd's youngest brother died at the age of seven from a brain tumor, an event that had a significant impact on Ohlin's interest in psychology. He became interested in psychology as a result of his brother's affliction and his exposure to some of the literature in the area. On graduation from high school in 1936, Ohlin went to Brown University, where he divided his time between his academic interests in sociology and psychology and participation on the track team. His interest in sociology was fostered by his roommate at Brown, an older friend of his from Belmont who was already majoring in sociology. Lloyd graduated from Brown with honors in 1940, with a bachelor's degree in sociology and a minor in psychology.

The chair of the sociology department at Brown specialized in criminology and, through contact with him, Ohlin became interested in the study of crime, which he says seemed to bring sociology and psychology together for him. Given his interest in the study of crime, it is not surprising that, when Ohlin's undergraduate work was completed, he went to study with Edwin Sutherland at Indiana University in their graduate program. The interaction with Sutherland was to have great influence on Ohlin's approach to criminology. While there, he was also exposed to the ideas of Nathaniel Kantor in the psychology department. Ohlin says that he found Kantor's "brand of psychology and social psychology quite fascinating" and credits Kantor as having great influence on his theorizing and work. Ohlin received his master's degree in sociology in 1942.

From Indiana, Ohlin went into the military, serving in the counterintelligence corps in the European theater from 1942 until November 1945. In January 1946, he married Helen Barbara Hunter, with whom he raised four children, Janet, George,

Robert, and Nancy. Helen is the daughter of Walter Hunter, who was the chair of psychology at Brown University. In March 1946, both Lloyd and his new wife started in graduate school at the University of Chicago. It was at Chicago while working on his Ph.D. in sociology that Ohlin met the other person whom he credits with influencing the direction of his career—Ernest Burgess.

In the fall of 1947, Ohlin accepted the position of sociologist–actuary with the Illinois Parole and Pardon Board because it allowed him to pursue his dissertation in the area of adult corrections. As a sociologist–actuary, he interviewed inmates, prepared case materials for parole board dockets, and conducted research in parole prediction. He was transferred to the Chicago office of the Board in 1950, where he served as a supervising research sociologist, doing research on parole board decisions, parole statistics, and prediction. He was also involved in the development of in-service training programs for correctional workers. Of course, during this time, he continued to work toward his Ph.D. In 1953, Ohlin left the Parole and Pardon Board to take a position at the University of Chicago as the Director of the Center for Education and Research in Corrections. Just prior to starting in this new post, he spent three months in Korea investigating problems of prisoner-of-war camps for the Human Resources Research Office of George Washington University.

The next three years were to be a very busy time. In 1954, he received his Ph.D. in sociology from the University of Chicago. He continued to fulfill his duties as the director of the center, supervising research on probation and parole organizations and adult correctional institutions, but he also became active in other roles. At the same time, he began what was to be a five-year relationship with the American Bar Foundation as a consultant on field research for their survey of the Administration of Justice in the United States. In 1955, he was employed as a part-time consultant to the Sheriff of Cook County, assisting in the reorganization of the correctional program of the Cook County Jail.

In 1956, Ohlin accepted a position that would propel him on his way to becoming a pioneer in criminology. Not that his work to that time had gone unnoticed or had not been of significant value, but his appointment as a professor of sociology in the doctoral program at the Columbia University School of Social Work would mark the beginning of the work with which he has become most associated and that led to what is considered to represent his greatest contribution to criminology. It was at Columbia that Ohlin began to shift his interest from adult corrections to the area of juvenile delinquency. In the fall of 1957, he and Richard Cloward began a comparative study of institutions for juvenile offenders at the school's newly established research center. It was this three-year project sponsored by the Ford Foundation that ultimately led to the development of differential opportunity theory and the publication (1960) of *Delinquency and Opportunity: A Theory of Delinquent Gangs*. During his early years at Columbia, Dr. Ohlin immersed himself in the study of delinquency, serving as a consultant for and member of the Ad Hoc Advisory Committee on Delinquency to process grants in the area of delinquency for the National Institute of Mental Health (1957–64), as a consultant to the Ford Foundation on grants in the delinquency area (1957–61), as a member of a board of national advisors to *Children*, a journal published by the U.S. Children's Bureau (1959–61), as Chairman of the Social Science Research Council Committee on the Sociocultural Contexts of Delinquency (1959–60), as a member of the Professional Council of the National Council on Crime and Delinquency (1959–63), and as a consultant to the Youth Center Study being conducted by Syracuse University (1959).

While working on the Ford Foundation study, Ohlin and Cloward were asked by the coalition of the Lower East Side Community Settlement House in Manhattan to help them develop a "saturation of service" project for youth. This project became both a testing ground for some of their ideas about differing subcultures and served as a pilot for what was to eventually become the Mobilization for Youth program under the Kennedy Administration. This project and the publication of *Delinquency and Opportunity* led Attorney General Robert Kennedy to ask Ohlin to serve as a Special Assistant to Abraham Ribicoff, the Secretary of Health, Education, and Welfare. His role would be to work with the President's Committee on Juvenile Delinquency, serving as an "in-house academic theorist on delinquency." Ohlin took a leave of absence from Columbia from 1961 to 1962 to accept the position. During this same time, Richard Cloward served as the Research Director for the Mobilization for Youth program.

Ohlin returned to Columbia in 1962 and assumed full-time duties as the director of the research center, along with his teaching responsibilities, and he remained at Columbia until 1965. During that time, in addition to his research and teaching, he participated in a variety of other roles. In 1963 and 1964, he was asked by the National Council on Crime and Delinquency to organize and begin to publish a new journal on *Research in Crime and Delinquency*. He served as the Vice-Chairman of the International Committee on Poverty Research and was a U.S. Delegate to the International Conference on Social Work in Athens, Greece, in 1964. From October 1965 to June of 1967, Dr. Ohlin took another leave of absence from Columbia to serve as the Associate Director of the President's Commission on Law Enforcement and Administration of Justice. He held that position until July 1967, when he joined the Harvard Law School Faculty as a professor of criminology.

During his years at Harvard, Dr. Ohlin continued to conduct research and write extensively in the area of juvenile delinquency. He remained at Harvard until the spring of 1982, when he taught as a Visiting Professor in the School of Criminal Justice at the State University of New York at Albany. In July 1982, Professor Ohlin retired from Harvard Law School as the Touroff–Glueck Professor of Criminal Justice, Emeritus. Since his retirement, Dr. Ohlin resides in Maine with his wife, where he keeps active doing research and writing. He served as the President of the American Society of Criminology in 1986.[1]

II. BASIC ASSUMPTIONS

The focus of most criminological theory in the fifties and early sixties was juvenile delinquency, especially gangs (Williams and McShane, 1988). Ohlin's work with Richard Cloward, on both theoretical and applied levels, became a very influential and highly visible part of the whole delinquency movement. Their work reflects strong ties to the Chicago School, with its attention to the relationship between the community and delinquency, but it also draws heavily from other sources. Their theory of differential opportunity represents an attempt to integrate a number of different theoretical approaches. It pulled together two quite divergent theoretical traditions

---

[1]All materials presented in the biographical sketch were adapted from an extract from *Current Biographies* 24(4): 1963; W. H. Wilson Company, New York; from information provided by Dr. Ohlin in personal communications on October 30 and December 7, 1988; and from an interview with Dr. Ohlin by John Laub (1983).

in the discipline at the time: Sutherland's differential association and Merton's anomie. (Their highly influential book, *Delinquency and Opportunity: A Theory of Delinquent Gangs* [1960], is dedicated to Sutherland and Merton.) Ohlin stressed symbolic interactionism, a la Sutherland, and Cloward brought in anomie, melding Midwestern with eastern orientations (Laub 1983). Differential opportunity theory also reflects the works of Shaw and McKay, Albert Cohen, Emile Durkheim, and Solomon Kobrin.

Given the range of approaches from which they drew ideas, Cloward and Ohlin's theory has been characterized in several ways. Mannheim (1965) calls their treatment of the factors contributing to a delinquent subculture "rigidly sociological." There is some level of general agreement with this characterization but, as discussed later, not everyone shares Mannheim's interpretation. Despite the general acceptance of the sociological characterization, there is disagreement as to what specific type of sociological theory differential opportunity actually represents.

Differential opportunity has most often been classified as a social structural theory. Schafer's (1969) claims that the seeds of Cloward and Ohlin's work go all the way back to Quetelet's "inclination toward crime" as it develops under certain social conditions, and of course there is the influence of the Chicago School, people like Shaw and McKay and Kobrin. There is also the strong connection to Merton and Durkheim and the strain perspective, which argues that certain social structural factors generate forces that drive individuals toward crime and delinquency (Vold and Bernard 1986). Shoemaker (1984) characterizes differential opportunity specifically as a strain theory, agreeing with Mannheim that Cloward and Ohlin were "wrestling with the problem of class as a decisive factor in delinquency" (1965, 152). This is not, however, class conflict in the more radical sense of ruling class dominance and oppression (Shoemaker 1984).

Whether one is discussing the ecological approach, strain theory, or some other version of structural theory, such explanations by definition refer conduct to some element of the situation, an element beyond the control of the individual. Structural explanations are bilateral: on one side is the generation of desires; on the other, satisfaction of these desires. The structural level of analysis focuses on causative forces in the ever-changing economic, political, and other systems of society that generate and satisfy human wants (i.e., that distribute wealth and power). These are structural elements in that they are integrated parts of the fabric of society that affect the individuals who comprise it (Allen, Friday, Roebuck, and Sagarin 1981, Nettler 1984). A structural theory, such as Ohlin and Cloward's, which emphasizes the causal role of opportunities, stresses choice less and pressure more than economic theories, but stresses power less and economic opportunities more than radical criminological theories (Nettler 1984).

Cullen (1986) offers some qualification to the strain characterization, saying that Cloward and Ohlin's work is more of a critique of the strain paradigm than a mere extension of it, and goes on to say that Durkheim and Merton's anomie offered plausible theories of structurally induced pressure or strain, but not a complete explanation of deviance or criminal behavior. An explanation of the origin of strain is not an explanation of the resulting behavioral patterns of adaptation. Durkheim and Merton addressed the sources of strain that create deviance, but left unexplained the circumstances that shaped responses to it. The differential opportunity approach extends or modifies anomie by trying to account for subcultural variations in adaptations made by individuals or groups when faced with opportunity barriers (Allen et al. 1981). Although it is true that the critique/extension of strain theory presented by Ohlin and Cloward has strong ties to the Chicago School (Cullen 1986), the most notable source of influence is not the structuralists, but the work of Edwin Sutherland, which serves to complicate the classification picture a bit. Sutherland's theory of differential association is considered to be a process or social learning theory. In the Edwin Sutherland chapter, the social psychological implications of differential association are discussed in some detail. So, along with attention to structural sources of strain, Ohlin and Cloward addressed the resulting differences in emotional, psychological, and behavioral responses of individuals and groups, leading some to claim that their theory is as much social psychological as it is sociological.

Both Schafer (1969) and Allen et al. (1981) portray Cloward and Ohlin's work as presenting an "Adlerian" view of juveniles and delinquency. Alfred Adler, a disciple of Freud, developed an approach called *individual psychology* (1956) that was more social and conscious than Freud's psychoanalytic theory (the Sigmund Freud chapter). Adler portrays humans as individuals striving to overcome inferiority and maintain superiority through the "innate aptitude of social interest." Social interest enables individuals to become responsive to reality, which Adler equates primarily with the social situation. Such a conceptualization makes reality more an internal than an external element, as social interest is seen as an innate and highly individualized potential that is developed in childhood and greatly affects adult behavior. For Adler, crimes are committed by individuals who must "goad" themselves into it. This situation implies that the criminal has some social interest but not enough; the criminal's social interest is underdeveloped and suppressed. The criminal "takes pains to subdue the relics of his social interest" (1956, 303). Adler believes that punishment and prison are not the ways to treat criminals, as they only reinforce the suppression of social interest. Crimes are symptoms of an attitude to life, and the approach to dealing with the criminal must focus first on identifying how this attitude has arisen and then on working to change it. Adler acknowledges that individual therapy is not possible with every criminal, but believes that group therapy (of the proper kind) can be of great help. Ultimately, he concludes, what must be instilled in criminals is that crime is cowardice, not courage.

Given the Cloward and Ohlin's penchant for using concepts and terms such as *frustration, aspirations, perceived discrepancies,* and *expectations,* it is easy to see how some might interpret differential opportunity as a social psychological approach. However, as Mannheim (1965) points out, Cloward and Ohlin's theory represents, more than anything else, a search for delinquent subculture. Consequently, it cannot be equated directly in its substance or assumptions with the highly individualized and internal orientation of Adler or other, more purely psychological, approaches. In their own words, Cloward and Ohlin (1960) characterize their theory as focusing primarily on the "social structural differentials in illegitimate opportunities." The problem of delinquency, for them, was fundamentally a problem emanating from the fabric of society. Although there are clearly some social psychological overtones to the theory, there appears to be a basic assumption that the expectations, aspirations, and so on of which they spoke were somehow constants, at least within groups. Nettler (1984) concurs with this observation, stating that Cloward and Ohlin's theory views all members of society as wanting very much the same thing. The theory does not emphasize individual (personality) differences (Haskell and Yablonsky 1978, Nettler 1984); people are conceived of as being pressured into different courses of action by the structure of life chances available. (This, incidentally, is what Hirschi, 1969, calls *strain theory.*)

Although there really is not a tremendous amount of direct similarity to Adler in the way Ohlin and Cloward address the etiology of delinquency, there does seem to be some fairly close correspondence in the area of crime prevention. Adler (1956) is convinced that every single criminal could be changed, but realizes that the time and effort required makes such a task unfeasible. In light of this, he believes that we could at least relieve those who are not strong enough to cope with their burdens. By this, he specifically means that great emphasis should be placed on eradicating unemployment and providing job training. He believes that teachers should be made "the instruments of social progress by training them to correct mistakes made in the family, i.e., to develop the social interest of children" (1956, 422). Also, we should avoid, in our social life, things that can act as a challenge to the poor or criminal, things that heighten the gap between poverty and luxury.

No matter how one ultimately classifies Cloward and Ohlin's theory, it is clear that their primary intent was to integrate some of the prominent theoretical notions of their time into a coherent theory of delinquency. Their theory represents an energetic attempt at combining Merton's class-oriented, structural approach with Sutherland's non-class-oriented, process approach (Williams and McShane 1988, Allen et al. 1981).

THEORETICAL ASSUMPTIONS

Our hypothesis can be summarized as follows: The disparity between what lower class youth are led to want and what is actually available to them is the source of a major problem of adjustment. Adolescents who form delinquent subcultures, we suggest, have internalized an emphasis upon conventional goals. Faced with limitations on legitimate avenues of access to these goals, and unable to revise their aspirations downward, they experience intense frustrations; the exploration of nonconformist alternatives may be the result. (Cloward and Ohlin 1960, 86)

One principle implication of this hypothesis is that social norms are two sided: norms defining legitimate practices also implicitly define illegitimate ones. The criminal who engages in criminal behavior does not invent a new way of life, because the "possibility of employing alternative means is acknowledged, tacitly at least, by the norms of the culture" (Cloward and Ohlin 1960, 145). However, Cloward and Ohlin argue that simple acknowledgment of the existence of "alternate means" is not sufficient to account for delinquency/crime, as many theories have incorrectly professed. A more direct accounting of the relative availability of illegal alternatives and their links to potential crime is necessary to understand fully the development of delinquent/criminal reactions and adaptations.

Motivations and pressures cannot fully account for the occurrence of deviant behaviors, anymore than they can for conforming behavior. The individual must have access to a "learning environment," and once learned, roles and behaviors must find the opportunity for application. Opportunities to fill given roles are not necessarily freely available. Access to such opportunities depends on a variety of factors, such as socioeconomic position, age, gender, ethnic affiliation, and personality characteristics. The conditions necessary to promote learning and performance of the roles is dependent upon the social structure of the community (Cloward and Ohlin 1960).

Cloward and Ohlin (1960) take issue with sociological and psychological theorists who erroneously assume that explanation of the motivational basis for deviant behavior patterns also explains the resulting response. "The social milieu affects the nature of the deviant response whatever the motivation and social position (i.e., age, sex, socioeconomic level) of the participant in the delinquent subculture" (160). They do not assume that deviance is simply an asocial primitive reaction and do not subscribe to explanations based on poor or incomplete socialization. It is not, they say, that delinquents do not know right from wrong; they understand the rules, but they respond differently to them. The delinquent subculture is fairly organized and normative in its own right. Cloward and Ohlin (1960) believe it is equally inappropriate to equate delinquent behavior with a "conflict subculture" simply because its nature is disturbing and attracts attention. Although it is true that delinquent behavior may be reactive, being generated by a sense of injustice and frustration, it is also true that delinquent behavior is highly adaptive or instrumental (Nettler 1984). It is this latter aspect that Cloward and Ohlin are especially concerned with describing and explaining.

From the perspective of differential opportunity theory, deviancy and conformity basically result from the same kinds of social conditions. (At this point, the notion of strain and frustration from efforts to conform or live up to expectations comes into to play.) Deviance ordinarily represents a search for solutions to problems of adjustment. Consequently, deviance/delinquency is not purposeless, although it may be random and disorganized in its appearance and occurrence. In other words, problems of adjustment are engendered by attempts at social conformity performed under adverse conditions. The resulting search for a solution to the adjustment problem may or may not be nonconforming or delinquent. Drawing on Durkheim and Merton, Cloward and Ohlin (1960) see these adjustment problems as inevitable because, whereas physical needs are satiable, social gratification is not. The inherently insatiable nature of social goals, coupled with a lack of fit goals and legitimate means for attaining them, is used by Cloward and Ohlin to account for the high concentration of lawbreakers among lower-class youths and to justify their heavy focus on the delinquent subculture.

PHILOSOPHICAL ASSUMPTIONS

Differential opportunity theory expressed the hope and optimism that had been fueled by post-war prosperity and a rising tide of liberalism in the United States. The climate of the late 1950s was one of expanding consumerism and increasing concern over the rights of individuals to their share of the American Dream, a dream seen as being represented by middle-class values. Urbanization reached all-time highs, and with it came heightened concern over the problems of cities, especially the plight of the lower class. Much of the attention to the urban lower-class situation was focused on delinquency and gangs, which came to be seen as indicative of the problems of the lower class.

Nettler (1984) calls differential opportunity the "social workers' favorite" because it looks at satisfaction of desires, not lowering of expectations, as the cure for crime. It was believed that satisfaction of desires of the lower class could be achieved by changing the opportunity structure. Such optimistic contentions found support with the "New Liberals" of the early 1960s. The Kennedy and Johnson administrations attempted to implement sweeping social welfare policies and programs based in part on differential opportunity and other theories of that ilk. Unfortunately, it is difficult to put even well-conceived theories into practice in our complicated social world, and, generally, the efforts to restructure segments of society did not work (Williams and McShane 1988, Vold and Bernard 1986). However, the apparent inability of differential opportunity theory to guide successful practice should not be accepted uncritically as proof of the total invalidity of the theory.

CONCLUSION

Shoemaker (1984) says that differential opportunity theory represents one of the three major conceptualizations in the subcultural perspective of lower class delinquency. (The other two are Albert Cohen's "middle-class measuring rod" theory and Walter Miller's theory of a lower-class value system.) Cloward and Ohlin were trying to resolve the conflicts between Merton's and Cohen's approaches and to integrate these ideas with those of the Chicago Ecologists and Sutherland (Vold and Bernard 1986). The theory that they developed was based on the assumption that Merton was correct in claiming that certain groups were disadvantaged in their quest for success, but it also directly addressed the problem of explaining the resulting deviant behavior patterns (Williams and McShane 1988). The explanation that differential opportunity offered was a hybrid of the previously mentioned approaches, infused with the hope and optimism of our post-war culture. In essence, the theory considered the ways in which rewards and punishments were handed out based on the legal and illegal opportunity structures that were in place in the neighborhood. It is the emphasis on the equality level built into these structures that demarcates the boundaries between Ohlin and Cloward's "opportunity structure" approach and other hypotheses indicative of the general subcultural perspective (Nettler 1984). Ohlin and Cloward present a positivistic and consensus-oriented explanation of delinquency, with a primary focus on reaching cultural goals (Williams and McShane 1988).

Nettler (1984) identified six fundamental assumptions on which differential opportunity theory is based:

- The theory is socially deterministic in that it is assumed that society leads lower-class youth to want things; society does things to people.
- The theory assumes that the gap between the desires of the lower class and their legitimate opportunities is greater than the gap between the aspirations of the middle class and their legitimate opportunities.
- Lower-class delinquents have "internalized conventional goals." The legitimate avenues to these goals are structurally limited.
- Lower-class youth do not and cannot "revise aspirations downward."
- The breach between promise and fulfillment generates intense frustration, which may lead to criminal conduct.

Shoemaker (1984) summarized the basic assumptions more succinctly, listing only two:

1. Blocked economic aspirations cause poor self-concepts and general feelings of frustration.
2. Frustration leads to delinquency in specialized gang contexts, the nature of which varies according to the structure of criminal and conventional values operating in the neighborhood.

According to Cloward and Ohlin (1960, ix), with differential opportunity theory, they were attempting to "explore two questions: (1) Why do delinquent 'norms' or rules of conduct develop? (2) What are the conditions which account for the distinctive content of various systems of delinquent norms—such as those prescribing violence or theft or drug use?"

III. KEY IDEAS

Although both Lloyd Ohlin and Richard Cloward have published on a variety of subjects, differential opportunity constitutes a statement of their general theory of delinquency and crime and is the primary source and originating point of their overall influence in criminology. Ohlin (in Laub 1983) calls *Delinquency and Opportunity* his "proudest work."

Generally speaking, Cloward and Ohlin (1960) were interested in why delinquent subcultures arise in certain locations in the social structure. However, they posit that there are at least five distinct classes of questions subsumed under this general question that must be answered to produce a comprehensive theory. They caution that although these questions are analytically distinct, they refer to empirical processes and conditions that are integrally related to one another. The questions are as follows:

1. What is the precise nature of the delinquency adaptation to be explained?
2. How is the mode of adaptation distributed in the social structure?
3. To what specific problems of adjustment might this pattern be a response (i.e., mode of adaptation)? In other words, under what conditions will persons experience tensions and strains that lead to the development of delinquent subcultures?
4. Why is one particular mode of delinquency selected rather than others?
5. What determines the relative stability or instability of a particular delinquent pattern?

To answer these questions, they drew on some of the most influential and prominent concepts in criminological theory at the time and tried to arrive at a comprehensive explanation of delinquent subcultures that developed among lower-class, urban, adolescent males. They were trying to integrate Merton's and Durkheim's structural conceptualizations with Sutherland's process approach and Shaw and McKay's cultural transmission aspects, along with selected components from other subcultural theories, such as Cohen's. They would also incorporate some of Kobrin's (1951) ideas, such as the concept of *integrated community,* which refers to the elements of social control and the level of organization of the criminal structure and its relationship with the conventional aspects of the community.

Shoemaker (1984) identifies two key concepts of differential opportunity theory: differential opportunity structure and specialized gangs. These are the most "original" aspects of the theory; however, a consideration of several other key ideas Cloward and Ohlin borrowed from other theories and modified to various degrees is essential to a more complete understanding of differential opportunity structure and specialized gangs, and to demonstrate more fully the level of integration and complexity that Ohlin and Cloward were striving for in their theory.

Our hypothesis can be summarized as follows: The *disparity* between what lower-class youth are led to want and what is actually available to them is the source of a major *problem of adjustment*. Adolescents who form *delinquent subcultures*, we suggest, have *internalized* an emphasis on *conventional goals*. Faced with *limitations on legitimate avenues of access* to these goals and unable to *revise their aspirations* downward, they experience intense *frustrations*; the exploration of nonconformist alternatives may be the result (Cloward and Ohlin 1960, 86; emphasis added).

ANOMIE/STRAIN CONCEPTS (ASPIRATIONS, EXPECTATIONS, AND FRUSTRATION)

Cloward and Ohlin see both deviance and conformity arising from the same kinds of social conditions. This conception provides the basis for the notion of strain and frustration resulting from efforts to conform or live up to expectations. Deviance, like conforming behavior, often represents a search for the solution to adjustment problems. Based on Durkheim's assumption that social needs are fundamentally insatiable, adjustment problems are seen as inevitable and frequent. Durkheim identified several states of society and its organization (e.g., economic crisis, industrialization, rapid technological advances) that contribute to such adjustment problems by creating "unrestrained aspirations" (Cloward and Ohlin 1960).

Aspirations are the desires or strivings that individuals have to attain certain goals. The different subcultural or strain interpretations present different views of the aspirations and goal structure of lower-class adolescents. Merton argues that lower-class youth strive for monetary success. Cohen sees them as striving for status in a middle-class world. Miller's typology generally casts lower-class youth as nonaspiring. Cloward and Ohlin flatly disagree with Miller, and argue that Merton's monetary success and Cohen's striving for status are separate types of aspirations that can operate independently of each other (Cloward and Ohlin 1960, Vold and Bernard 1986). They try to correct the problems that they see with the existing characterizations of lower-class aspirations by proposing four categories of lower-class youth that focus on the relationship between status and economic position (Vold and Bernard 1986). Cloward and Ohlin's (1960) four-type system is based on whether the aspirer envisages a change in group membership. Type I aspirers want both membership in the middle class and a better economic position. Type II aspirers want membership in the middle class, even though their economic position is not improvable. Those in type III have no concern for middle-class status; they just want to improve their economic condition. Type IV aspirers are content with their lower-class position; they are adjusted and stable.

Cohen believes that types I and II account for the most delinquents, as these types represent strivings for status that may become frustrated. Cloward and Ohlin argue that these types do not represent the main sources of delinquents, as individuals in these categories hold values consistent with the middle class (Vold and Bernard 1986) and, consequently, react differently to status discontent than do type III aspirers. Cloward and Ohlin (1960) also disagree with Cohen's contention that the educational system produces delinquency by its imposition of middle-class standards, as these standards are consistent with the values aspired to by types I and II. Type IV aspirers generally avoid problems, as they avoid contact with middle-class institutions. It is type III aspirers, say Cloward and Ohlin (1960), who are alienated from school because of a conflict regarding appropriate success goals. They are in conflict with middle-class values that they look down on, but they want economic improvement. Type III aspirers have the major input into the delinquent subcultures. These juveniles become delinquent because they "anticipate" that legitimate channels will be closed to them. Cloward and Ohlin further contend that class differentials in the value placed on education reflect, in large part, differences in availability of educational opportunities. Lower-class attitudes about education are adaptive. Expectations are scaled down to accord with realistic limitations on accessed opportunities. These limitations primarily take the form of social structural barriers, such as lack of facilities or economic means. If education is the legitimate and traditional route to higher position and access to educational opportunities is restricted, then pressure mounts to use alternative means. "The dilemma facing many lower class individuals is that their efforts to locate alternative avenues to success goals are futile, for these alternatives are often just as restricted as education channels, if not more so" (Cloward and Ohlin 1960, 104). It is at this point that unfulfilled aspirations and the resulting strain and frustration push people to seek illegal means.

Cloward and Ohlin (1960) claim that this situation is far more acute for males, as they must go into the marketplace to seek employment. (Obviously, this specific aspect of the theory may have been more applicable in 1960 than today.) They also claim that adolescents are more susceptible, as it represents a time for choosing a direction or occupation. Consequently, lower-class adolescent males make up the group that is most vulnerable to such pressures.

There are two ways in which to define *aspiration* irrespective of position in the social structure or in relation to that position. *Relative aspiration,* or *position discontent,* is the most relevant to differential opportunity theory. Lower-class status increases one's dissatisfaction and also restricts access to legitimate ways to change status, which adds up to pressure toward deviant behavior. Based on this conceptualization of aspiration, Cloward and Ohlin (1960) say that in order for their theory to be considered valid, it must be demonstrated that lower-class adolescent males are exposed to greater discrepancies in aspirations and opportunities than persons elsewhere in the social structure. However, they say that their hypothesis does not depend on demonstrating that a "large proportion" of persons in the lower class exhibit high levels of aspiration. It is sufficient to show that a "significant number" aspire beyond their means, if these same individuals contribute disproportionately to delinquent acts.

From Ohlin and Cloward's perspective, the social structure is primarily responsible for status frustration and the available alternative solutions to the adjustment problems it generates. They assume that the lower-class adolescent male is in an anomic situation that pressures him into one or another available subculture (Shafer 1969). This general orientation is drawn from Durkheim and from Merton's extension of Durkheim's work, both of which address the structural sources of strains that create deviance. Durkheim and Merton present a plausible theory of structurally induced strain, but their explanations are not sufficient to account for the various responses to the strain that can and do occur (Cullen 1986). Recognizing these limitations, Cloward and Ohlin looked to the ecological and process approaches of Shaw and McKay and of Sutherland. They acknowledge the fact that accounting for the development of pressures toward deviance does not explain why these pressures result in one deviant solution rather than another. In addition, the forces that account for selection of a solution may have little to do with whether resulting response patters are stable or unstable. Shaw and McKay's and Sutherland's works provide potential answers to how specific deviant adaptations develop and become persistent and stable (Cloward and Ohlin 1960).

SOCIAL ORGANIZATION AND STABILITY

Cloward and Ohlin (1960) believe that the social milieu affects deviant responses, no matter what the specific motivation or special position of the actor, and that both learning and performance are implied by the concept of opportunity. The conditions for learning and performance depend on the social structure of the community in which the individual lives. Cloward and Ohlin use the general concepts of stability and organization to explain the different behavioral outcomes of the varied structural opportunities. A community is stable when aspirations are relatively attainable. A stable order is one in which the legitimacy ascribed to the criteria for the distribution of social rewards does not challenge socially defined relationships between personal worth and location in the social hierarchy. Stability breaks down when aspirations become unlimited (Cloward and Ohlin 1960).

In addressing issues of community structure, Cloward and Ohlin drew from the work of Solomon Kobrin (1951), who introduced the concept of *integrated community.* He hypothesized that the degree of social control in a community depends on how well the criminal element is organized and the relationship it maintains with the conventional elements of the community. Ohlin and Cloward adapted this conceptualización to their explanation of the development of different types of deviant responses (i.e., different types of juvenile gangs). They generally conclude that violence surfaces under conditions of relative detachment from institutionalized systems of opportunity and social control, both legitimate and illegitimate. It develops in response to frustration over the situation and blocked opportunities and as a result of the absence of social control—that is, violence is more likely in less stable neighborhoods with no organized, adult criminal presence, but, as the level of integration pushes for stability in the neighborhood, theft becomes dominant over violence (Shoemaker 1984).

A criminal subculture is most likely to arise in a neighborhood characterized by close bonds between different age levels and between criminal and conventional elements. Out of these stable integrations, a new opportunity structure arises that provides avenues to success goals, and the pressures generated by restrictions on legitimate access to success goals is drained off. The high level of social control created by the stable relationship between the criminal and noncriminal elements limits expressive behavior and constrains the discontented by encouraging the adoption of instrumental, if criminalistic, life styles. Basically, the form of delinquency manifested is "conditioned by the presence or absence of appropriate illegitimate means" (Cloward and Ohlin 1960, 152), which refers to crucial differences in the social organization of lower-class areas.

DIFFERENTIAL OPPORTUNITY STRUCTURE

Ohlin (in Laub 1983) says that the notion of differential opportunity grew out of his and Cloward's work in corrections. The immediate source of the theory was a 1957 comparative study of juvenile institutions in New York that explored the inmate subculture in public and private schools for boys. The initial presentation of the ideas coming out of this study was published by Cloward (1959) in an article entitled "Illegitimate

Means, Anomie and Deviant Behavior," which served as the impetus for the more-detailed explication of the ideas that was to come in *Delinquency and Opportunity*.

Cloward and Ohlin (1960) acknowledge Sutherland's (1944) recognition of the fact that criminal behavior is partly a function of the opportunities available to engage in it. Differential association theory and cultural transmission theory assume that access to illegitimate means is variable, but do not recognize the existence of comparable differences in access to legitimate means. Later, Merton's anomie theory explores the role that blocked opportunities in the legitimate structure can play in criminality. Cloward and Ohlin (1960) combine these ideas, stating that each individual occupies a (different) position in both the legitimate and illegitimate opportunity structures. The concept of differential opportunity structure refers to the uneven distribution of legal and illegal means of achieving economic success in society, especially as access is divided disproportionately by social class or status (Shoemaker 1984).

Lower-class youth find themselves in the position of being more likely to have their legitimate channels blocked; this pushes them toward the illegitimate structure, which is often much more open to them. The exact nature and type of behavior that develops out of the illegal structure for the individual depends on the subculture of which he or she is a part, which, in turn, depends on the organization and stability of the neighborhood. Vold and Bernard (1986) believe that Cloward's 1959 statement (and the subsequent work it generated) constitutes the most significant attempt to extend and refine Merton's ideas. Cloward pointed out that although Merton's focus on the limited access of lower-class youth to legitimate means for attaining goals was correct, it was incomplete, because they did have access to illicit means. Williams and McShane (1988) call the addition of illegitimate opportunity structure to Merton's anomie theory "probably" the most important modification of it. However, the mere presence of such opportunities is not enough; the individual must know how to take advantage of them. Enter the works of Sutherland and Shaw and McKay, with their conceptualizations of criminal behavior as learned and normal.

Differential opportunity theory maintains a focus on goal–means discrepancies while stressing a role for both legitimate and illegitimate opportunity structures. The theory also addresses the processes by which the strain and other structural characteristics interact to create varied behavioral responses. By combining Sutherland and Merton, differential opportunity proposes that lower-class, male gang delinquency is "generated" from blocked legitimate economic opportunities through conventional institutions, and that the specific "nature" of the delinquency expressed is determined by "characteristics of the neighborhoods." These characteristics affect opportunities for engaging in illicit acts. The opportunity to commit illegal acts is unevenly distributed across the social structure, as is the opportunity for engaging in licit behavior.

DELINQUENT SUBCULTURES (GANG TYPES)

Cloward and Ohlin's work is a search for the origins of delinquent subculture (Mannheim 1965). Cloward and Ohlin (1960, 78) state that "pressures toward the formation of delinquent subcultures originate in marked discrepancies between culturally induced aspirations among lower-class youth and the possibilities of achieving them by legitimate means." The disparity between what lower-class youth come to want and what is actually available is the source of a major problem of adjustment and intense frustration. Faced with the constant limitations on legitimate avenues and seeking to solve their problems and alleviate their frustration, these lower-class juveniles may begin to explore "nonconformist alternatives," which is provided by the gang or delinquent subculture (Cloward and Ohlin 1960). In the terminology of the strain perspective, lower-class adolescents find themselves in an anomic situation, which pressures them into one or another of the delinquent subcultures available (Shafer 1969). "A delinquent subculture is one in which certain forms of delinquent activities are essential requirements for the performance of the dominant roles supported by the subculture" (Cloward and Ohlin 1960,7).

It should be noted that differential opportunity theory does not portray acts occurring among middle-class youth as being reflective of a delinquent subculture. The delinquent acts of middle-class adolescents do not receive support and approval from nondelinquent members of the class and from the predominant (conventional) norms. As middle-class delinquency is not caused by the existence of subcultures, it is neither as frequent nor as serious as lower-class delinquency. This interpretation was presented in direct opposition to Bloch and Nierderhoffer's (1958) contention that delinquency is primarily the result of the (general) difficulties of adolescence that are similar across social classes. Cloward and Ohlin (1960) postulate three different lower-class delinquent subcultures or gang types whose developments are determined principally by differentials in access to illegitimate means—the criminal, the conflict, and the retreatist. These different delinquent subcultures represent socialized modes of adaptation to the adjustment problems created by the lower-class situation; two of the subcultures consist of illegal behavior patterns and one represents an escape behavior pattern. (A great deal of similarity can be seen between Cloward and Ohlin's three subcultures and Merton's five adaptation styles.) Predominance of one or another of the subcultures is largely the result of the level of integration of conventional and organized illegitimate behavior systems and values and the integration of different-age offenders (Shoemaker 1984).

The *criminal gang,* as originally conceived by Cloward and Ohlin (1960), consists of juveniles involved primarily in theft, and develops in a neighborhood where adult crime is organized and adult criminals provide role models of success and serve as tutors. In neighborhoods conducive to the development of the criminal subculture, there is a stable relationship between adult criminals and noncriminals, and there is often cooperation with criminal justice agencies in terms of tolerance for some crimes (Shoemaker 1984).

Conflict gangs are characterized by a high level of violent behavior. Violence emerges under conditions of relative detachment from institutional systems of opportunity and as a result of lowered levels of social control, conditions endemic in less-stable and unorganized neighborhoods. Violence becomes a means for attaining status, and also serves as a release for pent-up anger generated by the frustration inherent in the anomic situation. In such neighborhoods and within the resultant delinquent subculture, the principle prerequisites for success are "guts" and the capacity to endure pain. Cloward and Ohlin (1960) call this the *warrior adjustment.* They do point out, however, that if new opportunity structures become available, violence is often relinquished. They also point out that this subculture has been erroneously equated with delinquent behavior in general because its nature is quite disturbing and attracts a lot of attention.

The *retreatist* is made up of what Cloward and Ohlin refer to as *double failures*. This type of subculture, which can develop in the same neighborhood as either of the other two types, is made up of individuals who did not make it in either the legitimate or the illegitimate opportunity structures. Shoemaker (1984) characterizes the retreatists as primarily drug users who have virtually totally withdrawn. He also states that not all retreatists adopt the roles of the subculture in the extreme; some adopt a lifestyle similar to Cohen's (1955) "corner boys." The exact form that retreatism takes in the individual depends on personality factors and specific associations and circumstances.

In conclusion, Cloward and Ohlin (1960) do not see lower-class juvenile delinquents as asocial or poorly socialized. In fact, they portray them as being quite the opposite—they are highly socialized, but into their own subculture, which is in its own right fairly organized and normative. The subcultures develop as collective solutions to shared problems. The youth within them are able to provide definitions, beliefs, and expectations for themselves and are able to establish achievable criteria of success (Allen et al. 1981). The level of stability and organization within a given subculture varies, and once formed, sometimes persists even after the forces that have given rise to it are no longer operating. By the same token, changes may also occur in the nature of the subcultural group and in the general prevalence of the type in various neighborhoods (Cloward and Ohlin 1960).

THEORY, APPLICATION, AND PRACTICE

The last key idea to be addressed, their general philosophy about the role of science, is an important one as it permeates the careers of both Ohlin and Cloward and was an instrumental factor in the development and nature of differential opportunity theory. It is not a specific concept like those discussed previously. They view science as a means for improving the human condition, and set out to apply its principles to some of the problems that exist in our society.

Ohlin (in Laub 1983) characterized his career as a "remarkable blend" of practical experience with research and academia. Early in his career, he worked extensively in the areas of corrections, parole, and juvenile delinquency. He worked with Donald Cressey at the penitentiary in Joliet, Illinois, and later did a study in Wisconsin on the probation and parole systems. He took the position of sociologist–actuary for the Illinois Parole and Probation Board in order to be able to gather prison data for his dissertation, but he was torn, as he was also interested in working with Shaw and McKay on the Chicago Area Project. Ohlin's dissertation research led to the publication of *Selection for Parole: A Manual of Parole Prediction* in 1951. This book presented some ground-breaking ideas about parole prediction and established the link between theory and practice that would be exemplified throughout Ohlin's career. A few years later, Ohlin prepared a paper that he refers to as his "swan song" on prediction. He had become disenchanted with prediction for parole, because he believed that the methods and statistical analysis had "outrun the data"; the statistical advances were not adding anything to predictive utility. In 1955, he presented *Predicting Delinquency and Crime* to the Third International Congress of Criminology in London and left the area of prediction (Laub 1983), but he never lost the applied and practical orientation that it represented. According to Ohlin (in Laub 1983), his experiences working in the correctional system had a profound effect on him, demonstrating that despite his commitment to research,

research alone does not provide complete understanding; for the whole picture, one must also stay close to practice.

In 1959, while both were at Columbia, Ohlin and Cloward were asked by the coalition of the Lower East Side Community Settlement House in Manhattan to help them develop a theoretical framework and research program for a "saturation of service" project for youth. In working on this project, Cloward and Ohlin first began to apply the ideas they had developed about differing subcultures (Laub 1983). Their practical experience and research in corrections led to the formulation of some general theoretical notions that could now be applied to a different set of real-world problems and would ultimately lead to their statement of differential opportunity theory.

After the publication of *Delinquency and Opportunity* in 1960, Cloward and Ohlin went in different directions. Ohlin continued to pursue the connection between theory and application, accepting Attorney General Robert Kennedy's offer to serve as Special Assistant on Delinquency to the Secretary of Health, Education, and Welfare, Abraham Ribicoff. Ohlin worked with the President's Committee on Juvenile Delinquency and Youth Crime at its inception in May 1961. Serving as an "in-house academic theorist on delinquency," he was involved in formulating new federal policy that became the Prevention and Control Act of 1961, based on a comprehensive action program developed by Cloward and Ohlin as part of differential opportunity theory. It called for improving the educational system, creating work opportunities, organizing lower-class communities, and providing a variety of services to individuals, families, and gangs (Laub 1983, Vold and Bernard 1986).

Ohlin believes that the programs under the Kennedy Administration were right on target. Unfortunately, he says, "the whole effort was escalated too quickly from the experimental stage and swallowed up in the war on poverty, building model cities, etc." (Ohlin, personal communication, October 30, 1988), which created a situation wherein the "rhetoric of expectations far exceeded the resources available" (in Laub 1983). This seems rather ironic, as it appears that in the haste to alleviate the anomic situation of the lower class, a new and even more intense anomie was fostered. In light of the impact that rising expectations (see Davis 1962) and relative deprivation (see Gurr 1970) have been shown to have, it is not surprising that the War on Poverty was lost.[2] Laub (1983) concludes that what happened during this period "radicalized" Cloward. Ohlin seems to concur, saying that he was always more optimistic than Cloward about the possibility of affecting change (in Laub 1983), but he also admits that both were somewhat naïve in their optimism about the readiness with which social and organizational changes could be accomplished. The analysis was basically sound, but the capability for such large-scale social action was not there (Ohlin, personal communication, October 30, 1988).

During this time, Cloward worked for a while as the Director of Research for the Mobilization for Youth (MFY) Program, and then moved away from criminology and into the politics of community change and social welfare. His interest and experiences in this area led to the publication of three books with Francis Piven (1971, 1977, 1982) examining the plight of the poor in contemporary American society (Laub 1983, Cullen 1986; personal communication, September 8, 1988).

---

[2]For more detail on the implementation of Ohlin and Cloward's plan, see Peter Marris and Martin Rein's (1974) *Dilemmas of Social Reform* (2nd ed.) New York: Pelican/Penguin Books. For a more general discussion of the failure of the "War on Poverty," see Stephen Rose's (1972) *The Betrayal of the Poor: The Transformation of Community Action.* Cambridge MA: Schenkman.

Ohlin took a sabbatical in 1964 and part of 1965, and then returned to the President's Commission on Law Enforcement and the Administration of Justice as the associate director, during which time he continued to try to implement criminological theory and research into policy. In 1967, Ohlin returned to academia, but he did not sever his ties with the applied and practical elements of the discipline. In 1969, he started a comprehensive study on the Youth Correctional System in Massachusetts that culminated in two publications addressing issues of delinquency control (see Miller, Ohlin, and Coates 1977, Miller and Ohlin 1985). He currently serves as a co-director of the Program on Human Development and Criminal Behavior, a project that attempts to develop plans for large-scale and long-term longitudinal studies (Ohlin, personal communication, October 30, 1988).

Throughout his career, Lloyd Ohlin remained a social, political, and criminal justice reformer, pursuing the need for changes through radical research and theory. He advocated radical change in corrections and other aspects of the criminal justice system. In recent years, he has become somewhat concerned with quantitative models that force the utilization of inadequate data, submerging the legitimate sociological perspective in the process. He is also concerned that the dynamic cultural and social processes that are the legitimate subject matter of social science theory and research are being replaced by an overly pragmatic focus on management and administration in the criminal justice system (Laub 1983).

CONCLUSION

In describing the publication of differential opportunity theory in 1960, Ohlin (in Laub 1983) says that he and Cloward wrote a very different book than either could have written alone. Ohlin brought to this book the Chicago tradition, with its focus on "the social–psychological dynamics of socialization," and Cloward brought the Eastern tradition, emphasizing the "structural and functional aspects." Out of this combination, the distinctions between social systems and personal experience became clearer. From the perspective developed by their collaboration, Ohlin and Cloward portrayed delinquency as adaptive and instrumental, but also as partly reactive (Nettler 1984). This focus on the adaptive nature of delinquency differentiated Cloward and Ohlin's orientation from earlier explanations (e.g., Cohen 1955). Differential opportunity theory characterizes delinquents as goal-oriented, capable of rational assessment of their economic situation, and able to plan their futures accordingly (Shoemaker 1984).

The environment that breeds delinquency is seen as one in which social disorganization and limited opportunities for legitimate success go hand-in-hand with illegitimate opportunities. In these lower-class neighborhoods there is also lessened social controls and "acute frustrations," all of which intensify tendencies toward aberrant behavior. Under such conditions, crime exists in individual and unorganized forms (Cloward and Ohlin 1960), but the major concern of the differential opportunity approach was to explore the link between social structural patterns of youth opportunities and the dominant patterns of subcultural formations of youth that occur in response to them (Laub 1983). Cloward and Ohlin's approach actually asked researchers and theorists to invert their typical reasoning—instead of focusing on a type of deviance and then trying to identify the specific stressor producing it, their approach was to first identify conditions creating strain and then specify the possible adaptations and the factors associated with the occurrence of each (Cullen 1986).

It certainly seems that Ohlin and Cloward understood the high level of complexity involved in the etiology of delinquency and made a legitimate attempt to accommodate it in their theory. The ultimate question is how well were they able to do so.

IV. CRITIQUE

Cloward and Ohlin's differential opportunity theory has generated a great deal of research and criticism. This is not at all unusual for ground-breaking works that attract a lot of attention, but it is still a little surprising to find that almost half of the total amount of information consulted took the form of some criticism or question about the theory. Many of the complaints are generally attributable to the *openness,* or sheer variety of situational elements deemed to be of etiological importance (Nettler 1984), of the fundamental assumption of structural explanations.

THEORETICAL AND EMPIRICAL CRITICISMS

There are a significant number of serious theoretical and empirical problems attributed to strain theories in general (Kornhauser 1978), and some of these have been translated into specific areas of concern with Cloward and Ohlin's application of the strain orientation (Nettler 1984). The problems relate primarily to three aspects of the theory: anomie, the relationship between aspirations and opportunity, and types of subcultures/specialized gangs.

ANOMIE

One advantage of differential opportunity over Merton's original formulation is that it is more testable (Allen et al. 1981), and many have tried to put it to the test. From reviewing the results of the various attempts to test the theory, Vold and Bernard (1986) conclude that there are two inconsistencies between the theory and the data: (1) Gang delinquents are not talented youths suffering from a sense of injustice over a lack of legitimate opportunities, as portrayed by Cloward and Ohlin. (2) Their typology is not well supported.

The first of these inconsistencies is relevant to the notion of strain. Kornhauser (1978) criticizes Cloward and Ohlin for failing to account adequately for the proposed source of the strain, the gap between aspirations and expectations. Vold and Bernard (1986) encounter the same problem in reviewing the research, finding no conclusive evidence for the necessary discrepancy between aspirations and expectations.

Cullen (1986) points out that differential opportunity theory was developed during the "heyday" of strain/anomic theories, and it fit the prevailing mood of the time. Consequently, most detractors focused on how Cloward and Ohlin applied Merton's paradigm and not on more fundamental criticisms of the theory itself. Scholars picked at parts of the theory that are most consistent with the strain perspective. Tests of the theory involve little more than assessing whether there is a disjunction between aspirations and perceived opportunities. The dominant etiological question examined has been whether frustrated aspirations are sufficient to cause delinquency, rather than the more appropriate question of how illegitimate opportunity structure influences the types of adaptation to strain. Even those who have attended to the subcultural aspects have adopted a more purely substantive focus, assessing whether the specific types of subcultures postulated exist. Cullen sees differential opportunity as a critique of the strain perspective rather than a simple modification of it; he believes that labeling differential opportunity as a strain approach led many to miss the main point of the theory, resulting in serious misinterpretations and leaving much of its true theoretical utility and power untapped. Cloward and Piven (1979) offer a similar observation, as does Ohlin in his 1983 interview with Laub.

ASPIRATIONS AND OPPORTUNITIES

A review of the literature supports Cullen's (1986) contention that most of Ohlin and Cloward's criticism relates to the strain issue, more specifically to their treatment of the source of the strain on lower-class youth. In the original statement of the theory, Cloward and Ohlin (1960) claim that there is support for class differences in absolute level of aspiration. According to Shoemaker (1984), even if there is such a difference, it alone is not sufficient to support the theory, as it predicts that most delinquent youths should possess high aspirations and low expectations. It has also been pointed out that differential opportunity postulates that the gap between the desires of the lower class and their legitimate opportunities is greater than the gap between aspirations of the middle class and their legitimate opportunities. This general assumption, says Nettler (1984, 207), is highly questionable, as "research lends evidence to the opposite possibility."

The fundamental assumption that blocked economic aspirations affect attitudes and lead to frustration has been tested in a variety of ways, but it has not been strongly supported. Interviews with lower-class youths failed to demonstrate the proposed relationships between aspirations and the outcomes of their being blocked. It is possible that this lack of supportive data may be explainable by the fact that there is a difference between aspirations and expectations not adequately addressed in some of the studies—in other words, what one desires and what one actually expects may be very different (Shoemaker 1984). Consequently, having one's aspirations blocked may be less problematic than having one's actual expectations thwarted. Operating from this premise, Elliot and Voss (1974) assess the actual and anticipated amounts of success and failure in regard to occupational and educational status, and their results do not demonstrate a relationship between failure and self-reported delinquency. In fact, if anything, slightly the opposite was found: lowered perceptions of occupational success followed delinquency, rather than preceded it.

Although Cloward and Ohlin predict that most delinquent youths should exhibit a combination of high aspirations and low expectations, in research conducted by Short (1964) and Short, Rivera, and Tennyson (1965), evidence to the contrary was found. In the 1964 study, which compared male, white and black, lower-class gang members with lower- and middle-class non-gang members, it was white, lower-class gang members who displayed the smallest discrepancy in aspirations in relation to their fathers' occupational levels. Cloward and Ohlin (1960) state that their hypothesis does not depend on demonstrating that a "large proportion" of lower-class youths exhibit a high level of aspiration; it is sufficient to show that a "significant number" aspire beyond their means, if these individuals contribute disproportionately to delinquency. Although Short (1964) did find that those who perceived that their educational opportunities were blocked had the highest rate of delinquency, a finding generally consistent with the theory, he also found that these same youths exhibited the lowest aspiration levels, a condition directly contrary to the theory. The findings of Short and colleagues in the 1965 study were basically consistent with the 1964 study. On reviewing the re-search addressing the relationship between aspirations and expectations, Vold and Bernard (1986) conclude that delinquents are most likely to be low on both. If no dis-crepancy can be established between aspirations and expectations, then there is no support for the existence of the purported resulting strain.

This conclusion calls into question a primary motivator of delinquency proposed by Ohlin and Cloward—that juveniles become delinquent as a result of their frustra-tion and sense of being subjected to unjust treatment. Their conceptualization of moti-vation and dynamics leading to delinquency rests on an assumption of equality—not equality of the opportunity structure itself, but of "aspiration, interest, motivation, ap-plication, and ability." They take for granted what one normally expects would need to be known about individuals in order to determine specific aspirations, interests, abili-ties (Nettler 1984), and emotional/cognitive responses. However, any sweeping accep-tance of uniformity of such variables within a group must be questionable, especially given the statistical fact that within-group variance is often greater than between-group variance. Nettler (1984), commenting specifically on the issue of purported uni-versal perception of unjust treatment reported by delinquents, states that it is not news that criminals claim to be victims of an oppressive society and criminal justice system, but it is surprising that social scientists accept such a rationalization as necessarily accurate.

. Generally, there are two possible ways to explain the findings concerning the rela-tionship between aspirations and expectations: (1) The relationship is not as it is hy-pothesized by Ohlin and Cloward, and (2) our methods for assessing it are inadequate. Although it is true that our methods are invariably flawed, it does not seem likely that the preponderance of evidence from such a wide array of studies is wholly invalid. However, is still to be established what exactly these findings mean in regard to the utility and value of differential opportunity theory in its entirety. To address this last issue more fully, it is necessary to examine some other aspects of the theory, both theoretical and otherwise.

Nettler (1984) proposes that the emphasis on equality clearly establishes Cloward and Ohlin's approach as one of "opportunity–structure" rather than one related to some other hypothesis. Nettler believes this classification is appropriate, because even though there are subcultural elements to the theory, it portrays all members of society as wanting much the same thing, but possessing differential opportunities to attain them. In other words, people are the same but are pressured into different courses of action by the structure of their available life chances. Nettler (1984, 208) concludes, however, that "while the opportunity–structure thesis as a whole sounds plausible, closer attention to its assumptions lessens confidence in its explanatory power." There have been three major questions raised about the opportunity–structure thesis:

1. Are the key concepts clear?
2. Does the theory accurately describe persistent offenders?
3. Are the recommendations of opportunity–structure feasible and effective? (Nettler 1984)

The two key concepts of the theory, aspirations and opportunity, are not clearly defined, because both have been borrowed from the common vernacular. Conse-quently, their meanings and interpretations are multidimensional, and the words themselves carry a variety of emotionalized connotations. The treatment of aspirations confuses what people say that they would like to have with what they believe they need and actually expect to get. Various attempts to assess aspirations have accepted what people say for what they really want; words have been equated directly with motives. Opportunity, within the context of the theory, is equally as vague. This vagueness has been perpetuated by the practice of using opportunity as a cause of conduct, and then using the alleged effects of that opportunity as a measure of it (i.e., that A causes B is proved by B as a measure of A). Such circular reasoning may be "comfortable for purposes of moral and political debate," but it does not meet the criteria for scientifically testing a hypothesis (Nettler 1984). Both Cullen (1986), who cites confusion over the term *opportunities* as one of the major limiting factors of the theory, and Vold and Bernard (1986) agree that Cloward and Ohlin's failure to define their concepts clearly created serious problems for and doubts about the theory.

In defense of Cloward and Ohlin, Cullen (1986) places some of the blame on others, stating that many scholars have inappropriately used a focus that is too narrow in interpreting opportunity. It has been treated like a single variable, when it is clear that Cloward and Ohlin use it to refer to various values, skills, and structural opportunities that allow social roles to be learned and performed.

Along with general concern over unclear definitions and operationalization of concepts, there are questions about the association between opportunity and criminality, especially in terms of economic opportunity (Allen et al. 1981). Even before the publication of *Delinquency and Opportunity*, Glaser and Rice (1959) found that the frequency of juvenile crime varies inversely with unemployment rates, whereas adult property crime varies directly with the rate of unemployment. It has been reported that juveniles do not exhibit immediate concern about future employment and economic goals. If this is the case, then it is doubtful that the blocking of legitimate economic opportunities is important in determining illegal activity by lower-class youths (Short 1964, Short and Strodtbeck 1965, Hirschi 1969). Such findings have led some to argue that it is not the absolute level of unemployment, but the "relative deprivation" that creates frustration and dissatisfaction (Allen et al. 1981). Gurr (1970) says that relative deprivation occurs when individuals believe that they are deprived in relation to those with whom they compare themselves. The greater the feelings of relative deprivation, the more intense the frustration.

Short et al. (1965) and Friday (1970) conclude that differential opportunity theory must be modified to include a stronger focus on perceived blockage of opportunities. This is similar to criticisms about the theory not using individualized variables when such an approach might be necessary for more complete understanding. A more individualized treatment would address the concern voiced by Reckless (1973) that Ohlin and Cloward do not indicate who would and who would not respond to illegitimate opportunities. The adoption of a more individualized focus might also provide answers to some of the questions raised by research on social mobility and career development, which indicates that careers depend more on how opportunities are used than simply on whether they are present. It appears that, had Cloward and Ohlin used concepts like aspiration, expectation, abilities, and so on in the more individual sense in which they are often conceived, they might have avoided some of the confusion and subsequent criticism. However, they would certainly have opened themselves and their theory up to a whole new host of criticisms usually levied at the more social–psychological accounts.

One other issue raised relates to the role of the criminal justice system in this process. Allen et al. (1981) point out that the research attempting to establish a relationship between the degree of opportunity and deviance has not controlled for the impact of contact with the criminal justice system. Consequently, most of these studies have not been able to examine the causal sequence sufficiently. It could be that various perceptions and actual gang behavior evolve out of such contact, either independently or in conjunction with blocked legitimate and accessible illegitimate opportunities. Differential opportunity may be more applicable as an explanation of maintenance of delinquent behavior and recidivism than of first offenses.

SUBCULTURES/SPECIALIZED GANGS

Cloward and Ohlin (1960) say that they were attempting to explore two questions: (1) Why do delinquent norms develop? (2) What conditions account for the distinctive content of the various systems of delinquent norms? In addressing these questions on a theoretical level, they relied heavily on the concept of delinquent subculture. In essence, differential opportunity theory represents a search for the origins of delinquent subculture (Mannheim 1965, Haskell, and Yablonsky 1978). In order to fully examine the criticisms concerning this aspect of the theory, it is necessary to discuss both the general conceptualization of subculture used by Cloward and Ohlin and their gang typology.

"A delinquent subculture is one in which certain forms of delinquent activity are essential requirements for the performance of the dominant roles supported by the subculture" (Cloward and Ohlin 1960, 7). This definition seems to suffer from the same affliction as the concepts of aspiration and opportunity; it is rather vague. It also offers an example of the source of the complaint lodged by Nettler (1984) that the reasoning is often circular. The existence of dominant subcultural roles is supported by the occurrence of certain forms of behavior that are in turn explained by the existence of subcultural roles. Another problem with the general notion of delinquent subculture is that Cloward and Ohlin (1960) argue that delinquent acts occurring among middle-class juveniles do not result from a delinquent subculture. They claim that there is no middle-class delinquent subculture because the delinquent middle-class youth do not receive support and approval from the nondelinquent members of the class or from the predominant conventional norms. Such a claim is hard to defend, and they offer no empirical support for it. As Mannheim (1965) points out, *Delinquency and Opportunity* does not present the results of any first-hand field work. In partial defense of Cloward and Ohlin's conceptualization of delinquent subculture, Spergel (1964) reports finding integration levels consistent with their formulation; however, integration is actually more relevant to the specific content of the subculture than it is to a general definition of the concept. According to Cullen (1986), this is the point at which differential opportunity differs from strain theories. Although strain theories may postulate the development of a subculture as an adaptation to the strain, they are incomplete because they do not account for the content of the resulting adaptation. Cloward and Ohlin were primarily concerned with explaining the form the subculture might take (Williams and McShane 1988, Mannheim 1965,).

The second of Nettler's (1984) three primary questions about the theory is, does the theory accurately describe persistent offenders? When one looks at the discussions of Cloward and Ohlin's gang types in the literature, two elements relevant to this question can be identified: (1) content or specialization and (2) motivation. In terms of the content or specialization, Spergel (1964) concludes that gang specialization does occur, but he was not able to identify the three types that Ohlin and Cloward postulated. He found no drug type (retreatist), and decided that the criminal type had two subcategories: theft and racket. Short and Strodtbeck (1965) and Wolfgang, Figlio, and Sellin (1972) also found some specialization in delinquent gangs, but not along the same content lines or as clearly as predicted by Cloward and Ohlin. Although one may interpret these findings as generally supportive of the notion of gang types, they do not support the existence of Cloward and Ohlin's specific types, nor do they offer conclusive evidence that delinquent gangs can be classified clearly based on their types of activities. In recent years, with the tremendous increase in juvenile gang involvement with large-volume drug trafficking, the lines between Ohlin and Cloward's original three types (if they ever did exist) have probably been completely eradicated. Many of these new entrepreneurs are also consumers, and the link between the drug trade and violence has been well established.

Rivera and Short (1968), similar to Kobrin, Puntil, and Peluso (1967), find that adolescent boys are not as isolated from or antagonistic to adults as Cloward and Ohlin had predicted. More specifically, Ohlin and Cloward adopt the same basic stance as Merton, focusing on economic goals (Short and Strodtbeck 1965). The earlier discussion of career orientation is also applicable here and is supportive of these findings; however, although it is true that much of the research in the 1960s did not present a picture of the juvenile gang member that was consistent with Cloward and Ohlin's characterization, it does seem feasible to conclude that the characterization of the juvenile gang member as calculating, rational, and strongly economically motivated may be more accurate today than it was then (Shoemaker 1984).

Vold and Bernard (1986) agree that there are two areas of inconsistency between the theory of differential opportunity and the data; one relates to the gang typology itself, and the other to the specific motivations of gang members. They go on, however, to state that neither component is essential to the theory overall and can be discarded with no substantial damage. They also claim that too much attention has been devoted to such subcultural elements, which are actually secondary to the structural components of the theory. (Of course, this point is quite debatable, as noted elsewhere in the chapter, including Cullen's conclusions.) The theory has often been evaluated using inappropriate groups. Bernard (1984) says that it is designed to explain seriously delinquent urban males in gangs, and when such a group is studied, the theory is supported.

Cullen (1986) argues, contrary to Vold and Bernard, that not enough attention has actually been paid to the subcultural aspects of Ohlin and Cloward's work, and furthermore, the studies investigating these aspects have adopted an almost purely substantive approach, trying to assess whether the types of subcultures postulated really exist. In regard to this part of the theory, as with the aspiration–opportunity issue, it has been argued by some that too much attention has been paid to the wrong thing and not enough to the real key elements. However, there is considerable disagreement as to what the wrong things are and what the key elements are.

In a couple of general comments, Mannheim (1965) calls the division of delinquency into three subcultures one of the more original features of the theory, but he considers the attempt to link these to the neighborhood milieu to be interesting but largely speculative. Unfortunately, the data collected since the publication of the theory have not yet provided a definitive assessment of Mannheim's conclusion. Cloward and Ohlin's "subcultural sociological typology" of delinquent subcultures fares no better than other sociological classifications, as it (too) is unable to discard psychological or social–psychological aspects (Shafer 1969).

APPLICABILITY AND PRACTICE

With respect to the issue concerning whether the recommendations of differential opportunity are feasible and effective, Nettler (1984) claims that a fair test of any hypothesis is whether it works when applied. In the case of Ohlin and Cloward's ideas, the principles of differential opportunity theory were implemented into policy and programs by the Kennedy and Johnson administrations, and the programs ultimately failed. However, for the utility of a hypothesis to be assessed validly, it must be established that the test was in fact designed and carried out appropriately. First, Cloward and Ohlin's plan called for preventive programs, not programs that attempted to change what already existed (Vold and Bernard 1986). In addition, they did not predict the eradication of crime simply through the process of providing more legitimate opportunities to some members of society. They pointed out that "extending services to delinquent individuals or groups cannot prevent the rise of delinquency among others" (Cloward and Ohlin 1960, 211). Therefore, they really were not advocating an all-inclusive mass change of the lower-class situation within the social structure. Nonetheless, by the time their recommendations were put into practice, they looked like change programs, and they very quickly were subverted to serve the interests of the bureaucracies administering them (Vold and Bernard 1986). Consequently, the programs that became part of Johnson's lost War on Poverty may not constitute a fair test of Ohlin and Cloward's theoretical concepts. Cloward, from his experience in the Mobilization for Youth project, became involved in the politics of community change and social welfare. His work in these areas was presented in three publications with Piven (Cloward and Piven 1979, Piven and Cloward 1971, 1977) that detail how the theoretical principles from differential opportunity have been successfully applied. Unfortunately, they have gone largely unnoticed by criminologists (Cullen 1986).

HEURISTIC VALUE

It is important not to lose the point that the main value of theoretical conceptualizations is not necessarily the ultimate establishment of their external validity. As George Kelly (1955) says, all theories have a limited lifespan. However, the thought and subsequent work that they generate need not know the same limits. On a general theoretical level, the Ohlin's and Cloward's ideas demonstrate to criminology the necessity for theories that are sufficiently complex and broad enough to address the full range of interacting variables involved in producing human behavior (Reckless 1973, Cullen 1986). They directed attention to the utility of some earlier ideas at a time when, as Ohlin (in Laub 1983) said, criminology had run out of theories and none were giving the payoff that was desired. They also showed the potential utility of integrating ideas from various sources in order to develop a more complete understanding.

Ohlin and Cloward are included in this book not just for the specific concepts that they developed or for their interpretation of someone else's work, but mainly because, thirty years after they published the major statement of their theory, people are still actively debating, interpreting, and conducting research about their ideas. The ultimate testimony to the value of an idea is not necessarily what is thought about, but how much thinking is subsequently done about it by others.

CONCLUSION

From a retrospective look at Ohlin and Cloward's work, in particular differential opportunity itself, it seems apparent that they comprehended the level of complexity involved in human behavior, and tried to accommodate it by drawing from a variety of sources and attempting to refine and integrate the different concepts. Of course, how successful they were in doing that is still being debated. In the process, they inevitably created some confusion, both in their interpretations and in the minds of many who attempted to assess them. The hybrid nature of their theorizing led different people to classify and interpret their work in different ways. Although to some extent this may be seen as a weakness, it can also be viewed as a strength. As with all theories, differential opportunity garnered some support and equally as much criticism, and as Cullen (1986) reminds us, it is possible that much of the criticism may be the result of misconceptions that have become self-generating preconceptions. In addition, despite the many criticisms that have been leveled at differential opportunity, the optimistic view of human nature woven into it has had an impact even on its critics, who acknowledge how appealing and plausible the theory is (Vold and Bernard 1986). Nettler (1978, 237) sums this up best, stating, "It may not be true, but it's a good story."

Whatever the final evaluation is, there is no doubt that differential opportunity theory is still an integral part of the criminological literature, and it may be that its true theoretical power has yet to be fully tapped (Cullen 1986). When John Laub (1983) asked Lloyd Ohlin how important *Delinquency and Opportunity* is for contemporary students and theorists, Ohlin replied that he did not think that it is outdated at all. He stated that *Delinquency and Opportunity* has been misinterpreted as offering a basic theory of individual delinquency, when in fact, it is really a theory of subculture formation—a narrower, more specialized problem. In particular, he believed that there were two aspects of the theory that have not been fully exploited: (1) the way in which opportunity structures create collective subcultural responses that condition individual experiences, and (2) the need to theorize and research further on ways in which operating criteria get established and applied to admit or deny access to legitimate and illegitimate opportunities to differentially selected groups.

References

Adler, A. 1956. H. L. Ansbacher, & R. R. Ansbacher (Eds.), *The individual psychology of Alfred Adler: A systematic presentation in selections from his writings*. New York: Harper Torch Books.

Allen, H. E., P. C. Friday, J. R. Roebuck, & E. Sagarin. 1981. *Crime and punishment: An introduction to criminology*. New York: The Free Press.

Bernard, T. J. 1984. Control criticisms of strain theories: An assessment of theoretical and empirical adequacy. *J. Res. Crime Delinq.* 21(4):353–72.

Bloch, H., & A. Niederhoffer. 1958. *The gang: A study of adolescent behavior*. New York: Philosophical Library.

Cloward, R. A. 1959. Illegitimate means, anomie, and deviant behavior. *Am. Sociolog. Rev.* 24(2):164–76.

Cloward, R. A., & L. E. Ohlin, L. E. 1960. *Delinquency and opportunity: A theory of delinquent gangs.* Glencoe, IL: The Free Press.

Cloward, R. A., & F. F. Piven. 1979. Hidden protests: The channeling of female innovation and resistance. *Signs.* 4(4):651–69.

Cohen, A. K. 1955. *Delinquent boys.* New York: The Free Press.

Cohen, A. K., A. Lindesmith, & K. Scheussler (Eds.). 1956. *The Sutherland papers.* Bloomington, IN: Indiana University Press.

Cullen, F. T. 1986. Were Cloward and Ohlin strain theorists? Delinquency and opportunity revisited. Revised version of paper presented at the meeting of the American Society of Criminology, Atlanta, GA.

Davis, J. C. 1962. Toward a theory of revolution. *Am. Sociolog. Rev.* 27:5–19.

Elliott, D. S., & H. L. Voss. 1974. *Delinquency and dropout.* Lexington, MA: D.C. Heath.

Friday, P. C. 1970. *Differential opportunity and differential association in Sweden.* Unpublished doctoral dissertation, University of Wisconsin.

Glaser, D., & K. Rice. 1959. Crime, age, and employment. *Am. Sociolog. Rev.* 24:679–86.

Gurr, T. R. 1970. *Why men rebel.* Princeton, NJ: Princeton University Press.

Haskell, M. R., & L. Yablonsky. 1978. *Crime and delinquency.* 3rd ed. Boston: Houghton Mifflin.

Hirschi, T. 1969. *Causes of delinquency.* Berkeley, CA: University of California Press.

Kelly, G. A. 1955. *A theory of personality: The psychology of personal constructs.* New York: W. W. Norton & Company.

Kobrin, S. 1951. The conflict of values in delinquency areas. *Am. Sociolog. Rev.* 16:653–661.

Kobrin, S., J. Puntil, & E. Peluso. 1967. Criteria of status among street groups. *J. Res. Crime Delinq.* 4:98–118.

Kornhauser, R. R. 1978. *Social sources of delinquency.* Chicago: University of Chicago Press.

Laub, J. H. 1983. *Criminology in the making.* Boston: Northeastern University Press.

Mannheim, H. 1965. *Comparative criminology.* Boston: Houghton Mifflin.

Merton, R. K. 1957. *Social theory and social structure* (rev. ed.). New York: The Free Press.

———. 1959. Social conformity, deviation, and opportunity structures: A comment on the contributions of Ohlin and Cloward. *Am. Sociolog. Rev.* 24:177–89.

Miller, A. D., & L. E. Ohlin. 1985. *Delinquency and community: Creating opportunities and controls.* Beverly Hills: Sage Publications.

Miller, A. D., L. E. Ohlin, & R. B. Coates. 1977. *A theory of social reform: Correctional change processes in two states.* Cambridge, MA: Ballinger.

Nettler, G. 1978. *Explaining crime.* 2nd ed. New York: McGraw Hill.

———. 1984. *Explaining crime.* 3rd ed. New York: McGraw Hill.

Ohlin, L. 1955. *Predicting delinquency and crime.* Paper presented at the Third International Congress of Criminology, London, England.

Piven, F. F., & R. A. Cloward. 1971. *Regulating the poor.* New York: Vintage Books.

———. 1977. *Poor people's movements: Why they succeed, how they fail.* New York: Pantheon.

Reckless, W. C. 1973. *The crime problem.* 5th ed. Pacific Palisades, CA: Goodyear Publishing Company.

Rivera, R. J., & J. F. Short, Jr. 1968. Significant adults, caretakers, and structures of opportunity: An exploratory study. In J. F. Short, Jr. (Ed.), *Gang delinquency and delinquent subcultures.* New York: Harper and Row, pp. 209–43.

Shafer, S. 1969. *Theories in criminology: Past and present philosophers of the crime problem.* New York: Random House.

Shaw, C. R., & H. D. McKay. 1942. *Juvenile delinquency in urban areas.* Chicago: University of Chicago Press.

Shoemaker, D. J. 1984. *Theories of delinquency: An examination of explanations of delinquent behavior.* New York: The Free Press, pp. 98–127.

Short, J. F., Jr., & F. L. Strodtbeck. 1965. *Group process and gang delinquency*. Chicago: University of Chicago Press.

Short, J. F., Jr., R. Rivera, & R. A. Tennyson. 1965. Perceived opportunities, gang membership, and delinquency. *Am. Sociolog. Rev.* 30:56–67.

Spergel, I. 1964. *Racketville, Slumtown, and Haulburg*. Chicago: University of Chicago Press.

Stephan, C. W., & W. G. Stephan. 1985. *Two social psychologies*. Homewood, IL: The Dorsey Press.

Vold, G. B., & T. J. Bernard. 1986. *Theoretical criminology*. 3rd ed. New York: Oxford University Press.

Williams, F. P., III, & M. D. McShane. 1988. *Criminological theory*. Englewood Cliffs, NJ: Prentice Hall.

Wolfgang, M. E., R. Figlio, & T. Sellin. 1972. *Delinquency in a birth cohort*. Chicago: University of Chicago Press.

Complete Bibliography

Lloyd Ohlin
Books

Cloward, R. A., & L. E. Ohlin. 1960. *Delinquency and opportunity: A theory of delinquent gangs*. Glencoe, IL: The Free Press.

Farrington, D. P., L. E. Ohlin, & J. Q. Wilson. 1986. *Understanding and controlling crime*. New York: Springer-Verlag.

Miller, A. D., & L. E. Ohlin. 1985. *Delinquency and community: Creating opportunities and controls*. Beverly Hills: Sage Publications.

Miller, A. D., L. E. Ohlin, & R. B. Coates. 1977. *A theory of social reform: Correctional change processes in two states*. Cambridge, MA: Ballinger.

Ohlin, L. E. 1951. *Selection for parole: A manual of parole prediction*. New York: Russell Sage Foundation.

————. 1956. *Sociology and the field of corrections*. New York: Russell Sage Foundation.

Ohlin, L. E. (Ed.). 1973. *Prisoners in America*. Englewood Cliffs, NJ: Prentice Hall.

Ohlin, L. E., R. B. Coates, & A. D. Miller. 1978. *Diversity in a youth correctional system*. Cambridge, MA: Ballinger.

Ohlin, L. E., & M. Tonry (Eds.). 1989. *Family violence*. Chicago: University of Chicago Press.

Miller, A. D., R. B. Coates, & L. E. Ohlin. 1980. Evaluating correctional systems under normalcy and change. In M. Klein & K. Teilman (Eds.), *Handbook of criminal justice evaluation*. Beverly Hills: Sage Publications.

Other Publications

Miller, A., & L. E. Ohlin. 1981. The politics of secure care in youth correctional reform. *Crime Delinq.* 27(4): 449–67.

Ohlin, L. E. 1954. The routinization of correctional change. *J. Crim. Law Criminol. Pol. Sci.* 45(4): 400–11.

————. 1955. Frustration in treatment experience. *Am. Correc. Assoc.* 41–50.

————. 1955. New trends in research in the organization of correctional agencies. *Am. Correc. Assoc.* 56–66.

————. 1956. [Review of Mannheim & Wilkins, *Prediction methods in relation to Borstal training*]. *Harv. Law Rev.* 70:398.

————. 1957. What are the delinquency problems in Cook County? In *Searchlight on delinquency in Cook County*. Chicago: Cook County Sheriff's Office.

————. 1958. Conformity in American society today. *Soc. Work* 3(2):58–66.

————. 1958. The development of social action theories in social work. *Education for social work*. Proc. Ann. Prog. Meet. Coun. Soc. Work Ed.

————. 1958. The reduction of role conflict in institutional staff. *Children* 5(2):65–69.

————. 1958. The U.S. crime problem and the correctional task. *Pris. Crime Preven. Miss. Nat.*

————. 1959. When is punishment effective? *J. Assoc. Psych. Treat. Prob.*

————. 1960. Conflicting interests in correctional objectives. *Soc. Sci. Res. Coun.* [Pamphlet].

————. 1964. Introduction. In I. Spergel, *Racketville, Slumtown, and Haulberg*. Chicago: University of Chicago Press.

_____. 1968. Challenge of crime in a free society. The effect of social change on crime and law enforcement. *Notre Dame Law.* 43(6):834–46.

_____. 1970. *A situational approach to delinquency prevention.* Washington, D.C.: U.S. Government Printing Office.

_____. 1970. *Situational perspectives on delinquency prevention.* Washington, D.C.: U.S. Department of Health, Education and Welfare.

_____. 1971. Partnership with the social sciences. *J. Legal Educ.* 23(1):204–08.

_____. 1973. Institutions for predelinquent children. In D. M. Pappenfort, D. M. Kilpatrick, & R. W. Roberts (Eds.), *Child caring.* Chicago: Aldine.

_____. 1974. Current aspects of penology: Correctional strategies in conflict. *Proc. Am. Philosoph. Soc.* 118:248.

_____. 1974. Radical correction reform: A case study of the Massachusetts youth correctional system. *Harv. Educ. Rev.* 44:74–111.

_____. 1975. Foreword. In D. Fogel, *We are living proof.* Cincinnati: W. H. Anderson.

_____. 1975. Foreword. In P. Lerman, *Community treatment and social control.* Chicago: University of Chicago Press.

_____. 1975. The President's Commission on Law Enforcement and Administration of Justice. In M. Komarovsky (Ed.), *Sociology and public policy: The case of presidential commissions.* New York: Elsevier, p. 93.

_____. 1975. Reforming programs for youth in trouble. In M. J. Begab & S. A. Richardson (Eds.), *The mentally retarded and society: A social science perspective.* Baltimore: University Park Place, p. 423.

_____. 1976. The prevention and control of delinquent acts. In N.B. Talbot (Ed.), *Raising children in modern America.* Boston: Little, Brown.

_____. 1977. The aftermath of extreme tactics in juvenile justice reform: A crisis four years later. In D. F. Greenberg (Ed.), *Corrections and punishment.* Beverly Hills: Sage Publications, p. 227.

_____. 1977. Preface. In B. C. Field, *Neutralizing inmate violence: Juvenile offenders in institutions.* Cambridge, MA: Ballinger.

_____. 1977. Tendances d'evolution penitentiaire aux Etats-Unis. *Revue de Droit Penal et de Criminologie* 57:845.

_____. 1978. Preface. In C. A. McEwen, *Designing correctional organizations for youth.* Cambridge, MA: Ballinger.

_____. 1979. [Review of *Criminal violence, criminal justice*]. *Harv. J. Legis.* 2:669.

_____. 1982. Population pressures and policy options for state prison systems. In *Criminal justice and corrections.* Washington, D.C.: National Governors Association.

_____. 1983. The future of juvenile justice policy and research. *Crime Delinq.* 29:463–72.

_____. 1987. Alternatives to the juvenile court process. In F. X. Hartmann (Ed.), *From children to citizens. Vol. 2: The role of the juvenile court.* New York: Springer-Verlag, pp. 219–26.

_____. 1987. A memoriam of Donald R. Cressey. *Criminol.* 12(5):5, 7.

Ohlin, L. E., & R. C. Cloward. 1969. The differentiation of delinquent subcultures. In D. R. Cressey & D.A. Ward (Eds.), *Delinquency, crime, and social process.* New York: Harper and Row.

Ohlin, L. E., A. D. Miller, & R. B. Coates. 1975. Evaluating the reform of youth correction in Massachusetts. *J. Res. Crime Delinq.* 12(1):3–16.

Ohlin, L. E., O. D. Duncan, A. J. Reiss, Jr., & H. R. Stanton. 1953. Formal devices for making selection decisions. *Am. J. Sociol.* 58(6):573–84.

Ohlin, L. E., & W. C. Lawrence. 1959. Social interaction among clients as a treatment problem. *Soc. Work* 4(3):3–13.

_____. 1958. The role of the inmate system in the institutional treatment process. *Proc. Natl. Assoc. Train. Schools Juv. Agen.* 54.

Ohlin, L. E., & J. Miller. 1976. The new corrections. The case of Massachusetts. In M. K. Rosenheim (Ed.), *Pursuing justice for the child.* Chicago: University of Chicago Press.

_____. 1979. The politics of correctional reform: An analytical approach to the nature of social change. *Penn. Assoc. Prob. Par. Correc. Quart.* 36:16.

Ohlin, L. E., H. Piven, & D. M. Pappenport. 1956. Major dilemmas of the social worker in probation and parole. *Natl. Prob. Par. Assoc. J.* 2(3).

Ohlin, L. E., & F. J. Remington. 1958. Sentencing structure: Its effect upon systems for the administration of criminal justice. *Law*

Contemp. Prob. 23(3): 495–507.

Ohlin, L. E., & H. S. Ruth, Jr. 1967. Combating crime: A bibliography. *Ann. Am. Acad. Polit. Soc. Sci.* 374:1–184.

Selected Bibliography

Richard A. Cloward

Cloward, R. A. 1959. Illegitimate means, anomie, and deviant behavior. *Am. Sociolog. Rev.* 24(2):164–76.

Cloward, R. A., & L. E. Ohlin. 1960. *Delinquency and opportunity: A theory of delinquent gangs.* Glencoe, IL: The Free Press.

Cloward, R. A., & F. F. Piven. 1979. Hidden protests: The channeling of

female innovation and resistance. *Signs* 4(4):651–69.

Piven, F. F., & R. A. Cloward. 1977. *Poor people's movements: Why they succeed, how they fail.* New York: Pantheon.

———. 1971. *Regulating the poor.* New York: Vintage Books.

CHAPTER 12
GRESHAM M'CREADY SYKES: B. 1922

—∼∽∾∿⌇—

I. BIOGRAPHICAL SKETCH

Gresham Sykes commands one of the most notable careers in contemporary criminology. Not only are his works distinct and exemplary publications, but his career has also been nicely balanced between wide-ranging teaching assignments and significant administrative posts. Information regarding his childhood in Plainfield, New Jersey, is sparse. However, his career as a high achiever is evident as early as 1942, when, at the age of twenty and prior to completing college, he entered World War II.

After four years of active duty in England, France, Belgium, and Germany, Sykes departed military service with the rank of Captain in the Corps of Engineers. Immediately after his military discharge in 1946, he married Carla Adelt, and that same year entered Princeton University; four years later, he graduated with a bachelor's degree in sociology. He distinguished himself by receiving Phi Beta Kappa honors and graduating *summa cum laude.*

During his undergraduate years, he held three scholarly grants: the Woodrow Wilson Fellowship (1950–51), the Northwestern University Fellowship (1951–52), and a summer fellowship (1951) from the Social Science Research Council. After graduation, Sykes went directly into the doctoral program in sociology at Northwestern University in Evanston, Illinois. Three years later, in 1954, he graduated with a PhD in sociology. His doctoral dissertation, entitled *Social Mobility and Social Participation,* concerned the function and structure of the Parent–Teachers Association (PTA), with particular focus on what type of person tended to participate in such voluntary organizations. In addition, Sykes found that a latent function of the PTA was that it acted as a mechanism for reducing conflict between parents and teachers (Sykes 1953a, 1953b).

Sykes' teaching career got off to an early start. Prior to completing the bachelor's degree, he taught as an instructor at Princeton University, and after completing his PhD, he returned to Princeton as an assistant professor in 1954, and he remained at his alma mater for four years. During these early academic years, Sykes quickly excelled through professional publications. In 1951, only a year after completing undergraduate school, he published "Differential Distribution of Community Knowledge" in the journal *Social Forces.* For the next thirty-five years, hardly a year elapsed in which an article, monograph, or book of his did not appear in print.

Contrary to some scholars discussed in this book, for much of his career Sykes was not one to remain isolated at a single university. After his initial teaching appointment at Princeton University, he moved to at least a dozen different institutions for varying periods of time. For several years, he must have been living almost out of a suitcase as he migrated between various professorial appointments. For this reason, it is rather difficult to determine his institutional affiliation when he was inspired to write some of his major works, or to determine from whom he received scholarly encouragement. At the same time, working in so many university environments must have provided wide exposure of his ideas to an extensive number of students.

Although Sykes did remain at Princeton for almost six years (1952–58), the subsequent six years saw him teach at six different institutions. Following Princeton, he taught for two summers at the Moran Institute of Criminology, after which he accepted a brief assignment at Columbia University as visiting professor. In 1958, he was appointed Associate Professor of Sociology at Northwestern University, where he remained for only two years. In the summer of 1960, Sykes moved west as a visiting professor at UCLA, returning east for a three-year stint as professor of sociology at Dartmouth College. Dartmouth saw fit to award Sykes an Honorary Masters in Arts degree in 1961.

In 1965, he participated in a summer seminar in Salzburg, Austria; and that same year, at age forty-three, Sykes finally settled in to one place for seven years — from 1965 to 1972, he was Professor of Sociology and Law at the Law Center of the University of Denver. Even during this time, however, he spent the winter semester in 1968 at the University of California at Santa Cruz. In 1977, he was Professor of Sociology at the University of Houston, and in 1973 to 1974, he was a visiting professor at the University of Iowa. Finally, in 1974, at age fifty-two, Sykes found a home at the University of Virginia in Charlottesville. In 1988, after a personal record of fourteen years at one place, he was named Professor Emeritus of Sociology.

Sykes published the first of his five books, entitled *Crime and Society,* in 1956. Two years later, while still at Princeton, he introduced *The Society of Captives* (1958). This work carved out a permanent niche for him in criminology and the rapidly expanding subdiscipline of penology or corrections. His timing could not have been better, because it had been eighteen years since a comparable analysis of a maximum-custody prison system had been published (see particularly, *The Prison Community,* Clemmer 1940). *The Society of Captives* saw great success in the United States and internationally, and was translated into Japanese in 1964. It was reissued in 1971 by Oxford University Press and remains available today. Sykes also authored *Law and the Lawless* (1969a), *Social Problems in America* (1971a), and *Criminology* (1978).

Sykes wrote or coauthored four notable monographs. The first and probably the most visible was published by the Social Science Research Council and entitled "Theoretical Studies in Social Organization of the Prison" (Sykes, Cloward, Cressey, et al. 1960), and was the result of the contributions of seven scholars participating in a correctional conference on prison organization in the late 1950s. For many years the small booklet was available free of charge from the Social Science Research Council, and undoubtedly appeared as supplementary reading in departments of criminology and corrections nationwide during the 1960s and 1970s. In 1980, Sykes wrote *The Future of Crime* under the auspices of the National Institutes of Mental Health. He maintained an avid interest in future directions of the discipline and addressed criminological trends in several publications (1971a, 1972, 1974a, cf. 1980). Two other lesser-known monographs that nonetheless reveal his other interests and activities include "Legal Needs of the Poor in the City of Denver" (1969b) and "Model Cities and Resident Participation" (1971d).

Sykes also produced about thirty articles or book chapters interspersed among his books and monographs. Unquestionably, a most significant contribution consisted of several articles coauthored with David Matza regarding the theoretical interpretation of delinquent behavior—"Techniques of Neutralization: A Theory of Delinquency" (Sykes and Matza 1957), and "Juvenile Delinquency and Subterranean Values" (Matza and Sykes 1961). Both of these works appeared in the *American Sociological Review* and met with great success. Since the appearance of these articles in print, virtually no text in delinquency or criminology fails to include a discussion of their original conceptualization. It appears that Sykes, following the pattern of many prominent thinkers in this book, produced his major writings early in his career. Sykes' written works cover a wide range of topics, from delinquency theory, to prison organization and inmate behavior, to evaluations of the future of the discipline. He clearly combined theory with applications of policy, especially notable in his discussions of prison riots (Sykes 1957a, 1957b, 1959a, Sykes and White 1969) and prison reform (Sykes 1968, Sykes, Cloward, Cressey, et al. 1960, Matza and Sykes 1961) and court congestion (Sykes and Isbell 1967).

In disseminating his ideas, Sykes took advantage of multiple outlets, not limiting himself to traditional journals in sociology and criminology. He published in literary magazines (*The Nation* 1959a, 1959b, 1971b) and law reviews (*The Denver Law Journal* 1969d, *The Toledo Law Review,* Sykes and Martinez 1971). Furthermore, he contributed a lengthy discussion on prisons and penology to the *Encyclopedia Britannica* (1974b).

Sykes' administrative career progressed at the same spirited rate as his teaching and publications. He served as director, chair, or executive officer of at least ten organizations. Noteworthy among these were his serving as department chair or director of four academic programs: the sociology departments at Dartmouth College, the University of Houston, and the University of Virginia, as well as serving as director of the Administration of Justice program at the University of Denver. Sykes sat on numerous state and national government advisory boards, particularly those concerned with penological issues, behavioral science research, and education.

Furthermore, Sykes served as criminology editor of *The Journal of Criminal Law, Criminology, and Police Science* from 1959 to 1964. In 1980, Sykes received the Edwin H. Sutherland award in criminology.

II. BASIC ASSUMPTIONS

It is often problematic to speak of basic assumptions underlying the thoughts and deeds of our more contemporary scholars. Certainly, as the discipline of criminology developed, increasingly diverse and extensive contributions to the existent body of knowledge emerged naturally. Consequently, determining the network of individuals who influenced modern writers becomes even more complex. Certainly, this is the case with Sykes, who continues to contribute to criminological thought after more than three decades. Nonetheless, analysis of his primary written works indicates at least three origins of apparent influence.

First, for many years Sykes maintained a fascination with the nature of knowledge and authority in organizations and society. An appreciation of the fundamental ideas of Max Weber—especially his theorizing about social and economic organizations Henderson, Parsons and Weber (1947) can be seen in his earlier writings as well as in *The*

Society of Captives. Sykes seems to have been influenced both by Weber's theoretical directions as well as by the concepts he used. Both examined authority networks in organizations. Perhaps more basically, Sykes, like Weber, developed the concepts of *rationalization* in social groups. Sykes argues that the ability to create ornate rationalization patterns provides a basic ingredient that enables individual or groups to behave in delinquent or criminal ways. Such ideas can be traced, at least indirectly, to Weber's explanations of such inventions as bureaucracies that can be understood as organizational systems that allow humans to rationalize the disuse of older and more primary human values (see the discussion of Max Weber by Robertson 1981, 299–300).

Second, as many students immediately following World War II, Sykes clearly built on the ideas and writings found in Robert Merton's *Social Theory and Social Structure* (1949) and Talcott Parsons' *The Social System* (1951). These prominent thinkers refined the fundamental Durkheimian statements demanding a functionalist view of society. Sykes' earlier writings advance functionalist concerns, as is apparent in his analysis of the distribution of knowledge throughout a community (1951), and his original work on the structure and function of authority networks in organizations, including prison settings (1953, 1956, 1958). Several of Sykes' colleagues at Princeton with similar intellectual bearings, namely Melvin M. Tumin and Wilbert E. Moore, had a more direct impact on him (Sykes 1958, viii).

A third basic assumption derives from his appreciation of the essential principles of Edwin Sutherland's work on cultural transmission or learning theory. There is no doubt that Sykes accepted sociological inquiry in the Sutherland tradition. Several of Sykes' more celebrated publications reflect a direct recognition of Sutherland's theory of differential association (Sykes and Matza 1957, Matza and Sykes 1961). Sykes certainly followed in Merton's and Sutherland's footsteps, and his basic assumptions hold close affinity to those underlying the thinking of the two earlier scholars.

III. KEY IDEAS

Sykes' works extend beyond the immediate boundaries of criminology. However, it appears clear that his principal contributions to criminology may be organized around three areas: (1) the prison system, (2) neutralization theory, and (3) future projections of crime and criminology.

THE PRISON SYSTEM

A review of the works that launched the names of individual scholars into prominence reveals several surprising points. A particular treatise, destined to become a classic document in the discipline, seems in many cases to emerge at the beginning of a career, as in the case of doctoral dissertations or books written soon after graduate school. To the individual contributors, this presents a bonus of early establishment of a career. Moreover, the written works, even if of future pioneering status, often appear, at least on the surface, to be unassuming and at times even of diminutive size. Cohen's *Delinquent Boys* (1955), Goffman's *Stigma* (1957), Whyte's *Street Corner Society* (1943), and Park, Burgess, and McKenzie's *The City* (1925) represent such examples. Sykes' *The Society of Captives*, a small, unpretentious book of 120 pages, fits this category of works that although creative in their own right, nonetheless appeared on the market at a time seemingly ripe for new interpretation of past issues.

The Society of Captives is not a definitive work on prisons and certainly not the first analysis of human captive populations. However, its publication in 1958, nearly two decades after Clemmer's *The Prison Community* (1940), introduced perhaps the first truly unbiased ethnography of a major maximum-custody prison. Besides Clemmer's study, the research project by Sykes built on other previous prison studies (see particularly Reimer 1937, Schrag 1944). With *The Society of Captives* we see a comprehensive view of the modern prison setting as a social system. The fundamental features of the book include the following:

1. Social structure of prison guards
2. Defects of total power
3. Pains of imprisonment
4. Inmate argot roles
5. Crisis and equilibrium within the prison

The Social Structure of Prison Guards

When Sykes began his study of the New Jersey State Prison in 1955, he anticipated resolving several specific hypotheses dealing with the causes and effects of various prisoner adjustment patterns to prison life. He soon learned that awareness of prison environments at that time was yet too little developed for such research questions. Sykes writes:

> An effort toward hypotheses testing was somewhat premature; there was far too little knowledge of the variety of roles played by criminals in prison and even less knowledge of how these roles were related to one another and to the social order which the custodians attempted to create in the pursuit of their assigned tasks. (1958, xviii–xix)

Sykes was convinced even prior to the research that the prison must be seen as a society within a society. All the mechanisms noted in other types of social systems, whether family or communities, would predictably be observed in the maximum-custody institution. What was different in the prison social system was the attempt to maintain total power over the inmate population. The prison was a bureaucratic organization, but one in which the bureaucrats carried guns in order to carry out their orders, at least in the minds of the community. However, the prison, according to Sykes, does not intend to annihilate its captives, either physically or psychologically, nor is it designed to "wring the last ounce of effort from an expendable labor force. Instead, it pursues an odd combination of confinement, internal order, self-maintenance, punishment, and reformation, all within a framework of means sharply limited by law, public opinion, and the attitudes of the custodians themselves" (1958s, xv).

Once the mission of the prison is established, the task remains of accomplishing it. Sykes outlines five dilemmas that prison guards face. First, by the very nature of the prison, the custodian necessarily adapts a "punitive orientation." The nature of the task of keeping offenders locked up forces such an image, because it involves such objectives as endless precautions, the constant counting of the inmates, the many regulations, and periodic searches (1958, 15). Prison officials are thus cast in a role of appearing to oppose reformation programs.

Second, Sykes found that given the fundamental principles of deterrence or retribution, a sense of inmate deprivation becomes appropriate, and necessarily demonstrates the advantages of obeying the law. This creates a collision course for those who believe in prisoner reformation. *The Society of Captives* emerged at the beginning of a resurgence of the rehabilitative ideal (Irwin 1980). Sykes was one of the first to document the tension felt by both custodians and advocates of inmate rehabilitation, both of whom were in pursuit of divergent goals. Goffman's work, especially his analysis of "total institutions," was being composed at about the same time as *The Society of Captives* (Goffman 1957).

Third, the prison guard had the difficult problem of maintaining prison labor forces and organizing inmate populations into a labor force capable of supporting itself. Such an attempt created thorny custodial problems and elicited outrage from private enterprise in the open community.

A forth dilemma confronting the custodians regards the maintenance of a crime-free population within the walls of a prison. This is difficult given the high level of movement of prisoners throughout the institution. Not all inmates can be kept in solitary confinement; consequently, the many woes found outside the institution also occur within the densely populated captive population. The custodians must therefore also be police officers and deal with such critical issues as internal disorder.

Finally, the question concerning exactly what role the custodian holds in the prisoner reform process remains unresolved. Although prison guards might not disagree with the ideological aims of prisoner reform, the task of implementing those reforms in a maximum-custody institution is found by Sykes to be problematic at best:

> The officials of the prison are indifferent to the task of reform, not in the sense that they reject reform as a legitimate organizational objective, but in the sense that rehabilitation tends to be seen as a theoretical, distant, and somewhat irrelevant by-product of successful performance at the tasks of custody and internal order. Within the walls, the occurrence of escapes and disorders is a weightier problem. (1958, 38)

The Defects of Total Power

Sykes is perhaps at his best in revealing what actually transpires inside the prison in respect to the authority structure. The common belief is that in a tight bureaucratic organization, lines of authority and who wields influence over whom are clear. However, according to Sykes, such is not the case in the maximum-custody prison. At least five features are noteworthy. First, contrary to what the ideal type of bureaucracy is supposed to accomplish, the prison is not a smooth example of the exercise of legitimate authority. If such were true, we would not see a proliferation of violence, fraud, theft, and aberrant sexual behavior—all commonplace in the prison setting. This is so despite the fact that the prison is viewed by society as the ultimate "weapon for the control of the criminal and his deviant actions" (Sykes 1958, 42).

Second, according to Sykes, the prison is distinguished by not fitting Weber's ideal-type bureaucracy because even with the prison's symbols of power and a system of order and regulations, there is no high probability that the rules will be obeyed. The inmate population is simply not an obedient group. Rebellious incidents are common. Inmates do not typically maintain a motive for compliance. This, of course, is particularly true when prisoners are already locked up on long sentences and are feeling near maximum punishment. What else is there to lose? Surely, there is no sense of duty to obey rules as supposed by Weber's ideal bureaucratic order.

A third defect of total power is that force or coercion is grossly inefficient as a means of eliciting obedience. This is particularly evident in a prison setting, where inmates are expected to perform a multitude of often-complex work tasks. It is well known today that the masses of prisoners actually hold sizable influence in large institutions compared to the smaller cadre of staff members. Sykes was perhaps the first to analyze this feature in detail.

Fourth, Sykes reveals that the custodial force may, indeed, not be willing to exercise authority in the sense expected by many unfamiliar with the inner workings of the institution. Just as police officers on the beat must ignore most of the infractions they know to persist, so the prison guard may also deliberately ignore disobedience. In a sense, "the guard shows evidence of having been 'corrupted' by the captive criminals over whom he stands in theoretical dominance" (Sykes 1958, 54). The custodial officer is much more likely to fall into a pattern of purposefully overlooking infractions because unlike the police officer, the prison guard is also locked within the confines of the institution.

The guard is torn between loyalty to the bureaucratic ideal of administrative rules and punishments and of getting along, while unarmed, with inmates in a potentially dangerous atmosphere. Sykes further notes that the guard, as a strict enforcer of the rules, is undermined by prisoners who can so easily retaliate by a series of infractions in the cell block, thus making the custodial officer look bad to higher administrators. Furthermore, "the guard knows that some day, he may be a hostage and that his life may turn on a settling of old accounts" (1958, 57). Sykes summarizes his view as follows:

> The lack of a sense of duty among those who are held captive, the obvious fallacies of coercion, the pathetic collection of rewards and punishments to induce compliance, the strong pressures toward the corruption of the guard in the form of friendship, reciprocity, and the transfer of duties into the hands of trusted inmates — all are structural defects in the prison's system of power rather than individual inadequacies. (1958, 61)

Pains of Imprisonment

As Sykes outlines the impact of prison life on the inmates, we are again reminded of Goffman's description of institutionalization. Both writers perceived similar effects of captivity. Sykes characterizes five types of *deprivation* suffered by the prisoner. These are deprivations of (1) liberty, (2) goods and services, (3) heterosexual relationships, (4) autonomy, and (5) security. In adapting to such personal stressors, the prisoner has two options: One, join with fellow captives and reap the benefits of mutual aid, loyalty, affection, and respect; doing so places the inmate in opposition to the prison staff. The second option is to pursue personal advantages without regard for other inmates. Sykes establishes two styles of reaction, one being *collectivistic,* or an inmate orientation, and the other an *alienated* response. The latter places the prisoner at odds with both the inmate population as well as with officials, who are viewed as simply another obstacle to overcome. Patterns of social interaction among inmates are scattered between these two extremes.

Argot Roles

Without a doubt, the analysis of language patterns within the prison population provided Sykes his most popular account of inmate life. Although argot roles may certainly be studied as a topic by itself, Sykes sees language more as another avenue of adapting

TABLE 1 Argot Roles in the New Jersey State Prison

"Argot" designation	*Functional Definition*
Rats	Inmates who squeal on fellow prisoners
Center men	Inmate who sides with staff
Gorilla	Inmates who take goods by force
Weakling	Inmate who submits to force
Merchants/peddlers	Inmates who sell objects for profit
Fish	New prisoners/strangers
Wolves	Aggressive homosexual (masculine role)
Punks, fags	Passive homosexual (feminine role)
Ball busters	Inmates openly defiant of officials
Toughs	Inmates hostile toward fellow inmates
Hipsters	Inmates who pretend to be tough
Real men	Inmates who serve time with dignity

Sykes 1958, 84–106.

to the unnatural life inside the prison, and simply as an alternate aspect of the overall prison social system. He discusses a variety of possible explanations for the emergence of distinctive language patterns among prisoners, most prominent among these was that special argot that functioned primarily to provide "utility in ordering and classifying experience within the wall in terms which deal specifically with the major problems of prison life" (1958, 85). Sykes uncovered interesting language patterns that provided a map of the inmate social system. Space limitation does not permit full discussion of the range of prison argot; however, Table 1 represents a quick review of the basic types.

Sykes sees the numerous argot types to be associated with the various "alienative" modes of response to the specific problems of incarceration. The "Rat," "Wolf," "Gorilla," or "Hipster" argot, for example, represents social roles in which the prisoner tries to adjust to the rigors of prisonization, often at the expense of fellow inmates. If some patterns of behavior result in alienative responses, others result in more "cohesive" adaptations to prison stresses. The "Real man" category represents a cohesiveness that embraces such social qualities as loyalty, generosity, and sexual restraint. Prison social order can be seen as an interplay between these two opposing forces.

Crisis and Equilibrium Within the Prison

The early 1950s saw a sizable amount of turmoil in the nation's maximum security prisons. Nearly two dozen prison riots occurred across the country that caught the various prison systems and correctional theorists somewhat by surprise. In *The Society of Captives,* Sykes offers one of the earliest, albeit brief, sociological discussions of prison discord. He does not attempt to explain the etiology of riots, but provides descriptions of roles, positions, and statuses of inmate and staff groups that typically fluctuate between crisis and harmony. In exploring the social structure of prison turmoil, he builds on the earlier typology of pains of imprisonment and argot roles. Sykes' focus on the extent of various argot roles, how each emerged, and their relationship to the prison administration allows a sharper conceptualization of the social organization of the prison community.

Sykes appears to accept the principle that the prison environment itself primarily generates conditions conducive to turmoil and crises, which may, over time, build to riot levels. Some years later, other researchers held that a good deal of prison disorder may also result from the diverse and conflict-prone nature of individual offenders who enter the prison in the first place (see particularly Irwin 1980).

NEUTRALIZATION: THEORY

A lesser-known work, the brief document "The Corruption of Authority and Rehabilitation" (1956), published several years prior to the release of *The Society of Captives,* may well be the best summary of Sykes' theoretical perspectives. Although the article obviously contains much of the information also outlined in the larger book, it nonetheless succinctly introduces several original ideas fundamental to what later received wide acceptance as "neutralization theory."

Simply put, neutralization theory argues that an individual obeys or disobeys societal rules depending on his or her ability to rationalize a particular infraction as appropriate. Accordingly, Sykes notes that "an individual justifies action by unconsciously distorting reality, and the ego-image is protected from hurt or destruction under the attacks of self-blame" (1956, 258). At this point, Sykes builds directly on Sutherland's earlier statements that criminal behavior is learned as "definitions favorably to violation of the law" (Sutherland and Cressey 1970, 77–80); that is, if an individual is taught in a social setting that it is appropriate in a given circumstance to steal, then the individual is likely to engage in crime based on an ability to rationalize wrongdoing. Sutherland mentioned the term *rationalization* but failed to develop it in his general theory of crime. Furthermore, Sykes first amplified the concept of rationalization in his discussion of the prison culture.

Corruption of Authority in Prisons

Although Sykes was concerned with the structure of authority relationships from the beginning of his scholarly writing, the tenuous nature of authority becomes clearest to him when he examines the relationship between prison guards and their prisoners. As revealed in *The Society of Captives,* this authority relationship is corrupted as a result of the nature of the prison social structure. Prisoners learn they can exert substantial pressure on the solitary guard; consequently, prisoners learn numerous means to circumvent the authority of the guard as a symbol of law and order to the prisoner.

Sykes suggests that if the prison becomes such an arena for learning how to rationalize overcoming the authority of the guard, then how can rehabilitation take place? The inmates' ability to influence the guard to overlook infractions is carried to the open community, where other symbols of authority (e.g., parents, police, employers) are seen as corruptible.

Rationalization of Delinquency by Youth

Sykes teamed with David Matza in 1957 to write "Techniques of Neutralization: A Theory of Delinquency." Following Sykes' earlier work, the writers develop a series of specific examples of how a youth might learn to neutralize violation of law. The authors enlarge not only Sutherland's theory of differential association (Sutherland and Cressey 1970), but also Cohen's explanation of the delinquent gang response (1955). For example, Cohen believed that working-class youth might respond to frustrated expectations by turning the norms of the middle-class upside-down.

The idea here, according to Sykes and Matza, is that a delinquent youth is aware of both sets of aspirations, but learns to rationalize one above the other. In fact, according to Sutherland, all individuals experience both good and evil to varying degrees, and the culture in which persons are reared determines to a major extent their ability to rationalize or neutralize deviant behavior as appropriate. More than fifty years have passed since Sykes and Matza's typology of five primary types of neutralization appeared in print, yet they remain as pertinent today as in 1957.

Denial of Responsibility

An individual may disavow personal accountability from wrongdoing by placing the blame on forces outside his or her personal control. Examples given by Sykes and Matza include unloving parents, bad companions, or being reared in a slum neighborhood. This particular technique may appear rather sophisticated, as in the case when a youth mimics, for personal benefit and for others, the textbook explanations of deviance learned from a professional counselor. Thus, a youth might argue, "Don't blame me; after all, I am suffering from an anomic environment."

Denial of Injury

This technique is comparatively straightforward and represents rationalization of deviance or crime by arguing that nobody was actually hurt as a result of the infraction. A sense of personal wrongfulness subsides as the offender is convinced that few people, if anyone, will miss the object stolen, or that vandalism was simply mischief (Sykes and Matza 1957, 667).

Denial of Victim

An offender may also avoid guilt feelings by a conviction that the deed was a result of rightful retaliation. Like the antics of Robin Hood, stealing or assault, for example, may be justified as appropriate under the circumstances. Arguing that someone deserves punishment meted out during the commission of a crime dehumanizes or denies the existence of a victim, and thus mitigates any sense of wrongdoing on the part of the offender.

Condemnation of Condemners

One may rationalize delinquency as appropriate by seeing the symbol of authority as corrupt—that is, the offender may rationalize, "Why should I obey rules if I see you, the law maker or rule enforcer, as more corrupt than I?" A malevolent or corrupt guardian, police force, or government allows the youth or adult to more easily neutralize his or her own feelings of guilt.

Appeal to Higher Loyalties

Legal requirements of the larger society may be sacrificed to demands of the small group. For example, one may violate the law by refusing to report the delinquent or criminal conduct of a friend or confidant. Loyalty to the fraternity may be greater than loyalty to the state. In addition, a parent may justify stealing in order to provide for a family. The important point is that the ability to neutralize deviance relates to the larger question of how tenuous the relationship is between those in authority and those subject to authority. If one spends the developing years in a social setting in which symbols of authority are not respected and there is no duty to comply with codes of conduct, a rationalization of infractions becomes more likely, as illustrated in the prison environment.

THE FUTURE OF CRIME

Sykes' insights into the future of crime and criminology are evident in his devotion of a sizable amount of time scrutinizing the abrupt and sometimes volatile social changes evident in the 1960s and 1970s. He was subsequently concerned with the way fluctuations in the sociopolitical mood of the times had an impact on crime and the justice system. Sykes resurfaced in the early 1970s as a scholar committed to understanding future directions of the discipline before such a topic was in vogue. At the beginning of the 1970s, he published several timely articles: "New Crimes for Old" (1971c), immediately followed by "The Future of Criminality" (1972).

Sykes argues, perhaps with more clarity than others of the time, that the earlier and rather traditional theoretical explanations of criminality no longer qualified as true explanations for much of the illegality appearing on the scene during that time period. Clearly, much reported crime could no longer be pigeonholed into the theoretical boxes that had long been associated with earlier eras. Specifically, for example, much of the deviance and crime begged for explanations other than those incorporated in cultural transmission, social control, or anomie theories. Sykes maintains,

> The trouble with these sociological explanations of criminality is due, not so much to their inadequacy in dealing with the more or less conventional crime for which they were designed, but to the fact that they have been overtaken by the rush of history, and are being used to interpret behavior patterns that are a new element on the scene. The position of the social scientist, like that of many others, is undermined by social change. (1971c, 594)

Sykes addressed several categories of illegal behavior that fell under the broad headings of (1) sport crime, (2) high-tech crime, and (3) political crime. Today, several decades later, these types are no longer newsworthy as novel categories of crime. However, to perceive such an emergent trend in 1971 was rather prophetic, given that the forecasting of future trends has become a pressing concern of criminology.

The reader is advised to consult the original publications for complete descriptions of what Sykes observed as "new" types of crimes. Briefly, however, in his first category, he believed that much crime and delinquency of this sort was committed purely as a game or sport, without any underlying motive to reap monetary rewards. He admits that others, such as Cohen, had earlier suggested nonutilitarian theft, but believed that the volume of crime falling in the sport category surpassed that noted among working-class gangs. A marked increase in auto theft as a type of adventurous, juvenile white-collar crime flourished in the 1960s and 1970s. Also, he saw a substantial increase in shoplifting among the more well-to-do, which tended to defy explanation using traditional economic or strain-type theories. Sykes writes,

> We are looking, I think, at a new kind of crime, in the sense that it doesn't fit much of the theorizing of criminology in the past. And, in fact, there are some writers who see in the future the possibility of a large increase in crime as sport, with relatively well-educated people using sophisticated techniques to create havoc in parts of the social system. (1971c, 596)

As a second category, Sykes recognized early the approaching wave of high-tech crime, such as tampering with long-distance phone lines, fixing national opinion polls, and modifying computer programs. Such a high-tech crime style allows the offender to remain detached from the victim, and at the same time to engage in crime for fun or illegal excitement.

Sykes also perceived a major growth in political crime, noting the more than 5000 bombings in the United States between 1970 and 1972. In addition, of eighteen persons on the FBI's "Most Wanted" list, ten were politically motivated offenders. He states,

> The kinds of acts that frequently involve political goals, such as violent anti-war demonstrations, the seizing of property, the destruction of records, and so on, have reached a new high and may be on the increase, despite the supposed cooling-off of the American scene at the beginning of the seventies. (1971c, 596)

Rather than try to use such traditional explanations as personality defect or economic strain of an impoverished social class, Sykes saw political crimes as a "denial of the validity of the political and social order. The offender becomes not a mere deviant from accepted rules, but a symbol for a competing system of power" (Sykes 1971c, 597, cf. 1972). In a Mertonian sense, these new crimes resulted not from innovation, but from a rejection of society's goals. Sykes saw such rejection much more widespread in the beginning of the 1970s than in earlier years. Crime had to be seen as more than a consequence of status frustration.

The proliferation of adventurous crime, high-tech fraud, and political terrorism involved value changes extending beyond simple economics and encompassing modifications in family, religion, work, and politics. Sykes saw the new styles of crime as a bitter rejection of America and everything it stands for. He argues,

> When this kind of alienation appears in society, we are likely to get a new kind of crime, or, perhaps more accurately, we should speak of new motives or additional motives for old kinds of crime. Trashing the establishment, or vandalism, acts of rage so diffuse in their targets that they appear virtually inexplicable—these become important symbolic gestures, not deliberate means to limited ends, but affronts to society as a whole. (1971c, 597, cf. 1972)

In such a condition, Sykes believed, law is not so much violated as ignored.

Sykes embraced the theoretical theme that gave meaning to the changing face of crime in his publication, "The Rise of Critical Criminology" (1974a). Essentially, it was not by chance that conflict theory flourished at the same time that Sykes was formulating the new categories of illegality. Rather than searching for the causes of crime in a defective personality or community, Sykes looked at the law and justice system itself as having become the target of criticism. In the same sense that many U.S. citizens blamed their own government as the culprit in the Vietnam War, so the new wave of crime could be seen as a consequence of disenchantment by citizens with a biased justice system or one gone astray.

Sykes was especially concerned that political dissent appropriate to a free society not be thwarted by a "get tough" policy of a post-Watergate era (Sykes 1980, 67, 69). Subsequently, the entire nature of the discipline of criminology began to adjust with the advent of "radical" or "critical" criminology. The justice system itself began to be again scrutinized by researchers, but from a different vantage point. In this regard, Richard Quinney's work, discussed elsewhere in this book, becomes particularly germane.

IV. CRITIQUE

Over the years, Sykes' key ideas remained relatively untarnished. His formative ideas regarding authority relationships in organizational hierarchies, as found in prison social systems, stand intact. From the advantage of hindsight, it appears that Sykes' conclusions represent the most definitive account of the impact of prison life on the inmate to arise in the late 1950s. His findings illustrate prison life at one point in time, rather than constitute a complete historical description. Consequently, it is clear that *The Society of Captives* provided a needed, and possibly the first truly unbiased ethnographic analysis of prison life in a maximum-custody prison in the post–World War II period.

After the *The Society of Captives*, holistic studies of major prison systems gave way to more detailed testing of hypotheses of specific aspects of prisoner life. Although not necessarily implying a criticism, post-1950s theorists claimed the problems of prisons do not result just from the strained social organization of guard–inmate relationships. Complications such as competing inmate gangs and rioting may derive from turmoil already existing outside the wall—that is, in the 1960s and 1970s, as urban populations increased dramatically in cultural heterogeneity, a new type of inmate emerged within prisons. As angry and politically energized ethnic groups began to appear in the open population, they ultimately found their way into the various prison populations (see Irwin 1980 for the best analysis of this point). Such a new mix of prisoners compounded the already strained organizational relationships in the maximum-security prison as described by Sykes.

Regardless of any subsequent complications, Sykes' work must be seen in reference to a time immediately following World War II and preceding the socially tumultuous late 1960s. The specific typology of prison argot and the way language patterns correlate with prisoner functions and social statuses remain distinctive and convincing.

Neutralization theory, as suggested by Sykes, originated from his research on guard–inmate authority relations. Inmates and guards alike, he found, learned quickly to rationalize breaking rules in the tight confinement of the prison. Joining with his student David Matza while at Princeton, he further refined the theoretical concepts of neutralization theory and produced a series of ideas and postulates well received by the criminological audience.

Heavy negative criticism of neutralization theory simply does not exist. What mild challenges one may find tend to follow the same reasoning directed against Sutherland's general learning theory. It is plausible and convenient to presume that individuals float or drift between law-breaking and acceptable behavior based on the ability to rationalize a particular deviant act as appropriate. However, Sykes and Matza were not precise as to why or how the neutralization process originated. A similar criticism of Sutherland's differential association theory asks the question, if criminal behavior is socially learned, from whom did the first person learn criminal behavior? If the ability to rationalize is also learned, we must presume then that such learning occurs in social groups and varies from one situation to another.

In a Jekyll–Hyde fashion, juveniles develop the ability to choose or to justify legal or illegal behavior by reflecting on the numerous adult models of behavior available to them. Among other factors, if a youth feels he or she can escape punishment or, like the prison inmate, has little to lose, then crime or delinquency may be more easily rationalized. Consequently, neutralization theory is occasionally discussed under the broader category of "control theory": that is, if the controls of behavior are seen to expand, and the risk of being apprehended and of losing face increases, then deviant or illegal acts become more difficult to rationalize. Accordingly, adults tend to be less deviant or criminal than youth because with advancing age and increased responsibilities, it becomes more difficult to justify getting into trouble with authorities (for further critique of these ideas, see Shoemaker 1984).

In the late 1980s, still relatively few criminologists designated the future of crime and criminology as a primary area of study or research. Nonetheless, concern with the manner in which law and justice systems adjust to the changing times increasingly appears as a topic at national conferences. Predictions of the ways crimes of the future may differ from those of today, or may be dealt with differently, must take into account Sykes' earlier projections. His booklet *The Future of Crime* (1980) is especially noteworthy in that it contributes predictions based on a careful synthesis of social science research rather than on nonscientific speculations, and is particularly valuable in that it offers the reader more than 200 footnotes and references.

After forty years in academia, Gresham Sykes continues to exemplify an optimal blend of qualitative science and theory applied to critical social issues.

References

Clemmer, Donald. 1940. *The prison community.* New York: Holt, Rinehart and Winston.

Cohen, Albert K. 1955. *Delinquent boys: The culture of the gang.* Glencoe, Ill.: The Free Press.

Goffman, Erving. 1957. *Characteristics of total institutions.* Symposium on Preventative and Social Psychiatry, Walter Reed Medical Center, Washington, D.C., April 15–17.

Irwin, John. 1980. *Prisons in turmoil.* Boston: Little, Brown, and Company.

Matza, David, & Gresham M. Sykes. 1961. Juvenile delinquency and subterranean values. *Am. Sociolog. Rev.* 26: 712–19.

Merton, Robert K. 1949. *Social theory and social structure.* Glencoe, Ill.: The Free Press.

Park, Robert E., Ernest W. Burgess, & Roderick D. McKenzie. 1925. *The city.* Chicago: The University of Chicago Press.

Parsons, Talcott. 1951. *The social system.* Glencoe, Ill.: The Free Press.

Reimer, Hans. 1937. *Socialization in the prison.* Proceedings of the Sixty-Seventh Annual Congress of the American Prison Association, pp. 151–155.

Robertson, Ian. 1981. Max Weber. In Arthur W. Frank (Ed.). *The encyclopedia of sociology.* Guilford, Conn.: DPG Reference Publishing, Inc.

Schrag, Clarence. 1944. *Social types in a prison community.* Master's thesis, University of Washington.

Shoemaker, Donald J. 1984. *Theories of delinquency: An examination of explanations of delinquent behavior.* New York: Oxford University Press.

Sutherland, Edwin H., & Donald Cressey. 1970. *Criminology.* New York: J.B. Lippincott.

Sykes, Gresham M. 1951. The differential distribution of community knowledge. *Soc. Forces* 29: 376–82.

———. 1953a. The PTA and parent–teacher conflict. *Harv. Edu. Rev.* 23(5): 86–92.

———. 1953b. The structure of authority. *Pub. Opin. Quart.* 17(1): 146–50.

———. 1956. The corruption of authority and rehabilitation. *Soc. Forces* 34(3): 157–62.

———. 1956. *Crime and society.* New York: Random House.

———. 1957a. Men, merchants, and toughs: A study of reactions to imprisonment. *Soc. Prob.* 4(2): 130–37.

———. 1958. *The society of captives: A study of a maximum security prison.* Princeton: Princeton University Press.

———. 1959a. Prison riots: A struggle for power. *Nation* May 5: 399–401.

———. 1959b. The luxury of punishment. *Nation* July 18: 31–33.

———. 1967. Feeling our way: A report on a conference on ethical issues in the social sciences. *Am. Behav. Scien.* 10 (June).

———. 1968. Criminals and non-criminals together: A modest proposal. *Pris. J.* XLVIII (2).

———. 1969a. *Law and the lawless.* New York: Random House.

———. 1969b. Legal needs of the poor in the city of Denver. *Law Soc. Rev.* 4(2): 255–77.

———. 1969c. Cases, courts, and congestion. In Laura Nader (Ed.), *Law in culture and society.* New York: Aldine Publishing Company.

———. 1971a. *Social problems in America.* Glencoe, Ill.: Scott, Foresman and Company.

———. 1971b. Today's campus: The eerie calm. *Nation* April 19.

———. 1971c. New crimes for old. *Am. Schol.* 40(4): 592–98.

———. 1971d. *Model cities and resident participation* (monograph). Denver Urban Observatory. University of Denver College of Law.

———. 1972. The future of criminality. *Am. Behav. Scient.* 15: 403–19.

———. 1974a. The rise of critical criminology. *J. Crim. Law Criminol.* 65: 206–13.

———. 1974b. Prisons and penology. In *Encyclopedia Britannica* 14: 1097–104.

———. 1980. *The future of crime.* U.S. Department of Health and Human Services. Washington, D.C.: Government Printing Office.

Sykes, Gresham, Richard A. Cloward, Donald R. Cressey, George H. Grosser, Richard McCleery, Lloyd E. Ohlin, et al. 1960. *Theoretical studies in social organization of the prison.* Social Science Research Council (Pamphlet No. 15), New York.

Sykes, Gresham M., & M. Isbell. 1967. Court congestion and crash programs: A case study. *Denv. Law J.* 44 (Summer).

Sykes, Gresham M., & Wilfred Martinez. 1971. Some lessons of Cleo. *Toledo Law Rev.* 2(3): 679–89.

Sykes, Gresham M., & David Matza. 1957. Techniques of neutralization: A theory of delinquency. *Am. Sociolog. Rev.* 22: 664–70.

Sykes, Gresham M., & Kyle B. White. 1969. Riots and the police. *Denv. Law J.* 46(1): 118–29.

The Theory of Social and Economic Organization by A.M. Henderson, Talcott Parsons, Max Weber; Oxford University Press, 1947.

Whyte, William Foote. 1943. *Street corner society.* Chicago: University of Chicago Press.

CHAPTER 13
ERVING GOFFMAN: 1922–1982

—*∿∿*—

INTRODUCTION

A chapter on Erving Goffman included in any book on criminological thought may at first seem out of place, especially because Goffman never wrote specifically about the discipline. In fact, according to some individuals who knew Goffman, he perceived of criminology as a vulgar trade, an applied field that was not elegant enough for him to study. When the authors of this book spoke to a former student of Goffman's, indicating we intended to include a chapter on him because of his influence on the discipline, the former student responded by calling our statement about Goffman's impact "contentious." However, although to date the work of Goffman has not been generally considered to have had a direct and significant impact on the development of criminological thought, except possibly in the area of labeling theory, he has indeed made important contributions to the development of thought that have direct applications to our field. Therefore, we include Erving Goffman among the pioneers of criminology.

I. BIOGRAPHICAL SKETCH

Very little information has been published about the early life of Erving Goffman. This appears to have been intentional; Goffman did not want, or possibly did not believe it important, to share with society the intimate details of his life. Goffman's position on providing biographical information about himself is aptly demonstrated in his Presidential Address prepared for the 1982 meeting of the American Sociological Association. Goffman states his address is different from most in that it is not "particularly autobiographical in character" (Goffman 1983, 2). He then proceeds to provide the reader with a succinct summary of his work, knowing that he is in the last stage of his life.

What has been published reflects, for the most part, his education and career as a sociologist. It is known that Goffman was born on June 11, 1922, in Manville, Alberta, Canada, the son of Jewish parents Max and Ann Goffman. In 1925, he received his bachelor's degree from the University of Toronto, and in 1949, he was awarded the master's degree from the University of Chicago.

From 1949 until 1951, Erving Goffman was a member of the faculty of the Department of Social Anthropology, University of Edinburgh. During this time, he was a member of the Shetland field research team. In 1951, he returned to Chicago to complete his work on his doctorate and was an assistant in the Division of Social Sciences from 1952 to 1953. The University of Chicago awarded him the Ph.D. in 1953. His dissertation, entitled *Communication Conduct in an Island Community* (1953), was based on his year of living and studying the people on one of the smaller of the Shetland Isles. It is reported that "twenty years after he had left the Shetlands he was still remembered with admiration, affection and disapproval as a hard man, a good friend, and a hard drinker" (Anonymous 1983, 13). From 1953 to 1954, Goffman was a resident associate in the Division of Social Sciences at Chicago, where he worked on several projects under the direction of E. Shils and E.C. Banfield.

In 1952, Erving Goffman married Angelica Schuyler Choate, who bore him one son, Thomas Edward. Goffman's wife unexpectedly passed away in 1964, and Goffman subsequently married for a second time, Professor Gilian Sankoff, a faculty member in the Department of Linguistics at the University of Pennsylvania.

From 1954 to 1957, Goffman was a Research Associate in the Visiting Scientist Program, Laboratory of Socioenvironmental Studies of the National Institute of Mental Health. During this time, he did research in a psychiatric ward in Bethesda, Maryland, as well as in St. Elizabeth's Hospital in Washington, D.C. His publication *Asylums: Essays on the Social Situation of Mental Patients and Other Inmates* (1961) was a direct outgrowth of his work in these psychiatric wards.

In 1958, he became an Assistant Professor of Sociology at the University of California at Berkeley, where he was promoted twice: to the rank of associate professor in 1959 and in 1962 to professor. He remained a member of the faculty of sociology at Berkeley until 1968, when he accepted the position of Benjamin Franklin Professor of Anthropology and Sociology at the University of Pennsylvania.

His dissertation on communication on the Shetland Isles informed his first book, *Presentation of Self in Everyday Life* (cited in Daniels 1983, 2). Published in 1956 by the University of Edinburgh Social Science Research Centre, it was first published in the United States in 1959. This first book has been followed by many others, all of which have added to Goffman's reputation.

In 1961, Goffman was recognized by the American Sociological Association for the contribution made by his *Presentation of Self in Everyday Life* and was presented with the McIver award. From 1977 through 1978, Goffman was awarded a Guggenheim fellowship. In 1979, the Section on Social Psychology selected Erving Goffman as the recipient of the Mead–Cooley Award and he received the George Orwell Award presented by the Harvard University Press. In addition to these awards, Goffman received honorary degrees from the University of Chicago and the University of Manitoba, and was elected a Fellow in the American Academy of Arts and Sciences.

In 1980, Goffman was voted president of the American Sociological Association, and was installed as president in 1981. Because of illness, he was unable to give his Presidential Address at the annual meeting of the organization in August 1982, but because he had written it for presentation, it was published posthumously in the *American Sociological Review* in February 1983 with the addition of a prefatory note.

Some of his students described Goffman as a very particular and opinionated individual who was difficult to get close to. He did not permit himself to be referred to as "doctor," and when discussing himself, he always identified himself as "student" (Lofland 1987, 18). There are those who identified themselves as "a close friend of Erving's, even though," as one person put it, "he might not have identified himself as a close friend of mine."

Of the numerous stories told about Goffman, in a 1987 *Urban Life* article on Goffman's legacies, John Lofland recites a number of them that provide insight into the man and a glimpse of his acerbic wit. An individual who attended graduate school with Goffman and remained a close colleague of his writes that Goffman was the "incarnation of cynicism."

One story told about Goffman attributes to him a line he used when in conversation with others. "In the time I'm talking to you, I could be writing a paper" (Lofland 1987, 20). In another vein, while he was in attendance at a department social gathering, Goffman is quoted as having said to an assistant professor who had been denied tenure, "After all, all of us aren't good enough to teach here" (Lofland 1987, 20). Lofland records another example of his acerbic wit: once when Goffman was speaking to a friend of his who was soon to marry a man twenty years her senior, Goffman is quoted as saying in the presence of the man, in "Jewish mother" fashion: "You have to be careful, because later on he will get older and you will have to take him to a home" (quoted in Lofland 1987, 21). Arlene Daniels appears to sum things up when she points out in her tribute to Goffman, "His resolute refusal to play the games of social manners often drove others into states of real fury" (1983, 2).

Goffman was not one to spare himself from similar attacks. When asked why he ran for president of the American Sociological Association, "he gave an instant one-word reply: 'Vanity'" (Lofland 1987, 21). He responded even more earthily when addressing "the kind of sociology he and others did: 'We are all just elegant bullshitters'" (Lofland 1987, 21). In his Presidential Address, Goffman pokes fun at himself and others who, by virtue of their position, are called on to give an address before a gathering of their colleagues. Goffman cites an "uneasiness" that is associated with a Presidential Address but then forges right ahead, taking the audience's time and stating, "Apparently, I am not uneasy about my unease about dwelling on my embarrassment" (1983, 2).

A self-deprecating comment attributed to Goffman was made after he joined the faculty at the University of Pennsylvania. When asked why he was not teaching more, he replied that "there was no need; anything he had to say was in his books" (Taylor 1968, 835).

A further and final glimpse of Goffman's view of himself and his colleagues is also provided in his Presidential Address, when he states: "Whatever our substantive focus and whatever our methodological persuasion, all we can do I believe is to keep faith with the spirit of natural science, and lurch along, seriously kidding ourselves that our rut has a forward direction" (1982, 2). Although Goffman could view himself and his colleagues in a humorous light, he was always serious about scholarship. Erving Goffman retained his position as Benjamin Franklin Professor at the University of Pennsylvania until he passed away on November 20, 1982, after a long struggle with cancer.

II. BASIC ASSUMPTIONS

In general, Goffman tended to disdain being identified by a specific category or label to describe his theoretical orientation. This position is consistent with the Goffman's attitude toward controlled biographical information about himself.

Approximately seventeen years before Goffman became a student at the University of Chicago, one of its most famous professors, George Herbert Mead, died. Herbert Blumer, a student of Mead's, coined the term *symbolic interaction* to represent Mead's concepts, and the work on symbolic interaction, particularly Mead's, was an important influence in the development of Goffman's thinking.

Mead's book, *Mind, Self and Society,* summarized Mead's views on individuals and interactions.[1] Blumer's definition of *symbolic interaction* refers "to the peculiar and distinctive character of interaction as it takes place between human beings" (1962, 180). Mead viewed the basic unit of analysis as people who are engaged in interaction. One of the purposes of Mead's work was to overcome the dualism of Man and Nature. For Mead, Man "constitutes society as genuinely as society constitutes the individual" (1934, xxv). The mind and the self are products of the social environment, and human behavior is seen as the product of social symbols communicated between individuals. According to this theory, symbols become an important part of Man's ability to form a definition of the situation. "It is in the process of communicating, or symbolizing that humans come to define both themselves and others" (Williams and McShane 1988, 39).

The definition and interpretation that one applies to the action of another helps determine how we behave. Oftentimes our response is not immediate, but rather, as Zeitlin explains, "based on an assessment of the meaning of the act" (1972, 215) we observe and experience. It is the symbols that we observe that help to mediate the exchange of human behavior.

At the University of Chicago, Goffman was a fellow student with Howard Becker who became involved with what has become known as *labeling theory,* in part an outgrowth of symbolic interaction theory. Becker and Goffman remained friends for a long time after their days as students and mutually influenced the development of each other's thinking.

Although Goffman does not directly acknowledge it, it appears he was also influenced by the work of Edwin Sutherland, Donald Cressey, and Lloyd Ohlin. In *Asylums,* Goffman footnotes both Sutherland and Cressey and their work on differential association, as well as Lloyd Ohlin's work, specifically referring to *Sociology and the Field of Correction* (Ohlin 1956).

Sutherland graduated from the University of Chicago many years before Goffman began attending school there, and when Goffman was a student, Sutherland's work was quite popular. In addition, Sutherland passed away in 1950, just before Goffman returned to Chicago to work on his doctorate. It is likely, then, that Sutherland's life and work was a topic of discussion at Chicago and that Goffman was aware of his work. Sutherland's work in differential association was grounded in part in symbolic interactionism, a subject Goffman was very familiar with. It is probable, then, that Goffman, when studying symbolic interaction, also studied differential association.

In 1953, Goffman wrote a review of Cressey's *Other People's Money,* demonstrating that although he himself did not work in the field of crime and criminology, he had an interest in it and kept abreast of at least some of the developments taking place. Goffman and Cressey were in contact, at least during the early to mid-1950s, and in addition to the review of Cressey's work in 1953, Goffman had a version of the first chapter of *Asylums,* "On the Characteristics of Total Institutions," published in a book Cressey edited entitled *The Prison.*

In her tribute to Goffman, Arlene Daniels (1983) suggests the work of some other individuals was influential in the development of Goffman's thinking. Durkheim's work, for instance, particularly as it relates to the use of social facts, was important for Goffman. In addition, the works of anthropologists Radcliffe-Brown and W. Lloyd Warner and of sociologists Louis Wirth and Everett Hughes played important roles in Goffman's intellectual development.

III. KEY IDEAS

Goffman was an extremely prolific writer who shared his thoughts with readers in approximately ten books, many of them printed and reprinted numerous times. A review of the common themes that appear in almost all of Goffman's work helps provide a general overview of his unique perspective.

Goffman's major concern in the majority of his works is to "promote acceptance of ... [the] face-to-face domain as an analytically viable one" (1982, 2). This face-to-face domain is identified as the "interaction order," which Goffman studies by using a microanalysis approach.

It appears that Goffman adhered to no particular theoretical approach in his work. His observational approach to describing in fine detail the interactions of individuals was his overriding concern; his emphasis was on process. In a review of Goffman's work, Laurie Taylor (1968) states: "While others were compiling the grand theory, he was to be found peering through cottage windows in the Shetlands, enjoying a smoke with catatonics in a closed ward, or making the scene in Las Vegas" (835). Goffman's work demonstrates a commitment to the "underdog," and if Goffman has a dominant theoretical orientation, it is more like Freud's in that he attempts to "construct a theory of human behavior from the apparent inconsequentialities of everyday life" (Taylor 1968, 835). Even then, his work is more the linkage of concepts than a coherent theory.

The use of a dramaturgical perspective, which incorporates a theatrical analogy to everyday life, is an important part of Goffman's work. An understanding of the dramaturgical perspective leads to a review of the first of Goffman's major works, *Presentation of Self in Everyday Life (1982, 2)*. As indicated previously and demonstrated by the bibliography at the end of this chapter, Goffman shared his ideas in his many publications. Much of what Goffman wrote has little direct relevance for criminology; however, within the vast array of his monographs, there are at least three that are of particular interest for students of criminology and deviant behavior: *Presentation of Self in Everyday Life, Asylums (1961),* and *Stigma (1963)*. It would be impossible to summarize Goffman's work in this short chapter, or even to attempt a complete discussion of the three books that have direct relevance. It is feasible, however, to try to cull from the three monographs the main points as they relate to criminology.

THE PRESENTATION OF SELF IN EVERYDAY LIFE 1956

Goffman's first monograph was *The Presentation of Self in Everyday Life*. Published originally in 1956 by the University of Edinburgh Social Science Research Center and in 1959 by Anchor Books, this monograph has become a cornerstone for most sociologists. When it was first published, it was described as one of the most vigorously effective and articulate contemporary contributions to the field of social psychology. The fact that Goffman was given the McIver Award for this work is testimony to its value as a contribution to the development of our understanding of human behavior.

A main perspective employed by Goffman in *The Presentation of Self in Everyday Life* is that of *dramaturgy,* which, as Goffman applies it, displays human behavior as part of a theatrical performance. Individuals are characters in a play acting out roles. In examining the interaction of individuals using a dramaturgical approach, Goffman shows that the "impression" that the actor gives to others becomes important. From

Goffman's perspective, the impression does not necessarily match the actual characteristics of the individual who is giving it. To paraphrase a line from Shakespeare's *As You Like It,* "All the world's a stage, and all the men and women merely players" (2002, II:vii, 139–40); this represents the way Goffman perceives face-to-face interaction. Specifically, Goffman states:

> On the stage one player presents himself in the guise of a character to characters projected by other players; the audience constitutes a third party to the interaction—one that is essential and yet, if the stage performance were real, one that would not be there. In real life, the three parties are compressed into two; the part one individual plays is tailored to the parts played by the others and yet these others also constitute the audience. (1959, xi)

The impressions that an actor gives are controlled, almost as if the person is playing a scripted part. The performance is important, because one must maintain credibility. For Goffman, a *performance* refers to "all the activity of an individual which occurs during a period marked by his continuous presence before a particular set of observers and which has some influence on the observers" (1959, 20). We have various "audiences" to which we present ourselves. In each case, because we normally want to leave a good impression, we manage our image. The question then becomes, how similar is the "true" or "natural" person to the one he or she portrays? There are similarities between Goffman's dramaturgical approach and Herbert Hyman's work in the area of reference group theory in terms of how individuals prepare their performances for different groups ("audiences"), depending on whether they are members or nonmembers. Alvin Gouldner describes the dramaturgical model as one that "advances a view in which social life is systematically regarded as an elaborate form of drama and in which—as in the theater—men are all striving to project a convincing image of self to others" (1970, 380). The emphasis is on what men are trying to be, not what they are trying to do.

As an example of how the dramaturgical perspective is used, we can look at an earlier work of Goffman's. In his very first published article, "On Cooling the Mark Out," Goffman (1952) discusses the way, when a confidence game takes place, it is necessary to go through various stages of the game with the person who is being taken advantage of. The dramaturgical approach is especially useful to us in understanding how the "con" works and the "sucker" is taken in. Goffman points to "talented actors who methodically and regularly build up informal social relationships just for the purpose of abusing them" (1952, 451). The act put on by the actors is designed to have the "mark" or audience believe that he or she is being assisted to win or gain something, usually money, through a fixed game or business venture. The con plays a role that if credible, helps relieve the mark of his or her money. An important part of the con is that the mark must not be made so angry after being duped that he or she decides to take some action against the operators of the con. This last stage of the con is the basis of the title of the article, "On Cooling the Mark Out," and requires the most creditable of performances by one of the operators. As Goffman's 1952 article makes clear, the presentation of self becomes the important factor.

When we are in the presence of others, we attempt to obtain information about them. Information "about the individual helps to define the situation, enabling others to know in advance what he will expect of them and what they may expect of him" (Goffman 1959, 1). When enough information is available for each of the participants to define the situation properly, the roles of each can be properly carried out. The impressions we wish to convey can be given. Information so that we can properly play our roles is obtained from a wide variety of sources. Behavior can be verbal or physical, intentional or unintentional. "The expressiveness of the individual ... appears to involve two radically different kinds of sign activity: the expression that he gives and the expression that he gives off" (Goffman 1959, 2). It is therefore possible for an individual to give misinformation intentionally by being deceitful.

Goffman notes that when performing a role, the "performer can be fully taken in by his own act; he can be sincerely convinced that the impression of reality which he stages is the real reality" (1959, 17). When a performer is taken in by his own performance, the "performer comes to be his own audience; he comes to be performer and observer of the same show" (Goffman 1959, 80–81). At the other extreme, as the operator in a con game, the performer is completely aware of his or her act and the fact that it does not coincide with the true or natural person. For Goffman, these extremes—belief and cynicism—represent the ends of a continuum with all possible combinations in between.

There are certain components, some more directly involved than others, that constitute a performance. One component is the *front,* which is "that part of the individual's performance which regularly functions in a general and fixed fashion to define the situation for those who observe the performance" (Goffman 1959, 22). This is the *expressive equipment* that an individual presents during a performance.

The second component is the *setting,* which involves the "furniture, decor, physical layout and other background items which supply the scenery and stage props" (Goffman 1959, 22) incorporated into the performance by the individual.

A third component, one that is more difficult to alter than the other two components, is the *personal front,* which includes the items we most intimately identify with the performer himself and that we naturally expect will follow the performer wherever he goes, such as age, race, gender, speech patterns, size, posture and looks. Personal front can be divided into two characteristic groups—appearance and manner. *Appearance* includes those "stimuli which function at the time to tell us of the performer's social status" (Goffman 1959, 24). *Manner* refers to "those stimuli which function at the time to warn us of the interaction role the performer will expect to play in the oncoming situation" (Goffman 1959, 24). There is an expected consistency between the manner and appearance of the individual as well as between the individual and the setting.

It should be noted that an individual might present the same front in different situations, to the point that the front becomes institutionalized. If this occurs, the front develops into a fact in its own right. Goffman says that "when an actor takes on an established social role, usually he finds that a particular front has already been established for it" (1959, 27). Maintaining the role and the front become prerequisites for each other. Individuals tend to pick an already established front rather than create a new one.

Oftentimes playing the role so that it is convincing means that other aspects of what is taking place elude the individual. Goffman presents us with a workable example of this by quoting Jean Paul Sartre: "The attentive pupil who wishes to be attentive, his eyes riveted on the teacher, his ears open wide, so exhausts himself in playing the attentive role that he ends up no longer hearing the lecture" (quoted in Goffman 1959, 33).

If individuals desire to be upwardly mobile, then they must present themselves in ways that demonstrate that they possess and "exemplify the officially accredited values of the society" (Goffman 1959, 35), often to the point that the appropriate behavior the individual demonstrates in that particular instance is greater than is generally part of the regular behavior of the individual. At the same time, to prevent downward mobility, the individual must perform in a manner that indicates that there are "sacrifices made for the maintenance of front" (Goffman 1959, 36). To maintain the front, it is necessary for an individual to conceal those features of his or her personality that undermine the image he or she is attempting to present. As Zeitlin states, "social interaction becomes a kind of information game in which each individual tries to manage his impressions while seeking to penetrate those of others in order to grasp their true feelings and intentions" (1972, 191).

The jockeying for position is an ongoing process, with each individual adjusting their front depending on the interpretation of the front presented by the individual with whom he or she is interacting. The image presented to or by us is extremely fragile, and is capable of being destroyed by a minor mishap. Oftentimes when engaged in interaction, individuals must be allowed to "save face" so that interactions can continue and the individuals can maintain their front. "To be a given kind of person, then is not merely to possess the required attributes, but also to sustain the standards of conduct and appearance that one's social grouping attaches thereto" (Goffman 1959, 75).

In the second chapter of *Presentation of Self in Everyday Life*, he addresses what happens when individuals act in concert as members of a team. Goffman uses the term *performance team* to represent "any set of individuals who co-operate in staging a single routine" (1959, 79).

When individuals become members of a performance team, each member of the team becomes somewhat dependent on the other members of the team for the accuracy of the performance. It follows then that a single team member "has the power to give the show away or to disrupt it by inappropriate conduct" (Goffman 1959, 82). This type of team creates out of each member a "conspirator" who, collectively with other members, puts on a show designed for some specific end. "Since each team is engaged in maintaining the stability of some definitions of the situation, concealing or playing down certain facts in order to do this, we can expect the performer to live out his own conspiratorial career in some furtiveness" (Goffman 1959, 105).

ASYLUMS 1961

In 1961, Goffman published his second book, *Asylums*, consisting of four essays, each designed to stand alone, two of which had been published previously. As indicated in the biographical sketch section of this chapter, this book is an outgrowth of Goffman's term as a visiting member of the Laboratory of Socioenvironmental Studies of the National Institute of Mental Health from 1954 through part of 1957. From 1955 to 1956, Goffman also worked at St. Elizabeth's Hospital engaged in field research.

From a methodological standpoint, Goffman raises some ethical questions when he discusses how he explained his presence to staff and residents on the wards at St. Elizabeth's Hospital. Goffman states:

> I started out in the role of an assistant to the athletic director, when pressed avowing to be a student of recreation and community life, and I passed the day with patients, avoiding sociable contact with the staff and the carrying of a key. I did not sleep in the wards, and the top hospital management knew what my aims were. (1961, ix)

It is clear that Goffman chose to deceive the residents and most of the staff with whom he had contact. The appropriateness of Goffman's behavior is something best left to others to debate and judge in another setting.

Goffman believed that "any group of persons—prisoners, primitives, pilots, or patients—develop a life of their own that becomes meaningful, reasonable and normal once you get close to it" (1961, ix–x). Therefore, Goffman, to study the life of mental patients, immersed himself in the everyday life of the residents of the wards at St. Elizabeth's Hospital. Part of his interest in the total institution is that it is "a social hybrid, part residential community, part formal organization" (1961, 12). Goffman is careful to inform his readers at the very beginning of *Asylums* that his "view is probably too much that of a middle-class male" (1961, x), and that he did not "employ the usual kinds of measurements and controls" (1961, x). Goffman also indicates that his study is only "in terms of a single articulation, inmates and staff" (1961, 112), and that a more detailed study that examines the role differentiation that occurs within each of the groups would be beneficial (Goffman 1961).

For the purposes of this study, the working definition of *total institution* is "a place of residence and work where a large number of like-situated individuals, cut off from the wider society for an appreciable period of time, together lead an enclosed, formally administered round of life" (Goffman 1961, xiii). These institutions have an encompassing character that controls contacts residents have with the outside and that regulates residents so that they rarely can choose when they come and go. Goffman points to "locked doors, high walls, barbed wire, cliffs, water, forests, or moors" (1959, 4) that limit the movement of residents.

Goffman identifies five general categories of total institutions:

1. Institutions established to care for persons felt to be both incapable and harmless—for example, homes for the blind, the aged, the orphaned, and the indigent.
2. Places established to care for persons felt to be both incapable of looking after themselves and a threat albeit an involuntary one, to the community—for example, TB sanitaria, mental hospitals, and leprosaria.
3. Those institutions organized to protect the community against what are believed to be intentional dangers to it—for example, jails, prisons, POW camps, and concentration camps.
4. Institutions purportedly established the better to pursue some work-like task and that justify themselves only on those instrumental grounds—for example, army barracks, ships, boarding schools, work camps, and colonial compounds.
5. Those establishments designed as retreats from the world that often serve also as training stations for the religious—for example, abbeys, monasteries, convents, and other cloisters. (1961, 4–5)

Total institutions differ radically from other types of social arrangements in that outside of the total institution, "the individual tends to sleep, play, and work in different places, with different co-participants, under different authorities, and without an over-all rational plan" (Goffman 1959, 6). In a total institution these three, normally separate aspects of a person's life—sleep, play, and work—are carried out in the same location with the same co-participants and under the same authorities. Most activities a person residing in a total institution engages in occur in a large group; very few activities are carried out in isolation. In the total institution, an individual's life is run by a very closely monitored schedule that occupies all parts of the day. All aspects of a resident's life are designed around the goals of the total institutions. In the case of the jail or the prison, custody is normally the primary goal. Therefore, head-counts are a common factor, as are accounting for silverware and tools, and the search of visitors and inmates both prior to and after a visit, especially in maximum-security institutions.

In all total institutions, there is a recognizable division between the large number of inmates and the small number of staff. In most total institutions, the inmates reside within the institution twenty-four hours a day with almost no integration with the outside world. The staff function inside the institution for a particular shift, while maintaining their social integration in the outside world (Goffman 1959). The relationships between members of these two groups, inmates and staff, are often formally regulated by rules, regulations, and policies. Goffman tells us that "social mobility between the two strata is grossly restricted" (1961, 7). One of the most telling features of a total institution is that discussions and decisions regarding the fate of the inmate normally take place without the input of the inmate.

Goffman points out the incompatibility between the total institution and the family. "Family life is sometimes contrasted with solitary living, but in fact the more pertinent contrast is with batch living, for those who eat and sleep at work, with a group of fellow workers, can hardly sustain a meaningful domestic existence" (1961, 11). The high divorce rate for those interred for extended periods offers some supporting evidence of the incompatibility of the total institution with the traditional family.

Goffman's notion that inmates bring to the institution a presenting culture has been examined by many criminologists and most probably relates to the present concept of "importation" variables. A *presenting culture* represents the way of life an individual has become used to when living in the world outside the total institution. It includes the values a person lives by that he has learned to take for granted. When an individual becomes an inmate, especially if his sentence is a long one, he or she undergoes what Goffman refers to as *disculturation*—an "untraining which renders him temporarily incapable of managing certain features of daily life on the outside" (1961, 13). The intent of the institution is to maintain the tension level between the opportunities the inmate has on the outside and the lack of control the individual has while imprisoned. The perpetuation of this tension acts to provide "strategic leverage in the management of men" (Goffman 1961, 13).

Once the individual enters the institution, he goes through a process that removes any support system he might have had. The inmate "begins a series of abasements, degradations, humiliations, and profanations of self. His self is systematically, if often unintentionally, mortified" (Goffman 1961, 14). As he proceeds through what Garfinkel (1956) has come to refer to as the *degradation ceremonies* and Goffman calls *mortification,* "he begins some radical shifts in his moral career, a career composed of the progressive changes that occur in the beliefs that he has concerning himself and significant others" (Goffman 1961, 14).

The realization that there is a physical barrier erected by the institution to prevent the inmate from leaving is one of the first steps in the process the inmate goes through that alters the concept of self. When a new inmate enters a total institution, there are admission procedures that Goffman refers to as "trimming or programming" (1961, 16) that shape and mold the inmate to fit the established routine. "The admission procedure can be characterized as leaving off and taking on, with the midpoint marked by physical nakedness" (Goffman 1961, 18). Most personal property is taken from the individual and cataloged, including the clothes the inmate wore to the prison. Often, the inmate is assigned a number that contributes to the stripping process by depriving him of one of his most important possessions, his full name (Goffman 1961). The scheduling of meals, showers, exercise, and so on by someone other than the inmate becomes a contributing factor to the alteration of the concept of self.

Much of what is lost, in terms of the concept of self, can be regained once the individual returns to society. Goffman points out, however, that there are certain losses that "are irrevocable and may be painfully experienced as such" (1961, 15). "Inmates ... suffer 'civil death' in that they lose their most precious civil rights, acquiring in their place only the meager 'rights' that are paternalistically granted from above" (Zeitlin 1972, 198). As examples of possible loss, Goffman notes that inmate "may face not only temporary loss of the rights to will money and write checks, to contest divorce or adoption proceedings, and to vote, but may have some of these rights permanently abrogated" (1961, 16). An inmate who has been divorced or had his children adopted by someone else while he was imprisoned is unable to return to the family situation he enjoyed prior to his incarceration.

Once an inmate begins his adjustment to life in a total institution, he begins to learn that there is a privilege system. Goffman suggests, based on his observations, that the privilege system "provides a framework for personal reorganization" (1961, 48). Goffman delineates the privilege system into three distinct parts: (1) house rules; (2) rewards; and (3) punishments. The *house rules* are "a relatively explicit and formal set of prescriptions and proscriptions that lays out the main requirements of inmate conduct" (Goffman 1961, 48). The *rewards* "are held out in exchange for obedience to staff in action and spirit" (Goffman 1961, 49). The *punishments* "are designed as the consequence of breaking the rules" (Goffman 1961, 50). Punishment can be permanent or temporary, or in some instances such that it prevents the inmate from competing for privileges.

Goffman identifies three features of the privilege system that are important for understanding how it works. The first feature is that "punishments and privileges are themselves modes of organization peculiar to total institutions" (Goffman 1961, 51). Second, "some acts become known as ones that mean an increase, or no decrease, in length of stay, while others become known as means for shortening the sentence" (Goffman 1961, 51). Third, "places to work and places to sleep become clearly defined as places where certain kinds and levels of privilege obtain" (Goffman 1961, 51).

In response to the privilege system, an inmate can select from a number of adaptations available to him. The choice of adaptation, according to Goffman, can be different depending on the inmate's phase of development in his moral career. The four different forms of adaptation are (1) situational withdrawal, (2) the intransigent line, (3) colonization, and (4) conversion. In *situational withdrawal,* the focus is on situations in his immediate presence to the exclusion of everything else. In the *intransigent line,* the inmate defies the staff and policies of the institution, refusing to cooperate. In the third form, *colonization,* the inmate accepts the few aspects of life on the outside that he is allowed to maintain and creates his whole world out of them. This adaptation allows for a relatively contented existence for the inmate. The final mode of adaptation, *conversion,* occurs when the inmate has completely accepted the role the institution has defined for him and performs the role of the "perfect inmate," at least from the perspective of the staff and administration of the prison. Goffman points out that inmates can shift between each of these adaptations and that none is necessarily permanently fixed (1961, 61–63).

In addition to the techniques of adaptation, the inmate can engage in "removal" activities that take him, figuratively speaking, out of his situation. These removal activities can be on the individual level or organized by the institution for the inmates. Goffman defines *removal activities* as "voluntary unserious pursuits which are sufficiently engrossing and exciting to lift the participant out of himself, making him oblivious for the time being" to the deprivation of his situation (1961, 68–69), and include such activities as dances, lectures, art classes, reading, and watching television alone. Removal activities are necessary for the inmate, because they provide a mechanism to "withstand the psychological stress usually engendered by assaults upon the self" (Goffman 1961, 70).

Given that total institutions are involved in people-work, and "have objects and products to work upon" (Goffman 1961, 74) which are humans, special problems arise that distinguish this type of situation from others. Goffman has observed that there are unique considerations that must be given to relatives of inmates because of the special problems they pose for the staff and administration of a total institution. Relatives help inmates to retain the status they held prior to entering the total institution, making it more difficult for the staff and administration to process the inmate through mortification. In addition, relatives are a particular problem because "while inmates can be educated about the price they will pay for making demands on their own behalf, relations receive less tutoring in this regard and rush in with requests for inmates" (Goffman 1961, 77) that inmates would not make for themselves and that cause embarrassment for all concerned. Relatives have difficulty understanding some of the procedures used when it comes to the handling of inmates, such as the placement of an inmate in isolation for protection from other inmates, or strapping an inmate down because he is suicidal. Although these actions may be in the inmate's best interests, they are not necessarily understood by the inmate's relatives.

For total institutions, there are problems inherent in the "constant conflict between humane standards on the one hand and institutional efficiency on the other" (1961, 78). As an example, Goffman cites the inmate's personal possessions, which are important for the establishment and maintenance of the concept of self, but the greater the ability of the staff to separate the inmate from his concept of self, the easier it is to manage the inmate (Goffman 1961, 78). Another conflict of humane standards versus institution efficiency is typically associated with people—work in situations where there is extensive long-term contact with the materials of the job—the inmates. "However distant the staff tries to stay from these materials, such materials can become objects of fellow feeling and even affection" (Goffman 1961, 81). Even though there is affection and feeling for some inmates by the staff,

> total institutions have a quasi-class character, for there is a basic cleavage
> between the inmates and the supervisory staff, the latter feeling "superior and
> righteous," the former, "inferior, weak, blameworthy, and guilty." Interaction
> and mobility between the two strata are severely restricted, while "social distance is typically great and often prescribed." (Zeitlin 1972, 198)

Staff members working at the lowest levels, the correctional officers, often serve the longest time in their positions and have the greatest amount of direct contact with the inmates, allowing them to see the inmate in a different light. However, because of their longevity, correctional officers become the carriers of tradition (Goffman 1961, 114). Upper-level administration and staff usually demonstrate a much higher rate of turnover. The correctional officer, the lowest level of staff, is also the one who "must personally present the demands of the institution to the inmates" (Goffman 1961, 114).

During his year as a participant observation at St. Elizabeth's Hospital in Washington, D.C., Goffman was able to observe the "audience" to which the institution appeared to be performing, and concludes that it is the visitor to the institution. "Sometimes the focus of concern is the visit to a particular inmate by a particular outsider" (Goffman 1961, 101). Staging the image presented to visitors, including the "right of the staff to limit, inspect, and censor outgoing mail, and the frequent rule against writing anything negative about the institution" (Goffman 1961, 103), helps maintain control over the inmates and contributes to separating the inmate from those on the outside, as is the often remote location of the facility, which makes it difficult for visitors to just "drop-in" on the inmate. Remoteness of the facility can "transform a family visit into something of a festive excursion, for which it will be feasible for the staff to make ample preparation" (Goffman 1961, 104), similar to that cited during World War II, when prisoners of war were given new blankets just prior to visits by the Red Cross or other inspection bodies. The new blankets were then immediately collected after the inspection and the other aspects of staging were returned to their normal state. Whatever the short-term effects of a visit by government agents to a total institution, "they do seem to serve as a reminder to everyone in the establishment that the institution is not completely a world of its own, but bears some connection, bureaucratic and subordinated, to structures in the wider world" (Goffman 1961, 104). There are three components of the social reality of the total institution as presented by Goffman: "that which is concealed from inmates, that which is revealed to inmates, and that which is shown to visitors" (1961, 106). All three components must be considered to constitute the whole because of their close connection, and even then, the social reality is not a very stable one.

In general, the number of goals that total institutions strive to achieve is not great, and Goffman suggests that prisons have four: (1) incapacitation, (2) retribution, (3) deterrence, and (4) reformation (1961, 83). The intent of reformation is to return the inmate to the outside world able to function in a normal and acceptable manner and become a contributing member of society. Goffman posits that although this might be a goal, it is seldom, if ever, realized. If the inmate is rehabilitated, it is more often than not in the manner that was intended by the staff and administration of the institution (1961, 71). Reformation aside, when an inmate is released back into society, it is often at the point where he has finally successfully managed to learn how to manipulate the privilege system. "In brief, he may find that release means moving from the top of a small world to the bottom of a large one" (Goffman 1961, 73). Return to society may also come with some continued restrictions for the inmate. If the inmate has been paroled, he or she must report on a regular basis to a parole officer, and may be required to avoid certain establishments and people. These types of restrictions can be especially cumbersome and difficult to adhere to if the inmate, when released, returns to his or her old neighborhood.

Goffman makes an overall observation about total institutions: "Many total institutions, most of the time, seem to function merely as storage dumps for inmates ... [although] they usually present themselves to the public as rational organizations designed consciously, through and through, as effective machines for producing a few officially avowed and officially approved ends" (1961, 74).

STIGMA

Goffman's *Stigma: Notes on the Management of Spoiled Identity* (1963) represents an important contribution to the literature in general, and sections of it have direct applicability for the development of criminological thought. From Goffman's perspective, the process by which one becomes stigmatized is a much-neglected area of study.

Goffman takes the term *stigma* from the Greeks, who originated the term to refer to "bodily signs designed to expose something unusual and bad about the moral status of the signifier. These signs were cut or burnt into the body" (1963, 1). Goffman expands on the Greek use of the term to include three types of stigma: (1) abominations of the body; (2) blemishes of individual character; and (3) stigma of race, nation, and religion (1963, 4). Abominations of the body represent physical deformities; blemishes of character signify weak-willed individuals who may have "domineering or unnatural passions, treacherous and rigid beliefs" (Goffman 1963, 4) and may be dishonest. Knowledge of these shortcomings is gleaned from official records that demonstrate "mental disorder, imprisonment, addiction, alcoholism, homosexuality, unemployment, suicidal attempts, and radical political behavior" (Goffman 1963, 4). The third form of stigma, that of race, nationality, and religion, is the type that can be "transmitted through lineages and equally contaminate all members of a family" (Goffman 1963, 4).

These categories of stigma and the attributes necessary for inclusion are established by society. We engage in "social intercourse in established settings . . . with anticipated others without special attention or thought" (Goffman 1963, 2). When a stranger enters our space, it is likely that we review his appearance in order "to anticipate his category and attributes, his 'social identity'" (Goffman 1963, 2). Once we have been able to categorize the individual, if he falls into one of the stigma categories we are able to adjust our behavior to respond appropriately to the individual.[2]

Individuals are imbued with both a "virtual" social identity and an "actual" social identity. As Goffman puts it, "Stigma ... constitutes a special discrepancy between virtual and actual identity" (1963, 3).

Those individuals who possess a stigma are often ill at ease with individuals identified as "normal," as, in turn, "normals" are with those who are stigmatized. The major difference between the two groups, a very important one, is that the normal individual is frequently in a position to alter the life chances of the stigmatized. As for the inmate who is stigmatized, because of his blemish of character, normals are able to reduce his life chances. When the former inmate is on the outside, the job possibilities often become negligible once his previous status becomes known. In *Asylums,* Goffman addresses this particular circumstance when he discusses the release of inmates.

> When the inmate has taken on a low proactive status by becoming an inmate, he finds cool reception in the wider world—and is likely to experience this at a moment, hard even for those without his stigma, when he must apply to someone for a job and a place to live. (Goffman 1961, 73)

The main task for the stigmatized is to present himself or herself in a way that conceals or mitigates his stigma and allows him to gain acceptance among the normals. Sometimes it is possible through surgery or training to remove a physical deformity, thereby allowing the individual to "pass." In terms of the blemish of character, individuals, depending on their blemish, can go through detoxification programs to rid themselves of an addiction or of alcoholism. As Zeitlin points out, this may result not in imparting normal status, but rather in transforming him or her "from someone with a particular blemish into someone with a record of having corrected a particular blemish" (1972, 212).

It is sometimes possible for an individual who is stigmatized to disguise the stigma. Such a person carries the added burden of hiding information about the stigmatization and deciding if and when to reveal it to normals.

In addition to his extensive work on face-to-face interaction in *Presentation of Self in Everyday Life, Asylums,* and *Stigma,* Goffman also produced a number of other works that found wide audiences. Daniels notes that

> in *Relations in Public* and in *Behavior in Public Places,* Goffman showed how
> the classic language of status, role, and obligation apply in understanding the
> most primary kinds of status. . . . In his later work (*Frame Analysis, Forms of
> Talk*), Goffman began to focus on the formal properties of communication to
> be found in sequences of events and in linguistics. (1983, 2)

IV. CRITIQUE

This review of Goffman's work suggests a useful linkage between some of his concepts and the development of criminological thought. There is certainly a direct link between Goffman's work and symbolic interaction and the development of labeling theory.

Goffman has been criticized by some for failing to ground his work in some theoretical perspective. Although Robert K. Merton (see the chapter on Merton in this book) delved into what is referred to as theories of the "middle range," Lofland (1987) describes Goffman's theoretical approach as one that is of the "lower range." Laurie Taylor in her review of Goffman's work suggests that "he has not so much a coherent theory as a set of linked concepts" (1968, 836).

In addition to criticism leveled at his lack of a coherent theory, Goffman's methodology has also been questioned. Kuper and Kuper (1985, 339) believe that Goffman's work is "rife with cultural preconceptions, and he depends on unsystematic observations. This limits the force of his work and diminishes its value as a model for further research and thought." Taylor believes that Goffman "lacks rigor because he assumes 'that a loose speculative approach to a fundamental area of conduct is better than a rigorous blindness to it'" (1968, 836). As Gouldner points out, there has been a suggestion by some students of Goffman's work, mostly the "rebellious young," that there is a "radical" orientation underpinning his writing. Goffman's work, if not radical in focus, has certainly been politicized by some, probably far more than Goffman would have liked.

One such interpreter is T.R. Young, who posits that Goffman's focus on the individual as "gamesman" shifts us away from looking at the "gamesmanship" of society (1971, 276). Young points out that Gouldner (1970), in his work *Coming Crisis in Western Sociology,* is able to understand Goffman's work and the dehumanizing system he describes, and therefore proposes an approach that allows us to "begin to take political action to transform it" (Young 1971, 276). Young argues that there is "political danger" in Goffman's work in that "his analysis will be helpful to gamesmen" (1971, 276) who wish to perfect their styles. Gouldner's work (1970) helps dispel some of this concern for Young.

In *Coming Crisis in Western Sociology,* Gouldner discusses Goffman's work and suggests that there is some ambiguity in Goffman's positions. Gouldner indicates that, in terms of the concept of dramaturgy, Goffman does not support the conventional hierarchicalization of functionalism that Talcott Parson's is best known for. At the same time, Goffman's "rejection of hierarchy often expresses itself as an 'avoidance' of social stratification and of the importance of power differences" (1970, 379). Gouldner concludes that this ambiguity often leads individuals to respond selectively, "focusing on the side of the ambiguity congenial to him" (1970, 379).

Gouldner, in his review of Goffman's work, classifies it as a kind of "microfunctionalism" (1970, 380); however, in general, within the category of functionalism, Goffman's work raises issues for Gouldner. Goffman does not ask many of the questions that should be asked if one is approaching understanding human interaction from a functionalist perspective, even a microfunctionalist perspective. For instance, Gouldner points out that Goffman "does not explain . . . why some selves rather than others are selected and projected by persons, and why others accept or reject the proffered self" (1970, 380). Goffman also does not address how power and wealth aid an individual's ability to project a successful image.

In a 1977 article, George Psathas, who claims that *Presentation of Self in Everyday Life* was one of the most important books he read after he finished his Ph.D., and that *Asylums* made him change the way he taught medical sociology, challenges Goffman to say more about the image of man. Psathas charges that Goffman is unfair and some of the things he says about man are "not so" (1977, 84). The general conclusion drawn by Psathas is that "Goffman's image of man is lacking in many important human characteristics" (1977, 84).

Psathas finds that "a major problem in *The Presentation of Self* is one of the analogy" to theater (1977, 86). When an individual plays a part in the theater, "his part may become a part of himself, but he knows he is not Hamlet nor Romeo—and though his performed character dies on the stage, he arises to take his bow and return to play the same part again" (Psathas 1977, 86–87). For Psathas, although Goffman paints an attractive picture, it does not accurately represent real life. "Performing and being are not identical" (Psathas 1977, 87).

Psathas is also concerned that Goffman "stops short" in his presentation because he "doesn't propose reforms, expose villains by naming them, analyze the institutional forces or the laws, propose ways to change these or attack the professions" (1977, 88). Goffman's model of man is fraught with problems and his "view of man is misleading and incomplete" (Psathas 1977, 89).

John Irwin, who has written more recently on the life of inmates, in part based on his own experience, rejects the description of the total institution presented by Goffman, particularly the relationships between the two groups—staff and inmates. In addition to challenging the work of Goffman, Irwin calls in question the work of Albert Cohen as it relates to the role of inmates (see chapter on Cohen).

Although there have been a number of individuals who can be classified as detractors when it comes to specific aspects of Goffman's work, in general, Goffman's work has been extremely well received. He has influenced the work of many students of sociology and criminology. Even today, his book *Asylums,* written nearly fifty years ago, is still published and used regularly in the college classroom. The same is true for Goffman's *Presentation of Self in Everyday Life.* One cannot deny the impact on the development of microanalysis that Goffman has had. In the field of criminology, Goffman has had an impact on the development of thought. Although as indicated at the beginning of this chapter, Goffman "looked down his nose at criminology" and did not necessarily intend to influence the development of criminological thought, his writings have had a lasting impact. Specifically, Goffman's work can be linked to the development of labeling theory, which is discussed in detail in the chapter on Howard Becker in this book. In addition, Goffman's work in the taking of roles and performing for audiences all relates to the development of labeling theory. In *Stigma,* Goffman talks about a category of stigma that includes individuals based on their race, religion, or nationality. Expanded, this can include individuals from lower-socioeconomic classes. The identification of these individuals as troublemakers, delinquents, and criminals is not a difficult step to take. The labeling of individuals in this manner helps stereotype our perceptions and expectations about their behavior. For a complete explanation of the development of the theory, the reader is referred to the chapter on Howard Becker as well as to the literature on labeling theory.

NOTES

1. It is interesting to note that George Herbert Mead did not write a single book on sociology. After his death in 1931, Mead's students put together what materials of Mead's they could find along with their lecture notes to produce *Mind, Self, and Society,* published in 1934. In addition to *Mind, Self, and Society,* Mead's former students collected material from Mead's scraps of notes and published two other books.

2. It should be noted for the reader that at the time Goffman was writing *Stigma,* the issues surrounding civil rights in this country were reaching a crescendo. Until this point, certain states required, among other things, separate bathrooms and drinking fountains, depending on the color of a person's skin, as well as the separation of races in public transportation. The view of the third category of *Stigma* was and still is very real in this country.

References

Anonymous. 1983. Professor Erving Goffman: Influential sociologist. *The Times,* January, 6: 13.

Blumer, Herbert. 1962. Society and symbolic interaction. In *Human behavior and social process,* Arnold M. Rose (Ed.). Boston: Houghton Mifflin.

Cressey, Donald R. 1953. *Other people's money.* Glencoe, IL: The Free Press.

Cuzzort, R.P. 1969. *Humanity and modern sociological thought.* New York: Holt, Rinehart and Winston, pp. 173–94.

Daniels, Arlene K. 1983. A tribute to Erving Goffman. *ASA Footnotes,* January.

Ditton, Jason (Ed.). 1980. *The view from Goffman.* New York: St. Martin's Press.

Dushkin Publishing Group.

———. 1974. *Encyclopedia of sociology.* Gilford, CT: The Dushkin Publishing Group, Inc., p. 120.

Garfinkle, H. 1956. Conditions of successful degradation ceremonies. *Am. J. Soc.* 61: 420–2 +.

Goffman, Erving. 1953. *Communication conduct in an island community.* Doctoral dissertation, University of Chicago.

———. 1959. *Presentation of self in everyday life.* Garden City, NY: Anchor Books, Doubleday and Company, Inc.

————. 1961. *Asylums: Essays on the social situation of mental patients and other inmates.* Garden City, NY: Anchor Books, Doubleday and Company, Inc.

————. 1963. *Stigma: Notes on the management of spoiled identity.* Englewood Cliffs, NJ: Prentice-Hall, Inc.

Gouldner, Alvin W. 1970. *The coming crisis of Western sociology.* New York: Basic Books.

Hall, J.A. 1977. Sincerity and politics: Existentialists vs. Goffman and Proust. *Sociolog. Rev.* 25(3): 535–50.

Kuper, Adam, and Jessica Kuper (Eds.). 1985. *The social science encyclopedia.* London, England: Routledge and Kegan Paul, p. 339.

Lofland, John. 1984. Erving Goffman's sociological legacies. *Urban Life* 13(1): 7–34.

Mann, Michael (Ed.). 1984. *The international encyclopedia of sociology.* New York: Continuum Publishing Co., p. 148.

Manning, Peter K. 1976. The decline of civility: A comment on Erving Goffman's sociology. *Canad. Rev. Sociol. Anthropol.* 13(1): 13–25.

Mead, George Herbert. 1934. *Mind, self, and society.* Chicago: University of Chicago Press.

Messinger, Sheldon E., Harold Sampson, and Robert D. Towne. 1962. Life as theater: Some notes on the dramaturgic approach to social reality. *Sociometry* 25: 98–110.

Ohlin, Lloyd E. 1956. *Sociology and the field of correction.* New York: The Russell Sage Foundation.

Psathas, George. 1977. Goffman's image of man. *Hum. Soc.* 1(1): 84–94.

Rogers, Mary. 1977. Goffman on power. *Am. Sociol.* 12(2): 88–95.

Rose, Jerry D. 1966. *The presentation of self in everyday life: A critical commentary.* New York: R.D.M. Corporation.

Ryan, Alan. 1976. Maximising, moralising, and dramatising. In *Action and interpretation: Studies in the philosophy of the social sciences.* Christopher Hookway and Philip Petit (Eds.), Cambridge: Cambridge University Press, pp. 65–81.

Shakespeare, William. 2002 (1597). *As you like it.* New York: Oxford University Press.

Stebbins, Robert A. 1967–8. A note on the concept role distance. *Am. J. Sociol.* 73: 247–50.

Taylor, Laurie. 1968. Erving Goffman. *New Soc.* Dec.: 835–37.

Wedel, Janet M. 1978. Ladies, we've been framed! Observations on Erving Goffman's "The arrangement between the sexes." *Theory Soc.* 5(1): 113–25.

Williams, Franklin P., and Marilyn McShane. 1988. *Criminological theory.* Englewood Cliffs, NJ: Prentice-Hall Inc.

Young, T.R. 1971. The politics of sociology: Gouldner, Goffman and Garfinkel. *Am. Sociol.* 6: 276–81.

Zeitlin, Irving. 1971. The social psychology of Erving Goffman. In *Rethinking sociology.* New York: Appleton-Century-Crofts, pp. 191–214.

Bibliography

Erving Goffman.

————. 1951. Symbols of class status. *Br. J. Sociol.* 2: 294–304.

————. 1952. On cooling the mark out: Some aspects of adaptation to failure. *Psychiatry* 15(4): 451–63.

————. 1955. On face-work: An analysis of ritual elements in social interaction. *Psychiatry* 18(3): 213–31.

————. 1955–6. Review of Tobati: Paraguayan town. *Am. J. Sociol.* 61: 186–87.

————. 1956. The nature of deference and demeanor. *Am. Anthropol.* 58: 473–502.

————. 1956. Embarrassment and social organisation. *American Journal Of Sociology*, Volume 63, Number 3 (November), pp. 264–271.

————. 1957. Alienation from interaction. *Hum. Rel.* 10(1): 47–60.

————. 1957. On some convergences of sociology and psychiatry: A sociologist's view. *Psychiatry* 20(3): 201–3.

————. 1957. Review of *Other people's money. Psychiatry* 20(3): 321–26.

————. 1957. Review of human problems of a state mental hospital. *Admin. Sci. Quart.* Volume 2(1): 120–21.

————. 1959. The moral career of the mental patient. *Psychiatry* 22(2): 123–42.

_____. 1961. *Encounters: Two studies in the sociology of interaction.* Indianapolis: Bobbs-Merrill.

_____. 1961. *Behaviour in public places: Notes on the social organization of gatherings.* Glencoe, IL: The Free Press.

_____. 1964. The neglected situation. Part II. *Am. Anthropol.* 66(6): 133–36.

_____. 1968. The staff world. *New Soc.* Nov. 21: 757–59.

_____. 1968. Marked for life. *New Soc.* Nov. 28: 795–97.

_____. 1969. *Strategic interaction.* Philadelphia: University of Pennsylvania Press.

_____. 1969. The insanity of place. *Psychiatry* 32(4): 357–87.

_____. 1971. *Relations in public.* New York: Harper and Row Publishers, Inc.

_____. 1974. *Frame analysis.* New York: Harper and Row Publishers, Inc.

_____. 1976. Replies and responses. *Lang. Soc.* 5(3): 257–313.

_____. 1977. The arrangement between the sexes. *Theory Soc.* 4(3): 301–31.

_____. 1978. Response cries. *Language* 54(4): 787–815.

_____. 1979. *Gender advertisements.* New York: Harper and Row Publishers, Inc.

_____. 1979. Footing. *Semiotica* 25(1–2): 1–29.

_____. 1981. *Forms of talk.* Philadelphia: University of Pennsylvania Press.

_____. 1983. The interaction order. *Am. Sociolog. Rev.* 48: 1–17.

_____. 1983. Felicity's condition. *Am. J. Sociol.* 89(1): 1–53.

Complete Bibliography

About Erving Goffman

Cioffi, Frank. 1969–70. Information, contemplation and social life. *Roy. Inst. Philos. Lect.* 4: 103–31.

Clarke, Michael. 1971. Total institutions: Some dimensions of analysis. *New Soc.* 1(4): 53–80.

Collins, Randall, and Michael Makowsky. 1972. *The discovery of society.* New York: Random House. (See specifically Chapter 12: "Erving Goffman and the theatre of social encounters.")

Cuzzort, Richard P. 1969. *Humanity and modern sociological thought.* New York: Holt, Rinehart and Winston. (See specifically Chapter 9: "Humanity as the big con: The human views of Erving Goffman.")

Gonos, George. 1976. Situation versus frame: The interactionist and the structuralist analyses of everyday life. *Am. Sociolog. Rev.* 42: 854–67.

Hall, J.A. 1977. Sincereity and politics: Existenialists vs. Goffman and Proust. *Sociolog. Rev.* 25(3): 535–50.

Manning, Peter K. 1976. The decline of civility: A comment on Erving Goffman's sociology. *Canad. Rev. Sociol. Anthropol.* 13(1): 13–25.

Messinger, Sheldon, Harold Sampson, and Robert D. Towne. 1962. Life as theater: Some notes on the dramaturgic approach to social reality. *Sociometry* 25: 98–110.

Psathas, George. 1977. Goffman's image of man. *Hum. Soc.* 1(1): 84–94.

Rogers, Mary. 1977. Goffman on power. *Am. Sociol.* 12(2): 88–95.

Rose, Jerry D. 1966. *The presentation of self in everyday life: A critical commentary.* New York: R.D.M. Corporation.

Ryan, Alan. 1976. Maximising, moralising, and dramatising. In *Action and interpretation: Studies in the philosophy of the social sciences.* Christopher Hookway and Philip Petit (Eds.), Cambridge: Cambridge University Press, pp. 65–81.

Stebbins, Robert A. 1967–8. A note on the concept role distance. *Am. J. Sociol.* 73: 247–50.

Taylor, Laurie. 1968. Erving Goffman. *New Soc.* Dec.: 835–37.

Wedel, Janet M. 1978. Ladies, we've been framed! Observations on Erving Goffman's "The arrangement between the sexes." *Theory Soc.* 5(1): 113–25.

Winkin, Yves. 1988. Erving Goffman: Les Moments Et Leurs Hommes, Seuil, Belgium: Minuit.

Young, T.R. 1971. The politics of sociology: Gouldner, Goffman and Garfinkel. *Am. Sociol.* 6: 276–81.

Zeitlin, Irving. 1972. The social psychology of Erving Goffman. Rethinking Sociology, New York: Appleton-Century-Crofts, pp. 191–214.

CHAPTER 14
HOWARD SAUL BECKER:
B. 1928

I. BIOGRAPHICAL SKETCH

Howard Saul Becker was born in 1928 in a middle-class Irish and Jewish neighborhood on the far west side of Chicago. Becker's father was a self-made man who had done fairly well in the advertising business. Consequently, the Beckers were comfortable, even during the Depression (personal communication, April 13, 1988).

Howard attended Austin High School in West Chicago, where, he says, he was a "smart kid" to whom grades came easy. He pursued his education because it was fun and so his "father wouldn't yell" at him. Despite the ease and fun that young Howard associated with education, his first (and, it appears, lifelong) love was the piano. At eleven, he started listening to "boogie-woogie"; at fifteen, he joined the Musicians' Union, and thereafter played professionally until the early 1970s in jazz clubs in and around Chicago. When asked about those who most influenced him, the first name Becker offered was Lennie Tiristano, a jazz piano player under whom he had studied (personal communication, April 13 and June 1, 1988).

As are so many of the significant contributors to criminology, Becker is a sociologist, but his entry into that discipline was somewhat accidental. He says that he can think of no significant events in his early life that could be credited with leading him in the direction of sociology (or criminology). Becker began taking classes at the University of Chicago while still in high school. [At that time, the University of Chicago undergraduate program was a general degree program (no major) that could be started in the third year of high school.] Consequently, Becker was young when he earned his bachelor's degree. Because of his son's youth, Becker's father encouraged him to go on for his master's degree, and because there was really no way to study jazz in college then, Becker considered English Literature. He changed his mind, however, after reading *Black Metropolis: A Study of Negro Life in a Northern City,* which roused his interest in ethnography and comparative science (personal communication, June 1, 1988; Debro 1970). In an interview with Julius Debro (1970), Becker said that he actually had it in his mind to be an anthropologist, but the distinction was not clear to him, so he signed up for sociology without knowing what he was getting into.

The sociology department at the University of Chicago was an exciting place to be in the late 1940s. There were 200 graduate students, many of whom, like Erving Goffman, James Short, and David Gold, went on to become quite prominent. There were also many top-notch sociologists on the faculty, such as Ernest Burgess, Everett Hughes, Lloyd Warner, and Herbert Blumer (Debro 1970).

Becker recalls that he went through his first year of graduate school in sort of a daze, but toward the end of that year, something occurred that provided some focus, not just in a temporary sense, but also for his future in sociology. He took a required class in advanced field studies with Ernest Burgess. During this time, Becker continued to play piano in various local clubs. For the class, he was required to either collect twelve interviews for an old-age study on which Burgess was working or do a thesis. Becker figured that if he took notes while he was working the bars, it would be considered fieldwork, so he started a diary. After he had compiled a considerable volume of notes, he showed them to Burgess, who sent him to Everett Hughes. Hughes' primary focus was occupation, and, according to Becker, he was happy to find someone doing work on a more nonconventional occupation (jazz musicians). Hughes urged and guided Becker in developing his notes into a master's thesis. This work was to become part of his now famous book, *Outsiders: Studies in the Sociology of Deviance (1954)* (to be discussed later). At this point, Becker decided that sociology was "pretty fun stuff" (Debro 1970).

Becker went through the graduate program at the University of Chicago rather rapidly, a fact he attributes to his lack of seriousness about sociology as a career: "I studied sociology like a hobby, and had very little anxiety about it" (quoted in Debro 1970, 160). He still considered piano playing to be his real profession. In 1949, he finished his master's thesis and married, two events that prompted him to decide that it was time to get out of school and go to work. However, Hughes encouraged him to apply for a fellowship; when Becker received one, he got involved with Hughes in a research project on schoolteachers. This project ultimately led to Becker's dissertation and a Ph.D. in 1951; all the while, he continued to play the piano in the bars around Chicago.

On receipt of his terminal degree, Becker says, "The question was, was I going to be the most educated piano player on 63rd Street or go to work as a sociologist?" (Debro 1970, 161). At twenty-three, Becker found that no one wanted to hire him in a teaching position, so he stayed in Chicago, where he knew he could work playing the piano. Ultimately, opportunities other than piano playing presented themselves, and Becker ended up serving as an instructor for two years at the University of Chicago. While there, he was also a research associate at the Institute for Juvenile Research, which piqued interest in studying marijuana use (Debro 1970), work that was heavily influenced by Alfred Lindesmith's (1947) book *Opiate Addiction* (personal communication, April 13, 1988). The criminalization of the drug provided early impetus for and became an integral part of his ideas about labeling and deviance.

In 1953, Becker received a Ford Foundation Post-Doctoral Fellowship to do personality research at the University of Illinois, but it ended in 1955, and he was looking for work again. Becker was not sure that he wanted to teach, and, as it turned out, he did not have to. Everett Hughes contacted him and asked if he would be interested in participating in a study of the Medical School at the University of Kansas; according to Becker, he went to Kansas City by default—he had no other offers (Debro 1970). On this project, he worked with Blanche Geer from Johns Hopkins University in Baltimore, and the two of them, along with Hughes and Anslem Strauss, published a book on the study entitled *Boys in White: Student Culture in Medical School* (1961). After the med-school study was completed, the research team stayed on to examine the undergraduate program at Kansas; at the same time, Becker continued to pursue his love of music, playing piano in the nightspots of Kansas City.

In the midst of working on the Kansas projects, Becker put together the first draft (1954) of *Outsiders: Studies in the Sociology of Deviance*. He says that the work represented what seemed to be the "natural way to pursue things from the sociological perspective." In 1954, his specialty was the social psychology of occupations or professions, and he approached deviance (at least an aspect of it) as the study of people whose occupation was either crime or watching criminals. After the completion of this draft, *Outsiders* sat for quite some time, not published until 1963 (Debro 1970). Becker says he does not really know why he left the manuscripts it for so long, but part of the reason was that it was not book length, being only ninety pages. Nonetheless, Irwin Deutsher read the manuscript and said that it should be in print, so Becker decided to include his empirical studies on musicians and marijuana use. He showed the now book-length manuscript to his friend Ned Polsky at the Free Press, and Polsky decided it was "worth a gamble" (personal communication, June 1, 1988). At the same time, Becker had no idea that *Outsiders* would become what William Chambliss (1988) called "an extraordinary influential book," or that so many would heed his call for a re-orientation of criminological thought and theory to recognize the role of labeling, or that he would come to be seen as the founder of labeling theory in criminology.

On completion of his work in Kansas City, Becker moved on to the Institute for the Study of Human Problems at Stanford University. He left the Institute in 1965 to accept a position in the sociology department at Northwestern University, a position he still holds today.

Becker has held a variety of important offices and has won numerous awards during his productive career. From 1961 to 1964, he served as the editor of *Social Problems*. He is a past president of both the Society for the Study of Social Problems and the Society for the Study of Symbolic Interaction. He has been a Guggenheim Fellow and the recipient of the Charles Horton Cooley Award from the Society for the Study of Symbolic Interaction, the Commonwealth award, the Cooley/Mead Award from the American Sociological Association, and the George Herbert Mead Award for a career of Distinguished Scholarship from the Society for the Study of Symbolic Interaction.

II. BASIC ASSUMPTIONS

Howard Becker has not written extensively in criminology itself, and he is quick to point out that he is not a criminologist (personal communication, April 13 and June 1, 1988). However, as a social scientist, his research and "theory" of deviance are quite relevant to criminology and have had considerable impact on criminological thought and theory. Becker's work exhibits a theme seen elsewhere in this book. It has crossed the (albeit often fuzzy) boundaries between sociology, psychology, and criminology. Despite the fact that it was Becker's ideas about deviance that have been most influential in criminology, he claims that his involvement with the deviance field has actually been minimal, and that he is more concerned with educational systems, social psychology, and qualitative methodology (Debro 1970). He characterized himself (Becker 1970) as an occupational sociologist as opposed to a professional sociologist (see the typology proposed by Horowitz 1968).

Becker differs from many of the others in this book in a very important respect — he is not at all a positivist. He does not adopt a deterministic view of the world or of human functioning and does not equate science only with the search for the cause(s) of things. He might be portrayed as being a somewhat left-of-center humanitarian and moral philosopher, but also as a philosopher of science whose ideas are deeply embedded in the notion of the relativity of human existence.

ASSUMPTIONS ABOUT BEHAVIOR (ACTION)

From Becker's perspective, human behavior is essentially social in nature. In his various works, three basic aspects of the sociality of human conduct can be identified: collectivity, relativity (subjectivity), and reactivity. These three fundamental concepts form the core of Becker's "theory" of deviance/crime that is discussed later.

Becker thinks of society as *collective action,* an emphasis that focuses our attention not only on the act and the actor, but also on all involved in any instance of behavior (Becker 1970, 1973). The acknowledgment of society as collective action is not trivial, according to Becker (1970), because such a conception precludes one from seeing society as a structure or an aggregation, or as an organization of forces or factors, or as a mechanism that produces rates, or in any number of other ways in which society has been characterized. The notion of collective action ultimately must refer to some view of people doing things together. Becker (1970) states that any conceptualization of society that does not have such a reference is "suspect," as the knowledge that events are "transactional or interactional" is unavoidable.

In the introduction to *Social Problems: A Modern Approach,* Becker (1966) states that social problems are often viewed by society's members as objective conditions that constitute a problem that something ought to be done about. However, to state that the problem is objective implies that an identifiable "normal state" must be maintained, which really cannot be the case. In actuality, social problems are what people think they are. Any set of conditions, even nonexistent ones, can be defined as a *social problem;* therefore, it is not just the conditions themselves that constitute or cause the problem. According to Becker, one difficulty with many of our definitions (scientific and otherwise) is that they have not identified the *area of life* in which the problem is being discussed (relativity).

An even greater weakness of our definitions relates to the subjective component. Who are the people who define the situation or event as a *problem*? It is important to remember, Becker says, that the problem is not necessarily the same to all parties. Every social problem has a history and develops through a series of stages, each reflecting changes in who defines the problem, the kind of definition given, and the resulting actions (reactions) adopted to solve it. To fully understand any social problem, it is essential to understand how it came to be defined as such. Social problems must be analyzed in social context because they are relative to the time, place, and subjective interpretations of the individuals involved. In *Outsiders,* Becker (1963, 1973) points out that the subjective view is the essence of the conception of *deviance.* The deviant or "outsider" appears so to some people, but not to others. He also points out that social rules are "continually constructed anew" in every situation.

The third aspect of (social) behavior is reactivity. Becker (1973) says that people act with an "eye to the responses" of others involved. The reaction to an act becomes a central component in collective action and, therefore, in understanding the act. Vold and Bernard (1986) refer to Becker's approach (and others like it) as "social reaction theory." Emphasis on social reactions to individuals and their behavior has its roots in symbolic interactionism (Williams and McShane 1988, Vold and Bernard 1986), which states that, through interaction, we establish meanings for events and people in our world. One of the most important meanings is one that we give to self, which is constructed primarily through interaction (reactions to self) with others (Mead 1934, Cooley 1902). Becker (1964) contends that, in pursuing various goals (i.e., exposing self to different reactions), people often become involved in activities that ultimately alter their views of self.

The necessity for addressing the interaction of these three components of behavior becomes most salient when one examines the area of deviance. Scientific research accepts commonsense assumptions that acts that break rules are inherently deviant, and that the people who commit such acts do so because they possess some characteristic that makes it inevitable. Scientists do not ordinarily question the label *deviant* when it is applied to particular acts by people, but rather take it as a given (Becker 1963). Some social models of deviance, such as rule breaking, erroneously assume that actors represent a homogeneous category (deviants) simply because they have committed some deviant act.

Becker seriously questions the validity and utility of pathological and homogeneous conceptualizations of deviance/deviants, and argues that there is no reason to believe that those who commit deviant acts are the only ones who have the impulse to do so (Matza 1969). He further insists that the study of deviance is nothing special, as it exists and occurs like any other human activity. People act deviant for much the same reasons used to justify and explain ordinary activity (Becker 1973). In the course of their research and theorizing, sociologists and other social scientists ignored the "central fact about deviance: it is created by society" (Becker 1963, 8). Deviance is not a quality of the act, but is a consequence of applications of rules and sanctions by others. This application or labeling process is far from infallible, which means that studies of deviance cannot assume that those so labeled represent a homogeneous group (Becker 1963).

Becker (1973) calls his approach an *interactionist theory of deviance.* In *Becoming Deviant*, David Matza (1969) referred to Becker as a Neo-Chicagoan because his approach places emphasis on the "secondary aspects of deviance" (i.e., the reactions to it). It is a processural theory based on the three aspects discussed previously and concerned with the way in which the labeling of behavior takes place (Becker 1970, Williams and McShane 1988). Becker's theoretical perspective required a different orientation to the study of deviance than had its predecessors (Williams and McShane 1988), which were theories dependent on statistical, pathological, or relativistic conceptualizations, none of which do justice to the reality of deviance (Becker 1963). From the labeling perspective, there is no deviance without some reaction to the act. Neither acts nor people are deviant until society identifies them as such by applying a label to them.

ASSUMPTIONS ABOUT RESEARCH AND THEORY

In *Sociological Work*, Becker (1970) offers two very fundamental observations about the research process in sociology: that sociology should be studied first-hand, and that he does not know if there is any particular causal order involved in the behavior being studied. Becker, in keeping with his call for close contact between the science and the subject matter, characterizes himself as a *naturalist* and primarily a qualitative researcher. Naturalistic or field observation, he insists, must be the major method of any truly interactionistic approach (Matza 1969, Becker 1973).

Becker's work started something of a revolution in criminological thought, and during such periods of "paradigm revolution" in scientific inquiry, older ideas and conceptualizations are often resurrected (Chambliss 1988). This is true of the orientation and approach promoted by Becker. He applied the research methodologies of people like Alfred Lindesmith, Everett Hughes, Lloyd Warner, and Herbert Blumer (i.e., the Chicago School) to his work on deviant behavior (Debro 1970, personal communication, April 13, 1988).

It is important to point out that even though Becker's methods are primarily qualitative, he was also influenced by some individuals of the more quantitative ilk, such as Ernest Burgess, William Ogburn, and Phil Hauser. He says that he did not regard the quantitative approach as "foreign" but as something that was just not to his interest. However, he expected such work to be done so that the information it could produce would be available (Debro 1970).

With his strong emphasis on first-hand qualitative methodologies, Becker (1973) was reacting to the reluctance of sociology (and criminology) to look at what was right in front of its nose. It was this lack of touch with reality that led to what Becker (1963) called the most persistent difficulty in the scientific study of deviance—the lack of solid data.

Just as some methods might take us too far from the phenomenon being studied, Becker (1973) believed that our theories often turn the collective activity of people doing things together into "abstract nouns" whose connections to people become very "tenuous." Under such circumstances, the search for causes is transformed into a chase of "invisible forces and conditions." Becker (1966) also argues that the theories in the social sciences (generally) have a conservative bias. Identifying these problems, however, does not mean that the theories are of no use. Social science has an advantage over lay and other professional approaches because it uses theories unavailable to others; its techniques, imperfect as they may be, provide a more complete understanding of the relevant facts and their interrelationships than does causal observation. The latter aspect of this conclusion is especially important in light of the fact that in our theories, we often argue not about various conditions, but about the relationships (especially causal) among them (Becker 1966).

The great trouble facing the scientific study of deviance is not technical but theoretical. Workable definitions of either particular actions or particular categories of deviance can be constructed, but our theories are unable to make the two coincide completely. According to Becker (1973), this is not necessarily surprising, as they do not do so empirically. The actions and categories that we have tried so diligently (almost blindly) to mesh neatly in our theories actually belong to two distinct but overlapping systems of collective action.

Sociologists (and probably many other social scientists) have created trouble for themselves with their "virtually unbreakable habit" of turning common events and experiences into mysteries. Becker (1973) says that he intended his own formulations to emphasize the logical independence of acts and judgments about them, while demonstrating the role that the interaction of various factors plays in the creation of deviance. One might argue that Becker, by focusing on the interaction process, attempts to demystify our thinking and theories about deviance and endeavors to move deviance theory out of the realm of individual pathology and root it firmly in the context of collective action. By highlighting the role that society plays in creating deviance/deviants, the interactionistic theories (as with any attempt at demystifying beliefs) have added considerably to the moral issues involved with the scientific inquiry into deviance/criminality.

Becker (1964) maintains that problems of deviance are problems of general sociology and should lead to general theories about personal and social disorganization.

Instead, he says, the study of deviance became a practical pursuit and, consequently, lost its connection with mainstream sociological theory and research. In other words, in the area of deviance, the social sciences have let the tail wag the dog. Policy and practice have dictated theory and research rather than the other way around.

Becker (1966) characterizes sociology and social science in general as the tension between the drive for understanding what is going on in the society in which we live and the "thrust toward a deeper understanding of the nature of man and society in the abstract." The scientific study of social problems represents the merger of these two interests. Social science, Becker says, can contribute to the understanding and solving of social problems in four ways:

1. By sorting out differing definitions
2. By locating assumptions of interested parties
3. By discovering strategic points of intervention in the social structure and processes that produce the problem
4. By suggesting alternative moral points of view

ASSUMPTIONS AND THEIR APPLICATIONS TO CRIMINOLOGY

Becker (1964, 1966) addresses, in detail, the broad issue of social problems, and when he lists examples of such problems, crime is first. There are several inadequacies in the scientific investigation of this important social problem, according to Becker. First, historically criminals and deviants have been slighted in research because of their subordinate status in various systems (Debro 1970). Echoing the much earlier observation of Sutherland, he also accuses criminologists of devoting their greatest efforts to minor areas of concern like juvenile delinquency and drug addiction, while continuing to ignore the phenomena that are by many criteria more important, such as antitrust violations, gambling, and employee theft (Becker 1970). Like Sutherland before him, Becker expresses serious concern with what he calls *conventional crime*, which is all activities that could lead to legal prosecution but are seldom subject to criminal sanction. These are acts for which the perpetrators are not and do not expect to be prosecuted; this is crime that is taken for granted by the community.

In terms of criminology's preoccupation with delinquency, Becker is not satisfied with the results that the plethora of studies in the area have yielded, because they have not actually told us what delinquents do on a daily basis. Commenting on this lack of relevant data, Becker argues,

> Just as we need anatomical descriptions of animals before we can begin to
> theorize and experiment with their psychological and biochemical function-
> ing, just so we need precise and detailed descriptions of social anatomy
> before we know just what phenomena are present to be theorized about.
> (Matza 1969, 167)

This leads to another historical problem: criminology's loss of connection with mainstream theory and research. Becker (1964) believes that the study of criminality had generally become a practical pursuit. Criminality had been studied to answer the questions of laypersons and elected officials—such as who is most likely to violate parole, or who is at high risk for becoming delinquent—and not to develop a complete understanding of the phenomena. This orientation began to show signs of change in the late 1950s and into the 1960s (a movement in which Becker himself was to become a prominent figure), as reflected in works such as Short and Nye's (1958) study on un-recorded delinquency, Kitsuse's (1962) article on the problems with theories and re-search on deviance, and Kitsuse and Cicourel's (1963) work on the use of official statistics. These and other projects like them began to raise serious questions about the process of becoming and being identified as criminal or deviant, and called into ques-tion the data (official statistics) on which many criminological theories were based. As Becker (1973) later pointed out, records, like the behaviors that they represent, are made by people acting together, and must be understood in that context. Therefore, by the mid-1960s, the link with mainstream theory and research was beginning to be reestablished. Becker (1964) cites two primary reasons for the shift in orientation: (1) The phenomena of deviance were being recognized in more conventional settings (e.g., prisons were seen as having the same characteristics as other organizations); and (2) the population of "deviants" had been expanded into other areas of society.

The "conventional style" of looking at deviance/criminality was to focus on the indi-vidual criminal or deviant, but the new approach looked at deviants and non-deviants as in-teracting in a complementary fashion. Deviance was seen as an interactive process (Becker 1964). The new focus placed the deviant and the non-deviant (the criminal and the criminal justice system) in an almost symbiotic relationship, with neither being able to exist without the other. In the new view, episodes of potential criminality are not dependent on just the acts themselves, but also on the allegations of wrongdoing. Within this perspective, there are no neat, clear-cut categories of crime (Becker 1973). Becker (1963) theorizes that peo-ple may perform criminal acts for various reasons, but whatever the reason, their fate actu-ally depends on whether they are caught and publicly labeled as criminal.

With regard to the issue of self-conception, the meaning attached to self is con-structed primarily out of interactions with others, and, although the maintenance of a non-criminal self-image is very important to most people, there are many ways to threaten this image, the ultimate being through the process of arrest and conviction, which results in the individual being officially declared a criminal to society at large (Vold and Bernard 1986). Once the label is declared, others begin to react to the label and not necessarily to the individual, which may have long-term, negative repercus-sions for the meaning of self and, in turn, may affect future behavior. Becker and oth-ers of the Social Reaction School took a giant step in the direction of deemphasizing the criminality of the person and emphasizing instead the social process of creating criminality and criminals. Labeling theory sensitized criminology to the fact that crimi-nality is as much a product of the way society reacts to the individual as it is of charac-teristics that the individual possesses (Williams and McShane 1988). As Chambliss (1988) points out, the labeling approach constituted a resurrection of Sutherland's con-tention that criminology cannot be just the study of criminal behavior, but must also at-tend to the reasons certain acts are so defined.

III. KEY IDEAS

As a sociologist, Becker is concerned with social problems and the social psychology of occupations and deviance. These interests led him to pay some attention to crime and criminals, and his ideas on those subjects have considerable impact on twentieth-century American criminology. Commenting on criminological thought, Becker (1970) takes issue with the traditional characterization of the criminal as someone who is "different" and whose behavior requires special explanation. He argues that this is quite the wrong approach, and uses the widespread and diverse nature of conventional crime to support his position. Criminology focuses on only a few subclasses of law-breaking acts against which criminal sanctions are invoked (no matter how crudely or spottily). These types of acts have become the target of the system and science alike, as their perpetrators are relatively unintegrated with society and so are easily separated, attacked, and studied.

THE PERSPECTIVE OR METHOD

Becker's general perspective has as great an influence on criminology as any of his specific concepts. However, it does not seem to be so much that Becker has something new to say, but rather, when and how it is said is the key. He published *Outsiders* during a time of intense and widespread change in our society. During such periods, older ideas and theories are often reexamined. Becker built on the works of Alfred Lindesmith (1947) and Thorsten Sellin (1938), and his ideas contained threads (whether intentionally or unintentionally) of Frank Tannenbaum (1938), Edwin Lemert (1951), Edwin Sutherland (1949), and Robert Merton (1957).

However, this "new criminology" is more than just a reincarnation of older ideas. The "critical criminology" of the 1960s and 1970s went beyond the empirical observations of the 1930s and 1940s, seeking to (re)establish a link between criminological theory and broader sociological theory. In a recent conversation, Becker said that he believes that his involvement and that of other "outsiders" in criminology was good for the discipline. Criminology had become very much a creature of the prison system and predicting delinquency, but he and others like him helped turn criminology back from a pure science orientation to a sociological one focusing on the process of deviance. They helped pull criminology out from under the legal perspective (personal communication, April 13, 1988).

Becker is credited with presaging the sociology of criminal law. His approach forced criminologists to recognize that their work took sides, and forced them to examine whose side they were on (Becker 1967). Chambliss (1988) believes that the most important innovation and direction fostered by this new perspective was that criminology began to take seriously the possibility that criminological inquiry was linked to conflict theory.

In *Outsiders*, Becker (1963) stresses the importance of accepting the subjective perspective. Subjectivity is at the core of Becker's orientation; deviance is in the eye (or label) of the beholder. This call for explicit attention to subjectivity echoes a point made earlier by Vold (1958), who had said that criminology faces the dual problem of explaining behavior as behavior, and the definition of behavior as criminal within the same perspective. The traditional perspectives in criminology had not done so; rather, they overemphasized the study of behavior and neglected the study of the ways in which behaviors come to be defined as crime (Jeffery 1956a, 1956b, 1959).

From this new perspective then, crime is created by a reaction to an act, and criminal is an ascribed status designation (label) assigned to an actor. Research on crime problems must pay close attention to the substantive nature of those reactions. Crime can no longer be seen as a static condition (Schur 1969) existing within the individual or environment alone. Becker (1973) calls for a naturalistic approach to the study of the phenomena of crime and criminality, centering on the interaction between those alleged to be engaged in wrongdoing and those making the allegations. The labeling perspective creates a "four-cell property space" with two dichotomous variables in which to place acts or events: commission/noncommission, and defined-as-deviant/not-defined-as-deviant (Cohen 1966). Labeling theory is not about one of these four cells, but about all four and their interrelationships. Such a perspective allows for the possibility that others are likely to define certain acts as deviant without making it a scientific judgment that the act is in fact deviant (Becker 1973).

Labeling is referred to previously as a perspective, as it is neither a theory in the strictest sense nor is it focused exclusively on the act of labeling itself. It is a way of looking at a general area of human activity. If Becker's ideas constitute a theory at all, he believes it should be called the "interactionist theory of deviance" (Becker 1973).

Richard Quinney (1965), whose work built on Becker's perspective, points to another aspect of the subjectivity issue. He observes that criminologists usually proceed from the premise that criminal law embodies important social norms that represent most of society, but this assumption may be somewhat erroneous. Criminal behaviors are not often considered deviant within the actors' group or subcultures. Consequently, criminologists should not take for granted, in terms of total correspondence, this relationship between laws and norms. The nature of such relationships is far from certain.

Becker's works and those of other proponents of the labeling perspective are a reaction to an unacceptable state of affairs in the study of crime and deviance. According to Becker, sociology accepted the notion that something was wrong with criminals; "the study of crime lost its connection with the mainstream of sociological development and became a very bizarre deformation of sociology" (Debro 1970, 166). The "theory" he proposed was not designed to explain why the criminal act occurred, but how the act came to have the quality of being deviant (Debro 1970).

In summary, there are two components to the labeling approach: why certain acts and/or individuals get labeled as criminal, and the effect of this labeling process on subsequent behavior. In other words, the process of labeling must be viewed as both an effect and a cause (Williams and McShane 1988). In order to examine the cause and effect natures of the labeling process, it is helpful to look at three more-specific concepts from Becker's approach: deviance, labeling or social reaction and its consequences, and moral entrepreneurs.

DEVIANCE (OR, HOW ONE BECOMES AN "OUTSIDER")

Science uses the term *deviant* to refer to rule-breaking behavior, but typically has studied only those individuals who have been so labeled (Becker 1966), ignoring the process by which the labels are developed and applied. The working assumption has been that "crime–not crime" are classes of behavior instead of simply labels associated with the process by which individuals come to occupy the ascribed statuses (Turk 1964).

The questions asked by Becker (1963) in *Outsiders* are essentially the same as those asked by other criminologists: What is criminality/deviance? How does one come to be criminal or deviant? However, Becker's answers were not the same. He states that

> social groups create deviance by making rules whose infraction constitutes
> deviance, and by applying those rules to particular people and labeling them

as outsiders . . . deviance is not a quality of the act the person commits, but rather a consequence of the application by others of rules and sanctions to an "offender." The deviant is one to whom that label has successfully been applied. (Becker 1963, 9)

This does not mean that acts like homicide and theft would never occur if they were not considered criminal. The point is that their nature, distribution, social meaning, and implications and ramifications are influenced significantly by patterns of social relations (Schur 1969).

LABELING AND ITS CONSEQUENCES

In 1937, Congress passed the Marijuana Tax Act, which was designed to eradicate the use of marijuana via the criminal justice process. This act and the enforcement of it served to redefine marijuana as a dangerous menace to American youth. Officially, it also served to label those who regularly smoked it as deviant and criminal (Becker 1963). The interactionist perspective Becker (and others) proposes calls attention to the fact that the behavior before and after the marijuana legislation was the same; what changed was the reaction of those with societal power (Clinard and Meier 1985).

By focusing on crime/deviance as a creation of society through its reactions to certain acts and individuals, the real issue is not why this person is a criminal; rather, the issues become: Who applies the label to whom? What are the consequences of the labels being applied? Under what circumstances are labels applied successfully? (Becker 1964). In addressing these three issues, labeling is by necessity treated as both a reaction or dependent variable, and also as a cause of deviance or independent variable. Once the label is applied, it raises a corollary question: What kind of person would break such an important rule? The answer is, someone who is different from us, someone who cannot or will not act morally, someone who might break other important rules (Becker 1963).

Whatever the reason for the original act, the individual's fate depends on whether he or she is caught and labeled publicly. Being caught and "publicly branded deviant" changes one's public identity, ascribing new status, and from then on, the label has an impact on whatever favorable impressions the person may create. Once the label of criminal is applied by criminal justice agencies, it overrides other labels so that the person is seen as primarily a criminal. *Criminal* is a "master status" to which most other labels are subordinate. The term also carries with it a number of connotations specifying "auxiliary" traits, such as not trustworthy. Treating people as though they are generally rather than specifically deviant may create a self-fulfilling prophecy. The ascription of deviant status denies the person access to ordinary means for carrying on the routines of everyday life, and so he or she develops illegitimate routines. Those labeled deviant may come to associate only with others who are so labeled, either through institutionalization or because non-labeled individuals will not associate with them. The labeled person is forced into criminal roles because of public stereotypes about criminals (Becker 1963).

Whereas the first step in a deviant career is the commission of some nonconforming act, the most crucial step in the development of a stable pattern of deviance is the experience of being caught and publicly labeled. The final step in the process is accepting the identity and all that it entails. The irony of this process is that through its reactions that force individuals to accept deviant status and socialize with other deviants, society ensures the continuation of behaviors it is trying to prevent (Light and Keller 1982). This scenario becomes even more problematic when one realizes that to be labeled as criminal, one need commit only a single criminal offense, and that the labeling process itself is highly fallible, being susceptible to both type I and type II errors.

MORAL ENTREPRENEURS

In the case of the Marijuana Tax Act of 1937, Becker (1963) contends that the legislation was not based on public concern, but on the Federal Bureau of Narcotics' effort at "moral entrepreneurship." Rules are the products of someone's initiative, and the people who exhibit such initiative are seen as moral entrepreneurs. There are actually "two related species" of moral entrepreneurs: rule creators and rule enforcers. For such entrepreneurial efforts to be successful, some must take the initiative to watch their fellows ("busybodies") and point out transgressions to the enforcers ("whistleblowers"). Given the strong sense of collectivity that characterizes a community, moral entrepreneurs, busybodies, and whistleblowers are all readily available (Becker 1963).

Such a system is fraught with problems. The whistleblowing and punishment aspects become quite selective, applied differentially among different kinds of people, at different times, and in different situations. Rule enforcers are faced with a double bind—they must demonstrate to others that the problem still exists, while also showing that attempts at enforcement are effective. This perpetuates the selective and discriminatory aspects of the process and gives the impression that the entrepreneurs are doing a good job while the problem actually gets worse (Becker 1963).

HISTORICAL UNDERPINNINGS

Strands of many different theories can be seen in Becker's interactionist theory; his approach is firmly rooted in the early conflict theories of people like Sellin (1938) as well as in symbolic interactionism and the Chicago School, and shares their attention to the effect of social setting and situational values on crime and deviance (Williams and McShane 1988, Chambliss 1988, Clinard and Meier 1985). Early in the twentieth century, Frederick Thrasher (1936) and Frank Tannenbaum (1938) both recognized the potential negative impact of officially labeling juveniles as delinquent. Then, in his book *Social Pathology* (1951), Edwin Lemert developed the concepts of primary and secondary deviance that were to become core elements in the labeling perspective. It is interesting to note that Becker (personal communication, April 13 and June 1, 1988), while acknowledging the contribution of Tannenbaum and Lemert (among others) to the labeling perspective, admits that when he wrote *Outsiders* he had not read Lemert at all, and that Tannenbaum's work had not had any real impact on his thinking.

Given that many of the basic tenets of labeling had been in print for some time, it might seem strange that it took the publication of *Outsiders* in 1963 to finally bring the orientation to some prominence in criminology. Up into the 1950s, the dominant sociological theories of criminality were, for the most part, structural (Shoemaker 1984), sharing their position of dominance to some extent with some other consensus and positivistic-type approaches; but starting in the 1960s, these approaches began to be profoundly challenged by theories (like Becker's) deriving from the conflict tradition. The existing theories were not being questioned because the delinquency that had been their primary focus had not changed; it was still present. What had changed was the "political climate" (Chambliss 1988) and the social awareness and conscience of an entire generation of Americans. Spurred by the Civil Rights Movement and the war in Vietnam, official policies and practices fell under closer scrutiny and sharper criticism than possibly at any other time in our history. The new and heightened social consciousness and the general changes in attitudes carried over into the sciences, especially the social sciences, and new questions were being asked (or old questions in new ways). Concern with crimes of the powerful grew (Chambliss 1988), and dissatisfaction with the focus on lower-class delinquency (Shoemaker 1984) initiated a new search for theories, explanations, and methods. Out of this search came renewed interest in the earlier conflict and social reaction conceptualizations, and it appears that this renewed interest found a vehicle for expression in the publication of *Outsiders*. The notion that deviance is created by the rulemakers and enforcers who are often biased against the poor and powerless became the central focus of criminology in the 1960s and 1970s (Shoemaker 1984).

Of course, others were offering very similar interpretations at the same time, people like Kai Erikson (1962), Kitsuse (1962), and Garfinkel (1956), and some question still remains as to why it was Becker who came to be seen as the standard-bearer of this new (old) movement. In trying to answer this question, Becker readily recognizes that others had said virtually the same things; but, he says, perhaps his work offered a clearer and simpler statement of the key ideas (Debro 1970). For whatever reasons, Becker's work epitomizes the labeling perspective and serves as the impetus for and a bridge to the later (often more radical) versions of conflict theory developed by David Matza (1969), Edwin Schur (1969), Richard Quinney (1965, 1970), Austin Turk (1964), and William Chambliss (1975).

In order to flesh out more completely the historical underpinnings of the labeling or social reaction approach, a brief discussion of the works of Frank Tannenbaum and Edwin Lemert is in order. Even though neither of these theorists is acknowledged as having had any direct influence on Becker's original statement, his work caused a resurgence of interest in and a rediscovery of these earlier theories.

Frank Tannenbaum

Tannenbaum (1938) in *Crime and the Community* explicitly addresses both the negative impact of labeling and the conflict components of the process that he called the "dramatization of evil." He states that delinquent behavior is not so much a product of the deviant's lack of adjustment to society, but more of his adjustment to a special group. Adjustment to this deviant group brings the individual into conflict with society, as he or she is now faced with two opposing definitions of appropriate behavior. If the individual is ultimately caught in a delinquent act, a "tag" is attached to him or her. This "tagging" process helps create further delinquency, because it causes people to react to the tag, and not to the person.

Edwin Lemert

Lemert, like Becker, is known for his theoretical writing on the labeling perspective. He too was a sociologist/anthropologist. Like Becker, he had backed into sociology, so to speak; he had originally planned to attend law school. After earning his bachelor's degree from Miami University of Ohio, Lemert spent a year as a welfare worker, and while attending graduate school at Ohio State University, he taught clinical psychology at Kent State University (Laub 1983). These experiences, along with exposure to the works of Mead, Shaw and McKay, and Sutherland, provided the foundation for his ideas, which were published in 1951 in *Social Pathology: A Systematic Approach to the Theory of Sociopathic Behavior.*

Even though the publication of Lemert's ideas predates the rough draft of *Outsiders* by three years and its actual publication by twelve years, Lemert states, "to be precise, labeling theory was devised by Howard Becker" (Laub 1983, 124). He further states that Becker's ideas about labeling took precedence over his in terms of popular acceptance and recognition and also in terms of the amount of criticism. He credits Becker with making it possible, via his editorship of *Social Problems* (1961–64), for others in the labeling theory area to get published. Lemert calls the approach developed by Becker, Erving Goffman, David Matza, and himself the "Neo-Chicagoan School" or "West Coast School" (Laub 1983).

Although he was a founding father of the labeling perspective, in an article entitled "Beyond Mead: The Societal Reaction to Deviance" (1974), Lemert broke ties with labeling theory, claiming it had become too psychological and had moved too far away from the interaction process. In the same article, Lemert made it clear that he was not part of the radical criminology movement either (Laub 1983). Lemert's problem with the strong emphasis on psychological factors in contemporary versions of labeling theory might be seen as a little surprising in light of some of the ideas expressed in *Social Pathology* and some of his other works.

The *primary deviant* person commits criminal behavior in the context of a non-criminal self-image. The antecedents of this original (primary) deviant act may be many and diverse, but the original reasons are only important for certain research purposes. From the sociological viewpoint, such deviations do not become significant until they are organized by the subject, transformed into active roles, and become social criteria for assigning status (Lemert 1967), which leads to the area of *secondary deviance.*

Criminal behavior generates negative social reaction, which endangers the person's noncriminal self-image. If the person cannot or will not stop the criminal behavior, then it becomes necessary to reorganize the self-image to incorporate criminal behavior, and possibly as a defense against the attacks of social reaction. It is this redefinition of self that opens the door to full participation in criminal life. Lemert (1951) further stated that the importance of the person's "conscious symbolic reactions" to his or her own behavior cannot be overstressed in explaining the shift in self-image. However, this is not meant to imply that the entire process is conscious.

Deviance is primary, or symptomatic and situational, as long as it is in some way dealt with (by the actor) as a function of socially acceptable roles. When the person begins to use deviant behavior or a role based on it as a means of defense, attack, or adjustment of the consequences of societal reaction, it becomes secondary. It is at this point that stigmatization of the deviance occurs in the form of labeling, name calling, or stereotyping (Lemert 1967).

Lemert's views on deviance and labeling have been greatly condensed and simplified here, but an attempt has been made to demonstrate the high level of complexity, symbolism, and abstractness that characterizes his approach. Given the relatively complex nature of Lemert's theory, it seems that Becker's explanation that his version caught on, at least in part, because of its clarity and relative simplicity, seems quite tenable.

CLOSING COMMENTS ON THE LABELING PERSPECTIVE

Gibbons (1982) very aptly points out that it would be misleading to claim that any single theoretical position can be identified as labeling theory, although a sizable body of sociological thought does share a set of common themes. Becker (1973) thinks that it is rather unfortunate that these approaches have been called *labeling theory,* preferring to call them *interactionist approaches.* Despite its diversity and no matter what the approach is called, its most fundamental premise is that criminality/deviance is a social process. The approach focuses on the interaction of the deviant with conventional society, especially with the official agents of social control, and on the reactions to the label and the consequences for the labelee (Clinard and Meier 1985). It is the consideration of the reactions of the labelee as well as society that justifies referring to the approach as *interactionist* (Shoemaker 1984).

There is no attempt to explain why certain individuals initially engage in criminal behavior; the attention is on the dynamics involved in socially defining acts and people as criminal, with the analysis being primarily centered on the reactions of others (Clinard and Meier 1985). The approach underscores the self-fulfilling nature of inferences invoked in the reactive proceedings of labeling or stigmatization. Labeling theorists in criminology have emphasized the criminogenic consequences of official stigmatization which forces individuals to embrace deviant roles (McCall and Simmons 1982). The theories further argue that informal as well as formal processes of social control have the effect of increasing criminal behavior (Vold and Bernard 1986).

IV. CRITIQUE

Like all those who challenge existing notions, Becker's ideas attract considerable criticism. Not all of the criticisms discussed here have necessarily been made specifically in reference to Becker's work alone, but all represent potential problems identified with the labeling or interactionist approach.

THE IMPACT OF LABELING

The single biggest criticism of this approach refers to the actual reaction to or impact of being labeled. Many studies have not found that delinquents or criminals have a delinquent or criminal self-image, as the labeling perspective predicts. Yochelson and Samenow (1976) find that most hardened criminals are unwilling to admit that they are criminals, but they recognize criminality in others easily. Cressey (1953) reports that embezzlers normally see themselves as upstanding citizens. Sykes and Matza (1957) find that delinquents lack criminal self-images. In *Law, Order, and Power,* Chambliss and Seidman (1971) state that it is a "truism" that all persons arrested perceive themselves as innocent. There are always circumstances that place their behavior "outside the definition of crime." Martin (1985) finds that convicted criminals, especially those who commit assaults, express positive self-concepts and describe themselves in terms that are not indicative of criminality. It can be concluded from the data on the impact of labeling juveniles, in terms of subsequent identities and behaviors, that the significance of labeling is questionable (Shoemaker 1984). One extensive review of the labeling literature demonstrates that it has not really been established that labeling leads to self-concept changes. In addition, there is little evidence that indicates that social characteristics of labeled deviants are major determinants of their fates in the criminal justice system, and there is a lack of firm empirical support for the notion of secondary deviance. Finally, it can be concluded that, overall, the existing evidence lends "relatively little support" to the sweeping allegations about the harmful effects of contact with the system (Wellford 1975).

Labeling theorists tend to pay little attention to the fact that not all individuals accept the stigmatization of the label passively (Edgerton 1967). There is some evidence that labels can be and often are shed (Prus 1975, Rotenburg 1974, Rogers and Buffalo 1974). Support for this notion is also gleaned from observations of people and events such as Oliver North and the Iran–Contra hearings, Richard Nixon and Watergate, and sports figures and actors, who are able to overcome a variety of transgressions both in our eyes and their own. The idea of the label persisting is also inconsistent with the data on the aging-out process in criminal behavior.

Interactionists have also been accused of overemphasizing the importance of official labeling from the opposite direction. Ronald Akers (1968) claims that labeling theory generally portrays deviants as resisting the label as long as they can, and that, from the impression given in the literature, a bad society singles certain people out on whom to hang a stigmatizing label, forcing them into deviance. Akers asserts that, quite to the contrary, it seems that in some cases a deviant identity may be actively sought out and formed before ever being labeled, either officially or unofficially (e.g., gangs). Official labeling may make it more difficult to change one's identity later, but it does not necessarily push one into deviance. In addition, there is no reason to believe that failure to label automatically leads to a law-abiding identity (Vold and Bernard 1986).

It has also been proposed that reducing the stigmatizing or labeling effects of criminal court could lead to an increase in criminal behavior. From this perspective, the basic question is not whether the labeling process creates crime, but whether it creates more than it eliminates (Vold and Bernard 1986). Tittle (1975) contends that it does not.

There are, however, some feasible responses to the studies that have found no criminal or delinquent self-images in various populations of labeled individuals. It is possible, in the case of some studies, such as those of Yochelson and Samenow (1976) and Martin (1985), that the use of personality or other psychological assessment devices (which very often are of questionable validity) or clinical interviews may not be effective in assessing changes that occurred over time, as these methods tend to be one-shot techniques administered after the fact. Such procedures may also be detecting defensiveness on the part of the respondents (see Martin 1985), as could be the case with Sykes and Matza (1957) in their investigation of delinquents. There may also be some problems in the conceptualization of self-concept as either criminal or not criminal. It seems more feasible to view self-perceived criminality as dimensional, rather than to categorize it as an either–or proposition. In terms of the Chambliss and Seidman (1971) observation about perceived innocence, it is reasonable to question whether perception of innocence in a particular case is equivalent to overall self-image. It is also likely that the immediate experiences of investigation procedures, incarceration, and going to court have a great impact on such perceptions. Denial is one of the most basic defensive mechanisms. Cressey's (1953) studies of embezzlers really deal with a different type of crime, and the sample population probably differs from the others discussed in terms of such variables as status prior to the incident.

Shoemaker (1984), while questioning the significance of labeling in his review, concludes that the assumptions of labeling theory are not totally indefensible. The data show the impact of labeling in two areas: (1) Juveniles were more affected than were adults; and (2) those less committed to antisocial behavior at the time of labeling were more affected. Shoemaker also makes the point that unofficial labeling has yet to be fully researched. Gibbons (1982) cites evidence that the master status of criminality may well affect the social niches that the offender comes to occupy. In a chapter added to the 1973 revision of *Outsiders*, Becker does not refute such criticisms directly, but says that the degree to which labeling has effects is an empirical question to be settled by specific cases, not theoretical fiat.

ETIOLOGICAL EXPLANATION

A number of researchers (Gibbs 1966, Akers 1968, Light and Keller 1982) criticize labeling theory for not providing an etiological explanation. In other words, the theory, although accounting for at least part of the process of criminal careers, does not explain initial involvement in crime.

A careful reading of the tenets and stated goals of the labeling approach undermines such criticism. On several occasions, Becker makes it quite clear that he is not attempting to explain why certain individuals engage in deviant behavior initially. In the 1963 edition of *Outsiders*, he clearly states that his interest is in those who commit deviant acts over time, those who have developed a deviant way of life and identity. Responding to this criticism in the 1973 edition, he points out that despite what some think about the theory's attempt to explain deviance by the response to it, the original proponents of the theory did not "propose solutions to the etiological question." He says that their aims were much more modest; they were to enlarge the study of deviance by adding the activities of others besides the alleged deviants to the phenomenological field. His own intentions were to emphasize the logical independence of acts and judgments about them. The theory was not designed to explain why a criminal act occurred, but how the act came to have the characteristic of being deviant (Debro 1970).

CONCEPTUAL TIGHTNESS AND EMPIRICAL SUPPORT

Several issues can be placed under the rather generic heading of conceptual tightness. Generally speaking, as with many other sociological formulations, one can attribute "more than a slight bit of conceptual flabbiness, ambiguity and the like to the labeling perspective" (Gibbons 1982, 195). The approach sometimes distorts the real world, characterizing deviance and social processes in exaggerated and misleading ways (Light and Keller 1982, Gibbons 1982). Becker's treatment of relativity presents an example of the lack of conceptual clarity and consistency. Becker (1963) talks about the common experience of being labeled an outsider shared by those who have been ascribed deviant status. Whether his actual intent was to represent this as a truly homogenous experience is unclear, but his discussion certainly could be interpreted that way, and such a representation is a bit inconsistent with the emphasis he placed on relativity. Of course, some have taken issue with the fundamental contention that deviance is a relative concept, arguing that there must be qualities of an act that make it deviant regardless of the definition, time period, and situation (Gibbs 1966, Alvarez 1968).

Compounding and contributing to the problem of conceptual ambiguity and flabbiness is the acceptance of assumptions and specific concepts without adequate empirical support (Shoemaker 1984, Wellford 1975, Gibbons 1982). Williams and McShane (1988) state that labeling theory does not meet the testability requirement, and observe that some criminologists are of the opinion that the ideas and concepts of labeling do not constitute a theory at all, but represent a sensitizing perspective.

Becker (1973) readily admits that his analysis contains ambiguities and some self-contradiction. In his defense, no approach is immune from such problems, and it falls to others in the scientific community to address these problems through critical analysis and empirical research. The motivation of such follow-up work is, in and of itself, a contribution of significant magnitude. Addressing specifically the concept of deviance, Becker (1973) acknowledges that much of the "heated discussion" over the labeling theory approach derives from the "equivocation of deviance," which has been made to stand for two distinct processes in two systems. By this, he is referring to the four-cell property space (discussed earlier) made up of two dichotomous variables, commission/non-commission and defined-as-deviant/not-defined-as-deviant. He admits that the term *deviance* has been loosely applied to all three cases (commission-not defined, commission-defined, non-commission-defined) in which deviance might be implicated. This sloppiness, he says, deserves criticism, but does not alter the point of the argument.

As for his ideas not constituting a theory, Becker (1973) agrees, saying that he has never thought that the original statements made by himself or others warranted being called *theories*—at least, not theories of the fully articulated kind that they are criticized for not being. This view is shared by other prominent figures in the development of the approach, as they do not refer to themselves as labeling theorists.

MORALITY

As is true of virtually all theories in the social sciences, especially those addressing emotionally charged areas of human functioning, the interactionists have been criticized on moral and ethical grounds. Charges have come from right, center, and left. The right accuses the interactionists of aiding the enemy by finding fault with and undermining our social institutions and of being subversive by supporting unconventional morality. Bordua (1967) went so far as to call the interactionist approach a "mischievous assault on social order." The centrists have claimed that the approach exhibits a "perverse unwillingness" to acknowledge rape, robbery, and murder as being deviant (Becker 1973).

Surprising as it may seem, some of the most vociferous attacks have come from the left. Mankoff (1968) and Liazos (1972) indict the interactionists for refusing to recognize that class oppression, racial discrimination, sexual discrimination, and so on, really are deviant. "Despite their best liberal intentions, these sociologists seem to perpetuate the very notions they think they debunk, and others of which they are unaware" (Liazos 1972, 111). Accusations of Establishmentarianism have also been made because the theories attack only the lower levels of oppressive institutions while leaving those higher up untouched (Gouldner 1968). As Becker (1973) puts it, the interactionists are seen as having failed to label institutions as being as rotten as they really are. So, both the left and the right complain about the ambiguous moral stance of the interactionists. It is difficult to respond to such impassioned attacks, but Becker (1973) makes an attempt. Fundamentally, the trouble is the result of equivocation over the notion of being value-free.

When an approach focuses its attention on undesirable actions of those officially in charge of defining deviance, it does not (and should not) necessarily in the process make empirical characterizations of the entire social institution. Becker further responds by saying that the attack on the hierarchy begins with attacks on definitions, labels, and conventional conceptions of who is who and what is what. Even though the focus has been on the immediate actors in the interaction process, the adoption of such a focus is not exclusive or inevitable, and the actual effect has been to cast doubt on authorities (for example the now infamous My Lai incident during Viet Nam). Becker defends the interactionists by saying that they have called attention to all of the participants in these "moral dramas" and have clarified phenomena under deviance, but in the process, they have also complicated the moral view of the deviance area.

CONCLUSION

Howard Becker states, "Good sociologists produce radical results" (Debro 1970, 171). By that criterion, Becker has certainly been a good sociologist. His work on the interactionist or labeling perspective has had a profound impact on the general study of deviance and on criminology. His approach forced us to expand the net of scientific inquiry beyond the individual offender to the entire justice system. His ideas demonstrate the value of dividing our theoretical and research attention among the offender, the rules, and those who make and enforce the rules. He also exposed us to the ever-changing processes of deviance and the role that these processes play in our official and unofficial conceptions of it.

There is no doubt that labeling insights have been important in the development of criminological thought, but, as is often the case, we must guard against diminishing their positive impact through overinterpretation and inappropriate application.

References

Akers, R.L. 1968. Problems in the sociology of deviance: Social definitions and behavior. *Soc. Forces* 46: 455–65.

Alvarez, R. 1968. Informal reactions to deviance in simulated work organizations: A laboratory experiment. *Am. Sociolog. Rev.* 33: 895–912.

Becker, H.S. 1963. *Outsiders: Studies in the sociology of deviance.* New York: The Free Press.

———. 1964. Introduction. In H.S. Becker (Ed.), *The other side: Perspectives on deviance.* New York: The Free Press, pp. 1–6.

———. 1966. *Social problems: A modern approach.* New York: John Wiley & Sons.

———. 1967. Whose side are we on? *Soc. Prob.* 14: 239–47.

———. 1970. *Sociological work.* Chicago: Aldine Publishing Company.

———. 1973. *Outsiders: Studies in the sociology of deviance.* Rev. ed. New York: The Free Press.

Becker, H.S., Geer, B., Hughes, E.C., & Strauss, A.L. 1961. *Boys in white: Student culture in medical school.* Chicago: University of Chicago Press.

Bordua, D. 1967. Recent trends: Deviant behavior and social control. *Annals* 369: 149–63.

Chambliss, W.J. 1975. Toward a political economy of crime. *Theory Soc.* 2: 152–53.

———. 1988. *Exploring criminology.* New York: Macmillan Publishing Company.

Chambliss, W.J., & Seidman, R.B. 1971. *Law, order, and power.* Reading, MA: Addison-Wesley.

Clinard, M.B., & Meier, R.F. 1985. *Sociology of deviant behavior.* 6th ed. New York: Holt, Rinehart & Winston.

Cohen, A.K. 1966. *Deviance and control.* Englewood Cliffs, NJ: Prentice–Hall.

Cooley, C.H. 1902. *Human nature and the social order.* New York: Charles Scribner's Sons.

Cressey, D.R. 1953. *Other people's money.* New York: The Free Press.

Debro, J. 1970. Dialogue with Howard S. Becker. *Iss. Crim.* 5(2): 159–79.

Edgerton, R.B. 1967. *The cloak of competence.* Berkeley: University of California Press.

Erikson, K.T. 1962. *Wayward puritans.* New York: John Wiley & Sons.

Garfinkel, H. 1956. Conditions of successful degradation ceremonies. *Am. J. Sociol.* 61: 420–24.

Gibbons, D.C. 1982. *Society, crime and criminal behavior.* 4th ed. Englewood Cliffs, NJ: Prentice Hall.

Gibbs, J. 1966. Conceptions of deviant behavior: The old and the new. *Pac. Sociol. Rev.* 9: 9–14.

Gouldner, A.W. 1968. The sociologist as partisan: Sociology and the welfare state. *Am. Sociol.* 3: 103–16.

Horowitz, I. L. 1968. Mainliners and marginals: The human shape of sociological theory. In I.L. Horowitz (Ed.), *Professing sociology: Studies in the life cycle of the social sciences.* Chicago: Aldine Publishing Company.

Jeffery, C.R. 1956a. The structure of American criminological thinking. *J. Crim. Law Criminol. Pol. Sci.* 46: 658–72.

———. 1956b. Crime, law, and social structure. *J. Crim. Law Criminol. Pol. Sci.* 47: 423–35.

———. 1959. An integrated theory of crime and criminal behavior *J. Crim. Law Criminol. Pol. Sci.* 49, 533–52.

Kitsuse, J.I. 1962. Societal reaction to deviant behavior: Problems of theory and method. *Soc. Prob.* 9: 247–56.

Kitsuse, J.I., & Cicourel, A.V. 1963. A note on the use of official statistics. *Soc. Prob.* 11: 131–39.

Laub, J.H. 1983. *Criminology in the making: An oral history.* Boston: Northeastern University Press.

Lemert, E.M. 1951. *Social pathology: A systematic approach to the theory of sociopathic behavior.* New York: McGraw Hill.

———. 1967. *Human deviance, social problems, and social control.* Englewood Cliffs, NJ: Prentice-Hall.

———. 1974. Beyond Mead: The societal reaction to deviance. *Soc. Prob.* 21(4): 457–68.

Liazos, A. 1972. The poverty of the sociology of deviance: Nuts, sluts, and perverts. *Soc. Prob.* 20: 103–20.

Light, D., Jr., & Keller, S. 1982. *Sociology.* 3rd ed. New York: Alfred A. Knopf.

Lindesmith, A.R. 1947. *Opiate addiction.* Bloomington, IN: Principia Press.

Mankoff, M. 1968. On alienation, structural strain, and deviancy. *Soc. Prob.* 16: 114–16.

Martin, R. 1985. Perceptions of self and significant others in assaultive and nonassaultive criminals. *J. Crim. Law Criminol. Pol. Sci.* 1(2): 2–13.

Matza, D. 1969. *Becoming deviant.* Englewood Cliffs, NJ: Prentice-Hall.

McCall, G.J., & Simmons, J.L. 1982. *Social pathology: A sociological approach.* New York: The Free Press.

Mead, G.H. 1934. *Mind, self, and society.* Chicago: University of Chicago Press.

Merton, R.K. 1957. *Social theory and social structure.* Rev. ed. New York: The Free Press.

Prus, R.C. 1975. Resisting designations: An extension of attribution theory into a negotiated context. *Sociolog. Inq.* 45: 3–14.

Quinney, R. 1965. Is criminal behaviour deviant behaviour? *Br. J. Criminol.* 5: 132–42.

———. 1970. *The social reality of crime.* Boston: Little, Brown.

Rogers, J.W., & Buffalo, M.D. 1974. Fighting back: Nine modes of adaptation to a deviant label. *Soc. Prob.* 22: 101–18.

Rotenburg, M. 1974. Self-labeling: A missing link in the "societal reaction" theory of deviation. *Sociolog. Rev.* 22: 335–56.

St. Clair, D. and Horace C. 1945. *Black metropolis: A study of negro life in a northern city.* New York: Harcourt Brace and Co.

Schur, E.M. 1969. *Our criminal society: The social and legal sources of crime in America.* Englewood Cliffs, NJ: Prentice-Hall.

Sellin, T. 1938. *Culture conflict and crime.* New York: Social Sciences Research Council.

Shoemaker, D.J. 1984. *Theories of delinquency: An examination of explanations of delinquent behavior.* New York: Oxford University Press.

Short, J.F., Jr., & Nye, F.I. 1958. Extent of unrecorded juvenile delinquency: Tentative conclusions. *J. Crim. Law Criminol. Pol. Sci.* 49: 296–302.

Sutherland, E.H. 1949. *White collar crime.* New York: Dryden.

Sykes, G.M., & Matza, D. 1957. Techniques of neutralization: A theory of delinquency. *Am. Sociolog. Rev.* 22: 664–70.

Tannenbaum, F. 1938. *Crime and the community.* Boston: Ginn & Company.

Thrasher, F.M. 1936. *The gang.* 2nd rev. ed. Chicago: University of Chicago Press.

Turk, A.T. 1964. Prospects for theories of criminal behavior. *J. Crim. Law Criminol. Pol. Sci.* 55: 454–61.

Vold, G.B. 1958. *Theoretical criminology.* New York: Oxford University Press.

Vold, G.B. & Bernard, T.J. 1986. *Theoretical criminology.* 3rd ed. New York: Oxford University Press.

Wellford, C. 1975. Labeling theory and criminology: An assessment. *Soc. Prob.* 22: 332–45.

Williams, F.P., III, & McShane, M.D. 1988. *Criminological theory.* Englewood Cliffs, NJ: Prentice-Hall.

Yochelson, S., & Samenow, S.E. 1976. *The criminal personality.* Vol. 1. New York: Jason Aronson.

Selected Bibliography

Becker, H.S. 1951. The professional dance musician and his audience. *Am. J. Soc.* 57: 136–44.

———. 1953. Becoming a marihuana user. *Am. J. Soc.* 59: 235–42.

———. 1960. *Outsiders: Studies in the sociology of deviance.* New York: The Free Press.

———. 1964. *The other side: Perspectives on deviance.* New York: The Free Press.

———. 1966. *Social problems: A modern approach.* New York: John Wiley & Sons.

———. 1966. Introduction. In C. Shaw, *The jackroller.* Chicago: University of Chicago Press, pp. v–xviii.

———. 1967. Whose side are we on? *Soc. Prob.* 14: 239–47.

———. 1968. Conventional crime. In M. Levitt & B. Rubinstein (Eds.), *Orthopsychiatry and the law.* Detroit: Wayne State University Press, pp. 199–212.

———. 1970. Practioners of vice and crime. In R. Habenstein (Ed.), *Pathways to data.* Chicago: Aldine, pp.30–49.

———. 1972. Labeling theory reconsidered. In P. Rock & M. MacIntosh (Eds.), *Deviance and social control.* London: Tavistock.

———. 1973. *Outsiders: Studies in the sociology of deviance.* Rev. ed. New York: The Free Press.

About Howard Becker

Debro, J. 1970. Dialogue with Howard S. Becker. *Iss. Crim.* 5(2): 159–79.

Lemert, E.M. 1951. *Social pathology: A systematic approach to the theory of sociopathic behavior.* New York: McGraw Hill.

Tannenbaum, F. 1938. *Crime and the community.* Boston: Ginn & Company.

Thrasher, F.M. 1936. *The gang.* 2nd rev. ed. Chicago: University of Chicago Press.

Wellford, C. 1975. Labeling theory and criminology: An assessment. *Soc. Prob.* 22: 332–45.

CHAPTER 15
EARL RICHARD QUINNEY: B. 1934

I. BIOGRAPHICAL SKETCH

There has been a substantial amount of material written about the life of Earl Richard Quinney, by Quinney himself as well as by some of his former students. Different from many of the pioneers detailed in this book, the specifics of Quinney's early life on a farm in Wisconsin have been well chronicled.

Richard Quinney, as he is known today, the son of Floyd and Alice Quinney, was born on May 16, 1934. Up until the time he left for college, Quinney lived on the family farm in Sugar Creek township in Walworth County in Wisconsin, approximately ninety miles north of Chicago. Quinney represented the fourth generation of Quinneys to farm the land in Wisconsin.

The first Quinney to work the Wisconsin land was Richard's great-grandfather John Quinney, who, with his parents, immigrated to the United States from Ireland in 1847 because of the Irish potato famine. The same year, Bridget O'Keefe set sail for America as well (Quinney 1984, 166), and both families settled in Yonkers, New York. Bridget and John met there and later married, and had two of their five children in that same area (Quinney 1984, 166).

In the 1860s, John and Bridget Quinney moved to the farmland of Wisconsin, at first renting the property they would later buy. Of their five children, one, a son named John, would live his seventy-nine years in Sugar Creek, farming the homestead and trading horses (Quinney 1984, 166). John Quinney married Hattie Reynolds, who bore him two children, one of whom was Floyd, Quinney's father.

Quinney's mother's family, on both sides, was English (Quinney 1984, 168). His mother, Alice Marie Holloway, was the only child of William Holloway and Lorena Taylor. She attended high school in Elkhorn, Wisconsin, and the State Normal School in Whitewater. After graduating from the State Normal School, she taught school at the Bay Hill rural school near Williams Bay. It was while teaching school that Alice Marie met and married Floyd Quinney. Alice and Floyd had two sons, Earl Richard and Ralph.

When the weather was appropriate, Quinney and his brother would ride their bicycles to school. Probably named after a combination of the cowboys and their horses that were popular at the time, the model of Quinney's bicycle was *Silver King*. In addition to his bicycle, Quinney had a pony named Sparkplug and later a bay riding horse named Lady, given to him by his cousin Howard. On Sunday mornings, the Quinney family would usually attend the Methodist church.

Quinney describes in vivid detail some recollections of his early years growing up on the farm and attending a one-room schoolhouse in an article entitled "A Place Called Home," published in the *Wisconsin Magazine of History* (1984):

[Dunham School] was a one-room building of red brick that stood on an acre of land surrounded by giant American elms. The girl's outhouse was along the south fence in back of the school; the boy's was to the north. A baseball diamond occupied the rest of the yard. (Quinney 1984, 170)

Each of the eight grades had only two or three students.

When Quinney finished the seventh grade, there were only five children attending Dunham School. Because of the small number of students, Dunham School was closed, and Quinney and his brother began attending the Island School in Richmond Township, still within walking distance. At his eighth-grade commencement, Quinney was asked to give a speech "representing all the grade schools in Richmond Township" (Quinney 1984, 172). The commencement speech was a first occasion for Quinney to wear a sport coat.

After graduating from the Richmond Township School, Quinney attended Delevan High School. Quinney acknowledges that attending high school in Delevan, five miles from the farm, represented the beginning of his separation from farm life. Each day, he drove the family truck to Delevan to attend school. Try as he could, his clothes and the fact that he drove a truck "let everyone know that he was from the farm" (Quinney 1984, 172). Adjusting to high school and interacting with the "town" kids was difficult for Quinney; in his second year,

[Quinney] developed sharp stomach pains that made getting to school a trial each morning. The pain finally settled in his right side—the obvious sign of appendicitis. Dr. Crowe agreed with Earl's persistent diagnosis . . .. Following the operation, his appendix was placed in a jar and studied. There was no inflammation; a perfectly good appendage had been removed. But somehow Earl began to feel better, and after the operation and recovery he returned to school with new confidence. (Quinney 1984, 173)

Once back at school, Quinney became involved in photography and began taking pictures as well as writing for the school newspaper. His interest in photography continues to this day, as exemplified recently by a grant he received from Northern Illinois University to take photographs of old structures in DeKalb County. Quinney also took up the trombone and played in the high school band. In his junior year of high school, Quinney formed a dance band that played at school dances.

When not in school, Quinney helped with the chores on the family farm. Young Quinney assisted with a wide variety of chores depending on the time of year. In addition to his work and study, Quinney spent time raising pigs to show at the Walworth County Fair, but instead of raising ordinary pigs, Quinney raised purebred Duroc hogs, which were sold for breeding purposes rather than for pork. This was a calculated endeavor designed to raise money for college. A fattened Duroc hog brought as much as seven or eight times the price of a nonregistered pig. The money for college would come in handy, but Quinney was careful not to disclose the source of his wealth.

In the fall of 1952, Quinney headed off to Carroll College, a small liberal arts Presbyterian school in Waukesha, Wisconsin. His plan was to graduate with a double major in sociology and psychology. Not able to separate himself entirely from his rural roots, Quinney considered studying biology as well as sociology and psychology. His intention was to be a forest ranger, but this interest began to disappear the more he "became involved in the human condition" (Trevino 1984, 8).[1] Outside the classroom, Quinney had a variety of interests. At one point during his career at Carroll College, he was elected president of the student body.

Before graduation in 1956, Quinney paid a visit to his biology advisor to discuss ways of combining his interests in sociology and biology into a career, and his advisor suggested hospital administration. Because of this, Quinney applied and was accepted into the master's program in hospital administration at Northwestern University.

In preparation for his entrance into the hospital administration program, Quinney worked in the credit office as a bill collector the summer before classes started at Wesley Memorial Hospital in Chicago, which made it clear to him that he did not want a career as a hospital administrator; Quinney greatly disliked having to put pressure on people to pay their bills (Trevino 1984).

Looking for an alternative, Quinney asked for a meeting with the chair of the Department of Sociology at Northwestern University. "The chair, Kimball Young, paternalistically welcomed Quinney to the program" (Trevino 1984, 9). During his nine months at Northwestern, Quinney worked with both Kimball Young and William Byron. It was because of his work with Byron's criminology classes that Quinney received his "first exposure to the academic study of crime" (Trevino 1984, 9). To culminate his master's study, Quinney wrote his thesis entitled *Urbanization and the Scale of Society.*

On completion of his masters degree. Quinney began looking at doctoral programs. His interests at this point were in the area of rural sociology, based in part on his rural roots, and after examining the programs at a number of schools, he settled on the University of Wisconsin at Madison. Madison was "the most logical choice given the fact that it had a good rural sociology program and that this geographical region represented a familiar place to which he still had some attachment" (Trevino 1984, 9–10). He was awarded a research assistantship and began his studies at Madison in the fall of 1957.

One year after he began his doctoral studies, Quinney married Valerie Yow, and their marriage produced two daughters, Laura and Anne. Valerie Quinney has held various faculty positions in the departments of history.

The Department of Sociology, which began in 1893, has a long and distinguished history. During Quinney's doctoral studies, the department could count among the faculty the likes of Howard Becker, Hans Gerth, Marshall Clinard, and Thomas Scheff. Such notable individuals as Simon Dinitz graduated in 1951, and C. Wright Mills had been a student in the department of sociology from 1939 to 1941. Austin T. Turk, a fellow student, received his doctorate in 1962, the same year as Quinney.

Given the caliber and interests of the faculty in the sociology department at the time, it was not long until Quinney changed his focus from rural sociology to general social theory. He developed a student–mentor relationship with Howard Becker, and took every class Becker offered (Trevino 1984).

When it came time for Quinney to sit for his comprehensive exams, "for some unknown reason [he] decided to concentrate on the field of criminology" (Trevino 1984, 13) for one of his substantive areas. Quinney spent six months reading in the areas of criminology and law to prepare for this component of his comprehensive exams. Quinney chose religion for his dissertation topic, and Becker became his natural choice for dissertation director. When Quinney was completing the first chapter, Becker died of a brain hemorrhage. "Not only did Quinney lose a friend in Becker, but he also lost a dissertation, a mentor and support in the department" (Trevino 1984, 13). Not uncommon in a situation like this, it took Quinney some time to rebound from these losses.

In the fall of 1960, without completing his doctoral work, Quinney took his leave of Madison and journeyed to St. Lawrence University in Canton, New York, to accept a temporary teaching position. Quinney was to be a replacement for Donald Newman, who was returning to the University of Wisconsin at Madison to teach in the law school. While Quinney was at St. Lawrence University, he decided it was time to select a new dissertation topic and dissertation director. With an introduction to Marshall Clinard from Donald Newman, who was Clinard's former student, Quinney identified a new mentor and advisor. Because Clinard had been in India doing research, Quinney had never met or studied under him when taking classes at Madison. In addition to requesting Clinard to direct his dissertation, Quinney's subject matter was crime, and his dissertation, *Retail Pharmacy as a Marginal Occupation: A Study of Prescription Violation,* was completed in 1962, when he was awarded the Ph.D.

Once Quinney completed his dissertation, he moved to the University of Kentucky, accepting a position as assistant professor. While there, Quinney became actively involved in the Civil Rights movement. "He, along with other faculty and graduate students, marched on the capitol city of Frankfort. They also demonstrated outside the federal courthouse building in Lexington" (Trevino 1984, 18). During this time, Quinney made the conscious decision to discontinue using his first name. Quinney had always disliked the name Earl, and he changed it to Richard so that his name "sounded less like the sound of the country" (Quinney 1984, 165). During his tenure at Kentucky, Quinney's first publication, "Occupational Structure and Criminal Behavior: Prescription Violation by Retail Pharmacists," was published in *Social Problems* (1963).

In 1965, Quinney accepted a position as associate professor in the department of sociology at New York University. The move to Greenwich Village, near the university, brought about a number of changes in Quinney's thinking, concerns, and even his dress—he began wearing "love beads, tie-dyed T shirts, and long hair" (Trevino 1984, 21). Given the events of the day, the public sentiment about the Vietnam War, and the problems with higher education, "Quinney and two other professors . . . awarded all of their students A's in all of their classes" (Trevino 1984, 28). In 1970, Quinney was promoted to the rank of professor. During his five years at New York University, Quinney collaborated with Clinard on the first edition of *Criminal Behavior Systems: A Typology* (1967) and completed work on and published *The Problem of Crime* and *The Social Reality of Crime.*

In 1971, he took a sabbatical from New York University and moved his family to the University of North Carolina at Chapel Hill, where he remained until 1974, when he was able to devote his time to reading and writing because of publication royalties. He completed one edited book, *Criminal Justice in America: A Critical Understanding* (1974), and wrote a second, *Critique of Legal Order: Crime Control in Capitalist Society* (1974). During his three years at Chapel Hill, he also did much of the research and writing of *Criminology: Analysis and Critique of Crime in America* (1975), and began, wrote for, and distributed *Bread and Roses,* a socialist newspaper. This was also a very productive time for Quinney—from 1971 through 1974, fourteen articles were published. Included in this long list of articles were an interview in *Issues in Criminology*

(1971); "The Ideology of Law: Notes for a Radical Alternative to Legal Oppression," *Issues in Criminology* (1972); and "Who Is the Victim?" in *Criminology* (1972). (For a complete list of Quinney's publications, see the references at the end of the chapter.)

In 1974, Quinney and his family moved to Providence, Rhode Island. Valerie Quinney had accepted a position as an assistant professor of history at the University of Rhode Island, and Quinney had accepted a visiting professorship at Brooklyn College and the Graduate Center of the City University of New York. To meet his obligations, twice a week, Quinney went from Providence to New York City, a commute that lasted for one year, after which he accepted a position as a visiting professor at Brown University.

In 1983, Quinney sent his letter of interest to the department of sociology at Northern Illinois University in DeKalb, Illinois, which was advertising an assistant-level position. In response to Quinney's inquiry, he was offered a position as a visiting professor for a year, with the understanding that the position would convert to a regular full professor position after the first year. The move from Providence was made with some mixed emotion, because there was no immediate opportunity for Valerie to become a member of the history department faculty. Since joining Northern Illinois University, Quinney has been and continues to be a productive member of the faculty. Quinney has returned to his roots in the Midwest, and has again taken up residence in the region in which he spent his formative years. After traveling long and far, he has come full circle, back to his roots.

II. BASIC ASSUMPTIONS

Quinney was born in 1934 during the Great Depression, at a time when the Midwest of the United States was slow recovering from its economic difficulties. The people of Walworth County were made up of hardworking farmers laboring on small family farms that had been in their families for generations. The Protestant work ethic was a dominant influence, and the people "were rewarded ethically and to a lesser extent materially" (Trevino 1984, 1) for their efforts.

When Quinney was growing up, the political climate favored the emergence of the Populist Party, which was formed in 1891 primarily to represent agrarian interests; to advocate the free coinage of silver and government control of monopolies, such as railroads; and to place restrictions on the ownership of land. Populist ideas focused on the interests of the common people, and "guided the Quinneys and their neighbors to engage in a cooperative effort in harvesting each other's land as well as purchasing and sharing a threshing machine" (Trevino 1984, 1).

It is not clear exactly what impact World War II had on young Quinney or his family, who were fairly well insulated on the farmland of Wisconsin. Although Quinney was far too young to participate in the war, he was certainly old enough to understand its meaning. Quinney recalls the day the war ended, the family completing the daily chores in record time, dressing up and traveling to Elkhorn to celebrate. He "could not remember having a feeling of anticipating a new world or of feeling that the old one had ended. But he had sensed that something in the lives of his family and their world would never again be the same" (Quinney 1984, 176). Carroll College, the small liberal arts Presbyterian school he attended after high school, was in keeping with the types of values Quinney had been imbued with and, although not a local school, was not far from his home.

It is not clear exactly where Quinney began to change in terms of his perspective, but it is possible that when he went to work in a hospital in Chicago, where he had daily experience with a large metropolitan area and dealt with people from all walks of life, that the change from Elkhorn, Wisconsin, was extreme. Although the experience in Chicago did not cause Quinney to alter the basic assumptions by which he operated, it did cause him to change his field of focus from hospital administration to sociology. After his summer job, Quinney stayed in Chicago to attend Northwestern University where he pursued his master's degree.

Quinney took his values about the farm and farm life to college and then to graduate school. His dissertation, which had to do with prescription violation, was based on a functionalist perspective. Quinney used Sutherland's work on differential social organization as well Merton's work on strain theory as the basis for his dissertation, from which Quinney published his first article, entitled "Occupational Structure and Criminal Behavior: Prescription Violation by Retail Pharmacists" (1962), which suggests that "structural strain is built into retail pharmacy . . . . the pharmacist must therefore make some sort of personal adjustment to the situation" (1963, 181).

It appears that Quinney did not begin to shift his basic assumptions about people and society dramatically until he graduated from the University of Wisconsin at Madison in 1962 and took a position at the University of Kentucky. Even then, the shift did not occur overnight. Once Quinney completed his degree, he began work with his mentor, Marshall Clinard, on the first edition of *Criminal Behavior Systems: A Typology* (1967) when Quinney was focusing on crime. He and Clinard state: "We feel that continued progress in criminology will largely depend on the study of types of crime" (1967, v). The publication of his work with Clinard demonstrates that Quinney was still adhering to a perspective that was primarily functionalist. In the first edition of *Criminal Behavior Systems* (1967), the authors had not "considered how certain offenses relating to each type had become defined as crimes nor the differences in the legal processing of each" (vii). In the second edition, published in 1973, the authors had enhanced their examination of offenses to include how crimes had become so defined.

For Quinney, there are two perspectives used to understand society: dynamic and static (Quinney 1970). From the vantage of the static perspective, "forces and events, such as deviance and crime, which do not appear to be conducive to stability and consensus" (Quinney 1970, 8) are the pathologies of society. Quinney suggests that the second perspective, the dynamic viewpoint, is more appropriate for understanding society. In the dynamic perspective, there are four assumptions about people and society: (1) process, (2) conflict, (3) power, and (4) social action. The first aspect of the dynamic perspective, *process,* is social process, which is a "continuous series of actions, taking place in time, and leading to a special kind of result" (Quinney 1970, 8). In terms of the assumption about *conflict,* "conflicts between persons, social units, or cultural elements are inevitable" (Quinney 1970, 9). The third assumption relates to *power* and its differential distribution: "[D]ifferential distribution of power produces conflict between competing groups, and conflict in turn, is rooted in the competition for power" (Quinney 1970, 11). Those groups with power are able to influence the development and implementation of public policy and do what is necessary to maintain their superordinated position. The fourth element or assumption of the dynamic perspective has to do with *social action.* A person's "actions are purposive and meaningful . . . human behavior is intentional, has meaning for the actors, is goal-oriented, and takes place with an awareness of the consequences of behavior" (Quinney 1970, 13–14).

Quinney told an interviewer in 1971 for *Issues in Criminology*:

> I don't think we need a criminal law with punishment to make people good. I'm assuming, as opposed to the traditional theory, that man is basically good rather than being evil or maybe being good at one time and then having fallen. Basically, man is good and given his chance to build decent institutions so he can live his life with others, man does not need formal authority over him. (52)

Given this basic assumption about people, it is easy to understand why Quinney would look to the legal order to explain crime: the political institutions of society cause people to "fall."

In 1973, when guest lecturing at Florida State University, Quinney delivered a presentation replete with tape recorder and theme song from the Lone Ranger television show that challenged the values that society had convinced people to adopt. The presentation, later published in the journal *Insurgent Sociologist* (1973a), is entitled, "There Are a Lot of Folks Grateful to the Lone Ranger: With Some Notes on the Rise and Fall of American Criminology." The presentation and its subsequent publication pointed to Quinney's dissatisfaction with the *frontier mentality* promulgated in the 1940s and 1950s that painted America as "a land of unlimited possibilities for everyone. Belief in limitless abundance—without material substantiation . . . was an ideology that worked against those who believed in it" (1973a, 7). Quinney accuses the Lone Ranger of being part of a larger myth that dominated during those years and that still has numerous adherents in many quarters. As Quinney grew in his thinking, he concluded that "the really bad guys were those who make the laws" (1973a, 9) because they were only protecting their own interests. When Quinney, on his Silver King, and his brother Ralph rode across the Wisconsin fields, they thought of themselves as part of the frontier. Quinney accepted all that the frontier mentality stood for—until he began to question it.

> Quinney posits about himself that: only years of liberal education and academic sociology could dull this sensibility. But as I free myself from this training, I find the underside of America. Only when we allow ourselves to break out of the conventional wisdom are we able to develop a critical understanding of crime and the legal order. (1973a, 11)

It was this type of thinking and these basic assumptions about people and society that guided Quinney to a radical conflict perspective.

III. KEY IDEAS

A chapter on Richard Quinney in a book on criminological thought is important because of his impact on the development of theory. For the past forty years there is no other individual who has had as much influence in propelling the discipline forward. Although many may reject his work, they have been forced to make note of his criticisms and reconsider their positions and policies. For those who have embraced his thinking, it has helped them formulate policy to reflect a better system.

Quinney's key ideas are a result of an evolution in his thinking that developed over a fifty-year period. At different points in his career, Quinney stretched the thinking and thoughts of criminologists beyond the boundaries of the day. Beginning with his work *The Social Reality of Crime* (1970), Quinney was one of the criminologists causing the shift in focus from looking for the causes of crime in the individual to examining the justice system for clues.

In the preface to *The Social Reality of Crime,* Quinney states that his "purpose . . . is to provide a reorientation to the study of crime" (1970, v), because the orientation we have been operating with is not "relevant to our contemporary experiences" (1970, 3). Historically, it was through the efforts of Cesare Lombroso and the Positive School of Criminology (see the Cesare Lombroso chapter) that the focus on the criminal became prominent. Looking for causes of crime in individuals is something criminologists have done since Lombroso published *Criminal Man* in 1871.

Recently, there has been a switch from the study of the criminal to the study of crime. "In the last few years . . . those who study crime have realized that crime is relative to different legal systems, that an absolute conception of crime—outside of legal definitions—had to be replaced by a relativistic (that is legalistic) conception" (Quinney 1970, 4). The question now being posed is, how are definitions of criminals constructed, and more importantly, how are they applied? The basis for this reorientation is, in part, an examination of legal systems and laws and their difference from one jurisdiction to another. In one jurisdiction, an individual can be identified and prosecuted for a behavior that in another jurisdiction would be ignored.

Building on the four basic assumptions of a dynamic perspective—social process, inevitable conflict, differential power, and purposive social action—Quinney develops a theoretical orientation that leads to a social reality of crime.

> Proposition 1: Definition of Crime—Crime is a definition of human conduct that is created by authorized agents in a politically organized society.
>
> Proposition 2: Formulation of Criminal Definitions—Criminal Definitions describe behaviors that conflict with the interests of the segments of society that have the power to shape public policy.
>
> Proposition 3: Application of Criminal Definitions—Criminal definitions are applied by the segments of society that have the power to shape the enforcement and administration of criminal law.
>
> Proposition 4: Development of Behavior Patterns in Relation to Criminal Definitions—Behavior patterns are structured in segmentally organized society in relation to criminal definitions, and within this context persons engage in actions that have relative probabilities of being defined as criminal.
>
> Proposition 5: Construction of Criminal Conceptions—Conceptions of crime are constructed and diffused in the segments of society by various means of communication.
>
> Proposition 6: The Social Reality of Crime—The social reality of crime is constructed by the formulation and application of criminal definitions, the development of behavior patterns related to criminal definitions and the construction of criminal conceptions. (Quinney 1970, 15–23)

A brief discussion of each of these propositions is in order. Proposition 1 addresses the issue of how behaviors are defined as crimes, and is based, in part, on the belief that criminal behavior is not an inherent quality of people; instead, crime is created by "agents of law" (Quinney 1970, 16), which include those who formulate and promulgate laws, such as legislators or other elected officials, as well as those who enforce the laws, such as police, judges, and corrections personnel. A logical conclusion, therefore, is that the greater the number of behaviors defined as criminal, the greater the amount of crime in society and the greater the number of people defined as criminals. Those identified as criminal do so because a law was formulated and applied.

Proposition 2 is concerned specifically with which behaviors are defined as crimes. Interest groups that are able to influence the development of policy make decisions that either protect and maintain the status quo, or increase and ensure their position of control. For Quinney, the formulation of law is a clear demonstration of the conflict in society. "Criminal definitions exist . . . because some segments of society are in conflict with others" (Quinney 1970, 17). In *The Social Reality of Crime* (1970), Quinney describes the way the conflict between segments of society leads not only to the formulation of laws by the segments with more power, but also to specific procedures for handling those segments with less power. This system, the formulation of laws and the administration of them, is somewhat fluid. Over time, the interests of society change, as do those segments with power, and the system is designed to have flexibility so it can bend but not break. According to Quinney, "the probability that criminal definitions will be formulated is increased by such factors as (1) changing social conditions, (2) emerging interests, (3) increasing demands that political, economic, and religious interests be protected, and (4) changing conceptions of the public interest" (1970, 18). If the segments of society that have the power to create criminal definitions and procedure become aware that there is impending change, then they can often respond with new laws and procedures to maintain the balance of power.

Proposition 3 is concerned with the actual application of criminal definitions. A number of factors influence whether a criminal definition is applied, such as the extent to which the behaviors of those in the segments of society with less power conflict with the interests of those with power. The more the segments of society with power feel threatened by those without power, the more frequently criminal definitions are applied. Quinney points out that the sanctions are not applied directly by the people who are members of the powerful segments of society; instead, the authorized agents—such as police, judges, and others—respond (1970). Other factors include the expectations of the visibility of the behavior and the general expectations of the community. Quinney incorporates some of labeling theory in his explanation of this proposition when he addresses the reaction the authorized agents have to those they define as criminal. Quoting from Turk, Quinney states: "A person is evaluated, either favorably or unfavorably, not because he does something, or even because he is something, but because others react to their perceptions of him as offensive or inoffensive" (1970, 20).

Proposition 4 discusses the issue of the development of behavior patterns as they relate to criminal definitions. Each person, regardless of the interest group or segment of society he or she identifies with, "acts according to normative systems learned in relative social and cultural settings" (Quinney 1970, 20). If a person is a member of a segment of society that has the power or ability to influence the development of policy, that person's normative behavior patterns are more likely to be in agreement with those that are deemed acceptable (noncriminal). The antithesis of this is that, for those who are members of a segment of society that does not have power, the degree to which their normative behavior pattern differs from that of the powerful segment is positively correlated with the degree of conflict and the application of criminal definitions they experience. From an individual perspective, "the probability that a person will develop action patterns that have a high potential of being defined as criminal depends on the relative substance of (1) structured opportunities, (2) learning experiences, (3) interpersonal associations and identifications, and (4) self-conceptions" (Quinney 1970, 21), all or in part dictated by the segment of society one regularly participates in.

In terms of criminal conceptions, Proposition 5 relates to how one becomes acquainted with the conceptions that are promulgated. Our conceptions of crime and criminals are formed through processes of communication. The mass media assists in this process by disseminating the conceptions of crime and criminals to the public. Conceptions are important, because a person "behaves in reference to the social meaning he attaches to his experiences" (Quinney 1970, 22).

Proposition 6 is a composite of the five previous propositions and summarizes Quinney's orientation. As indicated earlier, this construction is based on conceiving of crime as something that is not inherent in people, and on shifting our perspective to one that examines social relationships of different interest groups in society and their relative power in influencing policy.

Quinney's thinking was greatly influenced by Roscoe Pound's work, which led in part to *The Social Reality of Crime* (1970). Pound helped focus Quinney's attention on the study of law as a social control mechanism. The law, including its development and application, is a reflection of the values of society and, at the same time, influences society. Quinney addresses this when he declares that law is both a "social product and social force" (1970, 32).

In *The Social Reality of Crime* (1970), Quinney provides an expanded explanation of the role of law as a social control system. The explanation is an elaboration of the propositions that constitute his theoretical perspective. Law, as it is used in contemporary society, is a politically based product of those interest groups in a position of power that can create laws and see that they are enforced. "Law is a result of the operation of interests rather than an instrument that functions outside of particular interests . . . . Law incorporates the interests of specific persons and groups; it is seldom the product of the whole society" (Quinney 1970, 35).

Quinney posits that even supposed attempts to improve public awareness of the crime problem are actually in the best interests of the segments of society that have control. Even the establishment of crime commissions serves the interests of the segments that control society. The people appointed to crime commissions are of the type who propose solutions that continue to lead society down the same path: they look for causes of crime in the individual, rather than in the law and the administration of justice. The "realities of crime [that] are shaped by . . . periodic investigations of crime" (Quinney 1970, 304) are often those promoted by these commissions. As an example, Quinney cites President Johnson's 1967 Commission, which has had major long-term affects on the shape of criminal justice, and the people appointed to the commission:

> All the commissioners . . . had a vested interest in the analysis of the crime
> problem. In typical Johnson consensus style, the commission's composition
> was a careful balance of recognized constituencies . . . [and] . . . although the

group covered a range of opinion about crime, the report was non-controversial and clearly written within the bounds of the established political and legal order. (1970, 309)

In an interview published in *Issues in Criminology* (Goldwyn 1971), Quinney begins to go beyond his statements in *The Social Reality of Crime* (1970). Quinney talks about an "elite theory rather than a pluralist theory" (Goldwyn 1971, 47). The interests of the segments of society that have control are materialistic interests and the power is "capitalist, corporate power" (Goldwyn 1971, 47). When *The Social Reality of Crime* (1970) was published, Quinney had already moved beyond it in the evolution of his thinking. The text was actually written a few years before it was published, so when it finally appeared in print, Quinney was no longer positing the phenomenological approach it represented. In fact, the year it was published, Quinney delivered a harsh critique of it at the annual American Sociological Association meeting. The interview as well as a few of Quinney's articles was an indication of what Quinney was going to suggest with his next book, *Critique of Legal Order: Crime Control in Capitalist Society* (1973b).

By 1973, Quinney realized that it is necessary to go beyond his concept of conflict in *The Social Reality of Crime*, in which Quinney posits a segment analysis, whereas in *Critique of Legal Order: Crime Control in Capitalist Society*, he suggests a class analysis that is grounded more in Marxist theory. "To accomplish an adequate understanding [of the American legal order] I found it necessary to develop a critical form of thought . . . a critical Marxian philosophy" (1973b, v). By using a critical Marxist approach, Quinney believes, one is better able to understand "how the capitalist ruling class establishes its control over those it must oppress" (1973b, vi).

As in *The Social Reality of Crime*, Quinney states that it is necessary that we shed the constraints of the consciousness that presently bind society in order to search for a new consciousness that allows us to seek answers to the appropriate questions. Quinney believes that if we are capable of developing a new consciousness, it will most likely resemble a "Marxian theory of crime control in capitalist society" (1973b, 2). Quinney describes four types of modes or philosophies that characterize the approaches we can take to understanding the legal order: (1) positivistic, (2) social constructionist, (3) phenomenological, and (4) critical. A comprehensive review of Quinney's work indicates that when he wrote *Critique of the Legal Order: Crime Control in Capitalist Society* (1973b), he had passed through the first three phases and was in the midst of the fourth.

The positivistic philosophy permeates Quinney's earliest thinking before he entered his doctoral program. An adherent to the tenets of this philosophy is most interested in an "explanation of events" (1973b, 3). Positivists see themselves as "value-free," engaging in research without a moral commitment. Under the premise of the positivists, there is a blanket acceptance of the status quo.

The social constructionists assume that there is no objective reality. "Objects cannot exist independently of our minds, or at least . . . any such existence is important only as long as it can be perceived" (1973b, 5). The social constructionists, unlike the positivists, focus on the problematic nature of the legal order. "Crime and other forms of stigmatized behavior [are viewed] first as categories created and imposed upon some person by others" (1973b, 7). Crime is a construction, and the legal order is therefore a construction designed to maintain the authority of the ruling class.

The phenomenological philosophy is predicated on an orientation that "begins by examining the process by which we understand the world" (Quinney 1973b, 8). Not only do we know based on our personal experiences, but we can also discuss possible experiences. Included is a study of the development of human consciousness and self-awareness. *The Social Reality of Crime* is a demonstration of Quinney's movement through this philosophy, a questioning of the existing consciousness that has, according to Quinney, led us to a dead end.

A critical philosophy is examined and promoted in *Critique of Legal Order: Crime Control in a Capitalist Society* (1973b). The intention of this philosophy is to prevent the influence of any presuppositions. "The operation is one of demystification, the removal of the myths—the false consciousness—created by the official reality" (1973b, 11). We can only break with the status quo through a critical philosophy that examines the legal order. When using a critical philosophy, it is important to Quinney that students of society go beyond "merely looking for an objective reality," and that they become "concerned with the negation of the established order" (1973b, 13). Quinney asserts that it is difficult, if not impossible, for academic scholarship to find solutions to the problems of the legal order because it is caught up in the "conventional wisdom" and all its presuppositions.

Quinney addressed the work of Karl Marx and his relationship to criminal justice when he states, "Marx steered away from justice-talk because he regarded it as 'ideological twaddle,' detracting from a critical analysis of the capitalist system as a whole" (Quinney 1977, 26). Because Marx had very little to say specifically about crime control and criminal law, Quinney takes it on himself to adapt Marx's general ideas and to "develop a critical Marxian analysis of crime control in capitalist society" (1973b, 15). The following review of Quinney's explanation in *Critique of Legal Order: Crime Control in a Capitalist Society* describes how class analysis can be applied to an understanding of criminal law and crime control.

The study of the legal order, Quinney says, must no longer perpetuate the legitimization of the existing social order. We must look for the causes of crime in sources other than the individual. Theories of crime, instead of being theories of types of criminal behavior, must be assessed to develop theories of the legal order. Legal order theories address how the legal order participates in causing crime. The theory that is the foundation of most of our legal order comes from a positivistic philosophy and is designed to contribute to the maintenance of the social order. A new social order is needed to correct the imbalances and redistribute the power. Instead of attempting to resocialize the individual criminal, we must revamp the legal order.

Instead of asking questions about why an individual committed a crime, the question that must be asked is, how does one become labeled a criminal? As the legal order exists today, criminologists "have become the ancillary agents of power. They provide the kinds of information that governing elites use to manipulate and control those who threaten the system" (Quinney 1973b, 27). If criminologists do not question their basic assumptions, they then intentionally or unintentionally serve the interests of the state. The current system contains elements that "encourage the members' conformity to their role requirements" (Quinney 1973b, 47). Role requirements are defined by the ruling class through the development and implementation of laws. The justice system is the administrative arm of the legal order that enforces the laws, using—if necessary—physical force and violence. Quinney points out that it is imperative for the ruling class to operate this way given the positivistic philosophy. He cites statistics that indicate that "one percent of the population owns forty percent of the nation's wealth," which "still comes as a surprise to many citizens—an indication that the liberal perspective dominates" (1973b, 52). Control of the wealth means control of the means of production, tantamount to control of economic power, which dominates society. Therefore, there are, based on economic power, a ruling class and the subordinate class(es). The ruling class consists mainly of "the corporations and financial institutions of monopoly capitalism" (Quinney 1973b, 53).

According to the radical perspective, the division between the ruling class and the subordinate class(es) must be eliminated, because the division "establishes the nature of political, economic, and social life in capitalist society" (Quinney 1973b, 53).

Quinney presents numerous examples of the way academic criminologists are being used to further the status quo and perpetuate the division between the ruling class and the subordinate class(es). The types of grants funded by federal granting agencies contribute to the collection of information used to maintain the position of the ruling class. The types of research proposals funded are usually in keeping with behavior control technology. Quinney could not have foreseen two examples of this type of funded academic research: the house-arrest programs that incorporate electronic bracelets, and AIDS research, including HIV testing, as it relates to prisoners. In each of these cases, the ruling class uses the skills and legitimacy of the academic to serve its own end—the control of the dangerous classes. The house-arrest programs that use electronic bracelets are designed to keep the individual wearing the device under the control of the state. Usually, the individual is under a form of house arrest and is not supposed to leave a specified geographic area. The state expands its control over those of the subordinate class because with these electronic bracelets, it is able to maintain an awareness of where individuals are and what they are doing without having one of their representatives on the scene. Because this form of control is seen as less restrictive and less punishment oriented, it is marketable to the public. In addition, the reduced cost of this type of incarceration is appealing to the general public. The result is that the ruling class is able to place under direct control a much larger segment of the population without the great expense of building facilities and increasing the number of personnel required to watch over those incarcerated.

The AIDS research and HIV testing of prisoners is based in part on a perception of the American public's fear about the disease. Many people, because of their fear of contracting the disease, are calling for actions that would dramatically alter the rights of individuals, thereby providing the ruling class with increased control over the members of the subordinate class(es). It is in the best interests of the ruling to class to incite the general public to a greater fear of AIDS, even though medical experts agree the methods of transmission are limited, and actual chances of contracting the disease not as great as generally believed. The greater the level of fear the general public experiences, the more likely they are to acquiesce to methods and techniques that control the dangerous classes and strengthen the hold the ruling class has.

As society's complexity increased, the locus of crime control became more centralized. A pattern of centralization has been developing since the end of the nineteenth century, Quinney says, that can be observed in retrospect. The number of offenses that have become violations of federal laws has increased, as has the number of federal institutions that house those convicted. A recent example of this pattern centralization is the sentencing guidelines promulgated by a number of states and the federal government. The guidelines appear to address the issues of equity and fairness as they relate to sentencing, but Quinney, using a class analysis, suggests that this is another carrot designed to lead to the wrong questions. The U.S. Sentencing Commission occupies our attention with designing sentencing guidelines and diverts us from the real questions that must be asked about what behaviors are crimes and why. The U.S. Sentencing Guidelines also cause focus on a specific set of crimes that in reality are far less problematic than some of the crimes being committed daily by major corporations and the government. Crimes involving toxic waste, polluted water, the sale of adulterated food, and so on are far more serious in terms of the numbers of people affected and the cost to the American public than are such crimes as murder and robbery. We do not focus on these issues as much as we should because our attention is diverted. Because the media are controlled by the ruling class, it is a tool used for propaganda purposes to influence the thinking of the subordinate class(es). Under Quinney's critical perspective, the laws must represent the will of the people, not some ruling class. Quinney continued to expand this kind of analysis as he progressed in his intellectual development, and became more committed to a Marxist perspective.

In 1977, Quinney wrote *Class, State, and Crime,* in which he uses a structural Marxist approach to explain the legal order. A detailed explanation of the relationship between crime and capitalism is contained in chapter 2. In general, the thesis is that there is a structural class analysis when law and criminality are seen as required elements of a capitalist society. Because we operate in a capitalist society, capitalist justice is required. For Quinney, the capitalist order is at the end of its expansion and development, and is in the midst of a crisis that it is not likely to recover from. Marx rejects capitalism and calls for revolutionary action "based on the innate character of capitalism, on an understanding of capitalism as a whole and on its position in human history" (1977, 27). A transition from capitalism to socialism must take place. It is through a shift to socialism that society will be able to correct the justice system. "Only by going beyond capitalism to socialism, could the contradictions that produce the crime problem be confronted. Crime will continue to be 'inevitable' as long as a capitalist society exists" (Quinney 1977, 126).

Quinney summarizes his thoughts on the need to shift to a socialist society by stating:

> As we understand the nature of criminal justice under capitalism, and as we engage in socialist struggle, we build a society that ceases to generate the crime found in capitalist society. Criminal justice ceases to be the solution to crime. Socialist solutions are to be found in the nature of the society itself—a society that neither supports nor depends on a political economy of criminal justice. (1977, 144)

In 1984, at the American Society of Criminology in Cincinnati, Ohio, Quinney was presented with the Edwin H. Sutherland Award. As is customary, Quinney had an acceptance speech prepared that provided listeners with some insight as to what direction he was taking in his work (a published version of the speech appears in *The Legal Studies Forum,* Vol. IX, No. 3, 1985). The speech incorporated a tape recording of some contemporary music, including the strains of Willie Nelson's "On the Road Again." After the speech and a discussion among a number of people in the audience, the conclusion generally agreed on was that Quinney was saying goodbye to criminology. His interests appeared to have shifted to other areas, and he believed that until society was ready to alter the existing capitalist system, he needed to focus his energy elsewhere. The new focus was to be on the prophetic, including the incorporation of a religious orientation.

Beginning with Quinney's 1979 article "The Production of Criminology," one can pick up the threads of the transcendental or prophetic approach that Quinney was moving to. In the article, he compares the cultural production of criminology to the production of philosophy, religion, and art, and concludes that they are similar because they are all the production of human labor (1979). Criminology and art are human labors with a different approach from the traditional scientific–positivistic approach to understanding. Art, including criminology,

> as a way of seeing, feeling, and perceiving is prophetic in its form and content. Not only does it penetrate beneath the surfaces of social reality to the underlying structures, but it aspires to go beyond that reality in actual life. Art suggests how the world could be. It is a form of knowledge that has as its objective a transcendence of the everyday life of the existing order. (1979, 453)

In 1980, Quinney wrote *Providence: The Reconstruction of Social and Moral Order*, which includes chapters with titles such as "A Religious Socialist Order" and "The Religious Response to Capitalism." Quinney's thinking evolved to a point where he focuses on the prophetic imagination that "reflects the presence of the divine in history. Things of this world have their meaning not so much in themselves as in the spiritual, in the world of God revealed in the world" (1980, 113). Quinney closes *Providence* by stating, "Our historical struggle is thus for the creation of a social and moral order that prepares us for the ultimate of divine grace—the kingdom of God fulfilled. Peace and justice through the kingdom of God" (1980, 114).

Since the publication of *Providence* (1980), Quinney has continued to delve into the prophetic expanding his reading to include literature on Eastern religions. One of Quinney's most recent publications, *Crime, Suffering, Service: Toward a Criminology of Peacemaking* (1988), reflects his present approach to the problem of crime. It represents a very similar strain of thought to that which Quinney presented in a paper at the 1988 meeting of the American Society of Criminology in Chicago. Quinney sees crime as suffering, and the problem of crime can be resolved "only with the ending of suffering" (1988, 66). There must be a transformation of people that includes a movement to peace and justice. "Crime can be ended only with the ending of suffering (only when there is peace)—through the love and compassion found in awareness" (1988, 67). All this begins in the human mind, which must be unattached and compassionate. Working on creating a good society without simultaneously working to make ourselves better will not lead us to the solution to crime. "Without inner peace in each of us, without peace of mind and heart, there can be no social peace between people and no peace in societies, nations, and in the world" (1988, 73). With peace we can end suffering, and with the ending of suffering will come the end of crime. The need for peace is essential, because our present system of justice is "founded on violence. It is a system that assumes that violence can be overcome by violence, evil by evil" (1988, 74). Nonviolent criminology is a prerequisite to peace. We can achieve a nonviolent criminology "when our hearts are filled with love and our minds with willingness to serve"; we will then "know what has to be done and how it is to be done" (1988, 75).

As Quinney writes: "To eliminate crime—to end the construction and perpetuation of an existence that makes crime possible—requires a transformation of our human being. We as human beings must be at peace if we are to live in a world free of crime, in a world of peace" (Quinney 1988, 74).

IV. CRITIQUE

There are those who, because their basic assumptions are grounded in the positive philosophy, are unable to consider Quinney's approach work viable. The very basic domain assumptions of the positivists cause them to reject Quinney's work in the area of critical theory. To accept Quinney's work with its contradiction of the positivist philosophy necessitates the rejection of their own fundamental assumptions. In addition, there are theorists who line up to the left of Quinney in terms of their political stance, and they are of the opinion that Quinney has not gone far enough in his rejection of the positivist philosophy. Because most of the journals published in the discipline can be characterized as subscribing to a positivist mode of thought, people who subscribe to the positivist philosophy are more likely to write reviews and publish articles in these journals. It is thus no wonder that most of the reviews find some degree of difficulty with Quinney's work. This section examines a number of the general as well as a few of the specific criticisms leveled at Quinney's work. There have been some general comments made by a variety of reviewers that apply to *Critique of Legal Order: Crime Control in a Capitalist Society* (1973b), *Criminal Justice in America: A Critical Understanding* (1974), *Criminology: An Analysis and Critique of Crime* (1975), and *Class, State, and Crime* (1977). Critics maintain that Quinney does an elaborate job of pointing out the flaws in the existing capitalist structure and his calls for a socialist system, but fails to delineate exactly how the new system should look and operate (Friday 1976, Greenberg 1979, Regoli 1976, Schiller 1975).

A second criticism is that he fails to provide empirical evidence to substantiate his claims about the existing capitalist system. In a review of *Class, State, and Crime*, Greenberg (1979) argues that because of Quinney's failure to provide empirical support for his thesis, the text has at times "the quality of a religious tract rather than a work of scientific analysis" (111). In a review of *Critique of Legal Order: Crime Control in a Capitalist Society,* T.D. Schuby (1976) makes a number of comments about Quinney's failure to "present empirically verified data to support his contention" (493) about the role the capitalist system plays in operationalizing criminal behavior. Schuby identifies a number of historical examples that Quinney might have used as evidence to support his contentions, such as "the civil rights movement, the CIA counterinsurgent global operation, [and] the Vietnam War" (1976, 493). Quinney published *Critique of Legal Order* in 1974, and there are now additional examples of evidence, such as the Iran–Contra Affair, that could be used if Quinney were to publish a second edition of this work.

Most of the reviewers agree that Quinney takes far too narrow a view of the capitalist system and fails to credit it with any redeeming value. In one review of Quinney's work, Hills states: "Quinney's sledge-hammer assault on liberal and conservative orthodoxy leaves this reviewer with an impression that the author's analysis at times is more caricature than reality" (1976, 84). Reviewing *Class, State, and Crime* (1977),

Greenberg questions what Quinney has actually accomplished, and is of the opinion that Quinney's view of the state as serving only the interests of the ruling class is far too selective: "There is little recognition of the consequences capitalist states have had to make to subordinate classes; thus, there is no consideration of the possibility that some forms of state-organized crime control could correspond to a general rather than a class interest" (Greenberg 1979, 110). In addition, Greenberg believes that Quinney is naive to suggest that if society were to operate under a socialist system instead of a capitalist system, crime would disappear.

Other reviewers have raised questions about why Quinney does not examine existing socialist systems and explain why crime has not disappeared. Countries such as Cuba and the former Soviet Union are identified as operating under a socialist system, and all the evidence available indicates that they experience a substantial amount of crime. Greenberg states:

> It is evident that Quinney neglects crime and repression in societies he considers (on what basis is unclear) as socialist. This omission permits him to avoid the embarrassing questions they pose for someone who urges socialist revolution as an instant cure for both crime and repression. Thus the author who advocates a critical approach to crime and legal order appears as insufficiently critical of his own received orthodoxy. (1979, 112–13)

In a review of *Providence,* T.P. Schwartz finds much that he likes about Quinney's position, but finds the overall text not much more helpful than "the street corner Jeremiahs [who] tell us to repent" (Schwartz 1981, 1336). Schwartz views *Providence* as inspirational prophecy, and states:

> Only for some of us, sometimes, is it comforting and useful to relax all discriminations among hope, prophecy, prediction, perception, and objective reality. Is it prophecy, prescience, or simple wishful thinking to toll the bell on capitalism, civil religion, secularism, and atheism? Think about *The Wall Street Journal,* an election between Carter and Reagan, and ABC's telecast of an Oklahoma–Texas football game, and parts of *Providence* sound like whistling in the dark. (1336)

Addressing the same publication, John F. Wilson (1981) is disappointed that *Providence* does not properly equip society to grapple with the condition of contemporary American culture, no matter how problematic we believe it is. Wilson concludes his review by indicating that he is not surprised that Quinney does not provide answers, because the "thesis of the book is that we are utterly dependent upon providence."

Whether one agrees or disagrees with the approaches Quinney has taken during the course of his career, he has caused a considerable amount of serious discussion to take place. He moved the discipline forward in its thinking when he first wrote *The Social Reality of Crime,* and at the very least caused many to question their own perceptions of the justice system. Now, as Quinney moves forward in attempting to "spiritualize" Marxism, he has again raised important questions for the discipline. Quinney's criminological thought has been, and continues to be, important to the development of theory, and should be read by all those who consider themselves students of the discipline.

NOTES

1. Javier Trevino interviewed Richard Quinney extensively in completing his dissertation. Trevino presented his biographical material on Quinney to his colleagues at the 36th Annual Meeting of the American Society of Criminology held in Cincinnati, Ohio. It was at this same meeting that Quinney was honored by the society with the Edwin H. Sutherland Award for his contributions.

References

Clinard, Marshall B., & Richard Quinney. 1967. *Criminal behavior systems: A typology.* New York: Holt, Rinehart and Winston.

Friday, Paul C. 1976. Book review of Quinney's criminology: An analysis and critique of crime in America. *J. Crim. Law Criminol.* 67(2): 249–250.

Goldwyn, Eileen. 1971. Dialogue with Richard Quinney. *Iss. Criminol.* 6(2): 41– 54.

Greenberg, David. 1979. Book review of Quinney's *Class, state, and crime. Crime Delin.* 25(1): 110–13.

Hills, Stuart L. 1976. Book review of Quinney's *Criminology: Analysis and critique of crime in America. Crime Delin.* 23(1): 83–86.

Quinney, Richard. 1963. Occupational structure and criminal behaviors: Prescription violation by retail pharmacists. *Soc. Prob.* 11(Fall): 179–85.

———. 1964. Crime in political perspective. *Am. Behav. Sci.* 8(December): 19–22.

———. 1965a. Is criminal behaviour deviant behaviour? *Br. J. Criminol.* 5(April): 132–42.

———. 1965b. A conception of man in society for criminology. *Sociolog. Quart.* Spring: 119–27.

———. 1966a. A reformulation of Sutherland's differential association theory and a strategy for empirical verification. *J. Res. Crime Delinq.* 3(1): 1–22.

———. 1966b. Structural characteristics, population areas, and crime rates in the United States. *J. Crim. Law Criminol. Pol. Sci.* 57(1): 45–52.

———. 1970. *The social reality of crime.* Boston: Little Brown and Company.

———. 1973a. There are a lot of folks grateful to the Lone Ranger: With some notes on the rise and fall of American criminology. *Insurg. Sociol.* IV(1): 56–72.

———. 1973b. *Critique of the legal order: Crime control in capitalist society.* Boston: Little, Brown and Company.

———. 1977. *Class, state, and crime.* New York: David McKay Company, Inc.

———. 1979. The production of criminology. *Criminology* 16(4): 445–57.

———. 1984a. Journal to a far place: The way of autobiographical reflection. *Hum. Soc.* 8 (May).

———. 1984b. A place called home. *Wisc. Mag. Hist.* 67(3): 163–84.

———. 1985. Myth and the art of criminology. *Leg. Stud. For.* IX(3): 291–99.

———. 1988. Crime, suffering, service: Toward a criminology of peacemaking. *Quest* Winter: 66–75.

Regoli, Robert M. 1976. Book review of Quinney's *Critique of legal order: Crime control in capitalist society. J. Crim. Law Criminol.* 67(1): 125–26.

Schiller, Stephen A. 1975. Book review of Quinney's *Criminal justice in America: A critical understanding. J. Crim. Just.* 3(4): 337–38.

Schuby, T.D. 1976. Book review of Quinney's *Critique of legal order: Crime control in capitalist society. Crime Delinq.* 22(4): 492–93.

Schwartz, T.P. 1981. A review of Quinney's *Providence: The reconstruction of social and moral order.* Soc. Forc. 59(4): 1335–36.

Trevino, Javier. 1981. *Richard Quinney: A biography.* Unpublished manuscript, presented at the 36th Annual Meeting of the American Society of Criminology, Cincinnati, Ohio.

Wilson, John F. 1981. Review of *Providence: The reconstruction of social and moral order. Sociolog. Anal. J. Sociol. Rel.* 42(1).

Supplemental Readings

Bohm, Robert M. 1985. The dialectical potential of religion as a solution to the crime problem: A review of Quinney's providence and Shoham's salvation. *Human. Soc.* 9(2): 197–202.

————. 1983. *Contemporary Authors*. Vol. 9. Detroit: Gale Research Company.

Evory, Ann, & Linda Metzger (Eds.). 1973. *Criminal behavior systems: A typology.* 2nd ed. New York: Holt, Rinehart and Winston.

Friedrichs, David O. 1980. Radical criminology in the United States: An interpretive understanding. In James A. Inciardi (Ed.), *Radical criminology: The coming crises.* Beverly Hills: Sage Publications, pp. 35–60.

Jones, David A. 1986. *History of criminology: A philosophical perspective.* New York: Greenwood Press.

Milovanovic, Dragan. 1982. Contemporary directions in critical criminology. *Hum. Soc.* 6(Aug.).

Pepinsky, Harold E. 1985. An overview of Richard Quinney on law and crime. *Leg. Stud. For.* IX(3): 301–05.

Peskin, Stephen H. 1978. Book review of Quinney's *Class, state, and crime. Trial* 14(1): 60–61.

Stivers, Richard. 1981. Book review of Quinney's *Providence: The reconstruction of social and moral order. Qualit. Sociol.* 5(1): 64–65.

Stout, Kate. 1988. *Richard Quinney and the challenge of a radical pedagogy.* Unpublished manuscript, presented at the 36th Annual Meeting of the American Society of Criminology, Cincinnati, Ohio.

Richard Quinney: Bibliography

Books

Quinney, R. 1970. *The problem of crime.* New York: Dodd, Mead and Company.

————. 1970. *The social reality of crime.* Boston: Little, Brown and Company.

————. 1971. *Critique of legal order: Crime control in capitalist society.* Boston: Little, Brown and Company.

————. 1973. *Class, state, and crime: On the theory and practice of criminal justice.* New York: David McKay Company, Inc.

————. 1973. *Criminology: Analysis and critique of crime in America.* 2nd ed. Boston: Little, Brown and Company.

————. 1974. *Criminal justice in America: A critical understanding.* Boston: Little, Brown and Company.

————. 1975. *Criminology: Analysis and critique of crime in America.* Boston: Little Brown and Company.

————. 1979. *Capitalist society: Readings for a critical sociology.* Homewood, IL: The Dorsey Press.

————. 1980. *Class, state, and crime.* 2nd ed. New York: Longman Inc.

————. 1980. *Providence: The reconstruction of social and moral order.* New York: Longman Inc.

————. 1981. *Class, state, and crime.* 2nd ed. New York: Longman Inc.

————. 1982. *Social existence: Metaphysics, Marxism and the social sciences.* Beverly Hills: Sage Publications.

————. 1988. *The way of peace: On crime, suffering, and service.* Unpublished manuscript.

————. 1990. *Autobiography of an American sociologist: Journey to a far place.* Lewiston, NY: Edwin Mellen Press.

Quinney, Richard, & Piers Beirne. 1982. *Marxism and law.* San Francisco, California. John Wiley & Sons.

Quinney, Richard, & Marshall Clinard. 1967. *Criminal behavior systems: A typology.* New York: Holt, Rinehart And Winston.

————. 1973. *Criminal behavior systems: A typology.* 2nd ed. New York: Holt, Rinehart and Winston.

Quinney, Richard, & John Wildeman. 1977. *The problem of crime: A critical introduction to criminology.* 2nd ed. New York: Harper and Row.

Other Works

Quinney, Richard. 1963. Occupational structure and criminal behavior: Prescription violation by retail pharmacists. *Soc. Prob.* 11: 179–85.

———. 1963. Adjustments to occupational role strains: The case of retail pharmacy. *Southwest. Soc. Sci. Quart.* 44 (March): 367–76.

———. 1963. A conception of man and society for criminology. *Sociol. Quart.* 6 (Spring): 119–27.

———. 1963. Structural characteristics, population areas, and crime rates in the United States. *J. Crim. Law Criminol. Pol. Sci.* 57 (March): 45–52.

———. 1964. The study of white-collar crime: Toward a reorientation in theory and research. *J. Crim. Law Criminol. Pol. Sci.* 55 (June): 208–14.

———. 1964. Crime, delinquency and social areas. *J. Res. Crime Delinq.* 1 (July): 149–154.

———. 1964. Political conservatism, alienation, fatalism: Contingencies of social status and religious fundamentalism. *Sociometry* 27 (September): 372–81.

———. 1964. Crime in political perspective. *Am. Behav. Sci.* 8 (December): 19–22.

———. 1964. Mortality differentials in a metropolitan area. *Soc. Forc.* 43 (December): 222–30.

———. 1965. Suicide, homicide, and economic development. *Soc. Forc.* 43 (March): 401–06.

———. 1965. Professionalism and legal compliance. *J. Am. Pharm. Assoc.* NS5 (April): 190–92.

———. 1965. Is criminal behavior deviant behavior? *Br. J. Criminol.* 5 (April): 132–42.

———. 1970. Toward a sociology of criminal law. In Richard Quinney (Ed.), *Crime and justice in society.* Boston: Little Brown and Company, pp. 1–30.

———. 1971. The social reality of crime. In Jack D. Douglas (Ed.), *Crime and justice in American society.* Indianapolis: Bobbs-Merrill and Company, pp. 119–46.

———. 1971. Crime: Phenomenon, problem and subject of study. In Erwin O. Smigel (Ed.), *Handbook on the study of social problems.* Chicago: Rand-McNally, pp. 209–46.

———. 1971. Dialogue with Richard Quinney. *Iss. Criminol.* 6 (Spring): 41–54.

———. 1971. National commission on the causes and prevention of violence reports. *Am. Sociolog. Rev.* 36 (August): 724–27.

———. 1971. The ideology of law: Notes for a radical alternative to legal oppression. *Iss. Criminol.* 7 (Winter): 1–35.

———. 1971. From repression to liberation: Social theory in a radical age. In Robert A. Scott & Jack D. Douglas (Eds.), *Theoretical perspectives on deviance.* New York: Basic Books, pp. 317–41.

———. 1971. A transcendental way of knowing. In Nicholas M. Regush (Ed.), *Visibles and invisibles: A primer for a new sociological imagination.* Boston: Little, Brown, and Company, pp. 168–77.

———. 1971. Commentary. Response to Michael J. Lowy's *Modernizing the American legal system: An example of the peaceful use of anthropology. Hum. Organiz.* 32 (Summer): 213–14.

———. 1971. The social reality of crime. In Abraham S. Blumberg (Ed.), *Current perspectives on criminal behavior: Original essays in criminology.* New York: Alfred A. Knopf, pp. 35–47.

———. 1972. Who is the victim? *Criminology* 10 (November): 314–323.

———. 1973. There's a lot of folks grateful to the Lone Ranger: With some notes on the rise and fall of American criminology. *Insurg. Sociol.* 4 (Fall): 56–64.

———. 1973. Recent work in criminology. *Contemp. Sociol.* 5 (July): 414–16.

———. 1973. The production of criminology. *Criminology* 16 (February): 445–57.

———. 1975. Crime control in capitalist society: A critical philosophy of legal order. In Ian Taylor, Paul Walton, & Jock Young (Eds.), *Critical criminology.* London, England: Routledge and Kegan Paul, pp. 181–202.

———. 1978. The production of a Marxist criminology. *Contemp. Cris.* 2 (July): 277–92.

———. 1979. The theology of culture: Marx, Tillich and the prophetic tradition in the reconstruction of social and moral order.

Union Semin. Quart. Rev. 34 (Summer): 203–14.

————. 1980. Critical reflection on the meaning of social existence. In Scott G. McNall & Gary N. Howe (Eds.), *Current perspectives in social theory: A research annual.* Vol. 11. Greenwich, CT: Jai Press, pp. 117–32.

————. 1981. For a regional sociology. *Wisc. Sociol.* 19 (Spring–Summer): 35–37.

————. 1981. Leaving the country: A Midwest education in sociology in the 1950's. *Wisc. Sociol.* 19 (Spring– Summer): 54–66.

————. 1981. Nature of the world: Holisitic vision for humanist sociology. *Hum. Soc.* 6 (November): 322–339.

————. 1981. Myth and the art of criminology. *Leg. Stud. For.* 9(3): 291–99.

————. 1981. Voices from the east: Beyond the conventional wisdom of deviance and social control. *Quart. J. Ideol.* 10(1): 3–7.

————. 1981. The way of peace: On crime, suffering, and service. *Quest* (Winter): 66–75.

————. 1984. Journey to a far place: The way of autobiographical reflection. *Hum. Soc.* 8 (May): 182–98.

————. 1984. A place called home. *Wisc. Mag. Hist.* 67 (Spring): 163–84.

————. 1986. A traveler of country roads: Photographing a Midwest landscape. *Landscape* 29(1): 21–28.

————. 1988. A dark voyage. *Am. Theos.* 76 (January): 3–10.

————. 1988. Beyond the interpretive: The way of awareness. *Sociolog. Inq.* 58 (Winter): 101–16.

————. 1988. A winter's tale. *North. Ill. Univ. Fac. Bull.* 51(5): 3–8.

Quinney, Richard, & Ronald L. Akers. 1966. Differential organization of health professions: A comparative analysis. *Am. Sociolog. Rev.* 33 (February): 104–21.

Quinney, Richard, & Melvin DeFleur. 1966. A reformulation of Sutherland's differential association theory and a strategy for empirical verification. *J. Res. Crime Delinq.* 3 (January): 1–22.

Quinney, Richard, & Kate Dunnigan. 1978. Work and community in Saylesville. *Rad. Hist. Rev.* 17 (Spring): 173–180.

Quinney, Richard, & Clayton A. Hartjen. 1972. Social reality of the drug problem: The case of New York's lower east side. *Hum. Organ.* 30 (Winter): 381–91.

CHAPTER 16
TRAVIS HIRSCHI: B. 1935

I. BIOGRAPHICAL SKETCH

There can be no question that Travis Hirschi belongs in a work devoted to the pioneers of criminological thought. All one need do is pick up any book on juvenile delinquency or criminological theory and look in the index. Hirschi's works are made reference to as much as if not more than for any theorist. Empirical support for this observation has been established in several reviews of top contributors to the discipline (Wright, Bryant, and Miller 2001, Cohn and Farrington 1998, Cohn, Farrington, and Wright 1998). Hirschi's control theories, first in the form of social bond and more recently as low self-control, "developed into one of the most dominant etiological perspectives in criminology" (Gibbons 1994, 26). "Social control theory, specifically Travis Hirschi's version, has been the most popular of all criminological theories for the past thirty years" (Williams and McShane 2004, 275). "Hirschi's theory has become what most criminologists today refer to as control theory. It has come to occupy a central place in criminological theory" (Akers and Sellers 2004, 116). Although Hirschi is most credited for his development of control theory, it also must be recognized that he has made substantial contributions in the areas of IQ and other correlates of delinquency and methodology as well.

Despite Hirschi's renown as a criminologist and the copious coverage afforded his theories, very little has been written about Travis Hirschi the person. In his introduction to *The Craft of Criminology,* John Laub (2002) notes: "Travis Hirschi is one of the most cited criminologists of the twentieth century, yet it is remarkable how little is known about his life and career" (p. xi). This dearth of more personal information is most likely attributable, according to Laub (2002), to the fact that Dr. Hirschi "rejects the idea that personal background matters much in understanding a person's views on crime or anything else for that matter" (p. xi). In supporting this position, Hirschi noted that he adheres to the view of A.E. Housman, stating that "[M]y . . . philosophy is founded on my observation of the world, not on anything so trivial and irrelevant as personal history" (quoted in Laub 2002, xii). In a more recent communication, Dr. Hirschi was asked, given the emphasis placed on learning and childhood experiences in his theories, if he would reconsider this position. He clearly indicated that his view had not changed, politely saying, "I think we've agreed to remain rather far apart on the relevance of my personal history to an understanding of my theories" (T. Hirschi, personal communication, February 7, 2005). With all due respect to Dr. Hirschi's position, however, we now look, as best we can, at the background of this pioneer of criminological thought.

Most of the biographical material that follows has been drawn from Laub's (2002) introduction in *The Craft of Criminology,* which is the only substantial discussion published on Hirschi's life.

Travis Hirschi was the fifth of eight children born to Warren G. and Orra (Terry) Hirschi in Rockville, Utah, in 1935. Warren worked on survey crews as a transit man in Utah and Idaho. Neither of Hirschi's parents were college educated, both having gone through the eighth grade. Hirschi, however, is said to have "assumed from the beginning that he would go to college" (Laub 2002, xii).

As an undergraduate, Hirschi attended the University of Utah, majoring in sociology and history, and he is quoted as noting that "I knew from the beginning I was interested in deviance" (Laub 2002, xii). When asked as to how he knew this, Dr. Hisrchi replied,

> I believe <u>interest</u> in a field or topic <u>may</u> be explained by a combination of personal characteristics and experiences. . . . The sources of interest in crime and deviance can't be much of a mystery. Erving Goffman taught us that there are few "unblushing" males [and, by implication, no females] in America—that the pool of people potentially interested in stigma or deviant behavior is therefore very large indeed. And I don't mean to suggest that the commission of criminal acts is a necessary condition for such interest. Indeed, my theories are based on the assumption that we all imagine and are capable of inventing crime, and may therefore naturally wonder why some do and some do not engage in it. (Underlining in original; T. Hirschi, personal communication, February 7, 2005)

At this juncture in the communication, Dr. Hirschi took the opportunity to again address the issue of personal background and its lack of influence on the development of one's theory and therefore its irrelevance in understanding a theorist's work.

> Having said this, I continue to think that the content of one's theoretical or methodological views cannot or should not be approached in the same way. When we look back from some intellectual product (or, I am afraid, from some criminal act) to the person thought to be responsible for it, we are highly likely to be misled. As Nietzsche says, "success has always been the greatest liar—and the 'work' itself is a success; the [creator] is disguised by his creations, often beyond recognition; the 'work' . . . invents the man who has created it, [or] who is supposed to have created it." (Underlining in original; T. Hirschi, personal communication, February 7, 2005)

Finally, demonstrating a keen sense of humor, he concluded by saying, "I am thinking of writing a paper on this topic. If it is a 'success,' I'll send you a copy" (T. Hirschi, personal communication, February 7, 2005).

Hirschi completed his undergraduate studies in 1957 and stayed at Utah for his master's degree in sociology and educational psychology. During his time at Utah, Hirschi married Anna Yergensen (in 1955), with whom he would have three children, Kendal, Nathan, and Justine (Laub 2002).

In 1958, Hirschi was drafted into the Army and assigned to a research unit responsible for analyzing data from the Army's quarterly survey. This experience provided some valuable lessons about survey research and the use of survey data, "especially with regard to the clash between scientific data and ideology" (Laub 2002, xiv), lessons it appears that would have long-lasting impact on the paradigm that Hirschi would apply to the study of deviance.

After the military, Hirschi enrolled at the University of California at Berkeley. He was intent on studying crime, and initially applied to the School of Criminology; however, the only graduate program in criminology available at that time was a master's degree, and because he already had a master's degree, Hirschi entered the PhD program in sociology. As might be expected, a series of events and experiences occurred during his time at Berkeley that helped to further establish his approach as a criminologist. Probably of most note were his teaching assistantship in statistics and his interactions with Erving Goffman and Hanan Selvin. From Goffman, Hirschi learned that the focus in intellectual pursuits should be on the ideas and not the person. His work with Selvin helped to further develop his skills as a researcher and statistician, and also provided what might be considered the serendipitous event that firmly embedded Hirschi in the study of juvenile delinquency. Selvin had received a Ford Foundation Grant (of $2,500) to summarize the existing quantitative data on juvenile delinquency, but was not at all interested in the subject and turned the project over to Hirschi. In an interview with John Laub (2002), Hirschi indicated that simply summarizing the findings did not make sense to him, so he also provided a critique of the research. Selvin was very impressed with what Hirschi had done, and after some reworking, Hirschi, as a second-year graduate student, received his first book contract. It would take Hirschi another five years to complete the book, which was ultimately published (with Hanan C. Selvin in 1967) as *Delinquency Research: An Appraisal of Analytic Methods* (Laub 2002). (It should be noted that Hirschi actually wrote this work while also writing his dissertation, which would be published as *Causes of Delinquency*.)

In 1963, Hirschi was awarded a National Institutes of Mental Health pre-doctoral fellowship, which provided him the time to develop his dissertation project. Charles Y. Glock, who was the Director of the Survey Research Center at Berkeley, served as his dissertation chair, and other members of his committee were Irving Piliavin and David Matza (Laub 2002). According to Hirschi (1980), his dissertation project evolved out of his knowledge of the central ideas from the sociology and criminology literature and his research with Selvin critiquing the delinquency research. He devised what appeared to be an uncomplicated plan—he simply put the ideas together with the existing research findings. However, plans are never as simple in reality as they are on the drawing board, and the ideas that Hirschi found most exciting and consistent with the available data "had been treated as contrary to fact, passé and even 'appalling.' The only way to remedy this situation, it seemed, was to show the ability of the ideas to account for a single body of relevant data" (Hirschi 2002, ix). The initial strategy was to try to obtain a data set for secondary analysis, but large data sets were hard to come by in those days and researchers were reluctant to release them to others (Hirschi, 2002). Hirschi had tried to get access to the data set that the Gluecks had used for *Unraveling Juvenile Delinquency,* which he knew to be the best available on delinquency at the time, but the Gluecks declined, indicating that they were still working "intensively" with it (T. Hirschi, personal communication, May 22, 2006; Laub 2002). Ultimately, Glock put Hirschi in touch with Alan B. Wilson, the director of the just beginning Richmond Youth Project. Wilson permitted Hirschi to add items to the project's survey instrument, in exchange for Hirschi assisting on the project, and the rest, as they say, is history. (As a side note, Hirschi claims that despite his title of deputy director on the project, "my contributions were mainly clerical [and physical—boxes of questionnaires are heavy] rather than intellectual") (Hirschi 2002, x).

Hirschi's career as an academician formally started in 1966, when he accepted a position as an acting assistant professor at Berkeley. He remained at Berkeley for only one year and then moved on to the sociology department at the University of Washington at Seattle, where he stayed until 1971. From 1971 to 1977, he was at the University of California at Davis. After UC Davis, he was a Professor at SUNY Albany, from 1977 to 1981. In 1981, he accepted a position at the University of Arizona, where he remained until his retirement in 1997. Dr. Hirschi is currently Regents Professor Emeritus at the University of Arizona (Laub 2002).

II. INTRODUCTION

It should be noted that the format for the remainder of this chapter is slightly different from the others in the book. The discussion of Hirschi's influence in criminology is organized around two major theoretical contributions and the corresponding periods in his theorizing, which are referred to as Hirschi, Part I, and Hirschi, Part II. Part I relates to Hirschi's earlier contributions, his work on social bond theory,[1] in particular as it was presented in the seminal and classic *Causes of Delinquency* (1969). Part II covers his more contemporary theorizing, with Michael Gottfredson (1990), on *A General Theory of Crime*. As with the other chapters, the presentation of each contribution is constructed around the major themes of Basic Assumptions, Key Ideas, and Critique, but the two contributions are covered separately and in their respective entireties. After discussing each contribution, we discuss the relationships between the two theories and of the evolution of thought involved.

III. HIRSCHI—PART I: SOCIAL CONTROL THEORY

BASIC ASSUMPTIONS

Chapter II, "A Control Theory of Delinquency," in *Causes of Delinquency,* which Laub (2002) refers to as the work's "theoretical heart," begins with this statement: "Control theories assume that delinquent acts result when an individual's bond to society is weak or broken" (Hirschi 1969, 16). The central thesis then, restated, is that juveniles are freed to commit delinquent acts to the extent that their ties to the conventional social order are diminished or severed. Williams and McShane (2004) state that it is difficult to pin down the "intellectual heritage" of social control theories, but it seems that the modern versions developed primarily as alternatives to strain theory.[2]

In commenting on the rise of popularity of social control theory, Williams (1999) notes that "criminologists were looking for an alternative to perspectives that blamed society for criminal behavior without really giving up a social perspective" (p. 25). From these observations, we can begin to see why control theory is said to ask a different question than other theories of crime and criminality. "The question 'Why do they

---

[1]Laub (2002) notes that Hirschi is "not inclined to accept" this terminology, preferring *social control*. With apologies to Dr. Hirschi, we use the terminology here to avoid confusion, as the theory has become widely associated with that name.

[2]Williams and McShane (2004) offer an interesting piece of information, noting that, even though Merton did use the word *strain* in presenting his anomie theory, Albert Cohen (cited from a letter he wrote to Frank Williams), who is generally referred to as a strain theorist, claims that Hirschi, in *Causes of Delinquency,* "invented that theoretical classification."

do it?' is simply not the question the theory is designed to answer. The question is, 'Why don't we do it?'" (Hirschi 1969, 34).

In order to begin to more fully understand what social control theory is and why it asks this central question, we must first look at the assumptions on which the theory rests. There are three basic assumptions that can be identified with Hirschi's social control approach. The first relates to how the control theorists view human motivation, the second concerns the nature of human values, and the third focuses on the central factor in establishing and maintaining social bonds. The first two can be viewed as somewhat generic contemporary control theory assumptions; the third is more specific to Hirschi's version of social control.

Motivation: The Nature of Human Functioning
In describing the source of social control, Hirschi (quoted in Laub 2002, xxiii) said,

> It seems to me obvious in Durkheim and especially Hobbes. Control theory is inherent in attempts to solve the problem of order. Hobbes's question is this: Given our natural tendency to pursue short term private interests, how is society possible? The question does not assume that we are naturally evil. It assumes only that we have a tendency to act, and the ability to consider what will follow.

Contained in this quote are the two core aspects of the control assumption about human nature: (1) humans are not inherently evil, but more neutral; and (2) no special motives are required to explain delinquency or other forms of deviance.

In *Causes of Delinquency,* Hirschi (1969) discusses how early control theories addressed the question, "Yes, but why do they do it?" by simply stripping away the "veneer of civilization" to "expose man's animal impulses."

> These impulses appeared to him (and apparently to his audience) to provide a plausible account of the motivation to crime and delinquency. His argument was not that delinquents and criminals alone are animals, but that we are all animals, and thus all naturally capable of committing criminal acts. (p. 31)

We require no special motivation to explain a dog destroying a pillow or attacking another dog or a chicken stealing corn from another chicken. "It is simply the behavior of a chicken or a dog. . . . No motivation to deviance is required to explain his acts. So, too, no special motivation to crime within the human animal was required to explain his criminal acts" (p. 31).

Hirschi (1977, 329) states that control or restraint theories "assume that the potential for asocial conduct is present in everyone, that we would all commit delinquent acts were we not somehow prevented from doing so." He goes on to say that we are not born good or bad, but "amoral," and that morality comes about through "training" that is maintained by the ties that we have with others and institutions. As Gibbons (1994) notes, delinquent acts are often "intrinsically attractive" and may represent quick and convenient access to a desirable goal. Consequently, if not restrained in some way, most would pursue such acts.

Hirschi begins the article "Causes and Prevention of Juvenile Delinquency" by stating the following:

> Explanations of juvenile delinquency require considerations of two sets of elements. These are, on the one hand, the driving forces, the reasons or motives behind the act, on the other, the obstacles that stand in its way, the

restraints that inhibit its occurrence. In principle, it is possible to construct an explanation of delinquency that gives each set of elements, if not equal weight, at least some role in the outcome. In practice, equal treatment of motives and restraints turns out to be difficult. (1977, 322)

Later in the article, picking up on the latter aspect of this passage, Hirschi discusses the focus of control theories.

In control theories, the important differences between delinquents and non-delinquents are not differences in motivation; they are, rather, differences in the extent to which natural motives are controlled. Control theories thus focus on the restraints on delinquent behavior, on the circumstances and desires that prevent it. (p. 329)

Values: A Consensus View

The second central assumption relates to how social control theories view values.

Unlike the cultural deviance theory, the control theory assumes the existence of a common value system within the society or group whose norms are being violated. If the deviant is committed to a value system different from that of conventional society, there is, within the context of the theory, nothing to explain. The question is, "Why does a man violate the rules in which he believes?" It is not, "Why do men differ in their beliefs about what constitutes good and desirable conduct?" The person is assumed to have been socialized (perhaps imperfectly) into the group whose rules he is violating; deviance is not a question of one group imposing its rules on members of another group. In other words, we not only assume the deviant has believed the rules, we assume he believes the rules even as he violates them. (Hirschi 1969, 23)

Control theories in general, and social control theory in particular, assume the existence of "a dominant moral order," which is indicative of a consensus view (Williams and McShane 2004). Bernard (1987), in reviewing social control theory, concluded that Hirschi's definition of behavior rested firmly and exclusively in the acceptance of a common societal value system. Most versions of control theory assume a central value system; if they did not, the theories would have to assert that deviance results from "learning different moralities" (Clinard and Meier 1985). As we know, this is not the etiological position taken by control theory, and Hirschi did not place any credence in the relativistic conceptualization of deviance (Williams and McShane 2004). "Control theory must assume that there is one central value system so that variations in deviance can be attributed to variations only in controls" (Clinard and Meier 1985, 77).

In justifying this consensus assumption, Hirschi acknowledged the important role that "belief" plays in sociological theories, but offers an alternative conceptualization to what he terms the "most famous" view, that of *differential association.* Hirschi disputes the positions that delinquents either have beliefs or values that demand delinquent acts or that they are subject to substantial pressure to behave contrary to beliefs that forbid such actions; "the belief system neither requires or forbids delinquency" (1977, 337–38). Instead, the belief system makes the choice between delinquency and abiding by the law "a matter of expediency." Such a conceptualization helps explain why a delinquent acts as he does, but does not imply that he is at all compelled to act in that way.

In a critique of labeling theory, Hirschi offers additional support for the appropriateness of the consensus view.

> Compared to its antitheoretical competitors, "the theory of norms" is highly developed. This theory allows one to predict many of the norms of a society from its survival needs in general and its institutional structure in particular; it shows that many of the norms of societies are neither arbitrary nor ephemeral; it shows, to my satisfaction, that some forms of behavior are, within the context of a given system, necessarily deviant in the sense that most members of the system cannot be free to applaud or even to ignore them. (1973, 168)

The Importance of Parenting/Family

Perhaps placing central importance on parenting as a factor in the establishment of social bonds or as a restraint against delinquency does not seem to fit as a basic theoretical assumption. It may be that this element of social control theory is more aptly described as a key idea. However, from *Causes of Delinquency* (1969) to *A General Theory of Crime* (1990), at points in between (see, e.g., Hirschi 1977, 1983) and also subsequently (see Hirschi 1991, 1995), parenting and the family occupy a pivotal role in Hirschi's views on the restraint (or lack thereof) of delinquency as well as adult crime. Given the core role that these concepts/variables play in all of Hirschi's work and given the general consistency with which they have been treated, it seems apropos to at least mention them as part of a discussion of basic assumptions.

Laub (2002) states that, more than any other delinquency theorist, Hirschi brought the family, and most specifically family relations, back into the theoretical picture. In *Causes of Delinquency*, Hirschi (1969) reports an inverse relationship between delinquency and bonds or attachment within the family, and devotes an entire chapter (Chapter VI, "Attachment to Parents") to discussing the nature and importance of this finding. Early in that chapter, Hirschi makes the fundamental observation that "[A]lthough denied in some theories and ignored in others, the fact that delinquents are less likely than nondelinquents to be closely tied to their parents is one of the best documented findings of delinquency research" (1969, 85). He goes on to address various ways of accounting for the relationship, and notes that an empirical question is the determination of which accounting is most accurate. However, and a main reason for listing the importance of parenting as a basic assumption, he does not question the veracity of the relationship itself. It seems that he is satisfied that the essential role of parenting is a core truth, and he has treated it as such ever since.

In discussing family and attachments, Hirschi states that "[W]e may therefore assume that delinquency often says something about the quality of the relation between parent and child" (1977, 332). He goes on to highlight the "centrality of the family" in systems of control. Furthermore, he professes some bewilderment, not only at the fact that it had not been included in "most sociological theories of delinquency," but also with what he then termed as "recent efforts to justify its absence." Finally, in "Family Structure and Crime," Hirschi (1991) provides an assessment of what he believes the facts say about the role of childrearing in crime causation. Succinctly put, he concludes that the facts make it clear that family/childrearing has a consistent and stable impact on the likelihood of crime/delinquency and that this impact is established at ages as young as 6 to 8. Given the early onset and consistency, the differences in likelihood must be attributable to experiences in the family. He further concludes that such findings indicate that crime can actually be studied before its onset, by looking at what is happening within the family as children are being raised.

There may be some, including Hirschi himself, who could argue that what has been presented here constitutes coverage of empirically based fact, rather than an assumption, and this is a reasonable interpretation. However, we chose to include the focus on parenting as a basic assumption, as it has clearly been a central underpinning on which all of Hirschi's work has, to a great extent, rested. It appears that the foundational nature of the role of parenting has, in essence, been an assumption from which Hirschi's theorizing has proceeded; it has been one of his guiding truths. In addition, although it may be an assumption grounded in empirical observation, it is not an observation that everyone has apparently seen fit to acknowledge, at least not to the degree that Hirschi has.

Additional Assumptions

The three assumptions discussed previously constitute what might be seen as the most basic or general assumptions underlying social control theory. However, before moving on, it may be helpful to include a list of what Williams and McShane (2004) refer to as "Major Points of the General Social Control Theory Approach." These are provided to help flesh out the general control orientation and to add some specificity to the coverage of assumptions.

1. Human nature and behavior tends to be "self-interested."
2. "Human behavior must be restrained and regulated to benefit all."
3. There is an existing moral order in society, made up of rules and regulations.
4. Humans are bound to this moral order throughout life.
5. "The bond to the moral order is composed of elements that maintain and strengthen conformity."
6. Bond consists of elements like attachment, investment, involvement, and belief.
7. The elements of bond vary in their strength; when these elements are weak or absent, individuals are more free to deviate. (2004, 202)

KEY IDEAS

Control theories, generally speaking, cover quite a broad range of topics and can be specifically characterized in a variety of ways. Some scholars identify the individualistic approaches (e.g., psychoanalytic theory) of the latter nineteenth and early twentieth centuries as the beginning of control theory. Hirschi (1969) places the origins of control theory in Durkheim's work in the nineteenth century. Although the core ideas of control theory can be traced back quite a long way, most typically control theories of delinquency have been equated with self-concept approaches and mechanisms of social control such as family, school, and other institutions. Using this context, the origins of what we have come to identify as control theory can be historically placed in the work of theorists like Albert Reiss, Jackson Toby, and Walter Reckless, in the 1950s and 1960s (Shoemaker 2005). In the late 1960s, Hirschi provided his social control theory, which built on and extended these earlier works.

Hirschi did not envision individuals as being conforming or deviant. Instead, like Durkheim, he saw behavior as being reflective of varying levels of morality (Williams and McShane 2004). The theory he developed to explain this variation relied mainly on the roles of different constraints in controlling or regulating behavior. He identified the internalization of social norms (via attachment to others) and the need for approval and acceptance as central elements in regulating behavior (Hirschi 1969). Hirschi accepted the basic assumption that people are free to deviate, and theorized that the extent to which they do deviate or conform is determined by the level of bonds they have with society. As people are primarily motivated by self-interest, societal restraints are necessary to control criminal/delinquent behavior. The counterpart to this notion is, of course, that if these restraints are weakened or broken, then deviation from the norms becomes more likely. Hirschi's version of social control theory, therefore, begins from the fundamental proposition that "delinquent acts result when an individual's bond to society is weak or broken" (1969, 16). This basic proposition also explains why the focus of inquiry from the social control perspective is the Hobbesian question, "Why do men not obey the rules of society?"

Hirschi (1969, 16) notes that control "theories embrace two highly complex concepts, the *bond* of the individual to *society*" (italics in original). These two concepts form the basis for our discussion of Key Ideas. First, we examine the nature of bond, and then we look at how it relates, within social control theory, to society. The following passage from "Causes and Prevention of Juvenile Delinquency" (1977) should help set up the more specific discussions of social bond and societal constraints.

> Delinquent acts are acts contrary to law. Since the law embodies the moral values of the community (and insofar as it does not, the task of explaining delinquency is even easier), it follows that (1) delinquent acts are contrary to the wishes and expectations of other people; (2) they involve the risk of punishment, both formal and informal; (3) they take (and save) time and energy; and (4) they are contrary to conventional moral belief.
>
> If these assumptions are true, it follows further that those most likely to engage in delinquent acts are (1) least likely to be concerned about the wishes and expectations of others; (2) least likely to be concerned about the risk of punishment; (3) most likely to have the time and energy the act requires; and (4) least likely to accept moral beliefs contrary to delinquency.
>
> This, in brief form, is an example of control theory. It asserts that the delinquent is "relatively free of the intimate attachments, the aspirations, and the moral beliefs that bind most people to a life within the law" (Hirschi 1969, preface). Such theories assume that the potential for asocial conduct is present in everyone, that we would all commit delinquent acts were we not somehow prevented from doing so. Put another way, they assume that we are born amoral, that our morality has been added by training, and it is maintained by ties to other people and institutions. (Hirschi 1977, 329)

Social Bond

Social Control Theory proposes that individuals who are strongly bonded to social groups (e.g., parents/family, school, peers) are less likely to engage in delinquent acts. It therefore is essential that the concept of bond be clearly defined. It has been widely noted that Hirschi's conceptualization of social bond consists of four interrelated elements, which are described in every criminology theory text, as well as in a wide range of other sources. As we deem it necessary and appropriate to also provide some description, but as we do not want to present a description that becomes merely a reiterated conglomerate of other secondhand portrayals, we instead use Hirschi's (1969) original descriptions. The four elements of "the bond to conventional society" are attachment, commitment, involvement, and belief.

Attachment

> Durkheim said it many years ago: "We are moral beings to the extent that we are social beings.' This may be interpreted to mean that we are moral beings to the extent that we have "internalized the norms" of society. But what does it mean to say that a person has internalized the norms of society?

From this beginning, Hirschi (1969, 18) moves into his definition of *attachment.* He goes on to note that, as norms are shared by members of society, *violations* are actions "contrary to the wishes and expectations" of others. If one is not concerned about the wishes of others, or their opinions, "then he is to that extent not bound by the norms. He is free to deviate." Herein is the core of Hirschi's view of attachment: "[T]he essence of internalization of norms, conscience, or superego thus lies in the attachment of the individual to others" (1969, 18). Hirschi elaborates on this proposition and also highlights his heavy emphasis on the empirical process in a footnote to this quoted material. He states that the full meaning of internalization is not subsumed with attachment, but when attachment and beliefs are combined, they leave "only a small residue of 'internal control' not susceptible," at least in principle, to direct measurement.

Hirschi (1969) is convinced that attachment, as a concept, holds several advantages over internalization. It helps avoid, as he calls it, begging the question; attachment to others can be measured independently from that person's deviant behavior. It also provides a better model for conceptualizing variation in behavior, as unlike internalization and superego, it is not necessary to impute some internal shift that corresponds with and explains the change in behavior. He illustrates this with the example of a man being more likely to engage in deviant acts after a divorce. The man's changed behavior is not the result of his having lost his conscience in the divorce settlement, but is rather the result of having an important attachment broken. In other words, Hirschi moved the locus of *conscience* from an internal, personality aspect to being located in the (social) bond with others.

Commitment

Commitment   The second element of bond is *commitment,* which Hirschi (1969) identifies as the "rational component in conformity," meaning that when we consider deviant behavior, we must also consider the costs that are incurred with that behavior; what do we stand to lose on our investments in conventional behavior? "If attachment to others is the sociological counterpart of the superego or conscience, commitment is the counterpart of the ego or common sense" (1969, 20).

Sociological control theory assumes that decisions to commit (or not to commit) criminal acts are generally determined through rational thought processes. (This is not to say that errors in this calculation process cannot and do not sometimes become factors in deviant behavior.) Hirschi's conceptualization of commitment is predicated on the assumption that society is organized in such a way that criminal acts generally jeopardize the interests of the majority of people. In the normal course of living our lives, we acquire material things and social status; we become invested in conformity and conventionality. If we behave in a deviant manner, we risk our investments. "The person becomes committed to a conventional line of action, and he is therefore committed to conformity" (1969, 21).

Involvement   "Many people undoubtedly owe a life of virtue to a lack of opportunity to do otherwise. Time and energy are inherently limited" (Hirschi 1969, 21). *Involvement* as a restraint against delinquency, simply stated, relates to the notion that if a person is kept busy doing conventional things, he or she has no time or energy to devote to deviant behavior. Hirschi linked this directly to delinquency by noting that the "leisure of adolescence" can produce a set of values that leads to delinquency.

Belief   The final element of bond is belief. There has been some confusion, probably more so than with the other elements, about this element. There seems to be some inherent illogic, at least on the surface, with the social control treatment of belief. To address this confusion, it must be recognized that belief is very directly related to the underlying consensus assumption of control theory.

> We do not assume, in other words, that the person constructs a system of rationalizations in order to justify commission of acts he wants to commit. We assume, in contrast, that the beliefs that free a man to commit deviant acts are unmotivated in the sense that he does not construct or adopt them in order to facilitate the attainment of illicit ends. In the second place, we do not assume, as does Matza, that "delinquents concur in the conventional assessment of delinquency." We assume, in contrast, that there is variation in the extent to which people believe they should obey the rules of society, and, furthermore, that the less a person believes he should obey the rules, the more likely he is to violate them. (Hirschi 1969, 25)

The social control conceptualization of belief is, of course, dependent on the existence of actual variation in belief about the moral validity of societal rules. Hirschi (1969) claims that the presupposition that strength in moral beliefs varies across individuals is entirely consistent with the idea of a single value system. Social control theory does not propose that delinquents hold beliefs counter to conventional standards of conduct and morality, or that they do not believe that their delinquent actions are wrong. Rather, "[T]hey may well believe these acts are wrong, but the meaning and efficacy of such beliefs are contingent upon other beliefs, and, indeed, on the strength of other ties to the conventional order" (1969, 26).

Final Thoughts on the Elements of Bond
Before moving on to the second major key idea, a discussion of society, there are a few additional points about social bond that warrant some attention.

The first point relates to the relative importance of the four elements of bond. Vold, Bernard, and Snipes state categorically that "[T]he most important element of the social bond is attachment—i.e., affection for and sensitivity to others" (1998, 207–08). However, Wiatrowski, Griswold, and Roberts (1981) arrived at what would appear to be an antithetical conclusion, noting that no element is theoretically more important or superordinate, although one or another may appear more principal under varying conditions. In his original formulation, Hirschi (1969) did not offer any prioritization but rather deemed this to be a question for future research.

From review of the varied literature on social control theory, it does not appear that this question has been answered directly. However, when one looks at the plethora of studies that have been conducted to test social control theory, attachment clearly is the concept that has received the lion's share of empirical attention, if not support (Kempf's 1993 analysis confirms this conclusion). Also, in Hirschi's (1969) original study, there were more measures of attachment than of any other element. Taking these observations, in conjunction with what might simply be termed as a *logical analysis*, it could be concluded that Vold, Bernard, and Snipes (1998) were correct—attachment is the most important element.

If we take the liberty of looking at attachment in the developmental and personality psychology literature as being somewhat analogous to Hirschi's treatment and use that as the basis for our logical analysis, then we can conclude that attachment is, in fact, a foundational developmental concept. Without getting into a lengthy treatise, the essential role of attachment to caregivers in healthy development has been well documented across a somewhat diverse range of psychological literature. As early as 1917, Freud attributed depression to the loss of an object of love. This could be the loss of loved material objects, but most often it refers to separation from a loved person. In his classic work *The Moral Judgment of the Child,* Piaget (1932) highlighted the role of attachment in the development of moral reasoning.[3] In his widely cited works, Bowlby (1969, 1973) found that early childhood experiences with loss can predispose individuals to depressive and other psychological and emotional disorders in adulthood.[4] Finally, a wide range of cognitive theorists discuss the importance of social attachment for the development of a variety of cognitive processes and as a factor in behavior (for a review, see Flavell, Miller, and Miller 2001). In the psychological literature, attachment is seen as a process that begins literally at birth (or even before), and is foundational in and has major implications for a wide range of developmental processes. When attachments are ill-formed or when they are broken, a broad array of emotional, cognitive, and behavioral problems can result. Although Hirschi's specific conceptualization of attachment may be somewhat different, it would seem that, at its core, it is closely enough aligned with characterizations of attachment in psychology to make this a reasonable analogy (or to at least provide food for thought).

The second area is the interrelationships among the four elements. Space does not permit a detailed examination of research relating to the interrelationships of the four elements, but a few brief comments are in order. Hirschi (1969) stated that, generally, the more strongly a person is bonded to conventional society in any of the ways described in the four elements, the more strongly he or she is bonded in the other ways as well. He notes that there are six possible combinations of elements, and identifies three as being of particular importance: attachment and commitment, commitment and involvement, and attachment and belief. (We do not review his coverage here; the interested reader is referred to pages 27–30 in *Causes of Delinquency.*) A number of studies have been done looking at the interrelationships, the relative impacts, and the changing nature over time of the four elements. As noted previously, a review of this literature is

---

[3]Hirschi (1969) offers a quote from this work in his discussion of the relationship between attachment and belief.
[4]Note that Wilson and Herrnstein (1985) would likely take issue with this analogy, as they do not see Hirschi's definition of *attachment* as being at all like Bowlby's conceptualization.

beyond the scope of the current coverage. Interested readers are referred to Kempf (1993),[5] who provides a comprehensive review of the research, presented by the type/nature/focus.

SOCIETY

Hirschi (1977) states that one way in which control theories account for delinquency is by looking at the effectiveness of social institutions, such as family and school, in constraining delinquent conduct. Below, we examine the role of these societal constraints by looking first at "Parents and Family" and then at "Other Institutions."

Parents and Family

In his original formulation, Hirschi's (1969) emphasis was on indirect rather than direct parental control. This indirect control was manifested through the child's emotional attachment to the parents. Hirschi did not see direct parental controls, such as monitoring or supervision, as being as important, because, unlike emotional attachment, they are not operative at the times when delinquency is most likely to be occurring. So, for Hirschi, "relational controls," in the form of the parent–child attachment or bond, are the most central in inhibiting delinquency (Sampson and Laub 1993).[6]

"Control theory assumes that the bond of affection for conventional persons is a major deterrent to crime. The stronger this bond, the more likely the person is to take it into account when and if he contemplates a criminal act" (Hirschi 1969, 82). In support of this conclusion, Hirschi (1969) offers the observation that, although it is often ignored, one of the most well-documented findings in delinquency research is that non-delinquents tend to be more closely tied to their parents than are delinquents. The explanation for the centrality of this emotional bond in helping prevent delinquency rests on the fact that it is the bond that "presumably provides the bridge across which pass parental ideals and expectations" (1969, 86). Consequently, children who are alienated from their parents do not learn and have no feeling for moral rules. Because of this, Hirschi (1977) states that "delinquency often says something about the quality of the relationship between parent and child. . . . And, indeed, those least attached to their parents are most likely to commit delinquents acts" (1977, 332).

As unattached or weakly attached children do not care about the reactions of their parents, they have less to lose from involvement in delinquent behavior. Also, this lack of attachment has implications for other interactions and often results in a lack of respect for teachers, police, and other authority figures. Much of the power adults outside of the family have, in terms of exerting control, is actually based in the threat of reporting the child to the parents. If this threat is not salient, the sanctioning power of other social institutions is greatly diminished or removed (Hirschi 1977).

> Given the centrality of the family in the system of internal and external (psychological and structural) control, its absence from most sociological theories of delinquency is something of a mystery. The mystery is deepened by the

---

[5]While this work may appear to be a bit dated, it should be noted that, although some research continues to look at social control theory, much of the empirical assessment since 1990 shifted to the self-control aspects contained in *A General Theory of Crime,* which is discussed later in this chapter.

[6]Hirschi's views on the roles of indirect and direct controls would shift in his later theorizing, which is addressed in the discussions of *A General Theory of Crime* that follow.

recent efforts to justify the absence: "We do not accept . . . that delinquency may result from differential attachment to parents, and learning processes which result in children being differentially attached to moral authority in general—especially at a time when the hold of the nuclear family is, by all accounts, being weakened" (Taylor, Walton, and Young 1973, 184). One way of reading such statements is that the family is no longer important in the control of delinquency because the family is no longer important in anything. However, when we look at adolescents whose allegiance to their families is profound (the vast majority), we see the error in assuming that because the hold of the family has weakened for some it has weakened for all. In fact, once we admit variation in the effectiveness of family control, it becomes apparent that the family may become more important as a cause of delinquency as the number of "weak" families grow. (Hirschi 1977, 333)

Hirschi's point should be quite clear. At this phase in his theorizing, he saw parents and the family as being the essential elements in controlling delinquency. Put differently, he noted that variations in the efficacy of family controls can explain many of the main correlates of delinquency (Hirschi 1977).

Other Social Institutions

The coverage of other institutions is brief, serving only to highlight that Hirschi also postulated roles, for them in constraining delinquency, albeit to a lesser extent than parents and family. The two institutions that he addressed most directly and extensively were school and peers.

The chapter entitled "Attachment to the School" in *Causes of Delinquency* begins with the following statement:

Between the conventional family and the conventional world of work and marriage lies the school, an eminently conventional institution. Insofar as this institution is able to command his attachment, involvement, and commitment, the adolescent is presumably able to move from childhood to adulthood with a minimum of delinquent acts. (Hirschi 1969, 110)

Hirschi's (1969, 1977) fundamental observation about the relationship between school and delinquency was that those who do poorly in school are much more likely to engage in delinquent behavior than those who do well. The poor student is at greater risk for delinquency because he or she is less concerned about what the adults at the school think, and also is less likely to accept the belief in school as the "royal road to success" (1977, 335). Hirschi offers the rather stark conclusion that school has either become the major institution of social control in our society, or perhaps it is more the "major generator of delinquency." It is not that failure in school creates or represents a motive to commit specific delinquent or criminal acts, but rather it represents a "reduction in the potential cost of apprehension" for such acts (1977, 336).

Peers/Gangs

When adolescents are freed from ties to adult institutions, like family and school, they are free to and tend to gravitate toward others in a similar situation. This has lead to the long time (and correct) observation that peer groups or gangs are a "concomitant of delinquency." However, the social control view of this concomitancy is decidedly different from the social learning view. Social learning suggests that delinquency itself is learned or social in nature. It is a product of socialization or training, and therefore re-sults from strong ties to others. Social control sees it as basically the opposite — delin-quents are products of a lack of training and a lack of ties to others. Their behaviors are not social, but asocial. Gangs or delinquent peer groups do not consist of tightly bonded adolescents, but are more likely adolescents "caught in a common situation, they are to some extent forced together rather than attracted to each other" (Hirschi 1977, 336–37). What members in delinquent gangs tend to have in common is a low stake in conformity, and their relations "tend to be cold and brittle" (Hirschi 1969, 161).

In closing, we draw on Hirschi's summary of the findings presented in *Causes of Delinquency:*

1. The child with little stake in conformity is susceptible to prodelinquent influences in his environment; the child with a high stake in conformity is relatively immune to these influences.
2. The greater the exposure to "criminal influences," the greater the difference in delinquent activity between high- and low-stake boys. Although these criminal influences are beyond the reach of control theory, group-process theories are forced to work with material supplied them by the weakening of social bonds. (1969, 161)

CRITIQUE

Hirschi's (1969) approach in *Causes of Delinquency* has been characterized as unique in that not only did he present his own theory, but he also tested it using self-report techniques. "This 'testing' approach to assessing theories of crime and delinquency became the standard in the field" (Laub 2002, xxiii). The "combination of theory construction, conceptualization, operationalization, and empirically testing was virtually unique in criminology at that time and stands as a model today" (Akers 1994, 116). Of particular interest and concern to Hirschi was how his theory matched up, empirically, against strain theories (see footnote 2) and also cultural, social learning–type theories (Kempf 1993, Vold, Bernard, and Snipes 1998, Laub 2002). In fact, much of *Causes of Delinquency* is devoted to Hirschi's exploration and testing of the various chains of causation associated with these three theoretical perspectives (Vold, Bernard, and Snipes 1998). Over the years, Hirschi (1977, 1989) elaborated and clarified aspects of his theory, but he did not do any additional direct testing. He also made it clear that attempts to integrate aspects of social control with other theories constituted "effort without reward" (Kempf 1993, 166).

Although Hirschi may not have carried out any subsequent direct testing of his theory, others certainly have. Virtually every source that provides any depth of coverage of Hirschi's social control theory acknowledges that it has been one of the most extensively researched theories in all of criminology. Kempf (1993), in what has been the most complete review of research on Hirschi's social control theory to date, identified seventy-one empirical tests of the theory that were carried out between 1970 and 1991. Given the rather profuse amount of empirical attention that has been paid to social control theory, it is not surprising that the critiques cover a wide range of aspects and that the conclusions about the validity are equally diverse. The coverage consists of six basic areas. Some general observations about support are presented first, followed by brief discussions of three specific areas of critique: Weak Associations, Trivial Offenses, and Delinquent Peers. The section ends with a review of some other areas of critique, and then general conclusions about the overall validity of the approach are offered.

General Support

Over the years, there has been a fair amount of support for Hirschi's general views on bonding. Certainly, his own research (Hirschi 1969) provided support for the proposition that weaker bonds increase the probability of delinquency, and the reverse is also true. From their review of the literature, Akers and Sellers (2004) conclude that delinquency prediction studies consistently demonstrate that a range of family variables, and most especially parental discipline and childrearing practices, are "among the best predictors" of delinquency. Shoemaker offers a similar conclusion, stating that "the nature of parent–child interactions and the general atmosphere within the home . . . have been consistently related to delinquency" (2005, 191). Wiatrowski, Griswold, and Roberts (1981) report a strong inverse relationship between parent and school attachment and delinquent behavior. Finally, Sampson and Laub (1993) find support for attachments as constraints against criminal behavior, even into adulthood. (For additional support, see Hindelang 1973, Cernkovich and Giordano 1992, and Costello and Vowell 1999.)

However, it seems that despite this general support, there are still many questions about the veracity of social control theory. Empey (1978) concludes that although social bond theory seems to fare better than subcultural (i.e., strain) or differential association theory, the empirical evidence comes up short of supporting it as a full and complete explanation of delinquency. From her review, Kempf (1993) identified concerns about the scope or generalizability of social control theory, its ability to explain specific forms of delinquency, as well as general deviance, and its applicability across age, race, and socioeconomic groups. Some of these more specific concerns are explored next.

Weak Associations

Although relationships have been found between Hirschi's elements of social bond and delinquency, the problem of weak associations has been noted in the literature since the early stages of testing the theory (Empey 1978). Agnew (1991) found inconsistent and only "weak" effects for social control variables with longitudinal measures of delinquency. Kempf (1993) also notes this criticism in her review, and Greenberg (1999) identifies this same concern. Although acknowledging that the theory garnered some empirical support, Akers and Sellers conclude: "[H]owever, the magnitude of the relationships between social bonding and deviant behavior has ranged from moderate to low. High correlations and levels of explained variance are seldom found in the research literature on this theory" (2004, 121–22). They point out further that even in Hirschi's own research, the relationships found tended to be fairly modest (see also Krohn and Massey 1980, Agnew 1993).

Two other limitations are somewhat related to the general finding of weak associations—the restricted range of delinquent behaviors explained by social control theory (i.e., trivial offenses) and the confounding of the elements of bond with peer associations.

Trivial Offenses

Another criticism of social control theory is that its explanatory power is mainly restricted to less serious or minor forms of delinquency. Research generally shows that social bond factors account for "relatively minor forms of delinquency and for female lawbreaking more satisfactorily than they do for more serious instances of juvenile misconduct" (Gibbons 1994, 34). Krohn and Massey (1980) and Agnew (1991)[7] offer further support for this contention.

The data upon which social control theory is based are self report and therefore asked about less serious offenses (Wiatrowski, Griswold, and Roberts 1981). Also, many of the tests of the theory, especially those that have found support, focused on more trivial offenses, and often actually used non-delinquent samples (Kempf 1993, Vold, Bernard, and Snipes 1998). In light of these two factors, it is understandable that the theory is more attuned to less serious or moderate delinquency. However, according to Vold, Bernard, and Snipes (1998), Hirschi claimed that, had serious delinquency been included, it would have made the observed relationships even stronger. They (Vold, Bernard, and Snipes), however, balk at this notion, indicating that such an argument is valid only if the same causal processes are operating for both seriously delinquent youths and those who are essentially non-delinquent, which they conclude is not a defensible position.

There does seem to be some general level of agreement in the literature that social control theory may be more appropriate for explaining minor to moderate rather than serious forms of delinquent conduct. Kempf (1993) provides eight pieces of "advice from the literature" in regard to the future of social control theory, two of which relate directly to the issue at hand: serious crime must be included and crime-specific models must be developed. Whether the fact that social control theory is best at explaining less serious delinquency is most appropriately characterized as a criticism or more simply as an observed aspect of the theory is a topic for further debate. Such a criticism, and the accompanying recommendations, raises some questions about what theories ought to do, what any individual theory is actually capable of doing, and whether it is fair or appropriate to criticize a theory until these questions have been addressed fully. However, delving further into these issues here would take us too far from our focus.

Association with Delinquent Peers

An area of criticism that may be more threatening to the core validity of social control theory than the issue of trivial offenses relates to the impact of delinquent peers. As noted at the beginning of the Critique section, Hirschi was concerned with assessing social control theory as an alternative explanation to strain and social learning theories. He also acknowledges that modern versions of social control theory followed the oppositional development pattern by "simultaneously attacking strain and cultural deviance approaches while affirming its own sharply different view of the world" (Hirschi 1989, 37). This point is relevant here as, when such an oppositional framework is followed, evidence supporting one of the opposing theories, by definition, challenges the validity of the "new" theory.[8]

Scarpitti and Nielsen conclude that there has been "somewhat mixed support" overall for social control theory, but they note specifically that "hypotheses regarding

---

[7]Agnew (1993) found moderate relationships with more serious forms of delinquency, but reports that these relationships are mediated by social learning and strain variables.

[8]There has perhaps been some confusion about Hirschi's actual position on oppositional theory development. To clarify, he states that he believes "it to be the best way to proceed. . . . The oppositional approach has problems, but they are in my view outweighed by its virtues" (T. Hirschi, personal communication, May 22, 2006).

the role of peers in offending have particularly been criticized" (1999, 238). This observation finds support in numerous studies. In fact, even Hirschi's own research raised some questions about the role of peers from the beginning. Although he did find that, generally, weaker bonds are associated with higher delinquency, he also found that delinquents exhibited attachments to delinquent peers and that delinquency was most strongly related to having delinquent peers (Williams and McShane 2004, Akers and Sellers 2004). An additional finding was that attachments to parents and delinquent peers were independently related to delinquency, which Shoemaker (2005) interprets as being supportive of both social control and differential association theories.

In his comparative test of social control and differential association, Matsueda (1982) found that the effect of social control measures and delinquency of friends was entirely mediated by measures of definitions favorable to violations of the law. This led to the conclusion that differential association theory is supported over social control. In another test of social control theory, using path analysis, it was found that Hirschi's proposition about the link between attachment and delinquency is supported only when delinquent companions is included. The study identified consistently strong associations between delinquent acts and delinquent companions, even after social control variables were controlled for. The authors concluded, as had Matsueda, that their findings were more supportive of differential association than social control (Thompson, Mitchell, and Dodder 1984). A number of other researchers note problems with Hirschi's views on the role of delinquent peers (see, e.g., Hindelang 1973, Empey 1978, Krohn and Massey 1980, and Agnew 1993).

Other Areas of Critique

Before offering a final general assessment of social control theory, a few additional areas of criticism warrant mention. Williams and McShane (2004) offer an astute observation relating to social control theory (Hirschi's and other versions as well) being "methodologically bound" (see also Vold, Bernard, and Snipes 1998). From reviewing the various cases in the literature, it is often the case that studies with supportive results use self-report as the primary or only method of data collection, and studies that yielded non-supportive results were more likely to use methods other than self-report. (This criticism relates back to some of the areas discussed previously as well.) Picking up on this same theme, Kempf (1993) suggests that data appropriate for testing social control can be gathered using more than one method, and that the data must include multiple dimensions of each element of bond.

One final area that has drawn critical attention relates to the conceptualization (and also operationalization) of the elements of social bond. Generally, some (e.g., Agnew, 1985) identify the need for more refined and complete indicators of the constructs. In addition, more element-specific concerns have been raised. For instance, it has been noted that commitment and involvement are difficult to differentiate. Involvement actually appears to simply be the behavioral side of commitment, which makes these two aspects of the same thing, rather than distinct elements (Gibbons 1994). Although concerns are noted about all elements, the bulk of attention seems to be directed at attachment. Kempf (1993) cites a number of researchers (see Kempf 1993, 163) who call attention to the need for refinements in the sources of attachment. Wilson and Herrnstein (1985) go even further, indicating that *attachment* is not the appropriate term/concept to describe Hirschi's measure of parent–child relations. They state that actually "two fairly different things" are being assessed—one is the extent to which a person is concerned about approval from others, and the second is the extent to which others actually reward or punish the behavior. Given this, they conclude that Hirschi's approach can be assimilated into their "general behavioral model." From our reading of Hirschi's original presentation of attachment, we can see where some of the confusion may come from and also how Wilson and Herrnstein may have arrived at their conclusion. Hirschi variously refers to *attachment* as if it is primarily an external element (see the discussion of attachment under Key Ideas) and also as an internal/emotional element. It seems that in his concern with measuring the element of bond "empirically," he may have collapsed all of the aspects of a complex concept into only the most readily observable components (i.e., the conceptual and operational definitions are somewhat out of sync). There are likely ways to resolve this kind of conceptualization (and operationalization) issue, but that discussion is beyond the scope of this analysis. Also, this issue will be revisited, somewhat, in the coverage of *A General Theory of Crime* (Hirschi, Part II).

General Critical Conclusions

Shoemaker (2005) offers a rather positive assessment of the validity and viability of control theories generally, and of Hirschi's social control theory more specifically, concluding that there is "much empirical support." He acknowledges that many of the questions relating to control theories are yet to be answered, but observes,

> the research conducted thus far suggests that control theories are supported and worthy of continued investigation. This conclusion is particularly valid for the proposition that attachments and commitments to conventional institutions in society (the social bond) are associated with low rates of delinquency. (2005, 197–98)

Akers and Sellers (2004) also are positive, if somewhat less enthusiastic, in their general assessment. They indicate that "[O]n the whole, social bonding theory has received some verification from empirical research," but they go on to note that the associations found have tended to be moderate to low, and sometimes in the opposite direction of that predicted by the theory.

Some other researchers are less committed in their assessments, stating, or at least intimating, that the results of empirical tests of social control theory are mixed (see, e.g., Clinard and Meier 1985, Scarpitti and Nielsen 1999, Williams and McShane 2004). Still others have come to a more firm and negative conclusion. After their test of social control theory, Thompson, Mitchell, and Dodder (1984) conclude that their data "clearly do not support Hirschi's theory," and from his research, Agnew (1985) arrives at the conclusion that the importance of Hirschi's theory was "exaggerated." In a later statement, based on their review of the existing evidence, Vold, Bernard, and Snipes (1998) are quite to the point, stating,

> A number of criminologists have concluded that social control theories in general and Hirschi's social control theory in particular, is supported by empirical research. That conclusion, however, does not seem warranted either by general research on human behavior or by specifically criminological research focusing on the explanation of criminal and delinquent behavior. A more restricted but better-supported assessment is that social control theories are generally supported by one type of data—self report surveys—and that

they provide a good explanation of one type of crime, the less serious forms of juvenile delinquency. However, they are not as yet supported by studies that focus on more serious delinquency or on adult criminality. (1998, 217–18)

Kempf (1993) lists three criteria by which we may judge a theory of crime:

1. The subjective standard, which is the degree to which people agree with the theory
2. Its relevance to policy and its ability to effect program change
3. The scientific merits

Kempf concludes that social control has done reasonably well on the first two. It has been one of the "most heralded" theories of delinquency among the community of theorists. Also, it has been widely applied to policy and programs. However, Kempf cautions that policy decisions often "reflect feasibility and ease of program administration as much as they consider theoretical merits," and it is actually the latter, scientific merit, on which criminology should evaluate its theories. "By this important measure of scientific merit, social control theory has not fared well" (1993, 167). She concludes her review by stating:

Although the large number of studies reviewed should have proved otherwise, it is disheartening to conclude that Cohen was correct in asserting that Hirschi's theory of social control may be fertile but is not yet fecund. Criminology has done this theory a disservice. (1993, 173)

At this point, the logical question is, "Where does this leave us in regard to the validity of social control theory?" Before we attempt to answer this question, it is useful to look more carefully at what we are asking and whether what we are asking is actually the most viable question. It may be that (a big) part of the difficulty encountered when trying to assess the validity of any theory is that the question is often framed as an absolute (e.g., Is it valid or not? Is it more [or less] valid than some other theory?). Perhaps, in assessing any theory, we should not begin from a position of determining absolute rightness or wrongness, but more from a position of looking for the truth(s) offered from that theory. Instead of asking which theory is right and which is wrong, we begin from the assumption that each is true, but partial. The task then becomes not accepting the true and rejecting the untrue, but figuring out how to fit the partial truths together and how to integrate them. With such an approach, we can criticize the partiality of theories while still acknowledging and even honoring their basic truths; we are criticizing not so much the theory (or the theorist, which also often happens), but more its partial nature. (These ideas are adapted from Wilber 2000; see also Crittenden 1997.)

It would seem that some general comments about integration are now in order. Its proponents state that the purpose of integration (see, e.g., Liska, Krohn, and Messner 1989) is to improve explanatory power by combining the various partial truths of different theories while avoiding the decidedly destructive and, for the most part, counterproductive competitive approach. Of relevance here, however, is the fact that Hirschi (1989) himself has been quite clear and direct in his opposition to theory integration (see also Gottfredson and Hirschi 1990).

Therefore, if we adopt Hirschi's view, it seems that the preponderance of the evidence does not come down strongly on the side of social control theory; it is of questionable validity. However, if we adopt a more integrative view, social control theory provides some valuable truths and holds the potential for contributing to our overall understanding of delinquency, and possibly adult criminality as well. In this case, as with so many things, it seems that what we see depends greatly on where we are standing when we look, and to see more, we must look more deeply.

IV. HIRSCHI, PART II: *A GENERAL THEORY OF CRIME*

INTRODUCTION

Williams and McShane characterize the state of theory in criminology during the 1980s as a "period of doubt" resulting from "the massive effort to test theory" (2004, 313). They liken the situation to Kuhn's (1962) notion of "crisis," in which a discipline lacks clarity about its mission and direction, and even its fundamental questions. Out of this period of uncertainty, a heterogeneous view of crime emerged, generating a relatively large number of theories and different dependent variables, as well as a plethora of "'minitheories' proposing to explain singular forms of crime" (1962, 313). However, in the midst of this movement to ever further compartmentalize crime into its constituent manifestations, some theorists (re)turned to the notion that a general theory of crime was not only possible, but required.

> Not all contemporary criminologists agree that crime is heterogeneous and that separate theories are required in order to account for the myriad forms of lawbreaking. The most detailed statement of an opposite position has been made by Gottfredson and Hirschi (1990, 16), who contend that "the vast majority of criminal acts are trivial and mundane affairs that result in little loss and less gain." Additionally, they argued that criminality has much in common with accidents and with other forms of deviant behavior. According to these theorists, criminals, deviants and persons who are prone to accidents all exhibit low self-control, which is the major cause of their behavior. (Gibbons 1994, 67, Note 1)

Hirschi, in collaboration with Michael Gottfredson, put forth the "general theory of crime" (1990) as an explanation for not only all varieties of crime, but for other forms of deviant behavior as well. The theory maintains that all crime and other analogous behaviors are the result of low self-control (combined with opportunity), and that differences in self-control explain individual differences in the "propensity" to either commit or refrain from such acts. With the general theory of crime, Hirschi moves away from the multidimensional and external control that characterizes his classic social bond theory. The new theory consists of only one kind of control—internal self-control. Social controls, now, are relevant in explaining criminal behavior only to the extent that they influence the internal control process (Vold, Bernard, and Snipes 1998). The quintessential statement of the theory was presented in the book *A General Theory of Crime* (Gottfredson and Hirschi 1990), but there were several earlier publications that laid the groundwork (Hirschi and Gottfredson 1983, 1986, 1989, Gottfredson and Hirschi 1988), and some subsequent works have elaborated and clarified aspects of the theory (Hirschi and Gottfredson 1993, 1994, 1995, 2000).

BASIC ASSUMPTIONS

As had Hirschi's earlier rendering of control theory, the general theory of crime rests on the basic assumptions that people are, by nature, self-interested, criminals have no special motives (Williams and McShane 2004), and that there is a value consensus in society. Also, as was discussed under the basic assumptions in Part I, great importance is placed on parenting/childrearing. We do not reiterate the discussion of the assumptions from Part I, but some additional information is offered concerning the role of parenting. In addition, another assumption that underlies general theory is discussed more specifically—that criminality is stable over the life course.

The Stability of Criminality (The Distinction between Criminality and Crime)

One of the central assumptions that underlies the general theory of crime is that individual differences in criminal and other forms of deviant behavior emerge early in childhood and remain stable and consistent across the life course. Hirschi and Gottfredson quite explicitly state that "a fundamental assumption of control theory is that relative differences in the tendency to deviant behavior are stable over the life course" (2000, 58). This assumption rests on the core observation that crime and criminality are not the same thing. Laub and Hirschi identify the recognition of this distinction as "a key item in the development of self-control theory," which evolved out of "the age-invariance argument" (2002, 187).

In *A General Theory of Crime,* Gottfredson and Hirschi state:

> Individual differences in the tendency to commit criminal acts . . . remain reasonably stable with change in the social location of individuals and change in their knowledge of the operation of sanction systems. This is the problem of self-control, the differential tendency of people to avoid criminal acts whatever the circumstances in which they find themselves. (1990, 87; emphasis in original)

Gottfredson and Hirschi describe people who are more prone to commit criminal and other deviant acts as tending to be "impulsive, insensitive, physical (as opposed to mental), risk taking, short-sighted, and non-verbal" (1990, 90). These characteristics contribute to criminal behavior, in that they limit or reduce a person's ability to calculate the consequences of their actions. They further note,

> [S]ince these traits can be identified prior to the age of responsibility for crime, since there is considerable tendency for these traits to come together in the same people, and since the traits tend to persist through life, it seems reasonable to consider them as comprising a stable construct useful in the explanation of crime. (1990, 90–91)

This stable construct is what they refer to as "low self-control," which they claim can account for both the consistency of crime over time and the relationships among criminal acts and other forms of deviance. The general theory of crime proposes that temporal continuity in deviant behavior results from

> population heterogeneity in an underlying propensity for crime that is established early in life and remains stable over time. From this viewpoint,

the varied outcomes correlated with childhood antisocial behavior are all expressions of the same underlying trait or propensity. (Sampson and Laub 1993, 136)

This view has been referred to as *heterotypic continuity,* which promotes the position that childhood misbehaviors are connected to transgressions during adulthood, across "life domains that go well beyond the legal concept of crime" (Sampson and Laub 1993, 123).[9] More simply put, the general theory of crime posits that there are individual differences across people that are developed early in life and account for differential involvement in criminal and other kinds of deviant behavior throughout the persons' lives. These behavioral differences are very stable and consistent; those who are more prone to deviance/delinquency when young remain more prone to deviance/criminal behavior when older, despite general changes in the frequency of such behaviors associated with age.

One final issue that needs to be addressed before moving on to the next assumption is how the stability assumption relates to the distinction between criminality and crime. Hirschi and Gottfredson dispute the prominent claims in the literature that because delinquency declines over time, it is therefore unstable.

> The literature on maturational reform typically focuses on the decline in crime among those with high rates ("delinquents") and ignores a possibly similar decline in crime among those with low rates ("nondelinquents"). This oversight leads to the suggestion that delinquents tend over time to become nondelinquents, that the two groups, if they do not actually trade places, are at least eventually intermingled. This leads, as we have seen, to the conclusion that delinquency is unstable over time, and that it therefore cannot be explained by characteristics of persons that are stable over time. (2002/1986, 189)

They go on to state that the data, in fact, indicate that delinquency is "relatively stable over time, and it is reasonably stable during the years of decline in the crime rate" (2002/1986, 189). They conclude that one concept cannot account for both crime declining and delinquency remaining stable, and suggest that two concepts are required; they propose "crime" and "criminality."

> Crimes are short term, circumscribed events that presuppose a peculiar set of necessary conditions (e.g., activity, opportunity, adversaries, victims, goods). Criminality, in contrast, refers to stable differences across individuals in the propensity to commit criminal (or equivalent) acts. Accordingly, criminality is only one element in the causal configuration leading to criminal acts, and criminal acts are, at best, imperfect measures of criminality. It follows that the frequency with which individuals participate in criminal events may vary over time and place without implying change in their criminality. It follows further that differences in propensity within groups may remain in the face of change in the group's overall rate of crime. Finally, it follows that

---

[9]Sampson and Laub (1993) note that the more typical focus of criminological research has been *homotypic continuity*, which refers to "the continuity of similar behaviors or phenotypic attributes" across time.

criminality can exist without crime (both before it begins and after it ends). (2002/1986, 190)[10]

THE IMPORTANCE OF PARENTING/FAMILY (REDUX)

Gibbons (1994), in a discussion of the origins and development of criminal acts and careers, states that Gottfredson and Hirschi's (1990) low self-control explanation involves a "... core assumption that the past has largely determined the present."

He is highlighting the fact that the general theory of crime, as also was the case in social control theory, places central importance on parenting and family in the etiology of criminality. Earlier, it was noted that Hirschi concludes, in looking at the factors that most influence social bond, that family/childrearing has a consistent and stable impact on the likelihood of crime/delinquency, which is established as early as ages 6 to 8. Because of the early onset and the consistency, he further determined that the differences in likelihood must be attributable to experiences in the family. This foundational aspect of his theorizing carried over into the general theory, despite the shift in focus from external to internal control.

Earlier, the characteristics that Gottfredson and Hirschi (1990) use to describe those prone to criminal/deviant behavior ("impulsive, insensitive, physical [as opposed to mental], risk taking, short-sighted, and non-verbal" [1990, 90–91]) were introduced. These traits contribute to low self-control and thereby criminality, and as noted, they develop early and persist throughout life. Gottfredson and Hirschi attribute the development of these traits (i.e., low self-control/criminality) primarily to childrearing practices in the family; "[T]he major 'cause' of low self-control thus appears to be ineffective child rearing" (1990, 97). They continue:

> One thing is, however clear: low self-control is not produced by training, tutelage, or socialization. As a matter of fact, all of the characteristics associated with low self-control tend to show themselves in the absence of nurturance, discipline, or training. (1990, 94–95)

Low self-control results from family situations characterized by parents who fail to observe or recognize "deviant tendencies" in their children, and who also fall short in administering appropriate punishments (Gibbons 1994). "The disposition towards low self control arises from failures in supervision, discipline, and informal control in the family during the child's first eight years of life" (Brannigan 1997, 403).

Effective childrearing, however, is exemplified by adequate monitoring of the child's behavior, immediate recognition of deviant behavior, and appropriate and consistent punishment of misbehavior (Gottfredson and Hirschi 1990). Consistently and

---

[10]Without getting into a lengthy discussion, it seems that Hirschi and Gottfredson are observing that our typical approaches tend to confuse interior elements with or collapse them into exterior elements (i.e., equate the interior, intentional elements that help account for behavior simply with the occurrence or lack thereof of that behavior). The general and consistent tendency to do this is what some have referred to as

> the disaster of modernity, the disaster that was the "disenchantment of the world" (Weber), the "colonization of the value spheres by science" (Habermas), the "dawn of the wasteland" (T.S. Eliot), the birth of "one-dimensional man" (Marcuse), the "desacralization of the world" (Schuon), the "disqualified universe" (Mumford). (Wilber 1998, 76)

Although the conceptualization of this issue as expressed by Wilber (and others) certainly does not match up with the way Gottfredson and Hirschi ultimately pursue the issue, it is nonetheless an interesting take on what we see as the same basic concern. For more discussion of this view, see Wilber (1998, 2000).

appropriately applied external controls are eventually internalized by the child (i.e., socialization) (Vold, Bernard, and Snipes 1998), manifesting as high self-control/low criminality. In addition, "Gottfredson and Hirschi (1990) consider parental investment a cardinal element. Without it, it is unlikely that the components of parental management for the development of self-control will develop" (Gibbs, Giever, and Martin 1998, 43).

SUMMARY

The basic assumptions underlying the general theory of crime are the same as those that undergird Hirschi's social control theory, with two additions. An assumption relating explicitly to the stability of criminality (as an internal trait or characteristic) has been included. This was added primarily to account for the facts that, although involvement in deviant/criminal behavior changes over time, the relative propensities[11] across different individuals remain constant. Second, the role of childrearing has been retained, but with the emphasis shifted from establishing social bonds to affecting self-control. In addition, the importance or centrality of childrearing may have been intensified.

KEY IDEAS

Laub (2002, xxix–xxx) identifies seven "key ideas that are central to the general theory that distinguish it from early control theories, such as Causes":

1. The relationship between age and crime is invariant
2. The importance of distinguishing crime and criminality
3. Self-control is the locus of individual differences in tendencies to commit crime
4. Variations in self-control explain both crime and also analogous non-criminal acts (e.g., drinking, gambling, sexual promiscuity)
5. Differences in childrearing practices are the primary source for variation in self-control
6. Crime and deviance are stable over time
7. For everyone, crime declines with age

These key ideas clearly overlap in many respects. In addition, we have already covered various aspects of several of these key ideas under the "Basic Assumptions" of the stability of criminality and the importance of parenting. For ease of presentation and conciseness, the discussion of (the remaining) key ideas is condensed and combined into three more general areas: self-control, the generality of crime, and age and crime.

Self-Control
Self-control is the central concept around which the general theory of crime revolves and that provides the anchor for all of the key ideas. Given the foundational nature of this concept, much has already been said about it, especially low self-control. This section, although trying not to be too redundant, presents some additional points related to the role of self-control, and ends with a general summary of the concept as it relates to the general theory of crime.

Hirschi (cited in Laub 2002, xxxii) says that, in the general theory, self-control is conceptualized as "an attempt to understand the common element in a wide range of

---

[11]It should be noted that the use of the term *propensities* is not meant to imply that Gottfredson and Hirschi proposed anything resembling "an enduring criminal predisposition" that requires criminal conduct (see Hirschi and Gottfredson 1993, 49, for a full discussion of this issue).

behaviors." It is also the concept adopted to account for stable individual differences in criminal behavior, a decision that Gottfredson and Hirschi (1990) say they arrived at after considering many alternative explanations. Low self-control was used to

> describe the enduring "criminality" or "criminal propensity" that increases the likelihood that individuals will be unable to resist easy, immediate gratification that crime and analogous behaviors seductively, and almost ubiquitously, present in everyday life. (Pratt and Cullen 2000, 932)

Low self-control differentiates criminals/deviants from non-criminal/non-deviants, starting in childhood and extending across the life course. "Stability lies at the heart of the concept of self-control, and justifies our emphasis on early socialization" (Hirschi and Gottfredson 2000, 58–59). As noted previously, the primary factor in the development of self-control (either low or high) is childrearing, and once the level of self-control has been established, it remains relatively stable over the course of a person's life (Gottfredson and Hirschi 1990).

So, parsimoniously put, from Gottfredson and Hirschi's (1990) perspective, the problem of crime is a problem of low self-control. More specifically, there are certain "traits" associated with low self-control that affect one's ability to calculate the consequences of an act (Williams and McShane 2004). The "common element" that self-control represents in decision making (see previous) is, in essence, long-term cost (Hirschi, cited in Laub 2002). If one cannot accurately anticipate such costs, an important element of control on (many forms of) behavior is lost or severely limited.

As far as competing explanations of criminality, general theory "is quite clear about the probable relevance of a number of other key life experiences to delinquency and misconduct—the school, delinquent friends, drugs, and criminal justice interventions" (Brannigan 1997, 406). Gottfredson and Hirschi (1990, see especially chapter 7, "The Social Consequences of Low Self-Control") assert that many of the previously identified relationships between delinquency/criminality and factors like peers and school can actually be explained via low self-control. In addressing the findings on peer groups, they note that children with low self-control tend to avoid situations that require discipline, supervision, or other forms of constraint (e.g., school, work), and therefore "gravitate to 'the street' or, at least in adolescence, to the same-sex peer group" (1990, 157). Also, because of their characteristics, these children find it difficult to establish solid friendship bonds.

> Put another way, adventuresome and reckless children who have difficulty making and keeping friends tend to end up in the company of one another, creating groups made up of individuals who tend to lack self-control. The individuals in such groups will tend to be delinquent, as will the group itself. (Gottfredson and Hirschi 1990, 158)

Contrary to popular social learning views, they are not learning a lack of self-control from each other, but are forced together because of an already existing low level of self-control.

The purported etiological relationship between school and delinquency, Gottfredson and Hirschi (1990) note, has been based on the findings that offenders do not do well in school. The interpretation from both strain and labeling perspectives has been that this failure in school creates strain or frustration that may result in a deviant adaptation, or it sets up a self-fulfilling prophecy of deviance. Gottfredson and Hirschi, however, see the correlations between school performance and delinquency as resulting from individuals with low self-control not being able to function well in "the school's systems of rewards and restraints." They do not do well because they cannot adjust to the situation, and they cannot adjust because of their low self-control.

Another aspect that has not yet been fully addressed is the "elements of self control." The characteristics or traits that describe people with low self-control are discussed earlier in this chapter. Gottfredson and Hirschi (1990) also describe corresponding characteristics of criminal acts that match up with the characteristics of criminality. Criminal acts provide "easy or simple" and "immediate gratification." They are "exciting, risky, or thrilling." Such acts provide for "few or meager long-term benefits," require "little skill or planning," and "often result in pain or discomfort for the victim." These event/opportunity characteristics match up well with the traits that depict low self-control, in that such individuals tend to "respond to tangible stimuli in the immediate environment"; "lack diligence, tenacity, or persistence"; "be adventuresome, active and physical"; "be little interested in and unprepared for long-term occupational pursuits"; "have lower levels of and place less value on cognitive or academic skills"; and, "be self-centered, indifferent or insensitive to the suffering and needs of others" (1990, 89).

The last issue addressed here is the link between low self-control and crime. The relationship postulated by Gottfredson and Hirschi is "non-deterministic"; low self-control does not always bring about crime (Tittle, Ward, and Grasmick 2003).

> Our image of the "offender" suggests that crime is not an automatic or necessary consequence of low self-control. It suggests that many noncriminal acts analogous of crime (such as accidents, smoking, and alcohol use) are also manifestations of low self-control. Our image therefore implies that no specific act, type of crime, or form of deviance is uniquely required by the absence of self-control. (Gottfredson and Hirschi, 1990, 91)

Low self-control can and does lead to a wide range of behaviors (see the following discussion concerning generality of deviance), many of which may be deviant, but only one form of which is criminal behavior. The result is crime only when the appropriate opportunities are present and other factors to potentially counteract such behavior are not (Akers and Sellers 2004). From the perspective of the theory, there are limitless opportunities to commit one or another form of crime or analogous behavior. However, the opportunities to commit a particular crime may be much more seriously restricted. "Self-control and opportunity may therefore interact for specific crimes, but are in the general case independent" (Hirschi and Gottfredson 1993, 50).

SUMMARY

The level of self-control that a person develops is the direct result of childrearing, and once established early in life, that level remains relatively unchanged across the life course. Crime and analogous behaviors both are manifestations of low self-control; consequently, individuals with low self-control engage in such behaviors at higher rates than do those with high self-control, and these individual differences remain stable and consistent over time. In addition, there is a generality of involvement in deviant behavior and versatility in criminal behavior. (The latter two points are discussed in the following sections.)

THE GENERALITY OF DEVIANCE

"Ignoring the nature of crime, traditional theories of crime inevitably must also ignore the generality of deviance and must, in Gottfredson and Hirschi's view, create unnecessarily complex explanations for why people are motivated to commit crime" (Pratt and Cullen 2000, 931). As alluded to at the outset of this section, Gottfredson and Hirschi (1990) set out to provide a parsimonious and broad-ranging explanation, not so much simply of crime, but that encompassed crime.

> The theory, simply stated, is this: Criminal acts are a subset of acts in which the actor ignores the long-term negative consequences that flow from the act itself (e.g., the health consequences of drug use), from the social or familial environment (e.g., a spouse's reaction to infidelity), or from the state (e.g., the criminal justice response to robbery). All acts that share this feature, including criminal acts, are therefore likely to be engaged in by individuals unusually sensitive to immediate pleasure and insensitive to long-term consequences. . . . It also suggests, consistent with the idea of self-control, that individuals will tend to engage in (or avoid) a wide variety of criminal and analogous behaviors—that they will not specialize in some to the exclusion of others, nor will they "escalate" into more serious or skillful criminal behavior over time. (Hirschi and Gottfredson 2002/1994, 204)

Self-control is not, as noted previously, a personality trait that compels criminal or other acts; rather, it "is an orientation that shapes choice" across situations. When the opportunity presents itself, individuals with low self-control more likely opt for immediate gratification, whereas the behavior of those who have developed sufficient self-control are shaped by the anticipated long-term consequences, both for themselves and others (Gibbs and Giever 1995, 248).

Hirschi and Gottfredson acknowledge that there is considerable evidence of the "existence of reliable differences among individuals in the tendency to commit deviant acts" (2002/1994, 205). They further note that such evidence necessitates that this "latent trait" to deviance be conceptualized in a certain way.

> For example, we cannot make it conducive to specialization in some deviant acts rather than others, because that would be contrary to its generality (we cannot easily conceptualize it as "internalization of norms," because that would suggest the possibility of internalizing some norms and not others, an idea contrary to the finding of generality). . . . Reasoning in this way, and from examination of the diverse acts produced by or consistent with this "latent trait," we concluded that it was best seen as self-control, the tendency to avoid acts whose long-term costs exceeds their momentary advantages. (2002/1994, 205)

Further support is offered for the role of self-control in the generality of deviance, as self-control is maintained not by legal or formal social sanctions, which are often missing from situations, but through the "natural consequences" almost always present.

Hirschi and Gottfredson (2000) discuss the fact that control theories assume that people are free to follow their human nature by a lack of restraint. When this notion is translated into a specific theory, however, the restraints identified tend to be more general than the behavior they are invoked to explain. They note that few theorists have attempted to treat their dependent variable at the same level of abstraction as the independent variable. Building off of this observation, they state that in the general theory, "criminal and analogous behaviors" became "the conceptual equivalent of 'low self-control.'" (Although they do note that "the match is not perfect.") In other words, they were attempting to bring the dependent variable up to the same level of abstraction as the independent variable, especially in light of the widespread acceptance of the versatility hypothesis[12] of deviant/criminal behavior. "The variety of manifestations of low self-control is immense. In spite of years of tireless research motivated by a belief in specialization, no credible evidence of specialization has been reported. In fact, the evidence of offender versatility is overwhelming" (Gottfredson and Hirschi 1990, 91).

Some final points are in order concerning the generality of deviance idea. The first relates to the confusion revolving around the seriousness of criminal and other deviant acts. Such acts may differ greatly in terms of their relative seriousness and consequences for victims and offenders. The extreme variability in consequences and possible harm for others produces radically different responses, both in terms of formal/legal and less-formal/social sanctions. This clear and important distinction caused theorists to believe it necessary that our theories distinguish between trivial and serious acts. However, it is imperative that we differentiate between the consequences for others and the consequences for the offender; it is the consequences for the offender that are key in understanding the etiology of the act. Acts that generate long-term harm or risk for others and self are avoided by those with high self-control, whereas those with low self-control, because they do not attend to long-term consequences, are much more likely to engage in all such acts, trivial and serious. This is why increasing the penalties for criminal or other deviant acts has little or no effect on those most likely to commit them; they do not attend to the long-term consequences of their actions. "Because those with little concern for their own future will be even less concerned for the welfare of others, it seems to us we are on solid ground theoretically when we lump together acts that differ immensely in their consequences for victims" (Hirschi and Gottfredson 2002/1994, 217).

The final issue discussed here relates to the viability of a "general" approach. Hirschi and Gottfredson note that

> the charge that a theory is "too general" is hard to evaluate absent a context of competing theory. When specified in the statement "robbery is not murder" (or, more telling, in the statement "accidents are not crimes!") this criticism implies that these are such different events that they must have different explanations. But this is tantamount to a critique of the germ theory of disease that asserts that diphtheria is not whooping cough. The theory that diseases are caused by infectious agents is even more general than the germ theory. Is it "too general" because it includes viruses as well as bacteria? Obviously, a general theory is not damaged by the charge of excess generality. (2002/1994, 209)

It is not the assertion of a general theory that the events or phenomena they explain are identical, but rather that, within the domain of explained events, there are

---

[12]The *versatility hypothesis* refers simply to the observation that offenders do not tend to specialize in one or even a small set of criminal activities, but perform a wide range of criminal acts.

some identifiable commonalities. In other words, the general theory asserts that robbery and murder do have something(s) in common, which explains why they are more
likely to be committed by the same people. However, if it could be demonstrated that
it is more common for non-robbers than robbers to commit murder, this still does not
necessarily imply that the theory is too general, but denotes that it is incorrect (Hirschi
and Gottfredson 2002/1994).

AGE AND CRIME

In their 1983 article "Age and the Explanation of Crime," Hirschi and Gottfredson
first presented their view that the impact of age on crime and analogous behaviors is
invariant across cultural and social conditions and applies to all demographic groups.
The age–crime relationship, which has now been very widely discussed, shows that
crime increases strongly with age until the mid-to-late teen years, and then begins to
decline somewhat precipitously and consistently throughout the rest of the life
course. From their original age–crime hypothesis, they then derived others: the relationship could not be accounted for by any variables (or combination thereof) that
were available at that time; "the conceptual apparatus" that had been built around the
age effect findings was "almost certainly redundant or misleading"; and causes of
crime identified at one age may be appropriate for explaining crime at other ages
(Hirschi and Gottfredson 2002/1995, 241–42). In short, their observations about the
age–crime relationship became one of the cornerstones of the general theory, because
both

> stability and versatility effects can be derived from it. It gives new light to
> efforts to find diverse causes for crimes over the life course. It enables a gen-
> eral theory by showing that diverse acts spread over the life course must have
> common causes. It has profound consequences for research design, casting
> doubt on the utility and efficiency of longitudinal research, and showing the
> advantages of large-scale cross-sectional work focusing on the early years of
> life. It has equally significant implications for social policy, suggesting the lim-
> itations of deterrence, incapacitation, and rehabilitation as crime-control
> devices. (Hirschi and Gottfredson 2002/1994, 213–14)

The variable that they saw accounting for the age–crime relationship is self-control.

> The distinction between crime and self-control thus provides a device for
> solving one of the major empirical dilemmas of criminology: the fact that
> crime everywhere declines with age while differences in "crime" tendency
> across individuals remain relatively stable over the life course. Once this
> distinction between propensities and events has been made, it is hard to
> return to crime theories that operate without it. (Gottfredson and Hirschi
> 1990, 144)

CRITIQUE

Pratt and Cullen note that the general theory of crime "has been the focus of considerable academic attention and considerable controversy" (2000, 931). They further note
that *A General Theory of Crime* was the second-most cited of all criminology books

during the 1990s. Brannigan (1997) also recognized the significant impact of Gottfredson and Hirsch's (1990) work when he stated

> Over the past 15 years, we have witnessed a renaissance in control theories with tremendous implications for criminological research, methods, and policy. . . . At the center of the debate is a volume as important to our generation as Lombroso's *Criminal Man* was to his: Gottfredson and Hirschi's *A General Theory of Crime.* (1997, 404)

As might be expected from these observations, there has been a considerable quantity of research done assessing the validity of the general theory, and there has been a tremendous amount written both in support and also critical of the theory. The following critique focuses on four main areas of question and criticism: claims that the general theory is tautological; issues relating to life course/stability aspects; the role of childrearing; and issues relating to self-control itself. The general format is to first outline the criticism(s) and then describe the responses to that criticism. Given the scope and purposes here, the coverage is generally brief, touching only on the central elements in each area.

TAUTOLOGY

Generally defined, a *tautology* is the repetition of the same claim or point using different words, or in a more empirical sense, it is supporting an idea or hypothesis with that same idea or hypothesis stated differently. In 1991, Akers first criticizes the general theory of crime on the grounds that it is tautological. He notes that the hypothesis that low self-control causes the propensity toward criminal behavior is questionable (and actually tautological) because Gottfredson and Hirschi do not define *self-control* separately from *propensity.* In other words, he claims that they define self-control by the same thing that they say it causes; *self-control* and the *propensity to commit crime* are defined in the same way operationally, as observed criminal behavior. Akers has not relented in this criticism. He states that the "problem of tautology with self-control theory . . . has yet to be resolved" (Akers and Sellers 2004, 124).

In response to this criticism (which Vold, Bernard, and Snipes 1998 refer to as the "most sweeping criticism" of the general theory), Hirschi and Gottfredson recognize that Akers is still "convinced of its importance," and they "continue to disagree with his assessment" (2000, 56–57). Hirschi and Gottfredson (2000) identify two general forms of tautology: logical and empirical. In an earlier rejoinder to Akers's critique, Hirschi and Gottfredson adopted what might be considered a rather unusual position. Their following response is directed more at the charge of logical tautology:

> In our view, the charge of tautology is in fact a compliment; an assertion that we followed the path of logic in producing an internally consistent result. Indeed, that is what we set out to do. We started with a conception of crime, and from it attempted to derive a conception of the offender. . . . What makes our theory peculiarly vulnerable to complaints about tautology is that we explicitly show the logical connections between our conception of the actor and the act. (1993, 52)

They go on to indicate that they believe Akers's conceptualization of self-control is "fundamentally" different from theirs. Akers apparently sees self-control as a propensity to commit crime, whereas they do not recognize such a propensity at all. Self-control is not a "motivating force underlying criminal acts," but is instead a "barrier that stands between the actor and the obvious momentary benefits crime provides" (Hirschi and Gottfredson 1993, 53).

In terms of empirical tautology, they rather strongly note that "It has apparently escaped the attention of these critics that what they consider egregiously atheoretical or pointless and trivial tautologies are also known in the psychometric literature as tests of construct validity" (1993, 58).

Gibbs and Giever (1995), in addressing this same issue of empirical tautology, offer support for Hirschi and Gottfredson's position from the psychometric literature, citing that "the trait is reflected in or inextricably linked to the behavior" (Nunally 1978, 247). They do caution, however, that when measuring concepts like self-control with events, there is the potential problem of "vertical logic," which relates to the slippage or error attributable to the complexity of the link between the operational and conceptual definition.

Giving Akers (Akers and Sellers 2004) the final word—although he contends that "the tautology issue has still not been resolved," he recognizes that some research is moving in that direction by measuring self-control independently from crime propensity. We assume that he is referring to work such as that done by Tittle, Ward, and Grasmick (2003), in which it was found that cognitive measures of self-control predict crime/deviance as well as behavioral measures.

LIFE COURSE/STABILITY

Another aspect of the general theory that has garnered a fair amount of criticism is the claim that relative differences in the tendency to be involved in crime/deviance are stable across the life course. Some researchers have challenged this view, citing evidence that most delinquency is not "life-course-persistent" but is rather "adolescence-limited" (Moffitt 1993), and that most anti-social or delinquent children or adolescents do not ultimately become anti-social/criminal adults (Sampson and Laub 1993). This work is often referred to under the more general perspective of *multiple pathways*. Contrary to the claim that the path to adult offending is a clear and consistent one following from earlier deviance/delinquency, multiple pathways proposes that there are many separate ways or paths to offending. In other words, paths started in childhood do not necessarily lead to adult offending, and new deviant paths can be started in adulthood.

At the core of this disagreement is the observation that there are offenders who show themselves (as offenders) only at specific points in the life course. Prior to and after this particular time, the claim is that these offenders are not distinguishable from their non-offender counterparts. This, then, is offered as evidence that contradicts the invariant age distribution and stability aspects of general theory. Hirschi and Gottfredson (2000) have specifically responded to the multiple pathways criticism, stating that research that clearly locates these different and varied groups of offenders is hard to find. They do not profess much faith in the data that proclaim to have identified "late starters," noting that closer inspection likely shows that the late starters had either actually started much earlier or that they had never actually started at all. Although Hirschi and Gottfredson go into some detail on this issue and make reference to at least one study that seems to be supportive of their position, they do not provide any clear or definitive data of their own to dispute the multiple pathways data.

PARENTING/CHILDREARING

Surprisingly, given its foundational position, there does not seem to have been a lot of critical questioning surrounding the impact of childrearing as portrayed in the general theory. Having reviewed the literature (up to that point in time), Vold, Bernard, and Snipes (1998) concluded that none of the tests of the theory had actually examined the link between childrearing and low self-control. This lack of empirical scrutiny exists despite the highly controversial claim (at least as Vold, Bernard, and Snipes see it) that childrearing determines self-control, which is established and stable by age 8 or so. Vold, Bernard, and Snipes go on to state that a general assessment of the validity of the theory is not possible until this component of the theory is tested thoroughly.

An article published in that same year (Gibbs, Giever, and Martin 1998) also highlighted the dearth of data on this important component of the general theory, identifying only one study to date that had examined (and supported) this central proposition. One of the main purposes of the study reported by Gibbs, Giever, and Martin was to assess the relationship between childrearing and self-control directly. The basic finding (using path analysis) was that parental management has an impact on deviance, but the impact is mediated through self-control, which has a direct impact.

The other research that seems to relate, at least somewhat, to questions concerning the purported relationship between childrearing and self-control is that of Sampson and Laub (1993). Although they were looking more broadly at issues of stability, they made some observations that seem applicable here. They found that structural factors, such as poverty, are non-significant predictors of delinquency when included in models with variables relating to parental discipline, supervision, and so on. The macro variables predict parental effectiveness, however, indicating that structural influences are mediated by parenting factors, which they, in turn, have influenced. This finding, although it is somewhat supportive of childrearing as an influence on delinquency, does not seem to indicate the level or type of influence postulated in the general theory. In addition, Sampson and Laub assess the impact of family social variables on adult crime. The results of this analysis raise further questions about the link between childrearing and self-control (i.e., stable criminal/deviant behavior). They empirically addressed,

> whether family social control factors have a direct effect on adult crime or whether they are mediated by delinquency. . . . The answer . . . could not be any clearer. For both the delinquent and the control group samples, unofficial delinquency up to age 14 has significant positive effects on arrest at ages 17–25, 25–32, and 32–45. On the other hand, family and individual–difference constructs have, for all intents and purposes, no effect on adult crime. Indeed, 41 out of 42 coefficients reflecting the effects of seven family/individual factors on six adult crime outcomes are insignificant. (1993, 135)

It seems clear that this area requires considerably more research before final conclusions can be drawn.

GENERAL SUPPORT: THE RESEARCH ON SELF-CONTROL

In this section, the most fundamental empirical question pertaining to the general theory is addressed: "What role does low self-control play in crime and analogous behaviors?" Given the complexity of both the behaviors in question and also the explanatory concepts, it should not be surprising (although it may be somewhat dissatisfying) to find that the data are mixed. This is the consensus from almost everyone who has undertaken a general review of the literature, although the tone of the various presentations may be more or less positive or negative. However, although the data are mixed, there are some general conclusions that still can be drawn. There have been numerous studies using a range of methods and measures conducted to assess the general theory. Several solid reviews of the research on general theory have been published (see, e.g., Pratt and Cullen 2000, Curran and Renzetti 2001, Akers and Sellers 2004, Shoemaker 2005); therefore, the review presented here does not focus on the different and varied individual studies, but instead on the more general, aggregate conclusions that can be gleaned from them.

One of the most comprehensive empirical reviews has been that of Pratt and Cullen (2000), who conducted both a narrative review and a meta-analysis. A *narrative review* is summarizing the results of previous studies to assess the general level of support or lack thereof. From their narrative analysis, they concluded that, despite some problems and questions with various aspects of the theory, there is fairly consistent support for the proposed inverse relationship between self-control and crime/analogous behaviors.

A *meta-analysis* is a statistical analysis of the analytic results of a large number of studies for the purpose of developing an integrated picture of the empirical findings in an area (Glass 1976).[13] Pratt and Cullen's meta-analysis consists of 21 empirical studies containing 126 effect estimates that represent 49,727 individual cases derived from 17 independent data sets. From their analysis, they concluded that "low self-control is an important predictor of crime and 'analogous behaviors,'" and these general effects hold up across samples (2000, 931). It is also rather dramatically pointed out that for the significant relationship conclusion to be reversed, it would require an additional 422 studies finding no relationship between "attitudinal" measures of self-control and crime. They temper their conclusions with observations that self-control does not predict as well in longitudinal studies, which is contrary to what Gottfredson and Hirschi's (1990) predicted, and variables from other theoretical approaches, such as social learning, still garner support in studies when measured along with self-control.

In their review, Akers and Sellers (2004) note that, across a wide range of studies both in the United States and other countries, self-control variables account for variance levels ranging from 3 percent to 20 percent in explaining crime and analogous behaviors. In addition, the relationship between measures of parental control and

---

[13]For more information on meta-analysis, the interested reader is referred to the Meta Analysis of Research Studies available at http://www.edres.org/meta/.

adolescent self-control tend to be weak or moderate. Finally, they report that when measures of definitions favorable to violation of the law and differential peer association are added, the amount of explained variance doubles. Tittle, Ward, and Grasmick (2003) also recognize that, while the reported associations are consistent, they tend to be "usually only modest." Shoemaker (2005, 277–78), citing a wide range of research, notes that while Gottfredson and Hirschi's "ideas may be on the cutting edge," a number of studies have raised "doubts and qualifications regarding the applicability of low self-control as a predictor of delinquency."

One specific issue that should be addressed relates to Hirschi and Gottfredson's (1993) strong contention that behavioral measures of self-control are most desirable and appropriate for testing the proposed relationship with crime and analogous behaviors. Several studies have raised serious questions about the viability of this contention. Tittle, Ward, and Grasmick (2003) found that behavioral measures yield no better prediction than do cognitive measures of self-control. They further note that, contrary to the theory and unlike "cognitive type indicators," many crime-analogous behaviors are not highly interrelated, which creates difficulties in developing reliable behavioral measures. Their findings indicate that the exclusive use of behavioral measures would not provide stronger support for self-control theory, which is again contrary to what Hirschi and Gottfredson claim. Gibbs, Giever, and Martin identify a similar issue, concluding that "the problem may lie in the scope of the definition of self-control at both the conceptual and empirical levels" (1998, 45). They further conclude that their findings that parental management has an indirect influence through self-control, which then has more direct impact, "points to the usefulness of an operational definition for self-control that goes beyond the behavior it is supposed to explain" (1998, 66). Other researchers/reviewers also raise issues related to the appropriateness and viability of relying on behavioral operational definitions of self-control (see Pratt and Cullen 2000, Akers and Sellers 2004). Finally, this discussion of how best to operationalize self-control has relevance to the issue raised earlier (see footnote 10) about inappropriately equating or confusing interior aspects with exterior elements.

In conclusion, regarding the issue of self-control itself, it seems clear from the research that there is a relationship between low self-control and crime/analogous behaviors. Pratt and Cullen state that, with some caveats, their meta-analysis "furnishes some fairly impressive empirical support for Gottfredson and Hirschi's theory." The effect size generally found, when compared with other predictors of criminal behavior, "would rank self-control as one of the strongest known correlates of crime" (2000, 951–52). However, as has also been pointed out (see Tittle, Ward, and Grasmick 2003, Gibbs, Giever, and Martin 1998), it seems likely that self-control is a more complex concept, with more depth, than Gottfredson and Hirschi recognize. Because of this, Tittle, Ward, and Grasmick, although acknowledging the limitations of their own research, concluded that their data

> suggest that the general failure of self-control measures to predict criminal behavior to the degree envisioned by its proponents is probably not mainly because of the use of cognitive type measures. Instead, it may be from the neglect of theoretical specifications of the contingencies under which self-control is likely to have more or less effect. (2003, 363)

The responses to such criticisms have generally taken the form of reiterating their position that their theory does not claim that self-control is the only cause of crime, and that their conceptualization of self-control does not require one-dimensional measures of crime/analogous acts (Hirschi and Gottfredson 1993).

> Some critics appear to believe that the theory posits an isomorphic relation between individual acts and low self-control. It does not. As is true for all behavioral theories, our theory assumes multiple causation and considerable measurement error. (Hirschi and Gottfredson 2000, 65)

ADDITIONAL AREAS OF CRITICISM

Pratt and Cullen note that "Gottfredson and Hirschi's paradigm has been criticized on logical, ideological, and conceptual grounds" (2000, 951). As might be expected for a theory that has received the amount of attention that the General Theory has, criticisms have taken other forms besides those discussed here. The scope of the coverage does not permit detailed review of the remaining areas of critique, but some brief identification is provided.

Andrews and Bonta (1998) question whether Gottfredson and Hirschi actually presented a new theory or simply repackage some old and well-established ideas from the psychological literature on crime. Although he does not necessarily paint it in a strongly negative light, Gibbons (1994) characterizes the General Theory as being "relatively discursive," which is not typically considered complimentary when referring to a theory.

The theory also has been somewhat widely criticized for being too broad or encompassing, trying to explain behaviors to which it just does not apply (see Akers 1991, Vold, Bernard, and Snipes 1998). Gibbons identifies this as the "major flaw" in the General Theory, and observes that "efforts to construct theoretical arguments that span virtually the entire spectrum of lawbreaking (e.g., Gottfredson and Hirschi, 1990) have not been markedly successful" (1994, 205). However, some (see, e.g., Williams 1999) see the generality and versatility aspects as major strengths of the theory.

Shoemaker (2005) and Brannigan (1997) explicitly identify as areas of concern and question the assumptions that age and gender differences are invariant. (For additional information on gender, see Jang and Krohn 1995, LaGrange and Silverman 1999, Nakhaie, Silverman, and LaGrange 2000; on age, see Bartusch, Lynam, Moffitt, and Silva 1997, Tittle and Grasmick, 1998, and Steffensmeier, Allan, Harer, and Streifel 1999.) Barlow (1991) and others (see Grasmick, Tittle, Bursik, and Arneklev 1993, and Polakowski 1994) question the posited relationships between self-control and opportunity. In addition, several references have already been made to the inability of self-control to subsume or wash out the influence of other causal elements, such as social learning variables.

CRITICAL CONCLUSION

Hirschi and Gottfredson begin their "Commentary" on the testing of their General Theory of Crime with the statement that "tests of theory are tests of the articulation of an idea and, if done properly, of the value of the idea itself" (1993, 47). In concluding this section, let us explore the overall verdict on the value of the idea that low self-control causes crime and analogous behaviors.

> In summary, although the general theory is not beyond criticism and qualifi-
> cation, the meta-analysis of the extant literature indicates that Gottfredson
> and Hirschi's core proposition that low self-control increases involvement in
> criminal and analogous behaviors is empirically supported. On the absolute
> level, therefore, it appears that low self-control must be considered an impor-
> tant predictor of criminal behavior and the general theory warrants a mea-
> sure of acceptance. On a relative level, it is unlikely that Gottfredson and
> Hirschi's perspective can claim the exalted status of being the general theory
> of crime. (Pratt and Cullen 2000, 953)

It also has been concluded that, in its current form, without further modification and development, perhaps the theory has garnered about as much support as is possible (Tittle, Ward, and Grasmick, 2003).

However, as Hirschi and Gottfredson so aptly recognize,

> Theories that challenge disciplinary perspectives should expect reciprocal
> challenge from disciplinary sources. . . . Theories that seek parsimony and
> large scope should expect challenge from those convinced of the complexity
> of the causes of human behavior. . . . And of course these days all theories
> may expect challenge from experts in the detection of ideology. (2000, 66).

FINAL REJOINDER

It seems only fair to give the authors of the theory one last word. Hirschi (2004) and Hirschi and Gottfredson (forthcoming) have tried again to respond to their critics. The level of coverage in these two works exceeds the available space here, but some of the highlights and general conclusions should be illuminating. (The interested reader is, of course, referred to the originals.)

Hirschi begins his response to the criticisms of *A General Theory of Crime* by noting,

> The central issues would appear to be the source and nature of stable individual
> differences in propensity and the common element in the large variety of delin-
> quent, deviant, and criminal acts. We (Gottfredson and Hirschi, 1990) have
> argued that the relevant individual level trait is best seen as self-control, and the
> commonality among the acts in question is that each provides immediate benefit
> at the risk of long-term pain. This combination of "maladaptive" act and trait
> has been recognized and much discussed by economists, philosophers, biologists,
> and psychologists. It has received little attention from sociologists, for the simple
> reason that its core assumptions are anathema to them. There is irony in this.
> Sociology claims criminology as a subfield, and the more prominent or popular
> theories of crime have their origins in that discipline. Thus, we have a discipline
> that is unable to recognize essential elements of crime and criminality telling us
> what we should think and do about them (e.g., Uggen, 2003). (2004, 537)

With this statement, Hirschi makes it clear that he (and presumably Gottfredson) generally see most of the criticisms that have been published of the *A General Theory of Crime* to be somewhat off base and off target. In the chapter from which this reaction comes ("Self-Control and Crime"), Hirschi elaborates extensively on the many ways in which these ill-conceived critiques have been manifested. He concludes that, overall, the theory that has been so laboriously and extensively tested actually may resemble the General Theory of Crime in terminology only. In other words, Hirshi claims that the theory tested by the critics is not actually the theory that he and Gottfredson presented.

However, not wishing to lay all the blame solely at the feet of the critics, Hirschi acknowledges some ways in which he and Gottfredson contributed to the difficulties attributed to their theory. Hirschi notes that the conceptualizations of and focus on the elements of self-control were an attempt (he says "in a moment of madness") to reverse the preferred theoretical practice of beginning with offenders and then inferring from them the nature of crime.

> Thus we discovered the Big Five (plus one), introduced language I did not understand, championed ideas contradicting our theory, and otherwise muddied the waters. But this state of affairs was not immediately recognized. On the contrary, our exercise was seen as a set of directions for constructing measures of self-control, and much research and analysis have flowed from it. . . . Fortunately, in this case at least, truth is indeed the daughter of time, and we can see the errors introduced by our excursion into psychology and by the measures of self-control stemming from it. (Hirschi 2004, 541–42)

Hirschi (2004) then goes on to identify four specific problems that result and discusses how they might be resolved, at least partially, by shifting the definition of self-control to the "tendency to consider the full range of potential costs of a particular act" (2004, 543; italics in original). This new definition, he claims, is consistent with how self-control was originally envisioned and highlights more clearly and directly that "self-control is the set of inhibitions one carries with one wherever one happens to go" (2004, 543). We leave to the reader further exploration of how Hirschi envisions that this newly stated definition helps clarify many of the empirical issues currently being generated by improper conceptualization and operationalization of self-control (2004, 545–49).

To summarize, the general tenor of these more recent responses (Hirschi 2004, Hirschi and Gottfredson, forthcoming) to the critics is to note that essentially the vast majority of the empirical tests of the theory have simply had it wrong. They have been testing not the General Theory proposed by Gottfredson and Hirschi (1990), but the version of the theory that the critics generated and then perpetuated.

THE CONNECTIONS BETWEEN SOCIAL CONTROL AND SELF-CONTROL

Before concluding this chapter, one more topic that warrants some discussion—the interconnections among the ideas presented in parts I and II. Claire Taylor (2001) observes that the exact nature of the connection between Hirschi's social and self-control theories is debated among scholars in the field. Given our coverage of both of Hirschi's monumental theoretical contributions, this should certainly come as no surprise; his work has, from the beginning, generated this kind of debate. For the purposes of the current discussion, we do not review the various specific points of similarity or departure outlined by Taylor in her review, but begin from her basic conclusion about the connection and then look at what Hirschi, himself, had to say about the matter. Taylor concludes:

> In spite of the connections between social and self-control theory, I believe that the inconsistencies between the two formulations of control, as set out by Hirschi (1969) and Gottfredson and Hirschi (1990) respectively, render them *theoretically incompatible* (p. 382). . . . My interpretation is that self-control theory *rejects important insights* from Hirschi's original formulation of social control and is therefore a less adequate explanation. (2001, 384; emphases added)

In discussing the connection between social control and self-control theories with John Laub (2002), Hirschi said that social control, as conceptualized in *Causes*, was intended to explain the age–crime curve or "maturational reform." However, after closer examination, it became apparent that age–crime changes were universal, and then the "justification for social control theory disappeared. Maturational reform is a problem only if it is differential. If it occurs at the same rate for everyone, it is not a problem." Laub inquired whether that then means that self-control theory "trumps" social control. To which Hirschi responded, yes, but only to the extent that the age curve is invariant. If it turns out that the age curve actually does show variation, then social control trumps self-control; "it is a purely empirical question. We are arguing today because we don't have adequate data." However, at some point, "[w]e should be able to say social control or self-control is right" (2002, xxxi).

In elaborating further on the differences between the two theoretical positions, Hirschi (in Laub 2002) notes that the contribution of self-control is not its disagreement with social control, but its enhancement of the substantive understanding of criminal activity. He says that being "an old positivist at the time," the mistake he made when formulating social control theory was to believe that dependent variables could and should be defined independently from the independent variables.

Laub (2002) relates Taylor's (2001) conclusion to the distinction between crime and criminality, indicating that this distinction, once made, makes the connection between social and self-control problematic. In response, Hirschi states that the "apparent discrepancy" can be resolved if social control is made a "species of opportunity." This way, you can have changes in behavior/crime without necessarily having a change in criminality; "social control deals with control of behavior without necessarily caring about criminal propensity—about self-control" (2002, xxxiii). If this observation is accurate, then the next big theoretical task for both versions of control theory is to develop more in-depth conceptual and operational definitions of opportunity (Laub 2002).

The final issue addressed in terms of the connections (or lack thereof) between social and self-control theories is the role of supervision, which Hirschi (in Laub 2002) identifies as one of the "big differences between Causes and *A General Theory*." (We note here that what Dr. Hirschi says next, at some level, may strike the reader as counterintuitive.) "In *Causes*, supervision is psychological, cognitive, something you carry with you. In *A General Theory*, it has become external, formal, actual" (2002, xxxiii–xxxvi).

> That is a fundamental difference between the two models. The Patterson, behavioral, watch and bonk idea of supervision found in *A General Theory* differs in important ways from the cognitive view of supervision found in

Causes. This may well be the place to look for reconciliation of the two perspectives—a place to force the issue . . . I'd say that the supervision described in *Causes* is nothing other than self-control. The child supervises himself. (2002, xxxiv)

A few comments on this somewhat perplexing observation by Hirschi seem to be in order. It appears that Hirschi's perspective on the real focus or core of self-control differs somewhat from many who have researched it. The main focus, especially of much of the confirmatory research, has been on the cognitive aspects of self-control. As was noted in the "Critique," the findings relating to cognitive measures of self-control are not consistent with Hirschi and Gottfredson's predictions. It seems that this may be an area in which some modification of self-control theory could or should be considered. It also brings up the question of whether what Hirschi was getting at in social control was actually more conceptually akin to what current researchers see as self-control. Finally, it remains to be seen whether we will in fact, as Hirschi says we should, "be able to say social control or self-control is right" (in Laub 2002, xxxi). Rather, it may ultimately be determined that the control approaches outlined in *Causes* and *A General Theory* are not really different, but are both parts of the same, more complex and deeper conceptualization of control, and that elements from both are essential for a full understanding.

CONCLUSION

It seems fitting to conclude this chapter with the same statement with which we started: "There can be no question that Travis Hirschi belongs in a work devoted to the pioneers of criminological thought." His contributions have been more than enough for two lifetimes. Despite the very lofty company he keeps in this book, it is reasonable to conclude that his contributions to the discipline of criminology may well be unparalleled. Dr. Hirschi authored two of the most influential theories in the history of the discipline, and in so doing, perhaps more than any other theorist, defined an entire perspective. He also provides the impetus for what we believe qualify (in the real Kuhnian sense)[14] as paradigm shifts. For more than three decades, his work consistently helped shape both the theoretical and research agendas of an entire discipline, and his influence spilled over into sociology and psychology as well. The heuristic[15] impact that his work has had on the discipline of criminology has been immeasurable, and is most certainly not remotely finished. In short, Travis Hirschi epitomizes the concept of a scholar–pioneer.

---

[14]Thomas Kuhn (1962) said that normal science proceeds by "exemplary injunctions." An *exemplar* is a model, a pattern, or a typical instance; an *injunction* is a specified act or set of acts. An *exemplary injunction*, then, is a standard or patterned set of actions. In science, this becomes an exemplary practice or technique or methodology that all agree is central to furthering the quest for knowledge in a given field or subfield. These injunctions are shared practices and methods that scientists agree disclose and address important issues in their fields. Kuhn also referred to *paradigms* as "conceptual boxes" that frame questions and guide research.

[15]*Heuristic* is "the art and science of discovery and invention. A heuristic is a way of directing your attention fruitfully." (Available at http://en.wikipedia.org/wiki/Heuristic). "A rule of thumb, simplification, . . . that reduces or limits the search for solutions in domains that are difficult and poorly understood" (Available at http://www.definethat.com/define/4356.htm). In specific reference to the work of scholars, *heuristic* generally translates as the amount of impact their work had on that of others (i.e., how much additional work/research/theorizing it generated).

References

Agnew, R. 1985. Social control theory and delinquency: A test of theory. *Criminology,* 23(1): 47–61.

———. 1991. A longitudinal test of social control theory and delinquency. *J. Res. Crime Delin.* 28(2): 126–56.

———. 1993. Why do they do it? An examination of the intervening mechanisms between 'social control' variables and delinquency. *J. Res. Crime Delin.* 30(3): 245–66.

Akers, R.L. 1991. Self-control as a General Theory of Crime. *J. Quant. Crimin.* 7: 201–11.

———. 1994. *Criminological theories: Introduction, evaluation, and application.* Los Angeles: Roxbury Publishing.

Akers, R.L., & Sellers, C.S. 2004. *Criminological theories: Introduction, evaluation, and application,* 4th ed. Los Angeles: Roxbury Publishing.

Andrews, D.A., & Bonta, J. 1998. *The psychology of criminal conduct,* 2nd ed. Cincinnati, OH: Anderson Publishing.

Barlow, H. 1991. Explaining crimes and analogous acts, or the unrestrained will grab at pleasure whenever they can. *J. Crim. Law Criminol.* 82(1): 229–42.

Bartusch, D.R.J., Lynam, D.R., Moffitt, T.E., & Silva, P.A. 1997. Is age important? Testing a general theory versus a developmental theory of antisocial behavior. *Criminology,* 35(1): 13–48.

Bernard, T.J. 1987. Structure and control: Reconsidering Hirschi's concept of commitment. *Jus. Quart.* 4(3): 409–24.

Bowlby, J. 1969. *Attachment and loss. Vol.1: Attachment.* New York: Basic Books.

Brannigan, A. 1997. Self control, social control and evolutionary psychology: Towards an integrated perspective on crime. *Can. J. Criminol.* 39(4): 403–31.

———. 1973. *Attachment and loss. Vol. 2: Separation.* New York: Basic Books.

Cernkovich, S., & Giordano, P. 1992. School bonding, race, and delinquency. *Criminology,* 30(2): 261–91.

Clinard, M.B., & Meier, R.F. 1985. *Sociology of deviant behavior,* 6th ed. New York: Holt, Rinehart and Winston.

Cohn, E.G., & Farrington, D.P. 1998. Changes in the most-cited scholars in major American criminology and criminal justice journals between 1986–1990 and 1991–1995. *J. Crim. Just.* 26: 99–116.

Cohn, E.G., Farrington, D.P., & Wright, R.A. 1998. *Evaluating criminology and criminal justice.* Westport, CT: Greenwood.

Costello, B.J., & Vowell, P.R. 1999. Testing control theory and differential association: A reanalysis of the Richmond Youth Project data. *Criminology,* 37(4): 307–330.

Crittenden, J. 1997. What is the meaning of "integral"? In K. Wilber, ed., *The eye of the spirit: An integral vision for a world gone slightly mad.* Boston: Shambhala.

Curran, D.J., & Renzetti, C.M. 2001. *Theories of crime,* 2nd ed. Boston: Allyn and Bacon.

Empey, L.T. 1978. *American delinquency.* Homewood, IL: Dorsey Press.

Flavell, J.H., Miller, P.H., & Miller, S.A. 2001. *Cognitive development.* Upper Saddle River, NJ: Prentice Hall.

Freud, S. 1956/1917. Mourning and melancholia. In E. Jones (Ed.), *The collected papers of Sigmund Freud. Vol. 4.* London: Hogarth.

Gibbons, D.C. 1994. *Talking about crime and criminals: Problems and issues in theory development in criminology.* Englewood Cliffs, NJ: Prentice Hall.

Gibbs, J.J., & Giever, D. 1995. Self-control and its manifestations among university students: An empirical test of Gottfredson and Hirschi's General Theory. *Just. Quart.* 12(2): 231–55.

Gibbs, J.J., Giever, D., & Martin, J.S. 1998. Parental management and self-control: An empirical test of Gottfredson and Hirschi's General Theory. *J. Res. Crime Delin.* 35(1): 40–70.

Glass, G.V. 1976. Primary, secondary and meta-analysis of research. *Edu. Res.* 5: 3–8.

Gottfredson, M., & Hirschi, T. 1988. A propensity–event theory of crime. In W.S. Laufer & F. Adler (Eds.), *Advances in criminological theory.* New Brunswick, NJ: Transaction Publishers, pp. 57–67.

————. 1990. *A general theory of crime.* Stanford, CA: Stanford University Press.

Grasmick, H.G., Tittle, C.R., Bursik, R.J., Jr., & Arneklev, B.K. 1993. Testing the core empirical implications of Gottfredson and Hirschi's General Theory of Crime. *J. Res. Crime Delin.* 30(1): 5–29.

Greenberg, D.F. 1999. The weak strength of social control theory. *Crime Delin.* 45(1): 66–82.

Hindelang, M. 1973. Causes of delinquency: A partial replication and extension. *Soc. Prob.* 20(4): 471–87.

Hirschi, T. 1969. *Causes of delinquency.* Berkeley: University of California Press.

————. 1973. Procedural rules and the study of deviant behavior. *Soc. Prob.* 21: 159–73.

————. 1977. Causes and prevention of juvenile delinquency. *Sociolog. Inq.* 47(3/4): 322–41.

————. 1980. This week's citation classic. *Curr. Cont.* 16: 12–38.

————. 1983. Crime and the family. In J.Q. Wilson (Ed.), *Crime and public policy.* San Francisco: Institute of Contemporary Studies, pp. 53–68.

————. 1989. Exploring alternatives to integrated theory. In S. Messner, M. Krohn, & A. Liska (Eds.), Theoretical integration in the study of crime and deviance: Problems and prospects. Albany: State University of New York Press, pp. 37–49.

————. 1991. Family structure and crime. In B. Christensen (Ed.), *When families fail: An empirical test of Hirschi's control theory of delinquency—the social costs.* Lanham, MD: University Press of America, pp. 43–65.

————. 1995. The family. In J.Q. Wilson & J. Petersilia (Eds.), *Crime.* San Francisco: ICS Press, pp. 121–40.

————. 2002. *Causes of delinquency.* New Brunswick, NJ: Transaction Publishers.

————. 2004. Self-control and crime. In R. F. Baumeister & K. D. Vohs (Eds.), *Handbook of self regulation.* New York: Guilford Publications, pp. 537–52.

Hirschi, T., & Gottfredson, M. 1983. Age and the explanation of crime. *Am. J. Sociol.* 89: 552–84.

————. 1986. The distinction between crime and criminality. In T.F. Hartnagel & R.A. Silverman (Eds.), *Critique and explanation: Essays in honor of Gwynne Nettler.* New Brunswick, NJ: Transaction Publishers, pp. 55–69.

————. 1989. The significance of white-collar crime for a general theory of crime. *Criminology,* 27(2): 359–71.

————. 1993. Commentary: Testing the general theory of crime. *J. Res. Crime Delin.* 30(1): 47–54.

————. 1994. The generality of deviance. In T. Hirschi & M.R. Gottfredson (Eds.), *The generality of deviance.* New Brunswick, NJ: Transactions Publishers, pp. 1–22.

————. 1995. Control theory and the life course perspective. *Stud. Crime Crime Preven.* 4: 1–13.

————. 2000. In defense of self-control. *Theoret. Criminol.* 4(1): 55–69.

————. 2002/1986. The distinction between crime and criminality. Reprinted in J.H. Laub (Ed.), *The craft of criminology: Selected papers. Travis Hirschi.* New Brunswick, NJ: Transaction Publishers, pp. 187–201.

————. 2002/1994. The generality of deviance. Reprinted in J.H. Laub (Ed.), *The craft of criminology: Selected papers. Travis Hirschi.* New Brunswick, NJ: Transaction Publishers, pp. 203–19.

————. 2002/1995. Control theory and the life-course perspective. Reprinted in J.H. Laub (Ed.), *The craft of criminology: Selected papers. Travis Hirschi.* New Brunswick, NJ: Transaction Publishers, pp. 241–53.

————. Forthcoming. Advancing the general theory of crime. In Erich Goode (Ed.), *Criminality and opportunity: Assessing the general theory of crime.* Cambridge: Cambridge University Press.

Hirschi, T., & Selvin, H. C. 1967. *Delinquency research: An appraisal of analytic methods.* New York: The Free Press.

Jang, S.J., & Krohn, M.D. 1995. Developmental patterns of sex differences in delinquency among African American adolescents: A test of the sex-invariant hypothesis. *J. Quant. Criminol.* 11: 195–222.

Kempf, K.L. 1993. The empirical status of social control theory. F. Adler & W. S. Laufer (Eds.),

New directions in criminological theory. New Brunswick, NJ: Transaction, pp. 143–85.

Krohn, M.D., & Massey, J.L. 1980. Social control and delinquent behavior: An examination of the elements of the social bond. *Sociolog. Quart.* 21(4): 529–43.

Kuhn, T. 1962. *The structure of scientific revolutions.* Chicago: University of Chicago Press.

LaGrange, T.C., & Silverman, R.A. 1999. Low self-control and opportunity: Testing the General Theory as an explanation for gender differences in delinquency. *Criminology,* 37(1): 41–72.

Laub, J.H. 2002. Introduction: The life and work of Travis Hirschi. In J.H. Laub (Ed.), *The craft of criminology: Selected papers. Travis Hirschi.* New Brunswick, NJ: Transaction Publishers, pp. xi–xliv.

Laub, J.H., & Hirschi, T. 2002. Introductory comments to the distinction between crime and criminality. In J.H. Laub (Ed.), *The craft of criminology: Selected papers. Travis Hirschi.* New Brunswick, NJ: Transaction Publishers, p. 187.

Liska, A.E., Krohn, M.D., & Messner, S.F. 1989. Strategies and requisites for theoretical integration in the study of crime and deviance. In S.F. Messner, M.D. Krohn, & A.E. Liska, (Eds.), *Theoretical integration in the study of deviance and crime.* Albany: State University of New York Press, pp. 1–20.

Matsueda, R. L. 1982. Testing control theory and differential association: A causal modeling approach. *Am. Sociolog. Rev.* 47(4): 489–504.

Moffitt, T.E. 1993. "Life-course-persistence" and "adolescent-limited" antisocial behavior: A developmental taxonomy. *Psychol. Rev.* 100: 674–701.

Nakhaie, M.R., Silverman, R.A, & LaGrange, T.C. 2000. Self-control and social control: An examination of gender, ethnicity, class and delinquency. *Can. J. Sociol.* 25(1): 35–59.

Nunally, J.C. 1978. *Psychometric theory,* 2nd ed. New York: McGraw Hill.

Piaget, J. 1932. *The moral judgment of the child.* New York: Harcourt, Brace.

Polakowski, M. 1994. Linking self- and social-control with deviance: Illuminating the structure underlying a general theory of crime and its relation to deviant activity. *J. Quant. Criminol.* 10(1): 41–78.

Pratt, T.C., & Cullen, F.T. 2000. The empirical status of Gottfredson and Hirschi's general theory of crime: A meta-analysis. *Criminology,* 38(3): 931–64.

Sampson, R.J., & Laub, J.H. 1993. *Crime in the making: Pathways and turning points through life.* Cambridge: Harvard University Press.

Scarpitti, F.R., & Nielsen, A.L. 1999. Introduction to chapter 18. In F.R. Scarpitti & A.L. Nielsen (Eds.), *Crime and criminals: Contemporary and classic readings in criminology.* Los Angeles: Roxbury Publishing Company, p. 238.

Shoemaker, D.J. 2005. *Theories of delinquency: An examination of explanations of delinquent behavior,* 5th ed. New York: Oxford University Press.

Steffensmeier, D.J., Allan, E.A., Harer, M.D., & Streifel, C. 1999. Age and the distribution of crime. In F.R. Scarpitti & A.L. Nielsen (Eds.), *Crime and criminals contemporary and classic readings in criminology.* Los Angeles: Roxbury Publishing Company, pp. 159–66.

Taylor, C. 2001. The relationship between social and self-control: Tracing Hirschi's criminological career. *Theoret. Criminol.* 5(3): 369–88.

Taylor, Ian, and Walton, Paul, and Young Jock. The New Criminology London: Routledge and Kegan Paul (1973)."

Thompson, W. E, Mitchell, J., & Dodder, R. A. 1984. An empirical test of Hirschi's control theory of delinquency. *Dev. Behav.* 5(1): 11–22.

Tittle, C.R., & Grasmick, H.G. 1998. Criminal behavior and age: A test of three provocative hypotheses. *J. Crim. Law Criminol.* 88: 309–42.

Tittle, C.R., Ward, D.A., & Grasmick, H.G. 2003. Self-control and crime/deviance: Cognitive vs. behavioral measures. *J. Quant. Criminol.* 19(4): 333–65.

Vold, G.B., Bernard, T.J., & Snipes, J.B. 1998. *Theoretical criminology,* 4th ed. New York: Oxford University Press.

Wiatrowski, M.D., Griswold, D. B, & Roberts, M. K. 1981. Social control theory and delinquency. *Am. Sociolog. Rev.* 46(5): 525–41.

Wilber, K. 1998. *The marriage of sense and soul: Integrating science and religion.* New York: Random House.

———. 2000. *A theory of everything: An integral vision for business, politics, science, and spirituality.* Boston: Shambhala.

Williams, F.P., III. 1999. *Imagining criminology an alternative paradigm.* New York: Garland Publishing, Inc.

Williams, F.P., III, & McShane, M.D. 2004. *Criminological theory,* 4th ed. Upper Saddle River, NJ: Pearson Prentice Hall.

Wilson, J.Q., & Herrnstein, R.J. 1985. *Crime & human nature: The definitive study of the causes of crime.* New York: Simon & Schuster, Inc.

Wright, R.A., Bryant, K.M., & Miller, J.M. 2001. Top criminals/top criminologists: The most-cited authors and works in white-collar crime. *J. Contemp. Crim. Just.* 17(4): 383–99.

CHAPTER 17
MARCUS KRUKE FELSON:
B. 1947

—⁄ᵛᵛᵛᵗ—

I. BIOGRAPHICAL SKETCH

Marcus Felson, one of the youngest discussed in this book, stands out among many as a living pioneer in criminological thought. He was a driving force behind the emergence of the "routine activities approach" that stimulated a paradigm shift in regard to how we think about crime, why it occurs, and under what circumstances. By linking practical solutions to his theory of routine activities, Felson has also become a leader in crime prevention and reduction.

Some of the precise details concerning Felson's early history understandably remain obscure. Nonetheless, available documents augmented by communication with Professor Felson reflect an eventful and colorful early life that began on August 15, 1947, in Cincinnati, Ohio.

Marcus was born to Benjamin and Virginia Raphaelson Felson, both of whom were clearly forceful influences on the life of a young boy growing up in a relatively well-to-do household just after the Second World War. Professor Felson acknowledges his parents in his book *Crime and Everyday Life* (1994) with the following passage:

> I dedicate this book to my parents who marched to their own drummers while remaining a team for more than half a century. My father, the late Ben Felson, made his unique contributions to radiology by gathering information as directly as possible from nature itself. My mother, always an independent woman, was one of the few of her era to graduate from college. In her seventh decade of life, she has gone back to the university again because she likes reading thick books, going to long lectures, and arguing with her professors on interesting substantive matters. To the extent that I have a critical mind, it comes from them.

Eight years later, in the third edition of *Crime and Everyday Life,* Felson expanded his acknowledgments with further comments about his mother and siblings:

> I am very grateful to my family members, especially for how they avoid being narrow-minded. My mother, 87 years old, still takes courses at the University of Cincinnati. My youngest brother, Ed, is a lawyer and jazz musician. My next brother, Rich, is a great social psychologist and quite a humorist. Among those older, my sister Nancy is a linguist and classicist, while Steve is an appeals lawyer and playwright. My wife, Mary Adelaide Eckert, is meticulous at everything she does, from putting together manuscripts to baking torts, tarts, or galettes. (2002, x)

Clearly, Felson's life was shaped by a large and functional family life with the added advantage of parents who appreciated formal education. In a personal statement about his early life, Felson discusses the influence received from his father. In particular, Ben Felson was not only a radiologist but also an accomplished author, with a groundbreaking book demonstrating new ways to record and interpret x-rays. Felson reports that his father was known for "pithy writing and was a well-known lecturer and medical humorist, as well as a famous academic radiologist" (M. Felson, 2004, personal correspondence). His father explored novel ways to interpret objects and their interrelationships as they appeared on an x-ray screen, a scientific approach later to be built on by Felson, who also studied new ways to unravel the linkages between people and objects and events in their natural social surroundings. Felson stated that "early exposure to medical research by my father helped me formulate the minimal elements of the routine activity approach to crime analysis in the late 1970s" (Felson, Weinstein, and Spitz 1965, cf. Felson 2006).

Felson attended Walnut Hills High School for six years from the seventh grade to graduation in 1965. In personal communications, he recounts: "I learned Latin, studied French and Spanish along with calculus. On my own time, I studied Italian. In high school I wrote for the school newspaper which I credit for first learning something about writing and editing." More than forty years after graduation from high school, he still credits his early secondary school teachers for their academic stimulation (Felson 1994, "Acknowledgments"). Years later and as a senior professor, Felson admits to "having a lot of chutzpah and occasionally lecturing in French, Spanish and haltingly in Italian" (M. Felson, 2004, personal correspondence). Felson also noted spending a summer in Mexico during high school years and as a young man working for a trucking company during summers where "I learned something about the practical world" (M. Felson, 2004, personal correspondence).

Immediately after high school, Felson entered the University of Chicago and graduated in 1969 with a bachelor's degree in sociology. The university was still benefitting from a long tradition as a leading academic institution and incidentally as the birthplace of human ecological research, which was later to inform much of Felson's thinking (see the chapter on Park). During his undergraduate years it is likely that Felson was introduced to ecological principles and naturalistic inquiry, which he later integrated into his own approach to interpreting how crime emerges in some circumstances or life routines more than others.

Promptly after completing the bachelor's degree Felson entered graduate study at the University of Michigan. By 1973, in a short span of four years, he completed both the master's and PhD degrees. His doctoral dissertation was entitled *Conspicuous Consumption and the Swelling of the Middle-Class,* chaired by David R. Segal. Felson excelled as a student with early academic awards, including the Rackham Prize and a grant from the National Institutes of Mental Health while at the University of Michigan from 1969 to 1971, when he received the best paper award from the American Association of Public Opinion Research. Significantly, prior to graduating with his PhD, Felson had already published in the prominent *American Journal of Sociology* with a paper titled "Neighborhood segregation and white flight to the suburbs" (1972). After graduate school, as with other prominent scholars included in this book, Felson hit the ground running with a continuous string of publications, presentations, research grants, and organizational activities beginning in 1972 and that continues to the present. Research and writing snowballed with each subsequent year from graduate school.

Felson spent most of his academic days at three different universities in widely dispersed regions of the United States. In 1972, just prior to receiving his PhD, Felson began as a lecturer in sociology at the University of Illinois at Urbana–Champaign, where he remained until 1984, having received tenure and associate professor status. While there, his ideas about situational factors of crime activity began to solidify and he began to gain recognition with the routine activities approach. Also in 1984, he accepted a position in the Department of Sociology at the University of Southern California where, in 1990, he was promoted to the rank of professor. Felson accepted several visiting professorships while in California, one at the University of Stockholm and another at Rutgers University. His willingness to accept invitations to lecture, often as keynote speaker, is impressive, and in a four-year period between 1991 and 1996 he was guest speaker at universities in sixteen different nations throughout Europe and Asia, often elaborating on how to interpret the ecological distribution of crime.

Felson has not been a solitary researcher locked in a dusty library; instead, he associates himself with persons of a similar mindset and from whom he undoubtedly receives stimulation and support for his own ideas. Many of his publications reflect a team approach to research involving collaboration with others, including Ronald V. Clarke, Lawrence Cohen, David R. Segal, and Kenneth C. Land. Among the many colleagues he acknowledges as influencing his thinking from Rutgers University are Leslie Kennedy, George Kelling, Sharon Chamard, Phyllis Schulze, and Michael Maxfield. At the University of Southern California, Malcom W. Klein, Lourdes Ongkeko, Leo Schuerman, and the late Sol Kobrin contributed to Felson's patterns of thought. In the earlier years at the University of Illinois, he was influenced by David Bordua, Jan Gorecki, and Ken Land. Felson also singles out Travis Hirschi as being most valuable through writings as well as personal interactions, and attributes both Michael Gottfredson and Cheryl Maxson, at the University of California at Irvine, as influencing his thinking, and remarks that both Paul and Patricia Brantingham of Simon Fraser University "welcomed and informed me over the years" (2002, x).

Felson's research took him to many geographic regions where he has been quick to share his ideas in a wide variety of academic and literary outlets and with the media. He provided interviews with seventy-five newspapers (including *Time Magazine*, *The New York Times*, and *The Wall Street Journal*) and such radio and television stations as CBS and CNN.

The evidence reveals Felson to be an academic dynamo and willing to burn the midnight oil. In addition to his regular teaching duties at Rutgers University, he has continued for more than twenty years as a Senior Researcher with the Social Science Research Institute, where he is Director of the Designing Crime-Free Environments project. Without question, Felson is best known for his ideas on how routine life activities can have an impact on whether one becomes an offender or, conversely, a victim of others. It is to these ideas that we now turn, beginning with a look at some of the basic theoretical assumptions that helped set the stage on which his pivotal ideas emerged.

II. BASIC ASSUMPTIONS

Unraveling the basic assumptions that underlie the Felson's thinking is perhaps the most difficult task, in part because his ideas pertain to a variety of viewpoints, some of which arouse debate. In addition, this section demands some interpretation of the writings of others and forces an innovative look at how some of Felson's principles emerged in a broader historical and scientific context. Three assumptions converge to form a backdrop to Felson's principles and to the routine activities approach, and are addressed separately.

MAKING DECISIONS

The most fundamental question at the heart of criminology is whether people are responsible for their actions—in other words, do individuals have the ability to make independent decisions without being influenced or compelled by outside forces? This has been a basic point of inquiry in social philosophy and behavioral science long before criminology arrived on the scene as an academic discipline. Felson's ideas about criminal behavior place him in the middle of the debate between free-will advocates and science. In fact, his ideas hold logical connections to both Classical and Positive schools of thought.

Felson begins with the assumption that crime exists in social reality. He tends to avoid the fray of how the motivational process works on an individual basis to persuade one to commit an illegal act, and does not concern himself with a search for individual defects, such as those based on physiology or personality. Instead, he emphasizes situational features in the environment that predictably embolden one toward rule-breaking. If an individual is, in fact, influenced by the situation to behave one way or another, it makes common sense to suppose that one makes decisions or choices to commit crimes. Felson would not go so far to say that an individual makes judgments in a vacuum or totally outside environmental stimuli, as in pure "indeterminism" or absolute free will.

One decides to commit a crime or not to commit a crime based, in part, on the impact of variables external to the actor. It is true that others place Felson's principles in the category of Rational Choice Theory; this is likely too much of a generalization and possibly misleading. Much of Felson's arguments are based on commonsense assumptions and the notion of making choices appears secondary. It is more of an understood assumption that choices are made or will be made. Moreover, the choices people make may not be all that rational, and may even border on irrational behavior. More to the point, Felson simply does not emphasize the psychological or personality attributions inherent in specific decision-making processes; instead, he places more emphasis on factors in the social, cultural, or situational environment that could have an impact on decision making. Rather than making the case that individuals make choices to engage in crime, Felson emphasizes that some people are more likely than others to confront problematic situations (1986, 119, cf. Cullen and Agnew 2003). Cullen and Agnew further suggest "the routine activities approach deals with the factors that influence the range of choices available to individuals" (2003, 269). If we assume that environmental situations influence decision making, we must attribute some of Felson's arguments to positivistic influences. More precisely, presuming the decision making process is willed by the individual, even if only partially so, Felson's principles appear closer to neoclassicalism (i.e., soft free will; see Williams and McShane 2004, cf.)

Some of Felson's contemporaries and even coauthors appear to pay more attention to the precise psychological nature of the decision-making process, sometimes involving the impact of cost–benefit features on the potential offender (Cornish and

Clarke 1986; cf. Clarke and Felson 1993). Regardless, Felson's routine activity perspectives are, on occasion, categorized under "rational choice" theory albeit not in the strict sense of individuals forming a priori judgments.

As discussed in detail in subsequent pages, numerous social and cultural features convene to make certain that personal decisions are more or less palatable (i.e., whether to engage in crime). Although it is conceded that individual decisions are made, the door is left wide open to consider a vast array of stimuli that place Felson's ideas on strong positivistic grounding. There are clear and measurable social structural features that converge to influence personal decisions to commit illegal acts. Illuminating the diverse ways decision making is influenced by situation (often emphasizing technological changes) is fundamental to Felson's career path.

MODERNIZATION

Make no mistake, Marcus Felson is a sociologist in the purest sense. His career has long emphasized the search for often overlooked social facts that can be shown to have an impact on crime rates. It appears clear from his early professional life that he was influenced by basic principles of Emile Durkheim (see the Durkheim chapter). Felson's work can be seen, in part, as an extension of modernization theory that Durkheim helped launch in the late-nineteenth century. Although an oversimplification, Durkheim demonstrated that personal and group behavior suffered as society fluctuated between folk and urban lifestyles. Paris life was different from the lifeways of villagers surrounding the city. Many basic social problems were amplified in the city to include suicide, poverty, disease, marital instability, and crime and delinquency. Even with crude measurement strategies, Durkheim unraveled the social dynamics of group life between the extremes of small, isolated French towns and highly mobile, metropolitan areas.

Any focus on the modernization process naturally directs one to examine the general impact of sociocultural change at the macro level. What are the features in the social and physical surroundings of people (folk or urban) that may have an impact on the nature of crime? Is the commission of some crimes facilitated by the result of specific changes that occur between, for example, the folk and urban extremes? Durkheim addressed such questions in his early work (1893). A century later, with the advantage of standing on the shoulders of earlier pioneers, Felson asks similar questions (see, particularly, his *Crime and Everybody Life,* 2002). What led to an increase in rates of theft as rural villages morphed into larger towns and, ultimately, cities? An inclusive response must address psychological, cultural, and interactional variables. Felson, however, begins with the situational features that often appear imbued with commonsense logic. Theft is rare and difficult to carry out in agricultural villages. How does one steal a cow, for example, when market exchange is based on barter and property is identified with its owner? With a change in the "medium of exchange" to coinage and currency, wealth was contained in smaller compartments (pockets) and personal larceny and highway robbery took on new appearances. If we fast-forward to today, automated teller machines, credit cards, and long-distance transfer of money represent technological changes (situational) in market environments (discussed at length in Felson 2002, 2006). As department stores emerged, leaving behind "mom-and-pop" corner general stores, theft became easier as shoppers were expected to tend to themselves in self-serve styled warehouses. Shoplifting became more prevalent as employees were spread thinner among the masses of shoppers. These variables, among many others, are the kind analyzed by Felson, who uses modern methods throughout his written works, yet not losing sight of their Durkheimian origins.

SPACE AND TIME

All persons are influenced by the unique pathways they take in establishing their daily routine through space and time. Some deviant and illegal acts tend to occur in some spaces but not in others, and at some times more than at other times. If one's daily round of life or "routine path" takes one into spaces and times that are conducive to crime, then one may be targeted more easily by offenders (i.e., more easily victimized). This fundamental if not commonsense principle has been at the heart of social ecology since the late nineteenth century. Animals must be careful when they visit the local watering hole used by other species of animals, or they themselves become victims of predators (compare ecological perspectives in Felson 2006). The watering hole may be safer at specific times of the day. The routine activities of plants and non-human animals were better understood at the beginning of the twentieth century than the sociological activities of humans. Not until Park and Burgess finally made the leap to human ecology (1921) did the daily movements of people in space and time become a topic of serious study. With the breakthrough finding of the concentric-zone theory, certain areas were identified as bad spaces that tended to remain so regardless of the biological or ethnic features of people residing in the space (see also Burgess 1916, as quoted in Felson 2006.)

Felson worked with numerous fellow researchers to identify the kinds of specific spatial features that were aligned with natural areas of crime and deviance. Earlier writers (e.g., Reckless Hayner, Cressey, Anderson) eloquently explored natural areas of crime; however, it is Felson's work, assisted by some of his close colleagues, that helps to provide a logical conceptual scheme to view how select variables converge to result in criminal or non-criminal behavior.

For example, if a big city bus station is a hot-spot of crime and deviance, what features make it so? At first glance, are there recognizable crime-producing features of the space? If specific features are criminogenic, then removing them should reduce levels of illegal conduct. Consequently, how can a bus station be redesigned to reduce levels of deviance (see Felson et al.'s "Redesigning Hell" 1996)? By building on traditional ecological principles, Felson's work enters the arena of crime prevention and victimology. It is not surprising that some writers discuss Felson in relation to the ecology of crime (Williams and McShane 1998, 236). This makes sense in that ecology is, at its base, concerned with the relationship between living organisms and their surroundings or "living space," and Felson admits to being strongly influenced by Hawley's landmark book on ecology (1950, cf. Felson 2002, 166). Ecological perspectives clearly encompass human "routine activities." Survival of all organisms is directly linked to their making the right movements in space and time: finding food, mate selection, staying out of trouble, and so on. Felson's most recent book (*Crime and Nature* 2006) was "in process" at the time of this writing and could be examined only briefly. However, as the title suggests, it is launched from ecological points of view and is saturated with ecologically based crime-prone scenarios. This work is discussed further at the very end of this chapter.

III. KEY IDEAS

After publication of the breakthrough theoretical model that set forth the routine activities theory, Felson extended the discussion over the next quarter century, providing refinements while stimulating others to further test and critique the original ideas. In this section, three aspects of the routine activities theory are addressed: fundamentals, crime prevention, and integrative nature.

FUNDAMENTALS OF ROUTINE ACTIVITIES THEORY

Routine Activities

Humans and most lower animals do not drift through space and time in random movements. Rather, the same movements tend to reoccur over time so that daily life, from moment to moment, becomes relatively predictable, even though at first glance things may seem chaotic. Such patterned activity becomes necessary in order to carry out select functions that include the full range of family, work, and play routines. In short, arriving at select mobility patterns can have survival value. Cohen and Felson argue that such activity represents micro-level assumptions that "provide for basic population and individual needs, whether of biological or cultural origins. Thus routine activities would include formalized work, as well as the provision of standard food, shelter, sexual outlet, leisure, social interaction, learning and child-rearing" (Cohen and Felson 1979, 593).

Although routine activities of an individual or a population can become efficient in accomplishing tasks, it is also true that such predictable activities can also have dysfunctional and problematic qualities by propelling persons into dangerous or even criminal circumstances. From early writings with Cohen and in numerous subsequent writings, Felson shows that a fluctuation in traditional routine activities can lead to an increase in criminal activity. The earlier work concerning the impact of routine activities emphasizes how predatory crime such as rape, robbery, and personal larceny with contact increased over several decades (between 1947 and 1974) with the change in routine activity of people from a relatively sedate and safe lifestyle to a more insecure and dangerous routine of life typical of modern urban areas (Cohen and Felson 1979, Felson 2002, Felson and Cohen 1980, 1981).

One's entire daily routine can be extremely complex. As a simplified and partial example, consider the college student. Most students tend to follow the same walkway on campus en route to their classes. The same students may frequent the same cafeteria and commonly choose similar foods from the menu, sit at the same table, and afterward visit the library each day. On weekends, the students tend to visit the same series of gathering places that may include clubs or bars and afterward travel the consistent route to their dormitories. These pathways, among many others, form part of their routine activity for university students. Should the students get sidetracked on their way home from a bar and decide to take a shortcut down a cluttered city alley full of overfilled dumpsters, they are changing their routine and placing themselves in unfamiliar and potentially dangerous circumstances. For instance, the students may become targets for persons lingering in the back alley, and at late night hours, few would be around to offer protection. Regardless of their motivations, they run a greater risk of trouble than if they stayed on their familiar campus path. This scenario, by itself, is not all that unusual; what is notable is the analytic framework refined by Felson to better understand such case studies. In the years since the initial 1979 report, Felson worked to measure the link between routine activities and crime rates more precisely, and to provide increasingly diverse and timely examples of the theoretical relationship between offenders and the changing community.

Components of the Theory   The routine activities perspective states that three elements must converge for crime to occur—motivated offenders who come into contact with suitable targets in the absence of capable guardians (Cohen and Felson 1979, Felson 2002, 21). The range of choices available becomes a function of the daily routine activity and the relative confrontation people have with motivated offenders and suitable targets. If offenders and targets happen to be thrust together in the absence of a capable guardian against an offense, the mix is complete for crime to occur. Closer scrutiny of each variable adds clarification.

The Motivated Offender   Early research on routine activities tended to deemphasize the position of the offender. Even though Felson acknowledged that an offender is critical to the commission of a crime, he did not belabor the question of why offenders are present, only that their presence is necessary and to be expected. The offender must be both present who holds both an inclination to break the law (i.e., motivated) and also have the ability to carry out the inclination (1979, 590). In the late 1970s, this was somewhat of a deviation from the historic and popular aim of criminology. From the beginning of the discipline, much attention was placed on why some persons committed crimes whereas others did not. How might the offender be at fault? Felson reversed the trend by featuring instead a return to ecological and distinct situational relationships between the offender and specific targets in light of the nature of persons who may be safeguarding the targets.

There is some logic behind deemphasizing the offender and accepting the role of the offender as a given. It has long been acknowledged that there are always offenders present in any social setting. In one of his earlier writings, Durkheim set forth the simple but timeless proposition that the presence of deviance or rule breaking is at least statistically normal (1895), and goes on to suggest that the absence of an offender in a social setting is abnormal, because no two people can reach absolute agreement with others. Someone will appear to break the rules, thus making deviance and crime inevitable (see the chapter on Durkheim). Half a century later, Sykes and Matza remind us that all people think evil thoughts, and that those defined as evil (i.e., lawbreakers) generally have a good side (1957, see also the chapter on Sykes).

This suggests a potentially endless supply of motivated offenders. To the same point, self-report data revealed for decades that a vast majority of youth committed illegal acts, including felonies, prior to age eighteen (Siegel 2003, 53–59). The fact that motivated offenders are typically available in social settings does not appear all that remarkable; of more concern, certainly to Felson, is why deviant and criminal acts tend to occur at a particular time and place.

Felson does not entirely ignore the possibility that offenders possess specific attributes. In his latest edition of *Crime and Everyday Life,* he credits self-control theory as being particularly helpful in explaining decisions of motivated offenders to commit or not commit crimes at a given moment (2002, 37–51, cf. Felson and Gottfredson 1984). Simply put, some persons are able to control themselves in crime-prone situations more easily than others. Even in his more recent writings, Felson's discussion of offenders is clearly in reference to how a particular environment stimulates one to engage in crime. This promotes the suggestion that given the right set of circumstances, someone in the social setting is motivated to violate the law.

Felson gives close attention to self-control theory and accepts the idea that selected persons, because of their social and cultural backgrounds, are more disciplined and controlled than others. Some individuals are quicker to react (e.g., engage in theft) than others when placed amid suitable targets. Felson was influenced by and worked with Hirschi, and clearly incorporates Hirschi's themes of self-control into his own work. It was Hirschi who wrote an endorsement to Felson's book *Crime and Everyday Life* (2002, see back cover). In addition, Felson and Gottfredson coauthored research findings on adolescent activities in "Adolescent Activities near Peers and Parents" (1984), prior to the release of the well-received book *A General Theory of Crime* (Gottfredson and Hirschi 1990). There appears to be no question that these authors influenced each other. Felson wrote: "I owe a debt of gratitude to Ron Clarke, Travis Hirschi, Michael Gottfredson, Maurice Cusson, and James Wise. In addition, the wives and families of the first four had to put up with hours of meandering discussion while they wined and dined me" (1987, 911).

Felson stated in the third edition of *Crime and Everyday Life*:

> We are all born weak, but parents and teachers try to teach us self-control to help us resist various temptations; to keep us studying or working, out of the kitchen, or away from the bottle; to help keep our mouths shut when the boss, customer, spouse, or teacher says something that temps a nasty reply; to avoid fights, drugs, and thefts; and to keep doing our homework. (2002, 42)

Self-control also applies to paying attention, setting goals, managing money, avoiding procrastination, and regulating one's own impulses, appetites, moods, and thought processes (Felson 2002, 43; also drawing on the work of Baumeister, Heatherton, and Tice 1994). To Felson, it is the motivated offender who more often than not reflects low self-control, but who must be seen in the larger context along with available targets and an absence of guardians. This basic recognition allows Felson to offer his own version of a tangible and comprehensive theory of crime discussed later in this chapter. By 1998, with the publication of the second edition of his book *Crime and Everyday Life*, Felson adjusts the concept of *motivated offender* to *likely offender*. The change avoids much of the necessity to continually be concerned with unraveling how and why individuals are psychologically motivated, or possess dispositions to commit crime in the first place (1998, 53).

Suitable Targets   Although it is said here with some caution, the heart of the routine activities theory appears to be the presentation of data surrounding suitable targets. It is true that routine activities theory stresses the interrelationship among offenders, targets, and guardians that converge to form an analytical framework. However, the position of offenders, as noted earlier, is relatively stable. They always seem to be present in social settings. Also, the position of the guardian, when compared to targets, discussed later in this chapter, is generally slower to change. It is the "suitable target" that is all over the map in diversity and that appears to be highly flexible. Stated most simply, as a culture increases in material abundance and diversity, the number of items to steal increases, along with the varied ways to engage in theft.

Other than occasional anecdotal notes, this rather uncomplicated assumption remained relatively dormant until Felson and several of his co-researchers realized that the fluctuation in suitable items to steal correlated with crime rates in more meaningful ways than many of the more traditional social welfare explanations of changing rates of lawbreaking (Cohen 2002, 12–14, cf. Cohen and Felson 1979, Felson and Cohen 1980, Clarke 1999, Felson et al. 1996).

Societal Change and Suitable Targets The extreme expansion in population size and mobility over the past few hundred years saw the demise of a bartering economy and a shift to the more efficient use of currency and coin as a medium of exchange. Both styles and prevalence of crime changed—theft became easier to carry out because wealth was personally held in wallets and purses. Currency in all its forms became a suitable target. Highway robbery flourished. In addition, not only could pockets be picked, but banks emerged that could be robbed more easily as well, and with greater payoff than stealing a herd of pigs or field of corn. It also became feasible for a motivated offender to counterfeit money. With the emergence of banks and checking accounts came the growth of crimes associated with check fraud that included writing bad checks and forgery.

As recently as the early 1960s, credit cards began to make their way into the economy. These could be stolen easily and used worldwide to purchase goods fraudulently. Felson writes:

> Changes in goods and money are very important for crime rates trends. One of the major causes of the mushrooming crime rates in the United States after 1963 was the proliferation of lightweight durable goods that were easy to steal. Easier use of checks and credit cards without careful identification produces increases in fraud. . . . I have argued before that Americans using far less cash helped to produce the declining U.S. crime rates since 1990. (2002, 32)

With advances in technology and particularly in transportation and electronics, a growing abundance of suitable targets emerged that could be marketed as "must have" items. Cohen and Felson argue that target suitability is a function of "value, visibility, access, and inertia." Expensive and movable objects such as motor vehicles and increasingly miniaturized electronic appliances are most apt to be stolen. *Access* pertains to the ability of an offender to get to the target and *inertia* refers to such factors as size and weight of a target or if it is attached or locked—for example, to a wall (2002, 28, cf. Cohen and Felson 1979, 595). The advent of the automobile and its proliferation provided a suitable target. Moreover, many accessories to the automobile became available to thieves, because any detachable part could be fenced for profit. As automobiles were driven into the city for work or leisure, they needed to be parked, which placed them at risk to theft or vandalism (Felson 2002, 59).

Others have discussed *hot products* as objects most likely to be stolen. Felson quotes Clarke, one of his frequent coauthors on related topics, to explain which goods are most craved by thieves and therefore most likely stolen. Features of hot products are that they are Concealable, Removable, Available, Valuable, Enjoyable, and Disposable (CRAVED; Felson 2002, 28, cf. Clarke 1999). Felson elaborates:

> To put it another way, the property offender has six problems to solve. He or she wants to be able to conceal it, remove it, have it available, find it valuable, enjoy it, and dispose of it readily. Jewelry and money are easily concealed on

one's person. A very common car is easier to conceal than an unusual model (such as a Rolls Royce) that is easy to spot. Small items and those on wheels are the easiest to remove. Light televisions are always more vulnerable than the heaviest models. If thieves had to carry the car on their backs, there would be no car theft. So we can see that the CRAVED model helps us get inside the minds of offenders and to explain what items invite theft. (2002, 28–30)

Suitable Targets and the Changing Nature of Capable Guardians   It is difficult to talk about the proliferation of crime targets without acknowledging the accompanying shift in prevalence and attributes of people who may be around to safeguard the targets. Throughout history, as the number of items to steal and people to harm increased, so did the nature of available protection decline. Although this linkage between suitable targets in an environment increasingly devoid of guardians is observable in the earliest rural to urban movement, it was the post–World War II era that was the focus of concern to Felson and his colleagues. It is not necessary to repeat here the abundance of data that became increasingly available to measure the change in targets and guardians (Cohen and Felson 1979, cf. 2002). However, a number of propositions emerge from the early findings. For example, as the U.S. population began to move progressively out of the small towns and into the larger cities, an increase was seen in single-person dwellings. Greater numbers of people were living alone in order to be closer to the better jobs, and more single people could be seen roaming the urban areas in search of work, play, and companionship. Such an increase in mobility meant more motorized vehicles on the streets and an increase in goods to care for the city folk as well as their vehicles. The cultural base increased in abundance and diversity. Living alone, away from the group protection of an intact family, means persons are more at risk of victimization. Incidents of burglary, robbery, and personal larceny rise as the distance away from the protection of a larger family increases. Married persons are at a lesser risk of being victimized than are single persons. Larger households are safer than smaller ones. The would-be offender commonly targets the most vulnerable or the target least likely to offer resistance.

Felson reports that the decades after World War II saw an increase in female college students and women joining the labor force. Households became increasingly unattended after 8 AM, a time when the percentages of persons traveling, whether for work or pleasure, increased. More people visited national parks and more people traveled overseas. The number of weeks available for vacation increased. The expansion of single households, combined with the number of women joining the labor force, and an increase in the number of empty houses during the day coincided with a bourgeoning crime rate (Felson 1987, 2002, Felson and Cohen, 1979).

Although the numbers of homes without guardians increased, so also did the number of smaller and lightweight goods, as shown by the properties of goods in the annual Sears catalogs. Household appliances became easier to burglarize. The 1950s saw commercial establishments radically alter in style to the benefit and profit of the motivated offender. In other words, the same two decades after the war saw a near end of the traditional "mom-and-pop" style stores that were widely replaced by warehouse oriented department stores. This shift was associated with a decrease in the number of clerks overseeing the merchandise. The age of self-serve store with watchful employees more and more absent greatly facilitated theft (Felson 2002, 58).

The automobile altered the nature and extent of capable guardians. Streets had to be widened, which in turn narrowed the sidewalks or made them disappear entirely. This meant fewer neighbors strolled along a street that a few years earlier could have provided a deterrent against burglaries. For decades Felson reiterated the point that capable guardians include more than the lonely police officer walking the beat. A first order of guardians must include family members, neighbors, and even work associates. With extreme urbanization and the ability to move freely about the city witnessed a major decline in safety among friends and close associates who were increasingly dispersed. One's own lifestyle or routine of spending more time alone facilitated victimization including crimes against persons and property (Cohen and Felson 1979, 600–02, cf. Felson and Cohen 1980, Felson and Clarke 1995, 1998, Felson 2002 [particularly Chapter 4]).

The relationship between urbanization and crime and the importance of guardians is seen by Felson in an examination of changing patterns of population density. Traditional explanations suggest that crime rises with an increase in density. Reduce the territory for a group of persons, or even animals in a cage, and the anxiety level rises predictably. Felson correctly sees the linkage between density and crime rates as much more complex. One must look at the nature of the space as well as the type of crime. Some lawbreaking flourishes as the population density declines, whereas other crimes emerge as density increases. Examining the relationship between suitable targets and capable guardians clarifies the impact of density.

For example, burglary declines as population density increases. Felson (2002, 61–63, cf. 121–43) explains this by noting that in the crowded section of the city, the apartment buildings and crowded flats do not provide ideal conditions for the successful burglar. Burglary is facilitated in those less-densely populated neighborhoods characterized by physically separated houses with trees and shrubs available for hiding, and in a locale where fewer capable guardians are present, particularly as seen in the daylight hours when many residents are away from their homes (2002, 61–63, cf. 121–43). As seen in Singapore, one of the world's most densely populated city–states, burglary is almost nonexistent because, to a great extent, about ninety percent of the population live in well-secured high-rise apartment blocks that are crowded yet neighborly (Austin 2005). The socially cohesive *cul de sac* may also present an exception to the rule whereby burglary would predictably be unusual with traffic patterns conducive to neighborhood residents only and where watchful neighbors would deter burglars (Felson 2002, Chapter 9). Other crimes thrive in the crowded sections of the inner city such as theft associated with automobiles parked haphazardly on narrow streets, pocket-picking, assaults, and the like.

Felson also connects the juvenile delinquency problem that peaked in the late 1960s and 1970s to the absence of capable guardians. This was most evident as youth returned from school without traditional chores and fewer persons being around to offer supervision as was common in pre–World War II days. Opportunity for deviance and delinquency overwhelmed a generation of youth who were maturing at earlier ages but who had more years to go before they could engage in adult activities. In comparison, in earlier times, youth married younger and entered the workforce even in teenage years, which reduced idle time for delinquency. Routine activity patterns of youth, combined with neighborhoods empty of capable guardians, must be seen as major variables in understanding youthful lawbreaking (Felson and Clarke 1998, cf. Felson 2002, 79–92, Smith 1970, 291–320).

ROUTINE ACTIVITIES AND CRIME PREVENTION

For much of the twentieth century, criminology emphasized a search to explain criminal behavior and either slighted the practical side of the discipline or gave it secondary status. There were theorists and there were practitioners and the two seldom met. A wedge formed between the two functions of theory and practice that can be discerned to this day. Perhaps as much as any scholar, Felson helped bridge the gap by providing a clear example of how theory can set a logical stage for the practical application of crime prevention. Simply put, Felson gave crime prevention a theoretical foundation. Given the analytical scheme of likely offenders, suitable targets, and capable guardians necessary for crime to flourish, the practitioner could logically argue that modifying any one element must have an impact on the end effect of crime. If likely offenders are denied suitable targets, the crime rate declines. Likewise, crime wanes if environmental surroundings are adjusted to retain capable guardians. Because it is likely that some targets are going to become increasingly good targets for thieves—computers are not going to get bigger and heavier—other strategies must be developed to make targets less suitable for theft.

Felson reviews the research of others that emphasize ideas for "designing out crime." In so doing, Felson presents findings to reveal how established crime prevention programs can be dissected to reflect a change in the way we deal with offenders, targets, and guardians. For example, a better theoretical understanding of the environment allows police to predict more efficiently the location of offenders or where they may carry out crimes later. Felson notes: "By studying exact time and locations of each serial offense, Rossmo (1995, 2000) puts environmental criminology or theory to work to determine where the offender probably lives, works, and has his recreation. This information aids in figuring out the identity of the offender and making an arrest" (2002, 125).

Felson discusses the physical aspects of crime prevention by emphasizing targets:

> Crime can be prevented by at least four physical methods: target hardening, construction, strength in numbers, and noise. For example universities harden targets when they bolt down computers, typewriters, television sets, projection equipment, and the like. As for construction, universities sometimes put up extra walls, fences, or other physical barriers to reduce unauthorized entry to university buildings, or simply to channel flows of people coming and going, which makes mild supervision possible. . . . Strength in numbers is important for helping people to protect themselves and their property. One designer of a high-rise building for the elderly put the recreation room on the first floor with good lines of sight to the door. Together, the residents were able to keep people from wandering in without permission. Noise refers to alarms, barking dogs and door locks which typically cannot be opened without attracting attention. (2002, 128)

If we agree that some persons will always be motivated to engage in wrongdoing, then it makes sense to highlight environmental settings that provide greater access to capable guardians. Having said this, Felson would be the first to admit that much of the groundwork was laid by other thinkers with similar ideas that helped inform his own research and writing. He remarks that the early work of Jane Jacobs (1961) is as fresh today as it was when first written:

> She saw the coming tragedy of urban renewal before anyone else realized what was happening. She explained why old urban neighborhoods, even if low in income, provided places for pedestrians, had vibrant lives, maintained local control of space, and protected people against crime. These neighborhoods were bulldozed to erect unnatural high-rise public housing complexes that become sterile environments and had crime problems built into their design. Jacobs remains a hero to students of crime prevention because she showed how designing for less crime is as easy as designing for more. Her concept went beyond buildings themselves, including the entire urban environment and taking into consideration the people using that environment. (2002, 120)

Other crime prevention scholars acknowledged by Felson, to name only a few, include Brantingham and Brantingham (1984, 1998, 1999), Jeffery (1971), Newman (1972), and Poyner (1991, 1993, 1998). These writers' works either build on aspects of Felson's routine activities perspectives or they provide earlier findings that can now be reconsidered in light of the relationships among offenders, targets, and guardians. Felson's book *Crime and Everyday Life* (2002) offers two chapters on the application of routine activities theory—"Local Design against Crime" (Chapter 9) and "Situational Crime Prevention" (Chapter 10)—present insightful summaries regarding the union of the theory and practice of crime reduction.

More important, the routine activities perspective provides a conceptual scheme that helps us understand the prevention of all kinds of crime. This includes violence and property offenses as well as white-collar crimes. The conceptual scheme composed of motivated offenders, suitable targets, and absence of capable guardians can logically be called on for meaningful analysis. For instance, violence can be thwarted by defusing provocative scenarios (bar drunks) before they get out of hand. This might require modifying a volatile setting so that capable guardians are efficiently incorporated into the locale or that problem patrons do not enter in the first place. Bar patrons can adjust their own behavior so as to not provoke drunk or near-drunk persons. The issue of how not to become a suitable target becomes significant. In short, the routine activities of persons anticipated to be problem customers must be adjusted, as must controlling the routine of patrons once they are on the inside (2002, 154–57). Similarly, some violence can be prevented or "designed out" by adjusting the surroundings (e.g., adding street lights or controlling the flow of persons through a public park to better provide an audience of observers that tends to frustrate likely muggers). If burglars look for cues in a neighborhood to suggest likely targets, then removing or disguising such cues makes the neighborhood safer. Such a commonsense approach to simple adjustments to daily routines (having a lawn mowed and newspaper delivery stopped while on vacation) applies directly to the theory.

Felson also addresses white-collar crime and explains how workplace routines provide opportunity for breaking the law. He defines *white-collar crime* as "crime of specialized access: a criminal act committed by abusing one's job or profession to gain specific access to a crime target" (2002, 95, cf. 1997). Felson points out that specialized access through the workplace cover such diverse offenses as: "fixing prices, short-changing customers, cheating pension funds, faking insurance claims, dumping toxic wastes, abusing prisoners, mistreating patients, manipulating stocks, and enticing bribes. Indeed, a specific work role can put someone in just the right position to do the wrong thing" (2002, 95). Examples are as limitless as the diversity of workplaces, but the theory still applies. Such crimes of specialized access and their prevention can be analyzed by unraveling the linkages between motivated offenders who possess special access to targets while being relatively hidden from view of guardians. The 1990s saw a trend in Felson's writing toward applications of routine activities theory; for instance, "How buildings can protect themselves against crime" (1995a); "Those who discourage crime" (1995b); and "Technology, business and crime" (1997). In addition, Felson led research teams to explore ways of "Reducing pub hopping and related crime" (1997), and a larger project, involving a university class of eleven student researchers, exploring the crime problem and its reduction in a large public transit network in New York City ("Redesigning Hell: Preventing Crime and Disorder at the Port Authority Bus Terminal," 1996). The bus station project is particularly relevant because it demonstrates the application of routine activities theory to practical solutions of crime and deviance in a densely populated, high-risk urban area.

INTEGRAL NATURE OF ROUTINE ACTIVITIES THEORY

Felson does not discuss theoretical integration specifically — at least, he does not belabor the concept. Nonetheless, even a cursory review of his writing forces one to conclude that the routine activities perspective reflects a substantial incorporation of ideas and theory laid down by others. Felson illustrates this, in part, by often returning to ecology as a starting point in introducing his thinking about crime. He writes:

> Offending is highly diverse, quickly shifting and sometimes surprising. The most relevant actors are often found in roles seldom associated with crime at all: designers of money machines, bank architects, bartenders, city planners, public housing managers, receptionists, automotive engineers, real estate developers, and hot dog vendors. The diversity and specificity of this list is understandable in ecological terms: Each plant species has its particular pollination agents — sometimes the bumble-bee, sometimes a special moth, sometimes the wind. The giant panda lives off a single species of bamboo growing densely, high in the mountains of western China. Human occupations are also highly specialized and interdependent in precise ways. Why should crime be any less specific than the rest of nature? Even if offenders are often generalists over time, they are responsive at any given moment to very precise crime chances. Thus, we must study crime by gathering its details like a naturalist, classifying offense circumstances like a taxonomist, and working out interdependent systems like a physiologist. (2002, 166–67)

One can only understand crime by first studying the details of the criminal act itself. What is the act that has offended others and what are the situational circumstances surrounding it? After understanding the specific and tangible features of a crime, one can then look backward to try to make some sense of what may have motivated an offender to break the rules in the first place. Ecologically speaking, norm breaking is a naturally occurring activity, but to have survival value as a behavior pattern it must take into account the nature of the target to be preyed on and the likelihood that someone will or will not interfere with the offender while the crime is carried out. Do situations in the immediate physical environment provide opportunity for illegal behavior to flourish? (On opportunity theory, see Felson and Clarke 1998, cf. Felson 2002, 35, 109.)

Such an ecological foundation for routine activities theory opens the door to recognizing the importance of other theoretical perspectives. Some offenders are more savvy than others because they learned from childhood how and where to engage in wrongdoing successfully. Felson accepts the idea that all persons are conditioned from an early age to respond one way or another to crime-prone situations. Although it seems oversimplistic, it is clear that the more successful offenders learn early that they must take into account the routine activities of potential victims. For example, the shoplifter, the mugger, the burglar, and the bank robber must all be selective in the search for suitable targets in locations free of capable guardians, not unlike a wild animal stalking its prey. Consequently, more-attentive parents teach their children what pathways to avoid en route to school or play to stay out of trouble. The principles set forth by Sutherland and other social determinists provide points of view complementary to routine activities theory. (See the chapter on Sutherland in this book; cf. Felson and Gottfredson 1984, Gottfredson and Hirschi 1990.)

Routine activities theory also builds upon neutralization principles set forth by Sykes and Matza (1957; see the chapter on Sykes in this book). Thus, some environmental situations and targets make breaking the law easier to rationalize than others. As detailed in previous pages, some targets are more suitable than others for theft. A thief makes choices. It is easier to rationalize burglarizing a remote and empty house near a wooded area than one in a well-lighted *cul de sac*. Neutralization theory was first developed as an extension of Sutherland's theory of differential association. (See the chapter on Sykes in this book.)

Albert Cohen makes the argument that the more well-to-do social classes adhere to lifestyles and traditions that shield them from the frustration felt by those of lower socioeconomic status. Essentially, the social class variable establishes a routine of life for the lower classes making success in school and later in life difficult; in some cases, this is resolved by joining a gang. A person's routine activities are influenced by the social class structure in which one is reared. Particularly as a youth, if you work hard, defer your gratifications, pursue hobbies, and keep your nose to the grindstone, you are less likely to find yourself in crime-prone situations. The broken-home situation of many poor families means less parental supervision and less exposure to building safe and crime-free lifestyles. Status-frustration theory dovetails with routine activity perspectives (Cohen 1955; see also the chapter on Cohen in this book; cf. Felson 2002, particularly his discussion on crime, growth, and youthful activities).

Robert Merton's views regarding the American dream pertains to routine activities perspectives even if indirectly. In "On the Evolving Synthesis of Differential Association and Anomie Theory," one of his final writings, Merton states that perceptions of and quests for the "American dream" are learned and a function of, among other things, the relative exposure of persons to illegitimate opportunity structures (Merton 1997, 517–25; see particularly his discussion of Cloward and Ohlin's "opportunity theory"; cf., Felson and Clarke 1998). Opportunity overlaps with situation as variables that influence behavior. This clearly highlights Felson's discussion of whether people or their possessions are viewed as suitable targets. People who achieve the American dream provide different targets compared to people who do not. A hobo presents a different target than does a wealthy person. In addition, people who may become "likely offenders" differ in regard to their relative success in achieving the American dream.

It has already been noted how routine activities changed with the movement of people from rural to urban locations. Such a migration pattern is characterized by more single persons becoming increasingly dependent on automobiles and goods and services suitable to a fast-paced routine of life. Durkheim discovered that the lifestyle of disjointed urbanites resulted in greater degrees of social pathology of all kinds, including poverty, crime, and even suicide. Felson's writing amplifies Durkheim's by linking more clearly the changing physical surroundings (suitable targets) and the growing absence of capable guardians to the overall impact of modernization (see the chapter on Durkheim in this book; cf. Felson 1987, and Cohen and Felson 1979).

Felson states that he has been working toward a single theory of crime based on three principles (see *Crime and Everyday Life*, 2002, 165):

1. The offender seeks to gain quick pleasure and avoid imminent pain.
2. The routine activities of everyday life sets the stage for these illegal choices.
3. Inventions force crime to change by altering daily routines.

The first principle shows a return to the axioms of Jeremy Bentham, but with a qualification that offenders go through a process of reasoning, even if rapid, that draws on social and environmental features as influential factors of decision making. Everyone is affected by such a process and some always emerge to take advantage of pleasures (even if illegal) rather than the pain of doing without. The second principle points out that all crime is launched from, and is a function of, the routine activities of both victims and offenders. The actors involved in a crime may not be consciously aware in all cases of the interplay of the elements of routine activities such as the importance of suitable targets or the relative presence of guardians, but their impact is real and measurable for virtually all misbehavior. In the third principle, Felson underscores the short- and long-term impact of invention on one's daily routine of life. Especially in regard to new technologies, we can witness the dramatic changes in the extent and style of criminal conduct. Much of Felson's work emphasizes this point, with attention frequently given to the influence of such inventions (e.g., telephones, automobiles, transistors, ATM machines, lightweight plastics, computers) on the efficiency and likelihood of crime.

Any criminal act can be addressed logically by using the three principles. When combined with the basic elements of the routine activities perspective, the theory offers a conceptual scheme that explains the unexpected fluctuations in crime rates after World War II, a time when many rehabilitative programs flourished and social and economic trends improved.

A few comments are in order regarding how the theory fared over the past several decades.

IV. CRITIQUE

Marcus Felson's theoretical perspectives and his specific work with others on the development of the routine activities approach have been generally well-received. Routine activities theory has enjoyed substantial longevity as an analytical scheme that has made its way into virtually all textbooks on criminological theory published since the over the past 25-years. Most writers have positive comments about the theoretical perspective and acknowledge the fruitful relationship between routine activities and crime prevention and victimology. Williams and McShane write,

> The routine activities perspective . . . initially viewed as a very practical look at crime, gained popularity and became a staple of the 1980s. One reason for its popularity was the easy connection with the burgeoning interest in victimology and a new ecological crime-prevention approach. The major reason, however, was the resurgence of assumptions about the nature of humans as rational beings. Either way, routine activity theory clearly has been an important contribution to criminology. (1998, 235–36)

As with the other pioneering theories presented in this book, and with science generally, criticism is both expected and profitable. A number of judgments of routine activities theory require a rethinking of some of the basic premises of the perspective. C. Ray Jeffrey argues:

> Felson presents a case for using social indicators to explain the impact of routine activities on crime rates. The more potential offenders, the more targets, and the fewer guardians, the higher the crime rate. . . . By increasing the number of potential victims or potential criminals, we can expect an increase in crime, but this is a description of events and not an explanation. It does not explain why some individuals become criminals and others do not, or why some convenience stores are robbed and others are not. (1993, 492–93)

Jeffrey prefers a more intensive focus on the specific traits or impairments of the individual offender as opposed to Felson's more singular emphasis on the social and situational features. Jeffrey continues that stepping-up the number of police in a city will not automatically lessen the crime rate; rather, a reduction in the number of police, but with modern training and technology and organizational structure, will decrease the crime rate.

Others criticize routine activities theory by reasoning that the fundamental variables of motivated offender, suitable target, and capable guardian are inadequately explained. At times the target and guardian become blurred. For example, if a target (person) were able to provide self-defense, would the victim also be occupying the role of capable guardian? (Massey, Krohn, Bonati 1989, 378–400). These critics add: "the routine activity had only limited application . . . suitable targets and capable guardians were considered confusing and ambiguous and it made them difficult to measure." A suggestion was made to alter the concept *motivated offender* to *potential offender* to have measurements that could be both subjectively and objectively measured (Massey, Krohn, Bonati 1989, 384). As mentioned earlier, Felson later used *likely offender* rather than the more problematic concept of *motivated offender.*

Similar arguments were made regarding the difficulty in explaining the meaning of selected variables. For example, Felson makes the point that when persons are pulled away from their homes, the homes become more easily targeted by offenders. Yet, children at school and office workers at their places of employment may find themselves in a more secure or protected environment than at home. In this regard, Miethe, Stafford, and Long saw some variables as being inadequately operationalized. They write: "Time away from the residence was considered equal despite its relative safety or inherent exposure to risk. Certain non-household activities might decrease victimization and increase guardianship" (1987, 185). The same critics also note that some violence may be difficult to explain using routine activity theory. It can be argued that a person may erupt into violence at home or at the workplace in a show of "spontaneity or impulse" regardless of the potential guardians in the immediate environment (Osgood et al. 1996, 635–55, cf. Miethe, Stafford, and Long 1987, 192). Similar criticism was levied against differential association theory (see the chapter on Sutherland in this book). Felson was apparently aware of these conceptual difficulties (see his response in "Linking Criminal Choices, Routine Activities, Informal Control, and Criminal Outcomes," 1986, 119–28).

Positive critiques of the routine activities theory can be seen with its use as a theoretical base for crime prevention and forecasting in an increasingly diverse variety of social settings. For instance, routine activities theory has been applied successfully to aggravated assault, illegal markets, and white-collar crime (Felson 2002, cf. Felson and Clarke 1997). Mustaine and Tewksbury (1999, 2002, 2003) used routine activities as a theoretical foundation for the study of rape. Other victimization studies have addressed the difficulty faced by college students who reflect a routine of life, often placing themselves as targets. College students, after heavy partying and alcohol consumption, are at risk and are associated with an increasing array of marketable goods appetizing to the enterprising thief (Fisher, Sloan, Cullen and Lu 1997, Fisher, Cullen, and Turner 2000, Henson and Stone 1999).

A most complete evaluation of the routine activities theory is offered by Akers (2000, 30–39, 2002). Among others, Akers reviews the findings of Messner and Tardiff (1985), Jensen and Brownfield (1986), Sherman et al. (1989), and Kennedy and Forde (1990). In summary, Akers suggests the jury is still out on the long-term viability of the theory, but recognizes that many of the tests of the theory are supportive while leaving the door open for continued caution and more complete evaluation. He writes:

> Even though it draws upon etiological theories, routine activities theory is only indirectly a theory of the commission of criminal behavior. It is primarily a theory of criminal victimization. That is, it does not offer an explanation of why some persons are motivated to develop a pattern of crime or commit a particular crime. It simply assumes that such persons exist and that they commit crimes in certain places and times at which the opportunities and potential victims are available. Routine activities theory does not explain why informal crime precautions may or may not be exercised by individuals in their homes or elsewhere, nor does it explain formal control exercised by law and the criminal justice system. It simply assumes that, if informal or formal guardians are not present or able to prevent crime, then crime will occur. (2000, 35)

However, Akers realizes that

> Felson and others have taken these commonsense and empirical realities and woven them into a coherent framework for understanding the variations in criminal victimization by time and place. The theory is well-stated, logically consistent, and has clear policy implications and powerful potential for understanding the impact of normal, even desirable, social structural changes on predatory crime. (2000, 36)

In general, the various evaluations of the theory by others appear to support the assumptions of the theory, but with the provision that additional work is needed to better measure the basic variables of the theory.

ADDENDUM

Early in 2006, Felson's book *Crime and Nature* was released by Sage Publications. This chapter had already been written, but a few words must be added at the last moment about the latest work. At the risk of sounding overly biased in praise, *Crime and Nature* provides original insights concerning how crime operates as part of a human ecosystem. By drawing on ecological concepts and theory that began with Robert E. Park and Ernest W. Burgess (see the chapter on Park in this book), Felson integrates taxonomies first used by animal and plant naturalists to better organize our thinking about human deviance and crime. This appears to be a first and long-needed attempt to offer a pure ecological setting for criminal offenses and victimizations. In short, Felson has done what Park and Burgess did in 1921 with their *Introduction to the Science of Sociology*. Park and Burgess connected human social behavior with animal and plant ecological theory for the first time. Felson, nearly a century later, unites the same ecological systems and subsystems of plants and animals to human "criminal" conduct. Some of the chapters and subchapters of the new book reflect the ecological arguments: crime's ecosystem; crime habitats; crime niches; crime competition; crime adaptation; crime symbiosis; crime mutualism; crime parasitism; and so on (see discussion in chapters 2 and 3, *Crime and Nature*, 2006). Routine activities theory becomes an important but secondary segment of the larger human ecosystem needed to understand the relationship between offenders and victims.

References

Akers, Ronald L., _Criminological Theories: Introduction, Evaluation, and Application._Third Edition, Los Angeles: CA., Roxbury Publishing, 2000."

Austin, W. Timothy, "Life on the Atoll: Singapore Ecology as a neglected dimension of social order," International Journal of Offender Therapy and Comparative Criminology_,49 (5): 1–13, 2005.

Baumeister, R., T. Heatherton, & D. Tice. 1984. *Losing control: How and why people fail at self-regulation.* San Diego: Academic Press.

Brantingham, P. J., & P. L. Brantingham. 1984. *Patterns in crime.* New York: Macmillan.

_____.1998. Environmental criminology: From theory to urban planning practice. *Stud. Crime Crime Preven.* 7(1): 33–60.

_____. 1999. A theoretical model of crime hot spot generation. *Stud. Crime Crime Preven.* 8(1), 7–26.

Clarke, R. 1999. Hot products: Understanding, anticipating and reducing demand for stolen goods. Paper No. 112, *Police Research Series*. London: British Home Office Research Publications.

Clarke, R.V., & M. Felson. 1993. Introduction: Criminology, routine activity and rational choice. In *Advances in Criminological Theory: Vol. 5. Routine activity and rational choice.* New Brunswick, NJ: Transaction Books, pp. 1–13.

Cloward, R., & L. Ohlin 1960. *Delinquency and opportunity.* New York: Free Press.

Cohen, A. 1955. *Delinquent boys: The culture of the gang.* New York: The Free Press.

Cohen, L., & M. Felson. 1979. Social change and crime rate trends: A routine activity approach. *Am. Sociolog. Rev.* 44: 588–608.

Cornish, D., & R.V. Clarke. 1986. *The reasoning criminal.* New York: Springer-Verlag.

Cullen, F., and R. Agnew, Criminological Theory: Past to Present_, Los Angeles, C.A., Roxbury Press, 2003.

Durkheim, E. 1893. *De la division du travail social*. Paris: Felix Alcan. (*The division of labor in society*; G. Simpson, Trans.). New York: Macmillan, 1933.

Felson, B., H. Weinstein, & H.B. Spitz. 1965. *Principles of chest roentgenology: A programmed text*. Philadelphia: W.B. Saunders Company.

Felson, M., 1972. Neighborhood segregation and white flight to the suburbs. *Am. J. Sociol.* 78 (November): 674–76.

————. 1986. Linking criminal choices, routine activities, informal control, and criminal outcomes. In D.B. Cornish and R.V. Clarke (Eds.), *The reasoning criminal*. New York: Springer-Verlag, 119–28.

————. 1994. *Crime and everyday life: Insights and implications for life*. Newbury Park, CA: Pine Forge Press.

————. 1995a. How buildings can protect themselves against crime. *Lusk Rev. Real Estate Devel. Urban Transform.* 1(1): 1–7.

————. 1995b. Those who discourage crime. In J.E. Eck and D. Weisburd (Eds.), *Crime prevention studies: Crime and place*. Monsey, NY: Criminal Justice Press, vol. 4: 53–66.

————. 1997. Technology, business and crime. In M. Felson and R. Clarke (Eds), *Business and crime prevention*. Monsey, NY: Willow Tree Press, pp. 81–96.

————. 1998. *Crime and everyday life*, 2nd ed. Thousand Oaks, CA: Pine Forge Press.

————. 2002. *Crime and everyday life*, 3rd ed. Thousand Oaks, CA: Sage Publications, Inc.

————. 2006. *Crime and nature*. Thousand Oaks, CA: Sage Publications.

————. 1987. Routine activities and crime prevention in the developing metropolis. *Criminology*. 25: 911–31.

Felson, M., M. Belanger, G. Bichler, C. Bruzinski, G. Campbell, C. Fried, K. Grofik, I. Mazur, A. O'Regan, P. Sweeney, A. Ullman, & L. Williams. 1996. Redesigning hell: Preventing crime and disorder at the Port Authority Bus Terminal. In R. Clarke (Ed.), *Crime prevention studies: Preventing mass transit crime*. Monsey, NY: Criminal Justice Press, vol. 6: 5–92.

Felson, M., R. Berends, B. Richardson, & A. Veno. 1997. Reducing pub-hopping and related crime. In R. Homel (Ed.), *Crime prevention studies: Reducing crime, public intoxication and injury*. Monsey, NY: Criminal Justice Press, vol. 7: 115–32.

Felson, M., & R. Clarke. 1995. Routine precautions, criminology, and crime prevention. In H.D. Barlow (Ed.), *Crime and public policy: Putting theory to work*. Boulder, CO: Westview, pp. 179–90.

————. 1997. The ethics of situational crime prevention. In G. Newman, R. V. Clarke, & S. Shoham (Eds.), *Rational choice and situational crime prevention: Theoretical foundations* pp. 197–218. Dartmouth, UK: Ashgate.

————. 1998. Opportunity makes the thief. Paper No. 98, *Police Research Series*. London: British Home Office Research Publications.

Felson, M., & L. Cohen. 1980. Human ecology and crime: A routine activity approach. *Hum. Ecol.* 8: 389–406.

————. 1981. Modeling crime rate trends: A criminal opportunity perspective. *J. Res. Crime Delinq.* 18: 138–64. (As corrected, 1982, 19: 1).

Felson, M., & M. Gottfredson. 1984. Adolescent activities near peers and parents. *J. Marr. Fam.* 46: 709–14.

Fisher, B., F. Cullen, & M. Turner. 2002. Being pursued: Stalking victimization in a national study of college women. *Criminol. Pub. Pol.* 1: 257–308.

Fisher, B.S., Sloan, J.J., cullen, F.T. & Lu, C. (1998); Crime in the Ivory Tower: The Level and Sources of Student Victimisation; "Criminology 36, 671–710."

Gottfredson, M., & T. Hirschi. 1990. *A general theory of crime*. Stanford, CA: Stanford University Press.

Hawley, A. 1950. *Human ecology: A theory of community structure*. New York: Ronald Press.

Henson, V., & W. Stone. 1999. Campus crime: A victimization study. *J. Crim. Just.* 27: 295–307.

Jacobs, J. 1961. *Death and life of great American cities*. New York: Random House.

Jeffrey, C. 1971. *Crime prevention through environmental design*. Beverly Hills: Sage.

_____. 1993. Obstacles to the development of research in crime and delinquency. *J. Crime Delinq.* 30 (4): 491–97.

Jensen, Gary, and D. Brownfield, "Gender, Lifestyles, and Victimization: Beyond Routine Activity," _Violence and Victims_, Summer, 1(2) 85-99, 1986."

Kennedy, Leslie W., and David R. Forde. "Routine Activities and Crime: An analysis of Victimization in Canada, Criminology, 28(1), 137–152, 1990."

Knutsson, J., & E. Kuhlhorn. 1997. Macro measures against crime: The example of check forgeries. In R.V. Clarke (Ed.), *Situational crime prevention: Successful case studies,* 2nd ed. New York: Harrow & Heston, pp. 113–21.

Martin, R., R. Mutchnick, & W. Austin. 1990. *Criminological thought: Pioneers past and present.* New York: Macmillan Publishing Company.

Massey, J., M. Krohn, & L. Bonati. 1989. Property crime and the routine activities of individuals. *J. Res. Crime Delinq.* 26 (4): 378–400.

Merton, R. 1997. On the evolving synthesis of differential association and anomie theory: A perspective from the sociology of science. *Criminology.* 35 (3): 517–25.

Messner, Steven F., and Kenneth Tardiff, "The Social Ecology of Urban Homicide: An Application of the 'Routine Activities' Approach," Criminology_, 23:(2), 241–267, 1985."

Miethe, T., M. Stafford, & J. Long. 1997. Social differentiation in criminal victimization: A test of routine activities/lifestyle theories. *Am. Sociolog. Rev.* 52 (April): 184–94.

Mustaine, E.E. and Tewksbury, R.A., 1999. "A Routine Activities Theory Explanation For Women's Stalking Victimization." Violence Against Women Vol. 5(1):43–62."

Mustaine, E., & R. Tewksbury. 2002. Sexual assault of college women: A feminist interpretation of a routine activities analysis. *Crim. Just. Rev.* 27: 89–123.

_____. 2003. College students' lifestyles and self-protective behaviors: Further considerations of the guardianship concept in routine activity theory. *Crim. Just. Behav.* 30: 282–301.

Newman, O. 1972. *Defensible space: Crime prevention through urban design.* New York: Macmillan.

Osgood, D., J. Wilson, P. O'Malley, J. Bachman, & J. Johnson 1996., Routine activities and individual deviant behavior. *Am. Sociolog. Rev.* 61: 635–55.

Park and Burgess, 1921: *Introduction to the Science of Sociology,* Chicago: University of Chicago Press.

Poyner, B. 1993. What works in crime prevention: An overview of evaluations. In R.V. Clarke (Ed.), *Crime prevention studies.* Vol. 1. Monsey, NY: Criminal Justice Press.

_____. 1998. The case for design. In M. Felson & R. Peiser (Eds.), *Reducing crime through real estate development and management.* Washington, D.C.: Urban Land Institute, pp. 5–21.

Rossmo, D. K. 2000. *Geographic profiling.* Boca Raton, FL: CRC Press.

_____. 1995. Place, space, and police investigations: Hunting serial violent criminals. In J. E. Eck & D. Weisburd (Eds.), *Crime prevention studies: Crime and place.* Monsey, NY: Criminal Justice Press, vol. 4: 217–35.

Sherman, Larry, and Patrick R. Gartin, and Michael E. Buerger, "Hot Spots of Predatory Crime: Routine Activities and the Criminology of Place," Criminology_. 27(1), 27–56, 1989."

Siegel, L. 2003. *Criminology.* Belmont, CA: Wadsworth/Thomson Learning, pp. 53–59.

Smith, T. 1970. *Principles of inductive rural sociology.* Philadelphia: F.A. Davis Company.

Sykes, G., & D. Matza. 1957. Techniques of neutralization: A theory of delinquency. *Am. Sociolog. Rev.* 22 (December): 664–70.

Theoretical Developments in Criminology. (Wall chart published by Prentice-Hall.) Criminal Justice Division, 445 Hutchinson Ave., 4th Floor, Columbus OH 43235–5677.

Tremblay, P. 1986. Designing crime. *Br J. Criminol.* 26: 234–53.

Williams, F. P., & M.D. McShane.1998. *Criminological theory.* Upper Saddle River, NJ: Pearson Prentice Hall.

_____. 2004. *Criminological theory.* Upper Saddle River, NJ: Pearson Prentice Hall.

CHAPTER 18
THINKING FURTHER

When we wrote the introduction to this book, we could only anticipate what lie ahead. Now that it is behind us, and on reflection, a number of points emerge that deserve comment. First, we represent three different academic backgrounds. Consequently, a sizeable amount of debate (if not outright quibbling!) occurred as we honed the original and lengthy list of potential pioneers down to only fifteen. Along with personal preferences, our decisions were influenced by time restraints and the need to keep the book to a manageable size. Regardless, once the final cut was made, the quibbling necessarily stopped. However, over the course of the next year, an occasional comment was still heard, typically from colleagues or reviewers, that a number of writers should be included. Some displayed disappointment that another eminent scholar had not made the list, and whereas others were surprised that one or more were considered by us to be pioneers at all.

We all agree that another volume would eventually be in order. The viability of this is particularly evident when one considers the impact of the passage of time and the fact that some pioneers may lose their prestigious status only to make way for rising stars. In addition, it has become evident that many criminological thinkers were quite instrumental in the growth of the discipline, however perhaps not of sufficient merit to capture the label of *pioneer*. As found in English literature, the possibility of designing a volume on often-overlooked but influential or minor writers may be appropriate for further understanding the discipline of criminology. Occasionally in this book, we note that an individual may rise to fame in academic life by relying on the works of others who remained behind the scenes. We can only conclude that reaching prominence in a particular field of study likely involves a complex interplay of factors, only one of which may be the substantive contribution of the particular scholar.

A second and perhaps more important finding was the ongoing realization that a complex organizational network has persisted over the decades that literally linked one pioneer to another. As the chapters unfolded, it became increasingly clear that major contributors of a same period most likely knew each other personally, occasionally worked together, and often passed through the same graduate program. Thus, it was revealing to learn that many of the pioneers were influenced by the same cluster of educators who were themselves influenced by a similar group of earlier pioneers. In the earlier stages of research, it occurred to us that a type of intellectual genealogy might be evident, whereby one could trace the influence of one idea on a series of individuals over time. For example, August Comte influenced Emile Durkheim, who had substantial impact on Talcott Parsons at Harvard University; Robert Merton studied under Parsons and influenced a young graduate student named Albert Cohen, and so on. Although it was not a specific aim of this book to establish such a genealogy, each chapter provides some of the building blocks for the construction of such a "tree."

Third, the first chapters to be written in this book were of pioneers long deceased. One anonymous reviewer appropriately referred to the early scholars as the "ancients." Writing about such pioneers as Lombroso, Durkheim, and Freud provided a different task than that presented by the more contemporary and living scholars. First, it is easier to accumulate biographical information on an ancient scholar. Certainly, their works are more widely disseminated, appearing in diverse sources from books and encyclopedias to anthologies of historical figures. Most important, the early pioneers addressed here were of sufficient prominence to have inspired one or more biographies. In such cases, the problem became one of sorting through multiple evaluations of biographers for most relevant information. With some highly celebrated personages, such as Sigmund Freud, it is difficult to avoid engaging in challenges of the interpretations from different writers. Furthermore, the authors of this book believe they have greater latitude in critiquing the works of the early pioneers, because there was little if any risk of misrepresenting a pioneer to family or friends.

Writing about the living scholars was surprisingly more difficult. Early publications were often found only with difficulty. Biographies had yet to be written, making the reconstruction of the early life of a contemporary figure more laborious. Such was the case, for example, with Erving Goffman, who died in 1982, and with Walter Reckless, who died in 1988, when the chapter on his life and work was still being composed. There is always the immediate concern that when examining the life and works of the living, one feels less license to probe, critique, and make creative guesses. When direct contact could be made with a contemporary pioneer, this dilemma was somewhat alleviated. A number of letters were exchanged or telephone contacts made between the authors and several of the contemporary pioneers. Regardless, we all agreed that later chapters presented special difficulties.

Each of us as authors gained considerable insight into the individual pioneer being examined and into the discipline of criminology at large while the book was in progress. When a particular chapter was underway and with diverse materials compiled on a particular pioneer, the authors became, if only temporarily, most keenly acquainted with and knowledgeable of that particular pioneer. Much like the stage actor, for a time each of us became, in part, the pioneer whose life and works we were trying to characterize. At any given time, for example, one of the authors might be walking, talking, and dreaming about Cesare Becarria, Robert Park, or Edwin Sutherland. The authors took this with some amusement, yet still realized it was necessary to fully appreciate a particular pioneer.

Fourth, it is not necessarily an easy task to identify clearly the key ideas and basic assumptions in every theory or set of ideas. It is often equally difficult to totally sort and separate the assumptions from key ideas, as there is by necessity a high level of interrelatedness and overlap among them. These difficulties make for hard decisions about what to include and what not to include, as well as where and how to present specific ideas. It is also possible to characterize and define the general notions of *key ideas* and *assumptions* in a variety of ways, all of which have their own inherent merits and limitations. In this book, there has been no attempt to adhere to a specific or uniform conceptualization of the notions of key ideas or assumptions. Although it is true that the failure to adopt a uniform definition of these concepts may create some sense of inconsistency and confusion across the chapters, it avoids the pitfalls that accompany after-the-fact tailoring of ideas and assumptions to fit a predetermined classification scheme. The pros and cons of both approaches can be debated, and we have discussed them among ourselves. We agree that the use of more structured and uniform definitions of what is meant by *key ideas* and *basic assumptions* may have been advantageous in some ways. However, we believe that to express the true "feel," intent, and nature of the assumptions and key ideas of each individual pioneer, more flexibility in characterizing them is required.

Consequently, we decided that the individual sets of ideas and how the pioneer expressed them would guide our portrayal of the assumptions and key ideas. Individuals do not develop their ideas in accordance with a rigid and predesigned structure. Accordingly, we agreed that presenting the ideas within a fixed structure would not adequately display the uniqueness and individuality of the thinker or the thoughts. In other words, we maintain that it is important that each set of ideas, like the pioneer, be perceived as having its own "personality." The decision to use this approach in writing the basic assumptions and key ideas sections of each chapter was a judgment call, and as such is subject to question and disagreement.

A final comment is in order regarding the value of this book to theoretical criminology: A number of goals were set forward when this project began. We wanted to develop a different kind of resource about some of the more significant figures (as we see them) in criminology and their most important ideas. Only time will tell how good a resource we have derived, but despite the overall evaluations and ultimate longevity of this book, we believe that some immediate value can be identified. Undoubtedly, we stimulated some readers to evaluate their own criteria of "pioneerhood." Our inclusions and exclusions have no doubt sparked at least a few debates on this subject. This work has taken a different approach than other books in organizing and presenting the material, and attempts to include information not typically included in such books. We hope that in the process we have been able to provide some different insights into the people who helped shape criminology and their ideas.

Of course, it is without doubt that we have not accomplished some of the things that we set out to do. It is inevitable that we will look back on what we have done and find many places where things could have been, or should have been, done differently. In all likelihood, the reader may have found instances where they would have presented material another way. Herein lies one of the more basic values of a work such as this—the generation of reaction and thought. The exact nature of the reactions and specific content of the thoughts is not nearly as important as the processes themselves. The most significant contribution of most, if not all, of the individuals included in this book is not the specific concepts and theories they developed, but the further thought and research that their ideas stimulated. If, at this point in the book, the reader is, as we are, thinking further, then we are satisfied.

CHAPTER 19
HAVING THOUGHT FURTHER

It is difficult to get a book started, and also difficult to end it. Chapter 18 Thinking Further was actually penned in 1988. As authors, we thought that at least a few words were in order from the present.

First, "modern-day pioneers" are ever more increasingly difficult to isolate from the pack. This is the result in part of the burgeoning numbers of criminologists in the United States and world. It is also entirely possible that worthy notables are making their mark not in criminology, but in closely aligned sister fields of study and simply do not receive the recognition they deserve. Each decade sees a vast increase in the numbers of intellectual outlets with hundreds of new journals now compounded by millions of web-based sources. In addition, the number of subdisciplines increased in the past several decades. When the first edition of this book was released (originally as a Macmillan publication, which was then sold to Allyn and Bacon, and is now published by Prentice Hall), there was little acknowledgment of "cyber-crime," "chaos theory," or "human genome breakthroughs." Today, there are simply more things to study and more researchers to publish their findings.

Second, the ever-growing numbers of academic criminologists and the expanding domain of subdisciplines may well be currently fermenting the next wave of pioneering thought and theory that have yet to emerge. However, we are remiss if we do not acknowledge the precarious nature of human progress and development. Looking back over the twenty-odd years that have passed since the publication of the first edition, it is sometimes hard to decide where we have actually come. At times it appears that we may be at the beginning of a new wave of development in thought and theory, the first substantial and meaningful transformation in our collective consciousness since that manifested in the theoretical and paradigm shifts of the late 1960s and early 1970s. At other times it appears that rather than beginning to rise on the swell of this new developmental wave, we may be caught in a riptide, swimming for all we are worth and yet never seeming to get much closer to the shore. Actually, it may be that we are at the fulcrum of both points. Having "looked further," we are both hopeful and despairing—hopeful that the new wave is nigh, and despairing that it will somehow never gain momentum and simply fade into the many little waves that constantly ascend and recede. Having looked further, we come to the conclusion that whichever of these "futures" ultimately manifests depends on the new generation of criminologists and social scientists and, in a broader sense, on the next wave of social and cultural development. However, each of us can and does have a hand in both of these spheres of influence, which is a responsibility that we are both humbled by and have come to cherish deeply.

Third, and on more of a personal note, we began the first edition as much younger and perhaps more zealous and passionate academicians. Now, as more senior faculty, all occasionally still teaching theory in their own way, we fully realize that a third edition will likely be left to younger faculty—those with fresh outlooks and renewed zeal and passion. We hope that what we have provided is a base to continue discussion as to who the "pioneers" are. With that, we also pass to you the responsibility to determine who will be the next "pioneers" to deserve their own chapters.

INDEX